69
72

Victorian Women

Edited by ERNA OLAFSON HELLERSTEIN,

LESLIE PARKER HUME, and KAREN M. OFFEN

Associate Editors: ESTELLE B. FREEDMAN,

BARBARA CHARLESWORTH GELPI, and MARILYN YALOM

Prepared under the auspices of the Center for Research on Women
at Stanford University

Victorian Women

A DOCUMENTARY ACCOUNT OF WOMEN'S LIVES
IN NINETEENTH-CENTURY ENGLAND, FRANCE,
AND THE UNITED STATES

STANFORD UNIVERSITY PRESS

STANFORD, CALIFORNIA

1981

*Acknowledgments will be
found on pp. 523–24*

Stanford University Press
Stanford, California

© 1981 by the Board of Trustees of the
Leland Stanford Junior University

Printed in the United States of America

Cloth I S B N 0–8047–1088–0
Paper I S B N 0–8047–1096–1
L C 79–67770

To our mothers

ELIZABETH DIXON BRYANT

HARRIETTE SMITH OLAFSON

ELLA MAE MCALISTER STEDTFELD

Preface

This book is a collection of historical documents by and about women in three different yet related Western cultures—England, France, and the United States—in the nineteenth century. The original collection of over a hundred documents was developed for use as teaching material in an interdisciplinary, team-taught course offered at Stanford University in 1978. This course, entitled "The Female Experience: Victorian Heritage, 1830–1880," was funded by the National Endowment for the Humanities and the Ford Foundation and was sponsored by the Center for Research on Women at Stanford. The teaching staff tested these documents in the classroom and received an enthusiastic response from students and colleagues. Their comments and criticisms were invaluable in helping us reshape the original collection into its present form.

The collection draws from a wide range of autobiographical and prescriptive source materials: diaries, letters, advice manuals, medical and legal records and case studies, inquiries by governmental investigative committees, and the published findings of nineteenth-century social scientists. Not only have we contributed materials from our own research, but colleagues from all over the United States have generously responded to our requests by sending original archival materials. Many of these documents have never before been published; some have been translated into English expressly for this collection.

We have been especially fortunate in being able to draw on our own Victorian heritages: the letters and diaries of two great-great-aunts, Frances Marion Eddy and Mary Ellen Castle Rankin, and one great-aunt, Mary Chaffee Abell. We thank our families for sharing these private papers with us.

We are indebted to many people and institutions for their help. The National Endowment for the Humanities, the Ford Foundation, and the National Institute for Education generously supported our undertaking. The Center for Research on Women at Stanford University gave us financial assistance, work space, and many other kinds of help. We would like to thank the staff of CROW, in particular Estella Estrada, Diane Middlebrook, and Marilyn Yalom, for their steady support for the project. Marilyn Yalom deserves special thanks for doing many of the French translations.

Numerous libraries helped us to compile these materials, and many librarians assisted our research. Jo Ann Hoffman and Jim Knox of the Reference Department of Green Library, Stanford University, David Rozkuszka of the Government Documents Section, and Florian Shasky of Special Collections consistently provided us with valuable assistance and freely shared with us both their time and their knowledge. The staff of Lane Medical Library at Stanford, especially Claire Still, took great pains to help us locate materials. We found a wealth of material in the Southern Historical Collection, University of North Carolina, Chapel Hill, thanks to the diligence of Jerrold Hirsh, Ellen Barrier Neal, and Carolyn Wallace. We wish also to acknowledge the cooperation of the staffs of the California Historical Society; the Reference Department and Bancroft Library at the University of California, Berkeley; the Schlesinger Library at Radcliffe; and the Beinecke Library at Yale.

The names of those who contributed or called our attention to certain documents have been mentioned in the source notes, but we would like to express special thanks to our colleagues and friends George Behlmer, Susan Groag Bell, Suzanne Case, Natalie Zemon Davis, Sandra Dijkstra, Yolaida Durán, Mary Felstiner, Jennifer Hastings, Helen Smith Jordan, Patricia Otto Klaus, Carolyn Lougee, Theresa McBride, Angus McLaren, Sue Macy, Michelle Perrot, Elizabeth Hafkin Pleck, Barbara Corrado Pope, Michelle Zimbalist Rosaldo, Joan W. Scott, Carroll Smith-Rosenberg, Laura Strumingher, Peter Stansky, Martha Vicinus, and Hugh West for their generous support, comments, and suggestions. Gary Sue Goodman deserves special commendation for her ingenuity and persistence in locating American documents. We are grateful also to Valerie Matsumoto, our resourceful research assistant.

At Stanford University Press William Carver, J. G. Bell, and Norris Pope gave both encouragement and assistance in transforming our initial collection of documents into the present book. Barbara Mnookin, our editor, proved not only inexorably accurate in her criticisms of the manuscript, but unfailingly patient in dealing with a multitude of authors.

This book could not have been completed without the cheerful cooperation of our children and of those who cared for them while we worked on it. We owe special thanks to Jaynese and Peter Davis, who tended Benjamin Hellerstein, and to Rebecca and Elizabeth Hellerstein, who looked after themselves with a competence beyond their years; to Alice Schaub and Lydia Treichler, who tended Parker Hume; and to Janet Barrett, Catherine Maxwell, Cristina Scerna, Alice Thomasson, and Katie Wilson, who tended Stephanie and Catherine Offen.

Finally, we would like to thank our husbands, David Hellerstein, George Hume, and George Offen, for their critical interest in the manuscript and for sustaining our spirits while we wrote it.

In order to preserve the authenticity of the documents, grammar and spelling have largely been retained in their original form. We have, however, occasionally made some changes in punctuation in the interests of clarity. In the headnotes we have given the dates of the authors or principal subjects of the documents when known, but to avoid cluttering the text we have omitted the dates of family members, friends, and associates.

E . O . H .

L . P . H .

K . M . O .

Contents

PART II. *The Adult Woman: Personal Life*

Contents xi

PART III. *The Adult Woman: Work*

Victorian Women

General Introduction

In the ferment about sex roles and the family that characterizes our own time, men and women still define themselves in terms of the Victorians, either living out ideas and defending institutions that came to fruition in the nineteenth century or reacting against these ideas and institutions and against Victorian "repression." Modern "objective" social science, born during the Victorian period, both incorporated and legitimized Victorian prejudices about gender, the family, work, and the division between public and private spheres. These inherited categories still influence the way we organize our information, not only about ourselves, but about cultures different from our own. For women especially, the Victorian heritage continues to affect their lives and their self-conceptions. Because of this, the Victorian woman has attracted both scholarly and popular attention.

The term Victorian was used in the late nineteenth century to refer to English life during the reign of Queen Victoria (1837–1901). In this book, following Carl Degler, Michel Foucault, and others, we extend its coverage to France and the United States as well. For all their differences, the three countries formed an Atlantic community, a transatlantic culture that tells us more about Victorian attitudes and institutions than we could learn from a single nation. Our transatlantic focus underscores the fact that in the nineteenth century, England and France were a much greater part of the American consciousness than now. Whether defining themselves against the Old World or trying to imitate it, Americans were deeply influenced by European ideas and culture, as the many American reprints of European publications suggest. In turn, the English and the French, whether intrigued or repelled, were keenly aware of the new civilization across the Atlantic.

In addition to the commonalities England, France, and the United States shared as members of the Atlantic community, these countries underwent similar changes in the nineteenth century. In fact, the tempo of change in all areas of life, from politics to household management, accelerated throughout the century. Industrialization transformed agriculture and manufacturing in England, and to a lesser extent, in America and France, by mechanizing production and concentrating the labor force. As the market economy penetrated the countryside, more people came into the cash economy wherein more goods were available. These twin processes resulted in a vast increase in material wealth, although at the cost of the proletarianization of artisans and peasants and an increase in class conflict, social dislocation, and social fear. For women, industrialization, by separating the home from the workplace, began to force an unprecedented choice between home and children on the one hand, and the continued possibility of earning a cash wage, however meager, on the other. This development tended to create a dichotomy between woman as homemaker and woman as worker, a dichotomy that survives in the twentieth century as perhaps the most enduring legacy of the Victorian period.

Demographic changes also profoundly affected women's lives. Life expectancy, especially for women, rose significantly between 1800 and 1900. For example, French women born in 1801 could expect to live only about thirty-five years; those born a hundred years later could look forward to forty-nine years of life. As population increased, the pressure of people on the land became more intense, contributing to two other demographic changes: a gradual decline in the birthrate, first in France and later in the United States and England; and European outmigration, a vast movement of Old World peoples to the Americas and other parts of the globe. This transoceanic mobility was accompanied by internal mobility, as hundreds of thousands of men and women left the countryside to settle in the cities.

The growth of democratic institutions from which women were excluded paradoxically helped to politicize women. Egalitarian and democratic ideas spread to both men and women of all social classes, a diffusion that was aided by rising literacy rates, improved communications, and demographic and social mobility. But although women were touched by these ideas, they were left out of the political process and denied the vote. Similarly, among the working classes, men organized themselves into unions and political parties, from which women were as a rule barred. English, French, and American women responded by founding feminist organizations to protect their rights and promote their interests.

In all three countries political instability and the concomitant fear of social anarchy contributed to the growth of state power and the attempt to use the agency of the state to impose social order and homogeneity on its citizenry. These developments, too, profoundly affected the lives of women. The Victorians witnessed the explosive expansion of state bureaucracies and the enactment of legislation aimed at regularizing and standardizing both public and private activities: governments made education compulsory, criminalized abortion, established or strengthened municipal police forces to control city populations, and passed laws that subjected both industry and labor to a host of regulations. State power and a corresponding secular view of reality grew at the expense of family institutions and village traditions, as well as of church, charity, and workers' associations. With the help of the school and the railroad, the state intruded increasingly on the lives of its citizens.

An obsession with surveillance and regulation characterized not only the activities of the state, but also those of the private citizen. Household manuals and books on child-rearing proliferated as Victorian authors strove to create ideal mothers and perfect household managers. Men in the professions of law and medicine banded together and adopted codes that governed admission to their ranks and regulated the behavior of their members; these codes, like protective labor legislation, had the effect of barring women from public activities in which they had formerly engaged. The Victorian compulsion to regulate, and the professional invasion of both the public and the private sphere, subjected women to a host of new strictures, both legal and prescriptive; not surprisingly, women often resisted and resented these demands.

An extreme polarization of sex roles accompanied the imposition of the ordering vision: this was probably the change that had the most impact on the lives of Victorian women. In both practice and prescription the male and female spheres became increasingly separated, and the roles of men and women became ever more frozen. Social scientists by and large sanctified the separation of spheres and consigned women to the domestic, private sphere. In France the maverick socialist Pierre-Joseph Proudhon relegated women to domestic drudgery; because of their inferiority, he argued, women should be subject to male authority. His compatriot Auguste Comte subscribed to a more elevated vision of women and eulogized their civilizing mission; yet, like Proudhon, he believed that women, because of their weak brains and bodies, belonged in the home. Across the Channel social anthropologists, armed with the evolutionary theories of Charles Darwin, gave patriarchy scientific underpinnings by declaring that both history and evolution sanctioned the subordination of women to men. Herbert Spencer, undoubtedly the most famous of the social Darwinists, argued that evolution had placed women in the home, and that the dictates of social survival necessitated rigidly defined sex roles and male domination. Patriarchy was now equated not only with nature, but with the forces of progress and civilization as well.

Novelists, moralists, and journalists—both male and female—agreed for the most part with the social scientists. Both Charles Dickens and Honoré de Balzac, in their extremely influential works, took women's special domestic mission for granted and applied to their female characters very different standards from those used for males. Authors of popular children's books like Hannah More and the Comtesse de Ségur taught young girls the virtues of passivity and obedience. Similarly, the arbiters of etiquette and writers of manuals, from Sarah Stickney Ellis to Catharine Beecher, decreed that woman's mission was very different from man's, and that her natural sphere was the home. Of course, the image conveyed by the literature diverged dramatically from the reality of women's lives: these exalted domestic angels bore scant resemblance to Georgia slaves, Lancashire mill workers, or even Parisian bourgeoises. Although the idea of separate spheres was not new to the nineteenth century, the obsessive manner in which all three cultures insisted on this separation seems peculiarly novel. As one nineteenth-century reviewer of Charlotte Brontë's *Jane Eyre* indicated, and as many female writers and activists were to discover, any woman who, however tangentially, rejected the role that Victorian culture thrust on her, seemed as noxious and threatening to her contemporaries as the political revolutionary or the social anarchist.[1]

[1] See footnote 1, p. 8.

Because of the contradictory demands placed on women by changes in the structure and style of personal interaction in all spheres of life, their role in family and society was, at best, fraught with ambivalence. Women confronted these changes most immediately within the family. Among many families in the middle and upper classes, the nineteenth century witnessed a transition from what has been called the positional family to the personal family.[2] In the positional family the child was controlled by the "continual building up of a sense of social pattern," that is, behavior was governed by reference to relative position, such as placement by sex, age, or hierarchy. On the other hand, the more modern personal family that emerged during the Victorian period emphasized the unique and autonomous quality of each individual. In contrast to the positional family, the personal family did not stress status, position, and fixed or ritual patterns of action in its child training. Instead, parents controlled their children's behavior in a manipulative and flexible manner and justified their authority by verbal explanation adjusted to individual circumstance.

The changeover from the positional to the personal family style, complicated enough in the case of boys, was particularly complex for girls, for throughout the century in all three countries the dominant culture decreed that women had a static position in society; they were viewed as instruments. Thus familial treatment of women tended to take a positional tone. But, paradoxically, the fulfillment of that position—dutiful yet companionable wife, communicative and loving mother—demanded that they become more personally oriented. That is, in their interaction with family members, women necessarily became more aware of themselves as persons, and they transmitted their sense of autonomy to their children, both male and female. Thus, with each generation women's sense of their own intrinsic significance grew, even as they fulfilled an instrumental role within a dominantly male culture.

As an alternative to the traditional approach that has fitted women's experience into preconceived structures of historical change and periodization, we have chosen to construct our collection around the stages of the female life cycle, from the announcement of the birth of a female child until her old age and death. This organization confronts readers with the Victorian vision that biology was destiny and asks them to grapple with the issue of biological determinism. It makes possible the exploration of the relationship between ideological formulations about women and lived experience, between image and reality. Within this life-cycle framework we have included a wide range of female experiences and have not restricted ourselves to a particular class or geographic region. The writings of some exceptional women such as Elizabeth Cady Stanton, George Sand, and Queen Victoria herself appear in the collection, but only to describe or illustrate experiences common to women

[2] Douglas 1973. We are grateful to Barbara Charlesworth Gelpi for calling our attention to this theory and suggesting its applicability to women in the nineteenth century.

or to provide clues about the institutions that influenced women's lives and minds.

By resurrecting the voices of these Victorians we want to provoke readers to take a fresh look at the nineteenth century. It is tempting to patronize the Victorians and tempting also, because they are so close to us in time, to think that we understand them better than we do. By making available the words of Victorian women from all social classes through all stages of life, we hope to give readers a new view of the nineteenth century and to broaden their understanding of women's history.

We believe these documents raise many important questions. Is there a female experience that transcends class, culture, and ethnicity? Is femaleness a unifying category or an important determinant of experience? In what ways did the social relations between the sexes change in the nineteenth century, and in what ways did they remain constant? How did Victorian women interpret their own experiences, and how did they react to these experiences and shape their own histories? These questions are complex; they may never be answered completely. Yet they can lead us to a broader understanding not only of women's history but of the nineteenth-century history of the West as well.

Part I
The Girl

Introduction

Barbara Charlesworth Gelpi

Jane Eyre, refusing to be Rochester's mistress, asks herself, as he tries to break her will, "Who in the world cares for *you*," and finds this answer, "*I* care for myself. The more solitary, the more friendless, the more unsustained I am, the more I will respect myself." Victorians might have applauded her rejection of adultery, but some could—and did—feel more than a little uneasy at its rationale.[1] In an era that saw selfless submission as woman's essential posture—whether in acceptance of family or marital status, or in acquiescence to established religious belief, or in attendance on children—Jane's assertion of a personal significance unrelated to any social function or relation was alarming. It brought the threat of some radical inconvenience to the smooth running of a world ordered along completely different lines.

Yet if the doctrine Charlotte Brontë puts into the mouth of her heroine seems to question or even defy the right of privileged men to control societies in which women serve as functionaries, it also, however paradoxically, is an expression of the nineteenth century's very spirit and idea—for women as well as for men. For the concept of personal significance, mysterious and complex as a factor in Western history, appears to be linked to cultural change, and such change characterizes England, France, and America throughout the century. Thus women of that time, while being urged to think of themselves only relationally, were also, by the very nature of the metamorphosing societies in which they lived, being challenged to the creation of themselves as persons with separate and interesting destinies.[2] These two virtually antithetical impulses shaped the early years of the Victorian girl.

[1] Charlotte Bronte, *Jane Eyre*, chapter 27. Elizabeth Rigby, reviewing the book in 1848, sounded the alarm in these terms: "Altogether the autobiography of Jane Eyre is pre-eminently an anti-Christian composition. There is throughout it a murmuring against the comforts of the rich and the privations of the poor, which, as far as each individual is concerned, is a murmuring against God's appointment—there is a proud and perpetual assertion of the rights of man, for which we find no authority either in God's word or in God's providence. . . . We do not hesitate to say that the tone of mind and thought which has overthrown authority and violated every code human and divine abroad, and fostered Chartism and rebellion at home, is the same which has written *Jane Eyre*." *Quarterly Review*, 84.167 (Dec.): 173–74.

[2] On the differences between a relational or, to use Mary Douglas's term, a "positional" orientation and a personal one, see the editors' discussion in the General Introduction, p. 4.

Birth of a Girl

The first problem encountered, even if unconsciously, by the girl who wished to believe in her own significance was the reaction to her birth. To be sure, the comments gathered to illustrate this reaction (Doc. 1) contain some samples of what appears to be unfeigned pleasure at the news that the baby is a girl; but in their general negativity they reflect the dominant feeling in all three countries virtually throughout the century: the appropriate reaction to a boy's arrival was joyous congratulation, to a girl's something closer to condolence. Priscilla Robertson, writing of England and of Europe, states, "At every stage, in every country, however subtly, boys continued to be favored over girls."[3] Lest we think of such attitudes as maddening but of no real significance coming so early in a baby's life, we should keep in mind the conclusions arrived at by both Lloyd de Mause and Sheila Johansson in their examination of statistics on infant mortality. De Mause, noting the suspicious preponderance of boys over girls throughout Europe until the seventeenth century, when the proportions became nearly equal, suggests that until that time a girl child, even a legitimate one, was in more danger of filicide than a boy. Since we now know that the human female has the biological advantage over the male in possessing a greater hardiness through all stages of life, even the fact that the infant mortality rates of the sexes were equal appears somewhat suspicious. Johansson points out as well that in England throughout the nineteenth century girls between the ages of five and nine had a higher death rate than boys, a strong hint that a girl received with less enthusiasm may also have been fed less adequately (Doc. 2) and nursed in illness less carefully.[4] It is worth noting, however, that in America the reaction to the birth of a girl was not as uniformly negative as in France and England.

Clothing

On arrival, the infant, if French, would in all likelihood have been bound up in swaddling bands (Doc. 5); she or he may have been swaddled in England or America as well (Doc. 51), for the age-old custom persisted in both countries, but diapers were more commonly used. The Biblical associations of the word swaddling may make the process sound rather charming to modern ears, but actually the bands, constricting as they did a baby's legs and sometimes its arms as well, were cruel. Yet in some situations swaddling may have been a safety device: women in predominantly agricultural France, for instance, who carried their infants with them while they labored at field work, needed a way of keeping the baby "put." Whatever the reason for their use, swaddling bands were without question a positioning device and as such may have had a psychological effect on the child's sense of its social place. The adoption of diapers in England and America toward the end of the eighteenth century may well coincide with the growing concern there for personal experience and meaning. At the same time, we should remember that

[3] Robertson 1974: 409.
[4] De Mause 1976: 6; Johansson 1977: 171.

diapers made easier a restrictive and demanding toilet training that some-times started when the infant was only a month old.[5]

Once out of infancy, middle-class girls and boys in all three countries generally wore skirts until they reached the age of five or so. This practice, begun only in the mid-sixteenth century, Philippe Ariès calls the "effeminiza-tion of the little boy,"[6] a phrase that suggests a certain fear of the boy's being overwhelmed by female influences, but might, from another point of view, call up the happy possibility of a shared experience and shared viewpoint in this early, formative period. Perhaps the clothes occasionally provided such a bond, but evidence suggests that by and large they did not: if boys wore skirts, they were not asked to treat either the garment or the body within it in the same way as their middle- or upper-class sisters who, as one Victorian woman put it, were dogged by "that horrid word ladylike from the nursery upwards."[7] So Athénaïs Mialaret (Doc. 2) had to watch her little brother, "still in petticoats," run off to join the rough play of the older brothers with a carelessness about his clothing denied to her. Moreover, the dragging, clumsy garments—vest, chemise, stays, petticoat, stockings, dress, pinafore—restricted the boys for only a certain, albeit a formative, time, making the freedom of casting them off an all the more significant liberation. Their sisters continued to wear them all throughout childhood, including the stays (a word as posi-tional in its connotations as the garment was in its effect), only to change at late adolescence to the still more restrictive corset and even longer and more clinging skirt.

The clothing of children was not always, however, so cumbersome. A portrait of William and Eliza Wilson, son and daughter of wealthy American southerners, shows them clothed alike in off-the-shoulder dresses, socks, and boots.[8] The difference between their sexes and the attitudes toward that dif-ference are nonetheless clear: William sits astride a rocking horse, whip in hand; Eliza stands beside him, a huge bunch of flowers cradled in the skirt of her dress. Worth remembering too is the identification of long frocks with the condition of childishness. A boy, by changing to manly breeches, began to take on some of a man's dignity. The woman's skirts, longer than the child's but otherwise very similar, served as an outward sign of the childlike depen-dence that was to be hers for life.

Clothing had social significance for both boys and girls in another im-portant way. One is struck time and again in Victorian writing by how strong the associations are between cleanliness, neat clothing, and class; fresh, whole, well-fitting garments were the badge of middle-class status and, for those in the working class who possessed them, a sign of upward mobility (Doc. 9). For the children of those still struggling to get or to regain a foot-hold in the middle classes or for those in desperate and hopeless poverty,

[5] Gathorne-Hardy 1972: 172.
[6] Ariès 1962: 53.
[7] Louisa Lumsden to Barbara Bodichon, quoted in Atkinson 1978: 105.
[8] See Humm 1978: 23.

there were only the garments cast off by adults. Making over such garments was one of the Breton housewife's tasks (Doc. 75), and Mary Abell, struggling to maintain her family's middle-class standards while coping with Kansas farm life, was forced to do the same for her children (Doc. 66).

If the child was motherless or the mother too busy to perform this task, the adult clothes often had to serve without any adjustment for size. Mary Carpenter (Doc. 15.iii), who opened a "ragged school" in the slums of Bristol, had this description of two pupils who appeared at its door: "They are little girls, one five and the other six years of age. They had only frocks on, no article of underclothes whatever, and one of them was obliged to hold this with both hands to prevent its falling off her. Their faces were dirty, and their hair matted and clung round their head in bunches for want of combing."[9]

Food

Without pasteurization for cow's milk, much less special infant formulas, breast milk was a virtual necessity if an infant was to have much chance for survival. The question, then, was not so much whether the infant would be breast fed as whether the mother or a wet nurse would provide the milk. Even at the beginning of the century doctors, aware of the higher mortality rates among babies sent out to the homes of wet nurses, strongly advised mothers to feed their own children. To this practical consideration was added a growing feeling for the importance of a personal relationship between mother and child, which nursing would do much to foster. In earlier centuries the convenience of a wet nurse had been for the wealthy a mark of their superior advantages, but now affluent mothers and those influenced by new theories on child rearing tended to nurse their babies themselves.

For all sorts of reasons, however, as the documents show, this pattern could vary. In the American South it remained customary for a wealthy white infant to be nursed by a black slave woman, with little or no concern for the plight of the slave's own infant (Doc. 53.iii). Or a wealthy mother in France or England whose milk proved inadequate might well have had to use the services of a wet nurse, sometimes with a similar lack of concern for the welfare of the nurse's infant (Doc. 50). And, then too, despite the new feeling for intimacy between mother and child, some well-to-do mothers were simply indifferent (Doc. 2).

Both greater security about their infants' chances for life and the privilege of a more intense relationship with them were luxuries denied working mothers, particularly working mothers in factories and shops, who of necessity hired wet nurses for their children in order to return to work. In France, particularly, wet nursing became an organized industry, a means by which rural women earned extra income and city workers returned to their income-

---

[9] Statement incorporated in *Report of the Commission appointed to inquire into the State of Popular Education in England* (1861), 1: 393, quoted in Kamm 1965: 160.

producing jobs. But the meeting of these necessities was more than offset by the system's true cost, a depressingly high death rate among the babies.[10] The use of wet nurses seems to have been less common among the working women of England, though not necessarily with any happier result. Sugared water filled out with bread, called "pap," was often the only recourse if breast milk was unavailable. The infant's digestive system could not absorb any nourishment from the bread, so that the child might well starve gradually, with cramps and diarrhea as the food's only effect. To quiet the hungry crying, laudanum ("Godfrey's Cordial") was routinely given, sometimes in doses large enough to cause death (Doc. 54.ii).

Once past these hazards, children in the working classes of all three countries shared their parents' food and eating hours. The diet was for the most part monotonous, as shown in the descriptions of the lives of the Breton peasants, the Manchester housewife, and the Santerre family (Docs. 5, 64.i, 75). Interestingly, for children of the upper and middle classes, particularly in England, the diet was also monotonous, not from necessity as it was for the poor, but on principle. Eating all that they were apportioned, often separately from their parents (Doc. 2) and on a very rigid schedule, these children were having instilled in them along with their food those qualities considered important to their society: frugality in the management of economic resources, asceticism in the husbanding of the body's resources, discipline and thrift in the use of time. It was taken for granted, however, that boys and girls would use these characteristics for very different ends: the boys for political and commercial achievement, the girls for the life of self-sacrifice taken to be their future lot as mothers.[11]

The picture is by no means so uniformly grim; in all three countries, but particularly in France and America, family meals in common were part of what was recognized at the time to be an increasingly personal and integrated family life. Even so, in all classes and in all three countries food and discipline were intimately combined. The dining table was a socialization center and the food itself a disciplinary tool. For good behavior or to celebrate the relaxation of a holiday there were sweets (Doc. 5); bad behavior was punished with bread and water or the withholding of food altogether.

Discipline and Surveillance

European observers found American children obstreperous; to English eyes French children were spoiled; the French, in their turn, found English children quite repressed and insufficiently loved. An outside observer's ironic commentary on all three cultures lies in the epithet of some Indian tribes for the white man: "a man who beats his children." And indeed, a nineteenth-century child, whether girl or boy, whether upper, middle, or lower class, could expect more physical abuse of various kinds than a child of our own

---

[10] See Sussman 1975 and 1977.

[11] The connections between these characteristics are interestingly brought out in Thompson 1967. The ways in which expectation modified discipline become evident in the chapters on the training of boys and girls in Ellis 1843: 280–361.

time. Slaps and switchings were common forms of punishment and real beating or caning not unusual. Nor can we by any means assume that lower-class
children were especially badly treated in this regard: a lower-class French
family like the Santerres could be gentle despite all the strictness of the
parents' discipline, whereas a middle-class American family like the Lovells
saw beating as a normal disciplinary measure (Docs. 3, 5). Thus, as Isabel
Hall's story shows (Doc. 8), crossing boundaries and exploring for oneself
carried strong and perfectly reasonable associations with physical danger. And
a childish ego in the nineteenth century also had much to endure in the way
of battering through verbal abuse or humiliation.

At the same time, concern for children was very much on the rise during
the nineteenth century, bringing with it among many the ability to empathize
with children's sufferings. As a result, the advisability of harsh punishment
became a matter for question, and by no means all nineteenth-century parents used such methods. But even the methods of the more moderate-minded
can be broadly characterized as "intrusive."[12] We have already noted such
intrusiveness in the stress laid on early toilet training. That homely concern,
however, is only the tip of the iceberg.

Intrusiveness motivates virtually all the nineteenth-century disciplinary
theories and their accompanying techniques, even those that may seem antithetical. For instance, in nineteenth-century America Charles Strickland
finds a dichotomy of disciplinary attitude between a rationalist theory based
on the principles of John Locke, which stressed the establishment of good
habits in the unformed child through kind but firm discipline, and a romantic
theory, given imaginative force by such literary creations as Charles Dickens's
little Nell and Harriet Beecher Stowe's little Eva, which saw the child as a
saint from whom adults should learn. Strickland's prime exemplar of the romantic approach is Bronson Alcott, whose journal on his children, begun nine
days after the birth of his first daughter, Anna (1831), and continued through
Louisa (1832) and Elizabeth (1835), states that "the child must be treated
as a *free, self-guiding, self-controlling* being" (emphasis his). Yet even if
Alcott's statement is in theory at the opposite pole from intrusiveness, his
continual *watching* of his children (and watching, or "surveillance," was the
constant stance of parents toward their daughters; see Docs. 17.i–ii, 19.ii) and
his treatment of recalcitrance with psychological manipulation make Alcott,
in Henry Ebel's good phrase, "a wrap-around father."[13]

In all three countries the relatively new child-centeredness of the nineteenth century did not mean that the child's needs or feelings were the parents'
primary concern; on the contrary, the child served as the fulfillment of parental
needs or ambitions, whether they were for higher social status or for affection.
Depending on their sex, however, children served in different ways and had,
so far as watchfulness goes, different treatment. A boy, it was believed, would

[12] The term is Lloyd de Mause's (1974).
[13] See Strickland 1973: 15; and Henry Ebel's "Commentary" on Strickland's
essay in the same journal, p. 54. See also Foucault 1977 for a discussion of the connection between surveillance and power.

be a comfort and a credit to his parents through careful early training, but his constant surveillance after a certain age was considered impracticable.[14] Not so a girl. Only by assiduous watching could her virginity—a prerequisite for a "good" marriage—and her docility—the chief characteristic of a "good" daughter—be maintained. There were, nonetheless, significant variations between the countries in the degree of surveillance believed necessary. Middle-class American girls were given more freedom to move around and even, as they grew older, to meet young men alone than their counterparts in England had. At the other extreme, French girls of the upper and middle class were watched constantly and their movements severely restricted (Docs. 19.i–ii).

Religion and Education

Closely connected with—indeed at times identical with—disciplinary training was childhood training in religious belief. It is a truism that religion was of the greatest possible importance in all three countries, particularly in the first half of the century. In France the Catholic Church re-established itself strongly after the Bourbon restoration; it was all the stronger, more militant, and more concerned for the teaching of Catholic doctrine because of its running quarrel with rationalist, anticlerical elements in the society, and well into the Third Republic it maintained its ascendancy. Meanwhile, a strong revival of evangelical belief, emphasizing adherence to the word of the Bible, a constantly self-scrutinizing conscience, and personal conversion to the teachings of Jesus, stirred both England and America deeply in the first decades of the century. But in this connection, it is important to note also that in France women were markedly more religious than men, and that in England and America matters of religious faith came through the century to be assigned to woman's "sphere."

Religious beliefs were inculcated by some form of rote learning: in France little girls and boys learned the doctrines of the Church by memorizing catechism questions and answers from their mothers and from nuns; if they were poor they were similarly drilled in the charity schools run under the Church's sponsorship. Catechism for some and the learning of passages from the Bible were the rote tasks of English and American children.

Strong, too, in all three countries was the presence of ritual. That may seem most obvious in the many religious rites of Catholic France—daily Mass for many, including children, and a yearly cycle of feast days, each with its special ceremonies—but the proper keeping of the Sabbath, so prominent a feature of evangelicalism in both England and America, was in its somber way also a highly ritual event. It is nonetheless fair to say that the strong personal component of evangelicalism gave ritual a less important role in England and America than it had in Catholic France. Since ritual involves a hierarchical "placing," a French girl may have been inclined, then, by the nature of her religious belief and practice to accept and, indeed, take pleasure in

[14] Ellis 1843: 315.

her societal position without the sort of personal questioning of goals and achievements that evangelical Protestantism tended to foster in English and American girls.

The difference in religious systems may also be related to the different degrees of surveillance considered necessary in the three countries. External authority had an important function in forming the conscience of a French girl, as Saint Thérèse of Lisieux's talk with her confessor shows (Doc. 22), and, by the same token, external wardens were set up to guard her, whereas an American or English girl was expected to develop a conscience and to heed interior admonitions that created a constant guard.

Stories are an age-old method of developing such an internal mechanism in the child, and in the first half of the century children's stories, whether by Hannah More, Lydia Maria Child, or the Comtesse de Ségur, were thumpingly moral. They tended nonetheless to lay their stress on *this* world as the arena in which good behavior is rewarded and bad punished. Hannah More's tracts (Doc. 9) served as models for American writers; in her story about Hester Wilmot, otherworldly piety makes for worldly success, or as Anne MacLeod writes, in summarizing the plot lines of such pious tales, "Good girls married well; good boys made their way successfully in business."[15]

To young children religion may well have been drab, boring, or repressive, but for many adolescent girls it became an emotional outlet and an escape from repression. A religious experience like that of Saint Thérèse, or even the more common experiences of being "born again" or formally confirmed in the faith, could change a young girl's sense of herself for life. Even those who were not susceptible to the fervent spirituality of their peers, as in Catharine Beecher's case (Doc. 21.i), formed their adult personalities in the dialectic between their feelings and the religious expectations for them of those about them.

If the importance of religion was an obsession in the first half of the nineteenth century, the importance of education became an obsession in the second half. Among many possible reasons for this increased interest, two stand out: first, the middle classes, growing quickly in number, began to see in education a means of achieving greater social mobility and thus of rising as well in prestige; and second, those with governmental power over countries in which ever larger sections of the population had a vote came to realize that education, previously feared and even repressed as a potential source of revolution, could in fact help to create a homogeneous, disciplined electorate. Neither of these reasons seems particularly relevant to young girls, since they would live as women in societies that denied them, as far as possible, entrance into the professions and refused them the vote. Be that as it may, and though many people continued to think a girl's education unimportant, some now saw it as a necessity, not for the girl's own sake, but for her future function: as a wife, she would be the chief companion of a man within a fami-

[15] MacLeod 1975: 38.

ly circle increasingly enclosed and domestic, and as a mother she would influence her sons in ways that might well mold their careers and their political opinions.

Concern for women's education, then, had somewhat new terms and a new impetus, but the rationale behind it in all three countries throughout the century was the relational one succinctly formulated by Jean-Jacques Rousseau a century earlier:

> A woman's education must therefore be planned in relation to man. To be pleasing in his sight, to win his respect and love, to train him in childhood, to tend him in manhood, to counsel and console, to make his life pleasant and happy, these are the duties of woman for all times, and this is what she should be taught when she is young.[16]

Whether she was an American slave girl denied all education lest she become sufficiently conscious of her situation to revolt against her masters (Doc. 15.i), or a working-class girl schooled as a servant or nursemaid to tend the wants of an affluent family, or a girl of the upper classes in preparation for life as an ornament, household manager, and mother in her husband's domestic circle—whatever a girl's imagined future situation, her function was seen as relational, and the education offered her of the sort deemed appropriate for that function. The fulfillment of personal needs or even the expression of personal talent was, for most of those considering these matters, of scarcely any consequence at all. Yet within those parameters, a dedicated few worked to *use* relational theories and the systems resulting from them in order to achieve a wider personal scope for women. In this endeavor they were helped by the fact that the dominant social theorists themselves were somewhat bewildered and divided even as they tried to fulfill their relational purposes. Bonnie Smith describes such theorists in France as walking a tightrope as they tried in a rapidly changing society to meet their own aspirations for "a more *au courant* woman without bringing her into rebellion against her restricted life."[17] Her insight has application to America and England as well. Yet we should realize that the same tightrope-walking act was required of those who searched for a way to see their societies' expectations for women fulfilled (which amounted to seeing them happily in their place) and at the same time hoped for the virtually subversive achievement of personal destiny for women through educational opportunity.[18]

In America, after the institution of "common" schools for boys and girls in the early 1800's in the East (Doc. 12), state-funded coeducation spread comparatively rapidly—first to the lower grades (1830's) and then through the secondary grades (1850's). Meanwhile, the opening up of the West brought a demand for teachers that men, having more lucrative chances available, were unwilling to fill. Catharine Beecher used this situation to suggest that young women would make the country's best (i.e., cheapest) teachers.

---

[16] *Émile*, chap. 1. The translation is Barbara Foxley's (London, 1974; p. 9).
[17] B. G. Smith 1975: 53.
[18] For a fine discussion of these conflicts, see Delamont 1978: 134–63.

Educational institutions were established to prepare them for this work, offering the possibility of some higher education. "Seminaries" they were called, for these young women were to be missionaries with a religious but also a decidedly socializing function. The years before the Civil War saw a few colleges founded for women as well, but it was in the postbellum years that educational opportunities for women on all levels grew most rapidly. By 1890 twice as many girls as boys graduated from high school, and there were numerous colleges open to them, state coeducational and private women's schools alike.

At the time women's education was beginning to make this leap forward in America, the question had only reached the talking stage in England. Indeed, the wording of an 1864 memorandum commissioning an investigation of middle-class schools left so obscure the question of whether girls' schools were to be included that the feminist and educator Emily Davies approached Matthew Arnold in his capacity as school inspector, asking his help in getting a clarification. His reply was that the new commission would almost surely be too busy to investigate girls' schools as well as boys'.[19] Happily, as it turned out, Arnold was wrong (Doc. 14), but it gives one pause that the apostle of Culture had not even thought of extending to girls and women the blessings of education's "sweetness and light."

Only after the commission's work culminated in the Education Act of 1870 was there the beginning of a state elementary school system in England. During the rest of the century it grew steadily, as did the opportunities for girls' secondary education. Under the direction of women like Frances Buss (Doc. 14), middle- and upper-class girls, though generally not educated with boys, were receiving an education equivalent to that of their male counterparts by the end of the century. In the same period Barbara Bodichon and others began the long process, lasting into the twentieth century, by which university degrees would become possible for women.

In France changes in girls' education began even later than in England. Through the first part of the century poor girls in the cities had received a highly structured and strongly disciplined coeducation in the *salles d'asiles*, the schools run by private charitable organizations closely tied to the Church. In 1837, 800 of these schools provided for 23,000 children. In barracks-like structures, with 200 or even 400 children in a room, the pupils were packed in rows on benches (tables were introduced only in 1881) and drilled in catechism, reading, and arithmetic. By the end of the century, however, these schools, now under state control, had improved a great deal, thanks to the guidance of the reformer Pauline Kergomard.

French middle-class girls, meanwhile, were often, though not always, educated at home until early adolescence (Doc. 58.ii), then sent to a convent or (for the minority) a private, nonsectarian school. There, constantly surveyed within a rigid schedule, they received a great deal of religious training and, ideally, learned skills of domestic management—with less emphasis on

[19] Kamm 1965: 200.

"accomplishments" than in England and thus more preparation, at least in practical if not in sexual matters, for marriage.[20] Republican anticlerical forces in France, as they began to gain power toward the end of the Second Empire, were moved to change these educational systems, both for the poor and for the middle class, not so much out of concern for women's education as out of resentment and the suspicion (quite justified in their terms) that in their indoctrinating role these systems obviously strengthened the Church. Beginning in the late 1860's supplementary courses were offered in the boys' *lycées* for teen-aged girls; by 1880 education was free and compulsory at the elementary level and available either by scholarship or by the payment of fees at the secondary level. At the new state *lycées* girls, educated separately from boys, received courses in a wide range of subjects, including science and mathematics, but *not* including the classical languages required for entrance to a university. The convent schools, meanwhile, stung by anticlericalist gibes on the poverty of their curriculum, made analogous and even parallel changes in their offerings (Doc. 10.ii).

As even this briefest of descriptions makes clear, the changes that took place in the education of girls would never have occurred had those with political power in each of the three nations not considered such changes productive and even necessary. Still, this belief in the social utility of education for women was balanced by a concern that they might turn their increased productivity to personal ends, thus in some way detracting from what was taken to be their primary social function: reproduction. The century's biological myths reflect this concern.

Puberty: Fears and Myths

The description of women's increasing educational opportunities in all three countries has moved quickly to the relatively happy ending of what was actually a long and not always happy story. Providing anything but the most basic education to girls met with considerable opposition, whose nature, grounds, and extent need closer analysis. Although educational institutions in the three countries were very different, the arguments against giving girls an education as demanding and eventually profitable as that of boys were surprisingly, even suspiciously, congruent. As in earlier centuries, many felt no compunction about scoffing at women's pretensions to learning. The classic work with that theme, Molière's *Les Précieuses Ridicules* (1659), continued to be very influential in France, and Tennyson's *The Princess* (1849), whose theme was interpreted on similar terms whatever its author's intentions, was a school text in both England and America. But though the bogey that scholarliness was unladylike was raised against both young women and their teachers in all three countries in the nineteenth century, the opposition's strongest argument was grounded not so much in social contempt as in a tenderhearted, if somewhat prurient, concern.

[20] Because they were not subject to state inspection or control, the deficiency of these schools is difficult to judge. It is Bonnie Smith's opinion (1975: 29) that the Lille convents fulfilled their practical if limited objectives.

The difficulty lay with young girls' bodies. Menstruation was seen as a perilous function, one that was essential, because it cleared poisons from the blood, but was also chancy, because the female reproductive system—imagined, significantly, as "an engine within an engine"[21]—was a fearsomely complex structure that had to be carefully regulated and constantly, intrusively watched (Docs. 17.ii, 18). The flow was to begin neither too early (a sign of excessive sexuality, probably masturbation, and a diet larded with the red meats and spices that were inappropriate for a young girl) nor too late (a sign of an overstimulated mind draining energy from the reproductive organs). The "right" time was between fourteen and eighteen, and fifteen or sixteen the ideal.[22] Country girls, whose age for menarche established what was taken to be the wholesome norm, in fact often suffered from dietary insufficiencies, as did girls among the urban poor. Ironically, daughters of the affluent were almost as deprived, kept for their supposed health's sake on bland, protein-deficient food though better fare was available. Constantly asserted, with gruesome anecdotes as proof, was the life-or-death importance of a careful regimen. Transgression could bring disaster (Doc. 18).

These theories, first promulgated by highly influential French doctors like Marc Colombat, were shared by their American and British colleagues. They reached wide public expression through the American doctor Edward H. Clarke, who in 1873, the year Harvard University allowed women to take its entrance exams (without thereby qualifying, however, for a Harvard degree), published Sex in Education to express his concern over the trend he saw developing. His book was enthusiastically reviewed in England by a fellow doctor, Henry Maudsley. On both sides of the Atlantic those involved in the struggle to get higher education for women had to answer these arguments, hampered by the fact that for a lady this topic, so obsessively central to Victorian thinking about young girls, was hardly discussable, much less printable. Moreover, even those who wanted to educate the female mind tended to subscribe to a belief in the fragility of the female body.[23]

The topic, rarely mentioned save through euphemisms and almost never appearing in literary works, cramped and confined every aspect of a young girl's life, just as at menarche she was cramped by a tight corset and long, heavy skirts—which, as sensible women tried to point out, were much more likely to cause an uncomfortable menses than interesting and invigorating studies would. It is not surprising that middle-class girls, watched so closely, yet (given the taboo nature of the subject) with so much unspoken tension, were commonly afflicted with neurasthenia, hysteria, and chlorosis (or green-sickness), ailments that were present for different reasons in the working class as well (Docs. 23.i–ii). Not surprising either is the fact that tuberculosis,

[21] The phrase is Edward H. Clarke's (1889: 59).
[22] Hall 1904: 472–79 summarizes theories about the "right" age and gives tables. See also Laslett 1973: 44.
[23] Clarke's arguments were rebutted nonetheless by Julia Ward Howe and others; see Howe 1874. In England Maudsley's article in Fortnightly Review recapitulating Clarke's arguments (vol. 21, 1874: 466–83) was answered in the following issue by Elizabeth Garrett Anderson.

which often found its victims among those weakened by poor diet, lack of exercise, and nervous tension, yearly accounted for about half the deaths among women aged fifteen to thirty-five in mid-Victorian England. (Doc. 24).[24]

This concern about the menstrual cycle did not extend itself to the working-class girl, whose services as domestic, factory worker, or farm laborer the society found exceedingly useful. She was not endangered, according to Clarke, because she did not go to work until after the menses were well established, and neither at that critical time nor later did she impair or aggravate her flow by brain work.

But it was not only intellectuality in young girls that could endanger their reproductive function. Sexuality was also seen as a threat. Nor, given the nature of the Victorians' priorities, was their attitude as irrational as it might at first seem. A strong factor in sexuality is its personal élan, a desire for joys that have no necessary connection at all with social utility and may indeed be socially disruptive. Just as Victorian society wanted to give a young woman educational experience but not the experience of being an educated person, so it wanted her to have (on the permitted marital basis and for reproductive purposes) sexual experience but not the experience of being a sexual person. Of course, the distrust of sexuality as asocial extended to young men as well, but the nature of masculine sexuality made the simple denial of its existence —the preferred strategy for girls and women—virtually impossible in the case of boys.

Perhaps connected with this ambition to discipline all sexual expression into pure reproduction—with both senses of "pure"—was the Victorian belief that masturbation was a dangerous practice leading to a spectrum of physically horrible diseases and ultimately to insanity. Boys suffered as much as or more than girls from the methods with which the practice was "cured." Psychological terrorizing and the binding or chaining of the "culprit's" hands were among the milder remedies. For boys there were also devices, castrative morally and certainly dangerous physically, that held the penis with sharp points and dug in bitingly if it became erect. The analogously extreme technique for girls was clitoridectomy, introduced in 1858 in England by Dr. Isaac Baker Brown and much practiced by him for ten years after that. In 1867 he was expelled from the Obstetrical Society, and clitoridectomy, one takes it, was no longer performed or went "underground" in England. It remained a not uncommon treatment in the United States into the twentieth century and was practiced to some extent in France as well.

Clitoridectomy is the nadir among the devices and techniques whereby the Victorian girl was socialized into the attitudes that her society thought appropriate to her position, but every aspect of her life—the clothes she wore, the food she was given to eat, the religious instruction she received, the education she was allowed, the medical treatment considered necessary for her— was directed toward a similarly positional end. How is it, then, that as we read

<hr>

[24] Johansson 1977: 169.

the documents of this section we hear the voices of such highly distinctive and strong personalities? Charlotte Brontë, Catharine Beecher, and Saint Thérèse, among many others, lived even as young girls with an intense feeling for the significance of their personal destiny and a concern for its fulfillment. How did the nineteenth century's relational theories about women have the practical effect of creating such individualists?

A possible answer to the seeming paradox may lie in the very intrusiveness from which the Victorian girl suffered, whether from her own parents or guardians or from the many professional and semiprofessional advisers with their prescriptive theories about her behavior. Their concern was to mold her to society's and her family's purposes, but the effect of that concern was, at least in part, to instill in her a belief in her own intrinsic significance. The evidence suggests that she saw herself as *interesting,* and so for that matter did the society as a whole, if one is to judge by its literature. The "primary question" that came to Henry James about Isabel Archer, his heroine in *Portrait of a Lady,* "Well, what will she *do?*"[25] lies behind the plots of any number of other Victorian novels as well. And "What will I *do?*" is the question one also hears underneath the other concerns that the documents of this section delineate.

[25] Henry James, Preface to *Portrait of a Lady.*

Documents 1-24

1. Announcing the female child

The French peasants of the Franche-Comté believed that it was bad luck for a household if an owl hooted upon the chimney, for it meant that someone would soon die—or that a daughter would be born. Although most blatantly expressed in peasant custom, this negative attitude toward girl babies was widespread in the nineteenth century, as the following selections reveal. If the Victorian girl child was not, in consequence, fed last and worked hardest, she nevertheless experienced the emotional impact of this secondary status.

The following selections show how female children were received in the nineteenth century. In the first selection the American feminist Elizabeth Cady Stanton (1815–1902) recalls the compassion she felt at the age of four for her newborn sister, an unwelcome girl. The second selection, by the French writer Ernest Legouvé (1807–1903), describes how daughters were received at birth by Breton peasants. In the third selection Frances Marion Eddy (1862–1956), a Michigan minister's daughter, writes in her memoirs about her mother's disappointment at her birth. Mémé Santerre (b. 1891), a French linen weaver's daughter, reports that she, too, had been an unwanted girl. The second four selections show how adult women dealt with the cul-

SOURCES: (i) Elizabeth Cady Stanton, *Eighty Years and More: Reminiscences, 1815–1897* (New York, 1898), p. 4. (ii) Ernest Legouvé, *Histoire morale des femmes* (Paris, 1849), p. 19. (iii) Frances Marion Eddy, unpublished reminiscences. The editors are indebted to the family of Frances Marion Eddy for permission to publish excerpts from these reminiscences. (iv) Serge Grafteaux, *Mémé Santerre* (Paris, 1975), p. 9. The editors wish to thank Professor Louise Tilly, University of Michigan, for making this document available to us. (v) Delphine Gay de Girardin, "La Fête de Noël," in *Oeuvres complètes de Madame Emile de Girardin* (Paris, 1861), pp. 361–62. (vi) Caroline Clive, *From the Diary and Family Papers of Mrs. Archer Clive*, ed. Mary Clive (London, 1949), pp. 167–68. (vii) Helen Smith Jordan, *Love Lies Bleeding* (Syracuse, N.Y., 1979), p. 370. The editors are grateful to Mrs. Jordan for giving us permission to publish excerpts from this privately printed book and to Henry Chaffee Abell, Inchelium, Wash., for permission to publish the family letters cited here and in Docs. 4 and 66. (viii) Letter from Mary Hallock Foote to Helena de Kay Gilder, May [23], 1877, Mary Hallock Foote Papers, Special Collections, Green Library, Stanford University. The editors wish to thank Professor Carroll Smith-Rosenberg, University of Pennsylvania, for directing us to this letter.

tural preference for boys. The first, a poem by the childless French writer Delphine Gay de Girardin (1804–55), tells of her intense longing to bear a baby, which for her meant a son. In contrast, Caroline Clive (1801–73), a British novelist and minister's wife, rejoices at the birth of a daughter. In the third selection Mary Chaffee Abell (1846–75), a Kansas homesteader, writes indignantly to her mother about a neighboring farmer's preference for sons. Finally, Mary Hallock Foote (1847–1938) expresses her gratitude that her new baby is a boy because he will escape the suffering to which women are prone.

(i) Elizabeth Cady Stanton

The first event engraved on my memory was the birth of a sister when I was four years old. It was a cold morning in January when the brawny Scotch nurse carried me to see the little stranger, whose advent was a matter of intense interest to me for many weeks after. The large, pleasant room with the white curtains and bright wood fire on the hearth, where panada, catnip, and all kinds of little messes which we were allowed to taste were kept warm, was the center of attraction for the older children. I heard so many friends remark, "What a pity it is she's a girl!" that I felt a kind of compassion for the little baby. True, our family consisted of five girls and only one boy, but I did not understand at that time that girls were considered an inferior order of beings.

(ii) Ernest Legouvé

Ask such a peasant about his family, he will reply, "I have no children, sir; I have only daughters." The Breton farmer whose wife has brought a daughter into the world still says to this day [1849], "My wife has had a miscarriage."

(iii) Frances Marion Eddy

I was, for one, an unwanted postscript that was added nine years after the birth of my immediate predecessor, Cora Virginia. I write the word "unwanted" advisedly, for my mother, years later after she became an invalid, confessed that she was "most unhappy" over the prospect of me but "hoped for the best" which for her, I divined, meant another boy.

(iv) Mémé Santerre

For the moment, I was a nursling who needed a name. . . . Mama, who was very disappointed in another daughter, the eleventh, cried a lot. My older brother consoled her. "Mother," said he, "she will be your cane in your old age."

(v) Delphine Gay de Girardin

"Noël"

This is the day that Mary
Gave birth to our Savior.
This is the day I pray

With ever more fervor.
This day my soul fights off
A pain that drives me wild.
Oh Mary, I'm a wife,
A wife without a child.

. . .

Please bless my humble tears;
I offer thee this vow:
The gold of all my jewels,
The gold above my brow.
The choicest of my crowns,
They shall all be thine,
If ever I receive
A son, an angel, mine.

(vi) The Clives

[Caroline writing, Oct. 29, 1843]
At a quarter before nine a little girl was born. I was beside myself when
I saw her and heard her loud crying. It is a bewildering thing to see a human
being, one's own child, where just before there was nothing, and I cried out
alternately, "My child, thank God, my child, thank God, thank God."
[Archer writing, Nov. 5, 1843]
I desire to record my hearty thanks to Almighty God for the prosperous
confinement of my dear wife and the birth of a daughter in my house. Caroline recovers fast and the child is quite healthy. . . . Caroline is delighted with
her baby.

(vii) Mary Chaffee Abell

Sarah North has a boy now five weeks old. I suppose Thomas is glad.
Chester told us before the family—that "It would have been a great disappointment to Thomas if it had been a girl." "Ahem!"

(viii) Mary Hallock Foote

I am glad baby is a boy for he will suffer in a different (less hopeless,
perhaps, since it is fate) way than women suffer. Certain things come as an
inheritance to women. A man *may* escape pain—a woman is prone to it as the
sparks fly upward.

2. Childhood on a rural French estate: Athénaïs Mialaret Michelet

*Athénaïs Mialaret (1828–99) spent her childhood on a large farm near
Montauban (Tarn and Garonne) in southern France. In these excerpts from*

SOURCE: Mme Jules Michelet, *The Story of My Childhood*, tr. Mary Frazier
Curtis (Boston, 1867), pp. 1–4, 9–11, 13–14, 16–18, 20–22, 25–30, 43. Originally
published in Paris in 1867. The editors wish to thank Barbara Corrado Pope, University of Oregon, Eugene, for bringing these memoirs to our attention.

her autobiography, published when she was thirty-nine years old, she describes her austere girlhood doing needlework and supervising a younger brother who was favored by parents and servants alike. At the time she wrote this work, she was the second, and deeply beloved, wife of the historian Jules Michelet, to whom she was thirty years junior.

Among my earliest recollections, dating (if my memory deceive me not) from the time when I was between the ages of four and five, is that of being seated beside a grave, industrious person, who seemed to be constantly watching me. Her beautiful but stern countenance impressed one chiefly by the peculiar expression of the light-blue eyes, so rare in Southern Europe. Their gaze was like that which has looked in youth across vast plains, wide horizons, and great rivers.

This lady was my mother, born in Louisiana, of English parentage. After her marriage, she had been transplanted from the shores of the Mississippi to Montauban. At the time of my birth, she had suffered from a fright, caused by an alarm of fire, and was, in consequence, unable to give me nourishment. I was put out to nurse with a good woman, who lived in the country.

My parents already had two children, older than myself. Both were born in America, and, for that reason, were all the dearer to my mother. My sister was six years older than I; my brother, three. These lovely children would, perhaps, have proved to be all-sufficient to their mother's happiness. I came into the world unwished-for; and no haste was shown to reclaim me from my nurse: I remained with her until I was four years old. During that long interval, two boys were born: each had been left a short time with nurses who proved to be unfaithful, and had soon been taken home again. Our house was already full, when my parents recollected me, and I was sent for.

Infant as I was, seated on my little chair, I had my task. To work was the only game I knew in my childhood. I learned sewing and knitting, and was soon able to hem my own chemises. I was forced to sew under my mother's eye; and I was more clumsy when I knew that I was observed. Often was I made to pick out what I had done. Sewing, therefore, ceased to amuse me. But I liked to knit: the rapid play of the needles was so pretty; and then, with my little stocking in my hands, I could wander about at liberty.

But I never went very far: the end of our garden alley was the permitted limit. Even the view was much restricted. The hedges round the place shut in the horizon; and the house was shaded by fruit-trees. I pined for my former freedom in the farmyard,—for the merry voice of my foster-sister, Susan; above all, for my affectionate nurse. They all spoiled me there, and treated me like a *princess*, which title I still retained at home.

Nurse loved me dearly: whenever she came to see me, she would talk of that happy time, and say, "The sun itself was not bright enough *then* for my darling." And what a change now!—not to mention the parting from the pets, and all the animals I loved; the good cow,—my second nurse; the gentle, docile donkey.

I had constant toil before me, strangely unbroken for so young a child. At six years of age, I knit my own stockings, by and by my brothers' also, walking up and down the shady path. I did not care to go further: I was uneasy if, when I turned, I could not see the green blind at my mother's window.

Our lowly house had an easterly aspect. At its north-east corner, my mother sat at work, with her little people around her: my father had his study at the opposite end, towards the south. I began to pick up my alphabet with him; for I had double tasks. I studied my books in the intervals of sewing or knitting. My brothers ran away to play after lessons; but I returned to my mother's work-room. I liked very well, however, to trace on my slate the great bars which are called "jambages." It seemed to me as if I drew something, from within myself, which came to the pencil's point. When my bars began to look regular, I paused often to admire what I had done; then, if my dear papa would lean towards me, and say, "Very well, little princess," I drew myself up with pride. . . .

My sedentary life began about this time; and I took up my labors at sewing, as soon as my school hours were over. I was not of a turbulent nature, in spite of the freedom in which I had been nursed, which seemed to have given me something of the robust and passionate temperament of the peasants who dwell by the Aveyron. Far from being disobedient, I desired to please, to be praised, and to be loved. I felt so drawn towards my mother, that I sometimes jumped from my seat to give her a kiss; but when I met her look, and saw her eyes, pale and clear as a silvery lake, I recoiled, and sat down quietly. Years have passed, and yet I still regret those joys of childhood which I never knew, —a mother's caresses. My education might have been so easy; my mother might have understood my heart,—a kiss is sometimes eloquent; and in a daily embrace she would perhaps have guessed the thoughts I was too young to utter, and would have learned how faithfully I loved her.

No such freedom was allowed us. The morning kiss and familiar speech with one's parents are permitted at the north, but are less frequent in the south of France. Authority overshadows family affection. My father, who was an easy man and loved to talk, might have disregarded such regulations; but my mother kept us at a distance. It made one thoughtful and reserved to watch her going out and coming in, with her noble air, severe and silent. We felt we must be careful not to give cause for blame. She was order itself, and so industrious. She had an English bearing, a fine presence; and, having been left an orphan early, and mistress of the house from eight years of age, she was accustomed to command, and to require exact obedience. She loved uninter-rupted labor and mute docility. . . .

The younger children were not admitted to the family table,—an honor reserved for the two elder ones. As for us, we were made to sit in a circle around one of the servants, who administered a mouthful to each in turn. Any one could see that Janille favored my brothers. Marianne, on the contrary, was very good to me. She would sometimes take me in her lap; but her un-failing favors were for my elder brother, without whom she could not live. Twice she was dismissed from our service, and twice she came back, suppli-cating to be allowed to stay where she could hear every morning the voice of her beloved tyrant. . . .

I had nothing to do with the housekeeping. My sister, who had no rural tastes, kept all her energies within the four walls of the house. She was by nature a housewife. It is due to her to say, that she managed all things with admirable order. There was but one failing,—things that had been once folded, and put away, could not be meddled with by anybody. Everybody's wardrobe was in the hands of this austere guardian. My little fineries for great occasions, when friends or relatives were invited to dinner, were always under lock and key; and I was ignorant, an hour beforehand, as to what toilette would come out from the closet for me. Having nothing of my own to take care of, I did not know what to do with my feminine instincts. As no one seemed to expect me to do any thing, I finally believed in my own insignificance.

My mother could spin like a fairy. All winter she sat at her wheel; and perhaps her wandering thoughts were soothed by the gentle, monotonous music of its humming. Her fine, smooth thread made our handkerchiefs and our chemises. My father, seeing her so beautiful at her work, secretly ordered a light, slender spinning-wheel to be carved for her use, which she found one morning at the foot of her bed. Her cheek flushed with pleasure; she scarcely dared to touch it, it looked so fragile. "Do not be afraid, dear Miss Emma," said my father; "it looks fragile, but it can well stand use. It is made of boxwood from our own garden. It grew slowly, as all things do that last. Neither your little hand nor foot can injure it." My mother took her finest Flanders flax, of silvery tresses knotted with a cherry-colored ribbon. The children made a circle round the wheel, which turned for the first time under my mother's hands. . . .

The clumsy rustic one, which she discarded, was claimed by my sister, who talked of making sheets. I dreamed of towels, and was allowed to try what I could do with some *tow*; but the bunches were thick and short, they tried to pass through all at a time, the wheel wouldn't wait for them, the bobbin wouldn't come, and it was decided on the spot that I could never make any thing finer than a rope.

Now came a great event in the family. The good woman who had been my nurse brought home to us a little brother, who was given into my charge. He knew no other language than that which he had learned from the peasants, and we had opportunities to talk *patois* together; for the little fellow loved to run away to the farm, where the farmer's wife reminded him of his dear nurse. Then I had a chance to go and fetch him; but I was forbidden to stay, as my parents very properly thought that my rusticity was sufficiently marked without my learning more of the dialect of the country. . . .

After comedy came tragedy. With all my care as nurse or sentinel, the little boy escaped from me too often. He seemed to have the notion, that, like his elder brothers, he would never obey *a girl*. . . .

He took it into his head, therefore, to go alone one morning to the pond. At ten paces from the shore, he came to one of the re-frozen openings: it broke, and he fell through. Did he call for help? did he struggle in the cold water? Nobody knows. When at last I ran that way to look for him, I saw him still upright in the well, but his head drooping on one side; and he seemed but half alive. I rushed towards him, and took him in my arms; but his weight, with the water dripping from his garments, and my useless efforts to move him, only broke a wider hole in the ice. In my anguish I uttered so loud a cry, that the farmer's wife came out. Her steady hand soon brought us to the shore; but my poor little Pichon gave no signs of life. The good, kind woman said, "Don't go to the house, miss: you will be severely punished. Come to my room, and we'll soon make baby warm again."

He was undressed, and made to swallow hot wine; no easy matter, for he was unconscious, and his limbs were stiffened. We warmed a great bed, which was so high I had to climb on a trunk to see it. When the woman put him in it, I was very sad; for I fancied that he would never come out of it alive. I watched his face; but in the obscure room, under the green-serge curtains, it looked strangely livid. I wanted to take him in my arms, to talk to him, beg him to open his eyes; but was only allowed to look at him. I suffered tortures of apprehension. At last he sighed, opened his eyes, and spoke to us. The farmer's wife laughed, she kissed and scolded us; but I could not enjoy the revulsion of feeling: distress had pained me too much. I shed floods of tears; and, long after, the impression haunted me. I was anxious and troubled, and was sensitive to every little accident that seemed to cast reproach on my maternal care.

If there had been no other boys in the house, Pichon might have been submissive to me; and he would have been happy by my side. I reflected on this, and at last came to think it would, after all, have been a pity. He would never grow to be a man; he would have less vigor, less force and courage, than he has now. It is the sister's part to suffer and to yield. I was not so resigned at six years of age, nor at seven; but was grieved to see the child, still in petticoats, escaping from my hands, and running to join his big brothers, trying to follow their lead, and to join in their rough sports. . . .

"Why did my mother choose three boys, rather than three girls, after I was born?" This problem was often in my mind. Boys only tear blouses, which they don't know how to mend. If she had only thought how happy I should be with a sister, a dear little sister! How I would have loved her,—scolded her sometimes, but kissed her very often! We should have had our work and play together, thoroughly independent of all those gentlemen,—our brothers.

My elder sister was too far from my age. There seemed to be centuries between us. I never remember seeing her at the study table. She was a young Creole, absorbed in her house and her needlework. Books tired her very much; and my father unwillingly abandoned her education to my mother. . . .

I became very thoughtful, and said to myself, "How shall I get a companion? and how do people make dolls?" It did not occur to me, who had never seen a toy-shop, that they could be purchased ready-made. I inclined to believe that mothers taught their daughters how to make them,—that, in fact, they made their own. I fancied, that, after making a great many dolls, my mother had fabricated her own little children. But how did she begin, and what was her first attempt like? I wished to know, but had not the courage to ask her. Pre-occupied and troubled, I saw no way out of the difficulty. My chin resting on my hand, I sat in meditation, wondering how I could create what I desired. My passionate desire overruled my fears, and I decided to work from my own inspiration.

I rejected wood, as too hard to afford the proper material for my dolly. Clay, so moist and cold, chilled the warmth of my invention. I took some soft, white linen, and some clean bran, and with them formed the body. I was like the savages, who desire a little god to worship. It must have a head with eyes, and with ears to listen; and it must have a breast, to hold its heart. All the rest is less important, and remains undefined.

I worked after this fashion, and rounded my doll's head, by tying it firmly. There was a clearly perceptible neck,—a little stiff, perhaps; a well-developed chest; and then came vague drapery, which dispensed with limbs. There were rudiments of arms,—not very graceful, but movable: indeed, they moved of themselves. I was filled with admiration. Why might not the body move? I had read how God breathed upon Adam and Eve the breath of life: with my whole heart, and my six years' strength, I breathed on the creature I had made. I looked; she did not stir. Never mind; I was her mother, and she loved me: that was enough. The dangers that menaced our mutual affection only served to increase it. She gave me anxiety from the moment of her birth. How and where could I keep her in safety? Surrounded by mischievous boys, sworn enemies to their sisters' dolls, I was obliged to hide mine in a dark corner of a shed, where the wagons and carriages were kept. It was winter time, and our meetings were precarious and rare. Her solitude made her dearer to me; and I had a more lively joy in her than if I had not been restricted to secret and mysterious interviews. But there were some occasions when I felt an absolute need to have her near me, as when a sad night closed a day of penitence. After being punished, I could conceive no consolation equal to taking my child to bed with me. When I drew her shivering from her miserable hiding-place, I would burst into tears, and cover her with kisses. To warm her, I tucked her into my little bed, with the friendly pussy who was keeping it warm for me. At bedtime, I laid her on my heart, still heaving with sobs; and she seemed to sigh too. If I missed her in the night, I became wide awake; I hunted for her, full of apprehension. Often she was quite at the bottom of the bed. I brought her out, folded her in my arms, and fell happily asleep.

You laugh at this; but you are wrong. If I had had any other friend, this one would have been less to me. I might have kissed and nursed her, but without deceiving myself as to her qualities. As it was, I liked, in my extreme loneliness, to believe that she had a living soul. Her grandparents were not aware of her existence. Would she have been so thoroughly my own, if other people had known her? I loved better to hide her from all eyes. When we were alone in the garden, we held endless dialogues. I scolded her a little; but I never punished her. To send her early to bed; to feed her with dry bread; or, worse still, to strike her little tender body,—seemed to be too cruel: it would have been punishment to myself to do it. . . .

One thing was wanting to my satisfaction. My doll had a head, but no face. I desired to look into her eyes, to see a smile on her countenance that should resemble mine. . . .

Then I made an heroic resolution,—to ask my brother's assistance boldly. The temptation was strong, indeed, which led me to brave the malice of so many imps. I stepped forward, and, with a voice which I vainly endeavored to steady, I said, "Would you be so kind as to make a face for my doll?" My eldest brother seemed not at all surprised, but took the doll in his hands with great gravity, and examined it; then, with apparent care, chose a brush. Suddenly he drew across her countenance two broad stripes of red and black, something like a cross; and gave me back my poor little doll, with a burst of laughter. The soft linen absorbed the colors, which ran together in a great blot. It was very dreadful. Great cries followed; everybody crowded around to see this wonderful work. Then a cousin of ours, who was passing Sunday with us, seized my treasure, and tossed it up to the ceiling. It fell flat on the floor; I picked it up; and, if the bad boy had not taken flight, he would have suffered, very likely, from my resentment.

Sad days were in store for us. My child and I were watched in all our interviews. Often was she dragged from her hiding-places among the bushes and in the high grass. Everybody made war upon her,—even Zizi, the cat, who shared her nightly couch. My brothers sometimes gave the doll to Zizi as a plaything; and, in my absence, even she was not sorry to claw it, and roll it about on the garden walks. When I next found it, it was a shapeless bunch of dusty rags. With the constancy of a great affection, I remade again and again the beloved being predestined to destruction; and each time I pondered how to create something more beautiful. This aiming at perfection seemed to calm my grief. I made a better form, and produced symmetrical legs (once, to my surprise, the rudiment of a foot appeared); but the better my work was, the more bitter the ridicule, and I began to be discouraged. . . .

Hope revived at Christmas time. I had heard it said that old Father Christmas came down the chimney by night, and left presents for little children. I remembered this when the time came, and set my little wooden shoe in the chimney corner of an unoccupied chamber; and in the *sabot* I placed my dolly, to give the good man a hint of my wishes. I desired that she might be gifted with beauty, and be at last the child I had dreamed of. On Christmas morning, regardless of the excessive cold, I ran to the lonely room, and found there only my daughter just as I had left her. She was almost frozen, however, and seemed to reproach me for what I had done; so I popped her quickly into my warm bed. . . .

A real sorrow turned my attention within to a greater degree than ever. After much searching, my unlucky doll was discovered. Its limbs were torn off without mercy; and the body, being tossed up into an acacia-tree, was stuck on the thorns. It was impossible to bring it down. The victim hung, abandoned to the autumnal gales, to the wintry tempests, to the westerly rains, and to the northern snows. I watched her faithfully, believing that the time would come when she would revisit this earth.

In the spring, the gardener came to prune the trees. With tears in my my eyes, I said, "Bring me back my doll from those branches." He found only a fragment of her poor little dress, torn and faded. The sight almost broke my heart.

All hope being gone, I became more sensitive to the rough treatment and the malice of Jacques [a schoolmate of her older brother] and my brothers; and I fell into a sort of despair. After my life with *her* whom I had lost; after my emotions, my secret joys and fears,—I felt all the desolation of my bereavement, and regretted even the anxieties and vicissitudes which had animated and supported me. I longed for wings to fly away. When my sister excluded me from her sports with her companions, I climbed into the swing, and said to the gardener, "Jean, swing me high—higher yet: I wish to fly away." But I was soon frightened enough to beg for mercy. . . .

I would have been a bird, if a good fairy had taken pity on me. Birds are so free, so happy, they sing all day long. If I were a bird, I would come and fly about our woods, and would perch on the roof of our house. I would come to see my empty chair, my place at table, and my mother looking sadly; then, at my father's hour for reading, alone in the garden, I would fly, and perch on his shoulder. My father would know me at once.

3. An American Quaker disciplines her daughter: Lucy Buffum Lovell

Lucy Buffum (1809–95), daughter of a Rhode Island Quaker abolitionist, married Nehemiah Lovell, a Baptist minister, in 1835. In the ten years of their marriage, Lucy bore seven babies, of whom only three lived. As a widow, she supported herself and her children by running a school in Fall River, Massachusetts. In this selection from her diary, Lucy describes the training of her first child, Caroline (b. 1837), and her concern about whether this daughter had died repentant. This episode of filial disobedience occurred when Caroline was only four years old; she died at the age of five.

Caroline was generally obedient and easily governed, but there seemed to be a nervous impetuosity in her nature that sometimes led her into disobedience. For example, if she was jumping over a cricket and I said, "Caroline, don't jump over it again," she would in an instant be over. The impulse seemed to have been given and her quick and active temperament nerved for the effort, and the prohibition was unheeded. But she was always sorry, and I made allowance for her peculiar temperament, which to a stranger might appear like indulgence. We never but once, except in the first instance, were obliged to correct her for refusing to do what was required of her. In all other cases it was for this impulsive kind of disobedience. We wished to train her

SOURCE: *Two Quaker Sisters: From the Original Diaries of Elizabeth Buffum Chace and Lucy Buffum Lovell* (New York, 1937), pp. 84–89.

to a habit of implicit compliance with our directions, and on this account we frequently had occasion to correct her in such a way as we thought would best promote this object.

One day I was sitting in the parlor with the dear babe in my arms and Caroline was playing in the sitting room adjoining. I perceived she had taken the shovel and was drawing the ashes out of the fire-place upon the hearth. I spoke to her and told her to come to me. But being very busy she continued a few minutes at work with the shovel. I rose and went towards her, and she seeing me, started at the same time to come to me. I felt afraid that I had been too lenient with her in former instances of disobedience, and thought I must now do something that would make an abiding impression upon her mind. I took her into another room and expressed to her my regret on account of her disobedience, and told her that I would have to whip her now as she had disobeyed in the same way several times and I feared she would again. At the same time I endeavored to show her how wrong it was for her not to come when I first spoke to her. She seemed very penitent, and as she always dreaded that mode of punishment very much, more I think than any other child I ever saw, she entreated me not to inflict it, saying she would try to re-member and obey *immediately* in the future. I considered her request and told her I would excuse her if she thought she should remember. As she never liked to have any one see her when she had been crying, I told her she might stay in that room until she had dried her tears so that she could look pleasant and then she might come out.

She got up into a chair by the window and I left her. After waiting some time, expecting she would come, and hearing nothing from her, I went to the room to inquire the cause of her staying so long. As I opened the door she came toward me with a sweet subdued look and taking my hand said in a low voice, "Mother, I think you better whip me. I am afraid I shan't remember." I cannot describe the feelings of that moment. To see that delicate little crea-ture, whose dread of physical suffering, and especially of this kind of suffering, was so great that her language when she had transgressed was frequently, "O, don't have to whip me," or, "O, don't have to whip me hard!" to see her re-questing me to do it was a trial to my feelings such as I had never anticipated, and was not prepared for. I told her I hoped she would remember, I did not love to punish her unless it was necessary. "O no!" said she sorrowfully, "I think you better whip me, I'm afraid I shan't remember." What could a mother do? I stooped towards her reluctantly to administer the correction she craved. At that moment the God of Abraham bade me stay my hand. "Would it not do as well," said I, "to ask God to help you remember?" "O yes! better," said she, and she knelt by my side, while I endeavored to commend her to the watchful care of Israel's gentle Shepherd. I do not recollect that she ever after-ward disobeyed me in this way.

One instance, however, of disobedience of a different kind is most pain-ful to remember. One in which she refused to do what was required of her. The circumstances were these. Polly Burr was spending a few days with us, and one morning when she first came into the sitting room, she, as usual, bade Caroline good morning. It was in the spring, and Caroline, as I said before, was feeble, and sometimes irritable in the morning. She loved Polly very much, but at this time did not return her morning salutation. I said to her, "Say good morning, Polly," not thinking but that she would readily comply. But she did not. I spoke again, when she said, "No," very decidedly. I told her if she did not say so I must put her into the bedroom, and let her stay there till she would. She still refused, and I took her into the bedroom, and after talking to her a little time, left her.

Presently I went to her again, but she refused to obey, and I thought it my duty to chastise her, which I did, but without any good effect, repeatedly. She did not seem angry, but on the contrary, very affectionate, would put her arms around my neck, and kiss me, and say, "Why don't I do it, Mother?" But there seemed to be a fixed determination not to do it. She did not cry excessively, but I never saw more of mental agony and internal conflict depicted on a countenance than hers had at that time. Once or twice she said, "O, it will kill me!" Not meaning the chastisement but the excitement of her feelings. I was distressed. I knew not what course to take. I thought of the famous story of Dr. Weyland's child, and feared she might hold out as long as he did. But she was so frail, I feared she would sink under such protracted resistance. Our breakfast was ready and all the family were waiting, but I felt that it was of the first importance that she should be brought to yield.

Her father was in the study, and overhearing, called me to tell me that I must not yield to her, as he feared my feelings would lead me to, after having repeated the correction so many times, and continued it so long. I told him how decided she appeared, and he came down and went into the room where she was with me. He talked, and then prayed with her, and then I asked her if she would obey. "No! I shan't!" said she. Words that I do not know that she ever used on any other occasion. We were pained to the heart. It seemed as if the enemy had her completely in his power, and was trying to effect her ruin. As a last resort her father said he would go out and procure a stick to whip her with; this we had never used, as she had always yielded without any trouble. And if we ever were obliged to inflict punishment it was not to make her do what we wished her to, but for something she had done which she ought not to do. Her father left the room on his painful errand, and she knew that a more dreaded punishment than she had ever suffered awaited his return. She sprang to me saying earnestly, "I will, I will." I immediately gently led her out, almost trembling lest she should shrink from it when put to the test. But she made an effort and as soon as she got where Polly was said, "Good morning, Polly," and I led her back, and when her father returned we were glad no further correction was necessary. I wiped away her tears and as breakfast had been waiting an hour or more we all sat down to the table. Caroline seemed unusually mild and lovely, a sweet submissive spirit seemed to influence all her conduct, and in the afternoon she said to me, "I was very happy this morning at breakfast."

This was to us one of the most painful events of her life. It showed us the depraved state of the unrenewed heart, even of a gentle, lovely, and generally obedient child. I trust we were led by it to pray more earnestly for the renewing influences of the Spirit of God. Never before this had we felt so much the need of it. And we cherish the hope that those prayers offered in weakness, though I believe in sincerity, were heard for her before the throne of grace. Though she never gave us, during health, any reason to hope that her heart had been renewed, yet such gentleness and patience were manifested during her last sickness, and such comfort and hope vouchsafed to us when she was taken from us, that we rest in the belief that, "The blood of Jesus Christ which cleanseth from all sin," was applied to her soul. And we hope one day to meet all our little ones among the redeemed in Heaven.

4. An American girl goes west with her family: Nettie Abell

Antoinette Marie ("Nettie") Abell (1866–88) was the first child of Mary Chaffee Abell (Doc. 66), the twenty-year-old wife of a Civil War veteran and Free Methodist preacher, Robert Abell. In 1868 the family moved from western New York to Illinois, where Robert continued to preach and to conduct revivals. They moved again in 1871, this time to become homesteaders in Kansas. When Nettie was almost nine, her mother died after several months of illness in the family's unfinished Kansas farmhouse, leaving five children— the youngest a baby just over a year old. With Robert Abell's help, Nettie cared for her four younger brothers and the household until her father remarried four years later. So thoroughly did she replace her mother during these years that Robert and the boys came to call her "Mary." The following extracts from the letters of Nettie's parents and a Kansas neighbor to family members in the East reveal the delight Nettie's parents took in her, even in times of poverty, homesickness, and bereavement.

[Robert Abell to Mary's sister Kate, Dec. 12, 1866, New York; Nettie is now five months old.]
Baby Nettie is well and just as sweet and pretty as ever. She has on a little grey sack and she looks so cunning. Just now Mary is trotting her, saying, "This is the way the ladies ride, the ladies ride, the ladies ride, etc." which seems to suit Baby Nettie a good deal.

[Mary Abell to her sister Kate, Jan. 18, 1869, Illinois; Nettie is now two and a half.]
It is now 1 o'clock p.m. Baby [Eddie] is taking his nap and Nettie is also sleeping. She is quite sick today. Has vomited six times this a.m. We thought she was troubled with worms and gave her a new kind of medicine yesterday

SOURCE: Helen Smith Jordan, *Love Lies Bleeding* (Syracuse, N.Y., 1979), privately printed. The letters from May 1875 to May 1876 are unpublished family papers in the possession of Mrs. Jordan. The editors are indebted to Mrs. Jordan for permission to quote from her book and her family papers.

which does not seem to agree with her. It tastes just like McLeam's Vermifuge—I have been opposed to her taking it all of the time—but Robert thought it would be good for her. I'll not give her any more of the miserable stuff. She has slept most all day. Is very pale and sick to her stomach all the time. I don't know what to do for her. She has been quite fretful for several days past—has been teasing to "go home" as usual. I told her not to do something the other day and she looked up at me and said "they sant buse 'ittle Nettie— Nettie Gandma going to send Nettie something *nice*"—so she has not forgot her Grandma's humoring her you see. Expect if she could *go home*—she would be the happiest little thing ever was. I should not be able to do any thing with her. She has been very much interested about learning the letters in "Aunt Katie's Book" for a week or so past. She has learned the names of quite a number.

[Mary Abell to her sister Kate, April 4, 1869, Illinois]
Thought I had finished your letter but I must tell you what Nettie has just been about. I told her to put the old cat out of doors—she and Eddie went into the back room with her and presently I heard Nettie laughing and Eddie saying "burn burn"—and guess what the little rogues had been doing— well Nettie had put the cat into the stove (one we use washing days) and had shut and was holding the door. There did not happen to be any fire in the stove which was lucky for the cat—if it had been washing day—poor puss might have fried hard. As it was she only came out considerably sooted up, the cat is maltese, yellow and white spotted or mottled, but a good deal of white on her. I am going to make an "Indian pudding" today and do some other cookings so goodbye.

P.S. Nettie steals the pins out of Robert's coat, when we have praying or in fact at any other time when she can get a chance. Robert told her to put one back the other day, and after making quite a fuss about it, she said with a doleful face "Oh papa! it is *so* heavy Nettie can't."

[Robert Abell to Mary's father, Jan. 18, 1870, Illinois; Nettie is now three and a half.]
Little Nettie and Eddie have just set their table and are now eating— for you must know that Nettie has a set of pewter dishes. To make out, she has gathered up all the tin cups she could find, little and big. Of course she must have something to eat. And of course she calls on mother for the necessary provisions. To meet the very reasonable call of Miss Nettie for the provisions aforesaid, cake, cookies, crackers, cheese and raisins are promptly dealt out to the uplifted hands of Master Eddie and Miss Nettie. Then chairs are placed at the little round stand that contains this careful preparation of means to end and the youngsters alone surround the festal board. Now, true to the family custom, each lifts the hands devoutly put together, while Nettie with tender voice speaks a few words of grace all her own. To wit: "O Lordy gospel, Amen." And with childlike zeal, little Eddie repeats. "O, Lordy gospel, Amen." Now in due order they without further delay seize upon the edibles before them of which a considerable share drops to the floor in crumbs. Of

course that is no part of their business, and they are kindly left for mother to attend to with broom and dustpan.

[Mary Abell to her parents and sisters, Sept. 21, 1870, Illinois; Nettie is now four.]

Nettie has not given up seeing Grandma yet—she has a wonderful opinion of her grandmother—says she don't whip little boys and girls but gives them lots of sugar and when she gets to grandma's she's never coming back again on any account. She was praying the other day and says among other things, "When I die I am going to heaven and have lots to eat and lots of fun up there"—Nettie was asking who gave us every thing nice, and I told her the Lord—"Yes" Eddie says, "he will give me some candy." Nettie got provoked about something the other day and said "I don't want to die and go to heaven, I won't die—want to stay with papa and Mamma, I ain't going to die—no—not in ten weeks, lots of ten weeks." She gets to praying sometimes and tells the Lord she's going to Granma's on the cars, and when she gets there she is going to see the geese, peacock—& etc.—I nearly die laughing to hear her, it is so comical to hear her going over with such a lingo. If she hears of anybody being dead she always asks "who killed him?" and a variety of other questions. She beats everything I ever heard of to ask questions. When I tell her the rain comes from the clouds she wants to know if it comes out of the holes. . . .

Friday evening—I will now try and finish this letter—the children are abed and asleep and I am glad enough, so I can get a little quiet. Seems to me they are the most active youngsters ever I saw—they must be doing something perpetually, they have a great mania for cutting paper for a few weeks past, and what a looking house they do make, they keep it looking at sixes and sevens most of the time, chairs turned down, and cradle quilts with all the other dry goods they can get hold of laid in utter confusion under foot. They make dens for bears, pens for pigs, and cages for monkeys and tigers—and they enjoy it hugely. Nettie teases me to tell her stories a great deal, it seems as if she would craze me sometimes. I tell her an imaginary one about her and Nellie playing visit with their dollies and setting their table etc., which pleases her more than anything else I can tell her—and to have to spin it out miles in length for that is all the better you know. And while I'm telling it she won't allow Eddie to say anything, nor Robbie [b. July 12, 1869] to make a whine—without having terrible times. I have been dressing her doll today—have got a china head to fit the body of my wax doll, have put that head away and now it must have a nice outfit.

[Mary Abell to her mother, Aug. 14, 1872. This letter and the others that follow are all from Kansas. Nettie is now barely six and going to school.]

Nettie has commenced piecing a quilt. She sews very nicely—has finished six blocks—wants Grandma to send her a lot of pieces and the girls. Rob bought Robbie and Eddie each a little hatchet while at Manhattan—axe one side and hammer on the other—and Nettie a set of dolls' furniture, the smartest lot of little things I ever saw. There are four chairs, a bureau, table, sofa and bedstead, writing desk, stand, center table, footstool, and cradle, they are as perfectly made as any thing you ever saw—that is her present for taking care of baby. Robt. got her a drawing book for the slate a while ago—pages painted black and pictures white. She is learning to read also.

[Mary Abell to her sister Kate, March 7, 1874; Nettie is now seven and a half.]

Robert and Nettie are digging a well—They have got eleven feet now. Shall I tell you how they manage. Robert has a box holding a bushel and a half with a string handle to it, to which is attached a long heavy well rope, which runs over pulleys. When he gets the box full of dirt he sings out to Nettie who leads off the horse, who draws up the dirt in fine style. Rob pulls out the pin that holds the box end of the rope—hitches another horse which is close by to a staple in the side of the box—and hauls off the dirt, comes back, changes riggings again and gets into the bucket and horse No. 1. lets him down into the well again. If you want an idea of how they get along—I kept tally today, and they hauled up 22 boxes this a.m. and 36 this p.m. Rob dug over three feet today. He has come to rock now but how solid he don't know. He had engaged men to help him, but when he went to see them they could not come. He gets along just as fast—as if he had a man and with only Nettie's help. One would hardly believe it. He says he can do 35 feet in that way. He has a long house ladder which he puts into the well to climb out with and will splice it and make it go that far. If we could only get water at that depth how little it would cost us. Nettie is quite tired out tonight she says it has kept her running all day. Eddie tends the baby for me in her place. Yesterday was a miserable day. Snow—rain—hail—mud—and a hard wind, but Nettie led the horse for Rob to work all day. I bundled her up good and warm, so she would not catch cold.

By the way John Abell's little girl May is dead. . . .

I have written a letter for Nettie to Nellie, that I shall mail at the same time I do this, but when that will be I do not know. This is a beautiful day. Eddie has led the horse today, so he relieves Nettie, and for both of them it will not be hard work—besides it makes it some easier for me, as Nettie can hold the baby some of the time—and Eddie can only rock him—cannot hold him.

[Mrs. C. C. Humphrey, a Kansas neighbor, to Mary's mother, the week of Mary's death, May 1875; Nettie is now almost nine.]

I had not been to church since I visited Mary; until I attended her funeral. . . . Mr. Humphrey sang for one hymn "Shall We Gather at the River." Nettie is out by the door singing it now.

[Mrs. C. C. Humphrey to Mary's mother, Aug. 21, 1875]

I have been so tired on the Sabbath have not felt able to write. Was sorry to omit it for I well know your anxiety to hear, how those little motherless ones are. Have not been able to go to see them; and have heard nothing in particular until about two weeks since. Merritt saw Mr. A. [Robert Abell] at

Bala. Willie [the Abells' year-old baby] was not well then had bowel complaint, it is not more than he may expect, with no one to watch him excepting Nettie; how I do pity her; she and Willie are my favorites. Nettie is so much like her Grandmother and Willie like his dear Mother. I feel anxious about them.

[Robert Abell to Mary's mother, Oct. 11, 1875; he addressed the letter to "Dear Grandma."]

So I address you in behalf of the children. Not because I write at their request, but because I am writing about them. I came home this evening about sundown, bringing a barrel of water. For my well, though 75 feet deep —has not reached deep enough for water. I notice all the children were white with flour pretty much all over. "Why!" says I, "what you got so much flour on you for?" "Oh, we've been making biscuit." I came into the house, and every last one of them but the baby was to work in the dough. They occupied both tables all over. Flour was scattered every where. Even the baby had had a hand in the business. For he too was white enough for a baker.

Nettie had got her biscuits in the oven. But before that she had given each youngster a patch of dough and they had gone into the cracker business— using the top of the stove for an oven. Of course they were happy. Likewise the table and floor must have been delighted for they seemed to revel in flour. I didn't expect Nettie's biscuits were good for much. She had never made any, although she had several times said with great confidence she knew just how to make them. Well, after they were baked—I found they were first rate. And she used baking powder instead of sour milk. That is just her way. She takes a notion to do a thing and she does not hesitate a moment to take the fullest responsibility in the work. Whatever it may be. Her confidence does not flinch in the least.

Sometimes she will try to make cake—and such cake! She has made several real good custard pies. Yet she does all this cooking without giving me a hint of what she is going to do. She has often teased me to let her make a pot pie. I never consented but today she went at it while I was gone. I happened home before it was done. She put some biscuit dough into boiling water with neither meat nor butter. I told her to put in a good lot of butter. Well, it tasted real good. . . . Nettie is a fine looking girl. I have always maintained she looked like you and she does. Her disposition is very cheerful *as yours is naturally*. She seldom frets at all. Seems nearly always happy and never at a loss for some enterprise to amuse herself. She *must lead* where ever she is. She is full of tact, and by unanswerable suggestions over-rules all opposers. . . .

I read this to the children and they were much pleased. I cautioned Nettie against being flattered. Told her, her papa was perhaps a little partial to his daughter.

[Robert Abell to Mary's mother, May 27, 1876]

If God will give me health I'll carry this load alone as long as possible. I and the children had prayers in the parlor on May 16.—the day—one year ago that Mary died. I took from the bureau drawer the box containing the two braids of her hair she ordered me to cut close to her head, the morning of the day she died. Beside them I laid her likeness. I brought the children to look at them and told them "one year ago today mama died. This was mama's hair." Then we sung and prayed and *wept*.

5. A French working woman recalls her childhood as a linen weaver: Mémé Santerre

Marie Catherine (Mémé) Santerre was born in 1891 in the French vil-lage of Avesnes (Nord) to a family of linen weavers and migratory farm la-borers. Her life story, from which the following selection is taken, was tran-scribed by a third party, and has been accepted by French historians as authentic in detail. Santerre's account not only documents the events of her own childhood of work and study, but also gives us clues about the religion, family economy, and quality of family life of these landless laborers.

I was born on December 23, 1891. My mother told me that on that even-ing a bitter, glacial wind swept through our neighborhood courtyard, stirring up clouds of powdery snow that stuck to the brick walls and blew in under the doors.—My mother had been in bed for an hour, since the first pains. She didn't get up again for nine straight days.

Papa had made the bed with the sheets reserved for births, finer, less coarse than those that ordinarily adorned their bed. . . .

My father sat silently, awaiting the arrival of the midwife, fat Zulma, who, before my birth, had already brought my twelve brothers and sisters into the world.

On the table glittered a *roue de brouette*—as we called the silver hundred-sou coins. In due time it would be used to pay the midwife. If all went well, she would also get a tip: a cup of real, strong coffee into which my father would break an egg.—It was only at such times that these two delicacies en-tered our house. Ordinarily we drank chicory and as for eggs, we never had those.—

Outside, the north wind, stronger than before, stirred up the sawdust that covered the floor of the sole room in our house, which served as kitchen, dining room, and bedroom. My father, who was a stickler for convention, had succeeded in constructing a cubbyhole in the false attic upstairs, where my three sisters and I were hoisted up in the evening to sleep. . . .

My birth, I've been told, was quickly accomplished. Zulma was experi-enced, and again that evening she earned her coffee. She traveled around the village and neighboring settlements delivering babies. She didn't lack for work; all the families had at least ten children.

I was quickly extracted from the maternal womb, washed, and swaddled

SOURCE: Serge Grafteaux, *Mémé Santerre* (Paris, 1975), pp. 7–13, 15–19. The editors wish to thank Professor Louise Tilly, University of Michigan, for sending us a copy of this document, and Kathryn Tilly, for assistance in the translation.

according to a complicated and precise technique that would, according to the midwife, prevent me from becoming deformed.

Then Mama's toilette was promptly taken care of, with close attention to the smallest details. Zulma didn't want her clients to die from giving birth and she was skillful at preventing infections. . . .

As the last-born, I was to have the privilege of saying "Maman," which was denied to my brother and sisters who had to say "My Mother" or "My Father." All of us had to address them formally. That was the custom in our province.—The formal *vous* was respected in all of the ten homes that were clustered around our court. . . .

Thus, I grew until I was three. I was breast-fed until I was seven months old. It was the only milk I tasted in my entire childhood except for the milk I got from time to time later on at school.

At the age of three, I was given chicory with a hunk of bread in the morning, just like the others. At noon we had boiled potatoes and white cheese that we spread on thick slices of bread. My mother seasoned it with salt and garlic. You could get a big bowlful of it for three sous. In the evening we drank bowls of soup.

Meat was reserved for Sundays, and not always then! Then we had a little *pou au feu* or some boiled beef liver, or spleen from which Mama made fragrant-smelling stews. . . .

[In the cellar, a] big half-dark room, lit only by several high windows, were the looms on which everyone in the village wove during the winter months for eighteen hours straight.

After school, which I attended for six years because, being the youngest, I was the most "leisured" and could be sent—after school, I too had "my" loom. I was still so tiny when I was first put there that I had to have specially constructed wooden leg-extensions in order to operate the pedals. My legs were too short to reach them.

We woke up at four A.M. A quick wash, with water that we had to bring from the court fifty meters away, where one well served all the families on our court, and hop! we went down into the cellar with two coal-oil lamps. During this time, my mother lit the round stove that heated the main room. It had niches where we could warm our frozen feet when, around 10, she called us to come upstairs and get our so-called coffee; having been up for many hours, it was a long time to wait after getting up for this hot beverage that seemed so delicious to us.

Even today, when I drink real coffee it tastes no better than the chicory I remember so well. Mama, while attending to the housework, scouring the floor, scraping the table with a shard of glass, throwing fresh sawdust on the tiles, and boiling potatoes, at the same time had to prepare the warps that we would weave on the next day. My sisters and I made handkerchiefs that we wove into big rolls of linen. My father, who was very skillful, saved for himself the big pieces of linen, which were difficult to complete and much sought after at the time.

Every Saturday, one after another, running in order to waste as little time as possible, we went to take our cloth to the merchant, a resident of the court like us, who collected the work and got money for it.

As far back as I can remember, I earned two francs a week, and when my handkerchiefs became faultless, which happened with time, the *patron* gave me five sous as a tip.—Later on, I earned up to five francs a week. I would return home and give the money to my mother. Then my sisters would go, one after another, then papa, to take their work.

We couldn't make ends meet with these earnings. We had to live all winter on credit. We paid up on our return from the season in the country, which took us far away from home for six months, to a farm in Seine-Inférieure.

In those days, my father cooked his own bread in the court's common oven. . . .

I loved my father a lot. During his lifetime, none of us received the least physical punishment. He commanded our respect through an austere behavior that, alas, was not typical of the other heads of families in our court. The only luxury in which he was known to indulge was a pint of beer when he had had a good week—which was rare.

He seldom raised his voice and I never heard him once be discourteous to my mother, whom he adored. Still, he was a simple man, raised in a strict manner by strangers because, as a child, he had lost his parents. When he was in one of his rare talkative moods, he said he was glad that we had not had the same fate as he.

He was never really uncompromising except on the subject of religion. He revered the priests and nuns. When they were expelled from France, he went into the streets and fought with the police.*

. . . We didn't have to be told twice to go to bed. However, before going to sleep, we did not forget to thank God for his gifts and we would recite the Lord's Prayer out loud, just as we always said grace before eating whatever food we had.—Even now, I am faithful to this prayer, which I have repeated all my life.

On Sundays we were up at seven. My mother scrubbed the whole family in a big tub of hot water with vigorous strokes of a brush well doused with green soap. Then we put on our best clothes and went to eight o'clock Mass. I was very proud in my blue dress and my white linen bonnet. The priest, who was very old, was very nice. He asked us to practice charity and to be courageous.

Courage we didn't lack but charity was more difficult. Still, if it came to helping those worse off, my parents never hesitated to contribute a few sous, even though it would mean scrimping a little the next week.

Scrimping, moreover, what did that mean? We were not aware that we lacked anything whatsoever. It was only later, much later, that I calculated

---

* In 1904, before the final separation of Church and State in France, the republican government forbade members of religious orders to teach in French schools. There were many popular demonstrations against this action in the Nord, where the Santerre family lived.—EDS.

exactly how many things there were whose flavors and forms I had never known.

Fruits, for example.—We never had them. They were too expensive! We couldn't even buy a simple apple. Sometimes at Christmas, we would get an orange, which we called the "fruit of paradise," no doubt because of its flavor, which was, for us, unusual and exquisite.

At Christmas, too, we found in our thread boxes, near the loom where we were going to work that day just like any other, a small Jesus made of spice cake that we nibbled away at for hours in order to prolong the pleasure. We went to bed late, very late, on Christmas eve.

When the bells pealed, we had to dress warmly and go out in the snow and cold to the church for midnight Mass.

"It is the Nativity, children. You should never miss it," said Papa.

This mass seemed beautiful to us. It was warm in the choir where dozens of candles flickered. And we went to see the crèche, where a baby slept in the midst of the sheep, cows, and goats that the farmers brought there. . . .

What struck me on returning to the house was, after the perfume of incense, the flat odor that permeated our one-room house, that smell that I have never forgotten and that was found even in the cleanest houses. It was the smell of the peat that burned with coal dust in the round stove. Years later, I can still taste it sometimes and, amazingly, it brings tears to my eyes. When I smelled it, I was happy, perfectly happy. . . .

A long time ago, long before I was born, death had stalked our household. It was Mama who told me about it when I asked her about the two sisters and the brother who were missing from our family.

"It was twenty-seven years ago, Marie. During the war of 1870. I had your brother and your two sisters! We were even worse off than we are today. The emperor was in power at the time. We had lots of work but it paid so poorly that sometimes we had no bread. And then one day, we heard that there was a war and your Papa had to go away to be a soldier. He went to Cambrai.— I stayed by myself."

My mother's voice trembled as she recalled this time. I told her to stop, that I wasn't interested.—But she continued, saying that I ought to know.

"I couldn't take care of your brother, whom I had placed with a kind neighbor, who was childless and eager to have him. My poor baby! One night, the neighbor came in screaming. She had just knocked over a basin of boiling water on the child. He died the next day. He was buried like a dog in the earth, without a coffin. I couldn't pay for one and your father was not informed. He didn't learn of his son's death until after his return.

. . . "Your two sisters fell ill," continued my mother in a colorless voice. "The doctor came only once. He said that they needed bouillon or they would die. I didn't see him again. It was the mayor who came to register the two deaths. They died just like that, calmly, quietly. At the end I gave them my breast to comfort them but I didn't have any milk. I was pregnant with your sister Louise.

"When Papa finally heard of his triple bereavement, he couldn't get leave.

There were some funny things happening near Sedan,* and no soldiers were allowed to leave. So he left everything, his barracks, his gun, and he left in the night to return home.

"When I saw him arrive one evening," Mama told me, "he was like a madman. I was penniless. He swore that he wouldn't leave again until he had woven a large piece of linen, so that I could live for several weeks while awaiting the birth of your sister. The police came to get him. They had a long chain with which they planned to drag him along behind their horse. I told them that he was downstairs working. They went down and when they saw your father weaving, they were struck dumb. He told them that he would not leave that cellar until he had finished the cloth and I explained it to them too.

" 'Well,' said the one who had three stripes, 'I think you are a good man. Stay here. Promise me that you will go back as soon as you have finished.' Papa gave his word and he rejoined the regiment at Cambrai. They never punished him. The military police had written to his commanding officer."

. . . After I learned how my two older sisters died, I didn't dare to grumble or complain. Whenever I had bread to eat I was entirely satisfied. As Papa pointed out, there were lots of children who had nothing! Thus we were very sincere when, before each humble meal, we thanked God for providing it.

On my sixth birthday, Mama hugged me, as she did each year to celebrate the day, and told me that I was going to go to school. My parents had held a council of war in order to reach this decision. "The others didn't go to school," said Papa. "She is the last and we should make an effort. She should at least learn the alphabet and the multiplication tables."

On the day after Christmas I went to class for the first time at the convent school, where there were no nuns because they had been expelled. The young ladies from the chateau taught the classes. Papa hadn't hesitated in choosing this school. He had flatly rejected the municipal school, which we called the "riff-raff school."

Each family in the village, depending on its political and religious convictions, sent its children to one school or the other. Since the total number of pupils was hardly large, it was easy to determine the majority opinion.

At the convent school, there were some ten pupils; there were five or six at the other.—We didn't mix with them, even after school. On the common, the grassy place near the church, we each played on our side, and when it came time for first communion, the pupils of the convent school were given first place in the procession.

We did a little bit of mathematics, some reading, and learned our catechism. I really liked my school, which was in a very warm part of the presbytery, and the young ladies from the chateau were very nice. They sometimes brought us a little bit of milk. And so we passed the winter. When spring came and we left Avesnes for the country, Papa, like the other heads of families that "emigrated," made contact with the religious school in the area of Seine-Inférieure to which we were moving, and I continued my studies there.

* In early September 1870 the Prussians defeated the French at Sedan and took the emperor prisoner, thus precipitating the fall of the Second Empire.—EDS.

This lasted for four years, the best years of my childhood. Then one day, my father told me that I had learned enough, and that, like my two sisters, I would have to work at the loom.

That was the end of my lazy mornings, when I got up at seven o'clock. I began an apprenticeship that was very hard for me, since I was only as tall as *une tiote botte.** For eight years, and even after that, when I was married I took my place in the big cellar, half-lit by the coal-oil lamps, which were eventually replaced by oil lamps. . . .

Thus passed my childhood years, with no other joys except the company of my family. The only landmark in these years was the day of my first communion. Oh, it was a day like any other, but so beautiful that I still remember it.

My godfather arrived just before Mass. He brought me a little apron, and my godmother gave me a piece of material for a dress. A white veil was put on my head, and I was given a candle, a big gilt candle, which I was only allowed to hold for a little while. Just long enough for the procession. After the ceremony we returned to the house, and Papa offered everyone beer. Then the veil, which had already been used by my sisters and was later used by my nieces, was carefully folded up and placed in the cupboard, wrapped up in silk paper. Then we returned to the cellar to weave until time for vespers.

When we returned, my mother let me wear my new apron. That was the greatest pleasure of the day. I was eleven years old. It was June, 1901, just before our departure for the country.

6. The exploitation of children

Many poor children, both girls and boys, had no "childhood." Expected to contribute to their families' income, they went to work at an early age rather than to school. Poverty, sometimes aggravated by parental indifference, increased their natural vulnerability as children and could lead to economic and even sexual exploitation. The following selections reveal different aspects of the "non-childhood" of Victorian girls. In the first excerpt young English girls testify before a Parliamentary commission about their back-breaking work in the coal mines. Their testimony, published in the press, aroused public outrage and led to legislation in 1842 that prohibited the employment of children under the age of ten in the mines. In the second selection the novelist Elizabeth Gaskell (1810–65; Doc. 71.i) writes to Charles Dickens to ask his help in rehabilitating a poor Irish girl who had been forced into prostitution. Dickens and the philanthropist Angela Burdett-Coutts had established a

* Literally, a tiny boot.—EDS.

SOURCES: (i) Great Britain, *Parliamentary Papers*, 1842, XVI, Children's Employ-ment Commission (Mines), p. 252. (ii) *The Letters of Elizabeth Gaskell*, ed. J. A. V. Chapple and Arthur Pollard (Cambridge, Mass., 1967), pp. 98–100. (iii) Victor G. and Brett de Bary Nee, *Longtime Californ'—A Documentary Study of an American Chinatown* (Boston, 1974), pp. 84–87.

home to give prostitutes a new start in life. In the last excerpt Lilac Chen (b. 1887), a Chinese-American, describes how her family sold her into domestic service in a brothel; her reminiscences reveal that the buying and selling of human beings was by no means confined to the antebellum South. Chen subsequently spent many years in San Francisco, working with the reformer Donaldina Cameron to rescue Chinese girls who had been sold into prostitution and slavery. Although these selections reveal much about the abuse of children in the Victorian period, they also bear witness to widespread attempts, whether by official agencies or concerned individuals, to protect those unable to defend themselves.

(i) The mineworkers

[Testimony of Ann Eggley, eighteen years old. As a hurrier, she pushed carriages loaded with ore from the bank face to the shaft. Fully loaded, these carriages, or corves, weighed about 800 lbs. The other jobs she mentions, winding and riddling, involved, respectively, helping to hoist the coal to the surface and sifting the coal through a sieve, or riddle.]

I'm sure I don't know how to spell my name. We go at four in the morning, and sometimes at half-past four. We begin to work as soon as we get down. We get out after four, sometimes at five, in the evening. We work the whole time except an hour for dinner, and sometimes we haven't time to eat. I hurry by myself, and have done so for long. I know the corves are very heavy they are the biggest corves anywhere about. The work is far too hard for me; the sweat runs off me all over sometimes. I am very tired at night. Sometimes when we get home at night we have not power to wash us, and then we go to bed. Sometimes we fall asleep in the chair. Father said last night it was both a shame and a disgrace for girls to work as we do, but there was nought else for us to do. I have tried to get winding to do, but could not. I begun to hurry when I was seven and I have been hurrying ever since. I have been 11 years in the pit. The girl are always tired. I was poorly twice this winter; it was with headache. I hurry for Robert Wiggins; he is not akin to me. I riddle for him. We all riddle for them except the littlest when there is two. We don't always get enough to eat and drink, but we get a good supper. I have known my father go at two in the morning to work when we worked at Twibell's, where there is a day-hole to the pit, and he didn't come out till four. I am quite sure that we work constantly 12 hours except on Saturdays. We wear trousers and our shifts in the pit, and great big shoes clinkered and nailed. The girls never work naked to the waist in our pit. The men don't insult us in the pit. The conduct of the girls in the pit is good enough sometimes, and sometimes bad enough. I never went to a day-school. I went a little to a Sunday-school, but I soon gave it over. I thought it too bad to be confined both Sundays and week-days. I walk about and get the fresh air on Sundays. I have not learnt to read. I don't know my letters. I never learnt nought. I never go to church or chapel; there is no church or chapel at Gawber, there is none nearer than a mile. If I was married I would not go to the pits, but I know some married women that do. The men do not insult the girls with us, but I think they do in some. I have never heard that a good man came into the world who was God's Son to save sinners. I never heard of Christ at all. Nobody has ever told me about him, nor have my father and mother ever taught me to pray. I know no prayer: I never pray. I have been taught nothing about such things.

Elizabeth Eggley, sixteen years old.—I am sister to the last witness. I hurry in the same pit, and work for my father. I find my work very much too hard for me. I hurry alone. It tires me in my arms and back most. We go to work between four and five in the morning. If we are not there by half past five we are not allowed to go down at all. We come out at four, five, or six at night as it happens. We stop in generally 12 hours, and sometimes longer. We have to hurry only from the bank-face down to the horse-gate and back. I am sure it is very hard work and tires us very much; it is too hard for girls to do. We sometimes go to sleep before we get to bed. We haven't a very good house; we have but two rooms for all the family. I have never been to school except four times, and then I gave over because I could not get things to go in. I cannot read: I do not know my letters. I don't know who Jesus Christ was. I never heard of Adam either. I never heard about them at all. I have often been obliged to stop in bed all Sunday to rest myself. I never go to church or chapel.

Eliza Coats, eleven years old.—I hurry with my brother. It tires me a great deal, and tires my back and arms. I go sometimes at half past four and sometimes five; it's dark when I go; it often rains and we get wet, but we take off our top clothes when we get in the pit. They never lace or ill-use me in the pit. I can't read; I have never been to school. I do nought on Sundays. I have had no shoes to go in to school. I don't know where I shall go if I am a bad girl when I die. I think God made the world, but I don't know where God is. I never heard of Jesus Christ.

(ii) A sixteen-year-old prostitute

[Excerpts from a letter from Elizabeth Gaskell to Charles Dickens, Jan. 8, 1850]

I am just now very much interested in a young girl, who is in our New Bayley prison. She is the daughter of an Irish clergyman who died when she was two years old; but even before that her mother had shown most complete indifference to her; and soon after the husband's death, she married again, keeping her child out at nurse. The girl's uncle had her placed at 6 years old in the Dublin school for orphan daughters of the clergy; and when she was about 14, she was apprenticed to an Irish dress-maker here, of very great reputation for fashion. Last September but one this dress-maker failed, and had to dismiss all her apprentices; she placed this girl with a woman who occasionally worked for her, and who has since succeeded to her business; this woman was very profligate and connived at the girl's seduction by a surgeon in the neighbourhood who was called in when the poor creature was ill. Then she was in despair, & wrote to her mother, (*who had never corresponded with her all the time she was at school and an apprentice;*) and while awaiting the answer went into the penitentiary; she wrote 3 times but no answer came, and in desperation she listened to a woman, who had obtained admittance to the penitentiary solely as it turned out to decoy girls into her mode of life, and left with her: & for four months she has led the most miserable life! in the hopes, as she tells me, of killing herself, for "no one had ever cared for her in this world,"—she drank, "wishing it might be poison," pawned every article of clothing—and at last stole. I have been to see her in prison at Mr. Wright's request, and she looks quite a young child (she is but 16,) with a wild wistful look in her eyes, as if searching for the kindness she has never known,—and she pines to redeem herself; her uncle (who won't see her, but confirms fully the account of her mother's cruel hardness,) says he has 30£ of her father's money in his hands; and she agrees to emigrate to Australia, for which her expenses would be paid. But the account of common emigrant ships is so bad one would not like to expose her to such chances of corruption; and what I want you to tell me is, how Miss Coutts sends out *her* protegees? under the charge of a matron? and might she be included among them? I want her to go out with as free and unbranded a character as she can; if possible, the very fact of having been in prison &c to be unknown on her landing. I will try and procure her friends when she arrives; only how am I to manage about the voyage? and how soon will a *creditable* ship sail; for she comes out of prison on Wednesday, & there are two of the worst women in the town who have been in prison with her, intending to way-lay her, and I want to keep her out of all temptation, and even chance of recognition. Please, will you help me? I think you know Miss Coutts. I can manage all except the voyage. She is a good reader[,] writer, and a beautiful needlewoman; and we can pay all her expenses &c. . . .

I have not told you one incident about the poor girl. Her seducer was lately appointed assistant surgeon to the New Bayley Prison; and as Pasley was not quite well she was sent for for him to see her. The matron told me when they came thus suddenly face to face, the girl just fainted dead away, and he was so affected he had to sit down,—he said "Good God how did you come here." He has been dismissed from his post in consequence. The chaplain will guarantee the truth of all I have said. She is such a pretty sweet looking girl. I am sure she will do well if we can but get her out in a *good* ship.

(iii) Lilac Chen

I was six when I came to this country in 1893. My worthless father gambled every cent away, and so, left us poor. I think my mother's family was well-to-do, because our grandmother used to dress in silk and satin and always brought us lots of things. And the day my father took me, he fibbed and said he was taking me to see my grandmother, that I was very fond of, you know, and I got on the ferry boat with him, and Mother was crying, and I couldn't understand why she should cry if I go to see Grandma. She gave me a new toothbrush and a new washrag in a blue bag when I left her. When I saw her cry I said, "Don't cry, Mother, I'm just going to see Grandma and be right back." And that worthless father, my own father, imagine, had every inclination to sell me, and he sold me on the ferry boat. Locked me in the cabin while he was negotiating my sale. And I kicked and screamed and screamed and they wouldn't open the door till after some time, you see, I suppose he had made his bargain and had left the steamer. Then they opened the door and let me out and I went up and down, up and down, here and there, couldn't find him. And he had left me, you see, with a strange woman. That woman, it was suppertime, took me to Ningpo, China, to eat, and I refused to eat, I wanted to go home, and then she took me after dinner to Shanghai and left me with another woman. That woman never asked me to work, and was very kind to me, and I was there I don't know for how long. Then a woman from San Francisco came, and picked me up and brought me over.

Oh, God has just been wonderful. Just think, I was in such close waters for damnation myself! This woman, who brought me to San Francisco, was called Mrs. Lee, and she kept the biggest dive in San Francisco Chinatown. Oh, she had a lot of girls, slave girls, you know. And every night, seven o'clock, all these girls were dressed in silk and satin, and sat in front of a big window, and the men would look in and choose their girls who they'd want for the night. Of course, I didn't know anything, never heard about such things, you know. And whenever police or white people came, they always hid me under the bed and pushed a trunk in front of me and then after the police had left they let me come out again. And I saw these girls all dressed in silk and satin, and they were waiting for their business, see. But I didn't know anything.

When this woman needed money, she had to sell me to another party. Everywhere I had been they were very kind to me, except this last place she sent me. Oh, this woman was so awful! They say she was a domestic servant before and was cruelly treated. She used to make me carry a big fat baby on my back and make me to wash his diapers. And you know, to wash you have to stoop over, and then he pulls you back, and cry and cry. Oh, I got desperate, I didn't care what happened to me, I just pinched his cheek, his seat you know, just gave it to him. Then of course I got it back. She, his mother, went and burned a red hot iron tong and burnt me on the arm. Then someone reported me to the home. But they described me much bigger than I was so when they came they didn't recognize me. And then the woman who had reported to the mission said, "Why didn't you take her? She's the girl." They said, "She looked too small," and then they came back again. But even then, they weren't sure that I was the one, so they undressed me and examined my body and found where the woman had beaten me black and blue all over. And then they took me to the home. Oh, it was in the pouring rain! I was scared to death. You know, change from change, and all strangers, and I didn't know where I was going. Away from my own people and in the pouring rain. And they took me, a fat policeman carried me all the way from Jackson Street, where I was staying, to Sacramento Street to the mission, Cameron House. So I got my freedom there.

After I helped Miss Cameron I had five dollars a month and I saved and saved and then went to China and thought I could find my village. I couldn't find my family, you know, never got there. But I felt I must come back to help Cameron House because they had helped to rear me—well, I tell you, all I've been through! And yet when I look back I'm so glad I heard about Jesus and know all about Him, and He took care of me. Just think of the narrow chance! So many girls were sold to be prostitutes, you know. And why should I be exempt? It is only the mercy of God.

The work I did with Miss Cameron was called rescue work. We would find the Chinese girls who were sold to work in the dives, or as domestic servants, and bring them to Cameron House so they could be free. Sometimes people reported to us or sometimes the slave girls themselves would slip a note under our front door and we would find it, and go to the place where the girl wanted to be rescued. Usually we had to go to the dives. When we went on the raid we always took several of our own girls with us to help. Generally I would follow Miss Cameron as interpreter and she and I would go into the house through a door or a window. Sometimes the slave girls got scared and ran out, so the other girls from the home had to wait outside and grab them when they tried to run away. Then when they caught the girl they would blow the police whistle, so we knew. After we got the girl, sometimes we had to go to court over thirty times to free her from her owner. They always get the best attorney and they're so smart, you know, these slaveowners. They had lots of money to spend and they always found out where the girls were. . . .

Poor Miss Cameron, she never knew about these dives when she was growing up, you know. Scottish people, especially the refined, never discussed these things, they never heard of it, you know. So nobody told her, she was so innocent. These slave girls used to have terrific sores, and she had to dress the sores, you know. She never wore gloves, you see, and really, it's just the providence of God kept her from these diseases.

7. French and American songs, rhymes, and games

Children's games and rhymes, collected in the French countryside by the folklorist Eugène Rolland (1846–1909), reveal an interplay of secular and religious influences. Intermingled with the notions that "being good" will lead to handsome clothes and a happy marriage are the familiar figures of the devil and the Virgin Mary with the Infant Jesus. The Holy Mother was an important model for Catholic girls in France, one that was lacking to the Protestants of England and the United States. The second selection is taken from the unpublished reminiscences of Frances Marion Eddy (1862–1956), the youngest of six children of a Presbyterian minister and his wife. It presents a different version of play in the setting of a tightly knit American family living in Niles, Michigan. The third and fourth selections are the accounts of two ex-slaves. Julia Blanks (b. 1862) of Texas remembers playing a game called rap jacket as a child, and Maggie Black (b. 1858) of South Carolina recalls dressing up in an improvised hoopskirt made of wild grape vines.

SOURCES: (i) Eugène Rolland, *Rimes et jeux de l'enfance* (Paris, 1883), pp. 76–77, 135–36. (ii) Frances Marion Eddy, unpublished reminiscences. The editors wish

(i) Two games from the French countryside

A round

I've thirty-two daughters to marry!
I've filled my whole attic with them.
Good Lord, I don't know how
I'll marry off all my children.

My daughter, my daughter,
I'm speaking to you.
My mother, my mother,
What is it you're saying?
I say that if you're good,
You'll make a happy marriage.

I say that if you're good,
You'll make a happy marriage.
You'll be dressed up fit to kill;
Now turn around the circle.

Now go on with the dance.
Hop three times and bow,
And finally you kiss
The one that you will love.

Child's game

Three little girls play the parts of the Holy Virgin, the devil, and a ribbon merchant. The others are ribbons.
The Holy Virgin, in a little voice: "Knock, knock."
The merchant: "Who is there?"
The Holy Virgin: "It's the Holy Mother with her child."
The merchant: "What does she want?"
The Holy Virgin: "A ribbon."
The merchant: "Why does she want it?"
The Holy Virgin: "To put on her child."
The merchant: "What color?"
The Holy Virgin chooses one of the ribbons, who runs away joyously, and the devil has to catch her.

(ii) Frances Marion Eddy

Except for a year out of school in 1873 because of a siege of scarlet fever that nearly ended my life, the in-between years were particularly auspicious for my development, for with fewer demands on their time and strength my

to thank the family of Frances Marion Eddy for allowing us to quote from these reminiscences. (iii) *The American Slave: A Composite Autobiography*, ed. George P. Rawick, 4: *Texas Narratives* (Westport, Conn., 1972), part 1: 97. (iv) *Ibid.*, 2: *South Carolina Narratives*, part 1: 57–58.

parents became my playmates of a sort. Father, a very dignified, no-longer young man, would play hop scotch and mumblety peg with me; taught me to play croquet creditably and with a sporting spirit; to shoot marbles, fly kites and draw a stiff bow in the noble game of archery.

My mother started me out with cats-cradle and bean-porridge-hot and played these two games on demand until her soul must have revolted, for she speedily progressed me to parcheesi and to bagatelle. She could tell a rattling good story herself, and often made my back shiver exquisitely with her dramatic rendering of "Little Henry." I really believe that my parents renewed their youth with me, for I had no playmates I would not willingly forsake if I could get either of them to companion me.

I was already taking music lessons, and by ten years old I could dash off a tune fairly well. When I arrived at that superlative moment of playing simple chords for an accompaniment while my parents sang "When You and I Were Young, Maggie," I felt that I had received my accolade! I remember so tenderly the charming way they would sing together old songs familiar to them when they, too, were young. There was a lovely lazy sort of a melody about "Mermaids Floating O'er the Main" and "Mingling Their Songs with Gondolier's Strain."

The welkin rang when the uncles came, for the four brothers formed a quartette that gave lusty information about hunting, warfare and many other things that stirred the imagination of a ten-to-eleven year old girl. John Brown; The Battle Hymn of the Republic; the songs of the Civil War period; the interesting rounds of Three Blind Mice and Scotland's A-Burning. Then there were the old Scotch border songs Bonnets of Bonnie Dundee and the Campbells Are Coming, into which all four brothers put an esprit that was contagious because it was the marching song of their clan.

This was in the evening when callers were all gone; and at the very end they would sing with reverence some old hymn in which the family present would join. This was always followed by prayer offered by one of the four brothers.

(iii) Julia Blanks

Games? I don't know. We used to play rap jacket. We would get switches and whip one another. You know, after you was hit several times it didn't hurt much. I've played a many time.

(iv) Maggie Black

Dey use'er wear dem big ole hoop skirt dat sit out broad lak from de ankle en den dey wear little panty dat show down twixt dey skirt en dey ankle. Jes tie em 'round dey knees wid some sorta string en le' em show dat way 'bout dey ankle. I 'member we black chillun'ud go in de woods en ge' wild grape vine en bend em round en put em under us skirt en make it stand out big lak. Hadder hab uh big ole ring fa de bottom uv de skirt en den one uh little bit smaller eve'y tim dey ge' closer to de waist. Ne'er hab none tall in de waist cause dat wuz s'ppose to be little bitty t'ing.

8. An American girl's parable of the family: Isabel Hall

Stories and games often taught middle-class girls the lessons of obedience and domesticity. Though we have few first-hand accounts from young girls of the time to tell us how such socialization affected them, the following composition by a nineteen-year-old Rhode Island girl, Isabel Hall (b. 1847), provides one glimpse of how a young woman's imagination might reflect such lessons. In this "vignette," which she sent to her aunt in 1866, Hall offers a cautionary tale about the dangers of girls' straying too far from parental protection.

There lived once upon a time, A family of mice, a father and mother and three little ones. They lived together very happily and peacefully, until one day the little ones thought they would like to see a little more of the world. Thair parents told them they would see the world soon enough, but this did not satisfy the little mice. So one day while thair parents were away marketing they all went together to take a little walk, but the cat soon spied them, then away they scampered to thair hole, but the cat was too quick for them and but two of them reached home in safety. When thair parents came home, these naughty little mice told them that while they were busy playing together thair companion ran out. Of course thair parents believed this not thinking thair little ones would tell a lie, so they commenced searching for the missing one, but never found it. Now you would think that the little ones in meeting so sad an accident would be contented to remain at home but such was not the case; thair parents one day being absent, they thought it would do no harm to take a peep about them, so away they went, but one of them, the youngest, being unused to being away from home fell down in the mud. The cat coming along just at that moment seized it and ran away. The other finding it useless to remain returned home very sad determined to tell its parents the truth, and stray from home no more. The mouse I am happy to say kept its resolutions, its parents gladly forgave thair child. It is the mother now of a happy family and whenever any of the children show a discontented spirit she always tells them of her ill-fated sisters. She lived happy in the love of her children and died peacefully at a good old age. This is the end of the three mice.

9. An English Sunday-school story: Hannah More

Hannah More (1745–1833), an admiring friend of the conservative states-man Edmund Burke, was horrified by the violence of the French Revolution and determined that no such upheaval should occur in England. A staunch Anglican, she came under the influence of the Evangelical movement and

SOURCES: Doc. 8. Isabel Hall, "The Three Little Mice," Anderson Family Papers, Special Collections, Green Library, Stanford University. Doc. 9. "The History of Hester Wilmot," part 2, in The Works of Hannah More (Philadelphia, 1832), 1: 236–41.

established a number of Sunday schools in the area around Cheddar in hopes of improving the religious education of the poor. More taught her pupils to read so that they could study the Bible and their catechism, but she was set against teaching them to write, for fear that the poor might use that skill to compose revolutionary tracts.

The two impulses of political conservatism and Evangelical commitment fused in More's 'Cheap Repository Tracts,' didactic stories written to instruct the poor in religious and social attitudes. Widely distributed in both England and the United States (where they were read by the young Catharine Beecher; Doc. 21.i), these tracts taught young girls that obedience, the acceptance of one's station in society, sobriety, and cleanliness brought happiness in this life and the promise of salvation in the next. "Hester Wilmot," written in 1797, is one of these tales.

Hester Wilmot, I am sorry to observe, had been by nature peevish, and lazy; she would when a child, now and then slight her work, and when her mother was unreasonable she was too apt to return a saucy answer; but when she became acquainted with her own heart, and with the Scriptures, these evil tempers were, in a good measure, subdued, for she now learnt to imitate, not her violent mother, but *him who was meek and lowly.* When she was scolded for doing ill, she prayed for grace to do better; and the only answer she made to her mother's charge, "that religion only served to make people lazy," was to strive to do twice as much work, in order to prove that really made them diligent. The only thing in which she ventured to disobey her mother was, that when she ordered her to do the week day's work on a Sunday, Hester cried, and said, she did not dare to disobey God; but to show that she did not wish to save her own labour, she would do a double portion of work on the Saturday night, and rise two hours earlier on Monday morning.

Once, when she had worked very hard, her mother told her she would treat her with a holy-day the following Sabbath, and take her a fine walk to eat cakes and drink ale at Weston fair, which, though it was professed to be kept on the Monday, yet, to the disgrace of the village, always began on the Sunday evening.* Rebecca [the mother], who would on no account have wasted the Monday, which was a working day, in idleness and pleasure, thought she had a very good right to enjoy herself at the fair on the Sunday evening, as well as to take her children. Hester earnestly begged to be left at home, and her mother in a rage went without her. A wet walk, and more ale than she was used to drink, gave Rebecca a dangerous fever.—During this illness Hester, who would not follow her to a scene of dissolute mirth, attended her night and day, and denied herself necessaries that her sick mother might have comforts: and though she secretly prayed to God that this sickness might change her

* This practice is too common. Those fairs which profess to be kept on Monday, commonly begin on the Sunday. It is much to be wished that magistrates would put a stop to it, as Mr. Simpson did at Weston, at the request of Mrs. Jones. There is another great evil worth the notice of justices. In many villages, during the fair, ale is sold at private houses, which have no license, to the great injury of sobriety and good morals.

mother's heart, yet she never once reproached her, or put her in mind, that it was caught by indulging in a sinful pleasure.

Another Sunday night her father told Hester, he thought she had now been at school long enough for him to have a little good of her learning, so he desired she would stay at home and read to him. Hester cheerfully ran and fetched her Testament. But John [the father] fell a laughing, called her a fool, and said it would be time enough to read the Testament to him when he was going to die, but at present he must have something merry. So saying, he gave her a song book which he had picked up at the Bell. Hester having cast her eyes over it, refused to read it, saying she did not dare offend God by reading what would hurt her own soul.—John called her a canting hypocrite; and said, he would put the Testament into the fire for that there was not a more merry girl than she was before she became religious. Her mother for once took her part, not because she thought her daughter in the right, but because she was glad of any pretence to show her husband was in the wrong; though she herself would have abused Hester for the same thing if John had taken her part. John with a shocking oath abused them both; and went off in a violent passion.—Hester, instead of saying one undutiful word against her father, took up a Psalter in order to teach her little sisters; but Rebecca was so provoked at her for not joining her in her abuse of her husband, that she changed her humour, said John was in the right, and Hester a perverse hypocrite, who only made religion a pretence for being undutiful to her parents. Hester bore all in silence, and committed her cause to Him *who judgeth righteously*. It would have been a great comfort to her if she had dared to go to Mrs. Crew, and to have joined in the religious exercises of the evening at school. But her mother refused to let her, saying it would only harden her heart in mischief. Hester said not a word, but after having put the little ones to bed, and heard them say their prayers out of sight, she went and sat down in her own little loft, and said to herself, it would be pleasant to me to have taught my little sisters to read. I thought it was my duty, for David has said, *Come ye children hearken unto me, I will teach you the fear of the Lord.* It would have been still more pleasant to have passed the evening at school, because I am still ignorant, and fitter to learn than to teach; but I cannot do either without flying in the face of my mother; God sees fit tonight to change my pleasant duties into a painful trial. I give up my will, and I submit to the will of my father; but when he orders me to commit a known sin, then I dare not do it, because, in so doing, I must disobey my Father which is in heaven.

Now it so fell out that this dispute happened on the very Sunday next before Mrs. Jones's yearly feast. On May-day all the school attended her to church, each in a stuff gown of their own earning, and a cap and white apron of her giving. After church there was an examination made into the learning and behaviour of the scholars; those who were most perfect in their chapters, and who brought the best character for industry, humility, and sobriety, received a Bible, or some other good book.

Now Hester had been a whole year hoarding up her little savings, in order to be ready with a new gown on the May-day feast. She had never got less than two shillings a week by her spinning, besides working for the family, and earning a trifle by odd jobs.—This money she faithfuly carried to her mother every Saturday night, keeping back by consent, only twopence a week towards the gown. The sum was complete, the pattern had long been settled, and Hester had only on the Monday morning to go to the shop, pay her money, and bring home her gown to be made. Her mother happened to go out early that morning to iron in a gentleman's family, where she usually staid a day or two, and Hester was busy putting the house in order before she went to the shop.

On that very Monday there was to be a meeting at the Bell of all the idle fellows in the parish. John Wilmot of course was to be there. Indeed he had accepted a challenge of the blacksmith to a batch at all-fours. The black-smith was flush of money, John thought himself the best player; and that he might make sure of winning, he resolved to keep himself sober, which he knew was more than the other would do. John was so used to go upon tick for ale, that he got to the door of the Bell before he recollected that he could not keep his word with the gambler without money, and he had not a penny in his pocket, so he sullenly turned homewards. He dared not apply to his wife, as he knew he should be more likely to get a scratched face than a sixpence from her; but he knew that Hester had received two shillings for her last week's spinning on Saturday, and perhaps she might not yet have given it to her mother. Of the hoarded sum he knew nothing. He asked her if she could lend him half a crown, and he would pay her next day. Hester pleased to see him in good humour after what had passed the night before ran up and fetched down her little box, and in the joy of her heart that he now desired something she *could* comply with without wounding her conscience, cheer-fully poured out her whole little stock upon the table. John was in raptures at the sight of three half-crowns and a sixpence, and eagerly seized it, box and all, together with a few hoarded halfpence at the bottom, though he had only asked to borrow half-a-crown. None but one whose heart was hardened by a long course of drunkenness could have taken away the whole, and for such a purpose. He told her she should certainly have it again next morning, and, indeed intended to pay it, not doubting but he should double the sum. But John overrated his own skill, or luck, for he lost every farthing to the black-smith, and sneaked home before midnight, and quietly walked up to bed. He was quite sober, which Hester thought a good sign. Next morning she asked him, in a very humble way, for the money, which she said she would not have done, but that if the gown was not bought directly, it would not be ready in time for the feast. John's conscience had troubled him a little for what he had done, for when he was not drunk he was not ill-natured, and he stammered out a broken excuse, but owned he had lost the money, and had not a farthing left. The moment Hester saw him mild and kind her heart was softened, and she begged him not to vex, adding, that she would be contented never to have a new gown as long as she lived, if she could have the comfort of always seeing him come home sober as he was last night. For Hester did not know that he had refrained from getting drunk only that he might gamble with a better chance of success, and that when a gamester keeps himself sober, it is not that he may practice a virtue, but that he may commit a worse crime. "I am indeed sorry for what I have done," said he; "you cannot go to the feast, and what will madam Jones say?"—"Yes, but I can," said Hester, "for God looks not at the gown, but at the heart, and I am sure he sees mine full of gratitude at hearing you talk so kindly; and if I thought my dear father would change his present evil courses, I should be the happiest girl at the feast to-morrow." John walked away mournfully, and said to himself, surely there must be something in religion, since it can thus change the heart. Hester was once a pert girl, and now she is as mild as a lamb. She was once an indolent girl, and now she is up with the lark. She was a vain girl, and would do any thing for a new riband; and now she is contented to go in rags to a feast at which every one else will have a new gown. She deprived herself of her gown to give me the money; and yet this very girl, so dutiful in some respects, would submit to be turned out of doors rather than read a loose book at my command, or break the Sabbath. I do not understand this; there must be some mystery in it. All this he said as he was going to work. In the evening he did not go to the Bell: whether it was owing to his new thoughts, or to his not having a penny in his pocket, I will not take upon me positively to say, but I believe it was a little of one and a little of the other.

As the pattern of the intended gown had long been settled in the family, and as Hester had the money by her, it was looked on as good as bought, so that she was trusted to get it brought home, and made in her mother's absence. Indeed, so little did Rebecca care about the school, that she would not have cared any thing about the gown, if her vanity had not made her wish that her daughter should be the best drest of any girl at the feast. Being from home, as was said before, she knew nothing of the disappointment. On May-day morning, Hester, instead of keeping from the feast, because she had not a new gown, or meanly inventing any excuse for wearing an old one, dressed herself out as neatly as she could in her poor old things, and went to join the school in order to go to church. Whether Hester had formerly indulged a little pride of heart, and talked of this gown rather too much, I am not quite sure; certain it is, there was a great hue and cry made at seeing Hester Wilmot, the neatest girl, the most industrious girl in the school, come to the May-day feast in an old stuff gown, when every other girl was so creditably drest. Indeed, I am sorry to say, there were two or three much too smart for their station, and who had dizened themselves out in very improper finery, which Mrs. Jones made them take off before her. "I mean this feast," said she, "as a reward of industry and piety, and not as a trial of skill who can be finest, and outvie the rest in show. If I do not take care, my feast will become an encouragement, not to virtue, but to vanity. I am so great a friend to decency of apparel, that I even like to see you deny your appetites, that you may be able to come decently dressed to the house of God. To encourage you to do this, I like to set apart this one day of innocent pleasure, against which you may be preparing all the year, by laying aside something every week towards buying a gown out of all your savings. But, let me tell you, that meekness and an humble spirit is of more value in the sight of God and good men, than the gayest cotton gown or the brightest pink riband in the parish."

Mrs. Jones for all this was as much surprised as the rest at Hester's mean garb: but such is the power of a good character, that she gave her credit for a right intention, especially as she knew the unhappy state of her family. For it was Mrs. Jones's way, (and it is not a bad way,) always to wait, and inquire into the truth before she condemned any person of good character, though appearances were against them. As we cannot judge of people's motives, said she, we may, from ignorance, often condemn their best actions, and approve of their worst. It will be always time enough to judge unfavourably, and let us give others credit as long as we can, and then we in our turn, may expect a favourable judgment from others, and remember who had said, *Judge not, that ye be not judged.*

Hester was no more proud of what she had done for her father, than she was humbled by the meanness of her garb; and notwithstanding Betty Stiles, one of the girls whose finery had been taken away, sneered at her, Hester never offered to clear herself, by exposing her father, though she thought it right, secretly to inform Mrs. Jones of what had past. When the examination of the girls began, Betty Stiles was asked some questions on the fourth and fifth commandments, which she answered very well. Hester was asked nearly the same questions, and, though she answered them no better than Betty had done, they were all surprised to see Mrs. Jones rise up, and give a handsome Bible to Hester, while she gave nothing to Betty. This girl cried out rather pertly, "Madam, it is very hard that I have no book: I was as perfect as Hester."—"I have often told you," said Mrs. Jones, "that religion is not a thing of the tongue but of the heart. That girl gives me the best proof that she has learned the fourth commandment to good purpose, who persists in keeping holy the Sabbath day, though commanded to break it by a parent whom she loves. And that girl best proves that she keeps the fifth, who gives up her own comfort, and clothing, and credit, *to honour and obey her father and mother,* even though they are not such as she could wish. Betty Stiles, though she could answer the questions so readily, went abroad last Sunday when she should have been at school, and refused to nurse her sick mother, when she could not help herself. Is this having learnt those two commandments to any good purpose?"

Farmer Hoskins, who stood by, whispered [to] Mrs. Jones, "Well, madam, now you have convinced even me of the benefit of religious instruction; now I see there is a meaning to it. I thought it was in at one ear and out at the other, and that a song was as well as a psalm; but now I have found the proof of the pudding is in the eating. I see your scholars must *do* what they *hear,* and *obey* what they *learn.* Why, at this rate, they will all be better servants for being really godly, and so I will add a pudding to next year's feast."

The pleasure Hester felt in receiving a new Bible made her forget that she had on an old gown. She walked to church in a thankful frame; but how great was her joy, when she saw, among a number of working men, her own father going into church. As she past by him, she cast on him a look of so much joy and affection that it brought tears into his eyes, especially when he compared her mean dress with that of the other girls, and thought who had been the cause of it. John, who had not been at church for some years, was deeply struck with the service. The confession with which it opens went to his heart. He felt, for the first time, that he was a *miserable sinner, and that there was no health in him.* He now felt compunction for sin in general, though it was only his ill-behaviour to his daughter which had brought him to church. The sermon was such as to strengthen the impression which the prayers had made; and when it was over, instead of joining the ringers, (for the belfry was the only part of the church John liked, because it usually led to the ale-house,) he quietly walked back to his work. It was, indeed, the best day's work he ever made. He could not get out of his head the whole day, the first words he heard at church; *When the wicked man turneth away from his wickedness, and doeth that which is lawful and right, he shall save his soul alive.* At night, instead of going to the Bell, he went home, intending to ask Hester to forgive him; but as soon as he got to the door, he heard Rebecca scolding his daughter for having brought such a disgrace on the family as to be seen in that old rag of a gown, and insisted on knowing what she had done with the money. Hester tried to keep the secret, but her mother declared she would turn her out of doors if she did not tell the truth. Hester was at last forced to confess she had given it to her father. Unfortunately for poor John, it was at this very moment that he opened the door. The mother now divided her fury between her guilty husband and her innocent child, till from words she fell to blows. John defended his daughter, and received some of the strokes intended for the poor girl. This turbulent scene partly put John's good resolution to flight, though the patience of Hester did him almost as much good as the sermon he had heard. At length, the poor girl escaped up stairs, not a little bruised, and a scene of much violence passed between John and Rebecca. She declared she would not sit down to supper with such a brute, and set off to a neighbour's house, that she might have the pleasure of abusing him the longer. John, whose mind was much disturbed, went up stairs without his supper. As he was passing by Hester's little room he heard her voice, and as he concluded she was venting her bitter complaints against her unnatural parents, he stopped to listen, resolved to go in and comfort her. He stopped at the door, for, by the light of the moon, he saw her kneeling by her bedside, and praying so earnestly that she did not hear him. As he made sure she could be praying for nothing but his death, what was his surprise to hear these words: "O Lord, have mercy upon my dear father and mother, teach me to love them, to pray for them, and do them good; make me more dutiful and more patient, that, adorning the doctrine of God, my Saviour, I may recommend his holy religion, and my dear parents may be brought to love and fear thee, through Jesus Christ."

Poor John, who would never have been hardhearted if he had not been a drunkard, could not stand this; he fell down on his knees, embraced his child, and begged her to teach him how to pray. He prayed himself as well as he could, and though he did not know what words to use, yet his heart was melted; he owned he was a sinner, and begged Hester to fetch the prayer-book, and read over the confession with which he had been so struck at church. This was the pleasantest order she had ever obeyed. Seeing him deeply affected with a sense of sin she pointed out to him the Saviour of sinners; and in this manner she passed some hours with her father, which were the happiest of her life; such a night was worth a hundred cotton, or even silk gowns. In the course of the week Hester read over the confession, and some other prayers, to her father so often that he got them by heart, and repeated them while he was at work.—She next taught him the fifty-first psalm. At length he took courage to kneel down and pray before he went to bed. From that time he bore his wife's ill-humor much better than he had ever done, and, as he knew her to be neat, and notable, and saving, he began to think, that if her temper was not quite as bad, his home might still become as pleasant a place to him as ever the Bell had been; but unless she became more tractable he did not know what to do with his long evenings after the little ones were in bed, for he began, once more, to delight in playing with them. Hester proposed that she herself should teach him to read an hour every night, and he consented. Rebecca began to storm, from the mere trick she had got of storming; but finding that he now brought home all his earnings, and that she got both his money and his company, (for she had once loved him,) she began to reconcile herself to this new way of life. In a few months John could read a psalm. In learning to read it he also got it by heart, and this proved a little store for private devotion, and while he was mowing or reaping, he could call to mind a text to cheer his labour. He now went constantly to church, and often dropped in at the school on a Sunday evening to hear their prayers. He expressed so much pleasure at this, that one day Hester ventured to ask him if they should set up family prayer at home? John said he should like it mightily, but as he could not yet read quite well enough, he desired Hester to try to get a proper book and begin next Sunday night. Hester had bought of a pious hawker, for three halfpence,* the Book of prayers, printed for the Cheap Repository, and knew she should there find something suitable.

When Hester read the exhortation at the beginning of this little book, her mother, who sat in the corner, and pretended to be asleep, was so much struck that she could not find a word to say against it. For a few nights, indeed, she continued to sit still, or pretended to rock the young child while her husband and daughter were kneeling at their prayers. She expected John would have scolded her for this, and so perverse was her temper, that she was disappointed at his finding no fault with her. Seeing at last that he was very patient, and that though he prayed fervently himself he suffered her to do as she liked, she lost the spirit of opposition for want of something to provoke it. As her pride began to be subdued, some little disposition to piety was awakened in her heart.—By degrees she slid down on her knees, though at first it was behind the cradle, or the clock, or in some corner where she thought they

---

* These prayers may be had also divided into two parts, one fit for private persons, the other for families, price one halfpenny.

would not see her. Hester rejoiced even in this outward change in her mother, and prayed that God would at last be pleased to touch her heart as he had done that of her father.

As John now spent no idle money, he had saved up a trifle by working over-hours; this he kindly offered to Hester to make up for the loss of her gown. Instead of accepting it, Hester told him, that as she herself was young and healthy, she should soon be able to clothe herself out of her own savings, and begged him to make her mother a present of this gown, which he did. It had been a maxim of Rebecca that it was better not to go to church at all than to go in an old gown. She had, however, so far conquered this evil notion, that she had lately gone pretty often. This kindness of the gown touched her not a little, and the first Sunday she put it on Mr. Simpson happened to preach from this text, God resisteth the proud, but giveth grace to the humble. This sermon so affected Rebecca that she never once thought she had her new gown on, till she came to take it off when she went to bed, and that very night, instead of skulking behind, she knelt down by her husband, and joined in prayer with much fervour.

There was one thing sunk deep in Rebecca's mind; she had observed that since her husband had grown religious he had been so careful not to give her any offence that he was become scrupulously clean; took off his dirty shoes before he sat down, and was very cautious not to spill a drop of beer on her shining table. Now it was rather remarkable, that as John grew more neat, Rebecca grew more indifferent to neatness. But both these changes arose from the same cause, the growth of religion in their hearts. John grew cleanly from the fear of giving pain to his wife, while Rebecca grew indifferent from having discovered the sin and folly of over-anxious care about trifles. When the heart is once given up to God, such vanities in a good degree die of themselves.

Hester continues to grow in grace, and in knowledge. Last Christmas-day she was appointed an under teacher in the school, and many people think that some years hence, if any thing should happen to Mrs. Crew, Hester may be promoted to be head mistress.

10. Three French views on the education of girls

Following the French Revolution, writers of conflicting religious and political convictions debated how best to educate girls for the needs of a new

SOURCES: (i) Albertine-Adrienne Necker de Saussure, The Study of the Life of Woman (Philadelphia, 1844), pp. 27–29, 71, 74–75, 128–30. Originally published in Paris in 1838. (ii) Félix Dupanloup, Studious Women, tr. R. M. Phillimore (Boston, 1869), pp. 6–7, 18–23. Originally published in Paris in 1867. (iii) G. Bruno [pseud. of Mme Alfred J. E. Fouillée], Francinet, 66th ed. (Paris, 1887), pp. 333–39. Originally published in Paris in 1869. The editors are grateful to Professor Linda L. Clark, Millersville State University, Millersville, Pa., for sending us a copy of this story.

era. Three of the most influential of these writers were the Evangelical Calvinist Albertine-Adrienne Necker de Saussure (1766–1841), the Roman Catholic bishop of Orléans Félix-Antoine-Philbert Dupanloup (1802–78), and the anticlerical republican Augustine Tuillerie Fouillée (1833–1923), who wrote under the pseudonym of G. Bruno.

A member of a liberal Genevan family, Necker de Saussure was already well known in France and abroad for her treatise on progressive education when she published 'The Study of the Life of Women' in the late 1830's. In this manual, in which Necker de Saussure insisted that the intellect of women should be cultivated in order to make them better wives and mothers, she provided a plan by which mothers could educate their daughters at home. Like the American Catharine Beecher (1800–1878; Doc. 21.i), she argued for a rigorous division of public and private spheres and, in the name of family tranquility and social stability, justified woman's continued subjection within marriage. However, she rejected the assumption that girls should be educated exclusively for a domestic role.

By mid-century the focus of debate had shifted from the home to the school. In the 1860's the French educational bureaucracy launched a campaign to wrest control of female education from the Catholic Church; this battle for the conquest of women's minds raged well into the twentieth century. By far the most important Catholic voice in this contest was that of Bishop Dupanloup, who vehemently opposed state-sponsored secondary courses for girls and threatened to excommunicate any Catholics in his diocese who allowed their daughters to attend them. Dupanloup's views on the aims of female education did not, however, differ significantly from those of his secular opponents, some of whom even praised his ideas as liberal and progressive. Indeed, Dupanloup's views, translated into many languages, inspired the reform of Catholic girls' education throughout the Western world.

To counter the Catholic teachings, the educators of the Third Republic embarked on an explicit program of "molding the female citizen." One of their most successful textbook writers, G. Bruno, was later revealed to be the retiring wife of a well-known psychologist at the Sorbonne. This didactic story from Bruno's 'Francinet,' a favorite reader for eleven-to-thirteen-year-old children of both sexes before the First World War, instructs girls to forgo developing any talents or gifts that would conflict with their domestic duties. In fact, many republicans were even stricter in maintaining the separation of spheres than the religious writers.

(i) Albertine-Adrienne Necker de Saussure

The same gospel which says "Women, submit yourselves to your own husbands," teaches [them] also that there is no inequality among human beings in the sight of God. "Ye are all the children of God by faith in Jesus Christ." "There is neither bond nor free, there is neither male nor female, for ye are all one in Christ Jesus."

But this part of our celestial nature which education should constantly seek to bring out, man has scarcely taken into account. He has had this life only in view, and has shut his eyes upon whatever limited his rights here. He has seen only the wife in the woman—in the young girl only the future wife. All the faculties, the qualities which have no immediate relation to his interests, have seemed to him worthless. Yet there are many of the gifts bestowed upon woman that have no relation to the state of a wife. This state, although natural, is not necessary—perhaps half the women who now exist, have not been, or are no longer, married. In the indigent classes, the girl who is able to maintain herself, quits her parents, and supports herself by her industry for a long time, perhaps for life, without requiring aid from man. No social arrangements oblige her to become dependent. It is therefore important, that education should unfold in the young girl the qualities which give the surest promise of wisdom, happiness, usefulness, and dignity, whatever may be her lot. . . .

We do not desire that her end should be within herself—we wish that women should devote their lives to produce the happiness of others, but we wish this also for man.

There is, in our opinion, neither perfection nor happiness in any human creature, without a self-sacrificing spirit; but the self-sacrifice imposed by those who profit by it, and imposed without their giving the example, we believe is neither so constant nor so sincere as to deserve the name: and if, in order to obtain sacrifices which morality or affection would render voluntary, we paralyze the intellectual, or wound the dignity of the sensitive being, I say that we do not do justice to God's work. . . .

If we would have the selfishness of men plainly exhibited, let us listen to Rousseau.

"All the education of women should bear a relation to men—to please, to be useful to them—to possess their love and esteem, to educate them in childhood, to nurse them when grown up, to counsel, to console, to make their lives pleasant and sweet; such are the duties of women and should be taught to them from infancy."

If Rousseau had said that the education of women should bear a relation to what surrounds them, to the beings with whom nature or love had entwined their fate, we would applaud this language. Why particularly designate men? Why teach young girls to consider their own sex as nothing? and why give to the necessity of loving the most dangerous tendency? . . .

It is then at the age of ten years that we begin the education of young girls: an age which still belongs to childhood sufficiently to represent it as a whole. And if some of our remarks seem to relate to an earlier period, mothers will readily carry them farther back. The defects to be prevented in the character of their daughters must hitherto have occupied them as much as the qualities to be formed: so injurious is the atmosphere which surrounds women from the very cradle, so much is the influence around them addressed to their most dangerous tendencies, and calculated to increase their force.

With respect to this fact, the course followed in our preceding work would have for real life some advantages. The sisters brought up with their brothers would be subject to the same rules and duties, justice and truth being the only means employed to guide them. In this common education, there must be more firmness, less flattery; the promises and menaces of opinion, to which boys are comparatively insensible, are rarely employed. The motives proposed to all the children are those of goodness, reason, and true moral philosophy, adapted to their comprehension.

Since the comparative weakness of girls is rarely manifested before the age of ten years, why should they be freed from the laws of natural equality? Why led to calculate upon accommodations and consideration from the other sex? Many sad disappointments are thus prepared for them. . . .

Obedience is so important an element in education, it is so truly the first duty of childhood, and the way to observe every other, that in this respect no difference can be made in the education of the two sexes. However, docility, that internal disposition which naturally leads to the fulfillment of this duty, may well be the object of peculiar cultivation in young girls. Whenever boys are placed under public instruction, they are rather governed by general rules than by the will of individuals. Women, on the contrary, are called to bear, very often, and perhaps throughout their lives, the yoke of personal obedience. Since such is their fate, it is well to accustom them to it; they must learn to yield without even an internal murmur. Their gayety, their health, their equality of temper, will all gain by a prompt and cordial docility. . . .

Hence we would exhort mothers always to exercise fearlessly the authority with which God has entrusted them, since this also is sacred authority. Even though they might obtain the accomplishment of their plans in some other way, it would be important to accustom their daughters to submission. We would suggest that long expositions of motives invite objections, and seem to show that resistance is expected. It is with little girls especially that it is important to prevent rejoinders, the habit of contradicting and of arguing on all occasions.

A man is less exposed to this defect; he has but to express his will, and all yields to it in his family. A woman, on the contrary, who decides on no subject independently, if she prolongs indefinitely an insignificant opposition, both vexes her husband and disturbs the peace of her own heart.

The sentiment of superior duty, the idea ever present to the mind, that we are obeying God in observing the laws that nature or a formal engagement have imposed, prohibits all rebellion, and preserves, to a woman, her dignity, in the very bosom of obedience. This is what designates in her the immortal being, whatever be her mission upon earth.

In cherishing this sentiment you will also cultivate in your daughter other qualities: you will endow her with patience, resignation, and all the gentle virtues that a woman is infallibly called to exercise. To the caprices of fortune will be added, for her discipline, those of mankind. A multitude of illusive hopes and disappointed expectations form a part of her fate. Her best plans will be overturned: her occupations interrupted, she will have to suffer in silence humiliations and distresses still more poignant. But when, gentle and patient, she shall have supported all such trials, a high degree of virtue will be developed within her.

[Here is Necker de Saussure's schedule for organizing the hours in a young girl's day.]

Religious duties: worship and various exercises, 1

Literary and scientific studies—intellectual cultivation: elements of calculation and physical science, languages, history and geography, exercises of memory, 4 [total]

Fine arts: music and drawing, 1.5

Material duties and occupations: physical exercise, 1.5; female work and domestic care, 1.5; liberty, meals, and family circle, 4.5

On looking over the above plan, we see at once that the larger portion of the time is appropriated to recreations or duties purely material, and the smaller portion to study. It seems to us, therefore, that we cannot be accused of requiring too much mental application from young girls. But we can never approve of any diminution of the time claimed for purely intellectual education. If, then, we wish to preserve intact the four previous hours employed to develop the magnificent gift of intelligence, it is essential to lose not a moment; long preparations, idle words, must be prohibited, and this alone would be a valuable habit. The power of promptly fixing the attention forms what is called presence of mind, and also gives nerve to the character.

Undoubtedly it would be chimerical to expect that mothers should carry through their administrations the same exactness which forms the principal merit of institutions. But it would be, we think, possible for them to establish a more regular order in the employment of time than they usually do. A mother of a family is called to perform a variety of duties, and is exposed to interruptions in her functions as a governess; but may she not often anticipate the interruption, substitute one employment for another, and have in reserve some occupation for her daughters during her absence? Translations, extracts, tables, or charts to copy, serve as a continuation to interrupted lessons. . . .

When good proportions in the disposal of the hours of the day have been observed, the interior equilibrium is easily preserved in the young girl. Then you may often see her return of her own accord to her religious reading, carry on some object of study, and yield with moderation to her recreations; but it sometimes happens that a state of preceding fatigue is discovered, by a desire to depart as much as possible from habits; and as what usually wearies young girls is the constraint imposed by education, they abandon themselves to an excessive vivacity;—whatever is out of the line of their previous existence, appears a recreation. This symptom, and some others, indicate the necessity of changing the course, and perhaps of multiplying the periods of repose; but nothing should induce the mother to let go the reins of education. One kind of order may be bad, but order itself is indispensable.

(ii) Monseigneur Dupanloup

What I should wish to see above all things is, not a race of learned women, but—what is necessary to their husbands, their children, and their households —intelligent, judicious women, capable of sustained attention, well versed in everything that it is useful for them to know, as mothers, mistresses of households, and women of the world; never despising any labor of the hands, and at the same time not only knowing how to occupy their fingers, but their minds also, and to cultivate their souls and their whole being. And I must add: that what is to be dreaded as much as the very worst of scourges is the frivolous, fickle, effeminate, idle, ignorant, pleasure-loving woman, devoted to dissipation and amusement, and consequently opposed to all exertion and to almost all duty; incapable of all studious pursuits, of all consecutive attention, and therefore not in a condition to take any real share in the education of her children, or the affairs of her husband and her household. . . .

The rights of women to intellectual cultivation are not only rights, they are at the same time duties. This is what renders them inalienable. If they were only rights, women might sacrifice them: but they are duties. The sacrifice, therefore, is not possible without a dereliction of duty. These are the premises of my present argument, and I state plainly that it is a duty in women to study and to instruct themselves; and that intellectual labor ought to have its separate part assigned to it, amongst their own special occupations, and their most important obligations. The primordial reasons for this obligation are important, they are of divine origin, and absolutely incapable of being rejected; they are these: In the first place, God never makes useless gifts; in everything that God does, there is a reason, an aim; and if man's companion is a reasonable creature; if, like man, she has been created in the image and resemblance of God; if she has also received from the Creator the gift of intelligence, the sublimest of all his gifts, it is in order to make use of it.

God has given us all hands, which, according to the commentators, represent vigorous and intelligent action, but on condition that we do not return to him empty-handed. In short, He has explained Himself categorically in the parable of the talents, in which He declares that a strict account will be required of the use of every talent. And I do not know of any Father of the Church, or of any moralist, who has thought hitherto that this parable did not concern women as well as men. There is no distinction made here, each will have to give an account of that which has been entrusted to him or her; and human as well as divine good sense shows plainly enough that women, not more nor less than men, have the right to bury or to squander the gifts conferred upon them by God for the purpose of making a right use of them.

I will then say with St. Augustine, that no creature to whom God has entrusted the lamp of intelligence ought to permit herself to behave like one of the foolish virgins, in imprudently letting her lamp go out for want of trimming it; thus allowing the light to be spent, which is first intended for herself, and next, for others beside herself; and, since the question is about wives and mothers, for her husband and her children.

In most of the books which treat of the merit, the destiny, and the virtue of woman, she is far from being considered in the light of *an intelligent and free being, who is created in the image of* GOD, AND WHO IS RESPONSIBLE TO HER MAKER FOR ALL HER ACTIONS; she is converted into the property of man, made only for him *who is her aim and end.* In all these books, woman is only a fascinating creature to be adored, and not to be respected, and, in fact, an inferior being, whose existence has no other aim but the pleasure of man, or to be of use to him, in the most frivolous manner, depending in the first place, on man, who alone is her master, her legislator, and her judge: considering her absolutely as if she had neither soul, nor conscience, nor moral liberty, as if God has nothing for her, and had not given her soul, wants, faculties, aspirations, in one word, rights as well as duties.

Much has been said, and rightly said, against the futility of women, their wish to please, and what is called their "*coquetterie.*" But, in the first place, about their futility—is [it] not produced, is it not propagated, by the fear of making learned women, of developing their intelligence too much, as if it could ever be too much developed in a serious point of view, as if real development, by means of which duty and its results are best understood, could possibly do harm? Is not a woman who has serious tastes forced to hide them, or to make excuses for them *by all the means that she might employ in palliating a fault?* . . .

I say it without any hesitation, Christian morality alone teaches woman, with a decisive and absolute authority, her real rights and duties in their necessary reciprocal relaton. Yes; until you have persuaded woman that she is created first of all for God, next for herself and for her own soul, and lastly for her husband and her children, but after God, with God, and always for God, you will have done nothing either for the happiness or the honor of your families. . . . The Christian woman looks upon herself as the companion of man, as his helpmate, as much in earthly as in Heavenly things . . . and she feels it is incumbent on her to console him and to conduce to his happiness. But she also thinks that the husband and wife ought to help each other to become better, and after having together formed children for eternity, to share with them the same happiness for ever and ever. For such a destiny *the education of women cannot be too consecutive, too masculine, or too serious.*

The contrary system rests on a *Pagan view of their destiny,* and also, as has been truly said, *on the idleness of men who wish to retain their superiority without effort.* The Pagan view is that women are only charming creatures— passive, subordinate, and only made for the pleasure and the amusement of man. But, as I have said, Christianity has far other ideas. In Christianity the virtue of a woman, like that of a man, ought to be voluntary, noble, active, and intelligent. She ought to know the whole extent of her duties, and all the divine knowledge which can be derived from them, for the benefit of her husband and her children.

The prejudice against the cultivation of the intellect in women is one of the most culpable notions of the eighteenth century—that century of licentiousness and impiety. . . . A superior woman obliges her husband to reckon with her. He is forced to be influenced by the controlling power of an intelligent mind, and he does not feel himself at liberty to follow all his caprices, and this is the reason why vicious husbands wished to have ignorant wives.

(iii) Augustine Fouillée (G. Bruno)

Francinet.—Sir, how happy I am to be able to read so well! Miss Aimée lent me a book that contains a beautiful story; yesterday I read it to Mama and my sister and that made them very happy.

M. Edmond.—What story was it, Francinet?

Francinet.—It was about Joan of Arc, sir. Mama thought it was really beautiful; when my sister heard the part about poor Joan's death, she wanted to cry, and she told me that she was very proud to learn that France had once been saved by a young girl.

M. Edmond.—She is right to be proud, my child. Joan of Arc is one of our purest glories.

Francinet.—Sir, that story made me think of something: in all the stories you have told us, it is always men who have invented everything and never women. Why is that? Little girls are certainly just as bright as little boys; you know that Mlle Aimée answers much better than I, and often understands more quickly than M. Henri.

Henri.—Oh! that's surely true. Aimée understands right away, and she doesn't get conceited for all that. That's why I'm very fond of my little sister.

M. Edmond.—Well, Aimée. Prove to us once again how quickly you understand and tell us why women are so rarely found among inventors.

Aimée, very embarrassed.—Goodness! It seems to me, sir, that in order to invent something, you have to be involved in it. I don't know whether women could have invented the locomotive, like Stephenson; but I know that they have never had the opportunity; for they have never been assigned to tend machines, and people would find it very funny to see them learning mechanics or mathematics.

M. Edmond.—Very well reasoned, dear Aimée. Woman's role in society is not at all the same as man's. A woman's life is entirely interior, and her influence on society occurs in a nearly invisible manner. This is not to say, however, that her role is any less important or her influence smaller; it is only more hidden, that's all.

Women exercise their influence first of all on children, and it is remarkable that many illustrious men owed the qualities that made them famous to their mothers' example and precepts. You remember Saint Louis. Well, he had as a mother a very energetic woman, Blanche of Castille. Everyone knows the words she spoke to her infant son: "You know, Louis, how much I love you; yet I would infinitely prefer to see you die than see you willingly commit an evil act. Judge thereby to what extent injustice is a great evil and what distance you should keep from it." These noble words bore fruit, and the young prince who had been raised in such a remarkable fashion became one of the most noble personages in all French history.

As you have rightly said, Aimée, even though women very rarely learn

mathematics and sciences, there have nevertheless been several exceptions to this rule, and certain women who have had the opportunity of learning these sciences have become famous. Would you like me to give you some examples?
—Oh, sir! exclaimed the two children, that would give us great pleasure!

[In the next chapter, M. Edmond tells the children the story of Sophie Germain (1776–1831), the celebrated mathematician. When he finishes, Aimée says:]

Thank you, sir, for telling us this interesting story. I am very proud that there was such an intelligent and learned girl. I didn't think women were capable of understanding anything having to do with mathematics. It seems as strange to me as Greek and Latin.

M. Edmond.—Dear child, what you say about Latin and Greek reminds me of another story that also has a little girl for its heroine. I am going to tell it to you.

[M. Edmond then recounts the story of Mme Dacier (1647–1720), a renowned classical scholar who translated the *Iliad* and the *Odyssey* into French, and he concludes:]

This is not to say, my dear children, that every little girl should learn Latin and Greek, or occupy herself with higher mathematics. I only wanted to show you that girls are capable of learning even very difficult things. All the more reason why they can and must learn the easier, very useful things that they are taught.

In this regard, our little Aimée sets an example of goodwill and intelligence, and I happily take advantage of this opportunity to compliment her.
—Sir, said Aimée blushing, you are very kind to me.

11. Female health and the education of girls in England and the United States

Like the French writers on female education, the English writer and schoolmistress Elizabeth Missing Sewell (1815–1906) believed that girls should be educated for their future roles as wives and mothers. But she differed from them in her obsession with female fragility and her preoccupation with the adverse effects of a male-style intellectual training on a girl's health. In contrast to Sewell, the American writer Eliza Bisbee Duffey (d. 1898), a staunch proponent of coeducation, dress reform, and outdoor exercise, blames female ill health on faulty socialization and presents a far more challenging view of women's educational potential. Duffey's argument is particularly interesting in its application of Darwin's theory of evolution to the debate about the education of girls.

SOURCES: (i) Elizabeth Missing Sewell, *Principles of Education, Drawn from Nature and Revelation, and Applied to Female Education in the Upper Classes* (New York, 1866), pp. 396–97, 450–51. Originally published in London in 1865. (ii) Eliza Bisbee Duffey, *No sex in education; or, An equal chance for both girls and boys.* . . . (Philadelphia, 1874), pp. 40–43, 100–101.

(i) Elizabeth Sewell

The aim of education is to fit children for the position in life which they are hereafter to occupy. Boys are to be sent out into the world to buffet with its temptations, to mingle with bad and good, to govern and direct. The school is the type of the life they are hereafter to lead. Girls are to dwell in quiet homes, amongst a few friends; to exercise a noiseless influence, to be submissive and retiring. There is no connection between the bustling mill-wheel life of a large school and that for which they are supposed to be preparing. . . .

It is very easy for studious men, who have never had to deal with delicate girls, to suggest a course of instruction which shall bring them on a level with their brothers. There is no doubt that girls can, up to a certain point, be made to learn just as much, and as well, as boys. Take a school of little boys and little girls, and compare them, and the probability is that the latter will be found the superior. There is a quickness, a kind of intuitive perception about them, in which boys are wanting. They develop at an earlier age, and more rapidly. But take those same boys and girls at seventeen and eighteen, and the boy will have advanced far beyond the girl. Even in those things which he does not know, he will show a power of ready acquirement, in which she will be wanting. Not one girl in a hundred would be able to work up the subjects required for an Indian Civil Service Examination, in the way which boys do. And for one very obvious reason, putting aside all others. Her health would break down under the effort. And health is the obstacle, which, even under the most favourable circumstances, must stand in the way of a girl's acquiring the intellectual strength, which, at this age, is so invaluable to a boy. He has been tossed about the world, left in a great measure to his own resources, and been inured to constant physical exertion. He has been riding, and boating, and playing cricket, and both body and mind have been roused to energy; and so, when he comes to study, he has a sense of power, which acts mentally as well as physically, and enables him to grasp difficulties, and master them. The girl, on the contrary, has been guarded from over fatigue, subject to restrictions with regard to cold, and heat, and hours of study, seldom trusted away from home, allowed only a small share of responsibility;—not willingly, with any wish to thwart her inclinations—but simply because, if she is not thus guarded, if she is allowed to run the risks, which, to the boy, are a matter of indifference, she will probably develop some disease, which, if not fatal, will, at any rate, be an injury to her for life.

This question of health must be a primary consideration with all persons who undertake to educate girls. It will be a perpetual interruption to their plans for study and mental improvement, but it is one which can never be put aside. Parents in private, and the intellectual world in public, will demand that girls should be brought forward, and taught all that an age which makes intellect its idol thinks fit to require, and the attempt to satisfy them must be met in one of two ways. Either by the over mental exertion which ends in a break-up of health, or by a superficial intellectual show which resembles actual knowledge and moral power only as the veneered table resembles solid wood.

Any strain upon a girl's intellect is to be dreaded, and any attempt to bring women into competition with men can scarcely escape failure.

(ii) Eliza Bisbee Duffey

As infancy begins to give place to childhood, then the distinctive training commences in earnest. The boy is allowed to be natural, the girl is forced to be artificial. Some girls break through all restraints and romp, but they are not the model girls whom mothers delight in and visitors praise for being "lady-like." Boy and girl as they are, with the same life pulsing in their veins and drawing its sustenance in precisely the same manner, with the same physical and mental needs, nature calls imperatively for an equally active life for both. They both want the air and the sunshine. They need equally to be hardened by the storms, tanned by the winds and have limbs strengthened by unrestrained exercise. But instead of this equality, while boys have their liberty more or less freely granted them, girls must stay at home and sew and read, and play prettily and quietly, and take demure walks. I am not speaking of girls in a single stratum of society, but of girls everywhere, from the highest down almost to the lowest, wherever the word "lady" is sufficiently reverenced and misunderstood. . . .

Girls, whose energies are still the most powerful, have no opportunity for working off their surplus vitality in rude and boisterous ways, for the restraint is never lifted from them. So they enter with the whole force of their natures into their studies, and, as every teacher will bear testimony, soon far outstrip their brothers. To be at the head of their class, to receive the highest mark of merit, is their ruling ambition. Their minds are prematurely developed at the expense of their bodies. This does not result because they are educated as boys, but because *both* are educated wrongly, and the girl far more wrongly than the boy, inasmuch and just so far as her education in the general discipline of her life differs from that of the boy. . . .

When we still further admit that in matters of fresh air, exercise and dress girls almost invariably labor under disadvantages which boys do not feel, I think there has been sufficient admitted to account for all failures (supposing there to be any) of girls in keeping healthful as well as mental pace with boys. It is pernicious habits in these respects which need looking after and correcting—these and the further and to my mind still more important fact that at the close of her school-days is removed a girl's mental stimulus, and she is left to collapse. Set these things right, and let girls find a "career" open to them, and education will take care of itself.

If there is really a radical mental difference in men and women founded upon sex, you *cannot* educate them alike, however much you try. If women *cannot* study unremittingly, why then they *will* not, and you *cannot make them.* But because they do, because they choose so to do, because they will do so in spite of you, should be accepted as evidence that they can, and, all other things being equal, can with impunity. Instead of our race dying out through these women, they are the hope of the country—the women with broad chests, large limbs and full veins, perfect muscular and digestive systems and harmonious sexual organs, who will keep pace with men either in a foot or an intellectual race, who know perfectly their own powers and are not afraid to tax them to their utmost, knowing as they do that action generates force. These are the mothers of the coming race. . . . The result will be truly "the survival of the fittest."

12. Memories of New England schooling: Elizabeth Buffum Chace

Elizabeth Buffum Chace (1806–99), sister of Lucy Buffum Lovell (Doc. 3), was an active abolitionist and suffragist and the mother of ten children. In this excerpt from her diary, Chace recalls her school days in Smithfield, Rhode Island. American girls and boys, unlike their European contemporaries, often shared the same classroom, where they were subjected to the rote learning of grammar, spelling, and composition.

The fathers and mothers in Smithfield had a lively interest in the education of their children, and a good school was maintained fifty-two weeks in the year, with no vacations.

Our text books were of a very primitive kind. In geography we had no atlases to use—and I believe the imperfect manner in which I learned localities is the reason why I have never been able to think of places in the right direction—but we did an immense amount of memorizing. There was no learning made easy for us. In grammar we were obliged to recite every word of Murray's large volume over and over, for a long time, before we were set to make practical application of it in the analysis or parsing of a sentence. We must repeat *of, to, for, by, with, in, into, within, without, over, under, through, above, below, before, behind, beneath, on* or *upon, among, after, about, against,* for months before we were permitted to tell what should be done with the smallest preposition of them all.

I remember when at twelve years of age I had recited *Murray's Grammar* through perhaps over a dozen times without a word of explanation or application from the book or the teacher, the master, as I was passing by him to my seat, handed me an open book, and pointing to a passage, said I might study that for a parsing lesson. Alas! it was no open book to me. The sentences which he indicated read: "Dissimulation in youth is the forerunner of perfidy in old age. Its first appearance is a token of growing depravity and future shame." I knew every rule in the grammar but I did not know how to apply one of them even to the first word. I carried the book out at recess, and a more advanced pupil gave me a clue. I put my memory in harness, and soon learned to apply the rules, of which hitherto I had no comprehension.

Still, for that time it was a good school, for we had to work out our own salvation by hard study. The master carried all the time in his hand, a ruler with a leather strap nailed over each end. If he caught an eye wandering from the book, or if he saw signs of restlessness or heard a whisper, he gave the

SOURCE: *Two Quaker Sisters: From the Original Diaries of Elizabeth Buffum Chace and Lucy Buffum Lovell* (New York, 1937), pp. 23–24.

offender a smart blow, particularly if it happened to be his own little mother-less boy to whom he was especially cruel.

Our curriculum was narrow but we made good readers and spellers, and those of us who had the gift, good writers, and we were well grounded in grammar.

13. Life at an English boarding school: Frances Power Cobbe

The only daughter of an upper-class Anglo-Irish family, Frances Power Cobbe (1822–1904) spent the first part of her life on a large estate near Dublin. After having been educated at home, first by her beloved mother and later by several governesses, she was sent at the age of fourteen to a fashionable and expensive school in the English resort of Brighton. The following excerpt from her autobiography depicts her experience at this school. It is a credit to Cobbe that despite the superficiality of her schooling, she went on to distinguish herself as a writer, reformer, and advocate of the feminist cause.

When it came to my turn to receive education, it was not in London but in Brighton that the ladies' schools most in estimation were to be found. There were even then (about 1836) not less than a hundred such establishments in the town, but that at No. 32, Brunswick Terrace, of which Miss Runciman and Miss Roberts were mistresses, and which had been founded some time before by a celebrated Miss Poggi, was supposed to be *nec pluribus impar*. It was, at all events, the most outrageously expensive, the nominal tariff of £120 or £130 per annum representing scarcely a fourth of the charges for "extras" which actually appeared in the bills of many of the pupils. My own, I know, amounted to £1,000 for two years' schooling.

I shall write of this school quite frankly, since the two poor ladies, well-meaning but very unwise, to whom it belonged have been dead for nearly thirty years, and it can hurt nobody to record my conviction that a better system than theirs could scarcely have been devised had it been designed to attain the maximum of cost and labour and the minimum of solid results. It was the typical Higher Education of the period, carried out to the extreme of expenditure and high pressure.

Profane persons were apt to describe our school as a Convent, and to refer to the back door of our garden, whence we issued on our dismal diurnal walks, as the "postern." If we in any degree resembled nuns, however, it was assuredly not those of either a Contemplative or Silent Order. The din of our large double schoolrooms was something frightful. Sitting in either of them, four pianos might be heard going at once in rooms above and around us, while at numerous tables scattered about the rooms there were girls reading aloud to the governesses and reciting lessons in English, French, German, and Italian. This hideous clatter continued the entire day till we went to bed at night,

SOURCE: Frances Power Cobbe, *Life of Frances Power Cobbe As Told by Herself* (London, 1904), pp. 60–68.

there being no time whatever allowed for recreation, unless the dreary hour of walking with our teachers (when we recited our verbs), could so be described by a fantastic imagination. In the midst of the uproar we were obliged to write our exercises, to compose our themes, and to commit to memory whole pages of prose. On Saturday afternoons, instead of play, there was a terrible ordeal generally known as the "Judgment Day." The two schoolmistresses sat side by side, solemn and stern, at the head of the long table. Behind them sat all the governesses as Assessors. On the table were the books wherein our evil deeds of the week were recorded; and round the room against the wall, seated on stools of penitential discomfort, we sat, five-and-twenty "damosels," anything but "Blessed," expecting our sentences according to our ill-desserts. It must be explained that the fiendish ingenuity of some teacher had invented for our torment a system of imaginary "cards," which we were supposed to "lose" (though we never gained any) whenever we had not finished all our various lessons and practisings every night before bed-time, or whenever we had been given the mark for "stooping," or had been impertinent, or had been "turned" in our lessons, or had been marked "P" by the music master, or had been convicted of "disorder" (e.g., having our long shoe-strings untied), or, lastly, had told lies! Any one crime in this heterogeneous list entailed the same penalty, namely, the sentence, "You have lost your card, Miss So-and-so, for such and such a thing;" and when Saturday came round, if three cards had been lost in the week, the law wreaked its justice on the unhappy sinner's head! Her confession having been wrung from her at the awful judgment-seat above described, and the books having been consulted, she was solemnly scolded and told to sit in the corner for the rest of the evening! Anything more ridiculous than the scene which followed can hardly be conceived. I have seen (after a week in which a sort of feminine barring-out had taken place) no less than nine young ladies obliged to sit for hours in the angles of the three rooms, like naughty babies, with their faces to the wall; half of them being quite of marriageable age, and all dressed, as was *de rigueur* with us every day, in full evening attire of silk or muslin, with gloves and kid slippers. Naturally, Saturday evenings, instead of affording some relief to the incessant overstrain of the week, were looked upon with terror as the worst time of all. Those who escaped the fell destiny of the corner were allowed, if they chose, to write to their parents, but our letters were perforce committed at night to the schoolmistress to seal, and were not as may be imagined, exactly the natural outpouring of our sentiments as regarded those ladies and their school.

Our household was a large one. It consisted of the two schoolmistresses and joint proprietors, of the sister of one of them and another English governess; of a French, an Italian, and a German lady teacher; of a considerable staff of respectable servants; and finally of twenty-five or twenty-six pupils, varying in age from nine to nineteen. All the pupils were daughters of men of some standing, mostly country gentlemen, members of Parliament, and offshoots of the peerage. There were several heiresses amongst us, and one girl whom we all liked and recognised as the beauty of the school, the daughter of Horace Smith, author of *Rejected Addresses*. On the whole, looking back after the long interval, it seems to me that the young creatures there assembled were full of capabilities for widely extended usefulness and influence. Many were decidedly clever and nearly all were well disposed. . . .

But all this fine human material was deplorably wasted. Nobody dreamed that any one of us could in later life be more or less than an "Ornament of Society." That a pupil in that school should ever become an artist, or authoress, would have been looked upon by both Miss Runciman and Miss Roberts as a deplorable dereliction. Not that which was good in itself or useful to the community, or even that which would be delightful to ourselves, but that which would make us admired in society was the *raison d'être* of each acquirement. Everything was taught us in the inverse ratio of its true importance. At the bottom of the scale were Morals and Religion, and at the top were Music and Dancing; miserably poor music, too, of the Italian school then in vogue, and generally performed in a showy and tasteless manner on harp or piano. I can recall an amusing instance in which the order of precedence above described was naïvely betrayed by one of our schoolmistresses when she was admonishing one of the girls who had been detected in a lie. "Don't you know, you naughty girl," said Miss R. impressively, before the whole school: "don't you know we had *almost* rather find you have a P—" (the mark of Pretty Well) "in your music, than tell such falsehoods?"

It mattered nothing whether we had any "music in our souls" or any voices in our throats, equally we were driven through the dreary course of practising daily for a couple of hours under a German teacher, and then receiving lessons twice or three times a week from a music master (Griesbach by name) and a singing master. Many of us, myself in particular, in addition to these had a harp master, a Frenchman named Labarre, who gave us lessons at a guinea apiece, while we could only play with one hand at a time. Lastly there were a few young ladies who took instructions in the new instruments, the concertina and the accordion!

The waste of money involved in all this, the piles of useless music, and songs never to be sung, for which our parents had to pay, and the loss of priceless time for ourselves, were truly deplorable; and the result of course in many cases (as in my own) complete failure. One day I said to the good little German teacher, who nourished a hopeless attachment for Schiller's Marquis Posa, and was altogether a sympathetic person, "My dear Fraulein, I mean to practise this piece of Beethoven's till I conquer it." "My dear," responded the honest Fraulein, "you do practice that piece for seex hours a day, and you do live till you are seexty, at the end you will *not* play it!" Yet so hopeless a pupil was compelled to learn for years, not only the piano, but the harp and singing!

Next to music in importance in our curriculum came dancing. The famous old Madame Michaud and her husband both attended us constantly, and we danced to their direction in our large play-room (*lucus a non lucendo*), till we had learned not only all the dances in use in England in that ante-polka epoch, but almost every national dance in Europe, the Minuet, the Gavotte, the Cachucha, the Bolero, the Mazurka, and the Tarantella. To see the stout old lady in her heavy green velvet dress, with furbelow a foot deep of sable, going through the latter cheerful performance for our ensample, was a sight not to be forgotten. Beside the dancing we had "calisthenic" lessons every week from a "Capitaine" Somebody, who put us through manifold exercises with poles and dumbells. How much better a few good country scrambles would have been than all these calisthenics it is needless to say, but our dismal walks were confined to parading the esplanade and neighbouring terraces. Our parties never exceeded six, a governess being one of the number, and we looked down from an immeasurable height of superiority on the processions of twenty and thirty girls belonging to other schools. The governess who accompanied us had enough to do with her small party, for it was her duty to utilise these brief hours of bodily exercise by hearing us repeat our French, Italian or German verbs, according to her own nationality.

Next to Music and Dancing and Deportment, came Drawing, but that was not a sufficiently *voyant* accomplishment, and no great attention was paid to it; the instruction also being of a second-rate kind, except that it included lessons in perspective which have been useful to me ever since. Then followed Modern Languages. No Greek or Latin were heard of at the school, but French, Italian and German were chattered all day long, our tongues being only set at liberty at six o'clock to speak English. *Such* French, such Italian, and such German as we actually spoke may be more easily imagined than described. We had bad "Marks" for speaking wrong languages, *e.g.*, French when we [were] bound to speak Italian or German, and a dreadful mark for bad French, which was transferred from one to another all day long, and was a fertile source of tears and quarrels, involving as it did a heavy lesson out of Noel et Chapsal's Grammar on the last holder at night. We also read in each language every day to the French, Italian and German ladies, recited lessons to them, and wrote exercises for the respective masters who attended every week. . . .

Naturally after (a very long way after) foreign languages came the study of English. We had a writing and arithmetic master (whom we unanimously abhorred and despised, though one and all of us grievously needed his instructions) and an "English master," who taught us to write "themes," and to whom I, for one, feel that I owe, perhaps, more than to any other teacher in that school, few as were the hours which we were permitted to waste on so insignificant an art as composition in our native tongue! . . .

Lastly, as I have said, in point of importance, came our religious instruction. Our well-meaning schoolmistresses thought it was obligatory on them to teach us something of the kind, but, being very obviously altogether worldly women themselves, they were puzzled how to carry out their intentions. They marched us to church every Sunday when it did not rain, and they made us on Sunday mornings repeat the Collect and Catechism; but beyond these exercises of body and mind, it was hard for them to see what to do for our spiritual welfare. One Ash Wednesday, I remember, they provided us with a dish of salt-fish, and when this was removed to make room for the roast mutton, they addressed us in a short discourse, setting forth the merits of fasting, and ending by the remark that they left us free to take meat or not as we pleased, but that they hoped we should fast; "it would be good for our souls AND OUR FIGURES!"

Each morning we were bound publicly to repeat a text out of certain little books, called *Daily Bread*, left in our bedrooms, and always scanned in frantic haste while "doing up" our hair at the glass, or gabbled aloud by one damsel so occupied while her room-fellow (there were never more than two in each bed-chamber) was splashing about behind the screen in her bath. Down, when the prayer-bell rang, both were obliged to hurry and breathlessly to await the chance of being called on first to repeat the text of the day, the penalty for oblivion being the loss of a "card." Then came a chapter of the Bible, read verse by verse amongst us, and then our books were shut and a solemn question was asked. On one occasion I remember it was: "What have you just been reading, Miss S—?" Miss S— (now a lady of high rank has fashion, whose small wits had been wool-gathering) peeped surrepetitiously into her Bible again, and then responded with just confidence, "The First Epistle, Ma'am, of *General Peter*."

It is almost needless to add, in concluding these reminiscences, that the heterogeneous studies pursued in this helter-skelter fashion were of the smallest possible utility in later life; each acquirement being of the shallowest and most imperfect kind, and all real education worthy of the name having to be begun on our return home, after we had been pronounced "finished."

14. A schoolmistress testifies about the education of English girls: Frances Mary Buss

Born to the family of an improvident artist, Frances Mary Buss (1827–94) began her teaching career at fourteen. Nine years later, in 1850, she founded the North London Collegiate School for Ladies, and, although much occupied with her duties as headmistress, managed to attend evening classes at Queens College in order to acquire the educational training she believed all teachers should have. Buss devoted her life to improving the standards of education for English girls and, in 1865, was called to give evidence before the Schools Inquiry Commission, which was investigating the state of education for the middle classes. In the following excerpt from her testimony, Buss denounces the deplorable state of female schooling in England and argues that both boys and girls should be given an intellectually rigorous education.

Will you have the goodness to state the nature of your school; is it a private school, or is it a proprietary school?—It is a private school. . . .

Is it a boarding school, or a day school, or both?—It is both.

What number of boarders have you?—18 has been the largest number.

SOURCE: Great Britain, *Parliamentary Papers*, 1867–68, XXVIII, Part 4, Schools Inquiry Commission, pp. 253–55, 257–58, 261.

What number of day scholars?—At this present moment 201.

What, may I ask, is the expense to a boarder for education and board at your school?—The expense including the general education would be between 50*l.* and 60*l.* a year.

What is the expense to a day scholar?—Nine guineas would be the average.

Are your boarders generally from the same class of society as your day scholars?—Yes.

The ability and willingness to pay the sum you have mentioned for a boarder seems to imply that they are the children of what may be called the upper division of the middle class?—I should think that they would be considered so. . . .

I presume your course of education is that which is usually taught in good female schools. Are there any peculiarities about it?—I scarcely know. I should think it is much what most schools profess.

Do you teach Latin at all?—Yes.

Do you teach modern languages?—Yes.

French and German?—French and German.

I suppose you teach English literature. Do you teach mathematics at all? —No; we have no pupils sufficiently advanced.

Do you pay much attention to arithmetic, and English composition and spelling?—Very much more attention has been paid to arithmetic since the Cambridge local examinations were established.

I fancy it is not a very easy thing to teach children to spell, is it? We are told it is almost the most difficult thing they have to do. How do you find that? —Very much depends on how long the child remains at school.

Do you pay great attention to it? Do you make it a point of great importance that a girl who leaves your school shall be able to spell well?—Yes. . . .

Your girls come up to you very ignorant?—Extremely ignorant.

Do they seem to be very little taught at all?—In the essentials, hardly ever. They seldom know any arithmetic, for instance. We have a large number of girls of 13, 14, or 15 come to us who can scarcely do the simplest sum in arithmetic. . . .

In your opinion should the education of a girl differ essentially from the education of a boy in the same rank of life, with regard to the subjects which are to be taught?—I think not, but it is rather difficult to ascertain what is the proper education for a boy.

You believe there is not such a distinction between the mental powers of the two classes, as to require any wide distinction between the good education given to a girl and that which is given to a boy?—I am sure that the girls can learn anything they are taught in an interesting manner, and for which they have some motive to work.

Do you encourage the study of accomplishments in your girls?—I think there is a large demand for accomplishments, but we try to make the accomplishments as real as possible.

I believe you find that there is a great wish on the part of parents that their daughters should have some knowledge of accomplishments?—Yes;

some knowledge of music and drawing, music especially. All the pupils learn drawing as a matter of course, and usually about two-thirds learn music. . . .

Do you attach importance to needlework in the education of girls?—Yes; every girl in the school learns plain needlework but no other kind of needlework, and a large quantity of plain clothing is made every year, which is always given away amongst the poor of the neighbourhood. I think it is most desirable that every girl should know how to use her needle.

I suppose, besides any indirect advantage there may be, it trains the eye and the hand a good deal?—Yes; I think it does.

Do you think any means could be taken for improving the class of school-mistresses by any system of certificates, or in any other mode?—I think most strongly that every one who teaches ought to go through some course of training in the art of teaching after having received a certificate of attainment. . . .

What is the lowest age at which girls come to you?—We have them from six to 18.

Do they often come to you from preparatory schools?—A very large number come to us at about 12 or 13 from other schools.

Are you able to say, comparing girls with boys, in what state of preparation they come to you? Do you think that the girls who come to you from preparatory schools are in a better or worse state of instruction than boys similarly circumstanced?—I do not know about the boys, I know that the girls could not be much worse prepared than they are.

Do they often come to you direct from home?—Yes, but more often from schools. . . .

The whole of their school time is mostly spent with you?—Yes; we have many girls who have been with us 10 or 11 years. Still there is a strong feeling in the neighbourhood, especially among the lower class of parents, to send the girls to us later, to what is called "finish," but we have declined to receive them latterly, except on a considerably increased payment. We then make them work alone, apart from the other pupils as much as possible.

What do you think the general defects in the state of education of the daughters of the middle class in London?—I think in the first place there are scarcely any good schools; in the next place, there are very few good teachers; and in the third place, there is no motive offered to the girls for study, nor to their parents to keep them at school.

Do you mean that you would wish to see some more public standard of attainments for girls?—Yes.

By public examinations and certificates?—Yes. These would guarantee the school to the parents, and give to the girls themselves a motive for work.

As to the condition of the instruction of the daughters of the middle classes in London, you have stated what you think are the defects in the machinery, but as to the result on their minds, what do you think are the chief points in which they are defective?—I think that such education as they get is almost entirely showy and superficial; a little music, a little singing, a little French, a little ornaments work, and nothing else, because many girls come to us who fancy they can speak French and play the piano, but have comparatively no knowledge of English or arithmetic.

Could they generally write English correctly?—Not the girls who came in at 12 or 13.

For their age they would not write, spell, or compose English well?—Not well.

With regard to the training of schoolmistresses, you have not considered whether you would have special establishments, schools or colleges, for training schoolmistresses?—No; I only know of one place at the present moment where a governess of the middle class can get training, and that is at the Home and Colonial.

That has just been begun?—No; it has been going on for some years, but on a limited scale; they receive 14, and most of the girls educated in our school, who have been intended for governesses, have been trained also at the Home and Colonial after leaving us.

You mean that for the improvement of schoolmistresses, not only a better education for girls of that class is required, but some special training for the duties of a schoolmistress?—Yes. It seems to me that far too often, in fact mostly, a schoolmistress opens a school simply because she must make a living, and that she has no knowledge whatever of teaching.

How do they come to you as to the elements of religious knowledge; in what state of preparation?—Very deficient mostly.

Are they as deficient in that as any other branch of knowledge?—Quite. . . .

(Lord Taunton) Have they generally been taught their Catechism?—Generally, but without understanding it.

Have they been taught to say their prayers?—Yes; but upon the whole we are disposed to think that the girls we have had to do with would in that respect be behind the girls of the National schools, certainly the girls of Sunday schools.

(Lord Lyttelton) What state of moral discipline do they come in; do they often come in a very untrained and uncontrolled state?—Yes, often; but we do not find any difficulty. The number of pupils is so large that public opinion regulates everything, and a troublesome girl very soon tones down.

With regard to the schools from which girls come to you: do you think better of them in respect of the general moral training than as to the intellectual instruction?—No, because I think in the very small schools the pupils have it their own way; it is so entirely a matter of necessity for the mistress to live that she is obliged to allow the children to do as they like, and the parents too. . . .

(Mr. Acland) I think you consider that the apathy of parents is one of the great difficulties you have to deal with, is it not?—We have not found it so of late years in our own case.

I mean, speaking generally, where the subject has not been so prominently brought under the attention of parents?—It may be so, because they do not see any results. In cases where a parent has small means, and has to choose between the education of his sons and daughters, it is clear more immediate results follow from educating the sons.

I think you hold a strong opinion as to the want of inducements to girls to carry on the improvement of their minds after they have left school. Will you explain your views on that subject fully?—I think the want of inducement is such as to make it almost impossible for girls to go on cultivating themselves when they leave school. They are not old enough and strong enough to work by themselves without any help or encouragement.

You think that the deficiency of inducement to girls applies not only to the time which they spend in school, but applies to the time after they have left school; would you state to the Commission any views which you have as to that, and then give the remedies?—I think a higher standard of examination than that of the local examinations is wanted, and that the exhibitions to the Ladies' Colleges might be founded. Also, if school education were better than it is, girls would have some real foundation to work upon. As it is now, their education is so bad that their minds have not been cultivated, and they have no desire for study.

You think they leave school without any taste for reading?—I think so.

Owing partly to their very bad education?—Yes.

And therefore that they are glad to be rid of it, as a thing which is unreal?—Yes; and they get no encouragement at home. They can read in a loose desultory way, but serious study is considered unnecessary and unsociable.

From the want of cultivation of their parents, in many cases?—I think so.

Do you think that the standard of a young woman's education is much depressed by mental qualities not being appreciated by persons of the other sex of their own age?—Yes; no doubt if young women were better educated it would re-act upon young men.

Do you think, in point of fact, that the want of appreciation of female cultivation by young men is due partly to their not expecting to find it, and thus to their trifling with young women, in a way which they would not if they had more respect for them?—Yes; and also to a want of education on their own part.

You think therefore that the improvement of female education is not only improvement for the young women themselves, but would have good effect on their brothers and young friends?—Most certainly. I have found in several cases, that girls have influenced their brothers at home to a very great extent.

15. 'They are not dumb brutes': Educating the poor and the oppressed

Before the advent of compulsory education, formal schooling was a luxury unknown to many Victorian boys and girls. As in the case of exploited

SOURCES: (i) "The Trial of Mrs. Margaret Douglass for Teaching Colored Children to Read, Norfolk, Viginia, 1853," in *American State Trials*, ed. John D. Lawson (St. Louis, Mo., 1917), 7: 45–48. Originally published in Boston, 1854. (ii)

children (Doc. 6), interested individuals, either organized in groups or acting independently, reached out to the children of the poor and the oppressed and tried to educate them. In the first selection, Margaret Douglass, a former slave owner, narrates how she established a school for free black children in Norfolk, Virginia. Douglass's school was raided one morning in 1853, and she was tried and sentenced to one month in prison for violating a state law that outlawed the teaching of reading and writing to blacks. In the second selection William Locke tells a Parliamentary committee about the activities of the English Ragged Schools, which were set up to give a rudimentary education to the most impoverished children in London and other major cities in Britain. In the final selection Mary Carpenter (1807–77), who devoted much of her life to the education of the poor both in England and in India, argues that little girls in the poorest classes suffer more than their brothers from "misery and vice." Although these selections show that education was problematical for many children, they also show that certain Victorian men and women, motivated both by pity and by a desire to preserve social stability, worked diligently to provide these unfortunate boys and girls with some schooling.

(i) Margaret Douglass

There is a well known barber living in the city of Norfolk, a genteel and respectable colored man, much respected in that community. Having some business with him, I one day called at his shop, into which he politely invited me. Casting my eyes around, they fell upon two little colored boys, with spelling books in their hands, which they appeared to be very attentively engaged in studying. I inquired if they were his children, and if they went to school. His reply was, that they were his, but that they did not go to school, though he was very anxious to have them learn. I then inquired if there were no day schools for free colored children. He smiled, and said, No, madam; and he believed that there was no one who took interest enough in little colored children to keep a day school for them. I replied, that this was a pity, but that there was certainly a large Sunday school connected with Christ's Church, to which he might send his children. His answer was, that his children did attend that school, but that they did not learn much; as they had no one to assist them in their lessons during the week; that he kept them at their books, whenever they had any spare time, and that they would occasionally pick up a little instruction from those who visited his shop. I inquired if he had any education himself. He said no, but that he indeed felt the want of it, and was very thankful to any one who would take the trouble to instruct his children. I then found that he had five children, three of whom were little girls; and that they were all very anxious to learn. Without further consideration or hesitation, I then offered to allow my daughter to teach his little boys, stating that she would do so with great pleasure. I told

Great Britain, *Parliamentary Papers*, 1852, VII, Report of the Select Committee on Criminal and Destitute Juveniles, pp. 307–10, 315–16. (iii) Mary Carpenter, *Juvenile Delinquents: Their Condition and Treatment* (London, 1853), pp. 85–88. The editors thank Dr. Norris Pope for suggesting this selection.

him to send them every day to my house, and that it need not detain them long from his business. He thanked me very kindly, and said that he would send them, although their time was very valuable to him, as they were obliged to wait upon the gentlemen who visited his shop. His eagerness for the instruction of his children deeply interested me, and, on my return home, I related the circumstance to my daughter, who readily assented to my proposal. Having no further business with this man, I saw no more of him, and had nearly forgotten the occurrence until he called at my house with his little girls. I received him politely, and spoke kindly to his children, who were neatly dressed, and very respectful, and appeared unusually intelligent. Their father then said, "Mrs. Douglas, I have told my little girls of your kind offer to instruct their brothers, and they are also very anxious to learn, and I wish to know if you would not prefer to have these two eldest, thinking that the boys might give your daughter too much trouble." I replied that it would be no trouble, but a pleasure to us, and that he might send both the boys and girls regularly every day, and that we would do all we could for their religious and moral instruction. I then inquired if they had any books. He replied, only such as had been given them at Christ Church Sunday school. "Very well," said I, "give them those books, and send them tomorrow." I felt certain that there could be nothing wrong in doing during the week what was done on Sunday by the teachers in that school, who were members of some of the first families in Norfolk, nor in using the very books that were given to the children there taught. I was particular also to ascertain that both himself and family were free, as I knew the laws of the Southern States did not permit the slaves to be educated, although at the same time, all the churches in Norfolk were actually instructing from books both slave and free colored children, and had done so for years without molestation.

On the day following the two little girls made their appearance alone, their father being unable to spare their brothers from his business. My daughter received her little scholars kindly, and endeavored to make them feel as comfortably as strange children can feel in a strange house. . . .

The two little girls continued to come every day, and were well behaved and very obedient. They soon became indeed a source of pleasure to us. They were very attentive . . . and with my daughter's unremitting attention, they made rapid progress. They were with us nearly a month, when my daughter remarked to me that she would be very sorry to part with them, as they learned very fast, and every day required more of her attention, and she feared that they would interfere with her other duties. Now, up to this time, I had not anticipated receiving any compensation for the tuition of those children, nor had I dreamed of establishing a regular school. What I had done had been merely from the impulses of common humanity, without a thought of reward. I casually asked my daughter which she would prefer, to teach those children, or assist me in sewing; and if she would be willing to take charge of a small class of free colored children. She replied that she was fond of children, and would be glad to teach them if she could establish a class.

"Very well," said I, "you shall do so: we will open a school on the first of next month, (which was June, 1852,) for free colored children." I thereupon sent word to Mr. Robinson, the father of the two little girls, notifying him of our intention, and stating that he might send us all the scholars that he could, and that the price of tuition would be three dollars per quarter. We were at once overrun with applications, and our little school was soon formed and well regulated, the children punctual in their attendance, and under good discipline. My daughter paid strict attention to them, and they made rapid progress in their studies. Our school numbered twenty-five pupils, of both sexes, and continued in prosperous existence about eleven months. We made no secret of the matter and never intended to do so, nor could we, had we desired to ever so much. . . .

I was totally ignorant of any existing law prohibiting the instruction of free colored children, but, at the same time, I was careful to have no slaves among our scholars. Everything passed on quietly for several months, in the ordinary routine of a child's school, with nothing to interest my readers particularly, until the descent was made on my school on the 9th day of May, 1853, between eight and nine o'clock in the morning, when the children had nearly all assembled. No note of warning had been given of this movement, and it was as unexpected as the sudden upheavings of an earthquake.

(ii) William Locke

Chairman.—I believe you are Honorary Secretary of the London Ragged School Union?—Yes, I am.

How long have you held that office?—From the first; from its establishment in 1844.

Is that the date of the first establishment of Ragged Schools in London? —No; Ragged Schools (though not so called) existed long before that. . . .

However, the Ragged School Union was originally established in 1844? —Yes, in 1844; and I may just state, that at that time some friends and I, engaged in Sabbath School teaching, found so many children excluded from the Sunday School in consequence of their filthy, dirty, and ragged condition, that we were very anxious indeed to have another class of schools for such children. We found about 16 of such schools in London at that time, and we thought it an excellent plan to have a Union, so that we might arrange plans, and assist each other in carrying out so desirable an object as that of gathering in the outcast and destitute who were idling or doing mischief in the streets.

Then that was the foundation of the Ragged School Union?—Yes.

What kind of progress have you made since that time?—Since that time the schools in London have increased from 16 to 110; the voluntary teachers have increased from 200 to 1,600; there were no paid teachers at first, and we have now 200; the children at first were only about 2,000 in number; we have now in our day and evening schools about 13,000, which does not include the Sabbath School children, who amount to about half that number.

At what ages do you take the children?—We take them, I may say, at any age, but usually from 4 to 16, and even above that; we have adult classes for some as old as 20, and even 30.

Have you a great many young ones?—About one half of the children are under 10 years.

Now in what condition are those children when they are taken into the Ragged Schools first?—Most of them are in a very ignorant, destitute, neglected condition; I could describe their condition from our reports as worthy of our tenderest sympathy.

Do you mean individual cases?—Yes.

You need not trouble yourself with that; but be good enough to give the Committee a general account?—Many of them are quite homeless; many of them are entirely neglected by their parents; many are orphans, outcasts, street beggars, crossing sweepers, and little hawkers of things about the streets; they are generally very ignorant, although in some points very quick and cunning. I could refer to a list which I hold in my hand which we have made up, which will give the information which you ask for. By it you will find we have "Children of convicts who have been transported; children of convicts in our prisons at home; children of thieves not in custody; children of the lowest mendicants and tramps; children of worthless drunken parents, a large class; children of stepfathers or stepmothers, often driven by neglect or cruelty to shift for themselves; children of those who, although suitable objects for a workhouse, prefer leading a vagrant life, pilfering when they can; sometimes in employment, but oftener engaged in practices of a doubtful or criminal nature; children of parents who, though honest, are too poor to pay even one penny a week for a school, and who cannot clothe their children so as to gain admission to better schools; children who have lost parents, or are deserted by them, or have run away from home, and live by begging and stealing; youths who, disliking the workhouse, have left it, and lead a vagrant life; youths who are at work during the day as ostler boys, labourers' assistants, and in other ways, or who go about selling articles in the streets, such as fish, fruit, and vegetables, and who cannot therefore attend a day school, even if free admission be offered; girls who are driven into the street by cruel and worthless parents, and live by begging and selling water-cresses, oranges, or lucifer matches; children of Roman-catholics, who come in large numbers to the Ragged Schools, and do not object to reading the Bible.

What is the condition of admission into your schools?—Destitution.

How are children admitted?—The children are admitted in many cases by personal application; they are admitted in many other cases by the teachers going round and seeking for them, and by the assistance of the City missionaries (agents of the London City Mission) who have been exceedingly useful to us from the very first, not only in finding scholars, but in helping to establish schools, and in getting the good-will of parents towards us and our operations. . . .

Now will you be good enough to describe to the Committee the daily routine of one of your schools?—The daily routine varies according to the kind of school; some of our schools, which are day schools, are very similar to British or National Schools, assembling at nine to 12, and then at two to four, dismissing the children then for the evening.

You have both day schools and evening schools?—Yes, and also Sunday schools; in the same building where the day school is held we have generally an evening class for boys, and also girls, who cannot attend during the day, having to work or beg in order to get food to eat.

What is the kind of instruction that is given in the schools?—In the day schools we have reading the Scriptures, singing, reading, writing, and arithmetic, and in some schools industrial classes; in the evening schools we have similar instruction; in many of the schools we now have industrial classes, both day and evening, for teaching the boys tailoring, shoe-making, and other handicrafts, and for teaching girls to sew, knit, &c. &c. . . .

What time do they come?—About nine in the day schools.

How long do they stay then?—Till 12; then from two to four or five; indeed, as I have before observed, the routine is very much the same as in the British and National Schools, as far as the day schools are concerned, only the children, from their peculiar character and habits, need peculiar treatment, and much zeal and labour to win them from their evil ways and numerous temptations.

Now, with respect to the evening schools?—Some assemble at six, some at seven, and generally continue from two to three hours, spending a good portion of time in religious instruction.

Is it part of your system to give food in any of your schools?—In many cases it is, because the children are so destitute that they cannot be taught until they are fed; in one school they feed about 200 twice or thrice a week, in order to keep them from starving. We have several schools in London where we not only feed them, but lodge them; but the latter in limited numbers.

How do you select those children?—The most destitute, those who are thoroughly destitute and homeless; those who seem to have no other means of support are fed, and those who are homeless are lodged, that is, where there is a dormitory; but there are hundreds of children that we cannot afford to give food to, or to lodge, from the limited amount of funds at our command. . . .

Do any of the children who come to these schools pay anything?—Nothing; all the Ragged Schools are quite free, being intended only for the destitute. . . .

That brings me to the subject of the results; can you state to the Committee any information with regard to the results of the Ragged Schools?—We have had many children, who were formerly very bad characters, reformed; we have many placed out in situations, and doing well, who were formerly quite a pest to the community.

Have you taken any pains upon that subject; do you consider it at all a part of your office to assist in obtaining places for these children?—We do; the schools in London are all managed by local committees, who take a great interest in the children, and who are very anxious indeed to place the children out in situations whenever they can manage to do so; besides, we have emigrated in all about 360, and by the letters which have been received from them from abroad they are all doing well; those children, whilst they were here, were earning nothing; many were vagrants or pickpockets, doing a deal of mischief, and cost the community a great deal of money by robbing tradesmen, and so on. . . .

Why should not this class of children be admitted into the actual primary National Schools that are established?—One objection is, that they are rude in their behaviour, filthy in their appearance, generally without shoes and stockings; another objection is, that they cannot even find the 2d. or 3d. a week which is needed for their education there; the first cause I have stated would go to drive away respectable children from the National Schools; as respectable parents would not allow their children to meet with the class of children that we take.

They speedily change in appearance, do they not?—Very.

Both by better food and better clothing?—Yes, we insist upon their being clean, and in most schools we provide a place for them to wash in.

So that after a child of this kind has been under your care, say twelve months, you could scarcely tell the difference between him and one who was in the National School?—No.

Do you suppose that you have no cases in your schools in which parents could afford to pay for their children's education in a National School?—We have many, but it is where the parent is drunken, careless, and altogether neglectful of his duty to his offspring; where the parent who ought to provide for his children, does not do so, and recklessly leaves them to grow up for crime.

In cases of voluntary neglect on the part of the parent, does not such a supply of education to the child act as an encouragement to the neglect of the parent?—So far it may do so partly, but I think that the child on that account is not to be neglected by the community, who, by a timely outlay when the child is young, may escape a vast outlay when he grows to be old.

(iii) Mary Carpenter

The master and mistress of a Ragged School, in a very low part of Bristol, have invariably found it more difficult to retain a hold over the girls in the most degraded families, or even to bring them under school discipline, than the boys; it is far more difficult to awaken their minds, or to give them a pleasure in learning, and the voluntary teachers who give occasional aid in the school make the same complaint; they have not unfrequently given up in despair the attempt to teach the girls, while the same individuals have been able to make considerable impression on the boys.

Let us, then, admit it to be a fact that young girls when low and degraded are worse than boys in similar circumstances. Why is this so? Why, from the very nature of things, must it be so?

The answer may be briefly this, that in the case of the girls there is a greater departure from what ought to be their education and training, even than in that of the boys. In order to perceive this, let us reflect what is the training of girls in a well-ordered family in the middle and the labouring classes of society. The little girl early serves her apprenticeship to future maternal duties, by bestowing motherly cares on her doll, and in a lower class becomes a little nurse of a younger child, even while she would seem to require fostering care herself; her affections and young powers are thus called forth; she soon shares the mother's household duties; even at 10 or 11 years of age she has acquired a habit of care and forethought which will enable her to take, if need be, the mother's place, and do what nothing but love could have taught her; in the mean time, an education has been given to her adapted to her future circumstances in society; she has, perhaps, been stimulated to progress by her brothers, whose attention to study has been more undivided, and mingling in well-ordered society of her own class, with a modest reserve, and yet with the freedom natural to purity and unconsciousness of evil, she is prepared to fill the station to which God may call her. But observe the girls of the pariah caste, or rather of those families where there is no fear or love of God, no regard to human law, no self-respect, no pleasures but those of animal gratification, no perception of anything pure or beautiful. There is no loving tenderness called out in the little girl, for she receives none; the next unhappy babe that enters the world after her, cannot call from her fondling caresses which she has never known; it is probably carried in the arms of a drunken or mendicant mother, as she has been, to draw its first impressions of life from misery and vice, until locked up at home with one or two older ones to exist as best it may; perhaps, happily for it, to meet with a premature death from the fire, or the scalding water, from which its young nurses could not protect it. But still the girl is kept at home to be the drudge, not the helpmate, of the mother, and is thus more exposed to the close contamination of the scenes which pass there; feminine delicacy there is none, nor anything to call out the higher parts of her nature; she cannot in general be spared to go to school; when she can obtain permission to do so, she is listless and indolent, for her powers are unused to any intellectual exercise. If sufficiently young, skilful teaching may incite in her a desire of knowledge, but otherwise the feelings of personal vanity, which exist most strongly in the most degraded, are the only ones which seem to call forth any real and lively interest in her; her intercourse with the other sex has given her no self-respect, and inspired her with none but the lowest feelings; she is prepared even in girlhood to fall headlong into an abyss, the dangers of which she cannot know till she experiences its horrors—the depths of which she cannot comprehend till she is plunged too deep to be extricated from it.

The boys in the same families have been equally neglected, but the greater vigour of their natures has carried them into the open air, and led them to quicken their faculties by active exercise, by observation of the objects around them, and by the self-reliance caused by the very neglect which has driven them at so early an age to depend on their own resources to obtain a living; hence, though equally unprincipled with the girls, and more prone to overt and daring mischief and crime, they have far more which can be worked on for good, and their powers having been awakened and strengthened even more than is usual in the higher classes of society, it is far more possible than in the case of the girls to excite to progress in a right direction.

16. An English girl longs for her friend: Charlotte Brontë

At the age of sixteen, the future novelist Charlotte Brontë (1816–55) was sent to the Miss Woolers' school at Roe Head to learn the "accomplishments" she would need as a teacher or governess. There she made two lifelong friends: Ellen Nussey, the recipient of the two letters in this selection, and Mary Taylor, who is mentioned in the first of them. Three years later, Brontë returned to Roe Head as an assistant teacher. These letters, written when she was bitterly unhappy in this work, show her turning to the emotionally stable Nussey for friendship and support. Lifelong friendships such as this were common in the Victorian period; female friends enriched each other's lives and sustained one another through many a trial. The frankness and intensity with which Victorian women wrote to each other leaves no doubt that the "bonds of womanhood" could be very strong indeed.

Sept. 26, 1836.—Last Saturday afternoon being in one of my sentimental humours I sat down and wrote to you such a note as I ought to have written to none but M. Taylor who is nearly as mad as myself; to-day when I glanced it over it occurred to me that Ellen's calm eye would look at this with scorn, so I determined to concoct some production more fit for the inspection of common-sense. I will not tell you all I think, and feel about you Ellen, I will preserve unbroken that reserve which alone enables me to maintain a decent character for judgment; but for that I should long ago have been set down by all who know me as a Frenchified fool. You have been very kind to me of late, and gentle and you have spared me those little sallies of ridicule which owing to my miserable and wretched touchiness of character used formerly to make me wince as if I had been touched with a hot iron: things that nobody else cares for enter into my mind and rankle there like venom. I know these feelings are absurd and therefore I try to hide them but they only sting the deeper for concealment. I'm an idiot!

I was informed that your brother George was at Mirfield church last Sunday. Of course I did not *see* him though I guessed his presence because I heard his cough (my short-sightedness makes my ear very acute). Miss Wytes[?] told me he was there, they were quite smitten, he was the sole subject of their conversation during the whole of the subsequent evening. Miss Eliza described to me every part of his dress and likewise that of a gentleman who accompanied him with astonishing minuteness. I laughed most heartily at her graphic details, and so would you if you had been with me.

Ellen I wish I could live with you always, I begin to cling to you more

SOURCE: *The Brontës: Their Lives, Friendships, and Correspondence in Four Volumes*, ed. Thomas James Wise and John Alexander Symington (Oxford, Eng., 1932), 1: 146, 153–54.

fondly than ever I did. If we had but a cottage and a compentency of our own I do think we might live and love on till Death without being dependent on any third person for happiness.—Farewell my own dear Ellen.

Feb. 20, 1837.—I read your letter with dismay, Ellen—what shall I do without you? Why are we so to be denied each other's society? It is an inscrutable fatality. I long to be with you because it seems as if two or three days or weeks spent in your company would beyond measure strengthen me in the enjoyment of those feelings which I have so lately begun to cherish. You first pointed out to me that way in which I am so feebly endeavouring to travel, and now I cannot keep you by my side, I must proceed sorrowfully alone.

Why are we to be divided? Surely, Ellen, it must be because we are in danger of loving each other too well—of losing sight of the *Creator* in idolatry of the *creature*. At first I could not say, 'Thy will be done.' I felt rebellious; but I know it was wrong to feel so. Being left a moment alone this morning, I prayed fervently to be enabled to resign myself to *every* decree of God's will—though it should be dealt forth with a far severer hand than the present disappointment. Since then, I have felt calmer and humbler—and consequently happier. . . .

I have written this note at a venture. When it will reach you I know not, but I was determined not to let slip an opportunity for want of being prepared to embrace it. Farewell; may God bestow on you all His blessings. My darling—Farewell. Perhaps you may return before midsummer—do you think you possibly can? I wish your brother John knew how unhappy I am; he would almost pity me.

17. Purity, intellect, and puberty: Advice for the middle classes

In these selections from advice manuals a Boston abolitionist, a Parisian physician, and a London homeopathist caution parents to protect their daughters from intellectual labor and the hazards of boarding school during the dangerous crisis of puberty. In the first selection Lydia Maria Child (1802–80) advises American mothers to maintain open and confidential relations with their daughters to guide them safely through their troubled adolescent years. (Interestingly, this famous author of 'The Mother's Book' was childless.) The second selection is from a work on the illness and hygiene of women by Dr. Marc Colombat (1797–1851), a Parisian professor of the relatively new speciality of obstetrics and gynecology. The American translation of this work, which was directed to both a professional and a popular audience, went

SOURCES: (i) Lydia Maria Child, *The Mother's Book*, 2d ed. (Boston, 1831), pp. 130–31, 148–52. Originally published in 1831. (ii) Marc Colombat, A *Treatise on the Diseases and Special Hygiene of Females*, tr. Charles Meigs (Philadelphia, 1850), pp. 544–47. First published in Paris in 1838. (iii) J. Compton Burnett, *Delicate, Backward, Puny, and Stunted Children* (Philadelphia, 1896), pp. 89–92. Originally published in London in 1895.

through numerous printings and had great influence. In it Colombat propounds the dominant opinion among the clinicians of the prestigious Paris Faculty of Medicine about the risks of menarche. In the third selection James Compton Burnett (1840–1901), an unorthodox but successful London physician and the father of thirteen children, debunks the notion of the "New Woman," and argues that menstruation adversely affects women's mental abilities. Although these three documents show striking similarities, the authors' views on the "difficult years" are by no means identical.

(i) Lydia Maria Child

The period from twelve to sixteen years of age is extremely critical in the formation of character, particularly with regard to daughters. The imagination is then all alive, and the affections are in full vigor, while the judgment is unstrengthened by observation, and enthusiasm has never learned moderation of experience. During this important period, a mother cannot be too watchful. As much as possible, she should keep a daughter *under her own eye*; and, above all things, she should encourage *entire confidence towards herself*. This can be done by a ready sympathy with youthful feelings, and by avoiding all unnecessary restraint and harshness. I believe it is extremely natural to choose a mother in preference to all other friends and confidants; but if a daughter, by harshness, indifference, or an unwillingness to make allowance for youthful feeling, is driven from the holy resting place, which nature has provided for her security, the greatest danger is to be apprehended. Nevertheless, I would not have mothers too indulgent, for fear of weaning the affections of children. This is not the way to gain the perfect love of young people; a judicious parent is always better beloved, and more respected, than a foolishly indulgent one. The real secret is, for a mother never to sanction the slightest error, or imprudence, but at the same time to keep her heart warm and fresh, ready to sympathize with all the innocent gaiety and enthusiasm of youth. *Salutary* restraint, but not *unnecessary* restraint, is desirable. . . .

Young girls learn many mischievous lessons from their companions at school. Among a mass of young ladies collected from all sorts of families, there will of course be much vanity, frivolity, and deceit, and some indecency. The utmost watchfulness of a teacher cannot prevent some bad influences. For this reason, I should myself decidedly prefer instructing a daughter in my own house; but I am aware that in most families this course would be expensive and inconvenient. However, I would never trust a young girl at a boarding school without being sure that her room-mate was discreet, well-principled, and candid. I should rather have a daughter's mind a little less improved, than to have her heart exposed to corrupt influences; for this reason, I should prefer a respectable school in the country to a fashionable one in the city. For the same reason, I should greatly dread a young lady's making long visits from home, unless I had perfect confidence in every member of the family she visited, and in every person to whom they would be likely to introduce her. There is no calculating the mischief that is done by the chance acquaintances picked up in this way. If there are sons in the families visited, the danger is still greater. . . .

In this country, girls are often left to themselves at the very period when, above all others, they need a mother's care. In France, mothers always visit with their daughters; and if restraint upon unmarried people is carried to excess there, we certainly err on the opposite extreme. We allow too much freedom, and we allow it too soon. I believe it is much better for a very young lady never to go about alone, or visit for any length of time from home, without her mother. . . .

There is one subject, on which I am very anxious to say a great deal; but on which, for obvious reasons, I can say very little. Judging by my own observation, I believe it to be the greatest evil now existing in education. I mean the want of confidence between mothers and daughters on delicate subjects. Children, from books, and from their own observation, soon have their curiosity excited on such subjects; this is perfectly natural and innocent, and if frankly met by a mother, it would never do harm. But on these occasions it is customary either to put young people off with lies, or still further to excite their curiosity by mystery and embarrassment. Information being refused them at the only proper source, they immediately have recourse to domestics, or immodest school-companions; and very often their young minds are polluted with filthy anecdotes of vice and vulgarity. This ought not to be. Mothers are the only proper persons to convey such knowledge to a child's mind. They can do it without throwing the slightest stain upon youthful purity; and it is an imperious duty that they should do it. A girl who receives her first ideas on these subjects from the shameless stories and indecent jokes of vulgar associates, has in fact prostituted her mind by familiarity with vice. A diseased curiosity is excited, and undue importance given to subjects, which those she has been taught to respect think it necessary to envelope in so much mystery; she learns to think a great deal about them, and to ask a great many questions. This does not spring from any natural impurity; the same restless curiosity would be excited by any subject treated in the same manner. On the contrary, a well-educated girl of twelve years old, would be perfectly satisfied with a frank, rational explanation from a mother. It would set her mind at rest upon the subject; and instinctive modesty would prevent her recurring to it unnecessarily, or making it a theme of conversation with others. Mothers are strangely averse to encouraging this sort of confidence. I know not why it is, but they are usually the very last persons in the world to whom daughters think of applying in these cases.

(ii) Marc Colombat

When a young girl shows, by the unfolding of her physical faculties, that she is approaching the completion of her full development, she needs the closest watching, and a management having a different object from that towards which her childish constitution tended. Whereas before puberty she existed but for herself alone, having reached this age, the spring time of life, when all her charms are in bloom, she now belongs to the entire species which she is destined to perpetuate, by bearing almost all the burthen of reproduction.

During infancy, the vital forces tend to act equally upon all her organs, but at the epoch of puberty, the chief efforts of the organism are in some sort concentrated upon the sexual parts, whose functions are executed only during the second period of life.

As at this period, the instinct of modesty often leads young girls to conceal their first menstrual haemorrhage, it becomes the duty of mothers to inform them of the revolution they are about to undergo, and to announce to them that the sanguine discharge, which they are to become subject to, is a natural function upon which their health will henceforwards depend. Young persons, kept in entire ignorance upon this point, and taking their new condition for some shameful infirmity, have been known to oppose the salutary efforts of nature, by means of lotions, injections, and other equally dangerous agents. The exact truth, therefore, should be told to girls just arrived at puberty, because, though it is dangerous to know too much, it is more dangerous to be entirely ignorant.

The general attention required by women at entering the brilliant and stormy crisis, which is terminated by the appearance of the menses, consist in fulfilling two principal indications: 1, to moderate the excitement and disorder resulting from the momentary plenitude of the circulatory system; 2, so to direct the efforts of nature, that they may exert their chief action upon the sexual organs, in which the vital forces ought, so to speak, to centre and terminate.

A carefully regulated regimen is of all means the most appropriate for fulfilling the first indication; the food of a young girl at puberty ought to consist principally of vegetable substances, of preparations of milk, of the tender meats, and of light and easily digestible substances. . . .

To fulfill the second indication, to wit, to place the genital organs, especially the uterus, in a condition favourable to their becoming the seat of the irritation which precedes the menstrual exhalation, we should advise gymnastic exercises, walking and riding, running, the games of battledore, the jumping rope, the hoop, and riding on horseback; lastly, frictions about the pelvis and inferior extremities, the use of flannel-drawers, etc., are additional means very useful for inviting the flow of the menses. If the important function delays its appearance too long, and particularly if the girl suffers any of the evil effects of amenorrhœa, we should resort to very warm hip-baths and pediluvia; to aromatic fumigations; to applications of cups to the thighs, and leeches to the vulva; and finally, to the various means pointed out under the head of essential amenorrhœa. At this period, in particular, we must forbid the wearing of corsets with busks and whalebones, and of tight clothing, which obstruct the free development of the pelvis, of the thorax, and of the neck, and which might prove the origin of most of the diseases whose sad picture we have just sketched.

It will be well, at the same time, to pay attention to the moral condition of the patient, and for this reason, it is of the highest importance to remove young girls from boarding-school, when they approach the age of puberty, in order to exercise a constant watch over them. We should prevent, as far as possible, the false emotions produced by the reading of licentious books, especially of the highly-wrought romances of the modern school, which are the more injurious, as all the faculties become, as it were, overpowered by the desire to experience the sentiment which these works always represent in an imaginary and exaggerated strain. Frequent visits to the theatre ought to be carefully avoided, because they, also, may give rise to sensations conformable to the moral condition, which is, naturally, at puberty, already too much exalted. These powerful, exciting agents, and still more frequently, the violent intimacies formed at boarding-school, tear the veil of modesty, and destroy, for ever, the seductive innocence which is the most charming ornament of a young girl. Endowed with an organization eminently impressionable, she soon contracts improper habits, and constantly tormented by an amorous melancholy, becomes sad, dreamy, sentimental and languishing. Like a delicate plant, withered by the rays of a burning sun, she fades and dies under the influence of a poisoned breath. The desires for happiness and love, so sweet and attractive in their native truth, are in her converted into a devouring flame, and onanism, that execrable and fatal evil, soon destroys her beauty, impairs her health, and conducts her almost always to a premature grave! . . .

From the epoch of puberty to the critical age, the menstrual discharge requires certain cares and precautions, which it is important to understand. While the haemorrhage is present, women ought to refrain from taking baths, and from washing the hands and genital organs with cold water; they should also avoid cold feet; they should not remain with the arms or neck uncovered, and must abstain from iced, exciting and alcoholic drinks, such as sherbets, coffee, tea, liqueurs, etc.; coïtus, also, ought to be proscribed, because the excitement determined by it in the genital organs, may occasion either metorrhagia, or more or less complete suppression, and secondarily uterovaginal inflammation. It is well, also, to avoid sitting upon cold and damp places, for example the earth, a stone bench, a grassy bank, etc. The napkins, or *chauffoirs*, employed to receive the fluid of the menses, as it escapes from the genital parts, ought always to be well aired, and in winter warmed before being applied. If the discharge is too abundant, it may be remedied by a vegetable and milk diet; by repose; by the horizontal position; by cooling and sedative drinks, as barley water, whey, weak lemonade, etc.; if the female is of lymphatic temperament, she must use, on the contrary, a tonic diet, composed chiefly of roast meats, feculent substances, and rich soups. When menstruation is entirely or partially suppressed, in consequence of some imprudence or unexpected occurrence, it is necessary to endeavour to recall it, by means of a warm infusion of balm and orange flowers. Rest in bed; warmth to the thighs and legs, maintained by bottles filled with warm water, are other means which should not be neglected. . . .

It is likewise very important that they should abstain, during the presence of the discharge, from all intellectual labour, and from severe study, which, by establishing high cerebral excitement, determine an unequal distribution of the vital forces, and cause an afflux towards the brain of the blood which ought to flow towards the genital apparatus. Before concluding what we had to say upon the attention to hygiene that menstruation requires, we will add, that so long as the function lasts, women ought to be the object of the most attentive kindness, and of a solicitude capable of preserving them, as far as possible, from the unhappy influences of the physical and moral causes which affect them more strongly then than at any other period. It is well to say, also, that if some amongst them become subject at these periods to caprices, to sadness and unequal temper, we should always bear these transient humours with indulgence, because they depend upon the action of the body upon the mind, and upon an active irritation, which is radiated from the uterus towards the other organs, and especially towards the brain.

(iii) James Compton Burnett

Only the Almighty can make a New Woman. Put broadly, up to the age of puberty, the girl, all other things being equal, beats the boy; with puberty the damsel throws away every month a vast amount of fluid power in the order of Nature. Let us call this *pelvic power*. Assuming the girl to be the superior of the boy up to the pelvic power stage,—which, indeed, any one can observe for himself, in his own sphere,—but once arrived at the stage of pelvic power, and the damsel is left behind in her lessons by her brother in the natural order of things, or else the girl's brain saps the pelvis of its power, when she will also lose in the race with the boy, because he will be physically well, while she, with disordered pelvic life, must necessarily be in ill-health more or less. The whole thing is a mere question of quantity of energy. . . . The New Woman is only possible in a novel, not in Nature. . . . I have very many times watched the careers of exceedingly studious girls who spent the great mass of their power in mental work, and in every case the pelvic power decreased in even pace with the expenditure of mental power. Not one exception to this have I ever seen, and all the lady students of the higher grades whom it has been my duty to professionally advise were suffering in regard to their pelvic lives and power.

18. 'Not yet a woman': Mary Alden Wilder Loomis

A young girl's "crisis" of puberty was taken very seriously, not only by physicians and manual writers, but by family members as well. The author of

SOURCE: Letter from Mary Loomis to Mabel Todd, March 30, 1893, Mabel Todd Papers, Yale University Library. The editors are grateful to Sharon N. White, Yale University, for making this letter available to us and to the Yale University Library for permission to publish it.

this selection, born Mary Alden Wilder (1831–1910), was a highly educated woman descended from an old New England family; after her marriage to Eben Loomis, a naturalist and astronomer, she lived for many years in Washington, D.C. Here she writes to her daughter, Mabel Loomis Todd, a writer, lecturer, and faculty wife who lived in Amherst, Massachusetts. Loomis was concerned about the menarche of Mabel Todd's daughter, Millicent, who was thirteen years old in 1893, when this letter was written. Loomis warns Todd against the dangers of studiousness for both girls and women and chides her for choosing to edit the poetry of Emily Dickinson instead of tending to Millicent's "crisis." The letter discloses that menarche could focus the attention of an entire family, from father to grandmother, on a pubescent girl.

You will not be looking for a letter so soon—but I must write you what has been troubling me for months—concerning Millicent's condition—When she was here—we all saw a great change in her spirits—She was so very sad— Of course we did not let her know we observed it—but tried to make her very happy—and cheerful. She is now thirteen years old and is not yet a woman! It is in our family to develop early in that respect—I was only eleven years old—and I remember as if it were yesterday—how fondly my Father walked the floor with me in his arms—when just before these periods—my head ached so that my eyes were bloodshot and I could not see the light. He would say in a voice of tender sympathy—"poor poor little child" and I did suffer! I was alone when Millicent's photograph came but when I first looked at the exceeding sorrow of her sensitive mouth—I cried most bitterly—for I read her feelings from that face and longed to take her away on a long trip—full of pleasure not where she would have excitement but to California or somewhere where she could feel the healing of Nature! where she could forget herself! Oh you can never do a wiser thing than to *leave all your work*—and take that dear precious child away to Bermuda—or anywhere else—to give her a great change—and you will *always* be glad you did it! Do not delay! You need not let her see your motive—only say you both—need a change! for *months* before this change came *to you*, your Father, G'ma and I watched you daily. Especially just before the time the menses came—we planned walks in the Catholic grounds—Rock creek—Etc. Your father became your *companion*—talked in the liveliest manner—and kept your spirits even and happy—we saw to it that your studies did not depress you. You were so tenderly watched all through this dangerous crisis—that it came to you very naturally—and without any special sickness—Our great sorrow over our dear Eliza's death [Mary Loomis's sister]—made us very careful. She died at eighteen—and *slipped* away from us making no sign! She *loved* her books and studies so that she kept her distress away from us—until *too late!* She was never regular—and became more and more *irregular* until her death. When at last Dr Wesselhoeft came he told us it was too late—and she lived only a few months—there was not *then* vitality enough to work on—

I waited until your book was ready for the press before writing you—but *everyone* who comes to our room sees the framed photograph [of Millicent] standing on Mother's bureau and they all exclaim—"How very sad and depressed the dear child looks!" (but I never allow that I see it—) to any one—not even to G'ma—whose growing weakness is even more than she can bear! But I *know* she must have a change. Do see that she has *hours* of cheerfulness with her young friends! She is dearer to me than life. I would do anything for her in my power and have prayed God—to give me the chance to work and die for her if need be—She has a deep soulfull Nature—full of affection. Work or study would never take the place of sympathy and love—Five years more—and she will be very likely making a home for herself—for *her strength is in her home life among her friends*—What she needs every day is a com-*panion*—a young pure natural young girl. These *yearning feelings* for affection are stronger now in this crisis than at any other time of her life! And *they must be satisfied* or she will suffer in health. Do ask David [Mabel's husband] to read this hasty scrawl—for I know he will agree with me—his judgment is always good. And please take this advice as coming from one who knows from sad experience how fatal it is to overlook these premonitions.

19. Forming the lady: Comportment and dress for young women

For young French and English girls of the middle and upper classes, schooling in comportment and dress formed an integral part of their upbringing. The advice manuals decreed that both the behavior and the appearance of the young girl should be appropriate to her station in life and distinct from that of the older woman. Although many of the formal rules of etiquette and fashion governed French and English girls alike, the English authors stressed internal states as the truest guide to correct behavior, whereas the French depended heavily on external controls and surveillance. In America, young girls were generally freer from such constraints on their behavior, but European etiquette manuals were still widely read in the United States.

(i) Mme Celnart

Everyone knows that no matter how much a young lady's dowry is, her manner of dress must always . . . be less elegant and less brilliant than that of married women. Expensive cashmeres, very rich furs, diamonds are forbidden her, as well as much other showy attire. . . .

Until the age of about thirty, a young lady can never go out without being accompanied. For her errands in the city, to shops, to visit intimate friends, to church, she may go with a maid; but when it is a question of ceremonial

SOURCES: (i) Elisabeth-Felicité Bayle-Mouillard (Mme Celnart), *Manuel de la bonne compagnie, ou guide de la politesse et de la bienséance* (Paris, 1834), pp. 39, 48, 134–36, 262. (ii) Louis Alquié de Rieusseynoux, *Le Nouveau Savoir-vivre universel* (Paris [ca. 1880's]), 1: 25, 255. (iii) Sarah Stickney Ellis, *The Daughters of England* (London, 1842), pp. 230–31. (iv) *The Habits of Good Society: A Handbook for Ladies and Gentlemen*, author anonymous (New York, 1864), pp. 300–302. Originally published in London in 1859.

visits, of *promenades*, of parties, of balls, she may appear only with her mother, or with a lady of her acquaintance who will take her mother's place. . . .

[When visiting], one does not leave the table before the end of the meal except for an unexpected call of nature. If this unpleasantness should happen to a lady, she asks a friend to accompany her; a young lady withdraws with her mother. . . .

The gait of a woman should be neither too fast nor too slow. . . . Her expression must be sweet and modest.

It is not in good taste for a woman to speak with too much animation or too loudly. When she is seated, she should never cross her legs. . . .

But what is especially insufferable in a woman is a restless, bold, domineering manner, for this manner goes against nature. . . . No matter what her worth, no matter that she never forgets that she could be a man by virtue of her superiority of mind and the force of her will, on the outside she must be a woman! She must present herself as that creature made to please, to love, to seek support, that being who is inferior to man and who approaches the angels.

(ii) Louise Alq

When getting into a carriage or going through a door . . . girls, until the age of twenty-one, go before their parents, because it is supposed that the parents must always have their eyes on them. On an outing, no matter where, children and young girls thus walk in front of their fathers and mothers. . . . A young girl never remains alone in the drawing room with a masculine visitor.

(iii) Sarah Stickney Ellis

The young girl cannot too scrupulously shroud her modest feelings from the unsparing test of fashion. The bloom of modesty is soon rubbed off by vulgar contact; but what is thus lost in the young female can never be restored. And let her look to the risk she incurs. What is it? On the one hand, to be thought a little less fashionable than her friends and neighbours—on the other, to be thought a little more exposed than a delicate woman ought to be. Is there any comparison between the two? Or is there one of the daughters of England, who would not rather be known to choose the former?

If possessed of any genuine feeling on these important points, a young woman will know by a kind of instinct, that a bare shoulder protruding into sight, is neither a delicate nor a lovely object; that a dress, either so made, or so put on, as not to look secure and neat, is, to say the least of it, in bad taste; and that the highest standard at which a rightly-minded woman can aim with regard to dress, is, that it should be becoming, and not conspicuous. In order to secure this last point of excellence, it is unquestionably necessary to conform in some measure to the fashion of the times in which we live, and the circle of society in which we move; yet, surely this may be done to an extent sufficient to avoid the charge of singularity, without the sacrifice either of modesty or good taste.

(iv) 'The Habits of Good Society'

An agreeable, modest, and dignified bearing is, in the younger period of a woman's existence, almost like a portion to her. Whatever may be the transient tone and fashion of the day, that which is amiable, graceful, and true in taste, will always please the majority of the world. A young lady, properly so called, should not require to have allowances made for her. Well brought up, her address should be polite and gentle, and it will, soon after her introduction to society, become easy "to be civil with ease."

. . . There is a way also of looking that must be regulated in the young. The audacious stare is odious; the sly, oblique, impenetrable look is unsatisfactory. Softly and kindly should the eyes be raised to those of the speaker, and only withdrawn when the speech, whatever it may be, is concluded. Immediate intimacy and a familiar manner are worse than the glum look with which some young ladies have a habit of regarding their fellow-mortals. There is also a certain dignity of manners necessary to make even the most superior persons respected. This dignity can hardly be assumed; it cannot be taught; it must be the result of intrinsic qualities, aided by a knowledge very much overlooked in modern education—"the knowledge to behave." It is distinct from pretension, which is about the worst feature of bad manners, and creates nothing but disgust. A lady should be equal to every occasion. Her politeness, her equanimity, her presence of mind, should attend her to the court and to the cottage.

Neither should private vexations be allowed to act upon her manners, either in her own house or in those of others. If unfit for society, let her refrain from entering it. If she enters it, let her remember that every one is expected to add something to the general stock of pleasure or improvement. The slight self-command required by good society is often beneficial to the temper and spirits. . . .

20. An English girl is seduced by Catholicism: Annie Wood Besant

From girlhood on, religion played a powerful role in the lives of many nineteenth-century women. Christian churches all provided rituals—first communion for the Catholic child, confirmation for the Anglican, and personal conversion for the Evangelical protestant—to usher children into membership in their religious communities. That adolescent girls were highly susceptible to the emotional attractions of religious experience was well known; however, when a girl traveled from one culture to another, as in the case of Annie Wood Besant (1847–1933), a middle-class English girl who visited France, the appeal of an unfamiliar religious tradition could heighten piety to the point of virtual seduction.

Throughout her life Besant was affected by the strong and conflicting re-

SOURCE: Annie Besant, *An Autobiography* (Philadelphia, 1893), pp. 51–52, 54, 65–67.

ligious experiences of her childhood. Her father, who died when she was five, was an agnostic; her mother was a deeply religious Anglican; and the spinster who "adopted" her after her father's death was of "low-Church" Calvinist leanings. At the age of fourteen, Besant visited Paris, where she came under the spell of the Catholic Church. There, all the emotion repressed by her English education found a new outlet in an intense religious faith. Besant never converted to Catholicism; in fact, as a consequence of a brief and unhappy marriage to an Anglican minister, she lost her religious faith for a while. By the time she wrote this autobiography, however, Besant had become a theosophist, deeply interested in Eastern mysticism.

In the spring of 1862 it chanced that the Bishop of Ohio visited Paris, and Mr. Forbes, then English chaplain at the Church of the Rue d'Aguesseau, arranged to have a confirmation. As said above, I was under deep "religious impressions," and, in fact . . . I was decidedly a pious girl. I looked on theatres (never having been to one) as traps set by Satan for the destruction of foolish souls; I was quite determined never to go to a ball, and was prepared to "suffer for conscience' sake"—little prig that I was—if I was desired to go to one. I was consequently quite prepared to take upon myself the vows made in my name at my baptism, and to renounce the world, the flesh, and the devil, with a heartiness and sincerity only equalled by my profound ignorance of the things I so readily resigned. That confirmation was to me a very solemn matter; the careful preparation, the prolonged prayers, the wondering awe as to the "sevenfold gifts of the Spirit," which were to be given by "the laying on of hands," all tended to excitement. I could scarcely control myself as I knelt at the altar rails, and felt as though the gentle touch of the aged bishop, which fluttered for an instant on my bowed head, were the very touch of the wing of that "Holy Spirit, heavenly Dove," whose presence had been so earnestly invoked. Is there anything easier, I wonder, than to make a young and sensitive girl "intensely religious"?

This stay in Paris roused into activity an aspect of my religious nature that had hitherto been latent. I discovered the sensuous enjoyment that lay in introducing colour and fragrance and pomp into religious services, so that the gratification of the æsthetic emotions became dignified with the garb of piety. The picture-galleries of the Louvre, crowded with Madonnas and saints, the Roman Catholic churches with their incense-laden air and exquisite music, brought a new joy into my life, a more vivid colour to my dreams. Insensibly, the colder, cruder Evangelicalism that I had never thoroughly assimilated, grew warmer and more brilliant, and the ideal Divine Prince of my childhood took on the more pathetic lineaments of the Man of Sorrows, the deeper attractiveness of the suffering Saviour of Men. Keble's "Christian Year" took the place of "Paradise Lost," and as my girlhood began to bud towards womanhood, all its deeper currents set in the direction of religious devotion. My mother did not allow me to read love stories, and my daydreams of the future were scarcely touched by any of the ordinary hopes and fears of a girl lifting her eyes towards the world she is shortly to enter. They were filled with broodings over the days when girl-martyrs were blessed with visions of the King of

Martyrs, when sweet St. Agnes saw her celestial Bridegroom, and angels stooped to whisper melodies in St. Cecilia's raptured ear. "Why then and not now?" my heart would question, and I would lose myself in these fancies, never happier than when alone. . . .

The hidden life grew stronger, constantly fed by these streams of study; weekly communion became the centre round which my devotional life revolved, with its ecstatic meditation, its growing intensity of conscious contact with the Divine; I fasted, according to the ordinances of the Church; occasionally flagellated myself to see if I could bear physical pain, should I be fortunate enough ever to tread the pathway trodden by the saints; and ever the Christ was the figure round which clustered all my hopes and longings, till I often felt that the very passion of my devotion would draw Him down from His throne in heaven, present visibly in form as I felt Him invisibly in spirit. To serve Him through His Church became more and more a definite ideal in my life, and my thoughts began to turn towards some kind of "religious life," in which I might prove my love by sacrifice and turn my passionate gratitude into active service. . . .

As I have said, my day-dreams held little place for love, partly from the absence of love novels from my reading, partly from the mystic fancies that twined themselves round the figure of the Christ. Catholic books of devotion —English or Roman, it matters not, for to a large extent they are translations of the same hymns and prayers—are exceedingly glowing in their language, and the dawning feelings of womanhood unconsciously lend to them a passionate fervour. I longed to spend my time in worshipping Jesus, and was, as far as my inner life was concerned, absorbed in that passionate love of "the Saviour" which, among emotional Catholics, really is the human passion of love transferred to an ideal—for women to Jesus, for men to the Virgin Mary. In order to show that I am not here exaggerating, I subjoin a few of the prayers in which I found daily delight, and I do this in order to show how an emotional girl may be attracted by these so-called devotional exercises:—

"O crucified Love, raise in me fresh ardours of love and consolation, that it may henceforth be the greatest torment I can endure ever to offend Thee; that it may be my greatest delight to please Thee."

"Let the remembrance of Thy death, O Lord Jesu, make me to desire and pant after Thee, that I may delight in Thy gracious presence."

"O most sweet Jesu Christ, I, unworthy sinner, yet redeemed by Thy precious blood. . . . Thine I am and will be, in life and in death."

"O Jesu, beloved, fairer than the sons of men, draw me after Thee with the cords of Thy love."

"Blessed are Thou, O most merciful God, who didst vouchsafe to espouse me to the heavenly Bridegroom in the waters of baptism, and hast imparted Thy body and blood as a new gift of espousal and the meet consummation of Thy love."

"O most sweet Lord Jesu, transfix the affections of my inmost soul with that most joyous and most healthful wound of Thy love, with true, serene, most holy, apostolical charity; that my soul may ever languish and melt with entire love and longing for Thee. Let it desire Thee and faint for Thy courts; long to be dissolved and be with Thee."

"Oh, that I could embrace Thee with that most burning love of angels."

"Let Him kiss me with the kisses of His mouth; for Thy love is better than wine. Draw me, we will run after Thee. The king hath brought me into his chambers. . . . Let my soul, O Lord, feel the sweetness of Thy presence. May it taste how sweet Thou art. . . . May the sweet and burning power of Thy love, I beseech Thee, absorb my soul."

All girls have in them the germ of passion, and the line of its development depends on the character brought into the world, and the surrounding influences of education. I had but two ideals in my childhood and youth, round whom twined these budding tendrils of passion; they were my mother and the Christ. I know this may seem strange, but I am trying to state things as they were in this life-story, and not give mere conventionalisms, and so it was. I had men friends, but no lovers—at least, to my knowledge, for I have since heard that my mother received two or three offers of marriage for me, but declined them on account of my youth and my childishness—friends with whom I liked to talk, because they knew more than I did; but they had no place in my day-dreams. These were more and more filled with the one Ideal Man, and my hopes turned towards the life of the Sister of Mercy, who ever worships the Christ, and devotes her life to the service of His poor.

21. 'Born again' in America

The Protestants of nineteenth-century America believed that it was essential for a person to experience conversion in order to lead a religious life; indeed, only those converted could rest assured of joining God's elect after death. The following selections reveal the tribulations of two young women who strove for conversion.

Catharine Beecher (1800–1878) was the eldest daughter of a fervent New England Calvinist preacher, Lyman Beecher. Shortly after completing the arrangements for his daughter's engagement to a young Yale professor named Fisher in early 1822, Dr. Beecher set out, in a somewhat tardy effort, to precipitate Catharine's religious awakening, which he considered an essential preliminary to her marriage. In May of that year Catharine's fiancé drowned in a shipwreck, and her father confronted her with the charge that this tragic accident was God's retribution for her lack of faith. The first selection, excerpts from the celebrated correspondence between Catharine, her brother Edward, and her father, offers an unforgettable glimpse into the intensity of religious life during the Second Great Awakening, and into this articulate young woman's spirited resistance to her strong-willed father and

SOURCES: (i) *Autobiography, Correspondence, Etc.*, of Lyman Beecher, D.D., ed. Charles Beecher (New York, 1865), 1: 474–506 *passim*. (ii) "God Struck Me Dead: Religious Conversion Experiences and Autobiographies of Negro Ex-Slaves," *Social Sciences Source Documents* (Fisk University, 1945), 2: 98–101.

his evangelical faith. *As the second selection shows, the conversion experience was by no means confined to the Calvinists of New England. Encouraged and sustained by her mother, a young black Alabama woman, whose name is not known, underwent the ordeal of conversion. At the peak of the experience, she found herself in heaven, where a voice told her that she "must go and help carry the world."*

(i) Catharine Beecher

[Catharine to Edward, March 7, 1822]
Last Sunday was sacrament day, and thirty-six were admitted to the Church, and ten or twelve baptized. It was very solemn. The revival is going on still, though not powerful. I fear it will pass over like others, and none of our family feel its influence.

I know it is what our dear father and mother most earnestly desire and pray for, but as yet their prayers remain unanswered. I feel as much as any one can the necessity of a change, and still can not feel sorrow for sin, and it sometimes seems to me I never shall.

[Dr. Beecher to Edward, April 1, 1822]
Catharine has been sick three days, the first in acute distress. I had been addressing her conscience not twenty minutes before. She was seized with most agonizing pain. I hope it will be sanctified.

[Dr. Beecher to Catharine, May 30, 1822]
On entering the city [New Haven] last evening, the first intelligence I met filled my heart with pain. It is all but certain that Professor Fisher is no more.

Thus have perished our earthly hopes, plans, and prospects. Thus the hopes of Yale College, and of our country, and, I may say, of Europe, which had begun to know his promise, are dashed. The waves of the Atlantic, commissioned by Heaven, have buried them all. . . .

And now, my dear child, what will you do? Will you turn at length to God, and set your affections on things above, or cling to the shipwrecked hopes of earthly good? Will you send your thoughts to heaven and find peace, or to the cliffs, and winds, and waves of Ireland, to be afflicted, tossed with tempest, and not comforted?

[Catharine to Edward, June 4, 1822]
Your letter came at a time when no sympathy could soothe a grief "that knows not consolation's name." Yet it was not so much the ruined hopes of future life, it was dismay and apprehension for his immortal spirit. Oh, Edward, where is he now? Are the noble faculties of such a mind doomed to everlasting woe, or is he now with our dear mother in the mansions of the blessed? . . .

My dear brother, I am greatly afflicted. I know not where to look for comfort. The bright prospects that turned my thoughts away from heaven are all destroyed; and now that I have nowhere to go but to God, the heavens are closed against me, and my prayer is shut out.

I feel that my affliction is what I justly deserve. Oh that God would take possession of the heart that He has made desolate, for this world can never comfort me. I feel to the very soul that it is He alone who hath wounded that can make whole.

But I am discouraged, and at a loss what to do. I feel no realizing sense of my sinfulness, no love to the Redeemer, nothing but that I am unhappy and need religion; but where or how to find it I know not.

[Catharine to Edward, July 1822]

When I began to write to you on the subject which now occupies my thoughts, it was with a secret feeling that you could do something to remove my difficulties. But this feeling is all gone now. I have turned to you, and to father, and to every earthly friend, and have again and again felt to my very soul that it is a case in which "the help of man faileth."

It is the feeling of entire guilt, willful and inexcusable, which gives all the consistency and excellency to the Gospel. Without this the justice of God is impaired, His mercy is destroyed, the grace and condescension of Jesus Christ is veiled, and the aid of the Blessed Spirit made void.

This feeling I can not awaken in my heart, nor is my understanding entirely convinced that it ought to exist, any farther than this, that I perceive in the Word of God that the guilt of man is considered as without excuse by his Maker. I give the assent which a shortsighted, fallible creature ought to give to Omniscience, but it is an assent to authority, not to conviction.

The difficulty in my mind originates in my views of the doctrine of original sin, such views as seem to me sanctioned not only by my own experience, but by the language of the Bible.

Suppose a man born with an ardent love of liquor, in circumstances, too, when temptations are on every side. He is withheld by parental authority in some degree, and is daily instructed in the evils of intemperance. He sees it and feels it, and resolves to abstain; but the burning thirst impels him on, and he swallows the maddening potion. Now should we not *pity* such a man as well as blame? True, he is guilty; but does not the burning thirst implanted by nature plead in extenuation? Do we not feel that he is unfortunate as well as guilty?

Now take your sister as a parallel case. I find implanted within me a principle of selfishness, as powerful and inveterate as the love of drink in the other case, in the existence of which I am altogether involuntary. To restrain the indulgence of this, I have had the instruction of parents, the restraints of education, the commands and threatenings of God; but these have all proved vain. I have gone on indulging this propensity year after year, and time has only added new strength to it.

Now the judgments of God have brought me to a stand. I am called to look back upon past life, and consider what I have done. It is a painful and humiliating retrospection. I see nothing but the most debasing selfishness and depravity in my heart, and this depravity equally displayed in all the actions of my past life.

But, alas! this extenuating feeling blunts the force of conviction. I see that I am guilty, very guilty, but I can not feel, neither can I convince my understanding, that *I am totally and utterly without excuse.* I see that I could have done otherwise, and that I had the most powerful motives that could be applied to induce me to do so, and I feel that I am guilty, but not guilty as if I had received a nature pure and uncontaminated. I can not feel this; I never shall by any mental exertion of my own; and if I ever do feel it, it will be by the interference of divine Omnipotence, and the work would seem to me miraculous.

When I have confessed my sins to God, there has always been a lurking feeling, though I sometimes have not been aware of it, that, as God has formed me with this perverted inclination, he was, as a merciful being, obligated to grant some counteracting aid. Now I perceive how ruinous this feeling is, how contrary to the whole tenor of the Gospel. But is there not a real difficulty on the subject? Is there any satisfactory mode of explaining this doctrine, so that we can perceive its consistency while the heart is unrenewed? . . .

I see that my feelings are at open war with the doctrines of grace. I don't know that I ever felt enmity to God, or doubted of his justice and mercy, for I can more easily doubt the truth of these doctrines than the rectitude of God.

I feel that my case is almost a desperate one, for the use of the means of grace have a directly contrary effect on my mind from others. The more I struggle, the less guilty I feel; yet I dare not give them up.

Thus my hours are passing away as the smoke, and my days as a tale that is told. I lie down in sorrow and awake in heaviness, and go mourning all the day long. There is no help beneath the sun, and whether God will ever grant His aid He only knows.

[Dr. Beecher to Edward (accompanying the foregoing), Aug. 2, 1822]
Catharine's letter will disclose the awfully interesting state of her mind. There is more *movement* than there ever existed before, more feeling, more interest, more anxiety; and she is now, you perceive, handling edge-tools with powerful grasp.

Brother Hawes talked with her, and felt the difficulties and peculiarities of her case. I have at times been at my wit's end to know what to do. But I conclude nothing safe can be done but to assert ability, and obligation, and guilt upon divine authority, throwing in, at the same time, as much collateral light from reason as the case admits of, and taking down the indefensible positions which depravity, and fear, and selfishness, and reason set up. In other words, I answer objections and defend the ways of God.

After all, we must pray. I am not without hope that the crisis approaches in which submission will end the strife. She is hard pressed, and, if not subdued, I should fear the consequences.

[Catharine to her father, New Year, 1823]

I find that my heart is wayward, selfish, impure, and vain, and I never so feel my weakness as when I attempt to regulate its evil propensities. Sometimes I lose that supporting hope that God will help me, and then I am ready to give all up in despair; and sometimes the world looks so charming, and my situation and employments are so pleasing, that my naturally cheerful spirits assume their native buoyancy, and then it seems as if I never should *persevere* in seeking religion.

[Catharine to her father, Feb. 15, 1823]

The question of my entire ability to keep the law of God can never be settled, even to the conviction of my understanding, unless by supernatural interference. Should arguments equally powerful with those advanced by you and Edward, and ten thousand times more so, be advanced to prove that I had physical strength to move the everlasting hills, it would be to no purpose. Consciousness would be that brow of iron that would resist them all.

I do feel as certain that I have not present ability to realize the being and presence of God, and to awaken emotions of love toward him, as I do of the existence or non-existence of any faculty of the mind; and it is not strange, nor do I think it wrong, while this consciousness exists, that a conviction that God does require these impossibilities should awaken hard feeling toward him, for we ought not to experience other feelings than those of aversion toward what seems cruel and unjust in any being.

The difficulty and the guilt consists in this consciousness of inability. The truth to be proved, then, is that, in certain cases, we must not rely upon our own consciousness, but trust to the interpretations that are given by fallible men of the Word of God.

If I say that I can not perceive that emotions of affection are at the control of the will, you say that, as you understand the Bible, God does require these things. Now, which is easiest to abandon, confidence in my own consciousness or in your interpretation of the Bible?

(ii) 'One of the elect children'

I was born in Huntsville, Alabama during slavery time. When the war broke out I was married and had one child.

My mother was a good old time Christian woman. Me and my sister used to lay in the bed at night and listen to her and my aunt talk about what God had done for them. From this I began to feel like I wanted to be a Christian. I got so that I tried to pray like I heard them pray. I didn't know what it meant. I hardly know what I said half the time. I just said something with the Lord's name in it and asked Him to have mercy on me.

The first time I heard God's voice I was in the blackberry patch. It seemed like I was all heavy and burdened down more than common. I had got so I prayed a lot and more I prayed it look like the worse off I got. So while I was picking blackberries I said, "Lord, what have I done; I feel so sinful." A voice said to me, "You have prayed to God and He will bring you out more than conqueror." The voice scared me a little but some of my heaviness left me. I looked about to see where the voice came from but I didn't see nobody. From this time on I tried to pray more. I got so I felt heavy and burdened down again. My mother noticed it and asked me what was the matter. I told her I had heard a voice and that I had been trying to pray. She clapped her hands. She said, "Pray on, daughter, for if the Master has started to working with you, He will not stop until He has freed your soul."

It wasn't long after this before I died. I waited on the Lord till my change came. I got my orders at hell's dark door. I was dressed up. He set my feet in the path, told me to go and I have been travelling ever since. Falling down and getting up I keep my eye on the bright and morning star. He told me I would have hard trials and great tribulations but I must fight on. I got a crown in glory that outshines the sun. I've been dug up, rooted and grounded and buried in Him and I am not hell-scared. Some say what they think but I am talking what I know. I know that my soul was freed from hell; my feet lifted out of the miry clay and placed on the rock of eternity.

When I died I just slept away. I got up feeling awful heavy that morning. I had almost made up my mind that I wouldn't pray no more. It looked like the more I prayed the worse off I got. But the God I serve is a time God. He don't come before time. He don't come after time. He comes just on time. I prayed that morning and said, "Lord if I am anything at all like I feel, I am the least of all. It looks like the whole world is against me." God bless your soul, when I said that I don't know what got into me. I burst out crying. Something began to well up on the inside of me. I cried for joy. Then came a voice that set my soul on fire. It said, "My little one! Your cries have been heard in Glory. This day you must die." When I heard this I started to run. Everything got dim before me. I began to moan on the inside, "Mercy! Mercy! Mercy! Lord." I fell in my tracks.

When I woke up in hell, I was travelling along a big road. Down on each side I saw the souls in torment. Many of them were people I had known in life. They were just roaming and staggering along. They were saying, "Oh, how long?" I met on the road a great host, some walking, some on mules, going down to hell. I cried and said, "Lord, have mercy! What is the meaning of this?" A voice said, "These are going down to destruction but I have delivered your soul." The next thing I saw was a little man before me. He said, "Follow me." I followed. We came to where the roads forked. One way was broad and the other was a little narrow path that led upward. I saw all kinds of animals and people. They looked like they wanted to devour me. By this time the little man had stepped over into the narrow path. The path and the big road didn't touch each other. I was scared to try to step over lest I should miss it and fall into the pit below. I cried out, "Lord, I can't make it." He said, "Put your right food forward and your left will follow."

As we went on I heard a great rumbling noise ahead. The little man called and said, "Angels come down." Soon there was a great multitude. He told them to call me. They all mourned, "Mama, Mama, you must help carry the world."

We went on and came to a gate. The gate opened. We went in. We stood before the throne of God. The little man said, "Here is one come from the lower parts of the world." God spoke but he didn't open his mouth. "How did she come?" "She came through hard trials with the hell-hounds on her trail."

Mary and Martha put a robe on me and dressed me up. I sat down to a table with a host of angels. They all went away though like a flash. A voice said, "You are born of God. My son delivered your soul from hell and you must go and help carry the world. You have been chosen out of the world and hell can't hold you."

When I came back to myself I was just like somebody foolish. I felt like I wanted to run away. I cried and shouted for joy so glad to be one of the elect children.

This is why I say that a child that has been truly born of God knows it. I can rise and tell you about God the darkest hour of midnight. The law is written in my heart and I don't need no book. He told me to ask through faith and He would grant it in grace.

22. A French girl becomes a nun: Saint Thérèse de Lisieux

Like Mémé Santerre (Docs. 1.iv and 5), Marie-Françoise-Thérèse Martin (1873–97), now known as Saint Thérèse de Lisieux, was the last and favored child in a large family. The Martins, however, unlike the Santerres, were literate and relatively prosperous: the father was a successful watchmaker and the mother a craftswoman. The death of her mother in 1877 darkened Thérèse's childhood. By 1883 she was suffering a mixture of convulsions, hallucinations, and comas. Some three years later, she made what seemed a miraculous recovery, but her symptoms did not disappear completely until after Christmas 1886, when she experienced the conversion described in this selection. Shortly thereafter, she petitioned to enter the Carmelite convent in Lisieux where her two older sisters, Pauline and Marie, were already nuns. Only fifteen when she entered the convent in 1888, Thérèse died nine years later of tuberculosis. She was canonized in 1925. The passages that follow are excerpted from an autobiographical memoir written as a feastday present for Pauline, her sister by blood, her "mother" in religion.

How did I find the freedom of movement to want Carmel? God had to perform a miracle on a small scale to make me grow up; grow up all in a moment. And the occasion he chose for it was Christmas, that night of illumination which somehow lights up for us the inner life of the Blessed Trinity.

SOURCE: *Autobiography of St. Thérèse of Lisieux*, tr. Ronald A. Knox (New York, 1958), pp. 126–27, 183–86, 201–2. Originally published in Lisieux, France, in 1957.

Our Lord, newly born, turned this darkness of mine into a flood of light; born to share my human weakness, he brought me the strength and courage I needed. He armed me so well, that holy night, that I never looked back; I was like a soldier, winning one vantage-point after another, like a 'great runner who sees the track before him.' My tears dried up at their source; they flowed, now, only at long intervals and with difficulty. Somebody had once said to me: 'If you cry like that when you're small, you'll have no tears left later on'; and it was true.

Yes, it was on December the twenty-fifth, 1886, that I was given the grace to leave my childhood's days behind; call it, if you will, the grace of complete conversion.

[Thérèse enters the convent, 1888]

To-day, as yesterday, the whole family was there; we all heard Mass and went to Communion. Together, we made our Lord welcome in his sacramental presence; there was sobbing all around me, nobody but myself was dry-eyed. My own sensation was a violent beating of the heart which made me wonder whether I'd find it possible to move when we were beckoned to the convent door. I did just manage it, but feeling as if it might kill me; it's the sort of experience one can't understand unless one's been through it. There was no outward sign of all this; all the other members of the family kissed me good-bye, and then I knelt down and asked for a blessing from the best of fathers, who knelt down too, and blessed me with tears in his eyes. I think the angels smiled down on us, rejoicing at the sight of an old man giving up his daughter, in the very spring-time of life, to the service of God.

A few moments more, and then the doors of God's Ark shut behind me, and I was being embraced by all those dear nuns who had so long been mothers to me, whose example I was to take henceforth as my rule of living. No more waiting now for the fulfillment of my ambitions; I can't tell you what a deep and refreshing sense of peace this thought carried with it. And, deep down, this sense of peace has been a lasting possession; it's never left me, even when my trials have been most severe. Like all postulants, I was taken off to the choir as soon as I'd entered; the light there was dim, because the Blessed Sacrament was exposed, and I was conscious of nothing at first except a pair of eyes—the eyes of dear, holy Mother Geneviève resting upon me. I knelt for a moment at her feet, thanking God for the grace of being allowed to know a Saint; and then I went on with Mother Marie Gonzague.

In all the different parts of the convent, everything charmed me; it seemed so completely cut off from the world; and above all, how I loved my little cell! But there was nothing agitating about this delight I experienced, it was quite calm; as if the breeze was too light to rock my little boat on the water's surface, the sky too bright to admit of a single cloud. All that difficult time I'd gone through had been worth it after all, and I could go about saying to myself: "I'm here for good, now, here for good!" There's nothing transitory about joy of this kind; it doesn't fade away with the honeymoon illusions of the noviciate. And indeed, I'd no illusions at all, thank God, when I entered

Carmel; I found the religious life exactly what I'd expected it to be. The sacrifices I had to make never for a moment took me by surprise—and yet, as you know, Mother, those first footsteps of mine brought me up against more thorns than roses! Suffering opened her arms to me, and I threw myself into them lovingly enough. In the interrogation which is made before a nun is professed, I declared in the presence of the sacred Host that I'd come there to save souls, and above all to pray for priests. Well, if you want to secure any object, no matter what it is, you've got to find the right steps for attaining it. And our Lord let me see clearly that if I wanted to win souls I'd got to do it by bearing a cross; so the more suffering came my way, the more strongly did suffering attract me.

For the next five years, it was this way of suffering I had to follow, and yet there was no outward sign of it—perhaps it would have relieved my feelings a bit if other people had been conscious of it, but they weren't. There'll be a lot of surprises at the Last Judgment, when we shall be able to see what really happened inside people's souls; and I think this way of suffering by which God led me will be a revelation to the people who knew me. Indeed, I can prove it; two whole months after I entered, our director, Père Pichon, came down for the profession of Sister Marie of the Sacred Heart; and he told me then that he was astonished at God's dealings with my soul; he'd been looking at me the evening before when I was praying in choir, and got the impression that my fervour was still the fervour of childhood, and the way by which I was being led was one of unruffled calm.

I derived a great deal of comfort from my interview with this holy priest, but it was through a mist of tears, because I found it so difficult to explain the state of my soul to him. All the same, I made my general confession, the most thoroughgoing I'd ever made; and at the end of it he used an expression which echoed in my inward ear as nothing else ever had. "In the presence of Almighty God," said he, "and of the Holy Virgin, and of all the Saints, I assure you that you've never committed a single mortal sin." Then he added: "You must thank God for the mercy he's shown you: if he left you to yourself, you wouldn't be a little angel any longer, you'd be a little demon." I'd no difficulty in believing that; I knew well enough how weak and imperfect I was. But my gratitude knew no bounds; I'd always been terrified that I might, somehow, have soiled the robe of my baptismal innocence; and an assurance like this, coming from a director after St. Teresa's own heart, so wise, so holy, seemed to me to come straight from our Lord himself. Some other words of his remained deeply imprinted on my heart: "My child, there's one Superior, one Novice-master you must always obey—Jesus Christ."

[Thérèse takes her final vows, 1890]
On the morning of September the 8th, I seemed to be carried along on a tide of interior peace; and this sense of peace "which surpasses all our thinking" accompanied the taking of my vows. This wedding of my soul to our Lord was not heralded by the thunders and lightning of Mount Sinai, rather by that "whisper of a gentle breeze" which our father Elias heard there. I set

no limit to the graces I asked for that day; I felt that I had the privileges of a queen, who can use her influence to set prisoners free, and reconcile the king to his rebellious subjects; I wanted to empty Purgatory, and convert sinners everywhere. I prayed so hard for my mother, for my dear sisters, for all the family; but especially for my poor father, now so sorely tried and still so holy. I offered myself to our Lord, asking him to accomplish his will in me and never let any creature come between us.

[Here, between the pages of the manuscript, was inserted the following *billet de profession*, composed by Thérèse and worn on her heart, according to custom, when she took her vows.]

Jesus, my heavenly Bridegroom, never may I lose this second robe of baptismal innocence; take me to yourself before I commit any wilful fault, however slight. May I look for nothing and find nothing but you and you only; may creatures mean nothing to me, nor I to them—you, Jesus, are to be everything to me. May earthly things have no power to disturb the peace of my soul; that peace is all I ask of you, except love; love that is as infinite as you are, love that has no eyes for myself, but for you, Jesus, only for you. Jesus, I would like to die a martyr for your sake, a martyr in soul or in body; better still, in both. Give me the grace to keep my vows in their entirety; make me understand what is expected of one who is your bride. Let me never be a burden to the community, never claim anybody's attention; I want them all to think of me as no better than a grain of sand, trampled under foot and forgotten, Jesus, for your sake. May your will be perfectly accomplished in me, till I reach the place you have gone to prepare for me. Jesus, may I be the means of saving many souls; to-day, in particular, may no soul be lost, may all those detained in Purgatory win release. Pardon me, Jesus, if I'm saying more than I've any right to; I'm thinking only of your pleasure, of your content.

23. Two case studies of hysteria in young Frenchwomen

Medical records are valuable for revealing details about women's lives that Victorian reticence prevented many women from discussing. The following case studies from standard medical works for practicing physicians epitomize the two dominant and conflicting French views of the nineteenth-century "disease," hysteria. In the first case Jean-Baptiste Louyer-Villermay (1776–1837), a distinguished Parisian authority on hysteria, describes an extreme case of hysterical paralysis, apparently provoked by the rigid parental surveillance of a love-struck young woman of the upper classes. The genital treatments applied by Louyer-Villermay and the other doctors in this case stemmed from the prevailing French medical view that hysteria was caused by reproductive disorders, menstrual irregularities, and suppressed sexual de-

SOURCES: (i) *Bibliothèque du médecin-practicien* (Paris, 1844), 2: 226–27. (ii) Pierre Briquet, *Traité clinique et thérapeutique de l'hystérie* (Paris, 1859), pp. 56–61.

sire. In contrast, Pierre Briquet, from whose great treatise on hysteria the second case study was taken, argued that the disease was primarily mental in origin. He theorized that hysteria had its source in an impressionable type of personality that was extremely common in women but could also occur in men, that hysteria attacked the poor more often than the rich, that it was exacerbated by harsh treatment and scanty food rather than by coddling and luxury, and that its manifestations were not necessarily linked to genital malfunction or sexual continence. The excerpt presented here comes from Briquet's long case study of Marie Gaudin, a twenty-six-year-old washerwoman. Both documents reflect the class bias of the French medical establishment: the demoiselle in the first case study is protected by anonymity, whereas the working woman in the second case is named.

(i) Jean-Baptiste Louyer-Villermay

A young female person of twenty-one years, endowed with a good constitution and regular in her menstrual periods, who had habitually enjoyed perfect health, met a young man several times in society who succeeded in inspiring a violent passion in her. The parents of this young lady objected to the match that she so ardently desired. From that time on, a slight disturbance in her health became noticeable, and her menstrual cycle became irregular. In the space of six months she experienced several hysterical attacks with convulsive movements, the sensation of strangulation, hysterical boils, choking, tingling in the uterus, etc. Medical treatment was limited to the prescription of a few leeches to the vulva.

Shortly afterwards, this young person found a letter from her sweetheart in her parents' possession, which they refused to give to her. She was immediately seized by an attack much stronger than the preceding ones, which was accompanied by a lethargic coma, an absolute loss of feeling and movement, and lockjaw and rigidity of the pharynx to the extent that swallowing was nearly impossible. Her regular doctor prescribed copious bleeding by means of six leeches applied behind each ear for this condition, but the symptoms in no way diminished, and three days passed without the slightest change. It was then that I was called. I found the patient unconscious and unable to respond to questions addressed to her; she appeared to be very ill and to understand nothing at all. Her face was slightly flushed and bright, her eyes fixed, her eyelids constantly closed, and her teeth clenched, and the obstruction in her swallowing remained the same. Respiration was troubled; the pulse was faint but regular and not far from its natural state. I prescribed an infusion of lime-blossom tea, an antispasmodic potion, and two blistering agents to the thighs.

The next day, the patient was in nearly the same state. She did, however, utter a few words, but they made no sense, although they did seem to relate to her attachment [for the young man]. Moreover, a general clamminess began to manifest itself. It was deemed advisable to apply a new blistering agent to the nape of the neck, and when the sweating had been completed, compresses of salty water and vinegar were applied to her head. In addition, her neck was rubbed with oil, camphor, laudanum, and ether; finally she was given injections and partial injections of camphor and asafetida.*

At the end of seven days, this young woman recovered the use of her senses, retaining only a vague memory of the crisis that she had experienced.

(ii) Pierre Briquet

Marie Gaudin, washerwoman. Born and raised in the country until the age of twelve; mother hysterical without attacks; father sickly, subject to stomach disorders since the age of twenty-five. One healthy brother, another brother with stomach disorders, a sister hysterical with attacks.

This girl received an average education; as a child, she was very feeble and impressionable, often subject to migraines and with an irregular appetite. Since birth she has been subject to very frequent attacks of convulsions. During childhood, they often took place several times a week, and they rarely occurred less often than every two weeks. In most cases they were provoked by the slightest emotion. Since she is intelligent, she has carefully observed these attacks, which continued until the age of twenty-six. . . .

Menstruation began at age twelve; she was then large enough, but weak and always sickly. The first menstruation was painful. Her period then appeared every fifteen or twenty days; it was continuous and abundant, lasting six to eight days. The first day was usually painful. . . .

At eighteen, a painful pregnancy with frequent vomiting, and because of many vexations, frequent attacks [of convulsions]; normal delivery; the child lives and is healthy. She took refuge in Paris at nineteen, in order to escape the reproaches made to her on account of her pregnancy. Since then, she has had many difficulties. At the age of twenty, rheumatic disorders in the joints and muscles. At the age of twenty-three, she felt impelled to marry, more from reason than from taste; her family opposed her inclination, and from this, new griefs and the appearance of headaches and an intense pain in the middle of her back and down the right side of her spine. . . .

Entered the Charity Hospital September 26, 1854.

Woman of twenty-five, rather thin, medium height, face without color, white skin, auburn hair, normal intellect, very frequent headaches of the temporal lobe that occurred both while she was at rest and while moving.

[Reporting that all her senses were severely impaired on the right side but normal on the left, Briquet continued:]

Almost complete numbness on the right side of the trunk of the body and on the right arm and leg. . . . The right breast is insensitive to pin pricks; the labia majora and minora are numb on the right side; there is little sensitivity on the right side of the vagina; clitoris is insensitive when not erect, but becomes acutely sensitive during erection, which can be produced easily without creating any pleasant sensations. . . .

Treatment.—Iron tonic, 20 centigrams; extract of *nux vomica*, 7 centigrams; mustard plasters to the epigastrium; double portions of food.

* I.e. vaginal douches of anti-spasmodic drugs.—EDS.

No observable change during the months of October, November, and December; a single attack of hysteria. . . .

Toward the middle of May, 1855, the patient experienced no noticeable improvement; she constantly experienced dizziness, headaches, indigestion. . . . The numbness on the right side persisted. . . . Weary, she lost courage and wanted to leave the hospital. . . .

This woman, having seen a neighboring patient seized by paralysis improve under the influence of the same treatment, was heartened, and taking advantage of her new attitude, we pursued the treatment energetically, supplementing it with massage of the limbs, iron tonic, Bordeaux wines, and a good diet. . . .

February 3, 1856. . . . Released from hospital.

This young woman returned to her family, where she was welcomed; her health improved; all nervous symptoms disappeared; and eighteen months after, I learned that she was in perfect health and no longer had any traces of weakness or numbness.

24. A young Englishwoman dies of consumption: Emily Shore

The daughter of an English minister and private tutor, Margaret Emily Shore (1819–39) began keeping a journal at the age of eleven. From her writings, she emerges as an extremely sensitive and precocious young girl, who was an acute observer of everything she encountered. Educated at home, she was an eager student of history, poetry, and natural science, and spent much of her time studying and drawing plants and animals. At sixteen Emily contracted tuberculosis, the notorious "consumption" that took so many lives in the Victorian period. The following excerpts from her journal chronicle the progression of her illness and depict the almost painfully matter-of-fact fashion in which she faced death. She wrote the last entry on May 27, 1839, two weeks before she died, at the age of nineteen.

March 7, 1836.—I have been confined to the house, and partly to my bed, by a cough—a thing which I have not for many years had, except before my last fever. So that, unless I get out very soon, I am afraid that I shall miss the first singing birds of passage. I see from the windows that several crocuses are in blow. I am likely to miss the first violets and primroses also.

June 6, 1836.—To me, all this spring and part of the summer are quite lost, and it might almost as well have been continual winter. From the first day of March up to my illness, I have not been altogether out of the house more than sixteen different days, including going to church and a few drives, and some occasions on which I merely stepped out of the house for a few minutes; and during the whole year I have been in a state of very indifferent health, not to speak of this month of fever. So that I have been quite debarred this year from rising at four or five o'clock, and walking in the woods at will to watch the

SOURCE: Margaret Emily Shore, *Journal of Emily Shore* (London, 1891), pp. 137, 139–42, 174–75, 219–20, 256, 263–64, 350–51.

birds and hear their songs. I shall not now recover my strength for many weeks; and my mind, even my memory, is equally enfeebled. The very slightest fever completely upsets all one's powers.

June 29, 1836.—I get stronger, but my cough gives way very slowly, and my pulse continues high and strong. There is certainly danger of my lungs becoming affected, but we trust that, if it please God, the sea will restore me to health and remove the possibility of consumption. I know, however, that I must prepare myself for the worst, and I am fully aware of papa's and mamma's anxiety about me.

July 5, 1836.—To-day was effected the chief object of our stay in town, the consultation with the physician. . . . Dr. James Clark is of middle height, rather thin, very dark, and of a grave and quiet demeanour, speaking very little. His aspect, however, is very pleasing and amiable. My illness has made me exeedingly nervous, and his presence agitated me greatly. I trembled all over, my heart throbbed, my pulse quickened, and the perspiration broke out from every pore. Dr. Clark examined me most minutely, tapped me, and tried his stethoscope on my chest, neck, back, side, shoulder. He said nothing about the result of his observations, but retired with mamma to another private conference. I, in the mean time, was left in a state of anxiety amounting almost to agony. I could by no means compose myself; the doctor's tapping had given me pain of the left side of my chest, and I had no small reason to apprehend the pulmonary disease had already begun. I prayed earnestly for submission to the Divine will, and that I might be prepared for death; I made up my mind that I was to be the victim of consumption.

At length mamma re-entered the room, and told me Dr. Clark's opinion, viz. that my lungs are by no means at present diseased, but that there is the greatest danger of it, unless extreme care be taken of me. This was much more than I had dared to hope, and I thanked God for it.

Dec. 25, 1836.—Yesterday I was sixteen years old, to-day I am seventeen; the sound of the words seem to effect a greater change than the actual space of time. I lay awake last night for a long time, kept awake by a little matter which has disturbed my equanimity and put me into a painful state of mind. I heard the midnight clock strike twelve; I counted every stroke, and when the last had sounded, I had completed my seventeenth year, and entered on another.

I look back on the year I have just finished with many mingled feelings, most of a painful nature. . . . When I have felt happy, I have also felt that something more was wanting to complete that happiness, and for that something I have ardently wished and longed. This feeling has always rankled within, with various degrees of intensity, sometimes so little acknowledged to myself (never to anyone else) that it has seemed no longer to exist, and for a time my life has glided on in calm and uninterrupted enjoyment. I remember that last year I had no outward impediment to happiness. All was prosperous around me, I could pursue unchecked all my favourite studies and amusements, and I grew more and more attached to the world and estranged from heaven. In this state I felt my danger. I felt as if no ordinary call could awaken me from my dream of happiness; I almost wished and prayed for affliction, if there were no other means of correction. And has not God answered this half-indulged wish? Has He not chastised me by withdrawing me from those things which chiefly formed the delight of my life? It is a striking, an impressive circumstance, in which I cannot fail to see His fatherly hand.

There is completely a world within me, unknown, unexplored, by any but myself. I see well that my feelings, my qualities, my character, are understood by none else. I am not what I am supposed to be; I am liked and loved far more than I deserve. I hate—yes, I truly hate myself; for I see the depths of sin within me, which are hidden from all other eyes. No one ought ever to feel satisfied with himself, with his progress in holiness; but they may feel peace of mind; and much must I be changed before I can reach this state! Yet I have now many advantages, which I hope to improve. I have more leisure for serious thought; I have a dangerous illness hovering over my head to warn me; I am, by my removal to Devonshire, removed also from the temptations to some of my chief faults.

Sept. 18, 1837.—In looking back on the beginning of my illness, I feel sure that one of the principal causes of it was overworking my mind with too hard study, which is no uncommon cause of consumption. For many months before I was actually ill, I tasked my intellectual powers to the utmost. My mind never relaxed, never unbent; even in those hours meant for relaxation, I was still engaged in acquiring knowledge and storing my memory. While dressing, I learnt by heart chapters of the Bible, and repeated them when I walked out, and when I lay in bed; I read Gibbon when I curled my hair at night; at meals my mind was still bent on its improvement, and turned to arithmetic, history, and geography. This system I pursued voluntarily with the most unwearied assiduity, disregarding the increasing delicacy of my health, and the symptoms that it was giving way.

Oct 1, 1837.—My cough is gradually returning with the approach of winter, more than it did last year. My short breath and palpitations of the heart on moving or lying down are very annoying; my heart beats so loud at night that it is like the ticking of a clock. I am subject, too, to pains in the chest and side; and altogether I am very weak and out of health. I feel as if I should never recover the strength of body and unwearied vigour and activity of mind I once possessed. God's will be done, it is meant for the best, though so early in life, when I have but just quitted childhood; it is a painful prospect, and a severe trial both in endurance and anticipation.

July 1, 1838.—I have been addicted of late to growing faint after breakfast. I do not much mind it myself, only that it alarms papa and mamma. Poor papa is so anxious about me, that one would think every cough I utter is my death-knell.

I suppose I am never to be strong again. It is nearly three months since I have walked into the Forest, and now I am always left behind when others go out. This evening I could almost have cried when I saw mamma, Aunt Charlotte, Cousin Susan, and the four children set forth joyously to ramble in some of the loveliest glades, and poor I was obliged to content myself with the dull drawing-room. It was a sweet, still summer's evening, such as is proper for the enjoyment of the Forest, and I would have given worlds to have gone too. However, I had a partner in misery, poor papa, who is at present equally unable to walk. So we remained quietly conversing at home, and certainly I enjoyed it very much. I grew envious again of the strong party, when they returned at nearly nine o'clock, extolling the beauties they had seen, and bringing in a handful of butterfly orchises, whose delicious fragrance scented all the room, and recalled me to those long-past days when I used to gather them at Woodbury.

July 14, 1838.—Here is a query, which I shall be able to answer decidedly at the end of this volume, most likely before. What is indicated by all these symptoms—this constant shortness of breath, this most harassing hard cough, this perpetual expectoration, now tinged with blood, this quick pulse, this painfully craving appetite, which a very little satisfies even to disgust, these restless, feverish nights, continual palpitations of the heart, and deep, circumscribed flushes? Is it consumption really come at last, after so many threatenings? I am not taken by surprise, for I have had it steadily, almost daily, in view for two years, and have always known that my lungs were delicate. I feel no uneasiness on the subject, even if my ideas (I cannot call them fears) prove right. It must be my business to prepare for another world; may God give me grace to do so!

May 18, 1839.—On the 4th of April I broke a blood-vessel, and am now dying of consumption, in great suffering, and may not live many weeks. God be merciful to me a sinner.

God be praised for giving me such excellent parents. They are more than any wishes could desire, or than any words can sufficiently praise. Their presence is like sunshine to my illness.

May 22, 1839.—I have suffered much with lying long, and have just been put on our hydrostatic bed. Relief wounderful. My portrait has just been taken; they say excellent.

I linger on in the same way, and do not yet sink. Alas! I can never see Richard [her brother] again.

May 27, 1839.—I feel weaker every morning, and I suppose am beginning to sink; still I can at times take up my pen. I have had my long back hair cut off. Dear papa wears a chain made from it. Mamma will have one too.

Part II

The Adult Woman: Personal Life

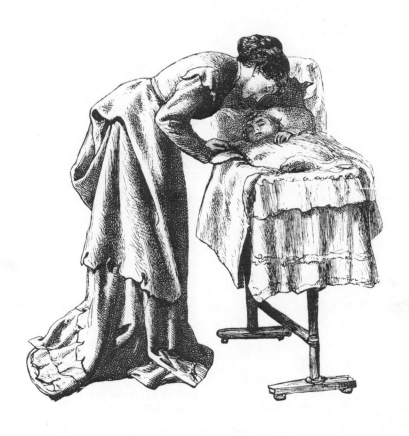

Introduction

Estelle B. Freedman and Erna Olafson Hellerstein

The doctrine of the separate spheres, as elaborated in literature, law, medicine, and religion, prescribed that women's personal lives center around home, husband, and children. The traditional separation between the male public sphere and the female private sphere took on new meaning in the nineteenth century as the distance between these worlds grew and as ever fewer jobs were performed in and around the household. Women at home became, ideally, specialists in emotional and spiritual life, protecting tradition and providing a stable refuge from the harsh, impersonal public sphere that men now entered in increasing numbers. Tennyson captured the ordering vision behind this sexual polarization in the words spoken by the old king in *The Princess*:[1]

> Man for the field and woman for the hearth:
> Man for the sword and for the needle she:
> Man with the head and woman with the heart:
> Man to command and woman to obey;
> All else confusion.

Not only in the middle classes, where the ideal predominated, but throughout each society, the dream of the "angel in the house" lent stability to a rapidly changing world.

The domestic ideal should not, however, be confused with the personal experiences of women, whether at home or in the workplace. Despite the rhetoric about the wife's "domestic empire" or the home as refuge, a woman's daily world was likely to be a single, poorly ventilated room in which an entire family ate and slept, and all too often worked as well. French peasants frequently shared dirt-floored hovels with their livestock (Doc. 75); women slaves in America, even those who worked in their master's comfortable

---

[1] *The Princess* (1849): part V, lines 427–31. Although this passage has often been quoted as epitomizing Victorian attitudes about the separate spheres, Tennyson himself did not defend these sentiments. In the poem, he made the king who uttered them a harsh, crude, and old-fashioned curmudgeon who, in the same speech, suggested that men should break women like horses. For a further discussion of this poem and of the angelic ideal in literature, see Christ 1977. F. Basch 1974 discusses the ideal of domesticity and Victorian criticisms of it in novels, poetry, and protest literature. Two classic studies of Victorian domestic ideology still worth reading are Houghton 1957 and Welter 1966.

household during the day, returned at night to care for their families in cramped and dark cabins (Docs. 53, 76); and the many women—and occasionally still entire families—who worked at home in the textile cottage industries had to eat and sleep amid the unwieldy looms, lint, and other detritus of their assorted trades (Docs. 5, 54.ii, 67).[2]

There were other obstacles to the achievement of the domestic ideal as well. Whatever the physical condition of their homes, women factory, field, and sweatshop workers had to spend as many as sixteen hours a day away from their households. Single working women who lived in urban boarding houses and domestic servants in narrow attic or basement rooms could do little to create cozy nests for themselves (Doc. 70). And certainly the women who migrated to the uncertain conditions on the American frontier had to fight heroically just to preserve the idea of the home in an alien land (Docs. 47, 62.i–ii, 78.iii).[3] Mary Abell, a Kansas homesteader who lived one winter in a prairie sod hut, wrote about this struggle in a letter to her sister back in comfortable New York State:

> Do you wonder that I get nervous shut up so week after week with the children in a room 10 x 11 for that is every inch of room we have. Em talks about being crowded, but let her try keeping house in the further bedroom with four small children. . . . I have to cook and do everything right here. Get milk—make butter, eat, sleep, etc. etc. The vessel under the bed a few feet from the stove does not thaw out week in and week out. (Doc. 66)

Even for the middle and upper classes, the private sphere over which women allegedly ruled slowly lost its isolation and autonomy as professionals like doctors and educators became the authorities on private matters such as childbirth, sexuality, and the raising of children. As the century wore on, more and more experts from the public world of the professions influenced home life with their standardized, printed advice, gradually displacing the traditional lore and rituals of female culture that women had customarily transmitted to each other orally and informally.[4]

These contradictions within the angelic domestic ideal and between this ideal and the real circumstances of women's lives are vividly revealed in the first-hand accounts of family life that follow. Not only do they illustrate the conflicts experienced by women, but they illustrate as well the ways different women responded to these tensions. In deciding whether and whom to marry, in living with husbands and children, and in friendships with their own sex, women of the Victorian era demonstrated both an awareness of the dilemmas they faced and an impressive resiliency in confronting them.

[2] On the living conditions for English working-class families, see Gauldie 1974. On the overlap of work and home and a review of literature on the subject, see Pleck 1976.

[3] On boarding, servants, and frontier women, see, respectively, Modell & Haveren 1973; McBride 1976; and Faragher & Stansell 1975.

[4] On the impact of the professions on women, see Wertz & Wertz 1977; and Ehrenreich & English 1978.

The Decision to Marry or Remain Single

In 1833 Stéphanie Jullien, a Parisian bourgeoise, wrote to her brother about a marriage proposal she had received: "*Mon Dieu!* Such indecision! Such perplexity! What should I do! I almost wish I were not so free, that I were restrained or controlled, so that I would not have the responsibility for my future unhappiness or happiness. Because the more I think about it, the more confused I become, the more I hesitate" (Doc. 28). Jullien, who almost seemed to long for a return to arranged marriages, was not alone in her anxiety, as the troubled musings in the courtship documents reveal (Docs. 27–29). The decision about marrying took on new weight in the nineteenth century as both the patterns and the meaning of marriage changed. In England and France the percentage of people who married gradually rose, while the average age at first marriage slowly fell, and life expectancy increased. The life expectancy of a French woman, for example, was only thirty years in 1800, compared with nearly fifty years in 1900. Americans had experienced a pattern of early marriage in the colonial period, but women's age at first marriage stabilized at twenty to twenty-three during the nineteenth century. At the same time, white American women shared in the increase in life expectancy that could lead to longer marriages. With marriages beginning earlier, and life spans getting longer, women in the Atlantic world could expect to spend more of their lives married than in the past.[5]

Victorian women may well have looked for greater emotional satisfaction from these lengthy marriages than their ancestors had, for a new emphasis on romantic love as a basis for union raised expectations for marital happiness.[6] Jullien wrote that she would never marry merely to give herself "a lot in life," and felt that she must love and desire her future husband for his sake as well as for hers. Helen Bourn, a young Englishwoman, warned her suitor about the importance of sincerity in love (Doc. 27). Moreover, Victorian women embarked on courtship knowing that a bad marriage could become a hell from which there was no exit. Indeed, divorce was not legally possible in France from 1816 to 1884; and law and custom continued to make even separation extremely rare in England and America (Docs. 60, 61.i–ii).

In addition, as Jullien complained, the choices on which women's future happiness depended now lay with them. Despite much regional and class variation, women in all three countries generally had more personal freedom in courtship and marriage than their grandmothers or even their mothers had. In the traditional "European marriage pattern," couples had characteristically

---

[5] For a concise summary of European demographic changes, see Tilly & Scott 1978: chap. 5. On America, see Wells 1979: 20, 22. See also Coale & Zelnik 1963; Wrigley 1969; Van de Walle 1974; and Johansson 1977. Consult as well the Part IV essay by Marilyn Yalom.

[6] Classic literary statements of this theme are presented in Taylor 1953; and Watt 1957. Such evidence is probably unrepresentative of the great numbers of peasants, slaves, and sweatshop workers who lacked the literacy and the time to read romantic novels and marriage manuals. Edward Shorter, in one of his more careful articles (1974), tries to show such a change among ordinary people.

waited until they could be certain of a house and some land before marrying, so that the average peasant woman had been almost thirty years old at marriage. Even these mature premodern brides had chosen their mates within the tight controls of kin and community. Although some remnants of this control survived into the Victorian period, the ex-peasants among the growing classes of industrial and wage laborers now courted more independently, with less participation by parents and community, and now founded and supported families on their own wages while relatively young (Docs. 35, 54.i–ii, 70).[7] Among the aristocracy and the bourgeoisie, arranged marriages were also becoming relics of the past; and though French demoiselles were still watched and chaperoned as in the past, young American women moved about quite freely, joked about courtship with their friends, and wrote love letters to their suitors (Docs. 17.i–ii, 19.i–ii, 29).[8]

The weakening of external controls on courtship was in fact a mixed blessing for women. To the extent that it lessened the surveillance over their romantic and sexual behavior, it brought greater personal autonomy; but at the same time it left them unprotected as they ventured into a larger world. Increases in illegitimacy rates in Europe suggest a new sexual vulnerability, particularly among migrants to the cities. Many of these illegitimate births resulted from coerced sexual relations by co-workers or neighbors, which would have been followed, in traditional societies, by marriage—village sanctions would have seen to that.[9] Now, however, men could take sexual advantage of women with impunity. Other evidence from the United States and Europe shows that rapes or seductions were often by social superiors: Lucy Brewer of Plymouth, Massachusetts, was seduced and abandoned by a respectable neighbor boy (Doc. 88); Suzanne Voilquin, a Parisian seamstress, had been raped by a "courting" medical student, only to be similarly abandoned (Doc. 35); Olive Ashe, a Vermont servant, was made pregnant by the farmer for whom she worked and died after a botched abortion (Doc. 43.iii).

Women's sexual and economic vulnerability, their desire for respectability and security, and their longing (in many cases) for children combined with the growing ideal of romantic love to place great pressure on them to marry. Spinsterhood was, in fact, rare in the nineteenth century—by the end of the century, more than 90 percent of all American women married, as did 85–88 percent of the women in England and France.[10]

The consequences of remaining single could vary greatly, depending on a woman's race, class, and nationality. The decision not to marry, for instance,

[7] Hajnal 1965. On early modern family life and family strategies in France, see N. Z. Davis 1977, which includes a very thorough bibliography. On 19th-century patterns, see D. S. Smith 1978: 94–96; and Tilly & Scott 1978: 93–98. See also Anderson 1971.

[8] For a comparison of European and American single women in the 1830's, see Alexis de Tocqueville's *Democracy in America*, vol. 2, 3d book, chap. 9.

[9] See Shorter 1975; and the criticisms of that work in Scott & Tilly 1975. See also Tilly, Scott, & Cohen 1976. In the U.S., however, illegitimacy rates were higher in the late 18th century and declined during the 19th. Smith & Hindus 1975.

[10] D. S. Smith 1974: 121; Tilly & Scott 1978: 92.

might mean independence for white, middle-class women like Catharine Beecher, Louisa May Alcott, and Harriet Martineau; such women could move about unchaperoned and become teachers, writers, lecturers, or social reformers (Docs. 21.i, 30, 71.ii).[11] And many single women found emotional support by living with family or friends. Eugénie de Guérin, who lived on her father's southern French estate, was insulated from worry by her comfortable economic position and had a tender relationship with her sister Mimi (Doc. 32). But most spinsters, without family means and social status, faced economic hardship and social marginality. Frances Marion Eddy, who gave up her dreams of college and a career in order to support her widowed mother, was more typical; for her spinsterhood meant hard work and considerable self-sacrifice (Doc. 31).

The consequences of marrying also varied widely among women. For a white woman in antebellum America or in Europe, marriage meant a loss of civil rights, including the rights to property, wages, and the custody of children. Under English law, as one critic, Barbara Bodichon, put it, her existence was entirely absorbed in that of her husband; and in the United States, a women's rights conference described married women as "civilly dead" (Docs. 33.vi, 33.viii).[12] In contrast, the slave woman in the American South had no civil rights from birth. Furthermore, her marriage, although it may have been performed according to complex Afro-American ritual, was not recognized by the state and entailed no transition in legal status.[13] In all three countries, marriage might come to mean primarily an economic partnership; however, for some, as we have seen in the Jullien case, marriage had to include the prospect of emotional and sexual satisfaction, in addition to financial security.

Marriage

Once married, nineteenth-century women found their personal lives beset with contradictions. On the one hand, the idea of the "angel in the house" called for a selfless, dependent creature who pleased and fascinated her husband and devoted herself to him without reserve (Docs. 25.i–ii). On the other hand, the realities of coping with a household, very likely with a job as well, and almost certainly with children, required sustained strength, skill, and creativity. To add further confusion, the marriage vows, reflecting the ideal of romantic love, evoked the image of loving partnership and mutual trust, yet the woman entered a "partnership" in which she had none of the legal and economic rights enjoyed by her spouse (Docs. 33.i, v–viii). How could she be an active, loving partner, yet remain a dependent angel?

It is possible that for many women such questions never arose. An angel rarely presided in the farm, factory, or slave family where marriage—indeed, where survival—clearly required a partnership in unremitting work (Docs. 5,

[11] The constraints on the activism of single women are discussed in Chambers-Schiller 1978. See also Schupf 1974.

[12] N. Basch 1979.

[13] On Afro-American marriage, see Genovese 1976: 475–81; Gutman 1977; and Burnham 1978.

66, 75). Middle-class women, too, although culturally and even physically constrained by the angelic ideal, were seldom idle, for all but the very rich had to work, if only in the home, tending the young, mending clothes, or nursing the sick.[14]

Despite all these difficulties, many women found personal happiness in marriage. For some simply fulfilling their marital duties and helping their families survive brought satisfaction (Docs. 47, 66). Married couples did attain loving partnerships in each country, especially in families where the "separate" spheres overlapped. Mémé Santerre reported that her father, a linen weaver who worked at home with his family, "adored" her mother; the aristocratic British Amberleys, engaged in a nursery battle to get their first-born son to breast-feed properly, were also clearly a loving couple who shared their trials (Docs. 5, 50). Even in the United States, with its more rigid separation of sexual spheres, the New England wife Persis Sibley Andrews found her husband a "sympathising partner," although she often expressed frustration at her inability to share his political life more fully; and the letters of Mary Ellen Castle Rankin, an American bride, shine with happiness (Docs. 34.i.–ii).

But even happy marriages did not satisfy all of women's needs, and many women turned outside of marriage for friendship and support. In the United States a strong female culture, which included both single and married women, could ease some of the strains of married life.[15] Through visits and letters married women found personal support from close female friends and relatives, especially when they faced life crises such as childbirth. Despite a devoted husband who brought her breakfast in bed during her first pregnancy, the California pioneer Georgiana Bruce Kirby wrote of her longing for the company of other women and the pleasure of her rare visits with distant neighbors (Doc. 47). The lifelong correspondence of the girlhood friends Mary Hallock Foote and Helena de Kay Gilder, whose marriages separated them by thousands of miles, brought great comfort at times of birth and death (Doc. 41).

For every one of the examples indicating the possibility for marital adjustment, another can be found to indicate how conflict in marriage could erupt, in all social classes, into extreme discord and even violence. The relative powerlessness of women in marriage left them vulnerable to physical and sexual abuse, as contemporary accounts of domestic violence, incest, and adultery illustrate.[16] Frédéric Le Play in his studies of European workers, for instance, recorded cases of wife-beating, drunkenness, and abandonment— and the case of at least one beaten French wife who regularly fought back (Doc. 102.i). Temperance advocates decried the effect of alcohol on family life, and claimed that drunken husbands neglected and abused their wives and children (Doc. 94.i), though court and prison records show that women,

---

[14] Branca 1974 and 1975. On the domestic tasks in the U.S., see, for instance, Kleinberg 1976.

[15] Smith-Rosenberg 1975.   [16] Pleck 1979.

too, could resort to alcohol and violence under economic and personal stress.[17]

Women's efforts to resist the power imbalances within the family and to control the world around them took both individual and social forms. French women had a reputation as wielders of power within the home through their responsibility for the family budget, and many middle-class women in England employed the same managerial leverage where they could. Some were able to impose their will on those around them by sheer force of personality, if not by manipulative charm, then by plain meanness or even sickness; in fact, invalided or hysterical women could wield formidable power. Some American historians have suggested that women gained power in the home by refusing marital sex so that they might exercise control over their own fertility. Such individual efforts had parallels in the social causes led by Anglo-American middle-class women in the last third of the century. Women's Christian Temperance Union members, voluntary motherhood advocates, and social purity reformers sought to convert men to the female ideals of temperance and chastity, standards that they believed to be in the interests of all women.[18] A direct call for egalitarian marriage appeared at mid-century in each country when the early women's rights advocates campaigned publicly to reform marriage and divorce laws, hoping to end the subjection of women in marriage (Docs. 33.vi, 33.viii, 61.i, 94.i).

Finally, some women simply took refuge from their husbands in adultery. The French doctor Auguste Debay, in a vastly popular marriage manual, counseled husbands to please their wives so as to keep them faithful (Doc. 37.1). And as the confessional letters of Louise Abber to the novelist Honoré de Balzac show, if adultery did not always make a woman calm and happy, it could at least provide her with some excitement and a sense of her own importance (Doc. 36).

Sexuality

Marriage entailed the right—and the duty—of mutual sexual access. The marriage ceremony of the Church of England required the groom to say to his bride, "With my body I thee worship" (Doc. 33.v). Indeed, Church and State recognized sex as of the essence of marriage, and counted the inability or the refusal to perform as among the few grounds for the annulment of the marriage contract. Nevertheless, Victorian sexual ideology was replete with anxious and conflicting advice. Bestselling manuals about conjugal health and happiness warned that insanity, disease, and even death could result from either sexual excess or sexual abstinence. The most blatant stereotypes of prudish Victorian attitudes, as epitomized by Queen Victoria's wedding-night advice to her daughter, "Lie still, and think of the Empire," have been

[17] On women's violent crimes, see Hartman 1977; and on women prisoners, Freedman 1981: chap. 5.

[18] O'Neill 1971: 40–42; Smith-Rosenberg 1972; Gordon 1974: 61–62; D. S. Smith 1974: 131–33.

modified by recent historical scholarship. The question of how women experienced their own sexuality remains, all the same, a controversial one.[19]

The sex manuals offered no monolithic advice for women. Although the
view of women's passionlessness held by the English physician William Acton
strongly influenced Anglo-American thinking, the works of some of his fellow
English writers, as well as of such other doctors as Auguste Debay in France
and Elizabeth Blackwell in America, place Acton's ideas within a larger context. These sexual theorists all believed that female sexuality differed from male
sexuality; yet each granted different properties to the female sex. Blackwell,
arguing from a feminist perspective, criticized the limited, phallic definition
of sexual passion employed by men and favored a more universal standard that
took spirituality and female sensuality into account. The French, in art,
literature, and medical advice, seemed generally more cognizant of women's
erotic potential; Debay nevertheless resembled the English doctor Acton in
advising women to defer to their husband's sexual interests. Debay's recom-
mendation that women should simulate orgasm for the sake of marital stability
indicates that the relatively greater interest of the French in female sexual
satisfaction should not automatically be interpreted as liberating for women
(Docs. 37.i–iii).

The passionless woman, then, was neither a simple nor a dominant cultural model in the nineteenth century, nor was it a model that necessarily
extended to women outside the middle and upper classes. Indeed, Victorian
moralists and social scientists alike often projected onto lower-class, slave,
or foreign women the sexual drives they denied the bourgeois wife. Most respectable Victorians distinguished their own social classes from the rest of
society on the basis of female virtue and purity, while at the same time leaving
poorer women—whether servants, slaves, or prostitutes—vulnerable to sexual
exploitation.[20] The French socialist Flora Tristan and the American union
organizer Leonora Barry, among others, pointed with indignation to this
double standard for rich and poor women (Docs. 87.i, 90.i).

Although the range of sexual norms may have been wider than some historians have suggested, the agents of sexual regulation nevertheless grew
stricter over the course of the century. The French case is instructive. Secular
prescriptive literature in France deemed sex not only desirable, but almost
compulsory; anticlerical republicans, in alliance with the increasingly influential medical profession, argued that good marital sexual hygiene fostered stable
families, and these in turn fostered a stable State. A similar drive for profes-

[19] On Victorian sexual ideology, see, for the U.S., Barker-Benfield 1973; Degler
1974; Haller & Haller 1974; Walters 1974; and Cott 1978. For England, see Cominos
1963 and 1973; Marcus 1966 (which should be approached cautiously); and F. B.
Smith 1977; and for France, McLaren 1974, and his more speculative 1975 article;
and Hellerstein 1980, chaps. 4, 5 (on French sexual morality). For a lighthearted
study, see Aron & Kempf 1978. See also Foucault's controversial 1978 work.

[20] On the sexualization of servants, see Davidoff 1979. On the distinction between
respectable and impoverished women, see Cominos 1963 and 1973; Marcus 1966; Pearsall 1969; and F. Basch 1974: chap. 3.

sional authority characterized the regulation of sexuality in England and America, where male doctors strove for greater status by exercising control over women's health. American doctors, for instance, began to condemn abortion in the 1860's as part of their quest for authority over public policy. By preventing women's access to contraception and criminalizing abortion, they restricted the married woman's ability either to avoid or to terminate her pregnancies, thus bolstering the ideology of motherhood as the goal of sexual experience.[21]

In the face of this drive to channel female sexuality into marital service, women's struggle for sexual autonomy sometimes took the form of avoiding sexual intercourse. In so doing, women were also protecting their physical health and well-being. As Blackwell explained, the results of sex could permanently harm a woman's health. Sexual intercourse evoked the fear of pregnancy and childbirth, and in the nineteenth century childbearing could cause tearing, uterine prolapse, and ulcerations. These and other "female troubles," such as anemia, vaginal infections, and venereal diseases, weakened women and could make intercourse unpleasant. Pregnancy and childbirth could also mean death; toxemia, hemorrhage, and puerperal fever were notorious killers. It is thus no wonder that some women avoided the marriage bed, and that others shared the secrets of contraception with their friends (Docs. 37.ii, 41). Physicians—and some women—claimed, moreover, that a woman's passion simply could not be gratified in intercourse with a man who was indifferent to female sexuality; and that likewise when a man relied on *coitus interruptus* for birth control a woman might well be left unsatisfied. Indeed, one French physician published case studies to show that women who were repeatedly interrupted while approaching or experiencing orgasm became nervous and even ill (Doc. 40.ii).[22]

Despite these deterrents to sexual expression, Victorian women sought sexual pleasure both inside and outside of marriage, and in many cases found it. Writers like Debay obviously knew that women experiencd clitoral orgasms. A late-nineteenth-century survey of American women's sexual practices showed that a sizable proportion of educated, middle-class women enjoyed their sex lives and regularly achieved orgasm.[23] The Frenchwomen Stéphanie Jullien and Louise Abber clearly saw sexual desire and sexual fulfillment as essential to their happiness in marriage; Abber complained that her husband was too brutal in his passions, and she wrote vibrantly about the intense joys of adulterous sex (Doc. 36).

Other women experienced sexual pleasure through masturbation or lesbian relationships. According to one American survey, nearly 70 percent of the female respondents who were adolescents in the late nineteenth century reported masturbating to orgasm, and about 20 percent of the educated,

[21] McLaren 1974, 1975; Branca 1975; Mohr 1978; Hellerstein 1980: chaps. 2, 4.
[22] Zeldin 1973: 87–115; Gordon 1974: 60–63; Knibiehler 1976a and 1976b; Stage 1979.
[23] Degler 1974. For a different interpretation of this survey, which was conducted by Dr. Clelia Mosher, see Smith-Rosenberg 1976.

middle-class women of the same era had had lesbian experiences at some time in their lives.[24]

Women's relationships with each other took various forms, ranging from intimate friendship, to homoerotic attraction, to explicitly lesbian partnerships. The passionate letters women friends exchanged and the crises precipitated by their marriages provide clues to the erotic content of these relationships (Doc. 38). It is impossible to know how many women friends who shared beds also shared their physical passions; but the intimacy of the letters and the self-reported homosexual experiences of some suggest that far more Victorian women than has been previously acknowledged knew the pleasures of lesbian sexuality. Some women who recognized their attraction to their own sex adopted men's attire in an effort to "pass" as the husbands of their lovers. But openly lesbian relationships rarely had public approval; indeed, the marriage of Annie Hindle and Annie Ryan was an exception within the marginal world of the American theater (Doc. 39.ii). By the end of the century doctors and psychologists had begun to label lesbianism as a pathological form of sexual deviance, thus making it more difficult for all women—whether lesbian or not—to express their loving feelings for each other openly.[25]

Motherhood

Even more than sexuality, motherhood was central to the identities of most nineteenth-century women. Indeed, as the personal experiences in the documents reveal, the bearing and raising of children dominated women's adult lives, and their experiences as mothers provided their greatest joys and deepest tragedies.

Yet for all this, women bore relatively fewer children as the century progressed. Although the population exploded in all three countries, marital fertility rates declined as more and more couples began to employ a variety of contraceptive techniques. The French were the first to use contraception on a population-wide basis; statistics reveal that the practice spread rapidly after about 1790. In the United States adult white women bore fewer children in each generation after 1800, and the total fertility rate dropped from 7.04 per adult woman in 1800 to 5.42 in 1850 to 3.56 in 1900. The British began limiting births on a statistically significant scale only after 1870.[26]

The evidence does not permit us to say precisely how and for what reasons couples in different social groups made the decision to limit family size.[27]

[24] Figures based on the answers of respondents over age 40 (in the 1920's), presented in K. B. Davis 1929: 101, 257, 307. The percentages were still higher for younger women.

[25] Klaich 1974: 55–67; Smith-Rosenberg 1975; Katz 1976; Sahli 1979; Schwarz 1979.

[26] D. S. Smith 1974: 123; Tilly & Scott 1978: 89–103.

[27] Demographic and historical analyses of family limitation appear in Banks 1954; Berguès 1960; Bourgeois-Pichat 1965; Biraben 1966; Noonan 1966, part 4; D. S. Smith 1974; Langer 1975; and Gordon 1976.

A falling birthrate does not, of itself, signify that women controlled their reproductive lives; the most common form of prevention was probably coitus interruptus, a technique that depends absolutely on male cooperation, and that can of course be performed without female consent. In some cases women may even have been deprived of babies they desired (Docs. 35, 40.ii).

Many women, however, clearly resisted childbearing: by sharing contraceptive information, by cooperating with their sexual partners in preventive measures, by abortion, by infanticide, and by deliberate neglect of the infant (Docs. 40–41, 43–44, 55). Such women had pressing reasons to avoid motherhood. Many working women knew that they could not support another child, and that their own labors in factories and fields would leave them little time for the joys of motherhood. Mothers of illegitimate babies faced dishonor and economic hardship; in England many could support themselves only as live-in wet nurses, so that their own babies often died of malnutrition and disease.[28] But even an economically secure married woman sometimes decided to avoid or terminate pregnancy when her own health was at risk or when another child would be inconvenient. When these women got "caught," they resigned themselves to bearing their babies, voicing their complaints about the misfortune in letters to friends and relatives (Doc. 46.ii).

In America the birthrate remained higher in the black population than in the white throughout the century, for a number of reasons.[29] For one thing, black women generally began childbearing younger than white women. Although slave families feared the sale of their children, and mothers knew that pregnancy would not reduce their tasks in the master's house or in the fields, slave owners encouraged breeding in order to increase their valuable human property (Doc. 42). It is possible, too, that slaves themselves desired more children because their families could offer them personal meaning in contrast with their institutionalized exploitation. After slavery ended, the majority of blacks remained agricultural workers for whom children were an economic asset. Since poverty and inadequate health care kept the black infant mortality rates extremely high, black women continued to bear many children to ensure the survival of their families.

For women in all three countries the experience of motherhood was profoundly affected by pervasive nineteenth-century changes—migration, professionalization, and the growth of the state. It appears that in the course of the century the typical family—whether rural or urban—went through a transitional stage of self-reliance as the older institutions that had traditionally buttressed the family were gradually replaced by new ones. Migration to cities, to the frontier, or to a new country meant the loss of supportive village networks and rituals, so that women, isolated from familiar settings, had to rely on themselves, on letters from distant friends and families, or on their

---

[28] Roberts 1976.

[29] For data on black women's higher rate of childbearing, see Grabell, Kiser, & Whelpton 1973: 390. On the importance of family life under slavery, see A. Davis 1972. See also Loewenberg & Bogin 1976; and Gutman 1977.

husbands, during pregnancies and while raising children. Although new or expanded services for the family, such as family physicians, advice manuals, and public schools, gradually replaced the traditional networks, in the interim, mothers (and to some extent, fathers) struggled alone. Parents improvised childbirth arrangements and taught, trained, and doctored their children in the time they could spare from wage labor and household work.

To be sure, many families were almost untouched by these changes, even by the end of the century. Even a good number of those who migrated managed to take kin and custom with them. The Kentucky-born Eleanor Brittain, for example, widowed in California and left with three children to support, was able to call for help on a cousin of her mother's who had migrated to a nearby town (Doc. 62.ii). The transitional self-reliant family was, then, an important but not a universal nineteenth-century family type.

Another factor also profoundly affected the experience of bearing and raising children: in England, France, and the United States alike, motherhood was celebrated with unprecedented intensity in the nineteenth century. Although the cult of motherhood and the idea of the child-centered family had taken shape through centuries of European development, in the Victorian era bureaucrats and politicians fostered the ideal of the personal family and stressed the social responsibilities of the "Republican Mother," breeder of citizens. The good mother, like the submissive and sexually pleasing wife, had her role to play in this new ideology by seeing to it that the family remained strong and intact, a bastion against social upheaval as well as a pillar of the state. Influential women writers, too, seeking a worthy role for women in a changing world, celebrated motherhood, as did Catholic and Evangelical authorities. Mother-educators did in fact play a critical role in all three countries until public education was equal to the task of turning out the desired literate, patriotic, and uniform citizenry.[30] No doubt this elevation of motherhood gave some women a tool for exerting moral influence. But it may be that, as with sexuality, women in the end lost a degree of autonomy as the standardizing influence of professional experts increased.

The gradual professionalization of medical care had its greatest impact on women during pregnancy and childbirth, but by no means all women were affected by it. Although physicians came to dominate in the birth chamber, developing in the process a new technology that included anesthetics, corrective surgery, and safer cesarean sections, many rural or migrant women continued to give birth and to learn about the care of their babies within traditional female cultures and rituals. Ironically, "modern" medicine reached the urban poor first, for they alone gave birth in hospitals, where they often served as teaching subjects and where the unhygienic practices that resulted from the contemporary ignorance of the germ theory of disease made deliv-

[30] Ariès 1962; Sklar 1973: 158–63; Ryan 1975: chap. 4; Kerber 1976; Pope 1976. For other literature about mothers and children, see the Part I essay by Barbara C. Gelpi.

eries too often fatal for both mother and child. Women of modest means typically continued to give birth at home or at maternity hospitals with the assistance of lay or licensed midwives, although physicians eventually succeeded in ousting most midwives from the birth chamber (Docs. 45, 101.ii). Well-to-do women like Caroline Clive and Kate Amberley struck a balance between old and new, giving birth at home with trusted doctors in attendance, while continuing to observe some traditional childbirth rituals (Docs. 48, 50). The direction of change, then, was away from female culture and ritual and toward the male professional birth attendant, but the change took place unevenly and with much regional variation.[31]

In raising children during this transitional period of familial self-reliance, mothers functioned as doctors and teachers to their children, provided emotional nurturance, and taught them a variety of skills. Rural or migrant mothers "broke up" their children's diseases with homemade or patent medicines and often taught them at home to read, write, and cipher (Doc. 66). For religious families, whether Catholic or Protestant, training for salvation was a prime parental duty: the American Quaker Lucy Lovell worried that maternal softness might foster depravity in her daughter, unlike the prosperous Catholic woman of Lille who saw herself as her children's "visible angel" and believed that the teaching of religious precepts was her most important duty as a mother (Docs. 3, 58.ii). In artisan and farm families, parents transmitted economic skills to their children: Santerre's parents taught her to weave, and the family spent long hours together at their looms (Doc. 5). Most mothers, even among the prosperous, taught their daughters household skills: Athénaïs Michelet was given her baby brother to care for, while her older sister learned to spin, cook, and manage the house; Nettie Abell, the daughter of indulgent "modern" American parents, had nonetheless been so thoroughly trained in cooking, sewing, and child care by age eight that when her mother died she could virtually take over the management of the household (Docs. 2, 4).

Mothers in the burgeoning urban working classes could rarely offer their children much in the way of tradition, teaching, or affection (Doc. 83). The French socialist Flora Tristan made bitter reference to the angelic ideal, pointing to the wretched conditions in the life of the French working class that made its achievement impossible (Doc. 58.i). Proletarianization had robbed working-class families of religious affiliation and of pride in traditional domestic or artisanal skills; and the press of factory and sweatshop labor left them little time or inclination for domestic grace and tender family life. The dream of domesticity nevertheless spread gradually to the lower classes, and in the 1860's, in one of the oddest contradictions of this contradictory century, many union and socialist spokesmen began to call for women's right to return

---

[31] Wertz & Wertz 1977; Ehrenreich & English 1978: 84–88. Traditional childbirth rituals among Native Americans are described in Niethammer 1977: 1–21. On the struggle between doctors and midwives, see the Part III essay by Leslie Hume and Karen Offen.

to the home just as middle-class women in all three countries were beginning their organized campaigns to free themselves from the stifling constraints of angelic domesticity and maternity.[32]

As the documents show, women often longed for children and were delighted with their babies. Victorine B——, a Parisian working woman, described the joys of caring for her baby and noted each minute change in his development; she wrote that her experiences as a mother were the happiest of her life (Doc. 56.ii). But just as the emotional experience of mothering differed from individual to individual, so the style of mothering varied from class to class and country to country. In general French and American middle-class women enjoyed a more intimate and tender family life than their counterparts in England, where a stable servant class provided a full supply of nannies and wet nurses. The English-style isolated nursery was an impossibility for the French because of their relatively lower living standard; all but the very rich lived in small apartments or modest houses and had to find ways to get along with each other in cramped quarters. And because the United States, apart from the South, did not have a servant class, most American middle-class women spent a good deal of time with their children, too. Except for a few months when she had a hired girl, Mary Abell tended her five children—affectionately and steadily, although she often complained about their noise and mess—helped only intermittently by her busy husband (Docs. 4, 66).

Many other women, in all three countries, were separated from their children because they had to work. English working women often had to leave their babies in the care of older children, who might well dose them with opiates to quiet their hungry squalling. French working women often put their babies out to nurse in the country, a situation from which a tragically high number of them did not return.[33] American slave mothers were forced to leave their babies with children or old women in the quarters, often so as to be free to care for white babies (Docs. 53, 54, 56). Not surprisingly, the infant mortality rates in such cases ran exceedingly high. Slaves and the poorest women, especially, were thus forced by circumstance to continue childcare practices that middle- and upper-class women, influenced by a growing sentiment of tenderness toward children, had foregone by the nineteenth century. As the bitter slave lullaby and the urgent letter from a Parisian working mother attest, their dilemma grieved and embittered such mothers (Docs. 53.viii, 56.i).

In fact, no account of nineteenth-century motherhood could be complete without mentioning the death of babies and young children. Death stalked the nursery, and such infectious diseases as diptheria and infant diarrhea could strike at any time. Accidents, too, especially where children were left alone or where mothers did wage labor at home, were tragically common. Infant death rates remained high throughout the century, and the fear of losing a child made decisions about feeding, wet nurses, medicines, and other aspects of child care urgent and anxiety-ridden for women in every social

[32] Perrot 1976.   [33] Sussman 1975; Wohl 1978.

class. Some found that their bereavements tested their faith in God; others took comfort that their families would one day be unbroken and reunited in Paradise (Docs. 3, 59.i–iii).

The End of Marriage

Under pressure for marital reform, divorce became somewhat more accessible to women toward the end of the century, although the divorced woman continued to suffer from a greater social stigma than her ex-husband. Nevertheless, divorce remained largely a privilege of the upper classes; it also remained almost entirely a male prerogative.[34]

The campaign to make divorce accessible took place within conflicting demographic and ideological trends. At the beginning of the century one marriage partner or the other was likely to have died before all the children had left home. But as men and women began to live longer and to have smaller families, more and more marriages continued long past the child-rearing years. With death parting fewer couples, the possibility of legal dissolution became a pressing issue. Divorce, however, conflicted with the domestic ideal and the cult of motherhood so heavily promoted by both religious institutions and the state. Thus, those who campaigned for the reform of divorce legislation now argued that divorce could actually help to ensure that homes were happy; on the whole, divorce reformers did not base their arguments on the woman's right to independence. The angel was to remain intact, even in the divorce court. Furthermore, reformers argued that the threat of divorce could shore up the marriage relationship by controlling both male and female behavior. The man who beat his wife, the woman who denied her husband his conjugal rights, would now face the sanction of public censure in the courts.

For all the gains in life expectancy, however, death rather than divorce still ended most marriages, in many cases when the marriage partners were still relatively young. When women died and left children behind them, their bereaved husbands were likely to be inexperienced in domesticity and child care, and many found it a struggle to keep their children with them and to care for them properly. Some were fortunate in having friends and relatives to help out. Robert Abell, for example, turned his four little boys and his household over to his eight-year-old daughter, and Warren Cranston fell back on parents who lived close by and took in his daughters (Docs. 4, 62.i, 66).

But because of women's limited job opportunities and low wages, the widow's struggle could be (as the widower's almost never was) a struggle for survival. Men in all social classes who knew they were leaving young wives alone to economic hardship expressed concern. "What can you do to make a living?" David Brittain asked his wife from his deathbed; Leander ——, a New York clerk dying of consumption, expressed a similar worry to his young wife (Docs. 62.ii, 70). Both men were troubled that their wives, left

[34] McGregor 1957; O'Neill 1973; Wells 1979: 21. For a guide to the reform literature about divorce in 19th-century France, see Offen 1977.

to support themselves, would have to endure not only poverty, but also the social disgrace of low-status jobs. Thus David asked Eleanor not to take in washing after his death, and Leander begged Almira, a sweatshop worker, not to degrade herself by becoming a domestic servant. David went so far as to wish he could take his "angel wife" with him, for he feared that in frontier America a woman and her children, left without a man's protection, might be vulnerable to bad men or adventurers. In fact, a year after his death, Eleanor had to horsewhip a man who tried to carry off her fifteen-year-old daughter.

Eleanor Brittain, an "angel wife" on the frontier who defended her home with a whip, embodies the contradictions between the Victorian domestic ideal for women and the realities of women's lives in the nineteenth century. Her life also gives some idea of the great range of the angelic myth, which surfaced not only in a deathbed declaration in the American West, but also in the rhetoric of the French working classes, in the speeches of English and American union organizers, and in the dreams of black female reformers (Docs. 86.i, 87.ii, 94.ii). As the documents make abundantly clear, the domestic dream spread and grew even among women who could not possibly attain it, while the women who already lived within its confines of dress and decorum struggled to free themselves from the parlor and get out into the world.

Documents 25-62

25. 'The Angel in the House'

The phrase *the angel in the house* is now much more famous than the poem from which it derives, but in Victorian England—and America—'The Angel in the House' (1854–56) by Coventry Patmore sold better than any other poetic work except Tennyson's 'Idylls of the King.' Its simple plot, inspired by Coventry's intense love for his wife, Emily Andrews Patmore (1824–62), describes the courtship and marriage of a young couple. Coventry originally intended to include a description of the bliss of domestic life in his poem, but after ten years of marriage and six children, Emily contracted tuberculosis, and he could not bring himself to complete the work. Although the poem tells us little in specific detail about the nature of Victorian domesticity, it is a very full expression of the idealization of womanhood that is central to the theory about woman's separate domestic sphere. The angel is introduced as purer than Eve, but she is not simply innocent; she exercises power in secret and subtle ways.

The angelic woman was not a British creation alone: the French literature of domesticity was replete with angels. Feminists took on the angelic ideal and charged that the self-sacrificing demands it placed on women were coercive. In the second selection Maria Deraismes (1828–94), a leading French feminist, gives a speech in Paris denouncing the angel. In the excerpt here Deraismes is taking issue with her fellow republican Jules Michelet, whose best-selling books on women romanticized love within marriage.

(i) Coventry Patmore

The Rose of the World

Lo, when the Lord made North and South
And sun and moon ordained, He,
Forthbringing each by word of mouth
In order of its dignity,

SOURCES: (i) Coventry Patmore, *Poems*, 4th ed. (London, 1890), 1: 23–24, 88–91, 123–24, 146–47. (ii) Maria Deraismes, "La Femme et le droit," public address given in the late 1860's, in *Eve dans l'humanité* (Paris, 1891), pp. 16–17.

Did man from the crude clay express
    By sequence, and, all else decreed,
He form'd the woman; nor might less
    Than Sabbath such a work succeed.
And still with favour singled out,
    Marr'd less than man by mortal fall,
Her disposition is devout,
    Her countenance angelical;
The best things that the best believe
    Are in her face so kindly writ
The faithless, seeing her, conceive
    Not only heaven, but hope of it;
No idle thought her instinct shrouds,
    But fancy chequers settled sense,
Like alteration of the clouds
    On noonday's azure permanence;
Pure dignity, composure, ease
    Declare affections nobly fix'd,
And impulse sprung from due degrees
    Of sense and spirit sweetly mix'd.
Her modesty, her chiefest grace,
    The cestus clasping Venus' side,
How potent to deject the face
    Of him who would affront its pride!
Wrong dares not in her presence speak,
    Nor spotted thought its taint disclose
Under the protest of a cheek
    Outbragging Nature's boast the rose.
In mind and manners how discreet;
    How artless in her very art;
How candid in discourse; how sweet
    The concord of her lips and heart;
How simple and how circumspect;
    How subtle and how fancy-free;
Though sacred to her love, how deck'd
    With unexclusive courtesy;
How quick in talk to see from far
    The way to vanquish or evade;
How able her persuasions are
    To prove, her reasons to persuade;
How (not to call true instinct's bent
    And woman's very nature, harm),
How amiable and innocent
    Her pleasure in her power to charm;
How humbly careful to attract,

Though crown'd with all the soul desires
Connubial aptitude exact,
    Diversity that never tires.

．　．　．

The Changed Allegiance

Watch how a bird, that captived sings,
    The cage set open, first looks out,
Yet fears the freedom of his wings,
    And now withdraws, and flits about,
And now looks forth again; until,
    Grown bold, he hops on stool and chair
And now attains the window-sill,
    And now confides himself to air.
The maiden so, from love's free sky
    In chaste and prudent counsels caged,
But longing to be loosen'd by
    Her suitor's faith declared and gaged,
When blest with that release desired,
    First doubts if truly she is free,
Then pauses, restlessly retired,
    Alarm'd at too much liberty;
But soon, remembering all her debt
    To plighted passion, gets by rote
Her duty; says, 'I love him!' yet
    The thought half chokes her in her throat
And, like that fatal 'I am thine,'
    Comes with alternate gush and check
And joltings of the heart, as wine
    Pour'd from a flask of narrow neck.
Is he indeed her choice? She fears
    Her Yes was rashly said, and shame,
Remorse, and ineffectual tears
    Revolt from his conceded claim.
Oh, treason! So, with desperate nerve,
    She cries, 'I am in love, am his;'
Lets run the cables of reserve,
    And floats into a sea of bliss,
And laughs to think of her alarm,
    Avows she was in love before,
Though his avowal was the charm
    Which open'd to her own the door.
She loves him for his mastering air,
    Whence, Parthian-like, she slaying flies
His flattering look, which seems to wear
    Her loveliness in manly eyes;

His smile, which, by reverse, portends
    An awful wrath, should reason stir;
(How fortunate it is they're friends,
    And he will ne'er be wroth with her!)
His power to do or guard from harm;
    If he but chose to use it half,
And catch her up in one strong arm,
    What could she do but weep, or laugh!
His words, which still instruct, but so
    That this applause seems still implied,
'How wise in all she ought to know,
    'How ignorant of all beside!'
His skilful suit, which leaves her free,
    Gives nothing for the world to name,
And keeps her conscience safe, while he,
    With half the bliss, takes all the blame
His clear repute with great and small;
    The jealousy his choice will stir;
But, ten times more than ten times all,
    She loves him for his love of her.
How happy 'tis he seems to see
    In her that utter loveliness
Which she, for his sake, longs to be!
    At times, she cannot but confess
Her other friends are somewhat blind;
    Her parents' years excuse neglect,
But all the rest are scarcely kind,
    And brothers grossly want respect;
And oft she views what he admires
    Within her glass, and sight of this
Makes all the sum of her desires
    To be devotion unto his.
But still, at first, whatever's done,
    A touch, her hand press'd lightly, she
Stands dizzied, shock'd, and flush'd, like one
    Set sudden neck-deep in the sea;
And, though her bond for endless time
    To his good pleasure gives her o'er,
The slightest favour seems a crime,
    Because it makes her love him more.
But that she ne'er will let him know;
    For what were love should reverence cease
A thought which makes her reason so
    Inscrutable, it seems caprice.
With her, as with a desperate town,
    Too weak to stand, too proud to treat,

The conqueror, though the walls are down,
  Has still to capture street by street;
But, after that, habitual faith,
  Divorced from self, where late 'twas due,
Walks nobly in its novel path,
  And she's to changed allegiance true;
And prizing what she can't prevent,
  (Right wisdom, often misdeem'd whim,)
Her will's indomitably bent
  On mere submissiveness to him;
To him she'll cleave, for him forsake
  Father's and mother's fond command!
He is her lord, for he can take
  Hold of her faint heart with his hand.

.   .   .

In Love

If he's capricious she'll be so,
  But, if his duties constant are,
She lets her loving favour glow
  As steady as a tropic star;
Appears there nought for which to weep,
  She'll weep for nought, for his dear sake;
She clasps her sister in her sleep;
  Her love in dreams is most awake.
Her soul, that once with pleasure shook,
  Did any eyes her beauty own,
Now wonders how they dare to look
  On what belongs to him alone;
The indignity of taking gifts
  Exhilarates her loving breast;
A rapture of submission lifts
  Her life into celestial rest;
There's nothing left of what she was;
  Back to the babe the woman dies,
And all the wisdom that she has
  Is to love him for being wise.
She's confident because she fears,
  And, though discreet when he's away,
If none but her dear despot hears,
  She prattles like a child at play.
Perchance, when all her praise is said,
  He tells the news, a battle won,
On either side ten thousand dead.
  'Alas!' she says; but, if 'twere known,

She thinks, 'He's looking on my face!
    'I am his joy; whate'er I do,
'He sees such time-contenting grace
    'In that, he'd have me always so!'
And, evermore, for either's sake,
    To the sweet folly of the dove,
She joins the cunning of the snake,
    To rivet and exalt his love;
Her mode of candour is deceit;
    And what she thinks from what she'll say,
(Although I'll never call her cheat,)
    Lies far as Scotland from Cathay.
Without his knowledge he was won;
    Against his nature kept devout;
She'll never tell him how 'twas done,
    And he will never find it out.
If, sudden, he suspects her wiles,
    And hears her forging chain and trap
And looks, she sits in simple smiles,
    Her two hands lying in her lap.
Her secret (privilege of the Bard,
    Whose fancy is of either sex),
Is mine; but let the darkness guard
    Myst'ries that light would more perplex.

      · · ·

The Married Lover

Why, having won her, do I woo?
    Because her spirit's vestal grace
Provokes me always to pursue,
    But, spirit-like, eludes embrace;
Because her womanhood is such
    That, as on court-days subjects kiss
The Queen's hand, yet so near a touch
    Affirms no mean familiarness,
Nay, rather marks more fair the height
    Which can with safety so neglect
To dread, as lower ladies might,
    That grace could meet with disrespect,
Thus she with happy favour feeds
    Allegiance from a love so high
That thence no false conceit proceeds
    Of difference bridged, or state put by;
Because, although in act and word
    As lowly as a wife can be,

Her manners, when they call me lord,
    Remind me 'tis by courtesy;
Not with her least consent of will,
    Which would my proud affection hurt,
But by the noble style that still
    Imputes an unattain'd desert;
Because her gay and lofty brows,
    When all is won which hope can ask,
Reflect a light of hopeless snows
    That bright in virgin ether bask;
Because, though free of the outer court
    I am, this Temple keeps its shrine
Sacred to Heaven; because, in short,
    She's not and never can be mine.

(ii) Maria Deraismes

Of all woman's enemies, I tell you that the worst are those who insist that woman is an angel. To say that woman is an angel is to impose on her, in a sentimental and admiring fashion, all duties, and to reserve for oneself all rights; it is to imply that her specialty is self-effacement, resignation, and sacrifice; it is to suggest to her that woman's greatest glory, her greatest happiness, is to immolate herself for those she loves; it is to let her understand that she will be *generously* furnished with every opportunity for exercising her aptitudes. It is to say that she will respond to absolutism by submission, to brutality by meekness, to indifference by tenderness, to inconstancy by fidelity, to egotism by devotion.

In the face of this long enumeration, I decline the honor of being an angel. No one has the right to force me to be both dupe and victim. Self-sacrifice is not a habit, a custom; it is an *extra*! It is not on the program of one's duties. No power has the right to impose it on me. Of all acts, sacrifice is the freest, and it is precisely because it is free that it is so admirable.

26. French dowry inquiries

Propertied French families—from the peasantry to the aristocracy—traditionally viewed marriage as a financial arrangement, where affection if it developed came only after the couple and their families had assured themselves of the economic and social suitability of the match.

The gentleman in the first selection, who writes to inquire about the

SOURCES: (i) George Sand Papers, G-37, Bibliothèque Historique de la Ville de Paris. (ii) Gouever letters in possession of Mlle Vaudoux, Villerable (Loir-et-Cher), France. The editors are grateful to Mlle Vaudoux for permission to use these letters and to Professor Judith Silver, University of New Hampshire, who arranged for us to use the letters and translated and annotated them.

dowry of Aurore Dupin (the future writer George Sand; 1804–76) on behalf of a friend who has never met her, follows the conventions dictated by his social class. This letter offers a vivid contrast between the delicacy of manners and discourse necessary for such an inquiry and the bald precision of the financial information requested.

The three letters in the second selection indicate that economic considerations were equally important among the French peasantry. In the first letter a local suitor, a coach driver at the nearby chateau, formally requests the hand of Célina Gouever, a woman in her early twenties living with her parents in a small village in central France; he obviously considers her a good catch since she will inherit her uncle's land and house. The second letter presents the negative reaction of her uncle, the local parish priest, and the third is Gouever's evaluation of another suitor a year and a half later.

(i) Aurore Dupin (George Sand)

Monsieur,

One of my friends who intends to establish his son, and who has heard people speak favorably of the granddaughter of Madame Dupin, owner of Nohant, desires to obtain some indispensable information. If I have been well informed, you, more than anyone else, are in a position to give me some specifics. I should like to know if Madame Dupin envisions marrying Mademoiselle her granddaughter in the near future; to know the dowry of this young lady, the fortune she may one day count on, whether this fortune consists exclusively of real estate, or if there is money invested, what the approximate amount is, and finally, whether Mlle Dupin's father left any debts.

Please, Monsieur, be so good as to respond to these different questions with the most scrupulous exactitude. I am addressing you confidentially; the discretion that I require of you is a sure guarantee of my own. If things were to take a favorable turn, M. le Vicomte and Mme la Vicomtesse de Montlevée could eventually give all the explanations required concerning Mlle Dupin.

Please accept. . . .

> Laisné de Ste. Marie
> rue Bannière No. 109
> Orléans—Loiret
> [March 3, 1821]

(ii) Célina Gouever

[Paul Noulin asks M. and Mme Gouever for the hand of their daughter, 1889.]

M., Mme Gouever

Undoubtedly, you found it strange that I presented myself three times in such a short period of time at your place. I've made my face known to you but you don't know me or my family. I shall ask for permission to get better acquainted.

That is why I am coming today to ask for the hand of your *demoiselle*.

My parents live in Savigny-sur-Braye and live on their income and my father is in the guano business. There are two children, my brother is married.

Since you are not acquainted with me I am taking the liberty of quickly tackling a difficult question.

My parents will add 2,000f to my present savings of 3,000f. Consequently I will then have 5,000f.

Knowing that you want your *demoiselle* to stay with you, I would accept that willingly.

I will furnish all the necessary information on my family background as well as on my immediate family. As for me you could ask the priest of St. Ouen and his mother who both know me, having known me at M. Martelliere's where I worked for six years. As for my family ask M. Prudhomme. I write as quickly as possible now because our masters are away for a month and I could visit more easily.

I hope that my letter will be well received and hoping to have a response.

Paul Noulin, driver

[Célina Gouever's uncle counsels her to reject Noulin's suit.]

Your dark, handsome, beardless suitor, mounted on his black horse, reminds me of two handsome beasts one mounted on top of the other. That is the impression he made on me when I read his letter. But I am wrong to speak like that because in truth the price he offers your parents for you, 5,000 and a few hundred francs, is obviously what you're worth, what do you think? Of course, I would not have offered as much.

What you should say to him is that the price is not suitable, that he should go to the fair; he seems to be a real horse trader.

[Célina Gouever writes to her uncle about a second suitor, Dec. 17, 1890.]

Now let us talk about la Roche.* You ask me how Mama handled it. First she spoke about their wealth, saying that theirs was greatly superior to ours. They replied to her that they weren't concerned with money. That it was the young girl they were asking for and not anything else. Mlle V.† and Mama decided that the young man should come and he came to make an offer fifteen days ago. Friday Mama saw her sister again. She told her that I hadn't yet made up my mind. She said that we would see a little later, that there was no hurry, that they should give me some time, and that she shouldn't give up hope. Just as we had thought, Lizot, on his way back from Thore, didn't hesitate to give his opinion. Everybody at Meslay tells me the same thing. My ears are still ringing from all the advice. Everybody who knows them tells me they are decent people and I couldn't find anyone better than this boy on every count, so that I am very confused. Even more confused than I was, what should I do? I haven't the faintest idea. O my poor uncle, there is nothing worse than being a *demoiselle* of marriageable age.

* The home of the suitor's family.—EDS.
† A female relative of the suitor. The Lizot mentioned below was a maternal relative of Célina's.—EDS.

27. 'I believed then that you would soon forget me': Helen Bourn

This selection from the family papers of a distinguished middle-class family from Norwich, England, presents the reply of Helen Bourn (1797–1871) to the renewed overtures of Thomas Martineau, whose suit she had rejected the previous year. It illustrates the formality, as well as the thoughtfulness, with which such serious matters as courtship could be conducted by members of the educated middle classes. Despite the reservations she expresses here, in 1822 she married Martineau, a younger brother of the well-known writer Harriet Martineau (Doc. 30). The marriage was brief, however, for he died of tuberculosis only a few years later.

My dear Friend

I fully intended to have replied to your letter yesterday but our time is not always at our disposal when we are visiting our friends (& regret exceedingly that it was not in my power); I know too well what are yr feelings to keep you unnecessarily in suspense, & yr letter deserves to be answered with candour & sincerity—I was indeed deeply grieved some weeks ago to hear of such unfavorable accounts of yr health—the idea seized my mind that perhaps it might in fact be occasioned by the disappointment of yr hopes respecting me— & I felt that if yr. illness terminated as I then feared, from the accounts I heard, that I should never forgive myself; it was under this impression that I wrote to yr Sister Rachel being convinced that from her I should know the truth—her reply was long in coming & I anticipated the worst—when it did arrive it was the greatest possible relief to me to find that yr health was so much improved, but her account of the state of yr mind interested & affected me & perhaps prepared me to receive more favorably than I should otherwise have done renewal of yr former proposals which the conviction of the depth & steadiness of yr attachment has aided materially—If I know my own heart it is warm & affectionate & unwilling to give pain to anyone.

How much I was distressed at refusing a compliance with yr wishes on a former occasion, but I believed then that you would soon forget me & find that happiness in some other connection which I had it not in my power to bestow—I did feel at that time that I was hardly doing you justice in not permitting a correspondence, as a means of attaining a more thorough knowledge of yr character; but I had been taught to consider it in the same light as an engagement, & I thought that if I consented to it & after some time perceived no change in my own feelings towards you, that it would be trifling with yr. best affections, & using you ill—& as I before told you I consider those feelings of too sacred a nature to be trifled with—

Esteem for your virtues & a deep admiration of your mental qualities is all that I can now give you—& judging from the enthusiasm of my character, I

SOURCE: Draft of a letter from Helen Bourn to Thomas Martineau, York, Nov. 29, 1821, from the private collection of Dr. Reinhard S. Speck, University of California Medical School, San Francisco. The editors are grateful to Dr. Speck for giving us access to these papers and permitting us to quote from them.

know it to be capable of much more—whether time & increasing intimacy is likely to produce any favorable change in my feelings is yet to be tried—but I feel that it is due to you to comply with yr [desires/wishes] as far as regards a more confidential communication of our thoughts & ideas on this most important subject—more I cannot promise at present, how it will terminate must yet be doubtful—but I can assure you that you will never have reason to complain of the want of sincerity & openness on my part.

There are some other difficulties existing in my mind of which I may hereafter speak to you—but I shall reserve them to some further communication —if you are still desirous of a continued intercourse.

Believe me my dear friend

Your's with great sincerity
H.B.

28. A Parisian bourgeoise contemplates marriage: Stéphanie Jullien

Not all nineteenth-century Frenchwomen accepted the mercenary view of marriage. In the following letters Stéphanie Jullien (1812–83), the only daughter in a large Parisian bourgeois family, expresses her anguish about choosing a suitor. In contrast to her brothers, all of whom had entered the liberal professions, Jullien's own role and security in life depended on marriage. Further, her father was pressing her to choose a husband and settle down, and in her indecision she sorely missed the counsel of her mother, who had died when Jullien was twenty-one. In these excerpts Jullien writes to her brother Auguste and her father about two suitors, the second of whom, Simon Lockroy, she finally accepted. It seems clear from these letters that Jullien not only sought economic security in marriage, but insisted on emotional satisfaction as well. Her wishes appear to have been realized, for her marriage to Lockroy was reportedly very happy.

[Stéphanie Jullien to her brother Auguste, March 6–7, 1833, Dieppe]
Mon Dieu! Such indecision! Such perplexity! What should I do! I almost wish I were not so free, that I were restrained or controlled, so that I would not have the responsibility for my future unhappiness or happiness. Because the more I think about it, the more confused I become, the more I hesitate. I get lost in my thoughts and can't make up my mind. Yesterday I decided to broach the subject to my aunt. She's so good, so affectionate with me, I think of her almost as a second mother. Besides, she has experience and she could help me to unravel my thoughts, to see what I have in my head, which I don't

SOURCE: Jullien Family Papers, 39 AP 4, Archives Nationales, Paris. The editors are grateful to Barbara Corrado Pope, University of Oregon, for making her translation of these letters available to us and for providing the information on Jullien's life and family.

even know myself. I left our small company of four or five people gathered in the salon, the music and the romantic ballads, and I went to my room with my aunt. We talked a long time. She promised the strictest secrecy. And when I told her everything and explained everything, she raised the same objections that you did. She was very opposed to the realization of the project in question and left me more indecisive than ever and almost persuaded me that it would be madness to accept. Moreover, she told me to wait for your letter, your advice. I have read and reread it and I am more confused than ever. This is not child's play, this is a matter of my whole life, of my future, of my happiness. *Mon dieu!* What should I decide? He is so young, and does not have a position. It's all so chancy. . . . Who can assure me that he will succeed? And if he loves me now, how do I know that he will always love me in the same way? Perhaps I'll be paving the way for lots of trouble if I accept, but if I refuse, what will I do? . . .

Thursday, March 7.—It's me again. Perhaps you are waiting for a positive response. *Mon dieu!* I am just more confused, more indecisive, wavering and irresolute, I just got a letter from Alphonse* to which I'm going to respond— but what should I say? As with you, that I don't know what to do or to say or how to balance things, that I am lost in my thoughts? I could, I think, ask the advice of the whole universe and yet nothing could make me decide. As for writing to Adolphe and papa,† I already know what they will say. Nothing that Adolphe could say would relieve the pain I would feel in refusing. And nothing that papa would say could keep me from thinking that accepting is madness. Yes, it's madness; the more I think about it, the more I am persuaded. But, shall I tell you all? That it is an act of madness that I am on the verge of undertaking. Because to refuse would be painful to me—very painful. (It takes all my confidence in you to add the word very.) But to accept? To decide my fate once and for all, my whole destiny? I don't dare do it. I recoil, I tremble. And then, two years. Two years! It's a long time when one is afraid, and anxious and suffering and hoping and despairing. Two years when the end of it is happiness or unhappiness, life or death. Two years when a day can change all one's ideas, and one's irresolutions, when life is so short, when I could die tomorrow. I am having trouble getting my thoughts together. Oh, when I had my good mother I could have waited five or six or ten years, all the time that anyone could have wished. I was so happy then. But now, now that I will return home alone and sad and in such an awkward position that I want every day to escape from it and the family dissensions. And now with papa's fortune running out. But to become engaged? How do I know that in two years he won't change his mind or that I myself will not want to marry someone else? When one is not tied to another the heart can change. The

---

* Alphonse was a year older than Stéphanie. They had spent much of their childhood together. It is probable that he was a friend of the suitor, Léon Forestier. —EDS.

† Adolphe, an elder brother, liked to advise the family on all financial matters. —EDS.

stronger the emotion, the more fleeting it is. And if I, cold and calm, if I refuse his entreaties and little by little I become attached to him, and then, he grows weary of me and draws away from me, then in two years I'll almost be an old maid, and he'll still be so young that he'll scarcely be of an age to marry. Is that reasonable? And what guarantees me that he'll succeed at getting a position? It may take him ten years to assure it; he might not even be able to present himself in two years. I'll wait, watching as the beautiful years of my youth slip away, losing little by little the hope and the means of being advantageously established. Then the situation that I will put myself in by promising to wait will be even more uncomfortable. There will be cause for fear, for jealousy.

But it is necessary to answer him. We can't leave him in this incertitude for two years. I believe it is great madness to accept and I don't have the heart to refuse. I'm telling you everything, Auguste, everything. You asked me to take you completely into my confidence; you seem to have some ulterior motive. But now you know everything that's going on inside me, maybe better than I. My aunt is dissuading me, dissuading me as much as she can. All of her reasons seem so cold. Calculation! Always calculation! As if wealth were happiness. No, but it does help. I feel that and must take it into account. *En voilà!* Enough! My indecision is probably tiring you out. Oh this indecision is a torment, a frightful torment.

[Stéphanie Jullien to her father, April 6, 1833, Dieppe]

M. Forestier came to the house and asked me if I would become angry if he offered to marry me. . . . I was quite embarrassed by the question and told him to talk to you about it. . . .

The three great obstacles against him are his extreme youth (he is only six months older than me) and his lack of fortune (he can only bring 20,000 francs to the marriage). If I marry, I want to be sure that, if I don't marry a very rich man, at least I'll marry a man who has enough wealth to keep me from the brink of want, from worries and cares. Finally the third objection, on which my aunt lays great stress, is that he hasn't made a position for himself; that it will take him many years to do so; that his extreme youth [does not inspire?] confidence; that no one knows if he has talent, if he has a capacity to succeed in his chosen profession. . . .

However, I must confess that I have some distaste in refusing. M. Forestier is the first man to present himself to me. It seems, according to what I am told, that he has some fondness for me. Then, too, in the situation that I find myself—without my mother—I will frankly confess to you that I want to get settled one way or another, to have a position, a future. When I was with my good *maman*, I did not want anything but to stay as long as possible. But now that I am deprived of her, I find myself in a false, awkward, troublesome position; I want to break away. Moreover, if I want to get married it's time I started thinking about it. Time flies and I have come to an age when, if I put it off too long, I'll lose the hope and the means of getting established. On the other hand, it would cost me a lot to marry an unknown. It is very difficult to get to know the character of a man, particularly now that I am alone and cannot get out much in society. I tremble to think of all the chances one takes in getting married. . . .

[Stéphanie Jullien to her father, Feb. 20, 1836]

You want an answer to your letter and I believe, in reality, that this is the best way to express a thousand things that one can lose sight of during a conversation in which one speaks only with difficulty and embarrassment. . . . I don't want to enumerate my anxieties about the future, the discord in my family that I felt more than anyone else, the vexations my mother endured and to which I was the only witness and consolation, the six months passed in anguish and despair over her deathbed. . . . I only want you to understand that I know grief. You men have a thousand occupations to distract you: society, business, politics, and work absorb you, exhaust you, upset you. But all these things also help you forcibly. As for us women who, as you have said to me from time to time, have only the roses in life, we feel more profoundly in our solitude and in our idleness the sufferings that you can slough off. I don't want to make a comparison here between the destiny of man and the destiny of woman: each sex has its own lot, its own troubles, its own pleasures. I only want to explain to you that excess of moroseness of which you complain and of which I am the first to suffer. My life has been sad, and my character shows it. But even now, when I do appear to be calm and happy, what anxieties, what worries about the future don't I have? I am not able to do anything for myself and for those around me. I am depriving my brothers in order to have a dowry. I am not even able to live alone, being obliged to take from others, not only in order to live but also in order to be protected, since social convention does not allow me to have independence. And yet the world finds me guilty of being the only person that I am at liberty to be; not having useful or productive work to do, not having any calling except marriage, and not being able to look by myself for someone who will suit me, I am full of cares and anxieties.

Is it astonishing that since any work that I could do would be *null* and *useless* for others as well as for myself, since it would not lead to anything, that I let myself be lazy, that I try to prolong my sleep in order to escape life? This laziness that you seem to reproach me for is really a means of discharging an excess of energy that has no outlet. If you believe that this *laziness* prevents me from doing anything, you are mistaken. I would quickly find courage and ardor again if I had some mission to fulfill or if some goal were proposed to me. But that is not the case. I don't have any calling, nor could I have one. That has been the most ardent of my wishes and no one will let me do it. I don't understand the reasons, and I'm not accusing anyone if I don't have a calling. I hope that one gives me the same benefit of a doubt, because it is not my fault. As for the sadness that I am accused of, one should not be astonished by it. This awkward position in which I find myself, my memories, my fears, my anxieties, often the delicacy of my health, are enough cause for it. . . . Would one be just if one reproached you for the annoyed and sad air that you often have?

I don't mean to say by all this that I don't have any faults. I have them, and I know they are very great. That is yet another reason why I hesitate to marry—for now it is time to talk about the matter at hand. I feel very keenly the urgent necessity of guaranteeing myself support. I have gone over and repeated to myself all the arguments that you have addressed to me. I know all the reasons why this party is so suitable and that it will be difficult, perhaps impossible, to find someone else as fitting. . . . That is why I hesitated for so long, that is why I did not say *no* three months ago. I have reflected a great deal, perhaps *too much*—although you appear to doubt it—and it is these reflections that make me irresolute.

I am asking for more time. It is not too much to want to see and know a man for ten months, even a year when it is a matter of passing one's life with him. There is no objection to make, you say. But the most serious and the most important presents itself: *I do not love him.* Don't think I am talking about a romantic and impossible passion or an ideal love, neither of which I ever hope to know. I am talking of a feeling that makes one want to see some- one, that makes his absence painful and his return desirable, that makes one interested in what another is doing, that makes one want another's happiness almost in spite of oneself, that makes, finally, the duties of a woman toward her husband pleasures and not efforts. It is a feeling without which marriage would be hell, a feeling that cannot be born out of esteem, and which to me, however, seems to be the very basis of conjugal happiness. I can't feel these emotions immediately. Indeed, considering the bustle and bother that this affair has caused, it would not be surprising if I never felt them. Let me have some time. I want to love, not out of any sense of duty, but for myself and for the happiness of the one to whom I attach my life, who will suffer if he only encounters coldness in me, when he brings me love and devotion.

I am, you say, cold and not very hospitable. How else could I be with someone that I do not love, that I would marry for reason's sake, in order to give myself *a lot in life*, who would be imposed on me by a kind of necessity? How could I be sufficient to his happiness? How could I hold onto him, if I do not love him and desire him?

I hesitate, then. I wait for duty's sake, for reason's sake, for necessity's sake. I don't think I'm being a prude or a coquette. I don't mean to turn anyone's head or inspire ill-fated affection. I only want to make sure that I don't risk my happiness and my virtue. I want to be sure that I will be able to fulfill my duties. If I am cold and reserved, it is because I fear becoming involved. I fear giving hopes to someone that perhaps will not be realized. As for the rest, I don't have *any* kind of inclination *for anyone at all*. I enter into emotional attachment with great difficulty, and for that reason my at- tachment can only be more solid and more desirable.

So I ask for more time, reflection and patience. If one does not want to accord it to me, I will immediately renounce an engagement in which I will not feel it possible to fulfill my duties. I am striving that my heart should be in accord with my reasons and my desires. I don't want to make a marriage for myself and *for another*, which will be the hell of which Dante spoke: "Abandon hope, all ye who enter here."

29. Varieties of courtship in America

On the whole, American women appear to have had a great deal more latitude in choosing marriage partners than their French or English counterparts. The following selections reveal a wide variety of courtship experiences, as well as the extent to which American women could and did exercise personal choice in marriage matters during the nineteenth century. The first selection comes from a courtship correspondence between Bessie Huntting (1831–62), a young Long Island schoolteacher, and Edward Payson Rudd, a partner in the New York publishing firm of Rudd & Carleton. They met in September 1858 and had become secretly engaged after only a week's acquaintance. The second selection is a letter from a young North Carolina Moravian woman, F. C. Masten, to her school friend, Mary Jane Smith. This teasing letter reveals the relatively informal—yet still controlled—nature of courtship among young people in the Moravian communities near Winston-Salem, where social life continued to center around the liturgical and musical celebrations of the congregations. In the third selection a former black slave from South Carolina, Violet Guntharpe, recalls in her old age her courtship by a young man named Thad.

(i) Bessie Huntting

[This is Huntting's first letter to Rudd after they pronounced themselves secretly engaged.]

Were you *here*, at this lovely sunset hour, **kind friend**, I know your *heart* would join in the anthem of praise, which meets my ear, and your eyes would brighten, with the view of these golden clouds, so very *like those* you were enjoying *last Sabbath eve*. Only the still, sacred quick of the country, enhanced by the cricket's low chirp give to the heart a holier, purer feeling of deep inward joy. *Sister* is playing and singing the sacred hymns *you so much* delight in, and I have stolen away, for a few brief *minutes*, to talk with one, who may wish to hear by this time of an absent spirit, and who *perchance*, may have allowed some thoughts to linger around her home—I almost regretted your absence, yesterday so charming was the *ride* I took, or more especially the sail across our beautiful bay. You, *hid* away among brick walls,

SOURCES: (i) Letter from Bessie Huntting to Edward Rudd, Sept. 26–27, 1858, Huntting-Rudd Family Papers, The Arthur and Elizabeth Schlesinger Library on the History of Women in America, Radcliffe College. The editors wish to thank Dr. Patricia King, Director, for facilitating our use of this letter. (ii) Letter from F. C. Masten to Mary Jane Smith, Dec. 6, 1885, in the possession of Jane Fruitt, Raleigh, N.C., and published with her kind permission. (iii) *The American Slave: A Composite Autobiography*, ed. George P. Rawick, 2: *South Carolina Narratives* (Westport, Conn., 1972), part 2: 217–18.

and office books, knew not how beautifully the sun was gilding, mountain, hill & vale, the air clear & bracing, was surrounded by no clouds to mar its beauty, & I enjoyed it keenly. You to, it may be, felt an inward satisfaction with the past and entuned more engagedly into the *duties* of life—I wondered to myself whether you were *alone*, or if Mr. Carlton had recovered sufficiently, to be there? I hope so, for the sake of both. . . . I could not help wishing for you today! so holy seemed this blessed Sabbath, though I *felt* that you *intensely enjoyed* every *moment* of its blessedness. I *rejoice* when I think of your engagedness in the cause, of our dear Savior, and may our correspondence (if continued) be a bond of union, helping each other on, in the pathway to Heaven. I was thinking *this noon*, of your *beginning* the Christian course, for you have only just *entered upon its glorious* warfare; for truly it is a *warfare*, in which we had no hope to win, did not *Christ* sustain, & urge us on. I *pray* you may be calm decided & consistent. Let us remember *words are not actions*; profession is not possession. While I pray for you—I almost faint at my own short-comings and weakness. I know I ought not to say one word. I am so weak & erring—but I do *earnestly desire* to see you such a Christian as Paul was—Full of *zeal* and energy, tempered by Love, and restrained by calm, impassive holiness. May we both assist each other & *strive* to "Live for Christ" and while the pleasures of life are to be enjoyed, we will not fail to perform its duties. . . .

Write me how this letter pleased thee

Monday night 11 O'clock. I wrote you a long letter, *kind friend*, at yesterdays twilight hour, for my thoughts rested on the memories of the Sabbath previous, but I laid it aside to join the loved circle. Sister Mary was playing & singing those good old hymns; sister Hattie assisting her while little brother & I were listeners with the most intense interest. It never seems like the Sabbath, unless we have sacred music after tea. My dear father loved it so— and I know you love it, and join in its rich notes of praise. . . . I welcomed your pennings by *to-day's mail*—the *outgushings* of *your thoughts* which *time* will sober, into deeper realities, for I know, you have not yet awoke from the *reverie* into which you have plunged for the last week. Will you therefore strive to be calm? for do you know how excited you were, when you jumped off the cars before we went into the tunnel? Look out, or your friends will accuse you of abstractedness when you are least aware of it. Remember, when the excitement wears away, you will see matters in *their real light* and as such, I wish you to see them—and would have you see them so now. The eye may not always be bright; nor the voice sweet & musical—better to know how it really is, than to imagine it different from its reality. You do not know yourself, though you think you do; I can read you better than you can read yourself. Therefore think deeply, and study your feelings. Do not feel hurt, that I speak thus *plainly*. But you know I told you a week was too short a time to *learn much*, of any person's character. A correspondence sometimes brings out more of the inner soul than long converse together. May ours prove such a communion. It is far better to find new beauties, at every unfolding of the flower, than to find it a single rose, that blasts with the early frost. Yet I appreciate every kind sentiment of your letter, and time shall reveal thoughts & feeling, as we know each other better. You saw enough of me to know, & I told you not to be too hasty. You must know my family and have an insight into the home-circle. . . . I have not yet mentioned your name to my dear mother. There has been no opportunity for me to do so, though sisters' inquired immediately if I *knew you* as soon as they saw the *book** was published by your firm—*Do you not almost* regret the storm that kept me a visitor at Mrs. Hutchins & gave you a new friend? Please not to mention my name at the Hotel for the *news* would spread, as there is a Mrs. *Goodrich* boarding there—and she is from here. You know how such things always go—and for the sake of both it is better kept at home. Today I have begun my school duties. I hope I may not find them disagreeable although rather confining— *You know I told you, you might dislike* your *name associated with a teacher.* Think of these matters and if a change comes over your dream, I shall quickly discover it in the tones of your letters. Your generous, noble and impulsive nature, will soon give token, should such a feeling take possession of your mind—Now only one day has elapsed and the *dream* (if such it be) is *still* there—but your feelings and the test of *time* & trial yet—I appreciate the noble gift you *lay* at *my disposal*, and while I would be its "guardian angel" I would see every affection of that loving heart, called forth. I have seen you, as the strong man, bowed down, and I bless you for the offering—were you satisfied with what you received in return? Do you remember what I told you Friday night that you had not asked for? . . . It was 11 oclock before our friends left and then I began this long epistle! may you not tire of it! but reply to it soon. and now I must say Good night wishing you every blessing— prosperity in your daily cares and toils—"blessings in your basket and in your store," but do not forget to take care of *yourself*. for you say "I have brought back to my home another true heart." *Then I have a right to claim a care over it*—You are not "quite certain of its happiness depending upon me"— for you may find it happier to be as you have been—I do want you to try yourself and you must not call this letter exacting or formal. I write as I talked with you *calmly* & *plainly*. Know thyself, fully & truly—and while I pray for thee, think kindly of your true friend.

Bessie H

(ii) F. C. Masten

I received your welcome letter promptly and read the contents at once and enjoyed *it all*. You asked me to write soon but I have waited untill now so I could tell you when Mr Delap will close his singing at Friedland. It will be the 4th sunday. I have heard that Mr Davis closes one at St's delight the 3rd sunday. I suppose you will *all* go. If so I hope you will have a *very nice* time and hope your *fellow* will be there. Then *I am sure* you will have a nice time. I dont suppose I will get to come but would like to. You must all come up to Friedland. You asked me how Josie and the singing teacher are getting

---

* Huntting was reading the novel *John Halifax* at the time.—EDS.

on. They have played quits, and Setta has not got any sweetheart like myself, and Annie still goes with Jim Ogburn occasionally, and Jim went to see his girl saturday eve.

You said you saw your fellow at Winston. I am sure you enjoyed that, and I wonder if it was some one whose initials are Mr. Levi Ring. You know there is no end to a ring. You must not get offended, you know I dont mean any harm. I think I will stop writing for the present for my sleeve is so tight that the blood cant circulate in my arm so I will finish later.

This monday eve. I will now try to finish this letter as Mother and I have finished our evening work and are sitting very close to the fire to keep warm. Miss Mollie I wish you were here to talk with us this evening and may be you would tell us when you are going to jump the broom.* I think you are bad that you wont tell me who your sweetheart is. If you dont tell me I shall take it for granted that it is Mr Ring. You told me in your letter that you would let me know about comeing up at Xmas. I hope you will come and then we can talk a great deal that we cant write. There will be a love feast at Friedland Xmas day. Have you made your new dress? If I am not mistaken I heard you had a new black cashmere. I have a new brown one for this winter but it is not made. I am going to be at Salem this week with Setia and Laura. They are very busy just now in finishing their work for the concert in the [Salem] academy and I am going to help them. I suppose you have heard how we are all niffed[?]. Mr. Glassgo got married and left us all to dance the pig trough.† I gues I will have to close for this time as I have nothing interesting to write. Please write very soon and give me all the news. This leaves me quite well excepting frost bitten feet. Tell Sonia to take good care of Mr. Blackburn. I suppose you will see Cousins Dora & Lou Crebus at the singing at St's delight. If they are there I know the Hunters will not be far away. Come, come, soon.

I will close as I said I would. I remain as ever your True Friend

F. C. Masten

(iii) Violet Guntharpe

My mammy stay on wid de same marster 'til I was grown, dat is fifteen, and Thad got to lookin' at me, meek as a sheep and dumb as a calf. I had to ask dat nigger, right out, what his 'tentions was, befo' I got him to bleat out dat he love me. His name Thad Guntharpe. I glance at him one day at de pigpen when I was sloppin' de hogs, I say: "Mr. Guntharpe, you follows me night and mornin' to dis pigpen; do you happen to be in love wid one of these pigs? If so, I'd like to know which one 'tis; then sometime I come down here by myself and tell dat pig 'bout your 'fections." Thad didn't say nothin' but just grin. Him took de slop bucket out of my hand and look at it, all 'round it, put upside down on de ground, and set me down on it; then he fall down dere on de grass by me and blubber out and warm my fingers in his

---

* A rural southern expression meaning to get engaged or married.—EDS.

† When a younger brother or sister got married before an older one, the older sibling was said to be left to jump the pig (or hog) trough.—EDS.

hands. I just took pity on him and told him mighty plain dat he must limber up his tongue and ask sumpin', say what he mean, wantin' to visit them pigs so often. Us carry on foolishness' bout de little boar shoat pig and de little sow pig, then I squeal in laughter over how he scrouge so close; de slop bucket tipple over and I lost my seat. Dat ever remain de happiest minute of my eighty-two years.

30. The advantages of not marrying: Harriet Martineau

The daughter of a prosperous manufacturer, Harriet Martineau (1802–76) was born in Norwich, England. Her parents, committed Unitarians, believed that all eight of their children should be given a good education so they would be equipped to earn a living, and Harriet proved a hard-working and gifted student. Unfortunately, the rigid discipline enforced in the Martineau household, and the rough treatment she received from her siblings, made Harriet an extremely morbid and unhappy child. Ill-health served only to exacerbate her gloomy spirits: she had no sense of taste or smell, and suffered from deafness.

One of the most famous women writers of the century, Martineau's first published works appeared in 1827—"two little eightpenny stories." Though she never entirely left off writing, for a time the financial difficulties caused by her father's death and the subsequent failure of the family fortune forced her to take up needlework to support herself. Then, in 1832, she published a series of tales designed to popularize the subject of political economy; these stories made her a "literary lion." Despite her persistently poor health, Martineau remained a prodigious author all her life.

Although Martineau died a spinster, at the age of twenty-four she briefly contemplated marriage to one of her brother James's fellow students. After much unhappiness, her fiancé went insane and died. In this selection, Martineau expresses relief that her courtship did not end in marriage and exults in the freedom and independence that she has enjoyed as a spinster.

And now my own special trial was at hand. It is not necessary to go into detail about it. The news which got abroad that we had grown comparatively poor,—and the evident certainty that we were never likely to be rich, so wrought upon the mind of one friend as to break down the mischief which I have referred to as caused by ill-offices. My friend had believed me rich, was generous about making me a poor man's wife, and had been discouraged in more ways than one. He now came to me, and we were soon virtually engaged. I was at first very anxious and unhappy. My veneration for his *morale* was such that I felt I dared not undertake the charge of his happiness: and yet I dared not refuse, because I saw it would be his death blow. I was ill,—I was deaf,—I was in an entangled state of mind between conflicting duties

SOURCE: *Harriet Martineau's Autobiography and Memorials of Harriet Martineau*, ed. Maria Weston Chapman (Boston, 1877), 1: 99–102.

and some lower considerations; and many a time did I wish, in my fear that I should fail, that I had never seen him. I am far from wishing that now;—now that the beauty of his goodness remains to me, clear of all painful regrets. But there was a fearful period to pass through. Just when I was growing happy, surmounting my fears and doubts, and enjoying his attachment, the consequences of his long struggle and suspense overtook him. He became suddenly insane; and after months of illness of body and mind, he died. The calamity was aggravated to me by the unaccountable insults I received from his family, whom I had never seen. Years afterwards, when his sister and I met, the mystery was explained. His family had been given to understand, by cautious insinuations, that I was actually engaged to another, while receiving my friend's addresses! There has never been any doubt in my mind that, considering what I was in those days, it was happiest for us both that our union was prevented by any means. I am, in truth, very thankful for not having married at all. I have never since been tempted, nor have suffered any thing at all in relation to that matter which is held to be all-important to woman,—love and marriage. Nothing, I mean, beyond occasional annoyance, presently disposed of. Every literary woman, no doubt, has plenty of importunity of that sort to deal with; but freedom of mind and coolness of manner dispose of it very easily: and since the time I have been speaking of, my mind has been wholly free from all idea of love-affairs. My subsequent literary life in London was clear from all difficulty and embarrassment—no doubt because I was evidently too busy, and too full of interests of other kinds to feel any awkwardness,—to say nothing of my being then thirty years of age; an age at which, if ever, a woman is certainly qualified to take care of herself. I can easily conceive how I might have been tempted,—how some deep springs in my nature might have been touched, then as earlier; but, as a matter of fact, they never were; and I consider the immunity a great blessing, under the liabilities of a moral condition such as mine was in the olden time. If I had had a husband dependent on me for his happiness, the responsibility would have made me wretched. I had not faith enough in myself to endure avoidable responsibility. If my husband had *not* depended on me for his happiness, I should have been jealous. So also with children. The care would have so overpowered the joy,—the love would have so exceeded the ordinary chances of life,—the fear on my part would have so impaired the freedom on theirs, that I rejoice not to have been involved in a relation for which I was, or believed myself unfit. The veneration in which I hold domestic life has always shown me that that life was not for those whose self-respect had been early broken down, or had never grown. Happily, the majority are free from this disability. Those who suffer under it had better be as I,—as my observation of married, as well as single life assures me. When I see what conjugal love is, in the extremely rare cases in which it is seen in its perfection, I feel that there is a power of attachment in me that has never been touched. When I am among little children, it frightens me to think what my idolatry of my own children would have been. But, through it all, I have ever been thankful to be alone. My strong will, combined with anxiety of conscience, makes me fit only to live alone; and my taste and liking are for living alone. The older I have grown, the more serious and irremediable have seemed to me the evils and disadvantages of married life, as it exists among us at this time: and I am provided with what it is the bane of single life in ordinary cases to want,— substantial, laborious and serious occupation. My business in life has been to think and learn, and to speak out with absolute freedom what I have thought and learned. The freedom is itself a positive and never-failing enjoyment to me, after the bondage of my early life. My work and I have been fitted to each other, as is proved by the success of my work and my own happiness in it. The simplicity and independence of this vocation first suited my infirm and ill-developed nature, and then sufficed for my needs, together with family ties and domestic duties, such as I have been blessed with, and as every woman's heart requires. Thus, I am not only entirely satisfied with my lot, but think it the very best for me,—under my constitution and circumstances: and I long ago came to the conclusion that, without meddling with the case of the wives and mothers, I am probably the happiest single woman in England. Who could have believed, in that awful year 1826, that such would be my conclusion a quarter of a century afterwards!

31. An American spinster: Frances Marion Eddy

The youngest child of a Presbyterian minister and his wife, Frances Marion Eddy (1862–1956; Docs. 1.iii, 7.ii), was born in Niles, Michigan. "Impressionable and impulsive" and extremely precocious, Eddy hoped to study at the University of Michigan, an ambition that her parents supported. Her father's death, however, forced her to abandon her educational plan and to become, instead, a music teacher so that she could support herself and her mother. When her mother suffered a crippling stroke, it was left to Eddy, as the only unmarried child, to devote herself to caring for the invalid.

By this time I was sixteen, growing so tall that it caused me acute chagrin on the dancing floor, as all the undersized boys seemed to leap for me as a partner. I was keeping the absurdest diaries; writing what I thought was poetry; taking an occasional flyer in story-writing (banal stuff) and already starting lessons on the pipe-organ. My father seemed to cherish the hope that I would eventually disclose some literary talent; my brother and sisters misguidedly believed that I was destined to be the real musician of the family; I alas, had no conviction that I could be either as I did not feel that it was in me to attain any heights except in stature. However I *did* very positively know that I possessed a great ambition to go to college, and finally plucked up courage to break the news to father. He was surprised but interested and

SOURCE: Frances Marion Eddy, unpublished reminiscences. The editors wish to thank the family of Frances Marion Eddy for allowing us to quote from these reminiscences.

asked me where I thought I wanted to go. When he learned that it was to Ann Arbor he became as serious about it as was I. Between us we decided on a Latin-English preparatory course, and to that end I started boning seriously.

I graduated from the Niles Senior High in 1880. At that time a diploma meant matriculation at Ann Arbor without further examinations. Members of the Ann Arbor faculty came to Niles for "orals," and our "finals" were sent *to* the graduating class *from* that University, and returned there for correction and rating. My papers brought me second honors.

My father's health,—never very good—began to fail noticeably, and in 1881 he developed Brights Disease. At his expressed wish I stayed at home, took a post-graduate course with an Ann Arbor tutor who vacationed in Niles; to my surprise, also, I annexed three music pupils, but I still thought I was going to college.

In our home life great economy was being practised; slowly and painfully it dawned upon me that college was out of the question. Immediately I concentrated upon my music and became a fair performer on both piano and pipe-organ. I acquired pupils almost magically, so it seemed to me, for I never solicited them, they just hovered. . . .

Immediately after the funeral of my father on March 8, 1883 we moved into a dear little house at the corner of Fourth and Oak streets. . . .

Mother and I tried to adjust our lives to a new scale of living, in a new environment where there was no gas, no sink, not even a pump—except out-of-doors. That summer in June 1883 I was twenty-one years old and felt as old as Methusaleh. The college hope had long vanished, for what little money there was left must be carefully invested and devoted entirely to the care and comfort of my mother.

My music class grew by leaps and bounds, because the two wealthiest and most influential women of the town spread over me the aegis of their patronage. . . .

All the time that I was outwardly absorbed in my profession, I was writing reams of stuff that luckily I never sent away for criticism or for publishing. Later I realized that it was pure exhibitionism because of my thwarted ambition for a college career; so I burned it all up in the kitchen stove and felt very much house-cleaned mentally.

I had been taking a correspondence course for four years from the Chatauqua Circle at Chatauqua, New York going there for what was called a graduation in 1885. On my return was invited to join a Niles Study Club comprised of women and men much older than I, but all having similar habit of mind because of our love of study. In this group were two lawyers, a minister, a scientist, and the superintendant of the Niles Public Schools. The women were two school teachers, a photographer, a clever housewife, (with a philandering husband), and myself. It was a stimulating experience for me and I remained in this group until the spring of 1887.

In May of that year my precious, courageous, little mother suffered a terrific apoplectic stroke, and for weeks we were not sure that she would live. Finally she struggled back, but was hopelessly paralyzed on the whole of her right side. . . .

She never could dress herself again, or care for herself in anyway, although she did learn to use her left hand for feeding herself. . . . At four o'clock in the afternoon [Oct. 20, 1893] the end came very quietly and I felt that my life, too, was all done; that the only reason for which I had come into the world was to comfort and care for my mother in her loneliness; that there was no more need on earth for me. I was thirty-one and very tired.

32. A French spinster describes her days: Eugénie de Guérin

Eugénie de Guérin (1805–48), a pious noblewoman from Languedoc, wrote the journal from which this selection is taken for her brother Maurice, a Romantic poet who lived in Paris. Later published in book form, it went through more than sixty editions in France alone and earned de Guérin the status among Catholics of a lay saint. In November and December 1834, when she wrote these lines, she lived on the family estate, Cayla, with her father and her sister Mimi. At twenty-nine, de Guérin did not need or wish to marry. As an exceptionally well-to-do spinster, she was free not only from the necessity of working for a living, but also from the demands of motherhood on her time and health. She spent her tranquil and uneventful days in prayer, reading, and performing good works among the local peasantry.

[Nov. 17]

Three letters since yesterday, three very great pleasures, for I am so fond of letters and of those who have written them to me: Louise, Mimi, and Félicité. That dear Mimi says such sweet charming things about our separation, her return, her weariness; for she gets weary of being far from me, as I of being without her. Each moment I see and feel that I want her, at night more especially, when I am so accustomed to hear her breathe close to my ear. That slight sound sets me to sleep; and not to hear it inspires me with melancholy reflections. I think of death, which also silences everything around us, which also will be an absence. These night thoughts depend somewhat on those I have had during the day. Nothing gets talked of but sickness and death; the Andillac bell has done nothing but toll these last days. It is typhus fever that is now raging, as it does every year. We are all lamenting a young woman of your age, the prettiest and most respectable in the parish, carried off in a few days! She leaves a young infant that she was still nursing. . . .

[Nov. 18]

I am furious with the grey cat. The wicked creature has just robbed me of a young pigeon that I was warming by the fire. The poor little thing was beginning to revive. I had meant to tame it; it would have got fond of me; and

SOURCE: *Journal of Eugénie de Guérin*, ed. G. S. Trebutien, 6th ed. (New York, 1893), pp. 2–24 *passim*. Originally published in 1863.

now all this ends in its getting crunched up by a cat! What disappointments there are in life! This event, and indeed all those of the day, have occurred in the kitchen; it is there that I have spent the whole morning and part of the evening since I have been without Mimi. It is necessary to overlook the cook. Papa too comes down sometimes, and I read to him beside the stove or in the chimney corner, out of the "Antiquities of the Anglo-Saxon Church." . . . With whom do you suppose I was spending this morning by the kitchen fire? With Plato: I did not dare to say so, but he chanced to come under my eyes, and I determined to make his acquaintance. I am only at the first pages as yet. He seems to be most admirable, this Plato; but one of his notions strikes me as singular, that of ranking health before beauty in the catalogue of God's gifts? If he had consulted a woman, Plato would not have written thus: you feel sure of that, don't you? So do I; and yet, remembering that I am a *philosopher,** I rather incline to his opinion. When one is in bed and really ill, one would gladly sacrifice one's complexion or one's bright eyes to regain health and enjoy the sunshine. And besides, a small degree of piety in the heart, a little love of God, is enough to make one speedily renounce such idolatries; for a pretty woman adores herself. When I was a child I thought nothing equal to beauty, because, I said to myself, it would have made Mamma love me better. Thank God this childishness has passed away, and the beauty of the soul is the only one I covet. Perhaps even in this I am still childish as of yore: I should like to resemble the angels,—this may displease God; the motive is still the same, to be loved better by Him. How many things occur to me, only I must leave thee! I have got to say my rosary; night is at hand, and I like to end the day in prayer. . . .

[Nov. 20]

I have just come away in good spirits from the kitchen, where I remained longer than usual this evening to try and determine Paul, one of our servants, to go to confession at Christmas. He has promised me that he would. He is a good youth, and he will do it. God be praised! my evening has not been lost. What joy could I but thus win every day some soul to God! . . .

[Nov. 21]

This day began radiantly: a summer sun, a soft air that invited one to take a walk. Everything urged me to do so, but I only took two steps beyond the door, and stopped short at the sheep-stable to look at a white lamb that had just been born. I delight in seeing these tiny animals, which make us thank God for surrounding us with so many gentle creatures.

[Nov. 24]

For the moment all is calm, within and without, soul and house: a happy condition, but giving me little to say, like peaceful reigns to the historian. This day began with a letter from Paul. He invites me to Alby. I cannot promise him this; I should have to leave home for that, and I am becoming sedentary. Very willingly would I take the vow of seclusion here at Cayla.

* De Guerin is making teasing reference to a conversation in which a local peas-ant boy called her a philosopher.—EDS.

No place in the world pleases me so much as home. Oh, the deliciousness of *home*! How I pity thee, poor exile, to be so far away from it; to see thy own people only in thought; not to be able to say to us either "Good-morning" or "Good-evening;" to live a stranger without any home of thy own in the world,—having father, brother, and sisters, in one place! All this is sad, and yet I may not wish thee anything else. We cannot have thee, but I hope to see thee again, and this consoles me. I am constantly thinking of thy arrival, and foreseeing how happy we shall be.

[Nov. 26]

I did not write yesterday; I did nothing but expect. At last she came in the evening—the dear Mimi! Now then I am happy. . . .

[Nov. 28]

This morning, before daylight, my fingers were in the ashes looking for fire enough to light a candle. I could not find any, and was just going back to bed when a little bit of charcoal that I happened to touch showed a spark, and there was my lamp lit. Dressing got over quickly, prayer said, and we were with Mimi in the Cahuzac road. That unfortunate road, I so long took it alone, and how glad I was to take it with four feet to-day! The weather was not fine, and I could not see the mountain; that dear district I look at so much when it is clear. The chapel was engaged, which was a pleasure to me. I like not to be hurried, and to have time before I enter in there to raise my whole soul before God. This often takes long, because my thoughts find themselves scattered like leaves. At two o'clock I was on my knees, listening to the finest teaching imaginable; and I came out feeling that I was better. The effect of every burden laid down is to leave us relieved; and when the soul has laid down that of its faults at the feet of God, it feels as though it had wings. I admire the excellency of confession. What ease, what light, what strength I feel conscious of every time that I have said "It is my fault!"

[Nov. 29]

Cloaks, clogs, umbrellas—all the apparatus of winter—followed us this morning to Andillac, where we stayed till evening between the parsonage and the church. This Sunday life, so stirring, so active, how much I like it! We come upon each other in passing, and then chatter while walking on together about the poultry, the flocks, the husband, the children. My great pleasure is to caress these last, and to see them hide themselves, red as fire, in their mother's petticoats. They are afraid of *las doumaiselas*, as of everything unfamiliar. . . .

[Dec. 4]

A rare and pleasant visit; Madame de F— has just gone away. We could only keep her a few hours, from ten to three. Her husband was with her, and carried her off in spite of our entreaties. The fact is, he himself was obliged to return, and he can no more do without his wife than without his eyes. Happy woman! to know how to make herself so indispensable! There she is now on the hill of Bleys—and here I am telling thee that she has been here —a great event at Cayla, a lady's visit, more especially at this season.

[Dec. 5]

Papa set out this morning for Gaillac; here we are sole "châtelaines," Mimi and I, till to-morrow, and absolute mistresses! This regency is not disagreeable, and I rather enjoy it for a day, but not longer. Long reigns are tedious. It is enough for me to rule "Trilby" [the cat], and to get her to come when I call, or to give her paw when I ask it. Yesterday a sad accident befell "Trilby." As she was tranquilly sleeping under the kitchen chimney, a gourd that was hanging up to dry fell upon her. The blow bewildered her; the poor pet came running to us as quickly as ever she could, to impart her distress. A caress cured her. Night has come. A knock makes itself heard! Every one runs to the door, crying "Who is there?" It was Jean de Persac, an old tenant, whom I had not seen for a long time. He was heartily welcomed, and set down upon his first entrance to eat and drink; after which we got him to talk of his present locality, and of his wife and children. I am very fond of such conversations and meetings. These faces of the olden time give peculiar pleasure; they seem to restore one's youth. I fancied myself yesterday back to the time when Jean used to take me upon his knee.

[Dec. 7]

Yesterday the evening was spent in talking about Gaillac, of these, and those, and a thousand things going on in the little town. I do not care much for news; but news of friends always gives pleasure, and one listens to it with more interest than to news of the world and of tiresome politics. Nothing makes me yawn so soon as a newspaper. It was not so formerly, but tastes change, and the heart detaches itself from something or other every day we live. Time and experience too disabuse; as we advance in life we at length gain the proper position whence to judge of our affections and know them in their true light. I have all mine now present before me. First I see dolls, toys, birds, butterflies, that I loved—sweet and innocent childish affections. Then come reading, conversation, dress in a slight degree, and dreams, beautiful dreams! . . . But I am not going to confess. It is Sunday. I have returned alone from the first mass at Lentin, and I am enjoying in my little room the sweetest calm in the world, in union with God. The happiness of the morning penetrates me, flows into my soul, and transforms me. . . .

[Dec. 9]

I have just been warming myself by every fireside in the village. This is a round that we make with Mimin from time to time, and which is by no means without its attractions. To-day it was a visiting of the sick; accordingly we discussed medicines and infusions. "Take this;" "Do that;" and we are listened to as attentively as any doctor. We prescribed clogs to a little child that had made itself ill by walking barefoot, and a pillow to its brother, who with a violent headache was lying quite flat; the pillow relieved him, but will not cure him, I think. He seems to be suffering from an affection of the chest, and these poor people in their hovels are like cattle in their stalls; the bad air poisons them. Returning to Cayla, I find myself in a palace compared to their cottages. Thus it is that, having habitually to look beneath me, I always find myself fortunately placed.

33. 'My wife and I are one, and I am he': The laws and rituals of marriage

Women embarked on marriage in a welter of prescriptive contradiction. Told in song and ceremony that they were entering a heaven in which they might expect worship, power, and adoration, women in all three countries were consigned through marriage to a civil purgatory, an indeterminate status in which they were virtual non-persons in the law. Barred from making contracts, bearing witness in court, and initiating lawsuits, they could nevertheless be prosecuted for most criminal offenses. Meanwhile, the religious and public pronouncements on their proper role as wives were often totally at odds: religion, notably Catholicism, counseled them to place God and children before their husbands, but the secular advice literature was unrelenting in the demand that conjugal love come first.

The contrasts between the sweetness of songs and ceremonies and the harshness of the legal and economic realities of marriage are clearly revealed in the following pastiche. The first four selections from France expose the contradictions between civil law and the new secular morality on the one hand and the Catholic vision of marriage on the other. The French Civil Code, promulgated by Napoleon in 1804, decreed that the married woman was subordinate to her husband; in contrast the author Marie-Catherine-Sophie de Flavigny, comtesse d'Agoult (1805–76), better known under the pseudonym Daniel Stern, recalls how her Catholic confessor taught her to put religion and children before her marital relationship. However different the voices of the pious aristocrat Louise-Mathilde de Montesquiou-Fezensac, comtesse de Flavigny (d. 1883), and the liberal dramatist Ernest Legouvé (1807–1903), they shared a vision of the married woman as self-sacrifice incarnate.

The two selections from England highlight the blatant discrepancies between the language of the traditional marriage ceremony of the Anglican Church and the actuality of women's position in civil law. An Englishwoman marrying according to 'The Book of Common Prayer' would hear her husband

SOURCES: (i) Henry Cachard, The French Civil Code, with the various amendments thereto, as in force on March 15, 1895, articles 212–17, 220, pp. 59–60. (ii) Marie de Flavigny, comtesse d'Agoult [pseud. Daniel Stern], Mes Souvenirs, 1806–1833 (Paris, 1877), pp. 213, 215. (iii) Louise-Mathilde de Montesquiou-Fezensac, comtesse de Flavigny, Recueil de prières, de méditatons, et de lectures (Paris, 1861), as quoted by Nicole Bothorel et al. "La Femme au xixe siècle," in Pierre Grimal, ed., Histoire mondiale de la femme (Paris, 1968), 3: 110. (iv) Ernest Legouvé, Histoire morale des femmes, 7th ed. (Paris, 1882), pp. 358–59. Originally published in 1848. (v) The Book of Common Prayer (London, 1903), p. 243. (vi) Barbara Leigh Smith Bodichon, A Brief Summary in Plain Language of the Most Important Laws Concerning Women; Together with a Few Observations Thereon (London, 1854), p. 6. (vii) Jonathan Stearns, Female Influence, and the True Christian Mode of Its Exercise: A Discourse Delivered in the First Presbyterian Church in Newburyport, July 30, 1837 (Newburyport, Mass., 1837), pp. 23–24. (viii) History of Woman Suffrage, ed. Elizabeth Cady Stanton, Susan B. Anthony, and Matilda Joslyn Gage (New York, 1881), 1: 70–71. (ix) The Ameri-

pledge her all his worldly goods; yet as the reformer Barbara Leigh Smith Bodichon (1827–91) indignantly reported, at marriage all of a woman's belongings—not only her clothes and jewels, but her body as well—became her husband's property.

Across the Atlantic the Presbyterian minister Jonathan Stearns (1808–89) warns women to stay in their place, reminding them that the stability of the nation depends on female delicacy and piety. The feminist reformers who gathered at Seneca Falls, New York, in 1848, however, questioned how much power could be exercised by a woman who was, in fact, civilly dead. The marriage of Harriet Jones, a former Texas slave, shows that no matter how joyous a plantation wedding might be, the freed slave woman, like the New England lady, promised obedience to her husband. The final selection, "Oh, Promise Me," a song by Clement Scott (1841–1904) that Americans began to hear at weddings in the late nineteenth century, equated marriage with paradise. Victorian women might well have complained that they had entered marriage believing in this beatific vision only to be rudely surprised.

(i) The French Civil Code

Of the Respective Rights and Duties of Husband and Wife

Husband and wife owe each other fidelity, support, and assistance.

A husband owes protection to his wife; a wife obedience to her husband.

A wife is bound to live with her husband and to follow him wherever he deems proper to reside. The husband is bound to receive her, and to supply her with whatever is necessary for the wants of life, according to his means and condition.

A wife cannot sue in court without the consent of her husband, even if she is a public tradeswoman or if there is no community or she is separated as to property.

The husband's consent is not necessary when the wife is prosecuted criminally or in a police matter.

A wife, even when there is no community, or when she is separated as to property, cannot give, convey, mortgage, or acquire property, with or without consideration, without the husband joining in the instrument or giving his written consent.

A wife may, if she is a public tradeswoman, bind herself without the husband's consent with respect to what relates to her trade, and in that case she also binds her husband if there is community of property between them. She is not considered a public tradeswoman if she merely retails the goods of her husband's business, but only when she has a separate business.

---

can Slave: A Composite Autobiography, ed. George P. Rawick, 4: Texas Narratives (Westport, Conn., 1972), part 2: 235–36. (x) Clement Scott, "Oh, Promise Me," in Old Favorite Songs and Hymns, ed. Richard Charlton Mackenzie (New York, n.d.), pp. 5–6. The title of this document is an informal nineteenth-century version of the English jurist Blackstone's formulation of the common law on marriage.

(ii) Marie de Flavigny, comtesse d'Agoult (Daniel Stern)

The young girl does not love, as she certainly knows, but she will love, her mother tells her; a well-born young girl always loves the man she marries; this is also the advice of her confessor. And then children will come, the true love of woman. . . . For the Catholic priest, marriage is nothing more, according to its definition in the catechism, than a sacrament destined to give children "to the Church," love being nothing but the passions of the flesh. The person of the husband, as the priest conceives it, is only of trifling importance; one does not inquire in the confessional if the fiancé is pleasant; and the bizarre thing is that one does not even worry much about his beliefs and his morals! He is desired by the family, that is sufficient. If he is a good Catholic, so much the better; if he is not—"Clotilda converted Clovis"*—and everything is said.

(iii) Louise-Mathilde de Montesquiou-Fezensac, comtesse de Flavigny

Lord, it is You who have given me,
In the husband with whom you have united me,
A guide for my inexperience,
A protector for my weakness—
Grant that, after the pleasure of pleasing you,
The attachment to my husband,
The care of making him happy
Will occupy me completely
Grant that by the abnegation of my will,
And deference to his least desires,
I will make his life agreeable and sweet.

(iv) Ernest Legouvé

Marriage alone can give to this feminine influence a character of continuity and of purity. . . . To live for another, to disappear in a glory or a virtue of which she is the principle, to dispense benefits while concealing the benefactress, to learn so that another may know, to think so that another may speak, to seek the light so that another may shine, there is no more beautiful destiny for woman, for all of this signifies devotion. And what more noble profession than that of devotion? What employment for life is more appropriate to all the qualities of woman? . . . Every wife who is truly a wife has for a career the career of her husband.

(v) 'The Book of Common Prayer'

Then shall they again loose their hands; and the Man shall give unto the Woman a Ring, laying the same upon the book with the accustomed duty to

---

* Clovis was a Frankish king of the fifth century whose wife, Clotilda, was reputed to have converted him to Christianity.—EDS.

the Priest and Clerk. And the Priest, taking the Ring, shall deliver it unto the Man, to put it upon the fourth finger of the Woman's left hand. And the Man holding the Ring there, and taught by the Priest, shall say, "With this Ring I thee wed, with my body I thee worship, and with all my worldly goods I thee endow: In the Name of the Father, and of the Son, and of the Holy Ghost. Amen."

(vi) Barbara Leigh Smith Bodichon

A man and wife are one person in law; the wife loses all her rights as a single woman, and her existence is entirely absorbed in that of her husband. He is civilly responsible for her acts; she lives under his protection or cover, and her condition is called coverture.

A woman's body belongs to her husband; she is in his custody, and he can enforce his right by a writ of *habeas corpus*.

What was her personal property before marriage, such as money in hand, money at the bank, jewels, household goods, clothes, etc., becomes absolutely her husband's, and he may assign or dispose of them at his pleasure whether he and his wife live together or not. . . .

The legal custody of children belongs to the father. During the life-time of a sane father, the mother has no rights over her children, except a limited power over infants, and the father may take them from her and dispose of them as he thinks fit.

(vii) Jonathan Stearns

Beware, then, how you forfeit your peculiar advantages. Beware how you do any thing to diminish that delicate and chivalrous respect, which the feminine character now commands from all who are not lost to every principle of honor. The refined and high minded woman, while she never presumes upon her privilege as an apology for selfishness and wrong, will rejoice to avail herself of every just advantage it affords her, in the cause of truth, benevolence and piety.

On you, ladies, depends, in a most important degree, the destiny of our country. In this day of disorder and turmoil, when the foundations of the great deep seem fast breaking up, and the flood of desolation threatening to roll over the whole face of society, it peculiarly develops upon you to say what shall be the result. Yours it is to determine, whether the beautiful order of society, a system of many members in one body, and all the members not having the same office, shall continue as it has been, to be the source of blessings to the world; or whether, despising all forms and distinctions, all boundaries and rules, society shall break up and become a chaos of disjointed and unsightly elements. Yours it is to decide, under God, whether we shall be a nation of refined and high minded christians, or whether, rejecting the civilities of life, and throwing off the restraints of morality and piety, we shall become a fierce race of semi-barbarians, before whom neither order, nor honor, nor chastity can stand.

And be assured, ladies, if the hedges and borders of the social garden should be broken up, the lovely vine, which now twines itself so gracefully upon the trellis, and bears such rich clusters, will be the first to fall and be trodden under foot.

(viii) The Seneca Falls Declaration

He has made her, if married, in the eye of the law, civilly dead.

He has taken from her all right in property, even to the wages she earns.

He has made her, morally, an irresponsible being, as she can commit many crimes with impunity, provided they be done in the presence of her husband. In the covenant of marriage, she is compelled to promise obedience to her husband, he becoming, to all intents and purposes, her master—the law giving him power to deprive her of her liberty, and to administer chastisement.

He has so framed the laws of divorce, as to what shall be the proper causes, and in case of separation, to whom the guardianship of the children shall be given, as to be wholly regardless of the happiness of women—the law, in all cases, going upon a false supposition of the supremacy of man, and giving all power into his hands.

(ix) Harriet Jones

I marries Bill Jones de year after freedom. It a bright, moonlight night and all de white folks and niggers come and de preacher stand under de big elm tree, and I come in with two li'l pickininnies for flower gals and holdin' my train. I has on one Miss Ellen's dresses and red stockin's and a pair brand new shoes and a wide brim hat. De preacher say, "Bill, does you take dis woman to be you lawful wife?" and Bill say he will. Den he say, "Harriet, will you take dis nigger to be you lawful boss and do jes' what he say?" Den we signs de book and de preacher say, "I quote from de scripture:

> Dark and stormy may come de weather
> I jines dis man and woman together.
> Let none but Him what make de thunder,
> Put dis man and woman asunder."

Den we goes out in de backyard, where de table sot for supper, a long table made with two planks and de peg legs. Miss Ellen puts on de white tablecloth and some red berries, 'cause it am November and dey is ripe. Den she puts on some red candles, and we has barbecue pig and roast sweet 'taters and dumplin's and pies and cake. Dey all eats dis grand supper till dey full and mammy give me de luck charm for de bride. It am a rabbit toe, and she say:

> "Here, take dis li'l gift,
> And place it near you heart;
> It keep away dat li'l riff
> What causes folks to part.

"It only jes' a rabbit toe,
But plenty luck it brings,
Its worth a million dimes or more,
More'n all de weddin' rings."

Den we goes to Marse Watson's saddleshop to dance and dances all night, and de bride and groom, dat's us, leads de grand march.

(x) 'Oh, Promise Me'

Oh, promise me that some day you and I
Will take our love together to some sky
Where we can be alone and faith renew,
And find the hollows where those flowers grew,
Those first sweet violets of early spring,
Which come in whispers, thrill us both and sing
Of love unspeakable that is to be;
Oh, promise me! Oh, promise me!

Oh, promise me that you will take my hand,
The most unworthy in this lowly land,
And let me sit beside you, in your eyes
Seeing the vision of our paradise;
Hearing God's message while the organ rolls
Its mighty music to our very souls,
No love less perfect than a life with thee;
Oh, promise me! Oh, promise me!

34. Two American women write about their happiness in marriage

Some women found great happiness with their husbands, as the diary and letters of these two American women show. Persis Sibley (1813–91), of Freedom, Maine, married Charles Andrews, an aspiring young lawyer and later a congressman, in 1842, when she was twenty-nine years old. With some regrets she left her parental home and close friends to make the seventy-mile, two-day move to Dixfield, Maine. The birth of her first child, Charlotte ('lotte), in 1843 left Andrews in ill health for several years, while her husband's business travels left her longing for his companionship. Yet in her diary Andrews privately comforted herself with the reflection that, in spite of the high personal costs, she had indeed found marital happiness.

SOURCES: (i) Persis Sibley Andrews Black Journals, 1845, Maine Historical Society. The editors are grateful to Sue Rice, Atherton, Calif., for making a typescript of this journal available to us, and to the Maine Historical Society for permission to publish these excerpts. (ii) Castle family correspondence in the possession of Susannah Loomis Sherman, Conneaut, Ohio, and published with her kind permission.

*Mary Ellen Castle (1837–92), the youngest child in a large Vermont fam-
ily that had emigrated to Ohio in the 1830's, had attended college in Indiana,
a rare privilege in her day. While a student, she fell in love with Professor
James Sanderson Rankin, eighteen years her senior, and married him against
her family's wishes. In this selection, a letter written in May 1860, during
the second year of their marriage while she was expecting the first of their
five children, Rankin writes to her absent husband of her intense love for
him, a love that sustained her through many subsequent hardships.*

(i) Persis Sibley Andrews

Jan. 1, 1845.—New Year's-day. I am spending it in solitude—no one to
wish me a happy-new-year—no one for me to speak to at all. Dear husband
went to Augusta nearly a week since—not with "axes to grind" of his own—
the rest of the villagers have gone to the Ball at Wilton—my girl has gone
home—boy not here this week; & little 'lotte & I stay here alone snow &
wind bound, but I can *think* unbound—think of other New Year-days far
back in the past—days of frolic & glee with numerous friends whose characters
& peculiarities I knew well—& just how to take them each, to make a jest go
off, & the laugh go round—days of gifts & tokens, received & confer'd—of in-
terchange of sweet friendships—of freedom from all perplexing care—Yes, they
were days of bliss in their way. But *now* I am the happy wife of the man I
prefer of all the world of men, & the joyful mother of a cherub that words
cannot describe. These are to me sources of heartfelt enjoyment that more
than recompense for airy delights buoyant freedom & luxurious abundance
of other days:—those alone wo'd not satisfy now that I have known these;—
but of my early friends I can never think without some regret that I am so
far from them all, for now I do not form new friendships as readily as I used
to—nor have I much opportunity if I did. I am devoted to my family & have
much poor health—& therefore am limited in my circulation (as papers say),
& a few of my dear relatives or old friends about me wo'd be very pleasant,
especially during the long absences of my husband. But go friends & relatives, one & all, for the sake of this same dear husband—if I cannot have
both. I left you all for him, & I wo'd do the same thing again. He is a gem
among the sands of worldlings, & improves in lustre by time & use. His mind is
clear & powerful beyond what I expected. He is capable of gigantic mental
effort & more than realizes all that I expected of him in this way. He is kind
& tender—accommodating to a fault. Indeed, his faults all grow out of his
disinclination to give pain in the least degree. He can't say—*no*. I mean his
faults to the world. Towards me he has but one fault—O that he co'd say
this of me. Well, I have loved him for the last six months with more reverence—respect—esteem & fervor—with more perfect trust & confidence
than ever before. I do not believe he wo'd try to hide a fault from me, & O
may I be enabled to retain his confidence as I have it now.

June 22.—Sabbath. Here I am in the same room where I was married
three years ago this day. My reflections upon this space of past time are
many—both sweet & bitter, but in *all* connected with *him* to whom I then

entrusted my happiness with a strange mingling of confidence & fear. I find but little of the latter & an abundance of the former to repay all the sacrifices I then made & the painful consequences. I believe few enjoy as rich an inheritance of domestic bliss. I have always been treated with tenderness & kindness & with great indulgence to my complainings in sickness. He has failings & I know them, but I *love* respect & esteem him more than I did then because I know him better. I have endured great suffering & loss of health that I never expect to regain, but I have ever found my husband a sympathising partner in my sufferings. I did well when I gave him my heart & hand. I bless God that he directed my deliberations to this decision.

Oct. 23.—I have had a "God Send". News from home. D. B. Fuller spent the night here. He was on business at Sangerville & rode up to see us. He is a confirmed *old bach*—& says he never loved any but me. How singular, for I never felt a throb of true love for him. I am highly favor'd in one respect. Whenever I see any of my old lovers I feel like streatching my arms toward Heaven & shouting from the depths of my loving heart Glory! Glory!! Thanksgiving & Praise be unto the Power that preserved me from yielding, when they tempted me with professions & wealth, & saved me to enjoy the bliss of reciprocal love with my dear Charles—tho' often we are pinched with scanty means.

(ii) Mary Ellen Castle Rankin

Wednesday, May 16, 1860.—Two days have passed away since I last felt your *good-bye kiss* and I am beginning to long earnestly for the sight of your dear face—and loving embraces; Yet my darling I am better content than I thought I could ever be away from you—and I will try not to be *unhappy* at all—I know it is much better for me to be *here* for several reasons. I can have some *exercise*, and that is what I *ought* to have, as hard as it is for me to *endure* it now—I have had so little to do all winter that I find I must begin very *gradually* now, but I *shall* be cautious darling and you must not fear that I shall do myself any injury—I shall be more *quiet* here too than I could be in Seymour [Indiana]—shall not see so many people. . . .

I wonder where you are tonight my own darling, and if you miss your *absent wife.*—Does your little room look desolate, or are you so very busy that you do not think of it?—I hope to get a letter from you by *tomorrow* night at farthest—write to me often dearest as I shall get the *blues* sometimes terribly—I *did* have such a *heart-ache* the last night I slept in your arms, I could not talk to you at all—but you must forgive my foolishness dearest— as you have often done before—and will have cause to do many times again— I am too tired to write more tonight—my heart is *full* of love to you *all* the time darling, I am still *your own* Ellen.

Thursday Evening, 7 P.M.—My dear I have but just time to say to you that *Pa* and *Ma* are here tonight—came this morning quite unexpectedly— They had written but the letter was not recd—both are well—I do hope I shall get a letter from you tonight darling it seems like a *long* time since you left—I will write you a *long* letter very soon—for this time receive this hasty scrawl, with a heart *full* of love from

Your loving wife,
Your own Ellen

35. A Parisian working woman tells about her marriage: Suzanne Voilquin

Young working-class women encountered formidable obstacles—from *venereal disease to economic insecurity—in pursuing the dream of domestic bliss, as these passages from the autobiography of Suzanne Monnier Voilquin reveal. Suzanne Monnier (c. 1800–1860) was the child of skilled artisans who had moved to Paris during the French Revolution. Raised at home by her mother, a devout Catholic, she learned to read and write at a convent school and was then apprenticed out to learn needlework. At the age of ten she was given full responsibility for raising her little sister, Adrienne. When her mother died and her father abandoned his family, Monnier was left to support herself and Adrienne by working as a seamstress and embroideress. Following her sister's marriage to a young printer and her own rape and abandonment by a medical student, Monnier set out to fashion a life for herself. In 1825 she married Eugène Voilquin, a construction worker. After eight unhappy years of marriage, the Voilquins, influenced by their involvement with the Saint-Simonians (a quasi-religious cult whose plans for social reform included ending the subjection of women), decided to separate; Suzanne later became a midwife. The following selection describes in unusually explicit fashion her marriage and its disappointments.*

Marriage, without the possibility of divorce, has serious consequences even when this indissoluble bond is formed with love by a naïve and pure young girl. But for me, whose blighted heart was capable only of maternal feelings, there were cruel battles to be fought within myself before I dared unite with the man whose name I would loyally bear.

I met Voilquin in a society of modest bourgeois and respectable workers to which my brother-in-law belonged. . . . We danced; the young poets of the group recited their poems; they drank to the health of the ladies; and so forth. Voilquin was one of the more handsome of the group. He composed gallant songs; his wit was inexhaustible; he made one dizzy with his liveliness and gaiety; his open, lively countenance predisposed people to like him. Before we appeared on the scene, all the young ladies of the society had flirted with him, but, as often happens in such circumstances, it was I, who care so little

SOURCE: Madame Suzanne V. . . . [Voilquin], *Souvenirs d'une fille du peuple, ou la Saint-Simonienne en Egypte, 1834 à 1836* (Paris, 1866), pp. 66–74. The editors wish to thank Elizabeth G. Altman, Cambridge, Mass., for giving us her unpublished annotated translation of this work.

for attracting men, whom he noticed the most. As soon as Mallard had introduced us to the group, Voilquin struck up an acquaintaince with my sister and brother-in-law, putting all his efforts into making a favorable impression on them. He succeeded, for after a short time my brother-in-law was singing his praises to me.

"The bearing and openness of this young man please me," he would tell me. "I believe he is a good, if somewhat frivolous, person. He is educated and comes from a respectable family. What more could you wish for? It would be sad to remain an old maid. Believe me, my sister, marry him and you will bring about Adrienne's delightful plan of the four of us forming together the jolliest and happiest group in creation. We have decided that we four should live together. Consent to this marriage, and we will at once begin looking for a lodging for the three of us to live in until the great event takes place."

For two and a half years my heart had thrilled only to the dreams of those little rosy angels that motherhood promised me. I thought that the only possible happiness would be to have children and to give them the overwhelming love that I held within me, and that made my life such a torment. I thought of it incessantly, but I wanted to surround the darling little creatures with every possible condition for happiness. To do this, I would have to give them a name and a father who recognized them as his own. From this standpoint I felt no reluctance in taking this self-confident and good young man as a husband. To compensate for the love I was unable to give him, couldn't I, I asked myself, enrich his life and make him happy by my constant devoted attention? He needed affectionate support because he had an inconsistent character that lacked a firm foundation, and this made him susceptible to every influence. The somewhat maternal feeling that I felt for him would remove all harmful obstacles from his path and give full rein to his good instincts. . . .

Thus, freely but without love, I accepted the offer of his hand and name. [But] my anxieties increased as the moment for our union approached. Should I tell my fiancé of my sorrows and past disappointments? Honesty advised me to confess everything, but prudence warned me to say nothing. Since it was Voilquin's nature to be expansive and outgoing it seemed to me that he would be unable to hear such a secret without divulging some part of it, thus exposing me to shame before my sister and brother-in-law. I would have preferred breaking off everything with him to that. I often thought of doing so, but that would have meant giving up the joy of becoming a mother. This hope alone could revive my soul. What should I do? Time passed while I hesitated indecisively. The banns were posted at Saint-Merry's and the day of the marriage was set. . . .

In the midst of these perplexities I turned to Father Lerat. I told myself that I would do whatever this kind, old priest advised me to do. Unfortunately, because of my long despondency, I had not seen him for two and a half years, but he nevertheless recognized me. I told him of our approaching marriage, and he at once asked me about my spiritual state. He asked if my thoughts were still occupied with the man who had caused me so much suffering.

"Oh no, my Father," I replied. "I have not thought of him since that time. Not only have I heard nothing more about him, but I never want to see him again." "Well, my child, get up from your knees. Your tears have purified you. Become a Christian wife and a good mother to your family. May God bless you, my dear daughter, as I bless you." Then he added as I withdrew, "Send your future husband to me. I will chat with him, and then give him the certificates of confession needed for your marriage. " . . . Despite the continuing murmurs of my conscience, I resolved to remain silent. The marriage took place.

For every young girl marrying under her mother's protective shield, the wedding day is a day full of troubled mysteries and charm, but it was for me, abandoned as I was, a day of anguish that increased to an indescribable point. As soon as our friends had left us, and we were finally alone together in the intimacy I so much dreaded, the ghost of the past appeared again. Under this pressure I would perhaps have betrayed my secret in a burst of honest candor had I not been seized by such a powerful feeling of suffocation that I lost consciousness. I don't know how long it lasted. When I came to I was touched by the attentions Voilquin lavished on me and by his intense emotion. I realized that it was too late to trouble his peace of mind. And again I swore to myself to compensate for the unconfessed wrong by consecrating myself to his happiness.

Several days later another intimate drama passed between us, a drama in which I was called upon to begin my role of self-abnegation and consolation all at once. Alas, it had fatal consequences for me, for it ruined the chance of happiness I had counted on from the union—the hope of becoming a mother. . . . A few days after our marriage, when I complained of various symptoms, I noticed that Voilquin questioned me intensely. My answers clearly troubled him. A few moments later he pretended to have some business to attend to and left immediately. He didn't return until late in the evening. When we retired to our room, without showing how upset I was, I pressed him with questions. Instead of receiving a reply I saw him turn pale, begin to tremble, become nervously agitated, stiffen with tension, and finally lose consciousness. This was so unexpected that it forewarned me of the seriousness of the problem, but my compassion for his state prevailed over all other considerations. While trying to revive him I told myself that such a good and loyal person as he could only respond with such powerful feelings to a wrong that was involuntary on his part. When he regained consciousness I spoke only words of tenderness and encouragement. He confessed to me that an inexperienced doctor had declared him to be cured of a serious illness for several months, but unfortunately he was not yet cured.* This morning, after our conversation, he had gone to consult another doctor who had given him proof that he was not over it. This certainty had nearly driven him mad, and he had hoped to calm himself by spending the entire day in the country. I finally came to accept everything, and this shared unhappiness served to bind us closer together. . . .

* Voilquin had a venereal disease.—EDS.

In my long practice of medicine [i.e. as a midwife] I have many times had to record the sad effects of either inexcusable thoughtlessness or lack of respect for a wife—for her beauty and, especially, for her role as mother. How many women and children whose health has been forever destroyed have finally died of this cause! . . .

As for me, in the first five years of my marriage I had to abandon the hope of becoming a mother because of it. Three times I felt a dear tiny being moving about in my womb only to die there before having seen the light of day. How many tears I shed in the silence of the nights as I saw my hopes disappointed again and again. Oh, to have felt near my heart this young life that I bore with so much love perish without my having heard that so-long-desired first cry. Believe me, you would have had to experience these sorrows to appreciate all their bitterness. Words are powerless to express to you the lassitude and disgust for life that each of these crises left deep in my heart. I even came to doubt divine justice. "Must I accept the ruin of my health," I asked myself, "the even more terrible loss of my child as expiations for a sin against society's laws and not against divine indulgence? If God is just, why these new sufferings? Wasn't I recently wronged in a cowardly way? Did I not cry and pray enough? If I was at fault, haven't I redeemed myself by work, courage, and devotion? Oh, sacred maternity, my beloved ideal! Why have you always eluded me? What can I cling to? This marriage to which I have given so much of my life, and from which I have received so little happiness in return, is it not to be blessed?" During such moments of discouragement or during the nights I was unable to sleep, I began to regret the loss of my Catholic faith. I told myself that if I still had the strong faith that had sustained my mother in her laborious and painful life, then perhaps I, like her, would be more resigned. But now that was no longer possible, and there was nothing left in me to control the internal flame that was destroying me.

36. An adulteress confesses to Honoré de Balzac: Louise Abber

Louise Abber was the pseudonym of an unknown woman of the wealthy Parisian bourgeoisie who in 1835 and 1836 wrote several confessional letters to the novelist Honoré de Balzac. Her first letter described her sheltered girlhood and the deep impression the sight of Napoleon and the great classical painter David made on her as a young girl. Had she been a man, she wrote Balzac, she would have become a soldier or an artist. She became instead a respectable wife, the mother of two children, and, after fifteen years of marriage, an adulteress. The letter from which this selection was taken chronicles the mixture of joy and guilt this nineteenth-century woman experienced in breaking her marriage vows; it also evinces the mannered self-importance of the Romantic generation. Abber clearly believed that her personal situation

SOURCE: *Lettres de femmes addressées à Honoré de Balzac. Première série* (1832–36), *Cahiers Balzaciens* (Paris, 1924), 3: 43–46.

was significant. This little drama of illicit sex was, for her, a historical event that she supposed would intrigue a great literary genius as a topic for a future novel. And in fact she was not wrong in this supposition, for adultery was a favorite theme of nineteenth-century writers.

A woman endowed with soul, heart, imagination, and the love of virtue, but also passionate, quixotic, and full of energy, was married to a man who did not love her. For fifteen years she suffered all the *frightful consequences* that a big city can impose on the unfortunate wife of a husband whose passions are excessively intense and all too physical.

(This woman owes it to the truth to state here that she alone in all the world suffered from her husband's life. He was considered delightful by everyone but her—but the passions!)

She remained pure, even in her thoughts, despite the efforts of several men, all of whom wanted to be something in her life. This woman is not at all pretty, she can circulate in a *salon* without being noticed; yet from the time she was thirteen years old, the men admitted to her circle of acquaintances loved her; she was never able to figure out why, but nothing could be more true. Until that time, she had only understood of love what she had read about it, and her severe glance always stopped the improper speeches that were addressed to her. Then a mysterious suffering took hold of her, she cried constantly, everything became dull and cold to her, an illness of the nerves and blood seized her, ennui and disgust with life came to weigh heavily on her heart and stop its beating. They said it was aneurism, poor people!

A man was then received at her home, his position admitted him to her intimate circle; he said he was unhappy, she pitied him, he said he was suffering, she suffered with his suffering, he loved her, she also loved him! A hundred times she wanted to break it off, said so, tried, but circumstances and her heart were both opposed. This frightful battle lasted two years!

It was the third of November last year—my God! she gave herself to him, without wanting to, without second thoughts, carried away by the agitation of her heart, her senses, by unknown new, strong, unbelievable sensations, and especially by the fear of seeing him kill himself or leave for a journey that would compromise his future and his life (ten years before she had almost been responsible for a bloody drama, the effects of which had darkened her entire life); she was afraid, she trembled; finally she forgot everything except for the love she felt for this man! She dishonored the respectable white hair of her father, she did not think of her thirteen-year-old daughter and her beautiful child of seven. In sum, she gave herself.

The hours that followed her error, ah! Monsieur, what pages to write! You understand so well—do I need to depict this desperate shame, mixed nonetheless with happiness, infinite happiness, for here it is my heart and my life that write, and they are expressing the utter truth.

For about six months my emotional life was tumultuous—despair, pleasures, tears, intoxication—but always accompanied by remorse that could not be vanquished! She was jealous, she hid her jealousy; impetuous and violent, she became sweet and fearful, and brought nothing to this liaison but the most absolute truth, without coquetry.

Knowing nothing of this passion she had never experienced, she was visited by too many good feelings, good intentions—even when the criminal feelings continued—to break with him; separate from him, no, for he wanted always to be something in her life, but finally this man was no longer the same; his character, which she had so admired, gave way to hard demands, sweet attentions to irritation, sweet endearments to words that were hard, offensive; finally, two months ago, after two hours of unbearable heartache, she became delirious for almost a day, she opened the gate of the garden in which she happened to live at the time . . . the Seine rolled by below . . . she restrained herself only when the mother in her revealed to her the stain she would place on the lives of her two poor children! . . . A fever, followed by convulsions, brought all her family together around her; what reproaches could she not address to herself?

He learned from her the cause of her illness, he wore a repentant air, but it was only an air; enough, I could say so much more about it!

Today the disenchanted woman cries, bemoans her transgression, hopeless, inconsolable.

Ah! Please, Monsieur, write of the experience of a woman guilty of such an offense, clinging to the affection of her father who, knowing how difficult her experience as a wife has been, praises her, thanks her for living a life he believes to be pure, and to the respect of her family, which she merits so little; of her daughter's presence, a perpetual reproach; of the remorse that torments her like a cancer, all of which make her life horrible. I beg you, write of this dreadful situation. What does one do when one has reached this point?

37. Three medical views on female sexuality

Nineteenth-century sexual prescription and practice were far more complex than the prevalent contemporary stereotype of Victorian prudery and repression suggests. The marriage manual by Auguste Debay (1802–90) from which the first selection is taken was one of the best-selling books in nineteenth-century France, reprinted 172 times in forty years. An ex-army surgeon turned medical popularizer, Debay conveys the dominant French secular vision of regular sexual exercise as a normal and necessary component of private hygiene and public health. In contrast, William Acton (1813–75), a British ex-

SOURCES: (i) Auguste Debay, Hygiène et physiologie du mariage, 153d ed. (Paris, 1880), pp. 17–18, 92, 94–95, 105–9. Originally published in 1849. (ii) William Acton, M.R.C.S., The Functions and Disorders of the Reproductive Organs, 8th American ed. (Philadelphia, 1894), pp. 208–12. Originally published in London in 1857. (iii) Elizabeth Blackwell, "On the Abuses of Sex—II. Fornication," Essays in Medical Sociology (London, 1902), 1: 46–47, 51–58.

pert on venereal disease, presents in this famous passage the classically Victorian concept of female passionlessness. Despite their different opinions about female sexual capacities, however, Debay and Acton agree that wives should consent unselfishly to sexual intercourse for the sake of male health, family harmony, and social stability. The third selection is taken from the writings of Elizabeth Blackwell (1821–1910), who in 1849 gained the distinction of being the first woman to earn a medical degree in the United States. Blackwell's view of female sexuality, based on fifty years' experience as a practicing gynecologist and obstetrician both in America and in England, is very different from that of her male counterparts.

(i) Auguste Debay

Marriage is the only means to channel the genital instinct and to subject it to a moral purpose; it alone can regulate and moderate venereal appetites. We will see below that it is as dangerous to suppress the genital instinct as to give it free rein. The general law of harmony requires a moderate exercise of all the organs in our physical structures. If one of the organs is condemned to absolute repose, the other organs soon suffer, and since the perfect equilibrium of all functions has been destroyed, health is affected and illnesses follow. The genital act is, therefore, a necessity for man and for woman; its absolute privation can only be harmful to the physical and moral health of the individual. . . .

During coitus, the pleasure experienced by the woman is due in large part to the titillation of the clitoris; friction exercised on the erectile tissue of the vagina and the *labia minora* contribute to and increase the amount of pleasure. The voluptuous spasm is less violent in woman than in man; on the other hand it lasts longer. One encounters a few women who, at the slightest contact, become delirious with pleasure, but most require prolonged and repeated caressing in order to reach venereal spasm. The former are nervous women of ardent imagination; the latter are lymphatic women, fat and endowed with a less impressionable nervous system. . . .

From twenty to thirty years of age, a married man may exercise his rights two to four times a week, leaving an interval of a day between times. To exhaust oneself with coitus repeated five and six times a day, as many young people do, is to court trouble later on.

From thirty to forty years, a man should limit himself to twice a week. From forty to fifty, once a week. . . . Continence is a necessity for those over sixty. . . .

The rules of health for women are almost the same as those listed above. . . . Although woman, by reason of the fact that her losses are less, can prolong the venereal act for a greater length of time than man and can repeat it more often, she should nevertheless be temperate in the pleasures of marriage, for such temperance will conserve the freshness of her charms, which would rapidly wither with excess. Solitary sensual pleasures, to which many women, discontented with their husbands, abandon themselves, are a dangerous proceeding that enervate women and predispose them to leukorrhea. . . .

A reasonable woman should always be contented with what her husband is able to do and should never demand more. Where an overly vigorous husband indulges too frequently in genital activity, it is the duty of a wise wife to use all the power she has over him to moderate his ardor, assuage his fires, and make him understand that venereal excesses are not only damaging to the conservation of his virile faculties, but even more deadly to children conceived in a state of exhaustion. . . .

The horizontal position, that is to say the man lying on the woman, is the natural and instinctive position for the union of the sexes in the human race. . . . The peculiar fancy that some wives occasionally experience to take the husband's place disturbs the natural order. . . .

Man loves to see his happiness shared; his sexual pleasures are increased by those experienced by woman, and when the frenzy of pleasure seizes her at the same time as it does him, it seems that life itself escapes from him and is extinguished in the midst of the sweetest sensuality. . . .

If one occasionally finds women who are too amorous, there are many more who sin by the contrary excess and introduce indifference and frigidity into the execution of their conjugal duty to cool off the husband, who is sometimes privately offended by this. When this happens over and over again, he may go to seek the sexual desire he is unable to find in his wife in the arms of a mistress. From that comes estrangement, desertion, reproaches, griefs, hard words, and all the disorders that follow.

It is true that man is brutal. Without bothering himself about the mental and physical state of his wife, he insists, he demands that she grant him what he desires. A refusal can provoke his bad temper and sometimes a tempest!

O wives! Follow this advice. Submit to the demands of your husband in order to attach him to you all the more. Despite the momentary aversion for the pleasures he seeks, force yourself to satisfy him, put on an act and simulate the spasm of pleasure; this innocent trickery is permitted when it is a question of keeping a husband. Believe me, grant with good grace and without hesitation that which would be demanded by force. You well know, alas! that man, seized by desires, is impetuous, sometimes brutal. Have the good sense to drown in your caresses the ardor of this genital fever; this is the only means to rid yourself of his importunities.

O wives! Follow my advice. It will assure you of peace and perhaps even happiness in marriage.

You husbands who wish to keep the respect of your wife, be for your part less despotic in your desires. Before demanding as the master what your appetites desire, bill and coo like a lover. Inquire into her physical state, her mood; respect her unpropitious days; do not trouble her with your desires in those moments of nervous irritation when the soul is sad and the senses are little disposed to pleasure. When you see indifference and repulsion, be wise enough to wait until later. Never take roughly and by force what is refused you; for be on guard! the woman, irritated, may go to seek in the arms of a lover what she does not find with her husband. Think about it, gentlemen; this point deserves your complete attention.

Always be pleasant around your wives; induce the awakening of their sleeping senses by sweetness and tenderness; begin by enchanting their ears with the harmonious notes of the language of love; employ stimulations to the soul and body at the same time, and when your caresses and your delicious preludes have dissipated indifference and inflamed their desires, oh! then you will no longer need to complain of coldness.

(ii) William Acton

We have already mentioned lack of sexual feeling in the female as not an uncommon cause of apparent or temporary impotence in the male. There is so much ignorance on the subject, and so many false ideas are current as to women's sexual condition, and are so productive of mischief, that I need offer no apology for giving here a plain statement that most medical men will corroborate.

I have taken pains to obtain and compare abundant evidence on this subject, and the result of my inquiries I may briefly epitomise as follows:— I should say that the majority of women (happily for society) are not very much troubled with sexual feeling of any kind. What men are habitually, women are only exceptionally. It is too true, I admit, as the Divorce Court shows, that there are some few women who have sexual desires so strong that they surpass those of men, and shock public feeling by their consequences. I admit, of course, the existence of sexual excitement terminating even in nymphomania,* a form of insanity that those accustomed to visit lunatic asylums must be fully conversant with; but, with these sad exceptions, there can be no doubt that sexual feeling in the female is in the majority of cases in abeyance, and that it requires positive and considerable excitement to be roused at all; and even if roused (which in many instances it never can be) it is very moderate compared with that of the male. Many persons, and particularly young men, form their ideas of women's sensuous feeling from what they notice early in life among loose or, at least, low and immoral women. There is always a certain number of females who, though not ostensibly in the ranks of prostitutes, make a kind of a trade of a pretty face. They are fond of admiration, they like to attract the attention of those immediately above them. Any susceptible boy is easily led to believe, whether he is altogether overcome by the syren or not, that she, and therefore all women, must have at least as strong passions as himself. Such women, however, give a very false idea of the condition of female sexual feeling in general. Association with the loose women

---

* I shall probably have no other opportunity of noticing that, as excision of the clitoris has been recommended for the cure of this complaint, Köbelt thinks that it would not be necessary to remove the whole of the clitoris in nymphomania, the same results (that is destruction of venereal desire) would follow if the glans clitoridis had been alone removed, as it is now considered that it is the glans alone in which the sensitive nerves expand. This view I do not agree with, as I have already stated with regard to the analogous structure of the penis. . . . I am fully convinced that in many women there is no special sexual sensation in the clitoris, and I am as positive that the special sensibility dependent on the erectile tissue exists in several portions of the vaginal canal.

of the London streets in casinos and other immoral haunts (who, if they have not sexual feeling, counterfeit it so well that the novice does not suspect but that it is genuine), seems to corroborate such an impression, and as I have stated above, it is from these erroneous notions that so many unmarried men imagine that the marital duties they will have to undertake are beyond their exhausted strength, and from this reason dread and avoid marriage.

Married men—medical men—or married women themselves, would, if appealed to, tell a very different tale, and vindicate female nature from the vile aspersions cast on it by the abandoned conduct and ungoverned lusts of a few of its worst examples.

I am ready to maintain that there are many females who never feel any sexual excitement whatever. Others, again, immediately after each period, do become, to a limited degree, capable of experiencing it; but this capacity is often temporary, and may entirely cease till the next menstrual period. Many of the best mothers, wives, and managers of households, know little of or are careless about sexual indulgences. Love of home, of children, and of domestic duties are the only passions they feel.*

As a general rule, a modest woman seldom desires any sexual gratification for herself. She submits to her husband's embraces, but principally to gratify him; and, were it not for the desire of maternity, would far rather be relieved from his attentions. No nervous or feeble young man need, therefore, be deterred from marriage by any exaggerated notion of the arduous duties required from him. Let him be well assured, on my authority backed by the opinion of many, that the married woman has no wish to be placed on the footing of a mistress. . . .

In strong contrast to the unselfish sacrifices such married women make of their feelings in allowing cohabitation, stand out others, who, either from ignorance or utter want of sympathy, although they are model wives in every other respect, not only evince no sexual feeling, but, on the contrary, scruple not to declare their aversion to the least manifestation of it. Doubtless this may, and often does, depend upon disease, and if so, the sooner the suffering female is treated the better. Much more frequently, however, it depends upon apathy, selfish indifference to please, or unwillingness to overcome a natural repugnance for cohabitation.

Other mental conditions may influence the female. Thus, the High Church enthusiast may consider it her strictly religious duty to be separated from her husband during the forty days of Lent; and . . . I have given an instance of a

* The physiologist will not be surprised that the human female should in these respects differ but little from the female among animals. We well know it as a fact that the female animal will not allow the dog or stallion to approach her except at particular seasons. In many a human female, indeed, I believe, it is rather from the wish of pleasing or gratifying the husband than from any strong sexual feeling, that cohabitation is so habitually allowed. Certainly, during the months of gestation this holds good. I have known instances where the female has during gestation evinced positive loathing for any marital familiarity whatever. In some exceptional cases, indeed, feeling has been sacrificed to duty, and the wife has endured, with all the self-martyrdom of womanhood, what was almost worse than death.

wife refusing to cohabit with her husband because she would not again become a mother. I was lately in conversation with a lady who maintains wom-
en's rights to such an extent that she denied the husband any voice in the
matter, whether or not cohabitation should take place. She maintained, most
strenuously, that as the woman bears the consequences—has all the discomfort of being nine months in the family-way, and thus is obliged to give up
her amusements and many of her social relations—considering too that she
suffers all the pains and risks of childbirth—a married woman has a perfect
right to refuse to cohabit with her husband. I ventured to point out to this
strong-minded female that such conduct on her part might be, in a medical
point of view, highly detrimental to the health of the husband, particularly if
he happened to be strongly sexually disposed. She, however, refused to admit
the validity of my argument, and replied that such a man, unable to control
his feelings, ought to have married a street-walker, not an intellectually disposed person, who could not and ought not to be obliged to devote her time
to duties only compatible with the position of a female drudge or wet-nurse.

I am not prepared to say what weight Sir James Hannen would attach to
such evidence in the case of a man seeking a divorce, and I am not aware that
counsel has as yet urged such conduct on the part of the female in extenuation of immorality on the part of the husband. Of one thing I am quite certain, that many times in the course of the year I am consulted by conscientious
married men, who complain, and I think with reason, that they are debarred
from the privileges of marriage, and that their sexual sufferings are almost
greater than they can bear in consequence of their being mated to women who
think and act as in the above-cited instances. I regret to add that medical
skill can be of little avail here. The more conscientious the husband and the
stronger his sexual feelings, the more distressing are the sufferings he is doomed
to undergo, ultimately too often ending in impotence.

(iii) Elizabeth Blackwell

One of the first subjects to be investigated by the Christian physiologist
is the truth or error of the assertion so widely made, that sexual passion is a
much stronger force in men than in women. Very remarkable results have
flowed from the attempts to mould society upon this assertion. A simple
Christian might reply, "Our religion makes no such distinction; male and
female are as one under guidance and judgment of the Divine law." But the
physiologist must go farther, and use the light of principles underlying
physical truth in order to understand the meaning of facts which arraign
and would destroy Christianity.

This mental element of human sex exists in major proportion in the vital
force of women, and justifies the statement that the compound faculty of sex
is as strong in woman as in man. Those who deny sexual feeling to women,
or consider it so light a thing as hardly to be taken into account in social
arrangements, confound appetite and passion; they quite lose sight of this
immense spiritual force of attraction, which is distinctly human sexual power,
and which exists in so very large a proportion in the womanly nature. The

impulse towards maternity is an inexorable but beneficent law of woman's nature, and it is a law of sex.

The different form which physical sensation necessarily takes in the two sexes, and its intimate connection with and development through the mind (love) in women's nature, serve often to blind even thoughtful and pains-taking persons as to the immense power of sexual attraction felt by women. Such one-sided views show a misconception of the meaning of human sex in its entirety.

The affectionate husbands of refined women often remark that their wives do not regard the distinctively sexual act with the same intoxicating physical enjoyment that they themselves feel, and they draw the conclusion that the wife possesses no sexual passion. A delicate wife will often confide to her medical adviser (who may be treating her for some special suffering) that at the very time when marriage love seems to unite them most closely, when her husband's welcome kisses and caresses seem to bring them into profound union, comes an act which mentally separates them, and which may be either indifferent or repugnant to her. But it must be understood that it is not the special act necessary for parentage which is the measure of the compound moral and physical power of sexual passion; it is the profound attraction of one nature to the other which marks passion, and delight in kiss and caress— the love-touch—is physical sexual expression as much as the special act of the male.

It is well known that terror or pain in either sex will temporarily destroy all physical pleasure. In married life, injury from childbirth, or brutal or awkward conjugal approaches, may cause unavoidable shrinking from sexual congress, often wrongly attributed to absence of sexual passion. But the severe and compound suffering experienced by many widows who were strong-ly attached to their lost partners is also well known to the physician, and this is not simply a mental loss that they feel, but an immense physical depri-vation. It is a loss which all the senses suffer by the physical as well as moral void which death has created.

Although physical sexual pleasure is not attached exclusively, or in woman chiefly, to the act of coition, it is also a well-established fact that in healthy, loving women, uninjured by the too frequent lesions which result from childbirth, increasing physical satisfaction attaches to the ultimate physical expression of love. A repose and general well-being results from this natural occasional intercourse, whilst the total deprivation of it produces irritability.

On the other hand, the growth in men of the mental element in sexual passion, from mighty wifely love, often comes like a revelation to the husband. The dying words of a man to the wife who, sending away children, friends, every distraction, had bent the whole force of her passionate nature to holding the beloved object in life—"I never knew before what love meant"—indicates the revelation which the higher element of sexual passion should bring to the lower phase. It is an illustration of the parallelism and natural harmony be-tween the sexes. The prevalent fallacy that sexual passion is the almost ex-clusive attribute of men, and attached exclusively to the act of coition—a fallacy which exercises so disastrous an effect upon our social arrangements—arises from ignorance of the distinctive character of human sex—viz., its powerful mental element. A tortured girl, done to death by brutal soldiers, may possess a stronger power of human sexual passion than her destroyers.

The comparison so often drawn between the physical development of the comparatively small class of refined and guarded women, and the men of worldly experience whom they marry, is a false comparison. These women have been taught to regard sexual passion as lust and as sin—a sin which it would be a shame for a pure woman to feel, and which she would die rather than confess. She has not been taught that sexual passion is love, even more than lust, and that its ennobling work in humanity is to educate and transfigure the lower by the higher element. The growth and indications of her own nature she is taught to condemn, instead of to respect them as foreshadowing that mighty impulse towards maternity which will place her nearest to the Creator if reverently accepted. . . .

Some medical writers have considered that women are more tyrannically governed than men by the impulses of physical sex. They have dwelt upon the greater proportion of work laid upon women in the reproduction of the race, the prolonged changes and burden of maternity, and the fixed and marked periodical action needed to maintain the aptitude of the physical frame for maternity. They have drawn the conclusion that sex dominates the life of women, and limits them in the power of perfect human growth. This would undoubtedly be the case were sex simply a physical function.

The fact in human nature which explains, guides, and should elevate the sexual nature of woman, and mark the beneficence of Creative Force, is this very mental element which distinguishes human from brute sex. This element, gradually expanding under religious teaching and the development of true religious sentiment, becomes the ennobling power of love. Love between the sexes is the highest and mightiest form of human sexual passion. . . .

This power of sex in women is strikingly shown in the enormous influence which they exert upon men for evil. It is not the cold beauty of a statue which enthrals and holds so many men in terrible fascination; it is the living, active power of sexual life embodied in its separate overpowering female phase. The immeasurable depth of degradation into which those women fall, whose sex is thoroughly debased, who have intensified the physical instincts of the brute by the mental power for evil possessed by the human being, indicates the mighty character of sexual power over the nature of woman for corruption. It is also a measure of what the ennobling power of passion may be.

Happily in all civilized countries there is a natural reserve in relation to sexual matters which indicates the reverence with which this high social power of our human nature should be regarded. It is a sign of something wrong in education, or in the social state, when matters which concern the subject of sex are discussed with the same freedom and boldness as other matters. This subject should neither be a topic of idle gossip, of unreserved publicity, nor of cynical display. This natural and beneficial instinct of reserve, springing from unconscious reverence, renders it difficult for one sex to measure and judge the vital power of the other. The independent thought and large observation of each sex is needed in order to arrive at truth. Unhappily, however, women are often falsely instructed by men, for a licentious husband inevitably depraves the sentiment of his wife, because vicious habits have falsified his nature and blinded his perception of the moral law which dominates sexual growth.

Each sex has its own stern battle to fight in resisting temptation, in walking resolutely towards the higher aim of life. It is equally foolish and misleading to attempt to weigh the vital qualities of the sexes, and measure justice and mercy, law and custom, by the supposed results. It is difficult for the child to comprehend that a pound of feathers can weigh as much as a pound of lead. Much of our thought concerning men and women is as rudimentary as the child's. Vast errors of law and custom have arisen in the slow unfolding of human nature from failure to realize the extent of the injury produced by that abuse of sex—fornication. We have not hitherto perceived that, on account of the moral degradation and physical disease which it inevitably produces, lustful trade in the human body is a grave social crime.

In forming a wiser judgment for future guidance, it must be distinctly recognised that the assertion that sexual passion commands more of the vital force of men than of women is a false assertion, based upon a perverted or superficial view of the facts of human nature. Any custom, law, or religious teaching based upon this superficial and essentially false assertion, must necessarily be swept away with the prevalence of sounder physiological views.

38. An American woman writes to her close friend: Mary Hallock Foote

The four letters (or parts of letters) that follow chronicle the early years of an intense friendship between two women that lasted half a century. The writer, Mary (Molly) Hallock (1847–1938), was raised in a genteel though far from wealthy Quaker family in Milton, New York. She studied art at Cooper Union in New York City, where in 1866 she met her lifelong friend Helena de Kay, who later married a poet and editor, Richard Gilder. Following her own marriage to Arthur Foote, a mining engineer, Molly went west and lived in a series of mining camps. While raising her children, she retained ties with the cultured East by publishing her graphics and stories about western life, and through her intimate correspondence with Helena.

After completing her artistic training, Molly Hallock returned to Milton

SOURCE: Mary Hallock Foote Papers, Special Collections, C. H. Green Library, Stanford University. The editors are indebted to Professor Carroll Smith-Rosenberg, University of Pennsylvania, for her guidance to various items in this correspondence; to Leslie Henner for the opportunity to consult her Stanford senior honors thesis dealing with these letters; and to Florian Shasky, Michele Leiser, and Pat Palmer of Special Collections, Green Library, for facilitating our use of the correspondence.

to live with her family. The first excerpt closes a letter written in 1869 in which she discusses her artistic work. Hallock wrote the second letter to make up with de Kay who, piqued that Hallock had bowed to family pressure to remain home rather than joining her in New York, had suddenly canceled a projected visit. Hallock later referred to this letter as "an awfully spoony letter." The last two letters were written after de Kay—despite her reservations about the effect marriage might have on her artistic career—had become engaged to Gilder. At this time Hallock was herself contemplating marriage to Foote.

[Mary Hallock to Helena de Kay, spring 1869, Milton, N.Y.]
Father is shutting the shutters ostentatiously and otherwise hinting that it is bedtime—Good night sweetheart—all send love to you and wish to see you—but I long for you—When you are here some stifling night like this we will creep out in the darkness and bare ourselves in the fountain. It splashes very temptingly now. Always lovingly thine, Molly.

[Mary Hallock to Helena de Kay, Sept. 23, 1873, Fishkill Landing, N.Y.]
My dear dear Girl
    Your letter came this morning just after Phil & I had been getting your room ready and making your bed—*our* bed where I thought I should lie tonight with my dear girl's arm under my head—It gave me a queer little sick trembly feeling that I've only had once or twice in my life—and then I thought I *must* see you—not to "talk things over"—I don't care about *things* —I only want you to love me—So I hurried & changed my dress & pulled my ruffle down low in front to please my girl, and rushed into the garden for a bunch of roses—your June roses, blooming late just for you—(We have been hoarding them and begging the buds to wait a few days longer for your coming)—then down to the Albany boat—I thought I'd either coax you to land—or go on with you as far as West Point.
    I wanted so to put my arms round my girl of all the girls in the world and tell her that whether I go to N. Y. or stay home, whether she sign herself "very truly your friend" or "your ownest of girls" I love her as wives do (not) love their husbands as *friends* who have taken each other for life—and believe in her as I believe in my God—Please don't mind about my decisions— they are not the real thing—It isn't whether we believe the same thing but whether we believe in each other and, dear Helena, I do believe in you and have faith in you in spite of the little jeer at "you people of faith"—You are not my "neighbor" but my chosen friend, chosen deliberately out of all the girls I have known—You believe that Love has its tides—Well there was a strong ebb tide this summer—I can't explain to you all that caused it now—many things combined—but it only shows me how much *you* (not your opinions, or words or deeds always) but you, the great heart & soul of you, are to me! *Little* streams don't have any tide—do you mind that?
    Now please don't call yourself very truly my friend again, will you honey? And love me just the same when I'm at home as when I'm in New York— All that my decision amounts to is this—that I must stick to the family and

to home-life—I'm *not* going to bury myself—I'm often coming down to you with my stuff—I'm going to have a room to myself and really work—I have never done justice to my home advantages—If I had great Genius it might be worth while to sacrifice my home, but hundreds & hundreds can do my Art work better than I can—*no one* can fill my home & family relations for me—Father & mother have done everything in the world for me—I am *not going* to live a life that will imply that while I love *them*, I must seek a more congenial & stimulating atmosphere than their society affords. If my Art cannot exist in my father's house where I belong, it will have to cease to be a part of me. But I think that my kind of work can be done at *home*—We will see. I didn't mean to enter upon this. . . . We will look in each other's eyes—we two—and I shall see my brown-eyed maid—mine—I can stand arguments & scoldings but "truly your friend"—I cannot stand from one who once called herself mine—As for the chill—I'm a donkey—If I didn't love you do you suppose I'd care about anything or have ridiculous notions & panics and behave like an old fool who ought to know better—I'm going to be sensible now & forever more—And I'm going to hang onto your skirts, young woman, genius tho' you may be. You can't get away from the love of your own M A H.

[Mary Hallock to "Cousin Richard" Gilder, Helena de Kay's fiancé, Dec. 13, 1873, Milton, N.Y.]

Do you know, sir, until *you* came I believe she loved me almost as girls love their lovers—*I know I loved her so.* Don't you wonder that I can bear the sight of you? I don't know another man who *could* make it seem "right." You must have been born to make her future complete and she was born to kindle your Genius. Isn't it wonderful how it flamed up at her touch—It was there but as unborn crystals are—as jewels in a dark room—She is the most inspiring being I ever saw who was herself so inspired. How can she be so passive and so active all at once!

[Mary Hallock to Helena de Kay, late December 1873, Milton, N.Y.]

Arthur Foote wishes me to meet his sister—She was his dearest woman before I came—I half dread to meet her, but now seems a good time to get over a doubtful experiment.

I was afraid to answer your last letter for fear of again indulging in untimely congratulations on a destiny which is so hard for you in its present aspect. It was because I feel so sure that the right way of living must in the end bring the surest peace & happiness, that I exulted over your sacrifice, forgetting the cost. It *is* right for you to give up personal ambition (I think) and follow the highest law of your nature—Cannot you feel at rest, now that the fight is over, and trust to the love that brought you thus far carrying you on to the end? Alas, I feel helpless to talk to you about it! I feel that perhaps every word of mine jars on your sensitive—tensely strung mood! We see the same thing, but on utterly different sides. Dear Helena I wish you would not speak as if my love for you were a thing of the past—taking it for granted that indifference is all you are to expect. Cannot I make you understand that the change which you speak of is not a *lessening* of my love for you, but the result of a revolution which must change the *nature* of *all* my relations. I did not love my mother less when your influence was stronger with me than hers— You know, dear Helena, I was really in love with you—it was a passion such as I had never known till I saw you—I don't think it was the noblest way to love you—When this new strange feeling came to me, for a few months all my old landmarks swam, in a strange troubled dream about me—There is tumult sometimes even in a shallow, hill-locked mill pond (for such I am perhaps). In that tumult many things *perished* among others that *passion* for you, but the *love* which is in my heart for all time, you must learn by testing it—I am not *first* with you—you are not first with me—Something has come to us both which stands alone and will not be denied—but it is no more sure & lasting than the mother & sister loves, and perhaps may prove less satisfying. It is to me a thing I have nothing to do with—it came to me unsought while my mind was fixed upon other people & other interests—it took possession of me un- awares—I would not believe in it, or realize that my world & my life were changing—I clung to the old & denied the new (in *my own heart*; this is all inside history) until at last came a sudden light & happiness—tremulous, unreal—it lasted only a day or two in the happening—but it has gone to the roots of my life—This is the change in me—it is the same with you, is it not? It involves no destruction of the old, but a clearer, quieter, healthier love in the New Year that is before us. May I come on Friday week, or will it tire you to see me—Do please trust a little more in the love of Thy sister M. A. H.

39. Passing women

The unconventional lives of the two women described in these selections may have been possible only in the marginal subcultures of the theater or the criminal underworld. The first selection is from a newspaper article about Jeanne Bonnett (1849–76), a French-born San Franciscan who supported her- self by catching frogs for sale to restaurants and by various criminal activities. Bonnett, a "passing woman"—a woman who passed as a man—was repeatedly arrested for wearing male attire. She had organized a thieves' ring of ex-prosti- tutes in San Francisco, and her unsolved murder in 1876 may have been due to her relationship with Blanche Buneau (Beunon), one of the prostitutes she freed from a pimp. The second selection tells the story of Annie Hindle, a British-born male impersonator and stage personality who, in 1886, formally married her dresser, Annie Ryan, in a religious ceremony in Grand Rapids, Michigan. The couple lived together in a small community with no undue attention paid to them by their neighbors until Ryan's death in 1892.

SOURCES: (i) "Jeanne Bonnett. The Mysterious Murder in San Miguel in 1876," *San Francisco Call*, Oct. 19, 1879. The editors thank Allan Berube, San Francisco, for contributing this document. (ii) "Romance of the Stage," clipping from the *Chicago Herald*, Dec. 27, 1892, in *Biographical Material*, 1: 542c, Clelia D. Mosher Papers, Stanford University Archives, C. H. Green Library.

(i) Jeanne Bonnett

Jeanne Bonnett . . . was a native of France about twenty-five years of age. She was medium height, with dark hair and regular features. In the last years of her life her face always wore a look of strong determination, which was seldom brightened by a smile. She was the eldest daughter of Paul and Marie Bonnett, who, in the early days of San Francisco, were members of the French Theatrical troup, which the French population then supported, When Jeanne reached a suitable age she appeared on the stage in juvenile parts, and soon became a great favorite with the audiences. . . . Had she but followed the course marked out for her she would probably have become a bright ornament in the profession of her parents, but when she reached the threshold of womanhood she evinced a disposition to "go it alone" . . . spurned the advice of family and friends, and hastened down the broad road to moral destruction. She became imbued with a spirit of that heroism so graphically depicted in dime novels, and at one time cursed the day that she was born a female instead of a male. Her ambition was to become the Captain of a gang of robbers, which would terrorize the community as did the brigands in Sicily.

To carry her ideas into effect she discarded those garments which fashion has decreed should be worn by the gentler sex and donned those worn by men. In this apparel, and with hair cut short, she had the appearance of a beardless boy of eighteen. She organized a gang of young boys who belonged to the criminal class and started them off in various parts of the city. . . . With the breaking up of this band Jeanne's fondest hopes were destroyed, and she turned man-hater, vowing to treat man only as she would a cur; at the same time declared that she would make herself, as far as lay in her power, the friend of those women of her nationality. She took to the mountains of San Mateo County, and there caught frogs, which she sold to the first-class restaurants in this city. From pursuing this occupation she acquired the name of "The Little Frog Catcher," and succeeded in earning a good living. The only companions she had while engaged in this pursuit were a few pot hunters and frog catchers who lived in the woods, and were ruled by her as if they were slaves.

[Blanche Buneau], the companion of Jeanne, was one of those women already described. She came to this city in company with one Arthur Deneve, a man who in France had been a ticket-seller in one of the minor theatres, and with whom she had lived as mistress. Upon their arrival here, he forced her to enter upon a life of shame, and to support him in idleness upon the proceeds. Before she had been here many months, she became the mother of a child, which shortly after birth was turned over to the tender mercies of a wet nurse. Jeanne had formed a resolve to step in between as many women of Blanche's character and men of Deneve's stripe as she possibly could, and cause a separation. At the time she met Blanche, she had already caused a number of these unfortunate women to dismiss their lovers and cut them off from an easy but disgraceful living. After some urging on the part of

Jeanne, Blanche consented to give Deneve her card, upon which she wrote the society letters P.P.C. (*pour prenne congé*).* Deneve ... raved and threatened, and swore vengeance against the one who had brought about the separation. He then sought to have Blanche change her resolution and return to him, but she was inexorable, telling him that he must go his way, and let her follow the path she had chosen for herself. Finding that neither prayer nor threat would move her, he, without her knowledge, and during her absence from the place she called home, disposed of all the household effects and pocketed the proceeds, a small amount only, as they were of but little value. He then had her child secretly removed, and entrusted an intimate friend with the name of the persons with whom he had placed it. When Blanche returned she found herself homeless, and was apprised of the removal of her child. Bad as she was, in a moral point of view, she had not lost her mother's natural love for her child, and she made a diligent but unavailing search for her offspring. This severe and unlooked-for blow had such an effect upon her that she took to drinking. When she recovered from the effects of the debauch she went to San Miguel [a village near San Luis Obispo, in northern California] and took room and board at the house of Mons. Logis, on the old county road. This place was a resort for women of her class. While there, she was visited by Jeanne, who was not a welcome guest, and who persuaded her to leave and accompany her to McNamara's house.

During Thursday, the 14th of September, Jeanne and Blanche had not been together very much, Jeanne having been to the frog-pond in the vicinity of the Seventeen Mile House. Upon her return, Blanche noticed that one of her eyes was discolored, and asked what had happened. Her reply was that she had fallen from her horse, on which she always rode man-fashion. . . .

At half past eight o'clock at night, the two women, who occupied the front bedroom in McNamara's house, got ready for bed. Jeanne summoned McNamara, and had him bring her a glass of brandy, and after he had brought it, was asked by Blanche to nail up the window-blind, which had fallen. This he did, and then went into the kitchen. Jeanne followed after him, went to the porch, returned in a few moments, and hastily undressing herself, sprang into bed, lying near the wall. Blanche then sat on the edge of the bed, about half-way between the head and the foot, and was in the act of stooping to unlace one of her shoes when there was the report of the discharge of a firearm, a crash of glass, a sudden darkening of the room, a cry of pain, and the exclamation, "Qu'est que c'est ça? Blanche, j'ai reçu une balle. C'est fini, je meurs. Je suis ma soeur." ("What is that? Blanche, a bullet has struck me. The end has come. I die. I go to meet my sister.") Blanche, affrighted, sprang for the door screaming for help, and then rushed into the barroom, where she met McNamara coming towards her and asking what had happened. Pointing to the bed-room, Blanche cried out, "Jeanne is dead."

* A colloquial version of *pour prendre congé*, to take a holiday. We have corrected the French spelling elsewhere in this piece.—EDS.

(ii) Annie Hindle and Annie Ryan

There was a funeral on the Jersey City Heights the other day and it brought together as mourners a dozen men and women who were once famous in an odd way on the American stage. They gathered in the little parlor of a pretty cottage; they sat for a little while around a handsome coffin; they talked in low and sad voices about the masses of flowers which were heaped upon the bier; they had a good word to say of the woman who lay dead among the palms, the roses and the smilax; and they seemed genuinely sorry for the chief mourner. She was a striking person in every way. Her face was masculine in all its lines; her eyes were gray, but lit with a kindly expression; her mouth was firmly cut, and though her lips quivered with emotion one could detect that this mourner was a woman of great mental force and capabilities. She was probably between forty-five and fifty years of age. . . .

When Annie Hindle was five years old, the woman who had adopted her and who gave the protege her own name, put her on the stage in the pottery district of Hertfordshire in England. The little girl sang well very early. There was a fearlessness in her manner that tickled her rough audiences, and they made a favorite of her from the very first. At the outset she sang tender songs with love as their theme, but as she grew and traveled to London she enlarged her repertory. One day, half in jest, she put on a man's costume and sang a rolicking ditty about wine, women and the races. A shrewd manager who listened to her saw a new field open to her. In a week Annie Hindle was a "male impersonator" and all London was talking about the wonderful accuracy of her mimicry. An American manager bargained with her, and about 1867 she came to New York, to triumph here as completely as she had triumphed in London. She was a blond, about 5 feet 6 inches, with a plump form, well-shaped hands, small feet and closely cropped hair, which, on and off the stage, she parted on one side, brushing it away from the temples, as men do. Her voice was deeper than an alto, yet it was sweet and she sang true and with great expression. She was the first out and out "male impersonator" New York's stage had ever seen. . . .

In the summer of 1886 Annie Hindle's dresser and faithful companion was [Annie Ryan] a pretty little brunette of twenty-five, a quiet demure girl who made friends wherever she went. She accompanied Hindle to and from the theatre and she was a most valuable help to the singer. One night in June, 1886, Annie Hindle and Annie Ryan left the Grand Rapids theatre where Hindle was then engaged, and drove to the Barnard House. In room 19 a minister of the gospel, Rev. E. H. Brooks, awaited the couple. There was a best man—jolly Gilbert Saroney, who oddly enough, was a female impersonator, but there was no bridesmaid. At 10 o'clock Rev. Dr. Brooks performed the marriage ceremony, and solemnly pronounced Annie Hindle the husband of Annie Ryan. The female groom wore a dress suit; the bride was in her traveling costume. The minister put a fat fee in his pocketbook, and Mr. Saroney, the female impersonator, and Miss Hindle, the new husband, opened a bottle of wine and smoked a cigarette or two. There was a sensation in Grand Rapids, of course, but the clergyman defended his action manfully. "I knew all the circumstances," he said. "The groom gave me her— I mean his—name as Charles Hindle, and he assured me that he was a man. The bride is a sensible girl and she was of age. I had no other course to pursue. I believe they love each other and that they will be happy."

The bride was happy and the clergyman was right—her happiness ended only with her death, for she it was around whose coffin Annie Hindle and her friends gathered the other day in the little cottage on the Jersey Heights. For four or five years Annie Hindle and her wife had lived in this cozy nest, which Hindle had built years ago with her savings. The neighbors respected them. The outer world did not disturb them with its gossip. That they could live together openly as man and wife, the husband always in female attire, and yet cause no scandal, is the best proof of the esteem in which those around them held them. No children were born to them, and perhaps that is why Annie Hindle, with tears in her eyes, told your correspondent that the best of her life is gone.

40. Contraception in England, France, and the United States

A graduate of Dartmouth medical college, Charles Knowlton (1800–1850) became famous with the publication of 'Fruits of Philosophy, or the Private Companion of Young Married People' (1832). The treatise, which advocated the use of birth control on medical, economic, and social grounds, challenged many of the accepted values and medical theories of the period; as a result, the author of this "scurrilous" publication was prosecuted, fined, and sentenced to three months in jail. The official reaction to Knowlton's work, however, did not in any way reflect the favorable public response to it: the book went through nine American editions. The work was published in England in 1834, but achieved little notoriety until 1877, when Charles Bradlaugh and Annie Besant, advocates of freedom of the press, were prosecuted for publishing it. As in the United States, the result of this prosecution was to popularize Knowlton's book, which now began to sell over 250,000 copies a year. In addition, the publicity given to 'Fruits of Philosophy' in the trial may have spawned a demand for new contraceptive techniques in England.

The French, by contrast, simply practiced birth control without writing or publishing much about it. Demographic studies suggest the widespread usage of contraception, probably coitus interruptus, even before 1800 in

SOURCES: (i) Charles Knowlton, *Fruits of Philosophy, or the Private Companion of Young Married People* (London, n.d.), pp. 33–36. (ii) Louis-François-Étienne Bergeret, *The Preventive Obstacle, or Conjugal Onanism*, tr. P. de Marmon (New York, 1870), pp. 3–4, 12, 20–22, 25, 56–57, 100–101, 111–13. Originally published in Paris in 1868.

France, more than two generations earlier than in any other country. In the second selection Dr. Louis-F.-E. Bergeret (b. 1814), chief physician of the Arbois Hospital (Jura), reports on the cases he has had to treat as a result of what he calls sexual or conjugal frauds, especially the "dangerous practice of Onan" (withdrawal). In his belief that severe illness and even death followed from such practices, Bergeret reflects the standard French medical opinion, but in spite of such warnings, the French birthrate continued to fall.

(i) Charles Knowlton

There have been several means proposed and practised for *checking* conception. I shall briefly notice them, though a knowledge of the *best* is what concerns us. That of withdrawal immediately before emission is certainly effectual, if practised with sufficient care. But if, (as I believe), Dr. Dewees' theory of conception be correct; and as Spallanzani's experiments show that only a trifle of semen even largely diluted with water may impregnate by being injected into the vagina, it is clear that nothing short of entire withdrawal is to be depended on.* But the old notion that the semen must enter the uterus to cause conception, has led many to believe that a partial withdrawal is sufficient, and it is on this account that this error has proved mischievous, as all important errors generally do. It is said by those who speak from experience, that the practice of withdrawal has an effect upon the health similar to temperance in eating. As the subsequent exhaustion is, probably, mainly owing to the shock the nervous system sustains in the act of coition, this opinion may be correct. It is further said that this practice serves to keep alive those fine feelings with which married people first come together. Still I leave it for every one to decide for himself whether this check be so far satisfactory as not to render some other very desirable.

As to the baudruche, which consists in a covering used by the male made of very delicate skin, it is by no means calculated to come into general use. It has been used to secure from syphilitic affections.

Another check which the old idea of conception has led some to recommend, with considerable confidence, consists in introducing into the vagina, previous to connexion, a very delicate piece of sponge, moistened with water, to be immediately afterwards withdrawn by means of a very narrow ribbon attached to it. But as our views would lead us to expect, this check has not proved a sure preventive. As there are many little ridges or folds in the vagina, we cannot suppose the withdrawal of the sponge would dislodge all the semen in every instance. If, however, it were well moistened with some liquid which acts chemically upon the semen, it would be pretty likely to destroy the fecundating property of what might remain. But if this check were ever so sure, it would, in my opinion, fall short of being equal, all things considered, to the one I am about to mention—one which not only dislodges

---

* William P. Dewees was a nineteenth-century American physician and professor of midwifery. Lazzaro Spallanzani was an eighteenth-century Italian anatomist and physiologist.—EDS.

the semen pretty effectually; but at the same time destroys the fecundating property of the whole of it.

It consists in syringing the vagina immediately after connexion, with a solution of sulphate of zinc, of alum, pearlash, or any salt that acts chemically on the semen, and at the same time produces no unfavourable effect on the female. In all probability, a vegetable astringent would answer—as an infusion of white oak bark, of red rose leaves, of nutgalls, and the like. A lump of either of the above-mentioned salts, of the size of a chestnut, may be dissolved in a pint of water, making the solution weaker or stronger, as it may be borne without producing any irritation to the parts to which it is applied. These solutions will not lose their virtues by age. A *female syringe*, which will be required in the use of this check, may be had at the shop of an apothecary, for a shilling or less. If preferred, the semen may be dislodged, as far as it can be by syringing with simple water, after which some of the solution is to be injected, to destroy the fecundating property of what may remain lodged between the ridges of the vagina, &c.

I know the use of this check requires the woman to leave her bed for a few moments, but this is its only objection, and it would be unreasonable to suppose that any check can ever be devised entirely free of objections. In its favour, it may be said, it costs nearly nothing; it is sure; it requires no sacrifice of pleasure; it is in the hands of the female; it is to be used *after*, instead of before connexion, a weighty consideration in its favour, as a moment's reflection will convince any one; and last, but not least, it is conducive to cleanliness and preserves the parts from relaxation and disease. The vagina may be very much contracted by a persevering use of astringent injections, and they are frequently used for this purpose, in cases of *procidentia uteri*, or a sinking down of the womb. Subject as women are to fluor albus [leukorrhea] and other diseases of the genital organs, it is rather a matter of wonder they are not more so considering the prevailing practices. Those who have used this check, (and some have used it to my certain knowledge, with entire success, for nine or ten years, and under such circumstances as leave no room to doubt its efficacy), affirm they would be at the trouble of using injections merely for the purposes of health and cleanliness. . . .

What has now been advanced in this work will enable the reader to judge for himself, or herself, of the efficacy of the chemical or syringe check, and time will probably determine whether I am correct in this matter; for I do know that those married females who have much desire to escape, will not stand for the little trouble of using this check, especially when they consider that on the score of cleanliness and health alone, it is worth all this trouble. A great part of the time no check is necessary, and women of experience and observation, with the information conveyed by this work, will be able to judge pretty correctly when it is and when it is not. They may rest assured that none of the salts mentioned will have any deleterious effect. The sulphate of zinc is commonly known by the name of white vitriol. This, as well as alum, have been much used for leucorrhœa. Acetate of lead would doubtless be effectual—indeed, it has proved to be so; but I do not recommend it, because I conceive it possible that a long continued use of it might impair the instinct.

I hope that no failures will be charged to inefficacy of this check which ought to be attributed to negligence, or insufficient use of it. I will therefore recommend at least two applications of the syringe, the sooner the surer: yet it is my opinion that five minutes' delay would not prove mischievous, perhaps not ten.

(ii) Louis-F.-E. Bergeret

One of the most powerful instincts nature has placed in the heart of man is that which has for its object the perpetuation of the human race. But this instinct, this inclination, so active, which attracts one sex towards the other, is liable to be perverted, to deviate from the path nature has laid out. From this arises a number of fatal aberrations which exercise a deplorable influence upon the individual, upon the family and upon society. I have observed such painful examples of this, I have been so struck by the disastrous consequences which have resulted from this cause, that I cannot resist the desire of giving publicity to my observations.

We hear constantly that marriages are less fruitful, that the increase of population does not follow its former ratio. I believe that this is mainly attributable to genesiac frauds. It might naturally be supposed that these odious calculations of egotism, these shameful refinements of debauchery, are met with almost entirely in large cities, and among the luxurious classes; and that small towns and country places yet preserve that simplicity of manners attributed to primitive society, when the *pater familias* was proud of exhibiting his numerous offspring. Such, however, is not the case, and I shall show that those who have an unlimited confidence in the patriarchal habits of our country people are deeply in error. At the present time frauds are practised by all classes. . . .

The laboring classes are generally satisfied with the practice of Onan, pederasty, or other modes *in vase indebito*. They are seldom familiar with the sheath invented by Dr. Condom, and bearing his name.

Among the wealthy, on the other hand, the use of this preservative is generally known. It favors frauds by rendering them easier; but it does not afford complete security . . .

Case X.—This couple belongs to two respectable families of vintners. They are both pale, emaciated, downcast, sickly.

The physiognomy of the husband is suggestive of the fair, flaxen sons of Germany, within whose blue eyes lurk the fires that consumed Werther.

The wife with her dark, though pallid complexion, her bright black eyes, flashing with passion, resembles the ardent daughters of the South.

They have been married for ten years; they first had two children, one immediately after the other, but in order to avoid an increase of family, they have had recourse to conjugal frauds. Being both very amorous, they have found this practice very convenient to satisfy their inclinations. They have employed it to such an extent, that up to a few months ago, when their health began to fail, the husband had intercourse with his wife habitually two and three times in the twenty-four hours.

The following is the condition of the woman: She complains of continual pains in the lower part of the abdomen and kidneys. These pains disturb the functions of the stomach and render her nervous. The pains are accompanied by abundant leucorrhœa and menorrhagia, which exhaust her. By the touch we find a very intense heat, great sensibility to pressure, and all the signs of a chronic metritis. The patient attributes positively her present state to the too frequent approaches of her husband.

The husband does not attempt to exculpate himself, as he also is in a state of extreme suffering. It is not in the genital organs, however, that we find his disorder, but in the whole general nervous system; his history will find its place in the part of this work relative to general disturbances. . . .

Case XIV.—Mrs. X—. Married young, she had a male child the first year. The father declares that his son must be the sole heir of his fortune, in order to perpetuate the fatuous tradition of the family; but being of very ardent passions, he has with his wife very frequent and fraudulent connections.

Five or six years pass in this way without any trouble; but, towards the age of thirty, this lady begins to feel heavy pains in the hypogastrium and kidneys. Very soon these pains become continued and intolerable. She cannot bear copulation; she is obliged to spend most of her time in bed; her existence is miserable, her nervous system excited, her moral nature deeply affected.

After a rather long treatment, which had somewhat modified her state, she goes to spend the summer season at the springs of Plombieres, and comes back much better.

I then advise her to become pregnant. This happens without delay, and gestation causes no inconvenience.

After her confinement, Mrs. X recovers perfectly; all lesions of the uterus have completely disappeared.

She has since had two more children, and her health has continued to be good. . . .

Case LV.—Mme. X—. Married very young; in the first year she has a boy, who is received with the greatest joy. The husband takes his oath that he will stop there, and remains faithful to it. He has been heard many times to ridicule plain people, who do not recoil from the prospect of a large family. This improvident defrauder was cruelly punished; his son died at the age of sixteen, of typhoid fever.

He immediately set to work to repair the misfortune; but his wife, during her long period of unfruitfulness which had been sullied by the continued frauds of her husband, had come to me to complain of acute pains in the womb. A new conception was sought in vain—all aptitude to pregnancy had vanished; there was sterility and despair.

Nevertheless, after two years of useless attempts and the use of all sorts of means to favor conception, I one day met the husband with a happy countenance; his wife was pregnant.

But his joy was of short duration. The uterine functions, revived for a moment, had not the strength to bear the fruit long enough; she miscarried at five months.

All subsequent attempts at fecundation failed, with an organ inert and powerless. . . .

Case XCI—A married couple present themselves before me with pale and haggard faces.

The woman is suffering from a very painful gastralgia.

The husband complains of all sorts of troubles, which may be summed up in a very distressing hypochondriasis.

They both complain of leading a miserable life. They are still quite young; the man is thirty, and the woman twenty-six. Married for nine years, they had several children very promptly; later, they began to employ fraudulent stratagems: both being very passionate, they have abused these without limitation.

Nevertheless—and I would call attention to this circumstance, as indicating how physicians may be misled by false answers from patients whose lips are sealed by a sense of shame from making painful avowals—on my first questioning the husband concerning conjugal frauds, he replied unhesitatingly in the negative, and protested even against such a suspicion. His provoked wife, however, cast in his teeth these two words: "You lie;" and then declared that I had put my finger upon the wound, and that she had for some time noticed that she had gastric pains, especially after fraudulent connection.

I then prescribed conception, and, after the woman should become pregnant, abstinence. Eight months afterwards I met them. They both looked very well; their physiognomy was quite changed; the abdomen of the woman indicated all the visible signs of a pregnancy approaching term.

The physician must then mistrust very much such affirmations from the mouths of husbands. They are disposed to deny, because in the employment of frauds they are generally the most guilty parties. . . .

Case CIV.—Woman aged sixty-one.

She is still very fresh looking.

Her husband, of the same age, is yet very vigorous, and her lover is forty-eight. She consults me for a profuse, greenish, tenacious leucorrhœa; vesical tenesmus; nothing organic in the uterus. She begins to declare, even before I had asked her a single question on the subject, *that it cannot be any bad disease.* "*You understand,*" said she, "*at my age it is impossible!*" She saw that I mistrusted her words; and when pressed by somewhat explicit interrogatories, she confessed that she had connection with a lover, and that though she could not tell why he was taking them, she found a box of pills in his closet; I asked her to show them to me: they were capsules of copaiba.*

* Used for the treatment of venereal disease.—EDS.

41. A pregnant American woman shares contraceptive advice with a friend: Mary Hallock Foote

Even though contraceptive information had been published by such writers as Charles Knowlton (Doc. 40.i) and circulated underground, it was not widely available. In fact, personal networks probably played a far more important role in spreading such information than printed materials. These excerpts from two letters written by Mary Hallock Foote (1847–1938; Docs. 1.viii, 38), an eastern woman transplanted to a mining camp in New Almaden, California, provide a rare glimpse into what was perhaps a nineteenth-century wife's most pressing concern. At the time of writing, Foote was twenty-nine years old and five months' pregnant with her first child, a son, born the following April. Her friend Helena de Kay Gilder had recently lost her own first child and had just given birth to another.

[Mary Foote to Helena Gilder, Dec. 7, 1876, New Almaden, Calif.]

I hardly dare tell you one thing which the future holds for us, lest it may trouble you. Don't let it—I pray you—for it has long since ceased to be anything but a happy though tremulous hope with me. One reason why I am so absorbed in finishing the S. L. [stone lithograph?] is because I must lay aside work by the 1st of May—

A child is coming to us—Its existence began almost when your darling went away—it has shared every thought of mine for you—Will you be able to include it in your love for me?

I was dismayed at first—but it seemed like fate—no precautions were neglected. The Doctor says change of climate alters everything—this feeling reconciled me at first, because it was simply inevitable—There was nothing to regret or to wish undone and I began to feel awed at this mystery of Nature which quietly sets aside our futile plans and carries out her own laws in spite of resistance.

It *is* awful, but what can we do. There *must* be some meaning in it— perhaps in the future, the lives of our children will reveal to us the meaning— In all ways I shall be comfortable—if I cannot get a good nurse, Lizzie [the hired girl] who is really wonderful in her faithfulness and intelligence will nurse me and we can easily get some one to keep things straight about the house. There is a good Doctor at Guadeloupe—My dear family are to send me *everything* the little one will need—Bessie & Sarah handing over their own surplus—I am thus saved all trouble or the necessity of sitting over sewing work; all the time I sit is needed for my blocks [probably printing blocks]—in the intervals I require exercise. I am, and have been so well that there was no excuse for morbidness, it is the wonderful climate—it fills me with life and vigor. With all these blessings how can I dare to complain— You must not have anxiety for me dearest. I don't know why I tell you—it is

SOURCE: Mary Hallock Foote Papers, Special Collections, C. H. Green Library, Stanford University.

selfish of me—but I feel as if I would like you to think of my child once in a while, before it comes—if you should hear of its existence first as a fact— you could only feel at first—surprise—I would like you to be glad.

It is a delicate thing to speak of in a letter but Mrs. Hague told me a sure way of limiting one's family—which is no injury to either father or mother—Her own two children came to her unexpectedly as proof that no reliance can be placed in the rule we trusted to. Her Doctor told her she must not have another child under a certain number of years and gave her the means of preventing any mistake. If you have provided for the future to your satisfaction there is no need to say more—but if you have any miserable un- certainty, pray let me tell you of this way—It seems to me to involve no possi- bility of bad consequences—

[Mary Foote to Helena Gilder, Dec. 21, 1876, New Almaden, Calif.]

I have followed your advice in one of the two ways in which you recom- mended me to be anticipating the evil day that is coming—as to the harden- ing of the nipples—but I do not know how you mean about using oil— Is it the abdomen that is to be rubbed? I begin to have a painfully stretched feeling—would oil relieve that?

I spoke to you about the advice Mrs. Hague gave me about the future. Of course I know nothing about it practically and it sounds dreadful—but every way is dreadful except the one which it seems cannot be relied on—

Mrs. H. said Arthur must go to a physician and get shields of some kind. They are to be had also at some druggists. It sounds perfectly revolting, but one must face anything rather than the inevitable result of Nature's methods. At all events there is nothing injurious about this. Mrs. Hague is a very fas- tidious woman and I hardly think she would submit to anything very bad— and yet—poor thing it is an absolute necessity with her. She is magnificently plump and strong looking—but really very frail—These things are called "cundums" and are made either of rubber or skin—. They are to be had at first-class druggists.

42. 'Look for some others for to 'plenish the earth': Rose Williams

Plantation owners in the American South valued female slaves for their ability to breed—reproduction played a vital role in the plantation economy, and a healthy young slave who could bear more slaves to work on the planta- tion brought a high price on the auction block. Slave women were sometimes forced by their owners to mate with other slaves "to bring forth portly chil- dren." As the recollections of Rose Williams show, it took exceptional courage and fortitude to resist such a demand.

SOURCE: *The American Slave: A Composite Autobiography*, ed. George P. Rawick, 5: *Texas Narratives* (Westport, Conn., 1972), part 4: 174–78.

What I say am de facts. If I's one day old, I's way over 90, and I's born in Bell County, right here in Texas, and am owned by Massa William Black. He owns mammy and pappy, too. Massa Black has a big plantation but he has more niggers dan he need for work on dat place, 'cause he am a nigger trader. He trade and buy and sell all de time.

Massa Black am awful cruel and he whip de cullud folks and works 'em hard and feed dem poorly. We'uns have for rations de cornmeal and milk and 'lasses and some beans and peas and meat once a week. We'uns have to work in de field every day from daylight till dark and on Sunday we'uns do us washin'. Church? Shucks, we'uns don't know what dat mean.

I has de correct mem'randum of when de war start. Massa Black sold we'uns right den. Mammy and pappy powerful glad to git sold, and dey and I is put on de block with 'bout ten other niggers. When we'uns gits to de tradin' block, dere lots of white folks dere what come to look us over. One man shows de intres' in pappy. Him named Hawkins. He talk to pappy and pappy talk to him and say, "Dem my woman and chiles. Please buy all of us and have mercy on we'uns." Massa Hawkins say, "Dat gal am a likely lookin' nigger, she am portly and strong, but three am more dan I wants, I guesses."

De sale start and 'fore long pappy am put on de block. Massa Hawkins wins de bid for pappy and when mammy am put on de block, he wins de bid for her. Den dere am three or four other niggers sold befo' my time comes. Den Massa Black calls me to de block and de auction man say, "What am I offer for dis portly, strong young wench. She's never been 'bused and will make de good breeder."

I wants to hear Massa Hawkins bid, but him say nothin'. Two other men am biddin' 'gainst each other and I sho' has de worryment. Dere am tears comin' down my cheeks 'cause I's bein' sold to some man dat would make sep'ration from my mammy. One man bids $500.00 and de auction man ask, "Do I hear more? She am gwine at $500.00." Den someone say, $525.00 and de auction man say, "She am sold for $525.00 to Massa Hawkins." Am I glad an' 'cited! Why, I's quiverin' all over.

Massa Hawkins takes we'uns to his place and it am a nice plantation. Lots better am dat place dan Massa Black's. Dere is 'bout 50 niggers what is growed and lots of chillen. De first thing massa do when we'uns gits home am give we'uns rations and a cabin. You mus' believe dis nigger when I says dem rations a feast for us. Dere plenty meat and tea and coffee and white flour. I's never tasted white flour and coffee and mammy fix some biscuits and coffee. Well, de biscuits was yum, yum, yum to me, but de coffee I doesn't like.

De quarters am purty good. Dere am twelve cabins all made from logs and a table and some benches and bunks for sleepin' and a fireplace for cookin' and de heat. Dere am no floor, jus' de ground.

Massa Hawkins am good to he niggers and not force 'em work too hard. Dere am as much diff'ence 'tween him and old Massa Black in de way of treatment as 'twixt de Lawd and de devil. Massa Hawkins 'lows he niggers

have reason'ble parties and go fishin', but we'uns am never tooken to church
and has no books for larnin'. Dere am no education for de niggers.

Dere am one thing Massa Hawkins does to me that I can't shunt from my
mind. I knows he don't do it for meanness, but I allus holds it 'gainst him.
What he done am force me to live with dat nigger, Rufus, 'gainst my wants.

After I been at he place 'bout a year, de massa come to me and say, "You
gwine live with Rufus in dat cabin over yonder. Go fix it for livin'." I's 'bout
sixteen years old and has no larnin', and I's just igno'nus chile. I's thought dat
him mean for me to tend de cabin for Rufus and some other niggers. Well,
dat am start de pestigation for me.

I's took charge of de cabin after work am done and fixes supper. Now,
I don't like dat Rufus, 'cause he a bully. He am big and 'cause he so, he think
everybody do what him say. We'uns has supper, den I goes here and dere
talkin', till I's ready for sleep and den I gits in de bunk. After I's in, dat
nigger come and crawl in de bunk with me 'fore I knows it. I says, "What you
means, you fool nigger?" He say for me to hush de mouth. "Dis am my
bunk, too," he say.

"You's teched in de head. Git out," I's told him, and I puts de feet
'gainst him and give him a shove and out he go on de floor 'fore he know what
I's doin'. Dat nigger jump up and he mad. He look like de wild bear. He
starts for de bunk and I jumps quick for de poker. It am 'bout three foot
long and when he comes at me I lets him have it over de head. Did dat nigger
stop in he tracks? I's say he did. He looks at me steady for a minute and
you's could tell he thinkin' hard. Den he go and set on de bench and say,
"Jus' wait. You thinks it am smart, but you's am foolish in de head. Dey's
gwine larn you somethin'."

"Hush yous big mouth and stay 'way from dis nigger, dat all I wants,"
I say, and jus' sets and hold dat poker in de hand. He jus' sets, lookin' like
de bull. Dere we'uns sets and sets for 'bout an hour and den he go out and I
bars de door.

De nex' day I goes to de missy and tells her what Rufus wants and missy
say dat am de massa's wishes. She say, "Yous am de portly gal and Rufus
am de portly man. De massa wants you'uns for to bring forth portly chillen."

I's thinkin' 'bout what de missy say, but say to myse'f, "I's not gwine live
with dat Rufus." Dat night when him come in de cabin, I grabs de poker
and sits on de bench and says, "Git 'way from me, nigger, 'fore I busts yous
brains out and stomp on dem." He say nothin' and git out.

De nex' day de massa call me and tell me, "Woman, I's pay big money for
you and I's done dat for de cause I wants yous to raise me chillens. I's put
yous to live with Rufus for dat purpose. Now, if you doesn't want whippin'
at de stake, yous do what I wants."

I thinks 'bout massa buyin' me offen de bloc and savin' me from bein'
sep'rated from my folks and 'bout bein' whipped at de stake. Dere it am. What
am I's to do? So I 'cides to do as de massa wish and so I yields.

When we'uns am given freedom, Massa Hawkins tells us we can stay and work for wages or share crop de land. Some stays and some goes. My folks and me stays. We works de land on shares for three years, den moved to other land near by. I stay with my folks till they dies.

If my mem'randum am correct, it am 'bout thirty year since I come to Fort Worth. Here I cooks for white folks till I goes blind 'bout ten year ago.

I never marries, 'cause one 'sperience am 'nough for dis nigger. After what I does for de massa, I's never wants no truck with any man. De Lawd forgive dis cullud woman, but he have to 'scuse me and look for some others for to 'plenish de earth.

43. Abortion experiences in England, France, and the United States

In the absence of reliable contraceptive practices, unwanted pregnancies were very common in the nineteenth century. For the prosperous married woman, an unexpected baby was an inconvenience and a threat to health, but for women of the poorer classes, whether married or single, it could spell economic and social disaster. In the excerpts in the first selection, Henrietta Maria Stanley, Lady Stanley of Alderly (1807–95), a member of the English aristocracy who had borne nine children in seventeen years, writes to her husband of the self-induced abortion they both desired. The second selection is a case study of a Parisian servant who, believing that she was pregnant, submitted to an unnecessary abortion performed by a midwife. The third selection is an account of a court case from Saint Johnsbury, Vermont, in which a doctor was tried for "producing criminal abortion" on a servant named Olive Ashe, who had been impregnated by a young farmer whom she had worked for. The girl died as a result of the operation, which was performed in the sixth month of pregnancy.

(i) The Stanleys

[Edward to Henrietta, Nov. 9, 1847]
My dearest love:

This your last misfortune is indeed most grievous & puts all others in the shade. What can you have been doing to account for so juvenile a proceeding, it comes very opportunely to disturb all your family arrangements & revives the nursery & Williams in full vigour. I only hope it is not the beginning of another flock for what to do with them I am sure I know not. I am afraid however it is too late to mend & you must make the best of it tho' bad is best. . . .

SOURCES: (i) Nancy Mitford, *The Ladies of Alderly* (London, 1938), pp. 142–45. (ii) Dr. H. Bayard, "Avortement. Simulation de grossesse. Tympanite. Ovarite," *Annales d'Hygiène Publique et de Médecine Légale*, 37 (Jan. 1847): 464–65. (iii) C. P. Frost, "Report of a Trial for Criminal Abortion," *The American Medical Monthly and New York Review*, 14 (Sept. 1860): 196–97, 201–2. The editors wish to thank Professor Carroll Smith-Rosenberg, University of Pennsylvania, for contributing this case.

[Henrietta to Edward, Nov. 9, 1847]
A hot bath, a tremendous walk & a great dose have succeeded but it is a warning. . . . I feel not too well which makes me idle.

[Edward to Henrietta, Nov. 10, 1847]
I hope you are not going to do yourself any harm by your violent proceedings, for though it would be a great bore it is not worth while playing tricks to escape its consequences. If however you are none the worse the great result is all the better.

[Henrietta to Edward, Nov. 10, 1847]
I was sure you would feel the same horror I did at an increase of family but I am reassured for the future by the efficacy of the means.

(ii) Marie Maudoin

In the month of July 1845, Marie Maudoin entered service as a domestic for a married couple named Mermet, merchants in the rue de Sentier. Her previous conduct had always been good, and she had been in the same household for eight years.

During the last days of the month of April 1846, Marie Maudoin began to complain of ill health. On Thursday, April 30, she asked a young woman named Besson, a working girl in the house, to lend her 30 francs, which she needed, so she said, that very evening, and when this young woman was not able to give her this amount, she made up her mind, against her better judgment, to ask her masters to advance her 30 francs in wages. She replied in an evasive manner to the questions addressed to her on this subject, limiting herself to saying that she had to have these 30 francs, and that she had to go to the suburb of Saint-Denis.* She left at nine in the evening and was gone for about a half hour.

On the first of May, Marie Maudoin felt sick; she went to bed early. The next day she was more seriously indisposed, complained of indigestion, fainted several times, and lost a great deal of blood. She was extremely pale.

A doctor was called. He suspected that Marie Maudoin had just had a miscarriage in the second or third month of pregnancy.

At first the Maudoin girl claimed that her illness was caused by a simple [menstrual] suppression,† followed by an abundant loss of blood caused by a foot-bath she had taken. Then, surrendering to the evidence, she admitted to a premature *accouchement*, and decided to make a confession, which, while revealing her guilt, pointed to the midwife Foriat as having been guilty of a far more serious crime.

Marie Maudoin declared that at the beginning of the month of April, believing she was pregnant, she had gone to the residence of the Foriat woman,

* Saint-Denis was one of the poorest and most crowded neighborhoods in Paris.—EDS.

† Medical theory held that menstrual delay or stoppage endangered women's health.—EDS.

rue du Faubourg-Saint-Denis, whose sign she had seen on the street. This woman, after having examined her, told her she was pregnant. After a fortnight she returned there; the Foriat woman confirmed that she was pregnant, adding that she would terminate it for 100 francs. Marie made the mistake of discussing this strange proposition; and in recognition of her feeble resources the Foriat woman reduced the amount to 30 francs. On April 30 Marie went there again with the money.

As soon as the midwife saw her, she understood the purpose of her visit. She went into a small room that opened onto the entry hall. Marie heard the noise of a drawer being opened and closed; the Foriat woman came back to her carrying something wrapped in cloth; the Maudoin girl felt herself punctured; she felt faint, and a few moments later blood began to flow. When the Foriat woman received the 30 francs, she told Marie that she would be rid of the baby in nine days at the latest, that she should take a bath and put her feet in water, and that she should bring her the blood-stained linens so she could have them laundered in such a way that the girl's masters would not notice anything. The Maudoin girl described the Foriat woman's apartment exactly, and when she was brought into her presence, she recognized her.

Iron needles of various sizes were seized by the authorities from a drawer in a piece of furniture placed in the small room off the entrance hall in the Foriat woman's apartment.

In the course of the court inquiry, the Maudoin girl stated *that she had believed herself to be pregnant, and that she had felt quickening.* We were charged by the president of the Assize Court to determine the condition of the accused.

[There follows a detailed description of the medical examination, which revealed evidence that there had been a pregnancy.]

In subsequent visits we confirmed the occurrence of menstruation, twice; the diminuition of the size of the abdomen; the empty state of the uterus; and the presence in the pelvis of a considerable ovarian tumor. This condition appeared to us to be the result of the operation that had been performed on the Maudoin girl.

After deliberating for half an hour, the jury returned a verdict of not guilty relative to the Maudoin girl, who was set free.

Furthermore, it found the Foriat woman guilty, though with extenuating circumstances. She was sentenced to eight years in solitary confinement.

(iii) Olive Ashe

An individual, a native of Ireland, styling himself Dr. W. H. M. Howard, and professing to be an English surgeon of great renown, was arraigned at the January Term (1859) of the Orange County (Vt.) Court, upon an indictment charging him with producing criminal abortion on Miss Olive Ashe, and also with causing her death thereby.

From the evidence adduced on trial, (the minutes of which have been kindly furnished me by the presiding Judge, Hon. James Barrett,) it appeared that Miss Ashe went to the establishment of Howard, at Bradford, Vt., about the middle of January, 1858, for the purpose of having abortion produced, supposing herself pregnant by a young farmer, by whom she had been employed as a servant during the previous summer; that a bargain was struck between the reputed father of the child and Howard, by which he was to perform the desired service for the sum of $100.

Her twin sister, who was with her during the whole of her stay at Howard's, testified that the doctor operated three times with instruments. These instruments she could not describe minutely, nor could she tell the number used. As the result of the first operation, in which he introduced one or more instruments into the body of her sister, there was a discharge of water, which she said lasted two or three hours or more. On the next forenoon he operated again; used two or three instruments; sister made no great outcry, but complained, and gave other evidences of considerable pain. This operation was followed by a discharge of quite a quantity of blood. At night of the same day he operated a third time. Sister did not sit up after the second operation. He used instruments at this time and also introduced his hand. The result of this operation was the delivery of the child, which was about two-thirds grown. Flowing continued a few days. This last operation was Saturday night, and sister lived till the next Friday evening, January 29th. The last two or three days of her illness were attended with delirium, picking the clothes, etc. . . .

The medical witness first called was C. P. Frost, M.D., of St. Johnsbury, Vt. The direct cause of death, in the opinion of the witness, was inflammation and sloughing of the cervix uteri, perhaps accompanied by haemorrhage. The inflammation and sloughing were caused by violence in the use of instruments applied to the neck of the womb in the attempts to induce abortion. [He] believed that instrumental violence was used, because of the depth of the slough at certain points, extending to the entire destruction of mucous membrane and muscular tissue. The inflammation and sloughing had obliterated or changed the direct evidence of violence. From the appearance of the womb, he judged the wounds were made at least three days prior to death, and probably a week or more. . . .

After a trial, lasting nine days, the jury brought in a verdict of guilty on the charge of abortion, and not guilty on that of manslaughter. After a hearing before the Supreme Court, on exceptions to the ruling of the Judge, Howard was sentenced to two years' imprisonment in the State Prison, where he is now serving out his sentence.

44. Infanticide

For the woman desperate to rid herself of an unwanted—and often illegitimate—baby, murder sometimes seemed the only recourse. By the mid-

SOURCES: (i) "Infanticide.—Asphyxie dans une fosse d'aisances.—Complicité d'une jeune fille" (Cours d'assises de la Marne), *Annales d'Hygiène Publique et de Méde-*

nineteenth century the "unnatural" crime of infanticide deeply troubled professional men and municipal officials in both France and England; they regarded it as an instance of social pathology to be studied, remedied, and of course punished. The following selections depict the extreme measures taken to dispose of infants. The first is an account of a French court case that was printed in the pioneering public health journal 'Annales d'hygiène publique.' The case recounts the story of a young girl who, in order to save her mother's honor, murdered her newborn sister. In the second selection, the Coroner of Nottingham supplies statistics from inquests held for infants who died in suspicious circumstances.

(i) La veuve M— and her daughter

A woman, widowed for eight years, became pregnant, and in spite of the precautions she took to conceal her pregnancy, the fact that she had given birth was noticed. She stated that she had indeed given birth the night of March 7–8 at three in the morning, and that, by mistake, her baby had been thrown into the cesspool. An investigation was therefore ordered and resulted in the discovery of the cadaver of a newborn infant of the female sex. Two physicians charged with performing the autopsy stated that it had been born at term and was born alive, that it had breathed, that it could only have lived a few instants, and that it bore no trace of wounds or organic lesions that could explain the death, a death that was in all probability the result of immersion in the cesspool and the resulting suffocation.

The daughter of Widow M—, young Alzira, age sixteen, who shared her mother's bed, having been questioned about what had taken place on the night of March 7–8, recounted with the greatest sincerity all the events that had followed the delivery, a story from which it emerged that death was deliberately dealt to the newborn child, and that it was she, following her mother's instructions, who had dropped the child into the latrines.

Toward three in the morning the mother had awakened her, complaining of being ill. On her return from going to find a light at a neighbor's, the daughter M— had found her mother standing and at her feet a baby. Her mother had returned to bed, had held the child on her knees, and had it drink a little sugar water. Then she had wrapped it in a kerchief, and handing the whole thing to her daughter, she had told her to go throw it into the cesspool. "I began to cry," added the young Alzira, "for I felt that what she asked me to do was not good; I think I even said this to her; but she insisted so vigorously, telling me that she would be dishonored in the eyes of the world, and that this dishonor would fall on us, that I gave up. I carried out my mother's order. As the pit is not, I believe, deep, I heard the bundle fall; the child did not utter the tiniest cry. I hurried back to my room where I found my mother nearly unconscious. As soon as she could speak, she asked me if I

cine Légale, 38 (July 1847): 462–63. (ii) Great Britain, *Parliamentary Papers*, 1862, XXII, 4th report of the Medical Officer of the Privy Council, pp. 192–93.

was really sure the child was in the pit. On hearing my affirmative response, she added, 'Keep my secret. I did it to preserve our honor.' "

(ii) The Nottingham inquests

Mr. Browne, the coroner for Nottingham, said, that he believed child-murder to be of much more frequent occurrence than is detected, and added that mothers in that town are very careless about their children, and that the mortality arising from this cause is very considerable. In illustration of this fact he referred to the large number of inquests which he has held on the bodies of infants found dead, and furnished a return here subjoined, together with the note which accompanied it:—

INQUESTS HELD IN THE TOWN OF NOTTINGHAM ON THE
BODIES OF INFANTS FOUND IN PRIVIES AND THE CANAL,
OR EXPOSED IN THE FIELDS OR OPEN PLACES,
FROM JANUARY 1856 TO OCTOBER 1861

Date		Sex			
1856:					
January	9	Male	child	–	Found dead in a privy
"	17	Female	"	–	"
February	16	"	"	–	" Verdict—Wilful Murder
March	6	"	"	–	Found near the footway in the meadows. Verdict—Wilful Murder
Sept. 15 & 19		"	"	–	Found in a field. Verdict—Wilful Murder
1857:					
March	14	Male	"	–	Found in a privy
"	18	"	"	–	Found in a chamber utensil
"	26	"	"	–	Found in one of the new streets of Nottingham, where it had been placed immediately after birth. Verdict—Wilful Murder
October	10	"	"	–	Found by the canal side. Verdict—Wilful murder
November	4	Female	"	–	Found in a privy
"	10	Male	"	–	Found in the meadows
1858:					
January	5	Female	"	–	This child was found in the general cemetery. A grave had been dug for an interment, and left for a time, and on the sexton returning to it he found the body of this child had been thrown in. Verdict—Wilful Murder
May	4	Male	"	–	Found under a bed. Died from want of attention at the birth
1859:					
February	28	"	"	–	Found in the canal
September	9	"	"	–	"

Date	Sex				
1861:					
February 19	"	"	–	Found in the church cemetery. Verdict— Wilful Murder	
June 26	Female	"	–	Found in a privy. Verdict—Wilful Murder	
October 8	"	"	–	Found in a privy	

[The coroner's accompanying letter follows.]

I now send you a return of the inquests held by me since the beginning of the year 1856, on the bodies of children found in privies, in the canal, or exposed in the fields or open places. Any other returns which you may wish for, and I can give, shall be made out for you.

I had last night an illustration of my view as to the state of morals amongst females employed in Nottingham warehouses. I held an inquest on an illegitimate child whose mother was a warehouse girl living away from her parents' house, though not at a great distance from them, in a hired room. A younger sister was living with her, and she (the sister) was also a warehouse girl, and the mother of an illegitimate child only a few weeks old.

45. A distinguished French midwife cautions against interference in the birth process: Marie-Anne-Victoire Gillain Boivin

In the following excerpts from a textbook used by the students of the Paris Midwifery School, Marie Boivin (1773–1841), midwife-superintendent of the Royal College of Health, and superintendent of the Paris Maternity Hospital, cautions against undue interference in the birth process. Boivin belonged to a unique French tradition of trained and licensed midwives who worked within the medical establishment and were closely associated with the great Parisian teaching hospitals. A research scientist, as well as a teacher, Boivin invented a new kind of speculum and was the first to demonstrate the nature of the hydatid mole, a tumor that produces the symptoms of pregnancy. As in England and America, most births in France still took place at home; the obstetrical patients on whom Boivin and her students practiced came from the poorest families in the city.

If daily practice shows that the terrible judgment that condemns women *to give birth only with pain* is not equally true for all women, if pain is not absolutely necessary in childbirth, why give up all hope of finding a way to ease the lot of those women who seem to be so condemned, indeed, to become mothers only amidst the torments of frightful agony?

SOURCE: Marie-Ann-Victoire Gillain Boivin, *Mémorial de l'art des accouchemens, ou Principes fondés sur la pratique de l'Hospice de la Maternité de Paris et sur celle des plus célèbres praticiens nationaux et étrangers*, 3d ed. (Paris, 1824), pp. iv, 406.

[In a table Boivin compares the record of two English physicians using instruments with the record of the midwives under her supervision at the Paris Maternity Hospital. These records, based on thousands of cases, showed a significantly higher incidence of cesarians and deliveries by instrument by the doctors: 1 in 43 deliveries vs. 1 in 62 for the midwives. Boivin then goes on to discuss these results.]

The conclusions that can be drawn from these results are too obvious to need explanation: we close by observing that *mechanical* deliveries (with instruments) are much more frequent in the practice of the Englishmen we have cited than they are in the practice of the Maternity Hospital, and this can be best explained by ascribing to them what Professor Dubois says in his lectures about those practitioners who build glorious reputations for themselves on the number of difficult deliveries they have encountered in their practice. "It is," says the professor, "because they want to perform the delivery peremptorily; they do not want to give nature, who is wiser than they, time to complete her work; they oppose her, thwart her, torment her, considering themselves fortunate that they were able to appear indispensable." "The abuse of the art," says Denman, "produces more numerous and more serious evils than all the imperfections of nature."

46. 'So very animal and unecstatic': Two queens write about pregnancy

As the following excerpts from the letters of Empress Eugénie and Queen Victoria attest, queens were granted no reprieve from the trials of maternity. Eugénie-Marie de Montijo de Guzman, comtesse de Teba (1826–1920), was from a Catholic aristocratic family of Spanish and Scottish stock. Educated in Paris, Eugénie was courted by France's new emperor, Napoleon III, whom she married in 1853. Eugénie's letters to her sister Paca, the Duchess of Alba, reveal her experience with a miscarriage, suffered just a few months after her marriage, and discuss the later stages of a successful pregnancy in 1856, which resulted in the birth of her first and only child, Louis. Her labor was extremely long and difficult and nearly cost the empress her life. At one point the doctors despaired of saving both mother and child; Napoleon III, when asked who should be saved if a choice had to be made, unhesitatingly replied "the mother."

Victoria of England (1819–1901) needs little introduction. Queen of England from 1837 until her death in 1901, Victoria became the living symbol of an entire epoch. Her marriage to Albert, Prince of Saxe-Coburg-Gotha,

SOURCES: (i) *Lettres familières de l'Impératrice Eugénie, conservées dans les archives du Palais de Liria et publiées par les soins du Duc d'Albe avec le concours de F. de Llanos y Torriglia et Pierre Josserand* (Paris, 1935), 1: 76–86, 122–23, 127. (ii) *Dearest Child, Letters Between Queen Victoria and the Princess Royal, 1858–1861,* ed. Roger Fulford (London, 1964), pp. 77–78, 93–94, 115, 120, 158–60.

epitomized domestic bliss, and their brood of nine children, born between 1840 and 1857, were considered the fruits of a virtuous "middle-class" model of happy family life. Victoria's childbearing experiences have left a firm imprint in the annals of Victoriana. After a series of difficult births, she made history by using an anesthetic (chloroform) for the births of her eighth and ninth children. She expressed her distaste for the physical discomforts of maternity in a remarkably frank correspondence with her eldest daughter, Victoria, the Princess Royal, who at seventeen married young Prince Frederick (the Fritz of the letters), later Crown Prince of Prussia.

(i) Empress Eugénie

May 1, 1853.—Today I have been in bed for fourteen days without moving and God only knows how much longer I will be here. I was very ill for 17 hours. The pains gave me a cold sweat. Finally, M. Dubois told me that I now know what it is like to give birth. The sharp pains stopped and at the very moment I had begun to have some hope, I had the misfortune of learning that I had suffered much in vain. I had been delighted at the idea of having a beautiful baby like yours. And I was in despair, but I thank God that this accident did not occur later; I would have had even more trouble. On the other hand, maybe it is better for my health for me not to recover too quickly. But I can assure you, I already lack the patience to stay in bed. *Adieu.* Your sister who loves you.

May 3, 1853.—They tell me that the Medinaceli will come this year. Since they love to dance so much, I will give a few little dances if they come. God willing, you will be in a state to dance too; I was so sick that it scares me to know you are pregnant. However, I would be very happy to be so again; when I say that I don't like children, I suppose it's due to jealousy. Especially to have some like yours, I would cut off my arm.

May 9, 1853.—I admit that your stories of last year made me laugh; I also look back very often and I don't laugh during those moments, for I see all that I have given up forever. . . . In exchange I have won a crown, but what does that mean except that I am the first slave of my kingdom, isolated in the midst of everyone, without a woman friend, and needless to say without a male friend, never alone for an instant; an unbearable life if I didn't have, as compensation, a man near me who loves me madly, but who is a slave like me, who has no other motive, no other ambition than the good of his country, and God only knows how he will be rewarded; at this moment, my sister, I thank God for not fulfilling a hope that filled me with joy, for I think with terror of the poor Dauphin Louis XVII, of Charles I, of Marie Stuart, and Marie-Antoinette. Who knows what will be the sad destiny of my child! I would a thousand times prefer for my sons a crown less resplendent but more secure. Do not believe, dear sister, that I lack courage. . . . You see that my thoughts are not very gay, but remember that I have been in bed for 22 days, for being in the *chaise-longue* is not exactly what you would call getting up. Moreover, I just got into that yesterday for the first time. I am beginning to be in a very bad mood because I ache in all my bones from always being in the same position. Today I wanted to try to stand up but I couldn't, so great is my weakness, resulting no doubt from loss of blood. You asked me about the cause of my accident. I swear to you that I don't know, nor does anybody else. It is true that I took a warm bath (not hot) but according to the two doctors, the misfortune had occurred earlier, for the child had already "come loose." I suppose you understand, for I can't give you any more explanation. As for myself I don't attribute it to anything because I don't know. Some time back I fell, but I didn't feel anything. Another day, my squire's horse ran away at Saint-Cloud, and I thought this man was going to kill himself by falling down an embankment onto the railroad track, but fortunately he steered the horse in another direction and only skinned his face in falling, but I had a dreadful fright. You see that I don't know what caused it. It is useless to look for reasons, so I will say, like the Moors: "It was written." Mama thinks it wouldn't have happened if she had been here. As if it were possible!—I have been cared for as you can imagine and, besides, I have had a model midwife who has satisfied me perfectly by her diligence and devotion.

July 1855.—You know already that I will go to Biarritz toward the 27th of July. I really need that, although I am somewhat better, though far from being recovered. Would you believe that the doctors told the Emperor that, happily, they got there on time, but if I had neglected it much longer, I would never have any children. Jobert will cauterize me again tomorrow. Truly, I spend my life being sick. Who would have predicted this when I was sixteen?

Feb. 14, 1856.—I have been somewhat unwell lately. No doubt, I had recently overtired myself and now I'm becoming a bit heavy. It makes me laugh to see my waist, but I can still make myself look presentable and in the evening, until only two weeks ago, you couldn't see anything different. I shall soon be obliged to make a fuss over the plenipotentiaries of the Congress,* and I fear that these dinners and concerts will not do me much good in my present state, since I have only a month to go. It is extremely annoying to live in public and never have the right to be sick, when unfortunately one is subject to the same maladies as everyone else.

(ii) Queen Victoria

March 24, 1858.—That you should feel shy sometimes I can easily understand. I do so very often to this hour. But being married gives one one's position which nothing else can. Think however what it was for me, a girl of 18 all alone, not brought up at court as you were—but very humbly at Kensington Palace—with trials and difficulties, to receive and to be everywhere the first! No, no one knows what a life of difficulties mine was—and is! How thankful I am that none of you, please God! ever will have that anomalous and trying position. Now do enter into this in your letters, you so seldom do that, except to answer a question.

* The Peace Congress summoned by Napoleon III to end the Crimean War. —EDS.

Now to reply to your observation that you find a married woman has much more liberty than an unmarried one; in one sense of the word she has,—but what I meant was—in a physical point of view—and if you have hereafter (as I had constantly for the first 2 years of my marriage)—aches—and sufferings and miseries and plagues—which you must struggle against—and enjoyments etc. to give up—constant precautions to take, you will feel the yoke of a married woman! Without that—certainly it is unbounded happiness—if one has a husband one worships! It is a foretaste of heaven. And you have a husband who adores you, and is, I perceive, ready to meet every wish and desire of your's. I had 9 times for 8 months to bear with those above-named enemies and real misery (besides many duties) and I own it tried me sorely; one feels so pinned down—one's wings clipped—in fact, at the best (and few were or are better than I was), only half oneself—particularly the first and second time. This I call the "shadow side" as much as being torn away from one's loved home, parents and brothers and sisters. And therefore—I think our sex a most unenviable one.

April 21, 1858.—I can not tell you how happy I am that you are not in an unenviable position. I never can rejoice by hearing that a poor young thing is pulled down by this trial.

Though I quite admit the comfort and blessing good and amiable children are—though they are also an awful plague and anxiety for which they show one so little gratitude very often! What made me so miserable was—to have the two first years of my married life utterly spoilt by this occupation! I could enjoy nothing—not travel about or go about with dear Papa and if I had waited a year, as I hope you will, it would have been very different.

June 15, 1858.—What you say of the pride of giving life to an immortal soul is very fine, dear, but I own I cannot enter into that; I think much more of our being like a cow or a dog at such moments; when our poor nature becomes so very animal and unecstatic—but for you, dear, if you are sensible and reasonable not in ecstasy nor spending your day with nurses and wet nurses, which is the ruin of many a refined and intellectual young lady, without adding to her real maternal duties, a child will be a great resource. Above all, dear, do remember never to lose the modesty of a young girl towards others (without being prude); though you are married don't become a matron at once to whom everything can be said, and who minds saying nothing herself—I remained particular to a degree (indeed feel so now) and often feel shocked at the confidences of other married ladies. I fear abroad they are very indelicate about these things. Think of me who at that first time, very unreasonable, and perfectly furious as I was to be caught, having to have drawing rooms and levées and made to sit down—and be stared at and take every sort of precaution.

June 30, 1858.—I delight in the idea of being a grandmama; to be that at 39 (D.V.) and to look and feel young is great fun, only I wish I could go through it for you, dear, and save you all the annoyance. But that can't be helped. I think of my next birthday being spent with my children and a grandchild. It will be a treat!

Jan. 25, 1859.—I am not going to speak today of my trials, but of your happiness, and I do hope that you will be able to spend your wedding-day in undisturbed happiness! I was more fortunate than you, on the first anniversary of my wedding day, I had shaken my burden off 6 weeks before, was as strong and well as if nothing had happened, and your christening took place in the evening for which also dear kind Uncle Leopold, who says he considers you as his grandchild, came over. How well I can see all before me! You, dear child, do understand now that a daughter's wedding must be a very trying day for the mother, far, far more so, than for the young, unknowing, confiding bride.

Jan. 29 1859.—God be praised for all his mercies, and for bringing you safely through this awful time!* Our joy, our gratitude knows no bounds.

My precious darling, you suffered much more than I ever did—and how I wish I could have lightened them for you! Poor dear Fritz—how he will have suffered for you! I think and feel much for him; the dear little boy if I could but see him for one minute, give you one kiss. It is hard, very hard. But we are so happy, so grateful! and people here are all in ecstasies—such pleasure, such delight—as if it was their own prince and so it is too! All the children so delighted! You will and must feel so thankful all is over! But don't be alarmed for the future, it never can be so bad again!

Feb. 2, 1859.—The delightful accounts of you give us the intensest pleasure and fill our hearts with gratitude and thankfulness!

Today is the anniversary of that dreadful parting, the most dreadful day for us and for you,—but which thank God! is past. Its bitter recollection is wiped out by the joyful feelings of having seen you, and seen you happy and contented; knowing you now in the possession of a child; with all those heavy trials, those cruel sufferings behind you and we poor absent parents looking forward to the prospect of meeting you again, and meeting and seeing you well and strong and happy, and without that load of anxiety and of uncertainty which we have carried about with us since last May! Don't you feel such a weight off your mind, such a sense of returning freedom and thankfulness? I always felt that intense happiness on first waking, so different to the mornings of anxious expectation, of dread and anxiety. It is not a pleasant affair God knows, for any one, but you, my own darling, have had the very worst beginning possible from suffering so much! How I do wish I could go to you now and read to you and beguile the dull hours—but you are now rapidly approaching the great day and I see you already before me on your sofa.

How I do long to see my little grandson! I own it seems very funny to me to be a grandmama, and so many people tell me they can't believe it! That dear, dear locket gives me such pleasure! Not only because it was the dear little darling's hair, but because it shows me that you thought directly of poor absent Mama, who quite pines at times to be with you.

I send you today a little cushion for your back when you are on your sofa, every stitch of which I have worked myself with the English colours which I trust you will like.

* The Princess Royal's first child, the future Kaiser (William II), was born on January 27.—EDS.

47. 'Every good woman needs a companion of her own sex': Georgiana Bruce Kirby

The geographic mobility of nineteenth-century Americans meant that many women were uprooted from their networks of family and friends; those who migrated to the sparsely settled and predominantly male world of the Far West acutely felt the strains of isolation. Georgiana Bruce (b. 1818), an Englishwoman who came to America as a governess, lived for several years in the Transcendentalist community of Brook Farm, Massachusetts, and worked as a prison matron at Sing-Sing, moved to California in 1850. There she turned to farming for a time, working with her close friend Eliza Farnham (1815–64; Doc. 96.ii), and then took a job as a domestic. In 1852 she married Richard Kirby, a tanner in Santa Cruz. During her first pregnancy she began the journal from which these excerpted entries are drawn. She writes about her joy at the prospect of motherhood and her happiness with her husband, but it is also clear that she sorely missed the companionship of other women.

Dec. 14, 1852.—It always puts me in good spirits to gallop up the hills and view the wild mountain scenery so on my return after taking in the clothes and all the wood that we chopped as the clouds looked ominous, I concluded that today for the first time in my life I would commence a journal. I think that perhaps I may die and my babe live, in which case it would be pleasant for the latter to have some record of my external and spiritual life during these important months; or should I survive this great trial of my physical powers and live to see my child grow up it will be interesting to me to see how far and in what manner my present and succeeding states of mind may have had influence in forming the character and consequently the external appearance of my child. . . .

Since I was a girl of 18 I have been ever conscious of the most intense desire to become a mother. The thought (in anticipation) on the condition in which I now find myself used to fill my whole being with joy. Often and often when alone with nature my soul has been lifted up as it were to higher spheres and so filled with a sense of harmony and melody that I was obliged to relieve myself by a long recitative, not, owing to my inferior vocal organs, at all worthy of the emotions that gave rise to it. It is not that I am especially fond of little babies, for I am not though I doubt not that this instinct will in due time become developed in me, but I do so earnestly love to watch the unfolding of character and intellect. I love so much to influence youth aright, to arouse moral ambition, to instil by precept and example a thorough respect for labor d. & h. [dirty & hard?] that my own child, be it boy or girl, may have some prominent noble trait, some beautiful spiritual gift, like music, for

SOURCE: Georgiana Bruce Kirby diary, typescript copy, California Historical Society Library, San Francisco. The editors are grateful to Karl Feichtmeir, manuscripts librarian, for his assistance. The original typescript is in Special Collections, Library of the University of California, Santa Cruz. The whereabouts of the original diary is not known.

instance, and no mean streak or fatal weakness. I desire that my child have a generous nature, good common sense and industry, at the very least.

My husband has so many excellent qualities that I am deficient in, and also so excellent a temperament that unless other causes have force enough to counteract the good I feel we have every reason to hope for the best.

For more than two months I have been suffering from the ordinary ailments of such a condition and they are such as do not conduce to healthy intellection [sic] action by any means. Mr. K. [her husband], kind and active and ever cheerful, gets up and prepares breakfast, brings me chocolate and toast or whatnot to bed, kills and dresses a chicken for my dinner or saddles the horse for me to take a short ride—then hurries off to the tan yard, two miles or so.

At night he often goes to the mission after closing work and is then sure to bring home a variety of articles with which to tempt my appetite or in some way contribute to my comfort.

Our rancho, with its hollows and gulches and noble sweep of hills, exactly suits me, but I have been used to mixing in pretty large circles and miss the pleasant and healthy excitement caused by the friction of mind on mind. I long for flowers and fruits and music too but one cannot expect every good in the present state of society. I have many as it is—unsurpassed beauty of scenery and climate, good health, neither poverty or riches, and the most devoted friend in my husband. . . .

The day before yesterday (Sunday) we went to see Mr. and Mrs. Sawin, who live up the coast maybe two miles from the mission. Owing to the first rains which lasted pretty much for three weeks, and to K's being so busy that he had to raise sheds and stables on Sunday instead of taking me on a "pasear" for more than three months previous to this, I had not been off the rancho or seen a woman and the Sawins are so friendly that I enjoyed this visit very much.

It is three miles from here to the mission and those women who have side saddles and horses at their command are yet so occupied by their housekeeping cares that they are unable excepting at distant intervals to leave home for a day. There are no sisters or aunts or grownup daughters to take their places while absent and if it should happen, which it has not as yet among any other class than the roughest Mission [illegible], that any such sisters, aunts or grown up daughters did exist, then before you could turn around they would be certainly snatched up and themselves immediately in the same plights as the rest of the women and quite as hardly as before.

Dec. 15, 1852.—I have seen the face of but one woman (Mrs. Sawin) in four months and a half and it is likely to be two months more before any one will have time to visit. No bright and beautiful thoughts and at the same time no fretfulness or anxiety. K. is so thoroughly kind that he has a tranquilizing effect on me, who am as a general thing inclined to be apprehensive of evil and too sensitive to the influence of others.

Feb. 3, 1853.—I am not sure that anything whatever could relieve or comfort me under my present very depressing condition of health, but if any thing could it would be a congenial female companion with whom I could chat and be merry, sympathize and advise. The being alone all day from eight in the morning to seven at night ensures a too great seriousness. There is nothing to call out any other faculties of the mind, fancy, imagination, affection, mirthfulness, nothing in fact to kindle or excite a worthy spirit life. I regret this more than I can express, dreading the effects on the little one.

Every good woman needs a companion of her own sex. No matter how numerous or valuable her male acquaintances, no matter how close the union between herself and husband, if she have a genial, loving nature, the want of a female friend is felt as a sad void. I have a fixed habit also of living nearly altogether in the future. Not that I am in the least discontented with my present circumstances; it is a habit that if I remember rightly grew out of my desire for knowledge when a young girl. I always hoped something would "happen" in a few years to enable me to attain the intellectual culture I so earnestly desired and which I found myself utterly unable in my cramped circumstances to arrive at.

Benevolence and affection always came in to interfere with the fulfilment of aspiration and so the years wore away in ceaseless yearning and this habit became fixed of looking far far away, even to the future of death when social duties and individual aspirations would never conflict.

Feb. 9, 1853.—Fine weather still lasts. I rode to the mission last Sunday, took tea at the Whitings and then went to pass the night at Mrs. Dryden's, the wife of the M. minister. She is in the like case with myself and as her husband was at San F. we slept together and had quite a cheerful time of it. The next day I saw at her house one or two other pleasant women. Mrs. W. is to come up this evening to pass a few days with me. I enjoyed the visit exceedingly and feel better in consequence. On the 6th sowed cauliflower, asparagus, rhubarb and onions and set out the strawberry plants.

Feb. 13, 1853.—We sowed celery, sea kale and set out the first little peach tree up by the house and the rose bushes around. I am better and had a two days visit from Mrs. Whiting which has quite made me forget myself and my ailments. She also is about to become a mother as are many other women in the mission and for the first time after being married many years. The place has become proverbial for its "fruitfulness". We are all in a state of partial anxiety about doctors and nurses. Those here, of the former class, are briefless, giving calomel to a confined woman and losing healthy patients frequently, and most of the latter being filled more or less with old women's superstitions as regards the treatment of new born babes.

48. A minister's wife gives birth to a boy: Caroline Clive

As a young woman, Caroline Meysey-Wigley (1801–73; Doc. 1.vi), a member of the Worcestershire landed gentry, began to write poems and essays and

SOURCE: *Caroline Clive: From the Diary and Family Papers of Mrs. Archer Clive,* ed. Mary Clive (London, 1949), pp. 133–34, 147–50.

to take an active interest in family financial affairs. Strong-minded and intelligent, she was content to remain single until, at age thirty-nine, she married the Reverend Archer Clive, rector of Solihull, a village near Birmingham. They were extremely happy together and became the parents of two children. A devoted mother, Caroline managed to continue her career as an author and published several novels. The following excerpts from the Clives' diaries describe Caroline's first pregnancy, the birth of their son, Charles, and the early months of his infancy.

[Caroline writing, 1841–42]

Undated.—The fourth month ended and I looked forward most anxiously to signs of quickening. I felt something while sitting in the ballroom at the Meriden archery which made me lift up my eyes and thank God. So there was something, whether it was my child or not. . . .

Oct. 11.—For one week there was decidedly no encrease of motion and almost stillness for several days, which made me uneasy. Since, and on Wednesday last, it had been very marked, more yesterday than ever I felt it. Lady Gordon, whom I asked to describe it, said like wind on the stomach. So did Mrs. Buckley. I said, like chickens moving in a basket; to which she agreed but substituted rabbits. . . . Regurgitated worse than ever. . . .

Jan. 20.—Several have been my falls, but I believe without injury, though always frightening me for my treasure. I fell down half a dozen steps backwards at Whitfield, and once fell sitting on some stone garden steps.

[Archer writing, 1842]

Jan. 31.—Yesterday morning, Sunday, January 30th, at about eight o'clock, Caroline told me that she had perceived symptoms which commenced the night before, of her confinement approaching. They increased after breakfast and I sent for Kimbell, who arrived just before morning church. He said there was no immediate haste and departed about his usual business to return in the evening. I went to church, having carried up Caroline to bed in the chintz room which we had previously fixed on for the lying-in hospital. I read morning prayers, but came out before the sermon and found the signs of labouring advancing. At two o'clock I sent the carriage to Birmingham for Hodgson and sent another messenger to hasten Kimbell's return, for the labour had begun. Kimbell arrived about half-past three. I stayed away from the evening church and remained in the dressing-room, while Caroline groaned away next door. At about half-past six the event was announced to me by Mary as to be expected any moment. I waited and listened anxiously. I prayed for Caroline's welfare, I tried to read my Bible and Lightfoot on the Articles of the Creed of the Holy Catholic Church, but I fear not to much profit. Again I listened. I fancied I heard the word "girl" said, and Mary ran in and told me the child was half born. After, there was a silence for two minutes and I fancied it was a still-born child. Then she rushed in again. I heard a faint cry, and she said, "Oh Archer, such a fine boy and quite safe and well." I shed tears of joy and humbly thanked God for this result. It was what both I and Caroline had desired, but what, upon comparing notes, we found that neither had ventured to ask in prayer. Mine had been offered daily for her safety and for her offspring, but I had felt it presumptuous to add male or female, or to say more than "Thy will be done": and hers had been the same. I am, I hope, duly thankful.

At this moment Hodgson arrived and came upstairs. The child cried lustily, was washed, brought in to me, and dressed. I took it in my arms and carried it to Caroline and knelt by her bedside and kissed her. That was a happy moment, and she wonderfully well and stout. At about eight I left the room. The nurses came to shift her and I went downstairs with Mary to dine, Hodgson remaining in the sickroom, and Kimbell departed. But how little did I know what was then taking place, or that my dearest wife was in extreme danger. About half-past eight I went up again and found Hodgson sitting at the bedside feeling her pulse and making her smell salts. A proper haemorrhage had taken place and she was quite exhausted. He had given brandy and sal volatile and did not leave her till past ten, when her strengthening pulse gave him assurance of her safety. Kimbell was again sent for and returned, and the two doctors slept here. She was fed frequently and slept a good deal. They visited her at three and again at five o'clock. She was going on well, and in the morning was quite comfortable. She has continued mending all the day, getting much sleep, and my boy is very healthy. I thank God and pray that these favourable appearances may continue, and go to bed tonight full of comfort and hope and thankfulness.

[Caroline writing, 1842]

Feb. 21.—Three weeks and a day since our boy was born. I did not care very much about him the two first days, except when Archer brought him to me first. He seemed to me scarcely alive, or really in the world. Since then I have grown to love him beyond everything except Archer, and to think his society, when he comes to feed upon me, perfectly delightful. He weighed seven pounds six ounces when he was born and measured twenty-one inches. He has dark blue eyes and brown hair, but is not the least pretty as yet. He is very well made and has nice little red hands, mottled, and white nails. His snub nose excites Archer's daily rebuke. He says it is the Clive nose as to the bottle, but wants the bridge. Bad as the pain of his birth was, I thought to myself several times that I wondered people imagined they were going to die in consequence. It did not seem at all like dying, and afterwards when I was really in danger I did not know what was going on. I merely remembered an inclination to sleep. Nothing else than the common wish to sleep after fatigue. Death would be very easy if I was near dying then—no parting, no quitting of the world; mere sleep without waking. It is something to be remembered that one has entered within the shadow of death.

My nurse is very quiet and lets me have my own way. She manages the boy very well, and I manage myself. I have done boldly and eaten fruit and vegetables though ordered not. They said my milk would suffer and disagree with the boy; but he was in torments of pain in consequence of a dose of castor oil which I took without any effect upon myself, and now I do well with my usual diet and it does him no harm. My doctors have taken leave of me, and I am sitting again in the library, dining at the usual hour and getting up to breakfast. The nurse has sundry superstitions. She asked me one day with apologies whether I had wished for anything during my pregnancy without succeeding in getting it. I said no, and enquired why she asked. She said the baby had a habit of licking his lips and rolling his tongue as if he wanted something, and she supposed my unsatisfied longing reappeared in him. The remedy she suggested was some sacramental wine, a *leetle* drop, and then he would be contented.

Feb. 27.—I went in the evening and was churched.* Just a month since I was confined. This day four weeks I was in misery and this day I was well, out of doors again, the mother of a fine healthy boy, and once more setting out in life—another stage—with my own dear husband.

Hodgson called to-day and said that for an hour he thought I should have died. I might have awoke perhaps, had I gone to sleep, but the greater danger of my sleeping was that it prevented the medical attendants from judging of my state. He said the brandy, the salts and sal volatile kept the machine going.

He examined the boy and pronounced him perfect in every respect. I heard from Archer to-day for the first time that there had been some doubt about one ankle, but as it was a mere doubt, Archer resolved not to tell me and succeeded in impressing on the nurse his wish that I should not hear of it. It is wonderful how he refrained from telling. Archer can keep a secret to himself in the most perfect manner of anybody I know. He never even talks round it.

Hodgson asked if I loved the child and said he had seen many instances in which there seemed no maternal feeling. He had frequently known the mother very indifferent to the infant being still-born. She was vexed perhaps if its life was of importance for an heirdom but not for itself.

He said "Don't cut his nails, it makes them grow square." Mrs. Hands [the nurse] thought, however, that it was the use of scissors which was forbidden and when I saw a bit of broken nail and Archer offered her scissors to remove it, she said "Oh no, Sir, I never cut them. I bite them if they want it, or tear them. Mr. Hodgson told us scissors were wrong," she added, triumphing in being able to say she and the doctor were of one mind.

March 9.—Mrs. Hands told me that Mrs. Harding's precaution against thrush was, when she was expecting a baby, to catch a frog and keep it in water till the baby came into the world. If any symptoms of thrush appeared, the frog was sewn into a muslin bag and its head put into the child's mouth, who was induced, if possible, to suck it. The rationale, as set forth by Mrs. Harding, was that the frog's breath drew away the thrush. "The frog always dies," added Mrs. Hands.

---

* An Anglican church ritual, performed after childbirth, in which thanks is given for the safe delivery of mother and child.—EDS.

I was afflicted with bad dreams till we got into our room again, dreaming constantly that Archer was away, or going on a long journey without me, or not writing, and that he was not my husband and I did not know how to see him and thought he was going to marry somebody else—just as it used to be before we were really married. But I have had none since I can put out my hand and find him there.

March 22.—On the 16th (Archer's birthday) our boy was christened. His names are Charles Meysey Bolton and his sponsors, Mrs. Henry Clive, Charles Wicksted and Mrs. Christopher Musgrave.

The ceremony was performed after the morning service and he cried only enough to satisfy his nurse who said she must have pinched him if he had been totally silent because children who don't cry when christened die soon after. Mrs. Musgrave was in mourning, another unlucky sign. Mrs. Hands said she did not suppose dress really brought ill-luck and yet it was true she knew a young woman once, married in a black gown, and certainly she never had any good fortune from that time.

April 29.—Very few events. The boy goes on very well and has had a wet-nurse since last Monday morning. I nursed him for the last time Sunday 17th, eight days before we succeeded in getting him another cow, but I did him more harm than good at last, and he only cried and kicked the last two days of my attempts. The Cow is the mother of a Calf seven weeks old, who went first to a woman with a baby of thirteen months and next to a dry nurse, when the thirteen month baby insisted on returning to its mother. Both of these processes were prohibited for our child, but the poor little plebian does perfectly well.

49. Childbearing in America

No nineteenth-century woman awaited the birth of a child without experiencing some fear that she or her baby would not survive. The state of the obstetrical arts was by no means satisfactory, and relatively simple complications could bring on infirmity or death to rich and poor women alike. Moreover, women worried about the period of dependence following childbirth and fretted about who would manage house and family. In these three selections Laura Lenoir Norwood (1815–94) of Hillsboro, North Carolina, pregnant with her fifth child, expresses her concerns in a letter to her mother; Persis Sibley Andrews (1813–91; Doc. 34.i) of Paris, Maine, confides to her

SOURCES: Letter from Laura Norwood to her mother, May 1, 1845, Lenoir Family Papers, Southern Historical Collection, Library of the University of North Carolina at Chapel Hill. The editors are grateful to Ellen Barrier Neal for bringing this document to our attention, and to the SHC and Martha William Daniels, Camden, S.C., for permission to publish it. (ii) Persis Sibley Andrews Black Journals, 1847, Maine Historical Society. (iii) Notebook containing an account of the death of Ann B. Pettigrew, June 30, 1830, Pettigrew Family Papers, Southern Historical Collection, Library of the University of North Carolina at Chapel Hill.

diary her anxiety and her subsequent relief at the birth of her second healthy child; and Ebenezer Pettigrew, member of a prosperous planter family from Tyrrell County, North Carolina, painfully records the death of his wife in childbirth.

(i) Laura Lenoir Norwood

You asked me about the *time* of my approaching confinement. I am pretty certain that the proper time is not before the middle of June, but as I have always been two or three weeks sooner than I calculated on I shall expect said event about the *first* of June. It would be a great comfort to me to have Sarah or some of you with me, but suppose I can't hope for that. Annie wrote to me in the winter that she wanted to come down this Spring, but I have heard nothing more on the subject since I do wish that she would come and I think she has a very good chance now. Sister E told me she would come up and stay a week with me, if I would send her word when I needed her—I shall feel very much tempted to send for her, though if I am as well as I have generally been after such events could get along without anyone—though it might not be so well for me on the whole. My heart almost sinks within me at the thought of feeding another child & yet I can't feel reconciled to the idea of getting a nurse. I never would have had one if my children had not done so badly on feeding, and now I feel ten times more averse to it than ever. I never mentioned to you what a narrow escape we made with the last nurse I had for little E—. Her husband who belongs to Ma had been sick some weeks of *rheumatism* he said—but finding it necessary at last to call in the Doctor, he pronounced the disease to be quite a different affair from rheumatism, and advised Mr N to send off the nurse immediately*—we did so forthwith and I understand she has not seen a well day since, though she did not complain before leaving here. Eliza will be able to give me some assistance after a while, but not at the time it will be most needed—for I suppose I shall be 3 months ahead of her at least—and I think it much more important for an infant to have breast milk for the first 2 or 3 months of its life than afterwards—but it is not worth while to fret about it and I will try not—when the time comes we must do what seems to be best under the circumstances and trust to providence.

(ii) Persis Sibley Andrews

April 8.—My last stitch is taken & I am now ready for the event for w'h I am looking daily. I have done considerable embroidery, made much more parad[?] than I did before so that my drawers are really beautiful—entirely satisfactory to myself. And now may the God of Mercy give me strength—as the time draws near I fear & tremble. My feelings are peculiar—as I anticipate the bright future—a fine son—or even daughter & speedy restoration to health I am filled with the most lively emotions of joy—aye *delight* in the prospect, but I have suffered much in the last four weeks & often find myself indulging

---

* This seems to suggest that the nurse's husband, and thus the nurse, had syphilis, which could be transmitted to an infant by breast-feeding.

in forbodings of evil—of years of ill health as was the case before & all & the worst ills to be feard in the case. God help me.

May 9.—It seems like a dream:—the month that has past since "Fast": but 'tis not all a dream. Here is my beautiful little daughter & we all love her with a heart full of the fondest affection—*then* she was not; & this fond love of parents & sister we had not known.

I was confined 13th April, w'h was Tuesday, before 2 o'clock in the morn'g, after having been sick 20 hours—very sick but a short time. Sent for my friends Mrs. N. Marble & Mrs. G. K. Shaw & the physician, Doct. Brown about eight o'clock Monday eve'g. Upon the whole, they called it a pretty *comfortable time.* I was not much disappointed in a daughter, tho' I wished for a son. I felt all the time that I wo'd rather have another daughter than never have any other child. The Nurse Miss H. Chesley came early the same day & is yet with me. She is one of the most skilful & experienced in the State—Aged about 43—healthy & smart & has nursed 200 women—is proud of her calling & has a genuine love for infants that amounts to passion. I sho'd have had a good getting up had I not been attacked with canker in the mouth & throat of the most violent & obstinate character. It affected the nerves of the face so that they pained me like ague, & the cheeks swelled much—blood flow'd to the head & the inflamation became high—then it seized upon the brain—I suffered several days the most distracting nervous headache & my physician feared brain fever. For many days I co'd not open my mouth—nor co'd I quite shut it—& for ten days I took no nourishment except simple drinks & that with the greatest difficulty, & I am still much afflicted with sore mouth.

The babe appears smart & healthy. She has a little round solid head & snug body, looked very small to my nurse, but upon weighing her found her just six pounds to the surprise of all. She has a very pretty forehead—high like her fathers—blue eyes light eyebrows lashes etc.—thus we think she will be complected like him. She does not look much as Charlotte did—has not near as much hair—nor is it as dark. All agree in calling her an uncommon handsome child of her age—& I really think they must be sincere—tho' I know this is no indication that she will be pretty a few months hence. The first day I proposed to call her Elizabeth for hus-' Mother, he was rather desirous to have her named for me & proposed Persis Elizabeth, & tho' this is not the *kind* of name I fancy most—I did not object & unless we change our minds this will be her name. . . .

It has been a matter of surprise with me that so much interest has been manifested by the ladies—*every* married lady in the village having called since I was confined—all classes—ten or twelve who never called before. Something owing to custom of the place perhaps, but I wo'd fain believe the longer we live here the more friends we have.

(iii) Ann B. Pettigrew

Mrs. Ann B. Pettigrew was taken in Labour after returning from a walk in the garden, at 7 o'clock in the evening of June 30, 1830. At 40 minutes after 11 o'clock, she was delivered of a daughter.* A short time after, I was informed that the Placenta was not removed, and, at 10 minutes after 12 was asked into the room. I advanced to my dear wife, and kissing her, asked her how she was, to which she replied, I feel very badly. I went out of the room, and sent for Dr. Warren.

I then returned, and inquired if there was much hemorrhage, and was answered that there was. I then asked the midwife (Mrs. Brickhouse) if she ever used manual exertion to remove the placenta. She said she had more than fifty times. I then, fearing the consequences of hemorrhage, observed, Do, my dear sweet wife, permit Mrs. Brickhouse to remove it: To which she assented. After an effort, Mrs. B. exclaimed, "There, you have pushed away my hand, and nearly broke off the cord." A second effort was made, and the cord, with some small quantity of flesh, was brought away. I held one of my dear wife's hands, and I do not believe that she put her hand down. But, I believe, the cord was broken at the first attempt. After the second unsuccessful attempt, I desired the midwife to desist. In these two efforts, my dear Nancy suffered exceedingly and frequently exclaimed: "O Mrs Brickhouse you will kill me," and to me, "O I shall die, send for the Doctor." To which I replied, "I have sent."

After this, my feelings were so agonizing that I had to retire from the room and lay down, or fall. Shortly after which, the midwife came to me and, falling upon her knees, prayed most fervently to God and to me to forgive her for saying that she could do what she could not. After remaining in that posture about ten minutes she fainted, and lay dead I think for an hour.

Several times, when I went in the room, my dear wife would hold up her hand which I would take, but, Alas! my feelings were too agonizing to remain. O my God! do I live when I say I had to leave the room. The servants were so agitated that, at one time, they were obliged all to be taken away, and no one remained by my dear wife but her old and well tried friend Mrs Warrington, who never left the room. The placenta did not come away, and the hemorrhage continued with unabated violence until five o'clock in the morning, when the dear woman breathed her last 20 minutes before the Doctor arrived.

So agonizing a scene as that from one o'clock, I have no words to describe. O My God, My God! have mercy on me. I am undone forever. These things occurred on the first day of July, and on the 2ᵈ at 10 o'clock, my earthly all was laid in the silent grave, from my sight forever. On the 12th, at 4 o'clock, my poor little dear children, Henry, Mary & Johnston set out for Newbern, with their Uncle Richard, to their dear relations, and, on the 24th, my dear little infant left her father's house for Dr Warren's, and I remained where I had spent so many happy, happy, days, Alas! without that dear, dear, woman and the sweet pledges of our love. My God, do I live while I write!

* This daughter was Ann Pettigrew's seventh child. She herself had a miscarriage and died in the first year of her marriage.—EDS.

50. An English mother's problems: The Amberleys

Most parents, even the very rich, were perplexed by the difficulties of rear-ing a new infant. In this selection from the papers of a prominent English family, Kate Stanley (1842–74) and her husband, John Russell, Lord Am-berley, describe the birth of their first child, Frank, and the subsequent diffi-culties they encountered during his infancy. These excerpts from their journal entries and letters show how close Kate and Amberley were to one another and how involved Amberley was in the care of his first child.

[Amberley writing, 1865]

Aug. 12.—Waking at 4 a.m. I was informed by Kate that she was in pain. It was slight, and she tried to prevent my leaving her. However, after a brief struggle, I got up & told her mother who, finding there was no doubt, at once sent for Merriman. The pains rapidly increased, & by 5 became terrible. From that time until delivery they never ceased. Merriman arrived at 6.30 & at 6.50 I heard him say "It's a boy," & heard its sweet little cry. Lady S. called to me it was a fine boy. I ran & told Maude who was waiting ready dressed. K. calm & happy after it. The baby was washed & brought to her. I thought it a very pretty child & felt very proud of it as a part of her. Very delightful to hear her talking to it. She was quite well all day but much exhausted.

Aug. 14.—Tho' perfectly well K. had much trouble today from baby not sucking. He would not or could not do it. Another baby took a little but K still suffered much pain in her breasts. In the evg. b.d. I sucked a little thinking it might do good, but I could not get much. Since I had to apply all my sucking power to get any milk it is no wonder the infant found it too hard for him. The milk was not nasty, but much too sweet to be pleasant; like the sweetest of syrup. It seems very badly managed by nature that little babies should not always find it as easy to suck as little puppies; but if this is one of the arrangements that was made in consequence of Original Sin of course we must not complain of it. Baby, though so obstinate, is a dear little fellow & it is a great happiness to look at his face & feel he is our own, mine & my darling wifie's.

Aug. 15.—Baby still refuses to suck. K. was not very happy or comfortable today having had a bad night & suffering much from headache. I was annoyed at the nursing not being successful & did not feel so happy as the first days. However Lady Stanley says she is sure to nurse with perseverance.

Aug. 16.—K not getting on well & the baby still not sucking.

Aug. 17.—In the evg after my walk I heard he had taken K.'s breast, wh. was a great comfort.

Aug. 20.—K. very low & weak; nurses her baby but has not enough to give it.

SOURCE: *The Amberley Papers*, ed. Bertrand and Patricia Russell (London, 1937), 1: 402–7, 413–16. The editors are grateful to Dr. Patricia Otto Klaus, Belve-dere, Calif., for guiding us to this document.

Aug. 21.—Lady Stanley appears to be dispirited about K., says she is too weak, & that baby is not flourishing as he does not get enough. K. cannot bear the notion of a wet-nurse & I dislike it nearly as much, but there seems no hope of her nursing now.

Aug. 22.—Papa, Mama, the boys & Agatha came today*; Mama admired baby & thought him very fine. I thought he looked pale, & am afraid we must get him a wet-nurse if he is to thrive. However, all who saw him seemed to be pleased with him. Dear K. struggled hard against the wet nurse, but in the evening declared her readiness to give up nursing if the child's health would be better with another woman. A terrible disappointment to her, for we both care very much about ladies nursing, but I doubt not her strong sense of duty will overcome the reluctance to relinquish this harassing attempt to feed her baby when nature does not provide the means of doing so.

Aug. 25.—Lady Stanley has found a woman (married three months, confined three weeks) who she thinks will do for a wet nurse.

Aug. 26.—Merriman came today & finally decided that K. must give up nursing. She was of course dreadfully unhappy but bore it very well. Indeed she has been wonderfully good & patient in all her trials. The wet-nurse was examined & approved. She came this evening. K. drove at 12 with Lady S. having been carried down stairs. She came home much exhausted & continued to feel extremely tired all day.

Aug. 28.—Our new wet-nurse was taken away by her husband, who had not been consulted about the arrangement. Inquiries were set on foot for another.

[Kate writing, 1865]
Sept. 5.—Mr. Merriman came & said the pain I felt was no mischief done only weakness & that I was to walk a little; so I went to luncheon for the first time—& drove with Mama to Astle & lay on the sofa on the lawn till 7. E Powell (the wetnurse) came—baby fought a good deal with her about sucking but took it in the evg. . . . A has been too dear & tender all the time of my confinement; full of care gentleness & thought for me, very low several times which made me sad when I did not feel strong enough to cheer him up. He is very dear too about his boy very fond of him & admires him as much as I do— My m. nurse Mrs. Cotton thinks baby has A's eyes but otherwise like me. He frowns too much but he has been so bothered since his birth—This is the 5th woman he has had poor darling—He weighed 9 lbs when born 10 lbs at a fortnight old & he was 23 inches tall altogether very large & very strong.

Oct. 21.—Amberley had a letter from his father telling him he was Prime Minister—Lizzie told me about Davies's brutal treatment of the baby.† I wrote to Mama to ask her advice.

Oct. 23.—I got a letter from Mama advising me to send away Davies at once—so I sent Lizzy out with the baby & Amberley saw her at 12 & told her she must go she came in & saw me & only said it was very unkind to her—

---

* Amberley's sister and brothers.—EDS.
† Lizzie was the wet nurse, and Davies the baby's regular nurse.—EDS.

She packed up & left at ½ 2—Lizzy told me many more things after she left of her nasty brutal conduct.

[Kate to Georgiana Peel, Amberley's half-sister, Oct. 24, 1865]

The *good trusted clever* Davies is gone for good—& such a good riddance I never knew of. I have been so deceived & with the very highest recommendations she had, it is too horrid—

My wetnurse (Lizzy) told me that Davies was very unkind to the child. The poor woman had lost her own baby & in her grief she could not help telling me all Davies did to mine feeling for a mother being ignorant of such things. I hardly could have believed it but all the other servants had been disgusted by it & told me the same—so I wrote to consult Mama & she said "send her away at once" which I did at 3 hours notice yesterday, as had she stayed she would have worried Lizzy's milk away with her fury—These are one or two of her horrid ways. It makes my blood boil for my precious little darling, to think what he has had to bear. I am too furious. When he cried she used to shake him—when she washed him she used to stuff the sponge in his little mouth— push her finger (beast!) in his dear little throat—say she hated the child, wished he were dead—used to let him lie on the floor screaming while she sat quietly by & said screams did not annoy her it was good for his lungs, besides she liked me to hear him scream as she thought otherwise I should think she had nothing to do & as soon as I came into the room she would take him into her arms & cant over him as if she loved him dearly. She hated being at Alderley because Mama & Mde [Kate's sister] used always to be coming into the room & to Mama she used to lie & when asked if Baby had been out say yes, when she had never stirred fr. the room—She thought she could manage me as she liked & that I would never find her out or find fault with her, & no more I think I should as I trusted her so implicitly. She would not let the wetnurse suckle him before he came to me, that he might scream & that I might know what a trouble he was—she sat in her room most of the day I find reading novels & never nursed the baby or spoke to it.

She said she meant to leave me in March anyhow as she hated the child & did not think the place grand enough—She said she had been accustomed to double her wages (25£) by the baby's clothes she got—She always put it on wet diapers though the nurse asked her to let her air them & so it often had a stomach ache, then she gave it an empty bottle in its cot to suck the tube & keep it quiet so making it suck in only wind—No wonder it cried & was so unhappy. I am so angry with her—Lizzy has had a child before & she quite understands the care of one & as this one is very strong & very well she will do till I can get a nurse & is far better than that wretch of a woman. I shall not get another in a hurry & without great investigations but shall feel afraid for Davies was so praised & so sensible & nice spoken to me—Of course I will never recommend her.

Karl complained to me also of her behaviour to Baby sweet little lamb I do so love it, & have it so much with me now & superintend its washing & dressing but Lizzy is so nice & loves it nearly like her own. She said she could not have gone on nursing it if she had seen it treated in that way any longer. I could write much more about her.

51. How an American mother coped with her first baby: Elizabeth Cady Stanton

Elizabeth Cady Stanton (1815–1902; Doc. 1.i) was one of the most influential leaders of the women's movement in the United States. A woman of tremendous energy, she managed to pursue her political activities while mothering seven children. In this selection from her memoirs she reminisces about her experiences in combating prejudices and mindless tradition in infant care after the birth of her first child in 1842.

The puzzling questions of theology and poverty that had occupied so much of my thoughts, now gave place to the practical one, "what to do with a baby." Though motherhood is the most important of all the professions,—requiring more knowledge than any other department in human affairs,—yet there is not sufficient attention given to the preparation for this office. If we buy a plant of a horticulturist we ask him many questions as to its needs, whether it thrives best in sunshine or in shade, whether it needs much or little water, what degrees of heat or cold; but when we hold in our arms for the first time, a being of infinite possibilities, in whose wisdom may rest the destiny of a nation, we take it for granted that the laws governing its life, health, and happiness are intuitively understood, that there is nothing new to be learned in regard to it. Yet here is a science to which philosophers have, as yet, given but little attention. An important fact has only been discovered and acted upon within the last ten years, that children come into the world tired, and not hungry, exhausted with the perilous journey. Instead of being thoroughly bathed and dressed, and kept on the rack while the nurse makes a prolonged toilet and feeds it some nostrum supposed to have much needed medicinal influence, the child's face, eyes, and mouth should be hastily washed with warm water, and the rest of its body thoroughly oiled, and then it should be slipped into a soft pillow case, wrapped in a blanket, and laid to sleep. Ordinarily, in the proper conditions, with its face uncovered in a cool, pure atmosphere, it will sleep twelve hours. Then it should be bathed, fed, and clothed in a high-necked, long-sleeved silk shirt and a blanket, all of which could be done in five minutes. As babies lie still most of the time the first six weeks, they need no dressing. I think the nurse was a full hour bathing and dressing my first born, who protested with a melancholy wail every blessed minute.

Ignorant myself of the initiative steps on the threshold of time, I supposed this proceeding was approved by the best authorities. However, I had been thinking, reading, observing, and had as little faith in the popular theories

SOURCE: Elizabeth Cady Stanton, *Eighty Years and More: Reminiscences, 1815–1897* (New York, 1898), pp. 112–18.

in regard to babies as on any other subject. I saw them, on all sides, ill half the time, pale and peevish, dying early, having no joy in life. I heard parents complaining of weary days and sleepless nights, while each child, in turn, ran the gauntlet of red gum, jaundice, whooping cough, chicken-pox, mumps, measles, scarlet fever, and fits. They all seemed to think these inflictions were a part of the eternal plan—that Providence had a kind of Pandora's box, from which he scattered these venerable diseases most liberally among those whom he especially loved. Having gone through the ordeal of bearing a child, I was determined, if possible, to keep him, so I read everything I could find on the subject. But the literature on this subject was as confusing and unsatisfactory as the longer and shorter catechisms and the Thirty-nine Articles of our faith. I had recently visited our dear friends, Theodore and Angelina Grimke-Weld, and they warned me against books on this subject. They had been so misled by one author, who assured them that the stomach of a child could only hold one tablespoonful, that they nearly starved their firstborn to death. Though the child dwindled, day by day, and, at the end of a month, looked like a little old man, yet they still stood by the distinguished author. Fortunately, they both went off, one day, and left the child with Sister "Sarah," who thought she would make an experiment and see what a child's stomach could hold, as she had grave doubts about the tablespoonful theory. To her surprise the baby took a pint bottle full of milk, and had the sweetest sleep thereon he had known in his earthly career. After that he was permitted to take what he wanted, and "the author" was informed of his libel on the infantile stomach.

So here, again, I was entirely afloat, launched on the seas of doubt without chart or compass. The life and well-being of the race seemed to hang on the slender thread of such traditions as were handed down by ignorant mothers and nurses. One powerful ray of light illuminated the darkness; it was the work of Andrew Combe on "Infancy." He had evidently watched some of the manifestations of man in the first stages of his development, and could tell, at least, as much of babies as naturalists could of beetles and bees. He did give young mothers some hints of what to do, the whys and wherefores of certain lines of procedure during antenatal life, as well as the proper care thereafter. I read several chapters to the nurse. Although, out of her ten children, she had buried five, she still had too much confidence in her own wisdom and experience to pay much attention to any new idea that might be suggested to her. Among other things, Combe said that a child's bath should be regulated by the thermometer, in order to be always of the same temperature. She ridiculed the idea, and said her elbow was better than any thermometer, and, when I insisted on its use, she would invariably, with a smile of derision, put her elbow in first, to show how exactly it tallied with the thermometer. When I insisted that the child should not be bandaged, she rebelled outright, and said she would not take the responsibility of nursing a child without a bandage. I said, "Pray, sit down, dear nurse, and let us reason together. Do not think I am setting up my judgment against yours, with all your experience. I am simply trying to act on the opinions of a distinguished physican, who says there should be no pressure on a child anywhere; that the limbs and body should be free; that it is cruel to bandage an infant from hip to armpit, as is usually done in America; or both body and legs, as is done in Europe; or strap them to boards, as is done by savages on both continents. Can you give me one good reason, nurse, why a child should be bandaged?"

"Yes," she said emphatically, "I can give you a dozen."

"I only asked for one," I replied.

"Well," said she, after much hesitation, "the bones of a newborn infant are soft, like cartilage, and, unless you pin them up snugly, there is danger of their falling apart."

"It seems to me," I replied, "you have given the strongest reason why they should be carefully guarded against the slightest pressure. It is very remarkable that kittens and puppies should be so well put together that they need no artificial bracing, and the human family be left wholly to the mercy of a bandage. Suppose a child was born where you could not get a bandage, what then? Now I think this child will remain intact without a bandage, and, if I am willing to take the risk, why should you complain?"

"Because," said she, "if the child should die, it would injure my name as a nurse. I therefore wash my hands of all these new-fangled notions."

So she bandaged the child every morning, and I as regularly took it off. It has been fully proved since to be as useless an appendage as the vermiform. She had several cups with various concoctions of herbs standing on the chimney-corner, ready for insomnia, colic, indigestion, etc., etc., all of which were spirited away when she was at her dinner. In vain I told her we were homeopathists, and afraid of everything in the animal, vegetable, or mineral kingdoms lower than the two-hundredth dilution. I tried to explain the Hahnemann system of therapeutics, the philosophy of the principle *similia similibus curantur*, but she had no capacity for first principles, and did not understand my discourse. I told her that, if she would wash the baby's mouth with pure cold water morning and night and give it a teaspoonful to drink occasionally during the day, there would be no danger of red gum; that if she would keep the blinds open and let in the air and sunshine, keep the temperature of the room at sixty-five degrees, leave the child's head uncovered so that it could breathe freely, stop rocking and trotting it and singing such melancholy hymns as "Hark, from the tombs a doleful sound!" the baby and I would both be able to weather the cape without a bandage. I told her I should nurse the child once in two hours, and that she must not feed it any of her nostrums in the meantime; that a child's stomach, being made on the same general plan as our own, needed intervals of rest as well as ours. She said it would be racked with colic if the stomach was empty any length of time, and that it would surely have rickets if it were kept too still. I told her if the child had no anodynes, nature would regulate its sleep and motions. She said she could not stay in a room with the thermometer at sixty-five degrees, so I told her to sit in the next room and regulate the heat to suit herself; that I would ring a bell when her services were needed.

The reader will wonder, no doubt, that I kept such a cantankerous servant. I could get no other. Dear "Mother Monroe," as wise as she was good, and as tender as she was strong, who had nursed two generations of mothers in our village, was engaged at that time, and I was compelled to take an exotic. I had often watched "Mother Monroe" with admiration, as she turned and twisted my sister's baby. It lay as peacefully in her hands as if they were lined with eider down. She bathed and dressed it by easy stages, turning the child over and over like a pancake. But she was so full of the magnetism of human love, giving the child, all the time, the most consoling assurance that the operation was to be a short one, that the whole proceeding was quite entertaining to the observer and seemingly agreeable to the child, though it had a rather surprised look as it took a bird's-eye view, in quick succession, of the ceiling and the floor. Still my nurse had her good points. She was very pleasant when she had her own way. She was neat and tidy, and ready to serve me at any time, night or day. She did not wear false teeth that rattled when she talked, nor boots that squeaked when she walked. She did not snuff nor chew cloves, nor speak except when spoken to. Our discussions, on various points, went on at intervals, until I succeeded in planting some ideas in her mind, and when she left me, at the end of six weeks, she confessed that she had learned some valuable lessons. As the baby had slept quietly most of the time, had no crying spells, nor colic, and I looked well, she naturally came to the conclusion that pure air, sunshine, proper dressing, and regular feeding were more necessary for babies than herb teas and soothing syrups.

52. Nursing advice for ladies

In this great age of advice manuals, professional experts intruded with their strictures into all areas of family life. In medicine the superior French and German medical faculties produced monographs and manuals that carried great authority throughout Atlantic civilization, and British and American translations of such works proliferated. In these two selections Alfred Donné (1801–78) and Eugène Bouchut (1818–91), both eminent Parisian physicians and professors of medicine, offer mothers advice about nursing and about selecting wet nurses. As with Dr. Colombat's rules for puberty (Doc. 17.ii), the emphasis is on regularity and constraint. In this mixture of medical and moral advice, mothers are cautioned to distrust their own impulses and to defer to the superior wisdom of the medical experts.

(i) Eugène Bouchut

In the first days following birth, the children may be frequently put to the breast, for it is a difficult matter to satisfy them; but after the first few weeks, a greater interval should be allowed to elapse between the hours of

SOURCES: (i) Eugène Bouchut, *Practical Treatise on the Diseases of Children and Infants at the Breast*, tr. Peter Huickes Bird, F.R.C.S. (London, 1855), pp. 12–13. Originally published in Paris in 1845. (ii) Alfred Donné, *Mothers and Infants, Nurses and Nursing* (Boston, 1859), pp. 35–58 *passim*, 104–6, 119–20. Originally published in Paris in 1842.

lactation. Women should not be inconsiderately zealous to discharge their duty of nurse, and always endeavour to calm the cries of the child by giving it the breast; they should, having the interest of the nursling at heart, take care of themselves, and not exhaust their strength by too frequent lactation.

During the day, mothers should suckle their children every hour, or every two hours, at least; during the night they should train their child not to wake them to take the breast. This is very easily accomplished; they soon acquire the habit, and experience no injury from it. The mother then, finds in sleep a salutary repose after the fatigues of the day. She may enjoy from six to eight hours uninterrupted sleep, by giving the breast, for the last time, towards eleven or twelve o'clock at night; and by recommencing the next day at six or seven o'clock in the morning. . . .

The mammary glands—which by their seat and form constitute the ornaments of the sex, become, by their functions, the source of a new existence, and are placed, by their structure, under the influence of the moral activity. We cannot, then, too strongly recommend to mothers who suckle their children, to endeavour to acquire the calmness and tranquillity necessary to the direction of a good education. But what words can one use to a woman whose heart thrills at the cries of her child, and whose mind is so deeply disturbed at them? Are we not fearful of seeing the heart get the better of the intelligence, and maternal passion triumph over reason? Nevertheless, the practitioner should deliver his firm and respectful dictum in the midst of these blind and exalted sentiments, which exercise the most disastrous influence on the health of the children.

The mother should be given to understand that the qualities of her milk are rapidly changed by violent mental emotions; and that tranquillity is absolutely necessary to her, in order that she may become a good nurse. What matter the cries of a child which has had the breast to a sufficient extent at the proper hour; which does not suffer, and which experiences no want? If it cries, it is by caprice; we must learn to resist it; then it ceases, and learns for the future not to cry without a motive. In this manner it becomes docile, and its cries assume much value from the time when it is known that they are always a manifestation of suffering.

(ii) Alfred Donné

ON NURSING BY THE MOTHER

Advantages of nursing by the mother; preference to be given to her.— There are, indeed, many mothers, whom I would not accept as nurses for other children than their own, whom I believe perfectly capable of nursing their own children, and often preferable even to the best hired nurses. . . .

If we were to allow the ability to nurse a child only to mothers of as robust strength and health as we require in hired nurses, we might nearly abandon the idea that ladies can ever nurse their children; for it is very rarely that we meet with these conditions in women who inhabit large cities, and particularly among those of certain classes of society. But there are so many compensations for their inferiority in this respect to hired nurses, that it is well to limit, in some degree, our requirements, and not to push severity to excess. Nothing is more common, in fact, than to see, even in Paris, women of medium strength, whose health is not always exempt from a crowd of those little ills which seem inherent to a certain social position, possessing, nevertheless, the qualities essential for a nurse, and performing this office with the greatest success, without experiencing any deterioration in their own health. It would be cruel, indeed, both for the mother and the child, to oppose the inclination to nurse, which these women experience, and to deprive the child of his natural nurse. . . .

Importance of putting an immediate stop to nursing in certain cases.—There are cases in which we cannot too soon put a stop to nursing. I have had an opportunity to observe [some] remarkable ones, which prove that, even if compulsion must be used, no hesitation should be felt in like circumstances to transfer the child from the mother to a hired nurse.

A very light-complexioned young mother, in very good health, and of a good constitution, though somewhat delicate, was nursing for the third time, and, as regarded the child, successfully. All at once this young woman experienced a feeling of exhaustion. Her skin became constantly hot; there were cough, oppression, night-sweats; her strength visibly declined, and in less than a fortnight she presented the ordinary symptoms of consumption. The nursing was immediately abandoned, and, from the moment the secretion of milk had ceased, all the troubles disappeared, the mother's health was restored, and, since then,—a period of now three years,—it has not ceased to be excellent, and no suspicious symptoms have again manifested themselves.

A woman of forty years of age, a door-keeper in the house I inhabit, having lost one after another several children, all of whom she had put out to nurse, determined to nurse the last one herself, which was born at the age I have mentioned. This woman, being vigorous and well-built, was eager for the work, and, filled with devotion and spirit, she gave herself up to the nursing of her child with a sort of fury. At nine months she still nursed him from fifteen to twenty times a day.

Having become extremely emaciated, she fell all at once into a state of weakness, from which nothing could raise her, and two days after the poor woman died of exhaustion. . . .

Nursing requires to be conducted with a certain method. It must take place at intervals as well-regulated as possible; the caprices which manifest themselves thus early must be wisely resisted, and bad habits must be avoided; and, when the mother is certain that her child has all which he needs, that he has nursed sufficiently, and that he does not suffer, she must know how to divert his attention, and even be able to bear his cries, without yielding to new importunities. This last point is so essential, that I do not fear to make of it a veritable axiom, in saying, that *every mother who cannot bear to hear her child cry, is incapable of bringing him up well.* . . .

OF PROFESSIONAL NURSES

Choice of a nurse.—If the mother does not intend to nurse her child, it becomes necessary to choose a nurse. In making the selection, suitable precautions are not always taken; much less, doubtless, through indifference or negligence, than in consequence of the general ignorance of the essential conditions to be required in the nurse, and of the evils which are to be feared. Our duty is to enlighten families, by attacking their very general prejudices, their want of attention to what is really important, and their frequently capricious requirements, as well as the trickery of nurses themselves, their defects, and the dangers they present. . . .

A certain family had taken all the ordinary precautions to procure a good nurse for a first-born child. The woman was young, ruddy, and apparently in perfect health.

At the end of a month several pimples were observed on the child's body. No great attention was at first paid to them; but they multiplied rapidly, and assumed such an aspect that it was thought necessary to call a physician. He immediately recognized the nature of the disease, and an examination of the nurse at once confirmed this sad result. She was herself infected, and had transmitted the disease to her nursling, either by her milk or by contact.*

The despair of the parents may be easily conceived. But this was not the end of their troubles and afflictions. The father wished to dismiss the nurse on the spot; but he was obliged to restrain his indignation and resentment, when he was informed that this nurse had herself become necessary for the cure of the child; that he must not only keep her, but treat her well to induce her to stay, in order through her to reach the child by treatment; that it was not possible to entrust a child, in that condition of disease, to another healthy nurse, to whom it would communicate the disease immediately, &c.

This hard alternative had to be accepted. But all sacrifices proved unavailing; no care could save the child, and it soon miserably perished.

Now, one single precaution had been neglected in this case,—the preliminary and complete examination of the nurse. . . .

Of the nurse's suckling the child during the night.—Nurses have not the same reason as mothers to suspend nursing during the night.

The reason of this difference must be obvious. Most ladies who undertake to nurse their children, are not strong enough to bear at the same time the fatigue of nursing itself, and that which results from the interruption or privation of sleep. It is, then, less for the purpose of sparing them, than with a view to preserve their milk, that I advise them to suspend nursing during the night. Rest being an indispensable condition in the secretion of milk, prolonged sleep becomes for them a greater necessity than for hired nurses of

---

* Is the venereal disease transmitted in such a case by means of the milk, or by contact and direct conveyance of the contagious principle? This question is not at all determined in the present condition of science. All that I can say is, that by no means, whether by the microscope or any other process of analysis, can the slightest trace of alteration in the milk in syphilitic women be detected.

a more robust constitution. The inconveniences, however, if any exist, are more than compensated by the advantages of nursing by the mother.

53. Slave motherhood

The slave women of the American South endured the most bitter maternal experiences, as the following reminiscences from elderly ex-slaves attest. Their babies could be sold away from them at any time, and even the mothers who were allowed to keep their children had to leave them in the care of young-sters or old women, or even alone on pallets in courtyards or hedges, so that they could return to work in field or house. Although some masters were scrupulous about protecting slave families and keeping them intact, others bred and sold slaves as if they were domestic animals. The slave lullaby in the eighth selection reflects the bitterness of black "mammies" who were forced to neglect their infants while pampering their white charges in the big house.

(i) Mary Gaines

One reason mother said she wanted to get away from their new master, he have a hole dug out with a hoe and put pregnant women on their stomach. The overseers beat their back with cowhide and them strapped down. She said 'cause they didn't keep up work in the field or they didn't want to work. She didn't know why. They didn't stay there very long. She didn't want to go back there.

(ii) Susan Hamlin

Lots of wickedness gone on in dem days, just as it do now, some good, some mean, black and white, it just dere nature, if dey good dey going to be kind to everybody, if dey mean dey going to be mean to everybody. Sometimes chillen was sold away from dey parents. De Mausa would come and say "Where Jennie," tell um to put clothes on dat baby, I want um. He sell de baby and de ma scream and holler, you know how dey carry on. Geneally (generally) dey sold it when de ma wasn't dere.

(iii) William McWhorter

My Aunt Mary b'longed to Marse John Craddock and when his wife died and left a little baby—dat was little Miss Lucy—Aunt Mary was nussin' a new baby of her own, so Marse John made her let his baby suck too. If Aunt Mary was feedin' her own baby and Miss Lucy started cryin' Marse John would snatch her baby up by the legs and spank him, and tell Aunt Mary to

SOURCES: All selections except the eighth are from *The American Slave: A Composite Autobiography*, ed. George P. Rawick (Westport, Conn., 1972), as follows. (i) vol. 9: *Arkansas Narratives*, part 3: 9. (ii), (iv) vol. 2: *South Carolina Narratives*, part 2: 12–13, 231. (iii) vol. 13: *Georgia Narratives*, part 3: 96–97. (v), (vi), (ix), vol. 4: *Texas Narratives*, part 1: 76–77, 86, 107. (vii) vol. 7: *Oklahoma Narratives*, pp. 187–88. (viii) John A. Lomax and Alan Lomax, *Best Loved American Folk Songs* (New York, 1947), p. 15.

go on and nuss his baby fust. Aunt Mary couldn't answer him a word, but my ma said she offen seed Aunt Mary cry 'til de tears met under her chin.

(iv) 'Mom' Ryer Emmanuel

Yes, honey, I been come here under a blessin cause my white folks never didn' let dey colored people suffer no time. Always when a woman would get in de house, old Massa would let her leave off work en stay dere to de house a month till she get mended in de body way. Den she would have to carry de child to de big house en get back in de field to work. Oh, dey had a old woman in de yard to de house to stay dere en mind all de plantation chillun till night come, while dey parents was workin. Dey would let de chillun go home wid dey mammy to spend de night en den she would have to march dem right back to de yard de next mornin. We didn' do nothin, but play bout de yard dere en eat what de woman feed us. Yes'um, dey would carry us dere when de women would be gwine to work. Be dere fore sunrise. Would giv us three meals a day cause de old woman always give us supper fore us mammy come out de field dat evenin. Dem bigger ones, dey would give dem clabber en boil peas en collards sometimes. Would give de little babies boil pea soup en gruel en suck bottle. Yes, mam, de old woman had to mind all de yearlin chillun en de babies, too. Dat all her business was. I recollects her name, it been Lettie. Would string us little wooden bowls on de floor in a long row en us would get down dere en drink just like us was pigs. Oh, she would give us a iron spoon to taste wid, but us wouldn't never want it.

(v) Charlotte Beverly

The white folks had interes' in they cullud people where I live. Sometimes they's as many as fifty cradle with little nigger babies in 'em and the mistus, she look after them and take care of them, too. She turn them and dry them herself. She had a little gal git water and help. She never had no chillen of her own. I'd blow the horn for the mudders of the little babies to come in from the fields and nurse 'em, in mornin' and afternoon. Mistus feed them what was old enough to eat victuals. Sometimes, they mammies take them to the field and fix pallet on ground for them to lay on.

(vi) Elvira Boles

I's seventeen, maybe, when I married to slave of Boles. Married on Saturday night. Dey give me a dress and dey had things to eat, let me have something like what you call a party. We just had common clothes on. And then I had to work every day. I'd leave my baby cryin' in de yard and he'd be cryin', but I couldn't stay. Done everything but split rails. I've cut timber and plowed. Done everything a man could do. I couldn' notice de time, but I'd be glad to git back to my baby.

(vii) Mattie Logan

My mother belonged to Mistress Jennie who thought a heap of her, and why shouldn't she? Mother nursed all Miss Jennie's children because all of her young ones and my mammy's was born so close together it wasn't no trouble at all for mammy to raise the whole kaboodle of them. I was born about the same time as the baby Jennie. They say I nursed on one breast while that white child, Jennie, pulled away at the other!

That was a pretty good idea for the Mistress, for it didn't keep her tied to the place and she could visit around with her friends most any time she wanted 'thout having to worry if the babies would be fed or not.

Mammy was the house girl and account of that and because her family was so large, the Mistress fixed up a two room cabin right back of the Big House and that's where we lived. The cabin had a fireplace in one of the rooms, just like the rest of the slave cabins which was set in a row away from the Big House. In one room was bunk beds, just plain old two-by-fours with holes bored through the plank so's ropes could be fastened in and across for to hold the corn-shuck mattress.

My brothers and sisters was allowed to play with the Master's children, but not with the children who belonged to the field Negroes.

(viii) 'All the Pretty Little Horses'

Hush-you-bye,
Don't you cry,
Go to sleepy, little baby.
When you wake,
You shall have
All the pretty little horses—
Blacks and bays,
Dapples and grays,
Coach and six-a little horses.
Hush-you-bye,
Don't you cry,
Go to sleepy, little baby.

Hush-you-bye,
Don't you cry,
Go to sleepy, little baby.
Way down yonder
In de medder
Lies a po' lil' lambie;
De bees an' de butterflies
Peckin' out its eyes,
De po' lil' thing cried, "Mammy!"
Hush-you-bye,
Don't you cry,
Go to sleepy, little baby.

(ix) Ellen Betts

Miss Sidney was Marse's first wife and he had six boys by her. Den he marry de widow Cornelius and she give him four boys. With ten chillen springin' up quick like dat and de cullud chillen comin' 'long fast as pig litters, I don't do nothin all my days, but nuss, nuss, nuss. I nuss so many chillen it done went and stunted my growth and dat's why I ain't nothin' but bones to dis day.

When de cullud women has to cut cane all day till midnight come and after, I has to nuss de babies for dem and tend de white chillen, too. Some dem babies so fat and big I had to tote de feet while 'nother gal tote de head. I was sech a li'l one, 'bout seven or eight year old. De big folks leave some toddy for colic and cryin' and sech and I done drink de toddy and let de chillen have de milk. I don't know no better. Lawsy me, it a wonder I ain't de biges' drunker in dis here country, countin' all de toddy I done put in my young belly!

When late of night come, iffen dem babies wake up and bawl, I set up a screech and out-screech dem till dey shut dere mouth. De louder dey bawl de louder I bawl. Sometime when Marse hear de babies cry, he come down and say, "Why de chillen cry like dat, Ellen?" I say, "Marse, I git so hongry and tired I done drink de milk up." When I talk sassy like dat, Marse jes' shake he finger at me, 'cause he knowed I's a good one and don't let no little mite starve.

54. Motherhood in English factory towns

Like American slaves, English working women had to fit pregnancy and motherhood into a life of virtually unceasing labor. As the statements of the Manchester midwife in the first selection reveal, factory women often worked up to the hour of delivery and returned to the mill after a brief confinement. Forced to work in order to feed themselves and their babies, these women either had to try to tend their infants while working at home or had to find someone—frequently a young child—to look after their children while they went out to a factory or sweatshop. In either case, babies were often dosed with opiate-based patent medicines to keep them quiet, as the reports from Nottingham in the second selection reveal. These two sets of testimonies from the 'Parliamentary Papers' show how far removed were the nurseries of the poor from those envisioned by Lydia Child (Doc. 57).

(i) Elizabeth Taylor

What is your age?—Fifty-two.

What is your occupation?—Midwifery.

Have you been attached for any time to the Manchester lying-in hospital? —Betwixt nine and ten years.

How long have you been in the habit of delivering women?—I began at twelve years old, in Manchester. . . .

At what age do you find that the factory women are generally delivered of their first child?—From eighteen to nineteen, most of them.

Are the factory women to whom you are called generally married?—I have a good deal of both sorts, both married and unmarried.

Do many of the factory women live with men without being married? —That I cannot tell. I attend many for love-children, but I cannot tell what becomes of them afterwards.

Are miscarriages more common among factory women than among the others whom you attend?—Much more frequent among the factory women.

In which class have you found still births most common?—I never took any particular notice.

Do you find that the children of factory women are as healthy when first

SOURCES: (i) Great Britain, *Parliamentary Papers*, 1833, XX Factory Inquiry Commission, 1st Report, pp. D3 13–14. (ii) Great Britain, *Parliamentary Papers*, 1843, XIV, Children's Employment Commission, part 1, pp. f. 45, 61–62.

born as those of other women?—No, certainly not; they are more delicate.

To what do you ascribe their being more delicate?—To the mother's being more delicate, from heat, and want of proper food.

How long do the factory women generally work up to the time of their being confined?—Many of them up to the very day; some up to the very hour, as I may say. Some have gone to work before breakfast, and I have had them in bed at two o'clock the same day. A girl has gone to work after her breakfast, and I have delivered her, and all over, by twece o'clock the same forenoon.

How soon do they go back to the factory after confinement?—Many at the end of a fortnight; three weeks they think a great bit.

Do any factory women complain of pain from working when they are pregnant?—Many complain of pains in their sides and legs.

When you attend a factory woman do you generally find that she has got tea, sugar, gruel, and other such things about her?—Very few of them have such things. . . .

During the winter, do you generally find they have got fire and candles upon such occasions?—No; very rarely. I have had to go to the watchman for a light.

Have they generally got baby-linen?—In a general way the English have, but the Irish not often. . . .

You often examine the persons of factory wives; do you often find any hurt or blemish?—I often find their feet and legs swelled.

Whom do you find most lean, the factory wives or the others whom you attend?—The factory wives are a deal more lean and more delicate.

What do they do with their infants?—Puts them out to nurse to any one they can get.

Do the children do well?—Some of them suffer very bad from this.

(ii) Drugging the babies in Nottingham

Elizabeth Smith, 26 years old:—Is married, and has two children; one is now alive, and the other died when nearly two years old; has been a lace runner about 13 years. The business has become much worse of late years; in the best season can earn about 5s. a-week; in the winter about 2s. 6d. if she sticks very close to it; the candles cost 6½d. a-week at this time. To earn 2s. 6d., must begin between seven and eight in the morning, and go on till about nine at night. Has breakfast before she begins; has about one hour to get the dinner ready, and eat it; and half an hour for tea. When a piece is to be finished, perhaps once in a fortnight, has to work on Thursday and Friday, till between 11 and 12; has not of late worked all Friday night, nor on Sunday.

Is near-sighted; the work tries the eyes very much; has sometimes a very bad mist, and also sparks. When she was nursing, kept the child upon her lap. It is very common to give Godfrey's cordial; has known several who have given it to their children. Lives with her husband and child in a low kitchen, (cellar,) and pays 10d. a-week. Her husband is a jobbing labourer; is now out of work; had yesterday no breakfast; a few potatoes and salt for dinner; and a bit of bread and coffee for tea; had a bit of bread and coffee this morning;

her husband had no breakfast; it is now a quarter past two, and she and her child have had no dinner, and do not expect to have any; her husband is gone to seek for work.

NOTE.—This poor woman lives in one of those wretched under-ground rooms, which are not uncommon in this particular part of the town. There were scarcely any articles of furniture, and everything had the appearance of great distress and misery. The daughter had lately had the small-pox. The privies, three in number, are used in common by several houses.

Sarah Johnson, 43 years old:—Has lived in Nottingham all her life. Knows it is quite a common custom for mothers to give Godfrey's and the Anodyne cordial to their infants, "it is quite too common." It is given to infants at the breast; it is not given because the child is ill, but "to compose it to rest, to sleep it," so that the mother may get to work. "Has seen an infant lay asleep on its mother's lap whilst at the lace-frame for six or eight hours at a time." This has been from the effects of the cordial; has never known an infant die suddenly from this cause; has seen many made "very poor creatures by it;" they get very thin: the joints and the head enlarge; they become remarkably listless, and they look vacant. The cordial is discontinued between two and three years old; at this age has known several to have the appearance of idiots. From three to four years old, the laudanum being discontinued, the children "generally begin to come round," if they get over the seasoning. In the present state of trade, it would be impossible for men to do without their wives labour-ing; they must work, however many children they may have: from the same cause, the children must go out to work as soon as they are able to use the needle. In Nottingham, the girls begin to work younger than the boys, because "it is rather more natural for them to handle the needle."

A. B.—Has been a chemist and druggist for many years in the town of Nottingham. A large quantity of laudanum and other preparations of opium, such as Godfrey's cordial, is sold by the chemists, especially in the poorer neighbourhoods of the town. Knows a chemist who sells as much as a gallon of laudanum a-week in retail; and also knows that several chemists in Not-tingham sell many gallons each in the year. A large quantity of solid opium is also sold; it is common, in many of the shops, to keep it ready prepared in small packets, like other articles in constant demand; these are sold at a penny or twopence each. Witness is obliged to prepare the laudanum of a greater strength than is prescribed in the Pharmacopœia, or the persons who purchase it would object. Godfrey's cordial, also called Anodyne cordial, and of which a very large quantity is sold in Nottingham, is prepared stronger of laudanum than is usual in the real Godfrey's cordial as sold in London.

The solid opium is consumed exclusively by adults, men and women, but more by the latter than the former, in the proportion of 3 to 1.

The laudanum is partly consumed by adults, and to a considerable extent by infants. Godfrey's, or the Anodyne cordial, is almost exclusively consumed by infants.

It is a common practice among a large portion of the poorest class of mechanics, inhabiting such places as "the Becks" and the "Meadow Platts," habitually to use opium in the fluid or solid form. Has some customers who take as much as an ounce of laudanum in a day; knows one woman who has taken that quantity in his shop.

Among the poorest classes it is a common practice of mothers to administer Godfrey's cordial and laudanum to their infants; the object is to keep them quiet whilst the mother is at work. A case occurred a short time ago of a mother coming into the shop with her child in the arms. Witness remonstrated against giving it laudanum, and told the mother she had better go home and put the child in a bucket of water,—"it would have been the most humane place of putting it out of the way." The mother replied that the infant had been used to the laudanum and must have it, and that it took a halfpenny worth a-day, or 60 drops. Does not know what has become of the child, but "supposes it is done for by this time." It is not uncommon for mothers to begin this practice with infants of a fortnight old; commencing with half a teaspoonful of Godfrey's, or 1 or 2 drops of laudanum. Has known an infant killed with three drops of laudanum, but nothing was said about it. Knows that many infants die by degrees, and that no inquest or other inquiry is made. Has known some odd cases where surgeons have been called to apply the stomach pump; but "infants go off quickly, they are not like grown people." A case of sudden death in an infant from laudanum occurred about three years ago, in which an inquest was held at the sign of the Fox, from Godfrey's cordial. Heard that four children of the same family had died in the same way. The infants which die in a more insidious manner become pale and emaciated and tremulous, and at last seem to sink from emaciation or a decline.

The system has considerably increased since witness has been in the business, which he attributes to the abject poverty of the people. Some females, lace runners, do not get more than half-a-crown per week. Mothers say they have not time to nurse their children, as they must work so many hours to obtain this pittance of a living, "if it be a living."

Mary Colton, 20 years old, lace runner:—Has worked at lace piece since she was six years old, for 14 or 15 hours a-day on the average; used to commence at 6 A.M. in summer, and left off at 10 at night; in winter, at half past 8 A.M., and worked till 10 P.M.; could earn from 4s to 5s. a-week. Was in the habit of sitting from 5 A.M. till 10 P.M. when the work was urgent; never went home to her meals till she was confined, some times had half an hour, oftener not. Was confined of an illegitimate child in November, 1839. When the child was a week old she gave it half a teaspoonful of Godfrey's twice a-day. She could not afford to pay for the nursing of the child, and so gave it Godfrey's to keep it quiet, that she might not be interrupted at the lace piece; she gradually increased the quantity by a drop or two at a time until it reached a teaspoonful; when the infant was four months old it was so "wankle" and thin that folks persuaded her to give it laudanum to bring it on, as it did other children. A halfpenny worth, which was about a teaspoonful and three-quarters, was given in two days; continued to give her this quantity since February,

1840, until this last past (1841), and then reduced the quantity. She now buys a halfpenny worth of laudanum and a halfpenny worth of Godfrey's mixed, which lasts her three days.

Can earn about 3s. a-week now, working from 9 A.M. till 10 P.M., having one hour for dinner, and three-quarters of an hour for tea. If it had not been for her having to sit so close to work she would never have given the child the Godfrey's. She has tried to break it off many times but cannot, for if she did, she should not have anything to eat.

Cannot either read or write; often wishes she had been sent to school, but never had anything to go in.

55. Baby farming in England: Police Serjeant Relf

In nineteenth-century England there were several ways to rid oneself of unwanted children. Abortions were available, although they were illegal, highly dangerous and often costly. A more extreme method was infanticide, which by the 1860's had come to be recognized as a national problem. A third option was "baby farming," a system by which the mother paid a third party to house and care for the child. In the absence of legal adoption the baby farm often seemed the most humane alternative to the desperate—often unmarried —mother. But whatever the intention of the mother, the farmed-out child frequently met with a gruesome fate, as the following testimony of a London policeman reveals. In his testimony to a parliamentary committee Relf described in grisly detail an unusually complete system for disposing of unwanted children; Mary Hall's house served as a lying-in hospital, and Hall placed those infants who survived with baby farmers. The outrage caused by the public disclosure of the horrors of the baby farm, together with the lobbying efforts of medical reformers, stirred Parliament, in 1872, to pass legislation to control the worst abuses of the baby farming system. Hall, however, was never punished for her crimes against children, although she was sentenced to two years' hard labor and fined £100 for fraudulently claiming that a baby was the child of a woman who was not in fact the mother.

Abstract Report, by Police Serjeant Relf, of the Case of Mary Hall
for Fraud.—P Division, 30 November 1870

I beg most respectfully to report for the information of Mr. Superintendent Gernon, the following abstract of the case of Mary Hall, lately residing at No. 6, Chapel-place, Cold Harbour-lane, Camberwell. . . .

This Mrs. Hall, and David, her husband, have resided at the above address since May, 1864, paying a yearly rental of £30, besides rates and taxes.

SOURCE: Great Britain, *Parliamentary Papers*, 1871, VII, Select Committee on Protection of Infant Life, pp. 229–32. The editors wish to thank Professor George Behlmer, University of Washington, for kindly offering us a copy of this document.

For three years prior to that date they lived at No. 4, Denmark-road, Camber-well, a short distance from Chapel-place. . . .

The first evidence I would direct your attention to is that of Mrs. Warren, who lives at No. 5, next door, and her servant, Elizabeth Culven. They prove undoubtedly that a great number of ladies were seen at Mrs. Hall's pregnant, sometimes five or more at a time; in addition to the servant hearing women groaning at night (as the head of her bed was next the wall), they usually, once or more a week, experienced a most sickening odour of something being burnt or boiled of a fleshy kind, and, strange to relate, never heard a child cry or saw one leave the house on any occasion during the whole time Hall has been there. This is confirmed by Mr. and Mrs. Tennant, who, during 1867–8, lived at No. 7. As to what she saw it is best stated in her own words. They are as follows:

"I have seen as many as six or seven women there at a time in the family-way. I have noticed bad smells from something or other being burnt. I have seen Mrs. Hall carry an infant from the garden into the house head down-wards. I never saw a live child leave next door. I have seen two small coffins taken away at night carried by a man. A little woman used to come after each confinement (a hunchback) and take away parcels since traced. Hall used to do the washing after confinements, and I have seen him throw lumps out of the clothes to two cats that he kept, and they eat it."

Having now seen what the residents next door have observed, it will be necessary to look into the house, and to do that it will be best to refer to the statements made by the servants employed by Mrs. Hall. . . .

Matilda Barrett, of 15, Thornhill-square, Walworth, the servant who gave evidence at the police court, [was] at Mr. Hall's from January till March 1870, and speaks of two women being confined, and their infants disposed of in the way detailed, viz., one thrown down a hole in the garden by Mr. Hall, the other took away by Mrs. Hall and Waters in a brown paper parcel. At the spot referred to by this girl, there is a hole about three feet deep filled up now with cinder ashes, lime, and a quantity of fatty sort of earth, in which were a great number of small maggots. The last domestic prior to Mrs. Hall's ap-prehension was her niece, Ellen Maria Crafter, age 13, now living at Greenstead Green, Kent; she was in Mrs. Hall's service for six months in 1870; during that time saw as many as five ladies in the house pregnant at one time. She knew a Mrs. Lester and Mrs. Cutting who were confined, and saw their babies alive the day after their birth; states these infants were taken away by Mrs. Hall, but she has no idea what became of them, as her aunt never told her.

We have here a total of 46 births, and yet between 1st January 1868, and when Mrs. Hall was taken into custody, only eight have been registered, and only in one case has Mrs. Hall been the informant. Having now obtained an insight into the system pursued at this private lying-in house, I will next refer to the females' statements that have been confined at 6, Chapel-place, as to what became of their offspring, and the amounts paid by these various per-sons for attendance, &c., and to find homes for their infants, to Mrs. Hall.

The earliest date of confinement in which the woman was discovered, relates to a female named Amelia Woodford, now living as housemaid in the family of Sir Benjamin Brodie, Brockham Warren, Reigate, Surrey, but then living at Oxford.

In March 1869 she was confined of a male child at 6, Chapel-place; the infant she had by her two days, when it was taken away by Mrs. Hall, who said "she had sent it to a good home in Gloucestershire"; £20 was paid by this woman to Mary Hall for putting the child out, and £15 for attendance, £7 of which yet remains unpaid. Mrs. Hall promised this poor girl that she would make arrangements for her to see her infant when she wished to, but some months ago wrote to tell her it was dead, but would not satisfy her to who had it, or where it was buried. . . .

The next woman of whom we have any knowledge is a Miss Cope (*alias* Mrs. Cutting), now living with her aunt at the Barley Mow Inn, St. George's-road, Brighton; this person was . . . delivered of a female infant at 6, Chapel-place, on 16th August 1870, at 6 a.m.; the child was taken away at once by Mrs. Hall, who told her she must not see it; but she did see it, but only for a minute. She paid Mrs. Hall £5 to adopt her babe, £19 for attendance, and was to pay her £27 more, making altogether £51. She has no idea what Mrs. Hall has done with her infant. . . .

I will now endeavour to show where infants go to from this lying-in house, and their subsequent fate when removed from the care and the proper food and nourishment of their mothers.

The earliest date of any child being removed from No. 6, Chapel-place to any other house (as far as we can trace) is 1866, then through seeing an advertisement in the "Daily Telegraph" relating to "adoption." Jane Morse, now residing in York House-lane, London-road, Gloucester, wrote to the address mentioned, and soon afterwards saw Mrs. Hall at her house, and received from that person two children; the first, a boy 15 months old, and an infant aged four weeks, and £7 with each; she took them home. The boy died six months after she received him, the latter (a female) is alive now. Also on 2nd March 1868, this baby farmer received from Mrs. Hall another female infant, five days old; that died five months after she had it; £10 was paid with this baby. It appears from the reports of the deputy chief constable of that district, that a medical man attended both the unfortunate children until their death. . . .

56. The problem of infant care for French working-class mothers

In nineteenth-century Paris and other major French cities, working-class women customarily placed their babies for a year or more to board with rural wet nurses so they could continue to supplement the family's income. By

sources: (i) Letter from the wife of Limoge, of the Hôtel de Ville Quarter (Paris), to the mayor of Beaubray (Eure), March 22, 1834, Archives Com-

1869 it was estimated that about 40 percent of the 55,000 children born in Paris that year were being nursed or cared for by commercial wet nurses in the countryside. An alarming number of these children were never seen again by their parents; the mortality rate among the infants placed by the Paris Municipal Nursing Bureau alone (where careful records were kept) rose above 40 percent in the 1870's.

In the first selection, a Parisian woman writes to the authorities, seeking news of her baby, who had been placed with a wet nurse some sixty miles from Paris. The second selection documents the emotional intensity of the working-class discussion in the 1860's about wet-nursing and child care. Its author, Victorine Brocher (1838–1921), a Parisian shoemaker's wife, was strongly committed to caring for her own son and had grand aspirations for him; despite her attentiveness he died in early childhood.

(i) Femme Limoge

Pardon me for interrupting you, but you must listen to a mother who is extremely anxious about her child, who was given to a wet nurse named Guille, the wife of Holot, living at Beaubray. She took [the baby] November 18, 1833. She wrote us December 5 that my son was sick with a miliary fever, and since that time I have received no more news of him. I have paid her wages every month at the [Paris Municipal Nursing] Bureau, and she has never acknowledged receiving any money. Would you please, Monsieur, have the goodness to answer me. You will do a great service to a mother who is in the greatest anxiety.

(ii) Victorine Brocher

How happy I was to be able to care for my dear baby myself! I have struggled a great deal, I have worked a great deal, but my dear angel lacked for nothing. With willpower one finds the strength to accomplish one's duty in life; willpower is a powerful lever that can conquer weakness and make great things happen.

How unhappy I would have been if my baby had been in strange hands.

I feel sorry for those mothers who cannot raise their own children, and I blame those who can do so and do not want to; they abdicate the first of their duties, the most sacred imposed on them by nature; they deprive themselves of many pleasures, in fact, the only unselfish ones. If they only knew how much happiness there is for a mother who follows day by day, hour by hour, the development of those dear little beings, so weak, so fragile! It is so satisfying to be on the lookout for their slightest gesture, their slightest transformation. From the first moment the child's dominant instinct is to seek food; he affirms his right to life, that fatal necessity; his vague glance wanders

munales de Beaubray, 5 Q 4, on deposit at the Archives Départmentales de l'Eure. The editors wish to thank George Sussman, Delmar, N.Y., for contributing this document and its translation. (ii) Victorine B. . . . [Brocher], *Souvenirs d'une morte vivante* (Paris, 1976), pp. 66–67. Originally published in Lausanne, 1909.

about everything in his environment, seems to seek a point of reference, a protection. He becomes used to objects, to good care, and as soon as his confidence is established, he reaps its benefits; he seems to say thank you with a sweet smile that penetrates to the core of your heart; that smile is something a mother never forgets. The first stammerings, the first sound of his voice surprises him. He is so astonished; he isn't sure that it is he himself who has produced the sound; he practices to make sure. Then come the first steps; how proud he is, the dear little one, when he discovers that he no longer needs help! I remember that when my son was strong enough to walk, only fear slowed him down; I held out a string so he could test his strength; he took it with his little fingers and headed out: as of that instant he was free. He was then fourteen months old and his first falls scared him a little. He fell ten times, twenty times, and then got up: he made it a game; he laughed until tears came. This is the only true happiness I ever tasted. Mothers who deprive themselves of this happiness do not know that it is the greatest happiness in life. How many wonderful dreams I had for my dear child. I wanted him to go to school, to be well brought up; how happy I would have been if one day chance had smiled on me and my son would have become a doctor; of course, I dreamed he would be famous. I taught him to be good to all the wretched poor, who suffer and die for lack of care and money. Or a professor . . . the doctor of thought, who strengthens the brain and creates intelligent men in the true sense of the word, without being pedantic.

Certainly I would never have imagined him as a general. I dreamed he would be good, that is, a man!

57. 'Gentleness, patience, and love': Lydia Maria Child

In sharp contrast to the suffering and occasional horror of child-rearing in indigent and working-class families, the middle-class nursery was an orderly and loving affair—at least in prescription. The following selection, although directed to relatively prosperous mothers, is representative of a large body of literature that advised mothers of their great responsibility toward their vulnerable babies. These advice manuals reveal the growing concern for the quality of infant experience and proclaim the right of children to a good start in life; such concerns also informed the nineteenth-century legislation to protect children from exploitation.

The author Lydia Maria Child (1802–80; Doc. 17.i) played a prominent part in Boston intellectual and antislavery circles. In 1828 she married against her family's wishes; the marriage was childless, and Child continued her writing career, publishing popular stories, advice manuals for women, and children's literature. She dedicated 'The Mother's Book,' from which this selection is taken, "To American mothers on whose intelligence and discretion the

SOURCE: Lydia Maria Child, *The Mother's Book*, 2d ed. (Boston, 1831), pp. 1–5.

safety and prosperity of our republic so much depend." Thus her message, directed toward more purely secular than spiritual ends, represented a dramatic shift away from the authoritarian child-rearing advice published by her Evangelical Calvinist predecessors. Her insistence on the "pure nature" of the infant and on the all-important role of the "self-governing" mother in shaping the baby's environment bespeaks the influence of Locke and Rousseau.

Few people think that the management of very young babies has anything to do with their future dispositions and characters; yet I believe it has more influence than can easily be calculated. One writer on education even ventures to say that the heaviness of the Dutch and the vivacity of the French are owing to the different manner in which infants are treated in those two countries.

The Dutch keep their children in a state of repose, always rocking, or jogging them; the French are perpetualy tossing them about, and showing them lively tricks. I think a medium between these two extremes would be the most favorable to a child's health and faculties.

An infant is, for a while, totally ignorant of the use of the senses with which he is endowed. At first, he does not see objects; and when he sees them, he does not know that he can touch them. "He is obliged to serve an apprenticeship to the five senses," and at every step he needs assistance in learning his trade. Any one can see that assistance tends to quicken the faculties, by observing how much faster a babe improves, when daily surrounded by little brothers and sisters.

But in trying to excite an infant's attention, care should be taken not to confuse and distract him. His soul, like his body, is weak, and requires to have but little sustenance at a time, and to have it often. Gentleness, patience, and love, are almost everything in education; especially to those helpless little creatures, who have just entered into a world where everything is new and strange to them. Gentleness is a sort of mild atmosphere; and it enters into a child's soul, like the sunshine into the rose-bud, slowly but surely expanding it into beauty and vigor.

All loud noises and violent motions should be avoided. They pain an infant's senses, and distract his faculties. I have seen impatient nurses thrust a glaring candle before the eyes of a fretful babe, or drum violently on the table, or rock the cradle like an earthquake. These things may stop a child's cries for a short time, because the pain they occasion his senses, draws his attention from the pain which first induced him to cry; but they do not comfort or soothe him. As soon as he recovers from the distraction they have occasioned, he will probably cry again, and even louder than before. Besides the pain given to his mind, violent measures are dangerous to the bodily senses. Deafness and weakness of eye-sight may no doubt often be attributed to such causes as I have mentioned; and physicians are agreed that the dropsy on the brain is frequently produced by violent rocking. . . .

Attention should be early aroused by presenting attractive objects—things of bright and beautiful colors, but not glaring—and sound pleasant and soft to the ear. When you have succeeded in attracting a babe's attention to any object, it is well to let him examine it just as long as he chooses. Every time he turns it over, drops it, and takes it up again, he adds something to the little stock of his scanty experience. When his powers of attention are wearied, he will soon enough show it by his actions. A multitude of new playthings, crowded upon him one after another, only serve to confuse him. He does not learn as much, because he does not have time to get acquainted with the properties of any one of them. Having had his little mind excited by a new object, he should be left in quiet, to toss, and turn, and jingle it, to his heart's content. If he look up in the midst of his play, a smile should be always ready for him, that he may feel protected and happy in the atmosphere of love.

It is important that children, even when babes, should never be spectators of anger, or any evil passion. They come to us from heaven, with their little souls full of innocence and peace; and, as far as possible, a mother's influence should not interfere with the influence of angels. . . .

Therefore the first rule, and the most important of all, in education, is, that a mother govern her own feelings, and keep her heart and conscience pure.

The next most important thing appears to me to be, that a mother, as far as other duties will permit, take the entire care of her own child. I am aware that people of moderate fortune cannot attend exclusively to an infant. Other cares claim a share of attention, and sisters, or domestics, must be intrusted; but where this necessarily must be the case, the infant should, as much as possible, feel its mother's guardianship. If in the same room, a smile, or a look of fondness, should now and then be bestowed upon him; and if in an adjoining room, some of the endearing appellations to which he has been accustomed, should once in a while meet his ear. The knowledge that his natural protector and best friend is near, will give him a feeling of safety and protection alike conducive to his happiness and beneficial to his temper.

You may say, perhaps, that a mother's instinct teaches fondness, and there is no need of urging that point; but the difficulty is, mothers are sometimes fond by fits and starts—they follow impulse, not principle. Perhaps the cares of the world vex or discourage you—and you do not, as usual, smile upon your babe when he looks up earnestly in your face,—or you are a little impatient at his fretfulness. Those who know your inquietudes may easily excuse this; but what does the innocent being before you know of care and trouble? And why should you distract his pure nature by the evils you have received from a vexatious world? It does you no good, and it injures him.

Do you say it is impossible always to govern one's feelings? There is one method, a never-failing one—prayer. It consoles and strengthens the wounded heart, and tranquillizes the most stormy passions. You will say, perhaps, that you have not leisure to pray every time your temper is provoked, or your heart is grieved.—It requires no time—the inward ejaculation of "Lord, help me to overcome this temptation," may be made in any place and amid any employments; and if uttered in humble sincerity, the voice that said to the raging waters, "Peace! Be still!" will restore quiet to your troubled soul.

58. Angels rich and poor: Motherhood in France

The satisfactory performance of the varied tasks of wife and mother, as the nineteenth century defined them, was by no means automatic. Indeed, if the many social critics of the 1830's are to be believed, women of the poorer classes in French society were miserably prepared to discharge their responsibilities toward those whose care was in their charge. Proletarianization had uprooted families from the supporting context of religion, kin, and tradition and had stranded them, faithless and isolated, in impersonal cities, where the most convenient institution was the neighborhood tavern. In the first selection Flora Tristan (1803–44), the first woman to campaign actively for the joint emancipation of women and the proletariat, describes the working-class mother. Tristan was uniquely qualified to comment on this subject; unhappily married to a printer and the reluctant mother of three children, she abandoned her family to spend years investigating the personal and political lives of the French and English working classes.

The second selection shows the angelic mother and Catholicism intact among the privileged classes years after Tristan found them moribund among the workers; it also reveals a new attitude of rational and all-pervasive parental surveillance toward children. This memorandum on child-rearing was written by an unknown female member of a prominent Lille family, the Bernards, who had become wealthy in the manufacture of cotton cloth. The family was deeply Catholic in belief and practice. Evidence suggests that the memorandum was written during the 1850's, and that the young mother died not long afterward, leaving the program she had drafted for her own guidance as a legacy to her children.

(i) Flora Tristan

In the life of the worker, woman is everything. She is the only good angel. If she is not there, everything is lacking. So people say: "It is the woman who makes or unmakes the home." It is so true that it has become a proverb. Yet, what education, what instruction, what direction, what moral or physical development does the lower class woman receive? None. As a child, she is left at the mercy of a mother and a grandmother who, themselves, have had no education. This one, according to her temperament, will be brutal and mean, will beat her up and bully her without reason. That one will be weak, careless, and will let her have her way in everything. (I am speaking in gen-

SOURCES: (i) Flora Tristan (Flore-Célestine-Thérèse-Henriette Tristan y Moscozo), *L'Union ouvrière*, 3d ed. (Paris and Lyon, 1844), pp. 51–62. The editors wish to thank Professor S. Joan Moon, California State University, Sacramento, for sending us this document and are indebted to Giselle Pincetl for permission to use her translation of this excerpt, which originally appeared in *Harvest Quarterly*, 7 (Fall 1977): 11–12. (ii) "Plan d'éducation d'une mère chrétienne," in Anatole de Ségur, *Vie de l'abbé Bernard* (Paris, 1882), pp. 426–30. The editors are grateful to Professor Bonnie G. Smith, University of Wisconsin, Parkside, for kindly offering us this document.

eral, of course; there are many exceptions to all I say.) The poor child will grow amidst the most shocking contradictions, one day irritated by blows and unfair treatment, the next day unnerved by a no less pernicious overindulgence.

Instead of being sent to school, the girl rather than her brothers is kept home because she can be taken advantage of in the household, either to rock the children to sleep, do the errands, take care of the soup, or whatever. At the age of twelve, she is sent out as an apprentice. There, she is also exploited by the woman employer and is often as ill-treated as she was at home. Nothing sours a temperament, hardens the heart, debases the character, like the continuous suffering a child endures because of unfair and brutal treatment. In the beginning, injustice wounds, distresses us, drives us to despair; eventually, we become irritated and exasperated. We think only of ways of avenging ourselves, and we end up by becoming, ourselves, hard, unjust, and mean.

This will usually be a poor girl's condition when she is twenty years old. Then she will marry without love, simply because one must marry if one wants to escape parental tyranny. What will happen then? I assume that she will have children, and, in her turn, she will be totally incapable of properly raising her sons and daughters. She will be as brutal with them as her mother and grandmother have been with her.

Women of the working class, I beg you to take note that by reporting here the facts regarding your ignorance and your incapability of raising your children, I do not intend to accuse you or your character. No. I accuse society for leaving you so uneducated—you the women, you the mothers who, on the contrary, need so much to be taught and trained in order to be able, in your turn, to teach and train the men and children entrusted to your care.

It is true that women of the lower classes are in general brutal, mean, and sometimes callous. But what causes a situation that is so inconsistent with the sweet, kind, sensitive, generous, disposition of women?

Poor working women! They have so many causes for irritation! First is the husband (one must admit that there are few happy working-class families). He has received a little more education; he is the master by law and, also, by virtue of the money he brings home. He believes himself (and is, in fact) much superior to the woman who brings home only a small salary for her day's work and who is merely a very humble servant in the house.

As a result, the husband treats his wife, at the very least, with contempt. The poor woman, who feels humiliated by each word and each look from her husband, rebels openly or secretly according to her character. This gives rise to violent, painful scenes which engender a constant feeling of anger between master and servant (one can even say slave, because the woman is, so to speak, the property of the husband). The situation becomes so distressing that the husband, instead of staying home and chatting with his wife, hastens to run away. And, since he has no other place to go, he goes to the tavern to drink cheap wine with other husbands as unhappy as he is, in the hope of drowning his sorrow.

While distracting himself in this way, he aggravates the difficulties. The woman, who is expecting the Sunday pay to feed her family during the week, is in despair when she sees her husband spend most of it in the tavern. Then her irritation reaches its peak, her brutality and meanness increase. One must have observed these workers' homes (especially the bad ones) to have an idea of the wretchedness felt by the husband, the suffering of the wife. From reproaches and insults, they go on to blows, and then tears, dejection, and despair.

Besides the bitter sorrow caused by the husband, there are pregnancies, illnesses, lack of work, and destitution—destitution always planted at the door like Medusa's head. Add to all this the ceaseless annoyance caused by four or five screeching, restless, tiresome children who whirl around and around the mother in a small worker's room where there is no space to move. Oh! One would have to be an angel come down to earth not to get irritated, not to become brutal and mean under the circumstances. Meanwhile, in such an environment, what happens to the children? They see their father only in the evenings and on Sunday, he is always drunk or in an angry mood. He speaks to them harshly and they receive nothing but blows and insults from him. Hearing their mother complain continually about him, they start feeling hatred and contempt for him. As for their mother, they fear and obey her, but do not like her. Such is human nature. We cannot like those who treat us badly.

Isn't it a great misfortune for a child not to be able to like his mother? If he is unhappy, who will dry his tears? If he makes a serious mistake, either through thoughtlessness or temptation, in whom can he confide? Having no desire to stay near his mother, the child will look for every excuse to get away from the maternal home. Bad company is easily found by girls as well as by boys. They start hanging about, then they go on to vagrancy, and often from vagrancy to theft.

Among the hapless creatures who live in houses of prostitution, and the unfortunates who moan in prisons, how many are there who can say: "If our mother had been capable of raising us, surely we would not be here." I repeat, woman is everything in the life of the worker. As a mother, she has an influence on him during his childhood. From her, and only from her, does he learn the first notion of the science of life which is so important to acquire, because it teaches us to live decently for our own sake and for the sake of others—depending on where fate has placed us. As a lover, she has an influence on him during his youth, and what a powerful influence a beautiful girl who is loved possesses! As a wife, she exerts influence on three quarters of his life, and finally, as a daughter she watches over his old age.

You will observe that the worker's position is very different from that of the rich. If the rich child's mother is incapable of bringing him up, he is sent to a boarding school or is given a governess. If the rich young man has no mistress, he can study art or science to occupy his heart and imagination. If the rich man has no wife he easily finds distraction in society. If the rich old man has no daughter, he finds old friends or young nephews who will gladly come and play cards with him. But the worker, who is denied all these advantages, has only the company of the women of his family—his fellow sufferers—for his joy and comfort.

This situation strongly points out the extreme importance of giving women a rational and solid education at an early age in order to improve the intellectual, moral, and material condition of the working class. . . .

All working class woes can be summed up in two words: poverty and ignorance; ignorance and poverty. I see only one way to get out of this labyrinth: start by educating women, because women have the responsibility for educating male and female children.

(ii) 'Plan d'éducation d'une mère chrétienne'

My mission with regard to my children is that of a visible Angel, whom God has placed in their midst to help them traverse life. I am the auxiliary of their Guardian Angel, preparing their souls to receive and understand the good thoughts he suggests to them, imprinting these on their fickle imaginations, and helping them to put these into practice. The goal of my mission is to help them reach Heaven. Having given them birth to life on earth, I must now give them birth to grace, a nobler task but a longer, more laborious, and often more painful one. . . .

Good and indulgent for everything childish, I want to be stern concerning every failing. Then I will punish, but calmly and with reflection. To encourage their goodwill, and as a stimulant, I will establish a notebook to record good marks. . . . Good marks will give them the right to choose an article of greater or lesser worth, according to the value of their good points, from a collection of rewards. I will take care to place among these objects several garments for the poor so that they will learn that they can find joy in giving to others. They must be left free to choose or to leave these objects. The act of withholding good marks will be a punishment in itself; in grave circumstances, when more severe punishment is required, being sent to bed without embracing me will be the punishment for such exceptional cases. As they go to nursery school when they are quite young and will be sent to boarding school later, my active part in their schooling does not amount to much. However, in my desire not to be wholly out of touch with it, I will have them recite their lessons to me every day, in order to help them comprehend the meaning, insofar as possible. This is an advantage they will scarcely encounter in class since there are so many children. To this end we will consecrate a few moments, after an amusement of forty-five minutes following dinner. As I will often be with them, I will strive to mold their judgment by teaching them to judge each thing at its true value, and in order to evaluate the results of our conversations, I will sometimes probe the children by allowing them to express their own opinion on certain events. . . . So that I can be with my children when they return from school, I will take care of as many household duties as possible during their absence. I will also avoid all serious work when I am with them, in order to preserve the sweetness and patience that I want to have with them. Advice on defects is far more effective and less wounding to one's pride when it is given in this context. I will also guard against giving the children any cause for jealousy, which can be a real source of trouble between brothers and sisters. To this end, I will avoid exciting emulation by comparing them with each other; rather I will read them edifying stories, and above all I will seek to make them behave well out of a love of duty. . . . The entire aim of the children's education is to make them understand, love, and practice their duties toward God, toward fellow humans, and toward themselves. While they are still little, I will tell them who created them, what Kingdom they must aspire to, what Jesus Christ did for them, and that in Heaven they also have a good Mother, to whom they were consecrated on the day of their baptism. As a safeguard against evil and a stimulant to goodness, I will make them understand that God sees all, hears all, always, always. . . .

At the age of six, they will begin attending Mass regularly on Sundays; before this age, they will only go occasionally as a reward. At the age of eight, they will be taken to the last part of the vesper service, but only for a short time, so that they become accustomed to it without becoming bored. I will explain to them the reasons for which the various feast days of the year were established and the spirit of the Church during these feast days. According to the solemnity of the feast day, they will take their small active role, whether by going to church, or by reciting a particular prayer for the occasion at home. I will take advantage of all occasions according to circumstances, to excite their confidence, their recognition, their love for God. Preparation for first communion will begin long before the event itself. It will become the prime mover for all good actions, the goal of all small internal combats. Several months before the date of this important occasion, I will send them off to boarding school, so that they may perfect their state of mind.

I will remind them that not only should they have a deep affection for their brothers and sisters, much tenderness, much goodwill, but that these feelings should be extended (in a more general manner, no doubt) to all other men, because in Jesus Christ we are all brothers. That among these brothers, some are God's chosen children, who come first in his heart because of their suffering. For these reasons, these chosen ones should also be of primary concern and sympathy to the children. I will remind them that their own interest is concerned, since they can only enter Heaven by helping these unfortunates. When I am with the little ones, who cannot understand my motives, I will not refuse the requests for alms of those poor souls who are not respectable. A coffer will be placed in the children's chapel, so that they can dispose of their own alms of their own free will, alone without witnesses. The small sums collected in this coffer will be given to a poor person in the neighborhood, possibly in the form of bread or clothing. When the children are bigger, I will sometimes take them, as a reward, to visit a poor household and will try hard to stir up their affection for the children of the poor. From their small savings they will give an annual subscription for the propagation of the faith and for the society of the Holy Childhood, with which they are associated. I will explain the goal to them so they understand that they owe their fellow men more than material alms alone; they must also, according to their capability, procure spiritual alms for their souls. All haughty and disdainful words will be punished, especially if they are addressed to a domestic servant: the children must then repair the damage they have caused by excusing themselves. . . .

My work, which is a work of each day and every instant, will only be accomplished on the day when, with God's grace, all my children will have become Christians in their hearts. Then I will owe them only the tenderness of my affection. Fortified by the counsel of him whom God has chosen to direct me, I will accomplish my mission with courage, confidence, and perseverance.

59. 'To a mother who also cries'

The fear that a child might die colored nineteenth-century motherhood. Infant mortality was high, and in the absence of life-saving drugs and vaccines, even older children were vulnerable to diseases such as scarlet fever, diphtheria, and smallpox. The following selections give a sense of the fragility of life in the Victorian period and show how devastating the loss of children could be. In the first excerpt Mary Botham Howitt (1799–1888), an English Quaker whose ambition was to live by writing, describes to her sister, Anna, the death of her two-year-old son, Charles. Howitt had lost three children at birth, and in the wake of these tragedies, Charles's death was particularly grievous. In the second selection Marceline Desbordes-Valmore (1786–1859), the most famous woman poet of nineteenth-century France, tries to console a friend whose daughter has just died: as a mother who had lost four children of her own, Desbordes-Valmore speaks with the voice of experience. In the third selection Carrie Fries Shaffner (1839–1922), a North Carolina doctor's wife, records in her diary her anguish at her ten-month-old Mary's death. Like many nineteenth-century women, she prayed that her next child might survive.

(i) Mary Howitt

April 1828.—How strangely and suddenly are my prospects changed, and my heart covered, as it were, with a thick cloud! I hardly know, my dear Anna, how to write; my thoughts seem tossed. I have much to say on one subject, and yet I almost fear encountering it. Alas! how much sorrow have I known since I last wrote! I have seen our dear little Charles cut off in a moment, in the midst of his childish beauty and winning ways, and, above all, with his heart overflowing with the most remarkable affection.

While in health, he was possessed of exceedingly strong passions and an

SOURCES: (i) Mary Howitt, *Mary Howitt—An Autobiography*, ed. Margaret Howitt (Cambridge, Eng., 1889), 1: 202–4. (ii) Marceline Desbordes-Valmore, "A une Mère qui pleure aussi," in *Les Oeuvres poétiques*, ed. M. Bertrand (Grenoble, 1973), 2: 536. Originally published in 1860. (iii) Carrie Fries Shaffner diary, 1866–67, Fries-Shaffner Papers, Southern Historical Collection, Library of the University of North Carolina, Chapel Hill. The editors are grateful to Ellen Barrier Neal of the SHC for this reference and to Dr. Louis Shaffner, Winston-Salem, N.C., for consenting to its publication.

impatient temper, though, to use a familiar expression, "cut down" in a moment by a word or look of reproof. Two days before the sad event which took him from our care, he became, to our surprise, totally changed. Never was martyr more patient or meekly submissive. My heart runs over with anguish when I recall his obedience in taking the most nauseous medicines almost hourly. Their effect was extremely trying, producing a nervous irritability beyond belief; yet he tried, at our desire, to compose himself, shutting his dear eyes and attempting to sleep, poor little fellow! as if with a desire to soothe us. He was parched with a burning thirst, and for twelve hours, while sleeping and waking, incessantly murmured, "Water, papa!" Dear, ay dearer than the blessed sunshine, as he has been in his health and joyfulness, never was he so dear as in those days of suffering. William was to him the soul of comfort, and the last word he articulated was "Papa!" Oh Anna! I hope thou may be spared the pangs of waking from a dream of confidence and proud hope, from delight in the present and joyful anticipation of the future, to a reality of suffering and death. It is indeed as much as human nature can support.

Thou can hardly imagine how the dear boy has impressed a memory on almost everything, and months must pass before we are restored to a quiet state of acquiescence with our loss. We miss his merry shouts and bursts of laughter, his vehement joy, which contrasted so much with his sister's [Anna Mary] quietness, his arch and mischievous little tricks, that kept us in a continual state of activity. Then his joy when he heard William's step, which he knew at any audible distance, and his actual scream of delight when papa promised him a walk. I wish thou had heard his voice, so loud, rich, and deep, always reminding me of the silver tone of a bell. Could thou but have heard him, in his merry health, singing to himself while he twirled round a bit of string or stick for a hand-organ, or played the little organ thou sent him, thou would have thought, as I often did, it was a voice which surpassed all music. It was a lovely sight to watch him and Anna Mary together, forming such a contrast. Dear, dear children, they have been my jewels, proudly worn and prized. Poor Anna Mary will miss him too. He was her man Friday, when for day after day she has acted Robinson Crusoe. It was wonderful to me to think how, at two years of age, he could comprehend the character; he marched about with a hearth-brush on his shoulder, pretending to shoot different things for game, sat down by Anna Mary and did as she bid him, like Friday himself. Then he has walked with two sticks, pretending to be an old lame man. His merry antics have amused me as much almost as they have him. Our house seems silent and forlorn, and there is a void in my heart, which no other child can ever fill.

Though, dear Anna, I have spoken yet only of sorrowful memories, I must not ungratefully forget the mercy which has been mingled with judgment. Never before—and my heart is full in writing it—never did I know the value of many a blessed promise in Scripture. From the pleasant books, in which, in the sunshine of my security, I took such delight, I have turned with distaste, and found in the beautiful and assuring words of Christ comfort and hope;

and dear Anna, without affectation, I can truly say, were the power to recall the dear boy given us, we would not do it. The blow has been a severe one; but there are some things that call for thankfulness in it, and assure me that there was a sparing and a merciful hand under all, so that I hope it may tend to our good, and not lightly be forgotten.

(ii) Marceline Desbordes-Valmore

"To a Mother Who Also Cries"

Who knows if the child who lives in your tears,
The child whose young charms still feed in your heart
(Lone heart that protects her from being forgotten),
Has not met my child at the threshold of God?

Who knows if their hands, joined for a moment,
Have not weighed in heaven our infinite pain,
And crying with love unique to that sphere,
Have numbered our tears as an offering to God?

Seeing you, Madame, at least I know this:
Tidings of comfort have entered my soul,
As if my dear child, in her loving power,
For my endless grief has sent me a sister.

If that be His will, then His will be done!
Nothing will alter the course of our fate—
But from the love-grief that brought us together,
Let us learn it is sweet not to forget.

(iii) Carrie Fries Shaffner

Dec. 31, 1866—It is nearly six months since I noted my acts & feelings here. It is impossible to portray them now. A week ago today we watched our little Mary breathe her last. On Wednesday 19ᵗʰ inst. I noticed that she coughed a little & appeared to have a cold, that night she had high fever. On Thursday morning we gave her a dose of calomel & thought that would relieve her as it had often done before. Sister Mary & Miss Norwood (who came to spend Christmas with Mother) spent the day with us, & baby rested in Sister's arms apparently quite comfortable the greater part of the afternoon. As night approached she seemed to feel more restless, & I went to bed with her about 8 o'clock. During the night had as much fever as on last night. My Dear Husband thought she was taking Pneumonia, & as soon as he told me so, my heart sank within me, for he had frequently remarked that she would never be able to stand an attack of that kind. Friday she was very languid, but still nursed occasionally. At night when I took her to bed she seemed more like herself than she had for several days & went to sleep very sweetly. Had but little fever during the night, & at 5 o'clock Saturday morning nursed very freely.—Mother came down early & nursed her while I attend to this house. Doctor thought her so much better that he went out into the country. I took her about 9 o'clock, & watched her closely for more than an hour. I then tried to arouse her, but not being able to do so, sent for Dr. Kulhn. He said there was no immediate danger. I however sent for Mother soon after, & when I told her our baby would not open her eyes, she replied, "Well Carrie I think she will soon open them in heaven." I sent for Dr. Kulhn again & he went for her Father. He was much surprised to see her so much worse, but seemed to have no hope for her. She continued in this stupor all night excepting two short intravals when she turned to look at the light. Mother Shaffner staid with her. Mother came down early on Sunday morning & staid with us all day. About 2 o'clock baby strangled while trying to cough. After this her pulse sank rapidly, & her Father thought she was dying until about 5 o'clock when she rallied a little again. Aunt Betsy & Cousin Willie staid with her all night. There was but little change. She was rather more restless than she had been. Towards morning she became more calm. About 10 o'clock she opened her eyes and followed her Father when he spoke to her. This was the last look on this earth. When she opened her eyes after this it was painful to see them. The brightness and luster which constituted their beauty was gone, & we knew they would never again notice us until they watch for our coming into a better home. At 15 minutes before four on Christmas eve our little Mary's spirit took its flight. The transit was so easy that we scarcely knew when she drew her last breath. Precious little darling. We try to be resigned. We know she is better cared for than she could have been with us, & when we remember that though she is 10 months old she could not sit alone, nor take hold of anything which she reached for, we must be thankful that she will not have to suffer any more. But Oh! how hard it is to say "Thy will be done." She died in Mother's lap, but after she was gone I took her in my arms & held her until they were ready to wash her. I washed her face & neck & then let her two Grandmothers finish her. About 7 o'clock they performed a Post mortem examination, as her Father was anxious to have one. He found every thing just as he expected: —Pneumonia principally on the right side.—We dressed her soon after, in the best clothes she had, & placed her in a metallic coffin. She looked so sweetly that every one remarked upon her beauty. She was still so plump, & her little hands & arms were perfectly natural.—Cousin Mollie, Miss Laura & John sat up with her last night, & today (Christmas) a great many persons came to see her.—

[The next entry, apparently written two days after Mary died, inexplicably follows the one for Dec. 31, which was a week after the death.]

Dec. 26.—Last night Nellie Laura Lavinia & Capt. Wheeler sat up. John & Uncle Henry closed the coffin about 1 o'clock. I will not dwell upon this. At 1½ Mr. Bahnson came to the house with quite a number of other persons, & after a hymn & prayer we proceeded to the church, where he delivered a very appropriate address. We then went to the cemetery where we placed our precious treasure in the vault beside her Grandfather. Thus another link which bound us to earth has been severed, & the incentive to strive to meet our dear ones grows stronger & stronger.

[The following entry was recorded nine months later.]

Sept. 19, 1867.—With the deepest gratitude we receive this second gift from our Heavenly Father & pray that he may permit us to keep it longer than the other. In wisdom He ordereth all things & so His holy will we will endeavor to submit patiently.

60. Mme Dudevant sues for legal separation from her husband

In 1835 Amantine-Lucile-Aurore Dupin, baronne Dudevant (George Sand, 1804–76; Docs. 26.i, 100), filed for a legal separation from her husband of thirteen years. This was the sole recourse open to a French woman or man who was unhappily married, since civil divorce had been outlawed in 1816; remarriage was, of course, impossible. This particular suit, however, was the subject of unusual public interest throughout France and abroad, since the plaintiff had recently gained world fame for her novels 'Indiana,' 'Jacques,' and 'Lélia,' and for her public flouting of social convention.

The first section offers a glimpse of early steps in the separation procedure, including a tentative agreement concerning child custody and property arrangements. The second section gives excerpts from witnesses' testimony at the final hearing, in January 1836, and concludes with the court's decision to grant the separation. In deciding the case in favor of Sand, the judges express their contempt for the husband who "permits his wife to live alone," implying that a man who abandons his marital authority in such fashion surely deserves what he gets.

[Resumé of the case, October–December 1835]

Oct. 30—Madame Dudevant presents a petition to M. the President of the Tribunal of La Châtre for authorization to file a claim for bodily separation from her husband.

Nov. 2—Pre-settlement hearing. M. Dudevant failed to appear.

Nov. 12.—M. Dudevant, understanding that he cannot contest his wife's claim, stipulates his personal and pecuniary interests in the following articles. . . .

Article 1: Madame Dudevant resumes the administration and use of all her goods, furnishings, and properties.

Article 2: M. Dudevant will return to Madame . . . the various buildings acquired during their marriage. . . .

Article 8: M. Dudevant, in addition to the assets and personal effects that are his own, and whose ownership and enjoyment he will preserve, will receive annually from Madame Dudevant the sum of 3,800 francs; this sum will be paid him in four equal parts, on the 1st of January, 1st of April, 1st of July,

SOURCE: *Précis pour Madame Dudevant, intimée; contre M. Dudevant, appelant,* May 3, 1836, George Sand Papers no. 760, Bibliothèque Historique de la Ville de Paris.

and 1st of October of each year. . . . Madame Dudevant will retain sole responsibility for the costs of educating and supporting Maurice and Solange, children born of the marriage.

Madame Dudevant will have free disposition of the education of Solange. She may leave her in the boarding school she presently attends, or she may remove her from it, either to place her in another or to keep her with her, according to her own wishes, without M. Dudevant placing any obstacles in her way—this he solemnly declares. He will in any case be free to see Solange as often as he likes, and Madame Dudevant promises to send her to him or to take her to him whenever he notifies her of his intention to spend the day with Solange.

As for Maurice, he will be left as a boarder in one of the *collèges* in Paris until his education is complete. He will spend his vacations and his holidays half with his father and half with his mother, or, in their absence, with whoever is chosen by either parent during the time he or she would have had custody of the child. . . .

Article 10: When the time comes to provide for the establishment of the said children, M. and Madame Dudevant, once they have reached agreement about the composition of the doweries and other advantages to be provided for the children, will each contribute thereto in proportion to their respective incomes. . . .

Made in duplicate at La Châtre, under the private seals of the two parties, November 12, 1835.

[Excerpts from the final hearing, January 1836]

First witness, Antoine André Bonphilippe (35 years old), gardener at La Châtre, deposes:

"I don't know if M. Dudevant has insulted or maltreated his wife; I only know that the girl called Claire told me several times at my place that her pregnancy was the work of M. Dudevant; the first time (she had just come back from Paris), I noticed that she was pregnant and teased her about it; she confessed as much to me; she was still in the service of Madame Chatiron. Another time, after giving birth, she came here with her daughter with the intention of presenting her to M. Dudevant; she was lodging with one M. Aubourg; she had me write a letter to M. Dudevant urging him to come to see her, but I don't think he came. She left the next day for Boussac, very annoyed. When I went afterwards to Boussac, the girl Claire often spoke to me of M. Dudevant and, showing me her daughter, told me she looked like him, and pointed out her eyes in particular as being similar to M. Dudevant's." He adds: "The girl Claire made the same confessions in front of Pierre Moreau, gardener at Nohant, in my presence, and Moreau told me that she had said the same to him several times."

Second witness, Pierre-Louis-Alphonse Fleury, lawyer at La Châtre, deposes:

"In 1827, I think, in the month of September, I took a trip along the banks of the Creuse with M. and Madame Dudevant and several other persons; we had arrived near Château-Brun; as we were taking the horses out of the stable to return home, M. Dudevant struck his horse on the head with several blows of his whip. When his wife made several remarks to him about how he was hitting the animal, he responded impatiently: 'It suits me to hit him, and if you continue your remarks, I'll give you the same.' Madame Dudevant withdrew without saying anything.

"For the five or six years that I have had continued relations with M. and Madame Dudevant, I've been witness to the brusque manner and caustic words M. Dudevant used with his wife. Whenever his wife wanted to take part in any discussion, he would shrug his shoulders, show his disdain for whatever she said, and add that she didn't have any common sense, that she only uttered nonsense, that she was mad. I remember, among other things, that in 1834, after Madame Dudevant's return from her trip to Italy, when I was one day at Nohant with M. Duvernet, the conversation during dinner turned to this trip. Madame Dudevant spoke of the fertility of the Italian soil, and especially of the plains that produced several harvests. M. Dudevant, after some discussion, replied that it wasn't true, that it was all lies, that she spoke like all scribblers who speak without seeing. The tone in which M. Dudevant pronounced these words revealed his intention to annoy his wife. We were very embarrassed by that scene.

"The same year, at the end of autumn, I was dining at Nohant with some other people; a bottle of champagne was upset by one of the guests. Madame Dudevant called for another from the servant, and M. Dudevant forbade the servant to obey his wife. I don't remember if he added that no order was to be received except from him; but he said that several times in my presence, under other circumstances."

· · ·

Fourth witness, Jeanne-Marie-Rose Petit (28 years old), wife of Joseph Bourgouin, tax collector at La Châtre, deposes:

". . . On the evening of [October 19], we were having coffee in the salon. Madame Dudevant's son asked for some cream. 'There isn't any more,' his father said. 'Go to the kitchen; just get out of here.' The child, instead of leaving, took refuge next to his mother. M. Dudevant insisted again that he should leave, and then Madame Dudevant herself said, 'Leave, since your father desires it.' An altercation arose between Madame and Monsieur— very calm on her part and very fiery on his. He went so far as to say to his wife, 'You get out too!' That's what he ordered several times. Madame Dudevant responded that she was in her own home, and that she intended to remain. After she asked her husband to declare what he would do if she didn't leave, he said: 'To begin with, I'll give you a h--- of a slap'; then he got up and approached Madame as if to slap her; he was prevented from doing so by the people present, who stood between them. . . . Unable to reach his wife, he retreated toward the door, uttering threats. To the gentlemen who followed him, he said: 'We'll see who's the master here.' I was told afterwards that he had gone to get his rifle; I thought he was going to get the servants. M. Dudevant returned to the salon, and a few minutes later Madame withdrew to her rooms."

. . .

Thirteenth witness, Catherine Mathelin (25 years old), washerwoman residing in Boussac, deposes:

"During the year and a half that I was in the service of Madame Chatiron, both in Paris and at Nohant, I didn't notice M. Dudevant mistreating or insulting his wife."

Asked if she had had relations with M. Dudevant and if the child to whom she had given birth could have resulted from these relations, she replied that she was not obliged to declare who the father of the child was, that it was perhaps he, perhaps another.

Asked if she had not said, either to André, called Bonphilippe, or to Pierre Moreau, gardener at Nohant, or to Madame Gilbert that M. Dudevant was the father of her child, she answered "No."

Asked if she had not said to André, called Bonphilippe, and to other persons that her child resembled M. Dudevant, she answered: "If I said it, since I wasn't in confession, I wasn't obliged to tell the truth, as I am obliged to tell it here. About two years ago, during vacation, I saw M. Dudevant and his son at Boussac, taking a walk with M. the subprefect and some other people; but I didn't speak to him or make him speak to me, although I went to the subprefecture after I had seen him."

Asked again if the child to whom she had given birth could have been fathered by M. Dudevant, she persisted in her first statement, saying that it could be his or another's.

. . .

Opinion

The undersigned Council members, who have read 1) the charges presented by Madame Dudevant to M. the President of the Tribunal of La Châtre on the 21st of last November; 2) the petition signed by the respondent's solicitor and served on the 14th of April, judge, on the basis of this petition, and without considering it necessary to pronounce judgment on the hearings that have taken place and without initiating new ones, that a separation should be granted. . . .

Society cannot allow a husband who is not the plaintiff to have the right, on the occasion of a suit brought against him, to cover with shame—and what shame! and what intolerable outrage!—a woman whom he should protect, if he himself has not taken the initiative in calling down on her the wrath of the law. Of course, one understands that a husband who, like M. Dudevant, permits his wife to live alone, far from him, in the capital, for several months of the year, *has disqualified himself from presenting the sole demand that could justify the language he is using today*; but then, such a man must accept the situation he has created for himself and not give vent to charges which, separated from the conclusion of Article 229 of the Civil Code, are nothing more than an insult of the highest order.

61. An indissoluble sacrament: Separation and divorce in England

In the first half of the nineteenth century an Englishwoman who found herself unhappily married—like her French counterpart—had virtually no chance of ending her marriage. Separations, granted by ecclesiastical courts, were almost unknown, and divorces could be obtained only by a private act of Parliament at the high cost of £800–£900. In theory either husband or wife could petition for divorce, but in practice only 3 percent of the actions were initiated by wives.

Caroline Sheridan Norton (1808–77), from whose writings the first selection is taken, played a leading role in the agitation to reform the divorce laws and make them more equitable to women. Granddaughter of Richard Brinsley Sheridan and a successful author in her own right, she married the Hon. George Norton in 1828. The marriage proved disastrous, and in 1836, after many violent scenes and quarrels, George accused his wife of adultery with the Prime Minister. Although she was judged innocent, Caroline's reputation was permanently tarnished. Separated from her husband, she was denied access to their three children; meanwhile, he took legal action to obtain the proceeds from her writings. These tribulations left Caroline bitterly conscious of the inferior legal status of married women and led her to condemn publicly the laws regarding divorce and child custody. In 1857, prodded by her protest and the activities of other feminists, Parliament passed the Matrimonial Causes Act, which established special civil courts to grant judicial separations and divorces. Frances Kelly, a minister's wife whose story is told in the second selection, benefited from this act; had it not been for this reform, she could never have escaped the control of the vindictive Reverend Kelly.

(i) Caroline Norton

A married woman in England has *no legal existence*: her being is absorbed in that of her husband. Years of separation or desertion cannot alter this position. Unless divorced by special enactment in the House of Lords, the legal fiction holds her to be *"one"* with her husband, even though she may never see or hear of him.

She has no possessions, unless by special settlement; her property is *his* property. . . .

An English wife has no legal right even to her clothes or ornaments; her husband may take them and sell them if he pleases, even though they be the gifts of relatives or friends, or bought before marriage.

An English wife cannot make a will. She may have children or kindred whom she may earnestly desire to benefit;—she may be separated from her husband, who may be living with a mistress; no matter: the law gives what she has to him, and no will she could make would be valid.

An English wife cannot legally claim her own earnings. Whether wages

SOURCES: (i) Caroline Norton, *A Letter to the Queen on Lord Chancellor Cranworth's Marriage and Divorce Bill* (London, 1855), pp. 8–13. (ii) Great Britain, *Law Reports, Courts of Probate and Divorce*, 33–55 Vict., 1869–72, II: 31–38.

for manual labour, or payment for intellectual exertion, whether she weed potatoes, or keep a school, her salary is *the husband's*; and he could compel a second payment, and treat the first as void, if paid to the wife without his sanction.

An English wife may not leave her husband's house. Not only can he sue her for "restitution of conjugal rights," but he has a right to enter the house of any friend or relation with whom she may take refuge, and who may "harbour her,"—as it is termed,—and carry her away by force, with or without the aid of the police.

If the wife sue for separation for cruelty, it must be "cruelty that endangers life or limb," and if she has once forgiven, or, in legal phrase, "*condoned*" his offenses, she cannot plead them; though her past forgiveness only proves that she endured as long as endurance was possible.

If her husband take proceedings for a divorce, she is not, in the first instance, allowed to defend herself. She has no means of proving the falsehood of his allegations. She is not represented by attorney, nor permitted to be considered a party to the suit between him and her supposed lover, for "damages." . . .

If an English wife be guilty of infidelity, her husband can divorce *her* so as to marry again; but she cannot divorce the husband, *a vinculo*, however profligate he may be. No law court can divorce in England. A special Act of Parliament annulling the marriage is passed for each case. The House of Lords grants this almost as a matter of course to the husband, but not to the wife. In only four instances (two of which were cases of incest) has the wife obtained a divorce to marry again.

She cannot prosecute for a libel. Her husband must prosecute; and in cases of enmity and separation, of course she is without a remedy. . . .

She cannot claim support, as a matter of personal right, from her husband. The general belief and nominal rule is, that her husband is "bound to maintain her." That is not the law. He is not bound to *her*. He is bound to his country; bound to see that she does not cumber the parish in which she resides. If it be proved that means sufficient are at her disposal, from relatives or friends, her husband is quit of his obligation, and need not contribute a farthing: even if he have deserted her; or be in receipt of money which is hers by inheritance. . . .

Separation from her husband by consent, or for his ill usage, does not alter their mutual relation. He retains the right to divorce her *after* separation,—as before,—though he himself be unfaithful.

Her being, on the other hand, of spotless character, and without reproach, gives her no advantage in law. She may have withdrawn from his roof knowing that he lives with "his faithful housekeeper": having suffered personal violence at his hands; having "condoned" much, and being able to prove it by unimpeachable testimony: or he may have shut the doors of her house against her: all this is quite immaterial: the law takes no cognisance of which is to blame. As *her husband*, he has a right to all that is hers: as *his wife*, she has no right to anything that is his. As her husband, he may divorce her (if truth or false swearing can do it): as his wife, the utmost "divorce" she could obtain, is permission to reside alone,—married to his name. The marriage ceremony is a civil bond for him,—and an indissoluble sacrament for her; and the rights of mutual property which that ceremony is ignorantly supposed to confer, are made absolute for him, and null for her.

(ii) Frances Kelly

KELLY *V*. KELLY

Judicial Separation—Cruelty—Undue Exercise of Marital Authority

If force, whether physical or moral, is systematically exerted to compel the submission of a wife, in such a manner, to such a degree, and during such a length of time, as to injure her health and render a serious malady imminent, it is legal cruelty, and she will be entitled to a judicial separation.

This was a suit for judicial separation instituted by Mrs. Frances Kelly, by reason of the cruelty of her husband, the Rev. James Kelly, the incumbent of St. George's Church, Liverpool.

The respondent filed a very long statement as an answer, in which, in effect, he denied he had been guilty of cruelty, and stated that in anything he had done he had only acted in the legitimate assertion of his marital rights. The marriage took place in 1841. The only child, a son, was born in 1845; and the parties ceased to cohabit in January 1869.

The petition was before the Court on the 19th, 20th, 24th, 25th, 26th, and 27th of November; and the Judge Ordinary took time to consider his decision.

[This document is dated Dec. 7, 1869, which means the judge spent more than a week coming to his decision. He issued the following statement in his finding for Mrs. Kelly.]

The peculiar and distinguishing feature of this case is the adoption by the respondent of a deliberate system of conduct towards his wife with the view of bending her to his authority. A man who sets about to achieve this end by purposely rendering a woman's daily life unhappy, is in danger of overstepping his rights, as he is pretty sure to fall short of his duties. The respondent in this case has, in my judgment, done both. Without disparaging the just and paramount authority of a husband, it may be safely asserted that a wife is not a domestic slave, to be driven at all cost, short of personal violence, into compliance with her husband's demands. And if force, whether physical or moral, is systematically exerted for this purpose, in such a manner, to such a degree, and during such length of time, as to break down her health and render serious malady imminent, the interference of the law cannot be justly withheld by any court which affects to have charge of the wife's personal safety. . . .

There is little variance or dispute about the leading facts. Towards the close of the year 1867 Mr. Kelly informed his wife that a sum of 5000l., which had been bequeathed to her by her sister, had been in great part lost by the investment he had made of it. Unable to obtain from her husband a clear idea of her rights, and those of her son, under her sister's will, she wrote to her brother-in-law, Colonel Thornbury, to see the will for her, and to explain it. This he did, and wrote her the result, telling her that the money was in law at the entire command of her husband, and that her son had no rights in the matter. Some further correspondence passed between the petitioner and Colonel Thornbury, and between the petitioner and her brother. These letters falling into the hands of the respondent, were vehemently resented by him, and were, directly or indirectly, the cause of much, if not most, that followed. About the same time the petitioner's son quarreled with his father, and was obliged to quit the house. The petitioner, to some extent, took the son's part, which increased the resentment of the respondent. From these circumstances the respondent took up the idea, which he afterwards allowed to fill his whole mind, that his wife was plotting and conspiring against him. He commenced opening her letters, and calling her a vile traitor and apostate. He told her that no modest woman would associate with her more than with a prostitute. That she had given her confidence to another man, &c. He refused to sit at meals with her; he insisted on occupying a separate bedroom; he told the servant to take orders from him, and not from his wife; he forbad her to visit the poor in the district, as she had been accustomed, and desired her not to attend the ministration of the sacrament. Some months passed in this way. The respondent kept apart from his wife all day, except at family prayers, and even then he appears to have had little or no communication with her, except in the way of rebuke and reproach. At length, in the month of May, 1868, the petitioner became ill, her appetite wholly failed, she lost the senses of taste and smell, and towards the end of that month felt a sensation of numbness in her arm, which gave reason to fear paralysis. She consulted Dr. Drysdale. He advised her to leave home; her husband refused; and, on the 29th of June, having become worse, she left her home without his consent.

I am satisfied, from the medical testimony, that at this time the occurrences which had taken place, and the isolation and the reproaches to which she had been subjected, had so preyed upon her nervous system and general health, that serious consequences were to be feared if she were not for a time withdrawn from the life she was leading. Mrs. Kelly stayed away nearly four months, which she passed with her relations. The respondent wrote her many letters, in which he enlarged upon her sin. He expressed no care for her health, and none that she should return. In October she returned; between that time and the January following (when she finally left home) she was purposely subjected to the following treatment. She was entirely deposed from her natural position as mistress of her husband's house; she was debarred the use of money entirely; not only were the household expenses withdrawn from her control, but she was not permitted to disburse anything for her own necessary expenses; every article of dress, every trifle that she required had to be put down on paper, and her husband provided it, if he thought proper. Having refused, on one occasion of going into the town, to tell her husband every where that she had been, an interdict was placed on her going out at will. At one time the doors were locked to keep her in; at another, a man servant was deputed to follow her; at another, the respondent insisted on accompanying her himself, whenever she wished to go abroad. On these occasions he appears to have occupied the short time they were together in, what he called, putting her sin before her, in strong, coarse, and abusive terms, applying to her the same epithets and language as would be applicable to a woman who had been guilty of adultery. He took no meals with her; he occupied a separate bed-room; he passed no portion of the day, however small, in her society. They met, as before, only at family prayers, and if he spoke to her at all, it was only to give some directions or to reproach her. Save on one or two occasions she saw no one. Those whom she desired to see were forbidden the house. She was absolutely prohibited from writing any letters, unless her husband saw them before they were posted. She was thus, as far as the respondent could achieve it, practically isolated from her friends. Meanwhile the care of the household was confided to a woman hired for the purpose, who was directed not to obey Mrs. Kelly's orders without the respondent's directions. In short, she was treated like a child or a lunatic, and in this light she was actually re-garded by the woman just mentioned when she first entered the service, and this, be it remembered, although she had passed the mature age of sixty years, and had been married to the respondent for seven and twenty years. With no occupation, debarred the society of her husband and son at home, and that of her friends abroad, withheld from the performance of her household duties, subordinated to servants, penniless, and so far as her husband could effect it, friendless, the daily life of this lady was little better than an imprisonment, the solitary silence of which was broken only by the language of harsh rebuke, foul words, and epithets of insult, indignity, and shame. What wonder that, under so grievous an oppression, her health again gave way? She could not eat; she hardly slept at all; she was subject to constant trembling and fainting; she awoke involuntarily screaming at night, and her nervous system was so shattered that the medical witnesses declared paralysis or even madness to be imminent. Now, upon this testimony, it is important to observe that there is no contradiction. The respondent did not, even upon his own oath, deny or qualify the petitioner's evidence as to her state of health. On this head (the most important in the whole case) the respondent confined himself to the suggestion that the miserable condition was brought about, not by his treat-ment, but by vexation at the discovery of her own treachery. Her actual con-dition and danger he did not call in question, and yet it is to a repetition of this treatment with its almost inevitable results, that the respondent expects this Court to order Mrs. Kelly's return. That it should be asked to break in upon his rights as a husband, by depriving him of his wife's society, or, I should rather say, of her presence under his roof, is to him a matter of surprise and indignation. For, as he has truly said, he has not beaten her. He has, indeed, on two or three occasions, made her feel that his superior physical strength was always ready to be exerted to constrain her movements, but he has in-flicted no bruises, and done no visible bodily injury. Such a view of the law, if correct, would be little to its credit, and to coincide with it would be to abrogate the first duty in these matters of the Matrimonial Court, the protection of the wife's health and safety. These, then, are the things which Mr. Kelley did, and these the results upon his wife's health.

The remaining question is, why did he do them? His answer, I believe, would be, to bring his wife to penitence and submission. But penitence for what? and submission to what? Although he has never in his numerous letters, so far as I can discover, stated with great clearness what it was that he wished her to do, it is I think to be sufficiently gathered from them that he desired her to admit that she had suspected him of fraud and had traitorously conspired with others to fasten that charge upon him. For this he would have her express remorse and contrition, suing for his pardon, and humbly confessing her guilt. Mrs. Kelley refused to do so, because she says she never had, in fact, suspected him of anything false and dishonourable, and never did take counsel with others to bring the charge of it against him. Writing on the 1st of August, 1868, she says, "I could not tell a lie in this matter. I did not design any treachery, and will never say I did." And further on, "I am sorry I did not ask your leave to see the will. I had a right to do so, but had I at all thought of its vexing you I would not have acted as I did. Surely, now that what has taken place cannot be recalled, it would be better to bury the past in oblivion; let bygones be bygones, forgive and forget mutually, and seek to spend the little time that remains of this life on earth together in peace. . . . I promise on my part to do all in my power towards this object, but my position must be such as not to cause a scandal. . . . If you will not do this, will you tell me what you do wish, and what is to be the end of it." Writing again on the 14th of September, 1868, she said: "I never thought you had done anything dishonourable, and certainly I never tried to prove it. . . . You are under a complete delusion as to my conduct. . . . My desire is to act towards you with the submission, obedience, and even affection of a wife."

It would be difficult for a wife to play her part in so critical and painful a situation in a more becoming manner. Surely, such language as this should have satisfied any reasonable man. It did not satisfy Mr. Kelly, because, as it appears to me, he had suffered his mind to become filled and mastered by notions utterly extravagant, both as to the authority of a husband, and the legitimate means of enforcing it. He invokes the theory of the law, that the wife should be subject to the husband, but he forgets to add the qualification, "in all things reasonable." He asserts that he is within the law, if refraining from physical violence, he only puts such pressure on his wife as shall force her to obey him. But again he should add, "provided the means used to exert moral pressure be reasonable." But what if reasonable means are insufficient, and a wife still holds out against her husband's lawful will? The answer is, that the law can neither do nor sanction more. The law, no doubt, recognizes the husband as the ruler, protector, and guide of his wife; it makes him master of her pecuniary resources; it gives him, within legal limits, the control of her person; it withdraws civil rights and remedies from her, save in his name. Conversely, the law places on the husband the duty of maintaining his wife, relieves her from all civil responsibility, and excuses her even in the commission of great crimes, when acting under her husband's order. By these incidental means, it has fenced about and fostered the reasonable supremacy of the man in the institution of marriage. In so doing, it is thought by some that the law is acting in conformity with the dictates of nature, and the mutual characteristics of the sexes. Be that as it may, the subordination of the wife is doubtless in conformity with the established habits and customs of mankind. With all these advantages then in his favour, the law leaves the husband, by his own conduct and bearing, to secure and retain in his wife the only submission worth having, that which is willingly and cheerfully rendered. And if he fail, this Court cannot recognize his failure as a justification for a system of treatment by which he places his wife's permanent health in jeopardy, and sets at nought not only his own obligations in matrimony, but the very ends of matrimony itself, by rendering impossible the offices of domestic intercourse and the reciprocal duties of married life. The cruelty of the respondent is established, and the Court decrees a judicial separation with costs.

62. Death on the American frontier

In the nineteenth century, marriages were frequently and unexpectedly ended by death, whether from diseases such as tuberculosis and diphtheria, or from accidents, starvation, murders, and wars. Even at the end of the century, both women and men died much younger than they do in the developed world today—in France and England, the average life expectancy for both sexes was still something under fifty years. Although many documents in this collection give evidence of the impact of those early deaths on families in the settled cities and villages of England, France, and the United States, the situation was quite different along the American frontier. There widows, widowers, and orphans found themselves, in many cases, thousands of miles from the family and community support that would normally have eased them through their bereavement. Moreover, the hardships and violence of frontier life killed many people before their time.

These selections document two such early deaths. The first tells the story of Susan Marsh Cranston (1829–57), an Oregon pioneer and the mother of three very young daughters, who died, apparently from lung disease, at the age of twenty-eight. As if she foresaw her fate, Cranston recorded in the journal she kept during the long crossing of the prairies the number of graves the wagons passed each day. In these letters to Susan's sister and brother-in-law,

SOURCES: (i) Letters of Warren Cranston to Susan's family, transcribed in 1940 by E. W. Davis, Susan Cranston's great-nephew, Bancroft Library, University of California, Berkeley. The editors wish to thank Professor Carroll Smith-Rosenberg for copies of some of these letters and the Bancroft Library for permission to publish them. (ii) Journals of Eleanor Fitzgerald Brittain Knowlton, VMS 128, The Manuscript Collection, California Historical Society Library, San Francisco. The editors wish to thank Karl Feichtmeir, manuscripts librarian, for directing us to this journal, and the California Historical Society for permission to quote from it.

Warren Cranston blames his wife's premature death on the conditions of frontier life. The letters depict the problems of a widower struggling to keep his children with him.

The second selection consists of excerpts from the journal of Eleanor Fitzgerald Brittain (1834–1907), daughter of an old and distinguished Kentucky family, who migrated to California with her husband, David, in 1857, losing a baby boy on the overland trail. David was shot in the course of a robbery in 1860, which left him invalided for life, and he eventually died of his wounds in 1869. Eleanor Brittain, left with $250 and three young daughters to support, had to protect herself and her girls in a rough and dangerous world. A skilled horsewoman who was quick with whip—and tongue—the spirited widow was a true frontier woman.

(i) Warren Cranston

[Warren Cranston to Susan's brother and sister, April 25, 1858]

My children are still at Father's. They have not been sick since their mother died. Mother says they are very good children to get along with. They are very well satisfied to stay at Father's. . . .

It is useless for me to harrow your feelings by speaking to you of my lonely condition or describing my feelings which are lonely indeed. I never expect to enjoy myself as I did when Susan was with me. There is a vacancy in my being or at least seems so. I cannot reconcile the idea of separation with Susan only in this wise, that although I am the loser, she is the gainer. She is free the toil, pain and anguish attendant to this life and gone I trust to heaven where pain and trouble are not known, where joys are said to ever abound.

[Warren Cranston to Susan's brother-in-law, Reuben Fairchild, July 25, 1859]

My children have had very excellent health as yet are living with mother and father. They are very good children and think a great deal of each other. Amelia would not come up with me and go to school unless Ella could go too. But Orpha said, Pa I will go with you. . . .

It has been over two years since Susan died and a long time it has been to me I assure you. I often times regret having come to Oregon, thinking perhaps had I not done so Susan might perhaps still be living. She always told me that she did not regret coming, but perhaps it is all for the best. It would be better for man if he could be reconciled to the mysterious workings of Providence. I cannot do otherwise than submit. My aim shall be to raise these little ones in such a manner that they will be as much respected as was their mother, but to do that I must be with them more than I have been since Susan died.

[Warren Cranston to "My Dear Sister," probably Susan's sister, Huldah Fairchild, Oct. 4, 1859]

I would like very much to have you come here to live. I would almost part with half my land if by that means I could live with you and my children.

The way I am now situated I am of necessity away from the children the most of my time. I want to be with them, but I cannot and carry on my farm. My sister's time is out and they will move next week and then I shall have to try batching. When I shall come back I cannot tell. Times are so hard that as yet I cannot raise the necessary amount to go and come which would be not less than $1000. I could raise that amount by selling off my [?]. But I would be too short when I got back. Should you take a notion to come here by the next migration, I will try and come back so as to cross the plains with you.

(ii) Eleanor Brittain

We are now [1865] just going to ascend the Sierra Mountains.* My life in Nevada is at an end. I never expect to make my home there again may have to go back on business. Now I have entered on my travels with a sick husban with the intention to go where ever he may desire to go as long as he lives or our money lasts and will show to him I am reconciled to the life I am now going to enter. In my previous life of hardships I never showed a morose disposition, and he would be quick to observe a change and it would make him unhappy. He is despondent on account of being disabled through life and has not much hope of ever being better. And I feel it my duty to be cheerful and every one so in camp. But I am often sad at heart when I think of my dear brother and my dear little baby boy being laid to rest beneath Nevada's soil, and Oh how lonely they seem to be. This is the only thing causes me to regret to leave Nevada. But I presume it will be my lot to be laid in some lonely grave without a board to mark the spot. I wish some kind friend would build a rookery over it to show some poor human is beneath. This is all I ask When I am laid to rest. So adieu. . . .

Now the year of 1868 has passed, and I have had many hard ships. But I have bore them without complaining. Now it is New Year, and I see no show for it to be a happy one. Mr. Brittain is bedfast most of the time. I now have had a cradle made large enough for him to lay in and be rocked for exercise. The children and I would rock him. There never was anything left undone that would give him any comfort. It is now the first of February, and I find I cannot do any longer alone. I paid Mr Cameron what I owed him and he went home. . . . Before he left he gave the three girls a nice dress and me one. Mr Brittain told me to show them to him and said you have been crying, now bring your dress, I know it is black. How thoughtful Tom was to get black. He new you would soon need it. And then he had me sit down by the bed. He asked me if I was getting scarce of money. I said I have enough to do with. He then asked me what can you do to make a living. I told him I could do anything that was honest and virtuous. He said he wanted to

---

* Brittain tended to scrawl things down in her journal, writing without care for such niceties as punctuation or capitalization. Because we feel this distracts the reader from the content of this remarkable memoir of the Old West, we have freely added periods, commas, and capitals to the original. Otherwise, the idiosyncrasies of the original (the misspellings, odd internal capitalization, inconsistencies, etc.) have been retained.—EDS.

make one request—that was never to take in washing and another that if at any time I was parted from either of our little girls and they would be sick and in distress for me to go to them if possible. I told him I would. Well the next thing he wanted me to do was to order his kasket and his burial suit which I did reluctantly, and he said you must burry me at your own expence. The masons would but I dont want be burried as a pauper, and the more you do the more My Brother Masons will do for you when I am gone. But I am affraid when you get sick no one will take the care of you as you have of me. I said I will have friends. He then told me to beware of the Gruwells. . . .

Now it is Friday March 20th 1869. Mrs McCarty is here. He had called me to come and sit by his bed. He said a few days more he would die and wished he had died at the time he was shot. I told him not worry. He then said you would have money to raise the children and live on. I told him we had made our money together, and if we have spent it we have many pleasures as well as sorrows in doing it. He then turned to Mrs McCarty and said I wish I could take my angel wife with me. She told him he ought to be glad that I was going to be spared to raise the girls. . . . It is now Sunday morning the 22nd of March 1869. He is no more. He was conscious up to the last— The town of Lakeport was small and every person came to bid him a last farewell. . . . I am now left a widow with three little girls, the eldest 14 years old, to raise and some debts to pay and very little means to do with, although the outside community believed I had plenty money. The first thing I did was to pay my debts, see what I would have left, then I had two hundred and fifty dollars left. My house was unfinished and no well. I knew I could not subsist on $250 dollars long and not earn something at some kind of labor. Finally I made up my mind I would try to get a third grade certificate. The Board of Education met the month of April. I went before them and was surprised when I was told I had got my certificate. The next thing was to get a school. I heard through a friend that there was a school in Morgan valley he thought I could get if I would go immediately. It was about 30 miles from Lakeport. I hired a livery team and Mr John Mathis . . . the Proprietor and an old Ky Friend of mine drove the team and trusted me for the pay untill I could earn the money. He and I went to see all the trustees. Staid all night at Mr John Capps, one of the trustees and a cousin of My mothers. Next morning I made arrangement to board with him. . . .

My school was for six months at fifty dollars a month. My board did not cost me much as I helped do the work. My Eldest daughter helped too. . . . My school was out in October. The children all learned well, and I loved them, and The Trustees Hired me for the next term. Now I am at home with my three girls and will get my wood and provisions in enough to do me untill my school commences in the spring and have a well dug and walled up.

It is now April 1870 and I am again ready to go to Morgan valley to take charge of my school at sixty dollars a month. I must try to get a place to board so I wont have to walk as I did the first part of last term. . . . Mr Capps told me while I was gone one of his neighbors who lived close to the schoolhouse had offered to let you have his house all to yourself, and furnish your provisions and wood if you would do his cooking and washing, and he would move his bed in a room in the Barn. He had a fine barn, and if I would give the Knoxville teamsters their suppers and breakfast twice a week I could have all that I could make off of them, and he would keep their teams and have that Profit—The schoolhouse was just a few yards from the place. I asked My cousin Mr Capps where his wife was. Capps said he was not a married man and was a Dane But a Gentleman. I told Capps I did not want to do anything that would give rise to Talk. He said it would not. Your children will be with you and you have the house to yourself and all you have to do is to furnish your Bedding. There is plenty of everything else to keep house with. So I agreed to go. . . .

My school is nice and everything is all right. But I have learned from a friend that they saw my daughter and a Lady in company with a Gentleman in Calistoga and from the discription he gave I new it was a Gruwell. So it brought to my mind what My Husban said beware of the Gruwells. This was about the middle of the week. I went to Lower Lake Friday and took the stage for my friends on St Helena mountain and got my daughter. Everything was all right then. I said nothing about why I wanted my daughter, Only she could go to school and be company for me and her sisters. I was home Monday morning for my school. I left my other two girls with my cousin, Mr Capps. Now I feel satisfyed to have my Three girls home under my care, and I am making a good living for us all. Well I hope to have nothing to worry me any more. If I did not take pleasure in my school and home dutyes I dont know what I would do, but they keep me from dwelling on my troubles which have passed well. . . .

It is now August. Orric Is cutting his hay and is quite busy. He always eats cold dinner. But I left my daughter Helene home in the Fore noons to fix him something warm. On this occasion which I am going to speak of she came running to the school. . . . I was anxious to know what was the matter. She called to me to run quick. Mr Orric's team has ran away, and He is cut all to pieces. I told Tommy Smith to dismiss the school and come down to the house immediately. When I got home he was laying on the floor in the front room in a pool of blood. Tommy Smith was just coming. I told him to get me a lot of water, and I taken a large sheet which I used to give Mr Brittain wet sheet packs and put blankets on a lounge which was in the room, then diped the sheet in a tub of water. Tommy wrung it out lightly, placed it on the blankets. Then I cut what few cloths was left on him off but while Tommy was fixing the pack I was holding an Artery which was cut in the left arm above the elbow. I bandaged it tight—then put him in the pack, then put cold towel to his head, kept him in the pack with hot bottles of water to his feet. . . . In this time a lot of men and women came. One fellow said, Orric I would not let this woman put water on me that way. Orric told him he was in my Power. I told the fellow to go way, that I knew what I was do-ing. . . . The women said to me how could you take that mans clothes off. Oh I would be Ashamed if I were you. Yes, I said, you would let him die on account of a little false modesty. Well the doctor is here. He is going to give Orric Chloroform and dress his wounds and amputate a finger or two. There was not a man that would stay in the room to help the Dr, so I helped him. The next day was Saturday, and The Dr came and dressed the wounds. Orric thanked him. The Dr told him to thank me, that I saved his life. . . .

It is now the middle of the second week of September and the day for the teamsters to be at the house for their suppers. I think it is Tuesday, and I have sent my two oldest girls home before I let the other children out. Just as I had dismissed the school I seen a Buggy pass with Two men. They were not going towards my house. I did not give them a thought untill Helene met me and told me one of them had come in to the yard and given Bruns a letter and said he would be back soon. I hurried in the house and asked her to give me the letter. It was only a few words Telling her to be ready he would be back for her soon. In a few moments he came rushing in to the back yard. I stopped him and said Mr Sam Gruwell, what do you want. Nothing but a drink of water. told him I knew better, and he said I did not. I told him I had his letter Trying to get my daughter to go with him. He told me in the hearing of the teamsters that it was a lie, that he did not want her nor none of the family. By this time he was in his buggy and still denied that he came for her. His whip was standing in the Buggy. I taken it and gave him Two keen cuts with it and told him I would whip him untill he acknowledged what he wanted. He said he did come for her and would have her at the risk of his life. The man that was with him had but one arm. I told him if he was not a cripple I would give him a few licks but I have compassion on cripples, my Husban was one. He told a friend of mine he was very sorry and would never go to help steal another womans girl. The teamsters told me to give it to them and if you want us we will help you, but the men drove away in a hurry. I went to my school the next day just as though I had no trouble—but everyone who heard of the trouble sympathized with me. I will soon have to go to Lake Port for a few days on account of getting my certificate If I should want this school again. But I have almost made up my mind to take my children and go East and stop this Gruwell from trying to get my daughter. She is too young. I don't know why a man wants to marry a girl not 16 years old.

Part III

The Adult Woman: Work

Introduction
Leslie Parker Hume and Karen M. Offen

> Once there lived a mother and a daughter who were both rather
> lazy. Neither of them was a bad woman, but they always felt
> that if they could get someone else to do their work for them,
> so much the better. It came to pass that the daughter married
> and according to the custom moved to live near her husband's
> family. All summer long she had a gay time and did not work
> at drying fish. When people asked her why she wasn't preparing
> for winter she replied, "Oh, mother always dries fish for me."
> The mother likewise was not working at preserving any fish, for
> she assumed her daughter was drying fish for both of them.
> When winter came it was a year of famine. These two women
> were the first to die.[1]

In the nineteenth century women worked: as children or widows, members of the English working class or slaves in the American South, married women or spinsters. The female experience of Victorian women was, in large part, a working experience. The labor of women—whether visible in the factory or invisible in the home, paid or unpaid—was of incalculable value both to their families and to the communities in which they lived. Over fifty years ago the American economist Sophonisba Breckinridge underscored this fact in her introduction to Edith Abbott's classic study *Women in Industry*: "Women have, of course, always worked. . . . Women have not, however, always worked for wages."[2]

Yet, paradoxically, Victorian culture was reluctant to recognize women as workers in a century that was above all else a century of work. The Victorians presided over the birth of industrial society and the coming of age of the working class; indeed, they came to define human experience in terms of work, and on both sides of the Atlantic their celebration of work rose to a crescendo. Whether in the bombastic lectures of Samuel Smiles or the stirring verses of Walt Whitman, Victorian writers extolled industriousness and zealously proselytized for the new "religion of work." The collective search for social order and stability, the dedication to nation-building, the shaping of a disciplined work force in the interests of economic expansion, the individual

---

[1] Tlingit tale, "The Lazy Woman," cited in Niethammer 1977: 130.

[2] Abbott 1924: vii, ix. For important contributions to the history of women's work in the pre-industrial and industrializing family economy, see Hufton 1975; Scott & Tilly 1975; and Tilly & Scott 1978.

WOMEN IN THE WORK FORCE IN ENGLAND, FRANCE, AND THE
UNITED STATES, 1850's–1910's
(*Thousands of people*)

Country	Total working population	Women in the working population	Working women as percentage of the working population	Working women as percentage of the total female population
England				
1851	9,377	2,832	30.2%	26.6%
1871	11,870	3,650	30.7	27.2
1891	14,499	4,489	31.0	26.4
1911	18,340	5,413	29.5	25.7
France				
1856	14,123	4,413	31.2	24.7
1872	14,686	4,348	29.6	23.7
1891	16,343	5,139	31.4	26.6
1911	29,931	7,719	36.9	38.7
United States				
1870	12,925	1,917	14.8	9.7
1890	23,318	4,006	17.1	13.1
1910	37,371	7,445	19.9	16.7

SOURCE: Paul Bairoch, *The Working Population and Its Structure*, vol. 1 of *International Historical Statistics*, ed. T. Deldycke, H. Gelders, J.-M. Limbor, et al. (Brussels, 1968).

NOTE: All figures in the table have been rounded. "Work force" or "economically active population" refers to paid employment. No comprehensive or reliable figures are available for the first half of the century.

quest for affluence, social position, and self-fulfillment, and the belief in the possibility of creating new Jerusalems on earth all encouraged the promulgation of the gospel of work.

As that gospel concerned women, however, it had a narrow application. Victorian prescriptive literature celebrated women's work *in the home* and applauded the notion of good household management. But the authors of these texts—many of whom were women—did not acknowledge, much less celebrate, women's work outside the domestic sphere. In fact, they promoted an ideology of domesticity that perpetuated the notion that the only appropriate working activities for women were domestic tasks. Like the French historian Jules Michelet, they believed that the term *ouvrière* (working woman) was an "impiety," an outrage.[3] How to account for this paradox? What happened to women and their work during the nineteenth century?

The explanation must be sought both in theory and in experience. During the Victorian period both the patterns of women's work and the cultural interpretation of work changed; increasingly, the word work came to mean something very different for men and women. With the growth of the market economy, more men worked away from their households than in the past and

[3] Michelet 1873: 23.

earned cash wages in a public world of work for pay. In contrast, most women's work continued to center around the home and much of it remained unpaid. Thus, the physical restructuring of work space—the great distances that separated home from factory and office—accentuated to the point of transformation traditional distinctions between the male and female spheres. It altered conditions of family life, intensified sex segregation in the Victorian labor force, and constricted women's work options. For women, the continuing overlap of home and workplace and the diversity of tasks within the household made it difficult either to categorize or to evaluate their work.

A new concept of work emerged during the Victorian period that further contributed to the devaluation of women's work. Increasingly, the Victorians recognized only "productive" wage labor as work; indeed, by the end of the century the very word work had come to be used in a new, specialized way—to define labor as the production of goods by wage earners working long hours in shops and factories located away from living quarters. This new perception of work in effect defined women out of the work force and made it possible to disregard their working activities: it created conflicts in women's feelings about their own work, enabled men to derogate or ignore women's working activities, and even isolated women from organized labor movements.[4]

The continuing influence of this nineteenth-century redefinition of work as productive wage labor has militated against a full appreciation of women's labor and obstructed our own century's view of women's work, both past and present. Women's work in fact historically encompasses all the tasks women perform. Women's "nonproductive" household activities, whether caring for children or cooking meals, along with their various cash-producing home industries, from taking in boarders or laundry to selling eggs or writing novels, must be viewed as legitimate aspects of women's work. Using this more comprehensive definition of work, let us now consider in more detail the range of tasks performed by Victorian women.

The Geography of Women's Work

Perhaps the most illuminating way to understand women's work and the ways in which the restructuring of male and female work space affected it is to compare two diagrams that portray the geography of women's work in the pre-industrial and industrial West. The organization of male and female space in pre-industrial times can be depicted as two concentric rings, designating locations where women and men performed their various work activities (Fig. 1).[5] At the center, representing the patriarchal household—the

---

[4] The Victorian redefinition of work has permeated the subsequent historical and sociological study of women's work, as David Potter pointed out some twenty years ago. See Potter 1959. Recent critics of the severe limitations this redefinition has imposed on historians of women's work include Madeleine Guilbert, Evelyne Sullerot, Michelle Perrot, Patricia Branca, Joan W. Scott, and Louise Tilly. Marxist-feminist analysts have attempted to break down the earlier dichotomy between production and consumption in the interest of understanding the complexities of women's work. See, for example, Mitchell 1966; and Bridenthal 1976.

[5] We have used the concentric ring device solely as a way to show the broad

basic social and economic unit—are clustered the traditional domestic tasks performed by women: housework, food preparation, and child care. A second set of activities carried out by women within the dwelling or its immediate vicinity is located in the same ring: the care of poultry, rabbits, dairy cows, and other domestic animals; the cultivation of fruits and vegetables; and sometimes the manufacture of goods, from cheese to cloth, for household use, barter, or sale. In a larger village or town the household might include a small shop.

At a short distance from the household lay the fields and forests and the public squares. All were the domain of men and as such are located in the second ring. Although women could be called into the grain fields to help sow the crops or pull weeds, they usually worked under the supervision of men, who plowed and reaped. Their cultures, prizing the physical strength required of the men who drove the plow horses or felled the forests, considered women's labors in the second ring to be auxiliary at best. Vast distances rarely separated field from home, so that both women and men worked near each other in the vicinity of the household, even though their tasks were segregated by sex. When women did travel from one location to another, to visit or to serve as apprentices, domestic servants, or midwives, their destination was usually another household, in which they performed tasks deemed appropriate for their age and marital status. All women, young and old, worked within the framework of the family economy: whatever they did was for the collective benefit of the family group.

In the nineteenth century, this traditional geography began to change, as illustrated in Figure 2. The expansion of the market economy, first in urban and later in rural areas, gradually transformed women's household-centered activities. Although the labels given these tasks often remained the same, their content changed dramatically: indeed, the increasing availability of commercial products, such as soap and matches, and the growth of municipal services, which brought plumbing and gas to the home, altered the very nature of housewifery.[6] As in the past, many women found ingenious ways to supplement their family income through home-based cash-producing activities—sewing and washing for others, or writing advice manuals for sale to commercial publishers. These activities did not alarm the Victorian public since they remained centered in the private sphere and were considered supplemental to women's primary domestic chores.

The commercialization of traditional female tasks brought women into a new arena (depicted in the figure by an intermediate ring) that emerged beyond the periphery of the household. Although many women continued to

---

spectrum of women's work activities in spatial terms of distance and destination. In using this device, which illustrates the increasing physical separation of women's work from the household, we do not intend to imply either than the concerns of family and work became separated in women's and men's minds, or that one can be studied without reference to the other. Such assumptions would certainly merit the criticism they have recently received. See, for instance, Pleck 1976; Kamerman 1979; and Rapp, Ross, & Bridenthal 1979.

[6] See Andrews & Andrews 1974; Oakley 1974; and Kleinberg 1976.

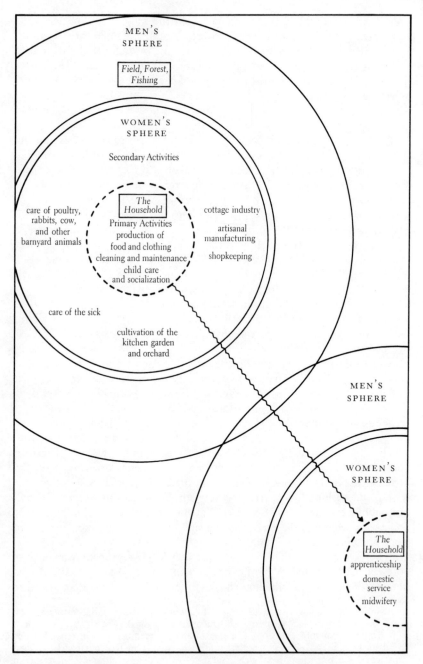

MEN'S
SPHERE

Field, Forest,
Fishing

WOMEN'S
SPHERE

Secondary Activities

care of poultry,
rabbits, cow,
and other
barnyard animals

The
Household
Primary Activities
production of
food and clothing
cleaning and maintenance
child care
and socialization

cottage industry

artisanal
manufacturing

shopkeeping

care of the sick

cultivation of the
kitchen garden
and orchard

MEN'S
SPHERE

WOMEN'S
SPHERE

The
Household
apprenticeship
domestic
service
midwifery

Fig. 1. The geography of women's work in pre-industrial times

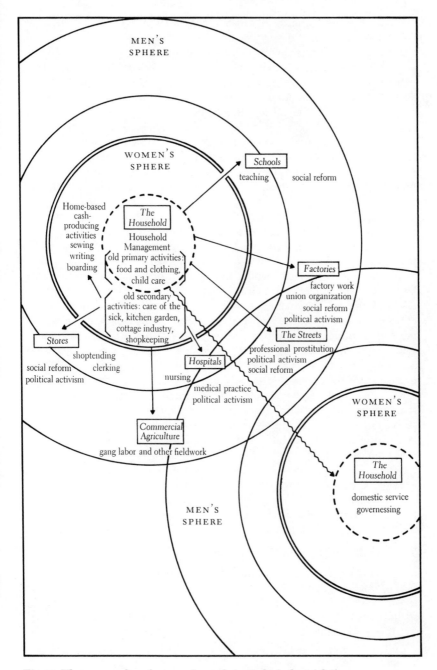

Fig. 2. The geography of women's work in early industrial times

work on their own farms or to assist neighbors on an occasional basis, a new commercial agriculture developed that enlisted their labor, whether as slaves, sharecroppers, or members of migrant agricultural gangs. Similarly, the department store, the urban offspring of the small village shop, provided employment for countless young women. Even some traditional female activities, such as the instruction of children and the care of the sick and infirm, slowly crept out of the household, as schools, hospitals, and other institutions increased in numbers. These institutions not only removed some burdens from the nineteenth-century housewife, but also provided new employment opportunities for single women, for these jobs conformed to traditional definitions of female work and were perceived by the Victorians as "safe" and quasi-household-centered work that did not jeopardize the single woman's future as wife and mother.

What alarmed the Victorians, however, were women's working activities that were distant from the household either in time or in space, that were not traditional, and that seemed somehow to threaten the family: these are depicted in the second ring. Controversy over women's work in these "public" arenas flared repeatedly throughout the nineteenth century, sometimes fueled by new socioeconomic conditions in which women's work for pay presented itself "in forms and conditions approximating those agreed upon for men."[7] Increasing numbers of single and married women found wage-earning employment in factories, the most visible, innovative, and awesome creations of nineteenth-century capitalism. Prostitution, in spite of its antique heritage, achieved a new notoriety in the Victorian period and provided a focus for much of the anxiety created by urban growth. As the century progressed a small number of highly educated "new" women asserted their right and their competence to enter the male professions of medicine, law, and theology. At the same time, there appeared a host of female social reformers who articulately criticized the male conduct of public affairs. However different the social backgrounds of these women, the prostitute, factory girl, doctor, and social reformer all proved deeply troubling to nineteenth-century society, and their working activities appeared iconoclastic to many of their contemporaries.

Bearing in mind this geographic overview of women's work, let us now take a closer look at each of these rings, returning first to the household and moving out to the factory and the street.

The First Ring: The Household

The theme of the home as a refuge from the turmoil of modern life runs throughout Victorian literature; the British social and art critic John Ruskin spoke for many of his contemporaries when he eulogized the home as "the shelter, not only from all injury, but from all terror, doubt and division."[8] Yet if sentimentally envisaged as a haven, the Victorian home was in reality a workplace, and, as in the past, many of women's working activities were centered there.

[7] Sullerot 1968: 11.
[8] Ruskin 1865: 59.

Throughout the nineteenth century domestic activities continued to absorb the working energies of married women from all classes. Economic and cultural changes, however, altered the woman's role as household manager. The affluence brought by commercial and industrial growth both increased the complexity of the middle- and upper-class household and freed wealthy women from the more onerous domestic chores. But a large house, ornate furniture, elaborate meals, and a domestic staff all demanded that the mistress of the house develop the organizational expertise of an army general. The Victorian matron was rarely a lady of leisure, even though she employed servants to clean and cook and could, following Isabella Beeton's instructions, purchase a sewing machine to manufacture the family wardrobe (Doc. 63.iii). Such splendid establishments were, in any event, rare. The more typical middle-class experience called for the lady of the house to do most of the work herself with the help of one maid-of-all-work.[9]

For working-class, rural, and black families, the survival of the family might well have depended on the judicious management and hard work of the wife. The Parisian and Manchester housewives of our documents (Docs. 64.i–ii) bore the sole responsibility for performing domestic chores that, in the absence of any labor-saving devices, were backbreaking. Like many women, Marie-Geneviève J— and Isabella Killick had to combine these chores with cash-producing work to help support their families (Docs. 67, 68.iv). And even in the most tradition-bound areas of rural France, agricultural wage labor could take peasant women away from their own households for more than a hundred days of the year (Doc. 75). Although at the opening of the nineteenth century many cash-producing tasks were still centered in the household, by 1900 commercial and industrial development had physically severed the workplace from the home in many areas; married women like Mrs. Smith of Nottingham and Ann Waldrop of Athens, Georgia, thus found it increasingly difficult to combine cash-producing work with household duties (Docs. 54.ii, 84.ii).

Though the arbiters of middle-class culture—authors of advice manuals such as Beeton, Cora-Elisabeth Millet-Robinet, and Eliza Leslie (Docs. 63.i–iii)—intended to help and guide the housewife in the performance of her domestic tasks, their prescriptions could in fact make housework more burdensome by setting rigorous standards that were difficult to meet. These intrusive advisers commanded women to devote all their energies to domestic management, thus to elevate the status of housework by "professionalizing" it; yet women who subscribed to their exacting canons were never awarded professional status. These changes in both the structure of their work and the cultural evaluation of their domestic duties could create tensions for women and in particular for less-affluent women.

This was especially true for the women who tried to meet the prescribed housekeeping standards in what was by necessity a workshop as well as a home. Long after the coming of the factory, cottage industry continued to employ

---

[9] See A. F. Scott 1970: 28–37; Davidoff 1973 and 1976; Branca 1975; Franklin 1975; B. G. Smith 1975; and Hellerstein 1976.

many women: spinning, weaving, lace-making, straw-plaiting, and other kinds of piecework were carried out in the household; and many urban women, such as the seamstress, the tailor's wife, and the trouser-finisher, manufactured fully salable items in their homes. The overlap of home and workplace enabled women to control the rhythm of their work and integrate their cash-producing and domestic labors, but it also increased dirt and confusion in the household. The word cottage may conjure up bucolic visions, but the accounts of Mémé Santerre and Elizabeth Smith (Docs. 5, 54.ii) attest to a darker, far grimmer reality.[10]

For middle- and upper-class women, too, the home could serve as a production center, the product in this case being literary works. During the first half of the nineteenth century the best English writing was nourished in rural parsonages or country cottages, as the careers of the Brontë sisters and Jane Austen attest; by contrast, in France literature tended to flourish in the metropolitan setting of Paris. In each country, however, there were many women who turned to writing to supplement their incomes; this was one of the few types of work in which a needy middle-class woman could engage without losing social status. Although most women authors worked in the traditional female sphere, the home, their vocation brought them into direct conflict with the cultural bias that defined writing as intellectual and therefore unwomanly. Some female writers adopted male pseudonyms to win a fair hearing for their work: Currer, Ellis, and Acton Bell (the Brontës) and George Sand come immediately to mind. Others, such as Catharine Beecher and Augustine Fouillée, justified writing on the grounds that their literary efforts would improve the moral tone of their nations. Still others, like Elizabeth Gaskell (Doc. 71.i), emphasized their domesticity to offset criticism of their "unwomanly" act of writing.[11]

During the course of the century both the nature of this female literature and the nature of writing as a female vocation changed. The explosion of the literary market enabled women authors to reach a wider audience: while Americans read Necker de Saussure (Doc. 10.i), whose earlier works had been promoted in the United States by the educational pioneer Emma Willard, the French read Harriet Beecher Stowe's *Uncle Tom's Cabin*, prefaced by George Sand. By the end of the century female authors were no longer at such pains to disguise their identities or justify their literary labors. In addition, some of them were far more explicitly feminist, and thus more critical of male-dominated culture, than their predecessors. By now, too, women had become more heavily involved in the world of publishing; they had begun to find work not only as writers and journalists, but as printers, publishers, and editors. Women's magazines and newspapers—Pauline Wright Davis's *The Una*, Bessie Rayner Parkes's *The Englishwoman's Review*, and Marguerite Durand's *La Fronde*—were a conspicuous phenomenon of the second half of the nine-

---

[10] For contrasting views on the advantages and disadvantages of the overlap between home and workplace, see Pinchbeck 1930; and Thompson 1963.

[11] For a discussion of 19th-century women writers, see Gréville 1884; Cone 1891; Wood 1971; Moers 1977; Showalter 1977; and Gilbert & Gubar 1979.

teenth century. Originally nourished in the private sphere of the home, the craft of the woman writer had given women access to the public sphere of the marketplace.[12]

Although most Victorian women worked in their own homes (even those who held some outside job), many moved into other people's households to work for pay as domestic servants or governesses. In England, and to a lesser degree in France, governessing was one of the few acceptable ways in which single women of the middle class could work for a living and still retain their claim to gentility. But as Nelly Weeton Stock discovered (Doc. 72), the domicile of a "gentleman" often proved less than a haven for the governess: neither servant nor family member, she found her position in the household ambiguous and uncomfortable, her wages minimal, and her tenure uncertain. Yet despite these drawbacks, the supply of governesses outstripped the demand, for few other employment opportunities were available to unmarried middle-class women.[13]

Like the governess, the domestic servant worked in the homes of others. In fact, in all three cultures throughout the nineteenth century, service became an ever-more-important source of paid employment for lower-class women: in England and the United States the number of female servants doubled in the second half of the nineteenth century (see the accompanying table). Both in France and in England service customarily attracted young, unmarried women like Elise Blanc and Hannah Cullwick, who came from rural backgrounds and for whom work in service generally ended with marriage (Docs. 73, 74). In America, by contrast, these jobs were typically held by black and immigrant women, both single and married, for whom there were few other employment options. The treatment of servants in the United States had a somewhat less monolithic character than in Europe; although the lot of an Irish maid in a Boston household might be similar to that of her counterpart in London, a Yankee hired girl in Maine, where girls were "scarce as gold dust" (Doc. 65.ii), could experience a more egalitarian relationship with her employer.

Domestic service attracted such large numbers of women because positions were plentiful and because most jobs demanded no initial skills. Moreover, for the young girl who was forced to leave home to find work, employment in service *seemed* to offer a secure form of migration—a place to live, food to eat, the opportunity to save one's wages, and the protection and surveillance of the mistress of the household. The reality of a servant's life, however, was often far removed from this ideal. As the statistics on both illegitimacy and prostitution suggest, the domestic servant was in a highly vulnerable position (Docs. 43.iii, 91). The servant was dependent on her employer; deference and subservience characterized her relationship with both master and mistress. The work was often onerous and dirty, the hours long, and the wages paid irregularly or infrequently. Furthermore, as Cullwick's

---

[12] For a sense of the magnitude of this change, see Dickinson 1891; Sullerot 1966; White 1970; and Showalter 1977.
[13] Peterson 1973.

PRINCIPAL OCCUPATIONAL SECTORS FOR WOMEN IN ENGLAND,
FRANCE, AND THE UNITED STATES, 1850's–1910's

(Thousands of Women)

Country	Personal and domestic services	Textiles	Apparel mfg. and related trades	Agri- culture	Com- merce	Pct. of working women in these 5 sectors
England						
1851	1,135	635	491	230	—	88%
1871	1,678	726	594	136	5	86
1891	2,036	795	759	81	26	82
1911	2,127	870	825	117	157	76
France						
1856	689	954[a]	[a]	2,159	—	91%
1896	692	493	953	2,760	505	85
1906	781	545	1,186	3,330	637	84
United States						
1870	982	109	197[b]	455	19	92%
1890	1,610	235	597	796	142	84
1910	2,530	403	865	1,176	465	73

SOURCE: Paul Bairoch, *The Working Population and Its Structure*, vol. 1 of *International Historical Statistics*, ed. T. Deldycke, H. Gelders, J.-M. Limber et al. (Brussels, 1968).

NOTE: All figures in the table have been rounded.

[a] Column 2 figure is a combined figure for these categories.

[b] Excluding boot and shoe manufacturing.

diary shows (Doc. 74), a servant enjoyed little job security. Under the circumstances, it is little wonder that by the end of the century many lower-class girls, by this time better educated and with more work opportunities open to them, preferred not to enter service (Docs. 70, 81).[14]

Although many Victorian women left the countryside to enter domestic service in the cities, large numbers of rural women found gainful employment in agriculture. Throughout the nineteenth century agriculture was the most important field of employment for women in France and the second most important in the United States. By contrast, in England the proportion of women employed in agriculture was relatively small; women sometimes worked at harvest time in agricultural gangs (Doc. 77), but the permanent agricultural work force was male. Although local or regional tradition had long defined certain kinds of agricultural pursuits as women's work, as agriculture became increasingly commercialized more than a few women worked side by side with men at the heaviest kinds of agricultural labor. Whether as slaves or sharecroppers, poor black women, like men, worked full-time in the cotton,

[14] Davidoff 1974 and 1979; Horn 1975; McBride 1976 and 1979; Guiral & Thuillier 1978; and Katzman 1978.

rice, and tobacco fields, just as English country women, like men, hired on as members of migrant agricultural gangs pulling mangolds. French peasant women worked long hours in the fields, and in a hard year even the mistress of a Kansas household could become a "hand" during the harvest crisis (Doc. 66). As long as women's labor remained vital to the survival of the family farm or the success of the plantation, the cultural sanctions against their performing heavy agricultural labor could be ignored. Yet when these sanctions were lifted, and women were needed both to till the fields and to care for children, their work was never awarded the same cultural recognition or pay. The expansion of commercial agriculture accentuated the traditional discrepancy between cultural prescription and the realities of female farm labor by changing the character of women's participation in the agricultural work force. By the end of the century, commercialization increasingly divorced field from household; moreover, by introducing new machinery—the tractors and combines that became the "playthings of men"—to the farm, it began to erode women's value as agricultural laborers.[15]

The Intermediate Ring: School, Store, and Hospital

Although the household continued to function as a workplace throughout the century, increasing numbers of young women crossed the divide that separated the home from the marketplace. However, their employment in the sorts of establishments designated in the intermediate ring did not arouse criticism or inflame the imagination of the Victorian public to the same extent as did their employment in the locations designated in the outer ring. Indeed, the growing needs of all three societies to staff new commercial and service institutions eased women's entry into the world of paid work. The fact that these new fields of employment grew out of tasks that women had traditionally performed in the household, and that the new employers, from school boards to department store magnates, made every effort to act *in loco parentis* effectively muffled whatever criticism women's increasing visibility as wage earners in these establishments might have aroused.

For single women primary school teaching offered one of the century's most important new job opportunities. Teaching was in effect an extension of a woman's traditional role as educator of the young and could be viewed as an apprenticeship for motherhood; with marriage, most women gave up teaching. Thus, the figure of the female teacher did not threaten the prevailing ideology of domesticity; in fact those teachers who did make education a lifelong career could justify their vocation, as Mary Lyon did, as a mission to improve domesticity (Doc. 79). Moreover, in the early years especially, many teachers held classes in their own homes; this was true of both Elizabeth Sewell's school at Ventnor, England, and Margaret Douglass's school in Norfolk, Virginia (Docs. 11.i, 15.i). Only gradually did women teachers move from the shadow of the private home into the light of the public classroom.

[15] On the changing relationship of women to modern agriculture, see the suggestive work of Boserup 1970. See also N. Z. Davis 1972; Ségalen 1973; Agulhon, Desert, & Specklin 1976; Roubin 1977; and Juster 1979.

If the forces of tradition helped women enter the classroom, it was the forces of change in the form of government-legislated compulsory education that opened the door wide for them, creating a demand for a cheap source of labor to staff the newly created schools. Female labor proved attractive because women were seen as less likely than men to complain about the conditions in which they worked and could be paid a third to a half as much. The educational hierarchy in effect reproduced that of the patriarchal family: the female schoolteacher worked under the direction of a male administrator.[16]

As the diary of Mlle N— (Doc. 80) shows, women teachers often experienced material and psychological discomfort, and a sense of loneliness and isolation. Yet for all these drawbacks, teaching(like governessing) offered a middle-class woman a "respectable" means of earning a living. Indeed, Lyon, Beecher, Buss, and the other middle-class women who founded the private schools of the early nineteenth century paved the way for lower-class women to staff the classrooms of the public primary schools; for poor but enterprising young women teaching came to provide a springboard to gentility. By 1900, the female schoolteacher had become a familiar and accepted figure in all three cultures.[17] Yet teaching, though it had given women access to the public sphere, appeared to decline in status as it became a "feminized" profession.

As in the case of teaching, cultural traditions and economic needs acted together to open sales work to women in the second half of the century. In moving from the small country shop to the far larger urban department store, women built on a tradition of female shopkeeping that existed in all three cultures. The dramatic expansion of the commercial sector of the economy spurred the transformation of this traditional type of work. The new emporiums cried out for a cheap, plentiful supply of shop assistants and clerks to sell their wares to urban consumers. Young women who had some education—particularly those who were unmarried and of lower-class background—were drawn to these jobs by the prospect of greater autonomy at work, better working conditions, and higher wages; yet as we learn from the stories of the New York shopgirls (Doc. 81), these prospects proved illusory. Like the more traditional forms of women's work, the new sales jobs did not pay particularly well; hours were long (in 1884 in England shop assistants worked some 75 to 94 hours a week), and for much of this time salesgirls were on their feet. Like the employers of domestic servants, European department store owners often acted as substitute parents, housing and exercising close control over their female employees. At the great Parisian store the Bon Marché, a formidable list of regulations governed the behavior of shopgirls; their counterparts in London complained about the heavy fines that could be as-

---

[16] On women and the development of the teaching profession, see Woody 1929; Holcombe 1973; Tyack 1974; Bernard & Vinovskis 1977; Meyers 1979; and Strober & Tyack 1979.

[17] Already in England by 1875, more than half of all primary school teachers (54%) were women; by 1914, they outnumbered men three to one. Holcombe 1973: chap. 3. On France, see Meyers 1979; and on the U.S., Tyack 1974; and Strober & Tyack 1979.

sessed for such sins as whispering after dark in their lodgings.[18] And like the educational hierarchy, the commercial hierarchy put women under the control of men. Although sales work offered an important new work option to women and provided an appealing alternative to domestic service or factory work, as a "feminized" profession its status remained low.

As with shopkeeping, nursing was a low-status, poorly paid female occupation that became a "feminized" profession in the nineteenth century. And as with teaching, cultural values, as well as social and economic need, sanctioned the development of this profession for women. Traditionally, most sicknesses had been tended to in the home, with the women in the family acting as nurses; nursing thus was an extended form of mothering and nurturing. Such hospitals as existed were usually also staffed by women. In the nineteenth century the institutional care of the sick in France continued to be left in the hands of female religious orders, but in England and America, the Crimean and Civil Wars overnight spawned a new profession for women in a secular context. But as with the teachers and shopworkers, English and American nurses worked under the direction of male supervisors, whether Army generals or doctors. In this role, they were applauded as "ministering angels," but when a Florence Nightingale or a Clara Barton (Docs. 82.i–ii) publicly declared that military and civilian authorities displayed incompetence in caring for the wounded, the "angel in white" quickly became a controversial and, indeed, a very political figure. To their contemporaries, these nurses could seem just as threatening as their sisters who labored in the locations designated in the outer ring.[19]

The Second Ring: Factory, Street, Consulting Room, and Public Platform

The entry of women into the labor force as teachers and shopgirls normally occasioned little controversy, but their appearance as factory workers, prostitutes, doctors, and social reformers provoked an uproar that could be heard from one side of the Atlantic to the other. The high visibility of women as workers in these extra-household settings (designated in the second or outer ring) may have sparked the furor, but more complex reasons underly the Victorians' discomfort. For one thing, the Victorians perceived these women as invaders of male workspace. Whether as factory workers or as doctors, they challenged the division of labor set down by the doctrine of the separate spheres and seemed to undermine the very foundations of the patriarchal family. For another, as in the case of urban prostitutes, they sometimes called into question Victorian notions about female sexuality and offended the moral sensibilities of their contemporaries. Finally, as reformers they challenged men for control of political affairs.

The explosive growth of the nineteenth-century textile industry brought women and children as wage laborers into factories, where they tended the new steam-powered looms. Typically the female mill worker was young and

[18] Holcombe 1973: 109, 112-14; Lesselier 1978; McBride 1978; Rotella 1979.
[19] Wood 1971; Holcombe 1973: chap. 4.

single; with marriage and the birth of children, most women left the mills. The women employed in the cotton and silk industries of Manchester and southeastern France (Docs. 83, 85) generally came from working-class or peasant backgrounds. But in New England middle-class prejudice against manual labor was less pervasive, and the mill owners first recruited the daughters of Yankee farmers. By mid-century, however, more and more immigrant women—many of them married—worked in the New England factories; and later, when the textile industry began to shift to the South, lower-class white women monopolized the jobs available in the new mills (Docs. 84.i–ii).[20]

Work in the mills opened up new employment opportunities for women, but these industrial workplaces were hardly as idyllic as the romantic name City of Spindles might suggest. Although government legislation gradually forced employers to improve working conditions, for much of the century the factory hours were long and hard: in Massachusetts in 1845 the average workday ranged from eleven to thirteen and a half hours; in England mill workers put in fourteen hours a day before the Factory Act of 1844 established a maximum workday of twelve hours for women. Though factory employment paid better than most of the other jobs available to these women (at Lowell a mill hand earned $2.00 a week in the 1840's, compared with a domestic servant's wage of $0.50 to $1.00), the working conditions were often unsanitary and the work itself both monotonous and dangerous (Doc. 83). Nor could remedial legislation change the fact that the factory imposed a work discipline on women and men in which the machines and their masters determined the rhythm of work.[21] Moreover, for all that factory labor seemed to hold out the promise of more autonomy to young women, strict contractual obligations and closely supervised living arrangements effectively limited the mill hand's freedom of action in much the same manner as parental controls (Doc. 85).

Although the proportion of women in textile factories remained relatively small throughout the century (see the tables on pp. 273 and 282), their rapid entry into these jobs provoked heated discussion.[22] The high visibility of women in the "dark Satanic mills" caused their Victorian contemporaries

[20] On England, see Neff 1929; Pinchbeck 1930; Smelser 1959 and 1967; Kovacevik & Kanner 1970; and Hewitt 1975; on France, Chatelain 1970; Reddy 1975; and Vanoli 1976; and on the U.S., Sumner 1910; Abbott 1924; Cantor & Laurie 1977; Foner 1977; and Dublin 1979.

[21] See Thompson 1967; Gutman 1976; and Perrot 1977a and 1977b.

[22] In England some 57,000 men and women were employed in the textile mills in 1818; by 1839 there were 146,000 women alone. By 1861 467,000 women were employed in the mills—over 60% of the total textile workers. Figures for France are unreliable, but the number of women employed in French textile mills in the 1860's has been estimated at between 400,000 and 450,000. The number of mill women in the U.S. was much smaller, though still representing some 60% of the textile work force; 62,661 women were employed in cotton alone in 1850, and their numbers rose to 75,169 in 1860. English and French figures are found in Pinchbeck 1930: 196 and Leroy-Beaulieu 1873: 28; French estimates in Leroy-Beaulieu 1873: 35; and American figures in Woody 1929, 2: 9.

a concern that mere numbers cannot explain. On one level critics in France and England complained that female factory workers were taking jobs away from men and undercutting male wages. This perception led many members of the International Working Men's Association (or First International, to use its more familiar name) to oppose wage labor for women and, subsequently, to block women's attempts to join their newly created trade unions. Paule Mink and other women who sympathized with the broader purposes of the International (Docs. 86.i–ii) hurried to counter such criticism with a strong defense of women's "right to work"; the problem of low wages could not be solved by pushing women out of the labor force, they argued; the only solution was to organize women workers. Though agitation to abolish wage labor for women so they could stay at home was sometimes well intentioned, it could also reflect men's fears that the extra-domestic employment of women in factories would erode patriarchal authority. This viewpoint, however, overestimated the potential for economic independence of women factory workers, whether daughters or wives, and overlooked the fact that most of these operatives, whether in Manchester, Lyon, or Lowell, worked in the interest of the family economy (Doc. 83).[23] As the debates of the First International also show, the movement to push women out of the factories and back into the home was influenced by the conviction that the female factory worker, removed from the protection of the family, was exposed and vulnerable, the potential victim of pernicious influences and unscrupulous male foremen. The convent-like accommodations that textile manufacturers in New England and southern France established for their unmarried female hands were designed specifically to protect the factory girl and avoid the "scandalous conditions" of Lancashire.[24]

Ultimately, the Victorians' fears about the deterioration in the quality of family life of factory women far outweighed their worries about the welfare of individual factory workers. In the England of the 1840's, where the controversy over women's employment in industry grew extremely heated, the champion of legislation to limit the factory workday, Lord Shaftesbury, bemoaned the "disorder, insubordination, and conflict" that characterized the family circles of married factory workers. Many of Shaftesbury's contemporaries shared his feelings and argued convincingly that a married woman who was gone from home twelve to fourteen hours a day had little time to give to housework or children. As for the single woman, they wondered, how and when could she ever find time to prepare herself for her future role as "angel in the house" (Doc. 58.i)? Shaftesbury spoke for all the rest when he gloomily asked: "Where, Sir, under these conditions are the possibilities of

[23] For contrasting views on the subject of female wage labor and female emancipation, see Shorter 1973; and Tilly, Scott, & Cohen 1976.

[24] An alternate approach was the construction of family-centered mill towns or worker-cities; among the most famous were Robert Owen's mill village at New Lanark, Scotland, and the worker-cities built by Protestant textile entrepreneurs in Mulhause, France.

domestic life? How can its obligations be fulfilled? Regard the woman as wife and mother—how can she accomplish any portion of her calling? And if she cannot do that which Providence has assigned to her, what must be the effect on the whole surface of society?"[25]

There is little question that these concerned Victorians were correct in thinking that work for wages outside the home made it hard for women to fulfill their domestic responsibilities. The position of a working mother with small children was particularly difficult, and as we saw in Part II, mortality rates were exceedingly high among the babies left to the care of older children or country wet nurses. At the same time, the Victorians' belief that a woman's place is in the home tended to make them hyperbolize the impact of such outside employment. Blinded by the ideology of domesticity, they lost sight of the reasons why women sought jobs away from home and could not recognize the fact that in an economy where cash played an increasingly vital role, family survival could depend on the wages that a wife or daughter earned by working in a factory or mill.

The nineteenth-century prostitute evoked as loud an outcry as the female factory worker, though obviously for different reasons. Investigations of Victorian sociologists and doctors (Docs. 89.i–ii) revealed that limited employment opportunities and underemployment drove thousands of poor women in cities to turn to prostitution in order to survive; for immigrants or servants out of work, poorly paid pieceworkers or dancers, prostitution offered a means of making ends meet or providing small luxuries. Yet however temporary a woman's commitment, prostitution could be hazardous. As the novels of Eugène Sue and Emile Zola underscore, disease, abuse, exploitation, and even death always threatened prostitutes.

Moral considerations shaped the Victorians' confrontation with the prostitute and prevented their accepting Flora Tristan's (Doc. 90.i) conclusion that most prostitutes were the innocent victims of gross economic injustice. Instead, many doctors, social scientists, and social reformers viewed "the great social evil" as a moral disease that threatened to contaminate their societies; as such, it must be eradicated or cured. In England and the United States crusaders embarked on a campaign to "rescue" prostitutes from a life of depravity (Doc. 6.iii). On both sides of the Atlantic politicians and doctors promoted legislation patterned on the regulations of the Paris Police Morals Bureau which recorded the names of all prostitutes and required them to register and submit to periodic physical examinations. These statutes positioned the "fallen women" and placed them under male control.

However reformist in intent, these laws made it increasingly difficult for women to move in and out of prostitution and had the effect of "professionalizing" it by making it a permanent career; this professionalization manifested itself in the proliferation of licensed brothels and the growth of the illegal white and yellow slave trades in the second half of the century.

[25] Cited in Hewitt 1975: 31.

Moreover, the legislation evoked much criticism and prompted some middle-class women to complain of the moral injustice of punishing the prostitute while leaving her equally culpable client free to seek the sexual services of other women. The flagrantly unjust treatment of suspected prostitutes (Doc. 91) drew public attention to the sexual double standard and stimulated the development of the feminist movement.[26]

Although an economic and cultural chasm separated the "two nations" of the prosperous and the poor, to the Victorians the small number of upper-middle-class women who entered the world of work as doctors or social reformers seemed almost as threatening to the social order as the female factory hands and the prostitutes. Traditionally, women had diagnosed illnesses, concocted medicines, cared for the sick at home, and delivered babies; yet as the male medical establishment took shape in the first half of the nineteenth century, women practitioners were shunted aside in the name of science. During the second half of the century pioneers like Elizabeth Blackwell and Madeleine Brès (Docs. 37.iii, 92) struggled to win the right for women to study to become doctors. Because of a strong tradition of professional midwifery, Frenchwomen had less difficulty breaking down the barriers to medical study than the American and British. In England and the United States the medical profession responded to female appeals with derision and hostility: the study of medicine was "too intellectual" for women and required a lifetime commitment that would leave them no time for home and family; the demands of internship and practice were too physically taxing; and then, just think, anatomy classes and operating procedures would expose them to male bodies. But the unvoiced concern that lay at the root of all the antagonism was the fact that the woman doctor squarely challenged Anglo-Saxon assumptions about the woman's and the man's separate spheres of labor. Although the number of women doctors remained small throughout the century and even these ministered mostly to female patients, they offered striking proof that women were capable of performing the same demanding work as men; in this respect, they confronted the doctrine of the separate spheres head-on and established a new cultural model for their societies.[27]

No less than the doctor, the social reformer provided a controversial example of the work women were capable of performing. Since women had been assigned the role of nurturers and moral guardians in the family, reformers such as Frances E. Willard could logically argue that they were responsible as well for the moral welfare of the commonweal (Doc. 94.i): "social feminism" was to become, then, the adjunct of "domestic feminism" as the angel in the house spread her wings to protect society at large.

[26] On the social ramifications of 19th-century prostitution in England, see Cominos 1963; Marcus 1966; Pearsall 1969; Petrie 1971; Sigsworth & Wyke 1972; Walkowitz & Walkowitz 1974; and Walkowitz 1977. On France, see Chevalier 1973; and Weston 1979; and on America, Riegel 1968.

[27] See especially Blackwell 1895. On England, see Manton 1965; and Donnison 1977; on the U.S., Walsh 1978; and on France, Lipinska 1900; and Charrier 1931.

By the middle of the century a growing number of educated middle- and upper-class women devoted their energies to volunteer activities outside the home. In England and the United States Protestant traditions encouraged them to employ this time usefully; and the "bonds of womanhood" created by their common experience in the private sphere often instilled in them a special desire to help other women.[28] Women thus entered into the temperance and abolition movements, worked to reform prisons and to improve the care of juvenile offenders, campaigned for "social purity," joined the socialist movement, and enrolled in a host of reform organizations—clubs, associations, and sisterhoods of all sorts (Docs. 93.i–iii, 94.i–iii).[29] Of course, many Victorians did not accept the argument that these activities were merely an extension of the woman's role in the home, and greeted what they regarded as an intrusion into the male sphere of political life with open hostility.

The entry of middle-class women into the public sphere through reform work quickly led to the development of a feminist political critique. Having seen the injustices and inequalities of their societies and having run head on into antagonism and obstruction in their efforts to right these wrongs, several reformers began to denounce the male domination of their societies and to demand political as well as civil rights for women. In America, for example, Elizabeth Buffum Chace and Elizabeth Cady Stanton moved from agitating for the abolition of slavery to agitating for women's suffrage. Similarly, in France Hubertine Auclert began by working to reform women's rights under the Civil Code and went on to spearhead the campaign for the vote (Doc. 95.i).

As a political movement, feminism was weaker and less cohesive in France and England than in the United States. A strong sense of class-consciousness militated against the development of English feminist organizations, and though feminist ideology fed on deep roots in France, a combination of class allegiances, religious differences, and laws prohibiting political association kept women divided.[30] In all three countries, however, the feminist movement found many recruits among women who had begun as activists in various fields of social reform. In transforming themselves from moral guardians of the home into arbiters of public morality, these industrious and seemingly omnipresent women chipped away at the wall that divided the male and female spheres; they showed both resourcefulness and creativity, often in the face of public opposition. Having extended the boundaries of the home to encompass

[28] See Cott 1977.

[29] See Lasch 1965; Conway 1971; O'Neill 1971; and Freedman 1980. The reforming impulses of women sometimes led them to take an active interest in the trade union movement. On their union activities, see Guilbert 1966; Flexner 1971; Middleton 1977; and Solden 1978. See also Boxer & Quataert 1978; and Tilly 1978.

[30] For a comparative interpretation of 19th-century feminism, see Evans 1977. See also on England, Strachey 1928; Banks & Banks 1964; Liddington 1977; Rosen 1974; and Hume 1979. On the U.S., see Flexner 1971; and Dubois 1978; and on France, Offen 1973; Bidelman 1975, 1976, and 1977; and Moses 1978.

the entire society, these reformers had come to enjoy their work as agitators far more than their assigned role of angel. They threatened to realize Princess Ida's egalitarian vision:[31]

> Everywhere
> Two heads in council, two beside the hearth,
> Two in the tangled business of the world,
> Two in the liberal offices of life,
> Two plummets dropt for one to sound the abyss
> Of science and secrets of the mind;
> Musician, painter, sculptor, critic, more.

[31] Alfred, Lord Tennyson, *The Princess* (1849), part II, lines 155–61.

Documents 63-95

63. Household management for ladies

Among the most novel aspects of nineteenth-century housekeeping was the widespread use of advice manuals; these books, written by women for women, poured from the newly established commercial presses of England, France, and the United States. The increasing technical complexity of the household, the replacement of oral tradition by the written word, and the new value placed on family life in the home all contributed to the attempt to professionalize household management. Women writers found in this situation an opportunity to earn money by converting their sisters to the rationalization of housework.

In France 'La Maison rustique des dames' (The Lady's Rustic Household), by Cora-Elisabeth Millet-Robinet (1798–1890), was the most popular book on domestic economy, appearing in twenty-one editions between 1844–45 and 1920. Though intended for country housekeepers, it seems to have been equally popular among city women. Millet-Robinet described the rural household as self-sufficient and portrayed its mistress as a powerful manager, overseeing the servants, paying wages, and looking after the physical and moral well-being of her employees and her family, all the while accomplishing her duty as a pleasing and charming companion to her husband. The American advice writer Eliza Leslie (1787–1858), a well-educated Philadelphia spinster, wrote her 'House Book' to guide the young married woman whose domestic apprenticeship had been neglected. Her book incorporated much practical information on all sorts of problems, from stained laundry to rodent control, with which the American housewife might have to contend without domestic help. In contrast, the celebrated 'Mrs. Beeton's Book of Household Management' of Isabella Mary Mayson Beeton (1836–65) underscores the far more urban character of English housewivery, by emphasizing knowledgeable consumption, the management of domestic servants, and the preparation of purchased foodstuffs. Beeton was only twenty-four years old when her enterprising

SOURCES: (i) Cora-Elisabeth Millet-Robinet, *La Maison rustique des dames*, 8th ed. (Paris, 1872), 1: 11–13, 47, 52. Originally published in 1844–45. (ii) Eliza Leslie, *The House Book; or a manual of domestic economy, for town and country*, 10th ed. (Philadelphia, 1849), pp. 3–5. Originally published in 1840. (iii) Isabella Beeton, *Mrs. Beeton's Book of Household Management* (London, 1880), pp. iii, 1–2, 5–8, 21–22. Originally published in 1861.

husband first published the book; nevertheless, women of the English middle classes accepted her as an oracle of household wisdom and rushed to purchase her book, which ran second in sales only to that Victorian best-seller, the King James Bible.

(i) Cora-Elisabeth Millet-Robinet

Obligations and Occupations of the Mistress of the House

The mistress of a house has many duties to fulfill. The order and perfection she brings to their accomplishment contributes greatly to the family's prosperity. She should recognize the importance of her task and not fear to confront it resolutely; she will derive pure pleasure from the sense of usefulness she receives from it. Boredom will never overcome her because boredom is born from idleness or from the utter uselessness of our occupations. When boredom has successfully been banished from one's existence, happiness is quite ready to take its place. . . .

If one wishes to give a young lady an education that would render her fit to manage the domestic economy of a farm, one should neglect nothing that would allow her to acquire pleasing talents and to enrich her mind. These talents will be as valuable to her in the country as in the city and, since they are found more rarely in the country they will attract more attention. Serious studies will give her confidence and permit her to discuss with her husband a great many subjects that interest men; if she wants to please her husband, for whom she will often provide the only company, she must make an effort to stay at his level. Since she will have to charm away their leisure hours, she may—in order to devote herself to the studies her position requires—neglect learning the insignificant intricacies of fine needlework and pay less attention to her toilette.

Perhaps one might think that agriculture and the cares requisite to a farm are very heavy subjects for a young lady to study; but is the study of grammar, of arithmetic, of history and geography any less serious? If agricultural instruction is considered equally important, it can be approached with no greater fear and pursued with the same perseverence, and this type of instruction will become a source of real pleasure.

Under these conditions a woman will be strongly motivated to study agriculture, first by the charm of novelty, and secondly by the pleasure of leading an active and useful life. The insignificant role allotted to women by contemporary custom prevents them from acquiring the importance in society that they could enjoy by becoming more energetic and effective. Thanks to the more serious role we assign them, their husbands will find them to be true associates. They will acquire an additional right to their husbands' love, and since the head of the family cannot have a better counselor than his wife, whose interests are so intimately linked to his own, the community will be richer in every respect.

In the country a wife has two households to govern: that of her family and that of the farm. They cannot be administered jointly; she must devote equal care and supervision to each. Even if directives sometimes have to be modified in order to be properly carried out, economy and order must prevail throughout both households.

The mistress of the household should have all the servant girls on the farm entirely under her immediate supervision. The farmyard—that is, the cowshed, the dairy, the pigsty, and the chicken coop—as well as the gardens, the orchards, and the sheep, are also her responsibility. She must be aware of all the jobs to be done on the farm in order to reinforce her husband in his supervision and to replace him in times of absence or sickness. Thus it is mandatory that she be familiar with every parcel of exploitable land and its place in the order of rotation; and that she keep an exact account of expenses and income from everything she manages in order to be able to judge the losses and profits easily, and to account for the expenses incurred in the management of house and farm.

A wife should also pay careful attention to all the duties involved in keeping all those who make up her household healthy; it is she who must dispense the medicines ordered by the doctor and see to it that his prescriptions are scrupulously followed. Thus, it is absolutely necessary for her to acquire some familiarity with family medicine; she can then treat uncomplicated cases, which will not get worse if they are well cared for at the outset, and she can then judge when the time has come to call for a doctor's assistance.

The distribution of alms should be carried out exclusively by the wife; this is, for her, a most sweet and just reward for all the troubles she takes.

The mistress of the household should keep a careful watch over the moral conduct of everyone in her house, gently recalling, by an appeal to reason, those who may stray from their duty and instigating their dismissal if they do not heed her observations. She should make sure that they all fulfill the duties required by their religion.

At once mistress of the house and of the farm, she should actively oversee everything that happens in both places; she must not be unaware of anything that happens, and when she has given orders, she must insist on their being carried out. To facilitate the work, it is best for her, whenever possible, to issue the orders for the next day's work the previous evening. By making surprise visits, the mistress of the household can keep all the servants on their toes; it is better to anticipate problems than to have to resolve them. . . .

Household expenses are much more difficult to account for in the country than in the city. They vary according to the season, the work, the size of the harvests, and the varying involvement of servants in the work. If . . . the husband provides a fixed sum each month for household expenses, the wife can keep an exact account; when she examines the accounts each month with her husband, he can then make any observations he considers suitable about the use of the money.

It would also be fair and reasonable if the wife could also scrutinize the other expenses of the farm so that she could also make judicious observations about these. In general women have a sense of detail that is lacking in men, and since in any agricultural enterprise there are an infinite number of details that multiply in every operation, a woman is very likely to give good counsel. . . .

The servants should be paid regularly and at the time of year customary for the region. However, it is preferable to pay them each month, or at least every third month, rather than once a year as is the custom in many provinces.

Capitalists and merchants will perhaps condemn this view, since they consider it advantageous to delay payment as long as possible; but in a private house, where money destined for a specific purpose ordinarily remains in a cashbox until it is used, it is wiser to pay what one owes as soon as possible. When money is at one's disposal, it is easy for it to be put to different use than that for which it was set aside, and this can become cause for embarrassment. Moreover, it is unfair to make servants wait a long time for salary that is due them. . . .

Workers' Account Book. In this book the mistress of the household writes down every evening the day's wages of the workers she employs. Every week she adds up the wages of each worker; she pays him, then she crosses out that week. If she does not pay, she still adds up the total in order to know how much she owes; but she doesn't cross anything out.

(ii) Eliza Leslie

The design of the following work is to impart to novices in house-keeping some information on a subject which is, or ought to be, important to every American female, so that they may be enabled to instruct unpractised domes-tics, or, in case of emergency, to assist personally in forwarding the indis-pensable work of the family. More than nine-tenths of these receipts are en-tirely original; all are expressly adapted to the meridian of our own country; and though they generally refer to the condition of families in what is termed genteel life, a large number of them may be found useful in houses where close economy is expedient.

It has been the design of the author to make her directions as plain and intelligible as possible, and therefore she has thought it best to explain every particular with unusual minuteness, as if addressed to persons who were totally ignorant of the subjects in question. In this, as in her Cookery Book, she has not scrupled, when necessary, to sacrifice the sound to the sense; repeating the same words when no others could be found to express the pur-pose so clearly; and being always more anxious to convey the meaning in such terms as could not be mistaken, than to risk obscuring it by attempts at re-fined phraseology or well-rounded periods.

Complaints are incessantly heard of the deterioration of servants; but may not one source of this growing evil be traced to the deterioration of *mistresses* in the knowledge and practice of all that is necessary to a well-ordered household. A great change has certainly taken place since the days when, during the presidency of her husband, Mrs. Washington, followed by a servant-man with a basket, went daily to Philadelphia market; and when the all-accomplished daughters of Mr. Jefferson made pastry and confection-ary in a room fitted up for that purpose in their father's mansion at Monticello.

While we regret the present system of education, in which all things are taught (or rather attempted) except that which to every American female must at some period of her life be absolutely necessary, we would not have our young married ladies discouraged if, on first assuming the charge of a house, they find themselves subjected to much perplexity and inconvenience from ignorance of their new task. A competent knowledge of household affairs is by no means difficult to acquire, and is within the reach of every woman of tolerable capacity, who has a proper conviction of its utility, and an earnest desire to profit by all opportunities of improvement in its pursuit. It is a homely but a true saying, that "where there is a will there is a way."

A neat and well-conducted house, with fires and lights always as they should be; and a table where the food is inviting, from being good both in material and cooking; also clothes well washed and ironed, are comforts that are not lightly prized by any married man; and it is but just that he who perhaps labours hard in his business or profession to procure the means of obtaining them, should not be disappointed in their application; particularly when the deficiencies are caused by the inertness or the mismanagement of the woman who should consider it her especial care to render his home agreeable to him.

Should this book have any effect in directing the attention of her young countrywomen to a subject of far more importance to their married happiness than the cultivation of showy accomplishments, or the unavailing pursuit of studies that to females are always abstruse; should it, on trial, be found a useful auxiliary to practised house-keepers, in furnishing them with additional hints, or new and easy modes of doing things that have always been done, its object will be accomplished; leaving the author with the gratification of knowing that she has not written in vain.

(iii) Isabella Beeton

I must frankly own, that if I had known beforehand that this book would cost me the labour which it has, I should never have been courageous enough to commence it. What moved me, in the first instance, to attempt a work like this, was the discomfort and suffering which I had seen brought upon men and women by household mismanagement. I have always thought that there is no more fruitful source of family discontent than a housewife's badly-cooked dinners and untidy ways. Men are now so well served out of doors,—at their clubs, well-ordered taverns, and dining-houses, that, in order to compete with the attractions of these places, a mistress must be thoroughly acquainted with the theory and practice of cookery, as well as be perfectly conversant with all the other arts of making and keeping a comfortable home. . . .

As with the commander of an army, or the leader of an enterprise, so is it with the mistress of a house. Her spirit will be seen through the whole establishment; and just in proportion as she performs her duties intelligently and thoroughly, so will her domestics follow in her path. Of all those acquirements, which more particularly belong to the feminine character, there are none which take a higher rank, in our estimation, than such as enter into a knowledge of household duties; for on these are perpetually dependent the happiness, comfort, and well-being of a family. . . .

Early rising is one of the most essential qualities which enter into good Household Management, as it is not only the parent of health, but of innumerable other advantages. Indeed, when a mistress is an early riser, it is almost certain that her house will be orderly and well-managed. On the contrary, if she remain in bed till a late hour, then the domestics, who, as we have observed, invariably partake somewhat of their mistress's character, will surely become sluggards. . . .

Cleanliness is indispensable to health, and must be studied both in regard to the person and the house, and all that it contains. Cold or tepid baths should be employed every morning, unless, on account of illness or other circumstances, they should be deemed objectionable. . . .

Frugality and economy are home virtues, without which no household can prosper. . . . The necessity of practising economy should be evident to every one, whether in the possession of an income no more than sufficient for a family's requirements, or of a large fortune which puts financial adversity out of the question. . . .

In marketing, that the best articles are the cheapest, may be laid down as a rule; and it is desirable, unless an experienced and confidential housekeeper be kept, that the mistress should herself purchase all provisions and stores needed for the house. If the mistress be a young wife, and not accustomed to order "things for the house," a little practice and experience will soon teach her who are the best tradespeople to deal with, and what are the best provisions to buy. Under each particular head of Fish, Meat, Poultry, Game, &c., will be described the proper means of ascertaining the quality of these comestibles.

A housekeeping account-book should invariably be kept, and kept punctually and precisely. The plan for keeping household accounts, which we should recommend, would be to enter, that is, write down in a daily diary every amount paid on each particular day, be it ever so small; then, at the end of a week or month, let these various payments be ranged under their specific heads of Butcher, Baker, &c.; and thus will be seen the proportions paid to each tradesman, and any week's or month's expenses may be contrasted with another. The housekeeping accounts should be balanced not less than once a month—once a week is better; and it should be seen that the money in hand tallies with the account. Judge Haliburton never wrote truer words than when he said—"No man is rich whose expenditure exceeds his means, and no one is poor whose incomings exceed his outgoings." Once a month it is advisable that the mistress overlook her store of glass and china, marking any breakages on the inventory of these articles.

When, in a large establishment, a housekeeper is kept, it will be advisable to examine her accounts regularly. Then, any increase of expenditure which may be apparent can easily be explained, and the housekeeper will have the satisfaction of knowing whether her efforts to manage her department well and economically have been successful.

Engaging domestics is one of those duties in which the judgment of the mistress must be keenly exercised. One of the commonest modes of procuring servants is to answer advertisements inserted in the newspapers by those who want places; or to insert an advertisement, setting forth the kind of servant that is required. In these advertisements it is well to state whether the house is in town or country, and indicate pretty closely the amount of wages that the mistress proposes to give. There are some respectable registry-offices, where good servants may sometimes be hired. Another plan, and one to be recommended under certain conditions, is for the mistress to make inquiry amongst her circle of friends and acquaintances, and her tradespeople. Shopkeepers generally know those in their neighbourhood who are wanting situations, and will communicate with them, when a personal interview with some of them will enable the mistress to form some idea of the characters of the applicants, and to suit herself accordingly. . . .

The treatment of servants is of the highest possible moment, as well to the mistress as to the domestics themselves. On the head of the house the latter will naturally fix their attention; and if they perceive that the mistress' conduct is regulated by high and correct principles, they will not fail to respect her. If, also, a benevolent desire is shown to promote their comfort, at the same time that a steady performance of their duty is exacted, then their respect will not be unmingled with affection, and well-principled servants will be still more solicitous to continue to deserve her favour.

The following table of the average yearly wages paid to domestics, with the various members of the household placed according to their rank, will serve to regulate the expenditure of an establishment:—

Men servants	When not found in livery	When found in livery
House steward	From £50 to £100	—
Butler	„ £40 to £60	—
Valet	„ £25 to £50	—
Cook	„ £25 to £50	—
Gardener (not in the house)	„ £40 to £120	—
Footman	„ £20 to £40	From £15 to £25
Under butler	„ £15 to £30	„ £15 to £25
Coachman	—	„ £25 to £50
Coachman (not in the house)	„ £65 to £78	—
Groom	„ £20 to £40	„ £12 to £20
Under footman	„ —	„ £12 to £20
Page or footboy	„ £8 to £18	„ £6 to £14
Stableboy	„ £6 to £12	—

Women servants	Without allowance for tea, sugar, and beer	With allowance for tea, sugar, and beer
Housekeeper	From £20 to £50	From £18 to £45
Lady's-maid	„ £16 to £25	„ £14 to £20
Head nurse	„ £15 to £25	„ £13 to £20

Cook	"	£16 to £45	"	£14 to £40
Upper housemaid	"	£15 to £25	"	£13 to £20
Upper laundry-maid	"	£20 to £25	"	£18 to £20
General servant, or maid-of-all-work	"	£8 to £16	"	£6½ to £14
Under housemaid	"	£8 to £14	"	£6½ to £12
Still-room maid	"	£9 to £14	"	£8 to £12
Nursemaid	"	£8 to £14	"	£6 to £12
Under laundry-maid	"	£12 to £18	"	£10 to £15
Kitchen-maid	"	£10 to £18	"	£8 to £15
Scullery-maid	"	£8 to £14		—

. . . All the domestics mentioned in the above table would enter into the establishment of a wealthy nobleman. The number of servants, of course, would become smaller in proportion to the lesser size of the establishment.

The following is a scale of servants suited to various incomes, commencing with—

About £1,000 a-year—Cook, upper and under housemaid, man servant.

About £750 a-year—Cook, housemaid, and footboy.

About £500 a-year—Cook and housemaid.

About £300 a-year—Maid-of-all-work.

About £200 or £150 a year—Maid-of-all-work, or girl for rough work.

If there be children in a family a nursemaid may be added to the servants as above enumerated, when the income ranges from about £350 to £1,000 a-year; but this expense may be saved if there be a daughter who is old enough, good enough, and careful enough to mind the younger ones in-doors and out-of-doors. In some cases a nursemaid is indispensable when the income is under £350 a-year, in order to allow the mistress to attend to other duties which cannot be neglected, especially if her family be both large and young. . . .

Having risen early, as we have already advised . . . and having given due attention to the bath, and made a careful toilet, it will be well at once to see that the children, where the house is blest with these, have received their proper ablutions, and are in every way clean, comfortable, and being well attended to. The first meal of the day, breakfast, will then be served, at which all the family should be punctually present, unless illness, or other circumstances, prevent.

After breakfast is over, it will be well for the mistress to make a round of the kitchen and other offices, to see that all are in order, and that the morning's work has been properly performed by the various domestics. The orders for the day should then be given; and any questions which the domestics desire to ask, respecting their several departments, should be answered, and any special articles they may require handed to them from the store-closet. . . .

After this general superintendence of her servants, the mistress, if the mother of a young family, may devote herself to the instruction of some of its younger members, or to the examination of the state of their wardrobe, leaving the latter portion of the morning for reading, or for some amusing recreation. . . .

Where the mistress makes her own and the children's clothes, it is necessary for her to possess a Sewing Machine—necessary because time is money. With the help of this useful invention, a lady can, with perfect comfort, make and mend every article used by herself and children, and do a great deal towards repairing and making her husband's clothes, and this without labour to herself, and at no expense beyond the first outlay. She can do all this without neglecting the duty she owes to herself of serious reading and recreation. . . .

Note—It will be useful for the mistress and housekeeper to know the best seasons for various occupations connected with Household Management; and we, accordingly, subjoin a few hints which we think will prove valuable.

As in the winter months, servants have much more to do, in consequence of the necessity there is to attend to the number of fires throughout the household, not much more than the ordinary every-day work can be attempted.

In the summer, and when the absence of fires gives the domestics more leisure, then any extra work that is required can be more easily performed.

The spring is the usual period set apart for house-cleaning, and removing all the dust and dirt which will necessarily, with the best of housewives, accumulate during the winter months from the smoke of the coal, oil, gas, &c. This season is also well adapted for washing and bleaching linen, &c., as, the weather not being then too hot for the exertions necessary in washing counterpanes, blankets, and heavy things in general, the work is better and more easily done than in the intense heat of July, which month some recommend for these purposes. Winter curtains should be taken down, and replaced by the summer white ones; and furs and woollen cloths also carefully laid by. The former should be well shaken and brushed, and then pinned upon paper or linen, with camphor to preserve them from the moths. Furs, &c., will be preserved in the same way. Included, under the general description of house-cleaning, must be understood, turning out all the nooks and corners of drawers, cupboards, lumber-rooms, loft, &c., with a view of getting rid of all unnecessary articles, which only create dirt and attract vermin; sweeping of chimneys, taking up carpets, painting and whitewashing the kitchen and offices, papering rooms, when needed, and, generally speaking, the house putting on, with the approaching summer, a bright appearance, and a new face, in unison with nature. Oranges should now be preserved, and orange wine made.

The summer will be found, as we have mentioned above, in consequence of the diminution of labour for the domestics, the best period for examining and repairing household linen, and for "putting to rights" all those articles which have received a large share of wear and tear during the dark winter days. In direct reference to this matter, we may here remark, that sheets should be turned "sides to middle" before they are allowed to get very thin. Otherwise, patching, which is uneconomical from the time it consumes, and is unsightly in point of appearance, will have to be resorted to. In June and July, gooseberries, currants, raspberries, strawberries, and other summer fruits, should be preserved, and jams and jellies made. In July, too, the making of walnut ketchup should be attended to, as the green walnuts will be approaching perfection for this purpose. Mixed pickles may also be now made, and it will be found a good plan to have ready a jar of pickle-juice for the making of which all information will be given in future pages, into which to put occasionally some young French beans, cauliflowers, &c.

In the early autumn, plums of various kinds are to be bottled and preserved, and jams and jellies made. A little later, tomato sauce, a most useful article to have by you, may be prepared; a supply of apples laid in, if you have a place to keep them, as also a few keeping pears and filberts. Endeavour to keep also two or three large vegetable-marrows—they will be found delicious in the winter, and may be cut and used as required without spoiling.

In September and October it will be necessary to prepare for the cold weather, and get ready the winter clothing for the various members of the family. The white summer curtains will now be carefully put away, the fireplaces, grates, and chimneys looked to, and the house put in a thorough state of repair, so that no "loose tile" may, at a future day, interfere with your comfort, and extract something considerable from your pocket.

In December, the principal household duty lies in preparing for the creature comforts of those near and dear to us, so as to meet Old Christmas with a happy face, a contented mind, and a full larder; and in storing the plums, washing the currants, cutting the citron, beating the eggs, and Mixing the Pudding, a housewife is not unworthily greeting the genial season of all good things.

64. Working-class housewives in England and France

These selections portray two different aspects of the lives of urban working-class wives. In the first excerpt Mrs. B—, a forty-year-old Manchester housewife, matter-of-factly responds to questions about the diet and living conditions of a skilled factory laborer's family. In contrast, Jeanne Deroin (1802–94), a Parisian seamstress and feminist, writes with indignation of the daily hardships typical of a French worker's wife. Unlike many nineteenth-century working-class women, the French and English housewives described here did not bear the double burden of working both inside and outside the home.

(i) Mrs. B—

This witness was accidentally met with, 13th May 1833. She was waiting for Dr. Hawkins, to consult him about her niece's health. I took her into a room, and examined her about the customs and comforts of operative families. She was not sworn. I consider her evidence to be a specimen, somewhat under the average, of the way in which an operative family lives.

Her husband is a fine spinner, at Mr. ——, where he has been from 1816,

SOURCES: (i) Great Britain, *Parliamentary Papers*, 1833, XX, Factory Inquiry Commission, 1st Report, pp. D1 39–41. (ii) Jeanne Deroin, "Le Travail des femmes," *Almanach des Femmes* (1852), reprinted in Adrien Ranvier, "Une Féministe de 1848, Jeanne Deroin," *La Révolution de 1848*, 5.26 (May-June 1908): 489–91.

CONSUMPTION BY THE WEEK, OF DIFFERENT ARTICLES, BY
HER HUSBAND, HERSELF, AND FIVE CHILDREN

	£	s	d
Butter, 1½ lb. at 10d.	o	1	3
Tea, 1½ oz.	o	o	4½
Bread she makes herself: buys 24 lb. of flour—flour, barm, salt, and baking cost	o	4	6
Half a peck of oatmeal	o	o	6½
Bacon, 1½ lb.	o	o	9
Potatoes, two score a week, at 8d. *a score*	o	1	4
Milk, a quart a day, at 3d. a quart	o	1	9
Flesh meat on Sunday, about a pound	o	o	7
Sugar, 1½lb. a week, at 6d.	o	o	9
Pepper, mustard, salt, and extras, say	o	o	3
Soap and candles	o	1	o
Coals	o	1	6
Rent	o	3	6
	£0	18	1
Alleged total of weekly income	£1	5	o
Deduct foregoing expenses	o	18	1
Leaves for clothing, sickness of seven persons, schooling, &c. a surplus of	£0	6	11[a]

[a] Read over this account to S. L., an operative, and a respectable witness on their side. He thinks it is somewhat below the average of comforts possessed by working families. The generality, he thinks, have tea and coffee for breakfast, instead of porridge, and that their dinners are generally fresh meat; and he says, that factory families may be divided into two classes, in respect of living,—those in which the parents work in mills as well as the children, and those in which only the children work in mills. The first class lives better than the second.—*May 26, 1833.*

Read over the whole to Thomas Worsley. He thinks the comforts rather above the average enjoyed in Stockport; but says that the operatives in good mills generally use fresh meat for their dinner most days.

Both S. L. and Mr. Worsley agree that the husband must earn at least 1l. 8s. at fine spinning, instead of 1l., as his wife states; and that his daughter must save him 4s. 6d. besides.

has five children. Her eldest daughter, now going of fourteen, has been her father's piecer for three years. At her present age, her labour is worth 4s. 6d. a week, and has been worth as much for these last four months; before, it was worth less. At present her husband's earnings and her daughter's together amount to about 25s. a week—at least she sees no more than 25s. a week;* and before his daughter could piece for him, and when he had to pay for a piecer in her stead, he only brought home 19s. or 20s. a week.

Rent of house, 3s. 6d. a week.

Breakfast is generally porridge, bread and milk, lined with flour or oatmeal. On Sunday, a sup of tea and bread and butter.—*Dinner*, on week days, pota-

* Whatever sum her husband may bring home, his earnings as a fine spinner at Mr. M.'s are certainly not less than 28s. per week.

toes and bacon, and bread, which is generally white. On a Sunday, a little flesh meat; no butter, egg, or pudding.—*Tea-time*, every day, tea, and bread and butter; nothing extra on Sunday at tea.—*Supper*, oatmeal porridge and milk; sometimes potatoes and milk. Sunday, sometimes a little bread and cheese for supper: never have this on week days. Now and then buys eggs when they are as low as a halfpenny apiece, and fries them to bacon.

They never taste any other vegetables than potatoes; never use any beer or spirits; now and then may take a gill of beer when ill, which costs a penny. Perhaps she and her husband may have two gills a week. Her husband never drinks any beer or spirits that she knows of beyond this. The house consists of four rooms, two on each floor; the furniture consists of two beds in the same room, one for themselves, the other for the children; have four chairs, one table in the house, boxes to put clothes in, no chest of drawers, two pans and a tea-kettle for boiling, a gridiron and frying-pan, half-a-dozen large and small plates, four pair of knives and forks, several pewter spoons. They subscribe 1d. a week for each child to a funeral society for the children. Two of the children go to school at 3d. a week each: they are taught reading for this, but not writing. Have a few books, such as a Bible, hymn-book, and several small books that the children have got as prizes at the Sunday school. Four children go to Stott's Sunday school.

Does your daughter, who pieces for her father, seem much fatigued when she comes home at night?—No, she does not seem much fatigued. She is coming of an age that perhaps she may be. She has a good appetite. Hears her complain of headach sometimes; does not hear her complain of not sleeping.

Do you think that people in your own way of life, spinners and such like, and their families, are better off than yourselves, or worse off, or just about the same?—Well, some's better, some's worse, some's the same. It is according to their work—whether they work upon fine or coarse work.

I want to know whether the most are like off to yourselves. Now, at Mr. —— mill, are most of the parents of children as well off, or better off, than yourself?—Well, they are most of them at his mill as well off as we ourselves, because it is one of the best mills in the town. There is not many better than his.

In answer to questions concerning herself, she said she should be forty years old on Whitsun Monday: that at fourteen years old she began frame-tenting, and worked at it for two years every day, from six in the morning till eight in the evening—sometimes from half-past five in the morning. She then went to stretching, at which she worked till twenty-five years old: at that she worked fourteen hours a day regularly every day. At twenty-five years old she married, and has staid at home ever since. Her father was a bleacher, her mother a spinner. Has eight brothers and sisters; but can't give no idea whether her brothers and sisters are bigger or less than her parents, because her mother took them all away to America when she was a child.

Should you say you were as healthy a woman now, as if you had not been a frame tenter or a stretcher?—Well, I don't know but what I am. I have not my health very well at present. I do not know that work injured it.

How many different mills were you in when you were young?—In four mills. Has heard different language at some from others; some very bad, some very well. A child may pick up much bad in mills. Better to put a child in a mill than let it run in the streets; it won't get as much harm in a mill.

Do girls run a chance of being bad by living in mills; in short, to be un-chaste?—I can't say. I never see'd nothing of bad wherever I worked. It is according to their own endeavours a good deal.

(ii) Jeanne Deroin

It is in the household that woman's work is the most tiresome and the least appreciated.

We are not speaking of a household where there is a live-in nurse and a maid for each child, and domestic servants to do all the work; we are speaking of the majority, of the proletarian household, where the mother alone cares for several children, where there is not always means to pay the laundress, where the wife must get up before dawn, often exhausted by having had to nurse her newest child through part of the night. She lights her stove and prepares her wash water, in order to wash her children's clothing and the diapers. Moreover, she hasn't enough of anything to be able to wait a week; the lodging is small, the basins inconvenient; the sink is either one floor up or two floors down, and the stairway is dark. Her husband gets up to go to work; his pants are torn and must be mended but a child cries or the clay casserole tips over; the woman runs; the husband gets impatient; the repair gets done. He leaves and the washing begins. The two biggest children get up and ask for their breakfast; the littlest ones cry to be gotten up; the sudsing finished, she hangs out the wash as best she can, wipes up the spilt water, makes the soup, dresses the littlest children and gives everybody breakfast; she puts some bread in the baskets of the bigger children and sends them off to school; she has not yet had time to sit down for an instant in order to nurse the little one who is crying loudly.

The landlord's wife enters: she is an early riser, a woman of order, a good housewife who does her own canning and makes her own jam, repairs her laces, cleans her own ribbons and embroiders her collars. Everything is neat and tidy in her quarters before nine o'clock. She rouses her maid and her domestic at five A.M. and supervises them, pushes them, prods them, so that the tasks get done promptly and well. Thus, upon entering, she is indignant at the laziness and disorderliness of her renter. The beds are not yet made, the room is not swept; the chipped bowls used for breakfast are still sitting unwashed on the floor; the poorly bleached diapers hang on the line, the torn caps and socks full of holes dry on the back of a chair. She concludes from all this that her renter doesn't get up early enough and doesn't work hard enough. She asks for the rent more severely than she might have otherwise and leaves, threatening to throw them all out if it isn't paid by the fourteenth.

Upset and already exhausted with fatigue, the poor wife nurses her infant, changes it and puts it back in the cradle, and leaves it in the charge of an obliging neighbor's children so that she can run to the central market to buy potatoes a bit cheaper. She returns in haste, loaded down, breathless and perspiring. She nurses the infant to stop its crying, puts her irons on to heat, peels her vegetables, irons the caps, mends the vests and pants, fixes the shirts, darns the socks, repairs the slippers, and prepares dinner.

The children come home from school: one has torn his blouse, the other has a bump on his head. She scolds the first one and bandages the second. During this time the potatoes have burned; her husband returns, and the soup is not yet poured over the bread. He is tired and in a bad mood, and displays his astonishment that a woman who has nothing to do but take care of her house is incapable of getting up dinner. He sulks or flies into a rage and, when dinner is over, he goes to bed. The wife undresses and puts the children to bed, washes the dishes, and is able to mend the most urgent items. But she has to interrupt her work every few minutes to calm the baby, whose cries are waking up its father, who gets upset at not being able to sleep and recover from the fatigue of the day. Often the poor baby has been changed with a diaper that is still wet; he gets colic, and the mother spends part of the night calming him. She scarcely gets a few hours of sleep and wakes up only to recommence the same life. And they say, in speaking of her, that only her husband works; she doesn't do anything. She has only her household and her children to take care of.

65. American women contend with household management

The work of married women in the nineteenth-century household could take many forms, ranging from administrative responsibilities to the performance of all the daily domestic chores. The following selections offer two different glimpses of this experience. The first is a letter from Anna Matilda Page King (1798–1859), a member of the antebellum Georgia cotton aristocracy, to her trustee. It reveals the extent to which a planter's wife could be familiar with the economic interests of her family while having to proceed through men in order to defend them. Under Anglo-American common law before the passage of legislation protecting married women's property, trusts like King's were the sole means of protecting a wealthy woman's personal property from possible confiscation by her husband or his creditors. The second selection, taken from the diary of Persis Sibley Andrews (1813–91; Docs. 34.i, 49.ii), provides insight into the satisfactions, as well as the difficulties, experienced by a rural New England housewife. In 1845, when Andrews wrote these pages, her daughter Charlotte was two years old and her husband Charles was frequently absent for weeks on legal business.

SOURCES: (i) Letter from Anna Matilda King to James Hamilton Couper, March 3, 1842, William Audley Couper Papers, Southern Historical Collection, Library of the University of North Carolina, Chapel Hill. The editors are grateful to Carolyn Wallace, Director of the SHC, for this reference and to Isaac M. Aiken, Saint Simon's Island, Georgia, for consenting to its publication. (ii) Persis Sibley Andrews Black Journals, 1845, Maine Historical Society. Typescript, courtesy of Sue Rice, Atherton, Calif.

(i) Anna Matilda King

My dear Sir   Waverley, 3ᵈ March 1842

It cannot be unknown to you that the unfavorable seasons for some years past, and the almost annual ravages of the Caterpillar have cut short the crop of Sea Island cotton on the coast of Georgia, and in some locations almost destroyed it. My husband has probably been one of the greatest sufferers from these successive disasters. At a time when negroes were selling from five to six hundred dollars round in gangs—he unfortunately purchased largeily; relying on the proceeds of his cotton crops to enable him to make payment, but the almost total failure in some years, short crops and low prices in others have prevented him from realizing the means to meet his engagements. The result is that his creditors have seized and taken from him all his property which in the condition of the country and at present Prices will probably not pay his debts: This may render it necessary for me to call on your friendly aid as one of my Trustees, to protect the property bequeathed in my Fathers will for the benefit of myself and children.

I do not impute any blame, or mismanagement to my husband, nor has his misfortunes, in the slightest degree impaired my confidence in his integrity, or his ability to manage property. Nor is it my desire to give you unnecessary trouble. I simply ask that you will stand the friend of my fathers child in case my husbands creditors shall after taking all his property attempt to seize that upon which I can alone rely for the support of a family of nine children most of them small and at that peculiar age when instruction and parental support are essential and necessary. I do not know that my husbands creditors will disturb me but in case they attempt it I desire permission to call on you and Mr Joseph Jones—my other trustee—to protect my property—as my husband cannot act and I can rely alone upon my Trustees.

It is my desire that my husband be left as your or my agent, in the management of my plantations and business generally.

If my memory serves me a copy of my Fathers will was sent to you soon after his decease. If you cannot lay your hand upon it I will send you another immediately.

I send you enclosed, a list of the 50 negroes left to me in the will, with their increase.

Pray let me hear from you as soon as convenient. Direct your letter to Waynesville.

My kind regards to Mrs Couper

Very respectfully
Your obt Servt, Anna Matilda King

(ii) Persis Sibley Andrews

[Each paragraph represents a different day's entry, which may or may not be complete. The period covered is early August to mid-December 1845. We have indicated all Sundays—or Sabbaths, as Andrews calls them.]

We have had a loom set up in our back kitchen & I am weaving my web of wool flannel myself. Father gave me a bag of wool. Costella [the hired girl] has spun the filling—I hired a woman to spin the warp, & I shall get 18 yds. of nice cloth pretty cheap. Mrs. W.* has a carpet to weave. It is not common now to make cloth in families, but we keep each of us a hired girl, & have but three persons beside, in either family, & both Mrs. W. & myself enjoying better health than usual—we have tho't to do a little something to convince the neighbors that we sho'd be smart women if we were not nearly always sick. . . . It has been the Hottest day of the Season & I have done my work—run after Charlotte (the harder of the two) wound my quills & woven three yeards.

I finished weaving my flannel this day. It is nearly 19 yds & quite pretty. Costella has been gone three days & I am alone, for I know not how long a time. Her mother & little sister are very sick at home, & I told her I tho't it her duty to go & take care of them—tho' I knew not how to spare her.

Sabbath.—I am quilting a small quilt—much work—pretty. Costella quilts well & fast. Colored greens for my rug—Good success but dont know when I shall put it in for school begins this week & I am to be Drawing Master.

I have color'd red & bark color—good success. Finished the quilt & Costella has gone to sleep with Lucy & I believe has taken the quilt with her—to dream under. . . . We have been regaled with pomegranites & apples this ev'g. We have little fruit in this County worth mention except wild berries. Blue berries & black berries are abundant & nice in their season. The blueberry is our staple for pies during six weeks ending with August & when abundant as this year we dry them for winter use.

Sabbath.—My health is good & I have many kinds of work on the stocks, & we have a good deal of company all of w'h, with the school, occupy my time pretty fully—& the few leisure moments I have I devote to drawing, in hopes to rub off the rust accumulated during years of non practice. . . . I am well & my family is well, & I am happy. Costella is a first rate girl & this is another great blessing.

Sabbath.—Harvesting is going briskly on—our crops come in abundant & good—except the potatoes w'h is a failure thro'out the State & indeed New England, in consequence of a disease call'd "potatoe rot" . . . . Our weeks work has been rippin hus-' old clothes (what he has not given away) washing & putting them away in good order—turning sheets—& a general "*mending*" of everything. I am never better pleased than with a weeks work of this kind.

The past week has been more eventful than some. Sabbath eve'g, last, Costella returned from a visit home saying—"Father has concluded to go to Mass. to work in that Stable again, where my brother is, & they all think it best for me to go with him. I can get $1.50 to 2.00 per week in the tavern." This was a poser. Charles was gone [and] I co'd not tell what I was to do. I became nervous—never shut my eyes to sleep for the night. Monday I suffered the most severe attack of nervous sick headache that poor mortal ever endured. Tuesday & Wednesday I did what sewing I co'd for Costella & at-

* The Andrewses shared a house in Dixfield, Maine, with a family named Washburn.—EDS.

tended my class. Wednesday eve'g she went home, & will leave for Mass. tomorrow.

[On Thursday Persis traveled to a nearby town to visit friends and found a new girl, Diantha, through neighbors.]

She knows how to care for children for she is the oldest of nine & this will give me opportunity to attend my class, w'h I co'd not do if I had not this Diantha, for girls are scarce as gold dust. Costella is the fourth girl who has left me to go to Mass. As soon as they get clothes up & a little money to bear expenses they are sure to go, for there they are paid more.

Charles has been absent another whole week—attending District Court at Paris. . . . I have been making a beautiful rug—had it in frame a little more than three weeks. It is about ¾ done, but I have put it away, to attend to the wants of my family—I may finish it before I move, but shall *not* at the expense of duty to my husband or daughter, but for this latter I shall get no great name, for the rug I shall be *famous* thro' all the County.

Husband has been at Augusta the past week—upon business with Governor & Council. I have been housecleaning morn'gs & making up my web of flannel eve'gs. The weather is fine—we must expect it cold soon. That nice old-maid, Deborah, whom I had engaged is taking care of a sick woman—my girl Diantha is too young—women to be had are not thorough, & I sho'd lose my reputation of good housekeeper if I leave my house uncleansed—therefore I co'd see no way of escape from this task, I took all care & tho't I sho'd not get sick, but when Charles returned he found me in a raging fever—suffering intense pain in every part of the body & if active measures had not been taken I believe I sho'd have had a hard fever.

Friday we butchered five hogs & Mr. W— set off with them for market. I had a woman & made soap same day, a barrel & closed up the whole concern—a good days work—well done. Yesterday I finished my rolls—spun five skeins of stocking yarn—doubled & twisted.

I am taken all aback again. I envy those independent ladies who can do their own work—alas! a precious few. Diantha's Mother is sick, & they have sent for her to go home—I am just up from a most unbearable sick headache. O—that my next girl might stay a thousand years if I must have this horrid nervous sick headache every time a girl takes it into her head to leave me without a moment's warning. What a fool I am. I shall get along some how—I always have, & I shall now.

66. 'Hard work is the watchword in Kansas': Mary Chaffee Abell

In 1865 Mary Abigail Chaffee (1846–75; Docs. 1.vii, 4), a school-teacher who wrote poetry and played the melodeon, married Robert Abell, a preacher and farmer fifteen years her senior. In the next nine years she gave birth

SOURCES: Helen Smith Jordan, *Love Lies Bleeding* (Syracuse, N.Y., 1979), privately printed. The editors are indebted to Mrs. Jordan for giving us permission

to five children, while the family moved west from upstate New York, first to Illinois and then to Kansas. In letters to her parents and sisters, Mary describes the changing fortunes of her family, from the relative prosperity of the years in New York to the bitter deprivation of the Kansas years. The contact with family back east provided more than emotional support for the Abells; in the hardest years, relatives kept the homesteaders alive with their gifts of food, clothing, and money.

[Mary Abell to her mother, March 1, 1868, Bergen, N.Y.]
I am rather lonesome today so I will write you a few lines not only to while away the time but because it is a real pleasure to write to my mother. . . . Mother Abell has been away visiting to one place and another all winter. I never saw a woman love to visit as well as she does, and she goes in the first society too. I have been with her some when I've been at home. I go quite as much as if I hadn't any babies and more than I used to at home I think. I always find some good souls who help to take care of babies, besides Robert is better than any woman. Ain't I lucky though? He's one of a thousand! Where will you find another man who will get up in the morning and sweep and get breakfast and take care of the children so that his wife may practice her music for an hour or two each morning. He does. And I am improving much. Have learned two new, and difficult pieces within the past two weeks. He makes me practice every morning. He has forbidden my sewing any more evenings for fear it will hurt my eyes. Says he will blow the light out as fast as I can light it if I attempt to sew. He says he will have all my sewing done, but I can't do that. . . . Now ma don't tell nor let any body read what I am going to write next, it is this—*I have got the queerest thing you ever heard of.* It is nothing more nor less than a wringer. I would not let it go for four times what I paid for it. Don't have to touch your hands to water nor stoop over at all. It hooks onto the mop pail and by turning the mop handle it wrings it quite as dry if not dryer than it can be done by hand. I can mop out of boiling water or hot lye without the inconvenience and without spilling a drop of water on the floor. When I color my carpet I'm going to have Rob fix me a hook onto a handle so I can wring out my rags from the dye without coloring my hands in the least. It will work just as nicely as can be. I want you to come and help me color if you will, for I know nothing about it besides you need not touch your hands to the barrel dye. I tell you it is nice. If you get a chance—buy one by all means. I paid three shillings for mine—the price was 50 cents.

Nettie is not nearly as fleshy as when I was home with her. I am giving her Scovilles' blood and liver syrup so high recommended for scrofula and disease of the blood and liver. She seems to feel better I think. Guess it will do her good at least it can do her no harm.

[Mary Abell to her sister Kate, June 29, 1871; this and all the following letters are from Kansas.]
Robert has got a piece of land that suits him, and so near market that we

---

to quote from this book and from the unpublished letter of C. C. Humphrey, May 1875, at the close of the section.

can get every thing just as cheap as we could in Lawrence. It seems so fortunate. Mr. Humphrey offers to let us have wood free by getting it for quite a while, he says it is rotting in the woods. Robert has gone to get a load today. Sarah's* husband says he will be glad to help us in any possible way—will let us have meat, turnips, potatoes and sorghum—for he as well as Mr. H. say they know just how hard it is to get along in a new country. There is a house to be built, fences to make—a well to be dug and a cow to be got beside a living—for the first year on a homestead brings in nothing—for the sod has to rot a year before a crop can be put in. I really cannot see how we are to get along—but in some way I hope. How I do wish you could all come out here. It is such a beautiful country—I did not know there was any thing so beautiful in the whole world as the country we passed over in coming here. You have no idea of it—I should never be content to live East now—things there would look very little. If father intends to farm it, it would be much easier out here—no hills, no thistles—no manuring to do—and I know his health would be better and all of you in fact.

[Mary Abell to her sister Kate, Aug. 14, 1871]
Say Kate don't you tell anybody, but how would you like another little nephew or niece, I just give you a hint of what you may expect in some less than a year—for you will not get mad about it like the rest of the folks.

I have not been feeling so well in over a year as now—and especially since I've been in Kansas. I've been feeling quite well for three or four weeks—you know I've been miserable ever since I've been here before. I feel scarcely anything of my rheumatism now. Say Kate you may tell Ma and the girls, *but nobody else on your peril.* I know you can keep a secret and when you make up that box just remember the "little fellow" ha, ha, my "old duds", are worn pretty thin and if any of you have anything that would do to cut up just send along and they will be very welcome.

[Mary Abell to her mother, Nov. 12, 1871]
The rain is falling out of doors and has been all day—but we are snug and warm in comfortable quarters. We never thought of having such a good house for this winter; we are indeed thankful you may be sure. I have commenced giving Alice Fullington music lessons, am going to give her three lessons a week. She is an only child, and they (her parents) are very anxious she should learn music as she has never learned much at school, she is seventeen years old and quite diffident—her father is wealthy, they are all pleased with the idea of my teaching her. I think she is going to do first rate. I could have a large class if I could manage any way to leave home and give lessons or have them come here. I can do nothing till I get my melodeon here. . . .

I had to lug all the water, and do most of the chores for several days. Carrying the water up the hill was the hardest work for me, but Rob is now able to attend to his wonted work himself—though his leg troubles him—pains him

* Sarah was a former neighbor in Attica who went west in 1866. She married Thomas North. Her parents, the Humphreys, also lived close by in Kansas.

a good deal of the time, he is lame in both knees now. He has picked corn two half days—was intending to work a good deal this fall, but he will be able to do scarcely anything. His school commences the first of Dec. . . .

I expect to earn money to get somethings after a little. I get all our provisions now by my sewing—Mother Abell sent us two lbs. of tea which will last us at least all winter—so the most we have to get in the grocery line will be sugar we have soda to last six months at least, the children have got to have new every day aprons, dresses—and must have doublegowns—they have worn their old duds patched and repatched all summer till they are good for nothing but paper rags. Indeed I cannot let them go looking so any longer. You see I have a good winters' work before me—with the "little sewing" I have to do. I shall take all the sewing I can get aside from Mrs. H's [Humphrey]. . . .

The calico you sent, I am very much obliged for. I needed it so much for the children, shall have to get twice as much to make up besides, for I must do my sewing for some months to come—I can not do much in that line after another "little stranger" comes, even if I could my eyes are always so weak, my limbs swell badly, but has not felt as bad for a few days. I've not been on my feet as much.

[Mary Abell to her mother, Dec. 31, 1871]

This is the last day of 1871. The 1st I spent in Attica* and I remember it quite well—I wish I were there this year, but it will be perhaps many years before I shall see you again—my cares increase instead of diminish. No sooner are the children a little out of the way than another comes—and so they come along. I have been quite nervous for a couple of weeks. More so than before this winter. The children worry me completely out by night—and none of them sleep any through the day, and it is a continual worry—when I am sewing as hard as I can all the time.

[Mary Abell to her sister Kate, Jan. 18, 1873]

Here we have been shut up all winter. Have not been anywhere since I was out to Miriams' last fall, do you wonder that I get nervous shut up so week after week with the children in a room 10 x 11 for that is every inch of room we have. Em talks about being crowded, but let her try keeping house in the further bedroom with four small children—a bedstead—bed on the floor—stove—table—big trunk, three chairs (stowed on the bed part of the time) and things that you can't get along without, and no sort of a store-room and half a window to light it all and then what about being crowded, and yet we are just in that predicament. I have to cook and do everything right here. Get milk—make butter, eat, sleep etc. etc. The vessel under the bed a few feet from the stove does not thaw out week in and week out—I wear felt over shoes and Robs Army blouse all the time and he wears his heaviest over-coat and then we can't keep warm. Rob has frosted his heels badly—cannot wear a boot on one of his feet.

---

* Mary and the children had spent several months in her parents' home while Robert went west by covered wagon.—EDS.

Our old cow has "come in", she has a beautiful little heifer calf, we have lots of milk now. The young cow is a splendid cow for butter as I ever saw.

[Mary Abell to her mother, Oct. 11, 1873]

I helped Rob in with the last of his hay Friday. Yesterday I cleaned all the lower part of the house excepting washing the doors and windows and mopping the other room floor. I was tired enough when night came. Nevertheless sat up till half past ten o'clock mending clean clothes for the little ones. They have all had the bowel complaint this fall, but are well and hearty again now. Baby has cut four double teeth at once. I felt motion soon after I wrote you last. Am over five months along, shall be sick the first part of Feb I expect—seems as if I have all I can tend to now. My head is much better, but I am bloated, and feel so uncomfortable most of the time. Have been at work all day even though it has been the Sabbath—washed the children all over, heads and all and put clean clothes on them—cut Robs' hair and whiskers etc. Everything has been neglected since I've been helping Robert. I have been his sole help in getting up and stacking at least 25 tons of hay and oats—some of the time I was deathly sick and faint while loading, but finally got through with it. My right limb is very bad. I have thousands of work to do this fall. Every one of the children has got to be rigged from head to foot for winter and I must do a new comforter and quilt, two thick quilts if possible. Have had several frosts. How I wish I had some of your grapes and apples. We have had the most luscious musk melons cut up in sugar and cream for six weeks— they were almost as good as peaches. We are the only ones in the neighborhood who have had a garden. Every one planted, but the dry weather killed everything. We have had an abundance of almost everything. Nettie has been a very good little girl, has taken all the care of the baby while I've been helping Robt. Did you get the letter I wrote home, telling you of Nettie receiving the tidy and .50 cents with which she was going to get her a doll?

[Mary Abell to her family, Oct. 16, 1873]

I feel very little like writing, but you will be wanting to know the whys of course. One of those dreadful prairie fires, accompanied by a hurricane of wind swept through here Tuesday night, the 14th and took everything but our house and stock (horses and cattle). All our hay and oats that Rob and I had worked so hard to get up and stack, harness, saddle, bridle, stable, 26 hens and chickens that I had had such work to raise—all the wooden part to the mower, hay rack posts planks all burned etc. At least a hundred dollars worth swept away in a few moments. The flames came rolling in, in huge billows—I rigged up in Robts' coat, boots and a flannel skirt with a wool comforter over my head and helped him fight fire—but no one could stand before this blinding smoke, heat and cinders. I burned the right side of my face raw. One of my eyes is half shut, it is so badly swollen. My back and hips are stiff enough. I worked about as hard as I could for two hours. The fire came so suddenly that we had not much time to think or act. The white cow got right into this fire—and badly singed—Robt. cut their ropes and let them run. The horses he tied to the wagon close to the house. Our house would have gone too, but for the dirt all around it—the fire came within a few feet, but the blaze did not touch it, neither was the privy burned. There were the three little scared-faces of the children at the window watching the fire. We left them asleep, but they never made a bit of fuss—afraid of waking the baby, and Nettie said the cat ought to have been let out but she was afraid to open the door, the wind was blowing the sparks of fire so she was afraid it might set something afire on the inside. Thoughtful wasn't she?

There is no way to do now but to move away for the winter and Robt. teach school. He went down to Milford to see if he could get the school he taught winter before last, last week, but Mr. Humphrey's folks wanted Flora to have it. . . . It seems hard to have things swept away as when folks have hard work to *live* here at the best. . . . Rob is blue enough—and who wouldn't be? I don't feel much like writing.

[Mary Abell to her parents, Nov. 28, 1873]

Well we have at last got a bedroom and living room fixed comfortable—without plastering a bit. Robert has done all the work, carpenter work included, himself. Don't know what we should have done but for the money Mary [Robert's sister] sent. The $5.00 you sent will furnish plenty of flour to last three months—so we are not in present distress either from cold or otherwise—though there are a great many other things to consider. Imagine yourselves for instance with nothing but land, house, and stock—for that's where we are. Not a tree, particle of water, grass, stable, fence or any thing else. Comfortable though right on the verge of winter—and the wherewith to get it with, about as vague. Eastern people may think us homesteaders are doing a fine thing to get 160 acres of land for nothing—all but the nothing. Oh, the suffering that the poor endure here, and privations you have not the remotest idea of, and poor means nearly *all* homesteaders.

[Mary Abell to her parents, Feb. 19, 1874]

Sarah North, her husband and three children were here and stayed all night one week before the baby was born. I sold Sarah the dress with overskirt Mary Eckley sent me last winter, Robert owed Thomas $8.00 for a plow—and I told Sarah if she wanted the dress for the debt she might have it. . . . They were both so well pleased with it—thought it was too much for the plow—said they never intended charging us anything for it—but of course that is not our way. It was a nice, pretty dress—but I'd rather pay a debt with it than to keep it. I sold the dress I made when at home to Mrs. Cole for $7.00 and the basquine that was Julia's [Robert's sister] for $8.00 to pay a debt, and get some flour and meal, and a grey dress that was Julia's we exchanged for a bedstead. So you see I am turning clothing to good account. The basquine was what I intended cutting up for Eddie's clothes to trim with those brass buttons, but it is better as it is. I am now going to let the dress pattern which I bought in Brockport when Eddie was a baby go, for 7 days work on a well—it is fine seeded Alpaca wine color—and 15 yards in the pattern—have also engaged 8 days work for the well for the brown dress of mine trimmed with black velvet—I shall take the velvet off and keep. The skirt is full having never been cut over—so the woman can take out enough for ruffles and peplum, if she wishes. It causes a twinge for me to let my dresses go, but that is probably the best way—you see I've already paid $26.00 in clothing—add $15.00 to that and it is quite a help. Though, if there had been any other way I should not have thought of it. I shall probably sell a couple more the one nearly white like the one Emma has—and that grey summer one, clouded like —neither have ever been cut over, which makes a nice full pattern. They will do us more good in that way than in any other—but my silk ones I shall keep —don't be afraid of my selling myself short. These have been packed away ever since I was married— . . .

Our neighbors all need clothing, and care more about it than I do, when I need more clothes we can probably afford them—you know Robert is very good about getting me things whenever I need them, if he possibly can. We shall have to sell one of our cows and a three year old steer in the spring to help pay a store debt. . . .

It is astonishing how we have got along this winter but, we have been provided for in some way as we've been in need. Rob has less than two dollars now —and we've but half a sack of flour, but shall trust in the Lord for the future —as we have in the past. . . . I tied a comforter the week before I was sick and although I worried so much over my work, I got it every bit done up before I was sick,* even to mending the last pair of stockings and making Nettie's doll a bedquilt and quilting it. . . .

O, mother, I wish you would get a new Union Primer and send by mail. Nettie's is so badly torn, Eddie can not read in it . . . and Eddie ought to be learning to read.

[Mary Abell to her sister Kate, March 7, 1874]
I am beginning to look old—and no wonder I look yellow instead of pale after my latter confinements, and work and care soon tell on a body's looks— though I hope I shall be relieved after a while. Robert don't look any older— men don't you know. I can't see that he looks any different from what he did when we were married i.e., when dressed decently, and his hair and whiskers in trim. He looks shaggy and bad enough though at other times. Well it is almost time for me to begin to get supper so I shall certainly have to stop writing—.

[Mary Abell to her mother, March 16, 1874]
I see by the Attica paper that the Chaffee family are becoming quite distinguished. I am not—though can boast over nothing but five children, the oldest only seven years old. My time except the tending to them is very limited. Hard work is the watchword in Kansas and no pay with the coarsest living.

[Mary Abell to her mother, May 4, 1874]
How much has father bought, and where situated. . . . You will have room enough now and lots of nice fruit, and one of these days when I go

---

* Mary refers here to the birth of her fifth child, Willie.—EDS.

home visiting in *grand style*, I shall not be afraid that there will not be room enough for all my babies. You need not laugh, at the idea, for if we can once get a foothold here and get to going we shall get ahead to use the Kansas phrase, *right smart*. We don't expect to have a fire every year, and I shall never go East till I can travel in as good a manner as when I came out here, and can go independent. We are hoping for a prosperous year this year. Rob's spring wheat is all up—his potatoes, over an acre all planted Early Rose, Peach Blow—and some other kinds. The garden all sowed but squashes and some melons. Our seed onions are up a finger high—peas, beets, and turnips also up. Rob is now ploughing for corn. Will have that all planted by the 15th of May. I cut all the potatoes and have sowed most of the garden. Mary Eckley sent us money enough to buy seed wheat, potatoes and corn and hay for the house.

[Mary Abell to her mother, Oct. 14, 1874]
Your letter containing $1. was received last week. Many thanks for it. I do hate to take it from you, for I know how hard your dollars come to you, at present I may need it most, and when prosperous times come, if ever, I can pay it back again. . . . You know how dreadful the drought was for you last year, well if you'd had a worse one this year and grasshoppers besides, where would you have been—but that's just where we and thousands of others are here in Kansas today—fire adding to the list of calamities in many instances.

Children run barefoot yet. I almost wonder they don't have the croup such damp cold weather as we have half of the time—but they don't seem to mind the cold much. I've made baby some shoes out of some old kid ones Nellie [her youngest sister] sent Nettie and they do him nicely. I have a great deal of work to do this fall in the way of rigging up the children for winter. I wish it would be a warm open winter.

I think of the meaning of the Lord's Prayer quite often lately, "Give us this day our daily bread" not even butter, meat, nor any thing else is added to it. That has got to be our fare now. I make bread every day but never realized the real importance of "daily bread" as now—no meat, fruit, vegetables of any description not even dried fruit—but little butter, but as yet plenty of milk and bread. Of course I can make gravy too. Our flour from our wheat is very nice, and so we shall not starve at any rate, nor lack *good* bread. I wonder what will befall us another year. Our trust in God almost gives out at times. Why he should allow such things is a mystery—and the burden falls on the portion of the people the least able to bear it. Those who have to struggle to make a living in the best of times. You never saw destitution, you may think you know something of it—but none of you have the least conception of what actual want, destitution and hard living is. When Robert preaches some men have no coats, and some no shirts, and cannot even buy thread to patch with. His text last Sabbath to them was, "Trust God, do good, dwell in the land and verily thou shalt be fed." But he preached to himself as much as to them, for he knows no better what he is going to do the coming winter to get along than they do.

[Mary Abell to her father, Nov. 21, 1874]

We've been obliged to tell the children that Santa Claus will not come here this year, everybody is so poor, and need food and clothes so much it wont pay him to bring any playthings. I shall try and sell butter to get them some candy etc. . . . I have aches and pains somewhere all the time, and with all am cross and nervous. If I was only where I could run home once or twice a year and get a rest—but I am here and here I must stay, how long? . . . The long dreary winter will wear away after a while and then we'll hope again for a crop.

[Mary Abell to her mother, Feb. 16, 1875]

Your two kind welcome letters have been received. I am sorry you worry about me so, but can't blame you. I am not as bad as I was in that coldest weather because I can sit up more, but I have no strength to do anything and the least little thing tires me all out. Baby has been quite sick for three days, and he is so heavy that the lifting and care of him has quite used me up. Today he is all around on the floor again, but looks peaked with that tired look in his little eyes. The little darling! How we should feel to lose him. I am not sure what the matter was, whether it was his teeth, worms or a severe cold that has just developed itself. I doctored him for worms and the lungs, think he is all right now. I never had such a dreadful place for a child to creep in before, a bare floor and such a cold house. The weather here is colder than with you, for with the cold is a fierce north wind which will freeze man or beast that happen to be out. The children had to wear their hoods nights. My eyelids froze together so I picked off the ice, the tops of the sheets and quilts and all our beds were frozen stiff with the breath. The cold was so intense we could not breath the air without pain. Had to cover our faces partially. We had not bedclothes enough to keep us warm and we piled on everything in the house that would answer any purpose. . . . I have not swept up all winter—and only been out of doors twice on warm days since last fall, and caught cold both times.

[Mary Abell to her mother, March 15, 1875]

Willie runs all over—I'm glad he can walk, 'twill be so much warmer than to creep. He's the smartest baby you ever saw—so fair, red cheeks, black eyes—fair hair and such white teeth—and usually so good. I cannot lift him now, nor much of anything, his father has taken care of him nights for a long, long time, changes him, undresses him and does everything Nettie can't. I'm good for nothing.

I would not dare to Dr. with McNeill. You must not lay it to Rob that I would not take the powders—when I've had nothing sweet to eat in Kansas— He's put me on bread and tea. We have no vegetables nor anything else, and I have no appetite nor flesh, beside he never told what the powders were for, nor what affect they ought to have, nor what they were composed of, and I'll never take a particle of medicine that I don't know what it is. I appreciate your trying to help me, but I am getting along slowly— . . . Dear mother, *don't worry.*

[Mary Abell to her mother, probably an addendum to the preceding letter]

Robert is going after wood tomorrow and will go to the P.O. for the first time in three weeks and I must write a few lines. Mother you need not worry at all about my being in the family way—for I've not the least symptoms, after ailing for nearly four months. . . . Indeed I've but little flesh or blood either. I suffer constantly from cold. I suffered with pleurisy in my left side and shoulder terribly for one week. I am now weak and good for nothing. Mary Eckley sent me money to buy shoes with, with which I got the medicine. . . . Mother Abell and Aunt Mary Wilcox have been around and gathered in their neighborhood of clothing, beans and dried fruit—five barrels and sent on with money to pay freight—$17.—gathered at the same time and sent on for Robt. to distribute among the destitute in our vicinity and how *destitute* people are—well educated, delicate women without chemises or drawers and everything else as scant. It is a dreadful time of want here. I wish father could get interested and get folks to making up barrels and boxes—unless people are helped I don't know what they are going to do—. . . .

We have five beautiful children and they are a great comfort to us. I'm sure I'd rather have them even in Kansas, than to have been buried ten years ago—I think Mother would change her mind about burying her daughters if she could see our dear little ones—besides mother set me a very poor example, she would have had quite an ample family if she had carried out all she set out for—don't blame your girls—nor their husbands either. But I must stop writing for I have a good deal to do even if I am sick—love to all. I've not written much that I wanted to, I'm so light-headed.

[This was Mary Abell's last letter home. She died in May 1875. The following is a letter to her mother from Mrs. Carrie Humphrey, a Kansas neighbor and an old friend of the Chaffee family. It was written shortly after Abell's death.]

I am at home staying with little Willie, Mary's baby, while the rest of the family have gone to sabbath school; Nettie is with them. 'Ere this reaches you; no doubt you will have received the sad news of dear Mary's death. It was no doubt startling to you; but I think it could not have been much more so than it was to me; not having heard anything from him, Mr. A. during her sickness; I cannot express the sadness I have felt that I was not informed of her situation; I told him he ought to let us know; I was not able to do much for her; but perhaps I could have influenced him to get other assistance to make her comfortable. . . . I have suffered a great deal with neuralgy and supposed that Mary was very much in the same way; and had no thought of her being consumptive; but think now it was quick born, and the neighbors think so.

When I was there feared she was in the family way and fancied she was worried on the account from a remark she made. She appeared unnatural and seemed to be in a study; and said if she had another she could not get along at all; said it did her good to see us and she felt much better. I got him to promise to bring her down if she was able to get ready, leaving all excepting Nettie and the baby; so that she could get some rest, and visit among the neighbors, but the next I heard she was not able to come. I think from what I learned that her nervous system was completely worn out and greatly deranged, she could not endure the noise of the children and even little Willie must be bundled up and kept out of her sight, it is a wonder that they did not get sick, it is Providential.

I hope and pray that you may have strength to endure this heart rending trial; trusting in the Lord who is able to sustain his people.

67. A study of cottage industry in Paris: la famille P—

The French engineer turned sociologist Frédéric Le Play (1806–82; Docs. 75, 102.i) spent over twenty years investigating the families of European workers. The result was a six-volume monograph that described in great detail the standard of living, work habits, religious beliefs, and moral values of fifty-seven workers' families. He divided his case studies into two principal categories: stable populations, made up of families that were relatively undisturbed by modernization, and disorganized populations, made up of families "led astray by novelty, scornful of tradition, in revolt against the ten commandments and paternal authority." Le Play characterized the family in the case study presented here as part of the disorganized population because the man and the woman were not legally married and were irreligious. The head of the family, a tailor, had taken on a "concubine-apprentice" to help him, as did many in his trade when young apprentices became increasingly hard to find. The tailor was a heavy drinker, which Le Play viewed as another manifestation of disorganization, but unlike many of the drunken fathers in these case studies, the tailor provided ample food for his family, took his consumptive child regularly to the doctor, and did not beat or scold his wife. One of Le Play's associates conducted the interviews and wrote this monograph in 1856.

The worker described in the present monograph lives in Paris not far from the Blanche tollgate (2d arrondissement). He belongs to the populous category of worker-tailors of suits; and the nature of his trade puts him in the group known as *apiéceurs* [pieceworkers]. With the worker lives a woman whom he has instructed in his trade and who has become an indispensable aide to him in his profession. Thanks to the help she gives him, he undertakes as extra work on his own account the making of suits for a clientele he has created for himself in the neighborhood. . . .

The industry to which this worker belongs formerly flourished in Paris; but it entered a period of decline when the merchants for ready-made garments, commonly called *confectionneurs*, began to multiply and to offer consumers much less expensive clothing. . . .

SOURCE: Adolphe-Jean Focillon, "Tailleur d'habits de Paris," in Frédéric Le Play, *Les Ouvriers européens*, 6: *Les Ouvriers de l'occident, populations désorganisées*, 2d ed. (Tours and Paris, 1878), pp. 387–414 *passim*.

Civil Status of the Family

The family consists of four persons, as follows:

1. François P—, born in Brussels (Belgium), 40 years old
2. Marie-Geneviève J—, born in A— (Loiret), near Orléans, 31 —
3. Charles P—, their older son, born in Paris, 3 —
4. Dieudonné P—, their younger son, born in Paris, 2 —

The worker is not married, but he has legally recognized his children by presenting them to the government official in charge of vital statistics and to the priest, who baptized them. Concubinage is not peculiar to this family: certain special causes make it common among the piecework tailors. The worker has had two other children who died very young by the same woman. At present François P—'s father lives on his savings in Brussels. The mother has been dead for five years. Marie J—'s father deserted his family after a disorderly life had brought them to the brink of misery. The mother lives in Orléans with another daughter, who is married and established; and even though she is sixty years old, she still works as a day laborer. Marie J— has two sisters, both married, and a brother who disappeared with the father and who shares his debauched habits.

Religion and Moral Habits

The worker had been obedient to the Catholic faith, pursuing the religious practices imposed on him by his father. But he has been moved to revolt by influences outside his family. Thus he has long since abandoned all religious observances and has never possessed any faith. In his eyes religion is, for some, a childish weakness; for many others, a hypocritical means employed to limit the freedom of the workers and to dominate them by superstition. Like his comrades, he thinks himself far above such shameful servitude. . . .

The conduct of the worker [is] extremely debauched, which is common among the workers in this profession. To the coarse disorders of drunkenness, he adds the more refined vices special to big cities. . . . Although he has always earned between five and seven francs a day when he wanted to work, he has left numerous debts in the cities he has passed through that he says he could not pay. Moreover, the ruses by which he has managed to dupe more than one creditor seem to him to be nothing but colorful episodes of his vagabond life. Such profligacy has not, however, alienated the worker's friends in the profession. Valued for his cleverness, he has the reputation of a bold bohemian, and none seriously reproach his behavior. . . . The precocious debauches of his youth have alienated the worker from all studies; he is badly educated, especially in comparison with some other workers in the same profession. He writes very poorly, and he has no taste for reading. . . . The worker described here has no strong political views of his own, but he is familiar with preoccupations of this sort; and he claims the ardor that his comrades have displayed in various popular demonstrations is an honorable trait. Moreover, he nurtures an envious disdain for the higher classes of society, and displays neither confidence, affection, nor respect for his employers. He complains about his position and seemingly has no inkling that he might be reproached for his dissipation. His heart goes out to those comrades with whom he has shared a life of debauchery and labor. He deplores the indifference of employers toward those whose infirmities make them incapable of working. Similarly, he believes that workers have an obligation to help each other in times of distress. Thus he and some of his friends came to the aid of an old comrade who had become paralyzed; and they all took turns bringing him his meals. This, plus the fact that the worker's very faults are intimately connected with a careless liberality, compensates somewhat for his vices. He is not stingy about household expenses and has resigned himself without reluctance to the extra expenses imposed on him by the ill health of his elder child. . . .

The woman who lives with the worker was shrewdly chosen for the trade he wanted her to exercise. Sweet, submissive, a hard worker, subjugated by the professional superiority of the worker who, in teaching her his trade, placed in her hands a precious resource for earning a living, she fulfills without complaint the task he has imposed on her. Forced by the very irregularity of her position to accept the tailor's established habits, she gives him free rein. Without complaint she tolerates the fact that he spends every evening out while she, alone with the sleeping children, continues her daily work until eleven at night. Moreover, she is well treated by the worker, who is neither ill-natured nor a scold. The past conduct of this woman does not seem to have been loose, and perhaps she was completely respectable until the day on which . . . she met the worker. Raised in unhappy circumstances, Marie J—, though she has completely forgotten the teachings of religion, has been saved from all envious thought by her intellectual inferiority and her good-heartedness. For the rest, she has been completely deprived of schooling. In this family without formal ties, the children receive care and affection, but it is all too easy to foresee that good character formation there will be impossible. The parents cannot offer their children a morality that they totally lack themselves. . . .

Health Care and Hygiene

. . . The woman has a puny look, though she is tall enough (1.69 meters).* Her pale face and thin figure proclaim the fatigue of a life of labor and of four successive births in five years. . . . Nevertheless she is healthy and her births have been successful; but she has the appearance of an anemic woman. . . .

Tasks and Activities

. . . During his work, the worker sits cross-legged on a large plank in front of the only window in the room where the family lives. He assembles the pre-cut pieces of the garments, does the arduous or difficult needlework, and smooths down the stitches with a hot iron. The other tasks, which require

* Something over 5′5″.—EDS.

less strength and skill, are left for the woman. In the summer the worker works eleven to twelve hours a day, and about ten hours in the winter. From this time one must deduct barely three-quarters of an hour for the morning and midday meals. Every day, he leaves work at dinnertime, at five in the winter, and at six or six-thirty in the summer. He never works evenings, or Sundays and holidays.

[The woman's] principal jobs are all performed with the worker. The woman helps him with the tasks of making suits, whether executed for the employers' accounts or for the family's accounts. Seated on a chair near the plank where the worker sits, the woman constantly receives from him pieces of work he has prepared, along with instructions for completing them suitably. The salary of an assistant in the woman's circumstances could be estimated at three francs a day; but on the one hand, by doing piecework, she raises her worth to four francs; and, on the other hand, she prolongs the workday after the evening meal until eleven at night. In these conditions the total number of hours she works must be estimated at twelve hours a day, 365 days a year. During these hours of labor, in addition to the work done with the tailor, the woman does household tasks. She cleans the room, makes the beds, dresses the children, and prepares food for the meals. Every week she washes the major household linens, the children's clothes, and even her dresses when they need it. She soaps these things at home in a glazed earthen dish, then she goes down to the courtyard near the pump . . . to rinse them in two tubs loaned to her by a neighbor. She uses the free moments that the slackening of work in times of unemployment allows to mend the children's clothes, her linens, and those of the worker. . . .

The children are much too young to be put to work or even to studying. If the elder has been sent to a school, it is so that he can be supervised during the day and thus leave his mother more freedom to pursue her usual work.

Food and Meals

The family has three meals a day, but these are not spaced as they ordinarily are for other Parisian workers who work at home. The main meal takes place around noon, following the Flemish custom. The worker calls it dinner.

Breakfast (8 o'clock): black coffee without sugar and 6 centiliters of eau-de-vie. The woman and children take café au lait with crumbled bread moistened in it.

Dinner (11 o'clock or noon): platter of meat, boiled beef, stew, or roast meat, dressed with vegetables and especially potatoes. When the price is not too high, fish is sometimes served at this meal. Dinner ends with a cup of black coffee. On Sundays and holidays the family eats out at a restaurant on the outskirts of the city. This can cost as much as 3 francs 50. . . .

Supper (5 o'clock in winter, 7 in summer): soup, some leftovers from dinner, cheese, and some fruits for the woman and children. The worker goes out every evening to a nearby tavern outside the city gates, where he dines with his comrades and spends the evening. This meal costs him 1.50 francs daily. . . .

Once a year a goose is bought when the price is judged not to be too high.

[The family's] diet is not unusual compared with that of other Parisian workers. The family usually drinks half a liter of wine per day; but for some time because of the high price of this beverage they have had to use water instead, which is flavored by steeping several morsels of licorice root in it. . . .

Housing, Furniture, and Clothing

The worker lives on the fifth floor of a handsome and very well-maintained building. The first four floors are lodgings occupied by persons of the bourgeois class. A small, narrow, steep staircase, which connects with the staircase for the lower floors, leads to the fifth floor; this is situated just under the eaves and consists of a corridor that opens into twelve rooms like the one in which the family lives. This room is nearly square, 4.6 meters x 4 meters; its height is 2.4 meters, but the paneling that covers part of the ceiling leaves an average height of only 1.98 meters.* In this single room, measuring at the most 36 square meters, the worker, his woman, and the children live all the time. . . . The door, customarily closed, does not allow fresh air to enter the room. The only ventilation comes from a dormer window and a [tiny] chimney. . . . These conditions are unhygienic and are only partially offset by the good condition of the building and the good ventilation that upper floors provide. . . .

The worker and his wife sleep in one bed, together with the younger child; at the foot of the bed is the crib of the elder. . . . A look at the income and expenses of the family reveals that by making better use of their resources, the family could find healthier and more comfortable lodgings. Annual rent is 140 francs. . . . The worker does not find this price high and wants to remain in this room, where he has lived for the last four years. . . .

[The furniture] attests at once to the negligence and sloppiness of the worker and to the cleanliness of the woman. It satisfies only the barest necessities, and does not even provide the most minimal comfort. . . .

History of the Tailor and the Woman

[The tailor's story is given first. We pick up here with the woman's history.]

This girl, named Marie J—, was born in a village 23 kilometers from Orléans; her father was a vinedresser and farmed a small plot that he owned in the country. The father's immorality ruined the family and led to the dissolution of the household after twenty years of marriage. The mother, abandoned since 1842, has managed to support herself and to raise two of her three daughters with her earnings as a day laborer. . . . Taken to Orléans in 1833, when her ruined father went there to look for some work, [Marie] made her first communion at the age of twelve, after only six months of catechism; and two years later she entered service in the homes of various people in the province. She came to Paris at the age of nineteen and served in two households until 1847. It was then that on the advice of an old woman who regularly employed her, she decided to take the job [with the tailor] and live in his room. This childhood, blighted by the misconduct and abandonment of a

---

* In feet and inches the dimensions given here are roughly 15′ x 13′ for the room, with a maximum height of 7′9″ sloping to an average of 6′5″.—EDS.

father, but still protected by the efforts of an honorable mother, explains well enough the faults and virtues seen in Marie J—; and if a miserable fate had not taken her away from the maternal roof and thrown her, ignorant and inexperienced, right into the big city, she would undoubtedly have remained a virtuous girl.

68. 'No men could endure the work': Women in English workshops

In the Victorian period many women continued to find employment in small—often home-based—workshops. Although in the course of the nineteenth century the hours and working conditions gradually improved in the larger industrial concerns (notably the textile factories), the women who were employed in the small craftshops or sweatshops could be worked at all hours, under any conditions, as the following four selections from England reveal. In the first selection, dating from the 1840's, C. D., a milliner, and Miss——, a dressmaker, testify to a parliamentary commission about the grueling hours and unhealthy conditions of their work in London. In the second selection Lucy Luck recalls in her memoirs how she left domestic service to work in the country as a straw plaiter. In the third selection Agnes Hafferman talks to a parliamentary investigator about industrial poisoning in a London artificial flower–making establishment. And in the fourth selection Isabella Killick tells a parliamentary committee in 1888 that her earnings as a trouser finisher provide the sole support for her invalid husband and three young children. Killick's revelations underscore the fact that even at the close of the Victorian period, women continued to serve as a cheap source of labor, competing for a limited number of unskilled jobs, and enjoying little or no bargaining power.

(i) The milliner and the dressmaker

Feb. 14, 1841. C.D.—Has been a milliner several years, and has been employed in 4 houses in London; the busiest season is from March to July. Witness works at ——. At this establishment a very considerable number of young persons are regularly employed, the greater part of whom are under 25. In the season many more are employed as day workers, and a few come from the country and London as improvers. The common hours at this establishment in the spring season are from 8 A.M. till 1 or 2 the next morning; often till 4 or 5. If they work till 4 or 5, they get up to work at 8 A.M. as usual. It very frequently happens that for 3 or 4 days in the week the hours are from 8 A.M. till 1, 2, 4, and 5 the next morning. It is almost invariably the case that the work is carried on all night, on the night before court days. On Saturday night

SOURCES: (i) Great Britain, *Parliamentary Papers*, 1843, XIV, Children's Employment Commission, pp. f 207–8. (ii) Lucy Luck, "A Little of My Life," *London Mercury*, 13 (Nov. 1925–April 1926): 354–73. (iii) Great Britain, *Parliamentary Papers*, 1865, XX, Children's Employment Commission, 4th report, p. 117. (iv) Great Britain, *Parliamentary Papers*, 1888, XX, Select Committee of the House of Lords on the Sweating System, pp. 149–51.

it is usual to work till 3, 4, and 5 on Sunday morning. If the young persons fall asleep at work they are aroused by the overlooker. When witness was an apprentice, has sometimes laid down on the rug and slept a few minutes, till she was called. In the intervals of the busy season the hours are from 8 A.M. till 10 P.M.

No particular times are allowed for meals, it is expected they should be taken as quickly as possible; if they should, in the season, remain up stairs for a few minutes, the bell is rung to bring them down. On an average, in the season, a quarter of an hour or less is all that is allowed for dinner. The food is good and sufficient; the proprietor wishes it to be so. Knows that there are several houses in London in which no meals are allowed on Sunday after breakfast; it is expected that they should obtain a dinner from their friends. Knows a young person who walked about the streets all day in consequence of being denied a dinner at her employer's. No exception is made in favour of those who have no friends in London.

All the workwomen, in the season about 50, work in one large room. In the season, with the sun in the day, and the lamps at night, this place is extremely hot and oppressive. Several young persons have fainted at their work. The sight is frequently affected. Witness's health suffers at the end of the season; this is universal. In consequence of this, it is necessary for the young people to go into the country to recruit the health for one or two months. Without this change it would not be possible for the young women to go through with the work. In this establishment the wages are stopped during the time the young persons are absent in the country; but this is an exception to the common custom. As the employers are generally anxious to get rid of any who are ill, the young persons, if taken unwell, are afraid of complaining, and consequently continue at their work to the serious prejudice of their health.

The salary for second hands, who principally form the establishment, is from 20l. to 30l. per annum, exclusive of board and lodging.

Is sure that no men would submit to the labour, which is imposed on the young dressmakers and milliners. Any protection to be effectual, should extend to the age of 25.

Feb. 11, 1841, Miss ——. Has been for several years in the dress-making business: has been 10 years "a first hand," which signifies the party who takes the superintendence of the business, as overlooker of the young persons, cutter out of the work, &c. The common hours of business are from 8 A.M. till 11 P.M. in the winter; in the summer from 6 or half-past 6 A.M. till 12 at night. During the fashionable season, that is from April till the latter end of July, it frequently happens that the ordinary hours are greatly exceeded: if there is a drawing-room or grand fete, or mourning to be made, it often happens that the work goes on for 20 hours out of the 24, occasionally all night. Every season, in at least half the houses of business, it happens that the young persons occasionally work 20 hours out of the 24 twice or thrice a week. On special occasions, such as drawing-rooms, general mournings, and very frequently wedding orders, it is not uncommon to work all night: has herself worked 20 hours out of the 24 for 3 months together; at this time she was suffering from illness, and the medical attendant remonstrated against the treatment she received. He wished witness to remain in bed at least one day longer, which the employer objected to, required her to get up, and dismissed the surgeon. At this house the hours are shorter, and altogether more comfortable than any other witness has been in.

The meals are always taken as quickly as possible, no fixed time being allowed in any house that witness knows. The general result of the long hours and sedentary occupation is to impair seriously and very frequently to destroy the health of the young women. Has seen young persons faint immediately after the work was over, the stimulus or excitement which had sustained them having ceased. The digestion especially suffers, and also the lungs; pain in the side is very common, and the hands and feet die away from want of circulation and exercise, "never seeing the outside of the door from Sunday to Sunday." It commonly happens that young persons who come from the country healthy and well become so ill that they are obliged to leave the business, either returning to their friends or going to other occupations, especially as ladies' maids. Her own health is so much impaired that she has spit blood during the last 6 years.

The two causes to which the present evils are to be referred are—1. The short time which is allowed by ladies to have their dresses made. 2. The disinclination of the employers to have sufficient hands to complete the work. Thinks there would not be the slightest difficulty in procuring any additional assistance that might be required whenever emergencies arose. The plain parts of the work could always be put out, and the remainder could always be finished at home with ease. Is sure there are some thousands of young women employed in the business in London and in the country. If one vacancy were to occur now there would be 20 applicants for it. The wages for the generality are very low: the general sum for journey-women is from 1ol. to 2ol. a-year, board and lodging being provided. Thinks that no men could endure the work enforced from the dress-makers.

(ii) Lucy Luck

By now [c. 1863] I had begun to bitterly hate service, and a fatherly old man who used the public-house where I had been told me of a place in Luton where they wanted a girl to learn the straw work and help in housework. Although this was another public-house, I thought it was a chance to learn a trade, so I went there. By the way, I stayed with this man's wife until I was ready to go. He was what was called a packman in the country, one who travels to different parts of the country with a pack on his back; that was how he came to hear of the place at Luton. As I said before, I went there, and the place was very well and they were very good to me, but they did not keep to their promise. They would not pay me more than two shillings a week, but said they would teach me the straw-work. You may think it strange, straw business going on in a public-house, but it was so, and I think the reason was, part of the business belonged to a sister and daughter. I sometimes did housework, sometimes served in the bar, and other times did the finishing of straw hats. They never attempted to teach me the making of them, but I was determined to learn, and would get a piece of straw and sit up half the night trying to do it. Now a girl with whom I had been out a few times told me of a woman who wanted two girl-apprentices for six months, and would supply food, but no money. I went with her to see this woman, and it was agreed that we two girls should go there. I did not know if I was doing right or not, but as I had been some time at my place, and the money so little, and they had not shown me how to do the work, except the finishing-off (lining and wiring); I wanted to make the hats, so I made up my mind and left. I had a good lot of clothes, but not much money, and so I started right into the straw trade.

Hats were very different then to what they are now. I thought I was going to do wonders, but I think my real troubles had now begun. I liked the work very much, and was quick at it. I could do the two leading shapes of the season in a fortnight, but this woman set us a task every day which was impossible to do. I have sat up all night sometimes, in bitter cold weather, not daring to get right into bed for fear I should get warm and lay too long. I have even been obliged to do the work on Sunday, and then perhaps not finish the amount, and whatever quantity I was short she reckoned I was so much money in her debt. As I say, it was impossible to do in the time what she gave us, and so my little money went, and when that was gone she had my clothes just for my living. I don't wish to boast, but I had kept myself respectable so far, and now this woman took in two other girls who had a most filthy disease, to sleep in the same bed as myself. Time went on like this for five months; at the end of this, the work began to get very bad. Mrs. P. came back one morning in a shocking temper, because she could not sell the work, and brought home a new-shaped bonnet which she gave me to do. The first time I did it, it was wrong. I did it again; it was wrong. I did it a third time; it was still wrong. The day was more than half gone, and I had not done half or a quarter of my day's work. I had only been taught just the two leading shapes, and it took much longer to do this new shape. But the season was over, and she had taken from me all I had got, and now she did not want me any longer. I threw the work down, and told her I would do no more, for I had got to that state of mind I did not care what became of me. That woman had taken all I possessed because I could not do the amount of work she set me, just for my food. I started out of that house that day, after having only been there for five months, with nothing but my mother's Bible and a few little things tied up in a handkerchief. The season was over, and I was homeless, penniless, and with only the clothes I walked in. She had turned the other girl away, who went there with me, some time before, because she was rather slow at the work. What to do or which way to turn I did not know. Some people would say it was my own fault; I should have kept to service. Well, perhaps it was, but remember I was never put to a decent place at the beginning.

I wandered about; I did not care what became of myself that day. I had had no dinner, and I had nowhere to go, but towards night I thought I would try to find the other girl who had been there with me. I found her at last, with an aunt and uncle, and I told them how I was placed, and they, although strangers to me, took me in. This man said he had an order for work that would last for two or three weeks, and I could stop there and help to do it, and he would pay me what I earned: So you see, a home was again provided for me before night. I stayed there and worked as long as they had any to give me, and even after that, when there was nothing to do, I was allowed to stay, although they had not much room.

The work was very bad everywhere at this time, and I wandered about, trying for work, sometimes getting just enough to get some food; but I could not get any more clothes, and my boots were almost worn from my feet, often causing me to get wet-footed. How often I was tempted to lead a bad life, but there always seemed to be a hand to hold me back. I don't want you to think I boast of myself, for I was not my own keeper, neither was I without faults; far from it. After a time, I got some work in a workroom, but I wanted a lot of improving before I could do it properly. So a woman in the same room undertook to see that I did my work correctly, and in time I was able to earn fairly good money now and then. I went to live with this woman, and on Saturday she would take my money and pay herself for looking to my work, and on the way home would meet two or three others, visiting different public-houses. Often when I got home quite half of my money was gone.

(iii) Agnes Hafferman

Sept. 1864.—I was employed eight months ago at an artificial flower maker's in Goswell Road. I was there for one year. About 50 females worked there; 10 or 11 of them were under 13; none under 11; I was 19.

Our regular hours were from 9 to 9, but in the season they were always longer. I should say that for six months out of the year we worked from 7 a.m. to 10 p.m. every night but Saturday, and sometimes we began at 6, and even 5 a.m., and worked till 12 at night. I worked about two dozen times from 6 a.m. to 12 at night; the younger ones were not so long at work; they did not ever come before 7 a.m. nor stay after 11 p.m.; their usual time in the season was from 7 a.m. to 10 p.m. We left at 9 p.m. on Saturday, and sometimes earlier.

All but the learners were on piecework. I only did the best work, but I never earned more than 10s. a week even when I worked three nights a week from 6 a.m. till 12 at night. I worked all the night through once or twice. Once was a Friday night; I went on till 5 p.m. on the Saturday before I went home; another time was a Monday night, and then I worked on till 10 p.m. on the next day. We used to be very tired indeed with the work in the season; the constant sitting hurts the chest; but I don't find that I am any the worse for it now. Face-aches were very common among us; I still suffer from that, but I think not so much as I did. The percussion-cap work at Messrs. Eley's is much better than artificial flower making, for the hours are regular and not half as long, and we have work all the year round, instead of having nothing to do for five or six months out of the year and working very hard for the rest.

It was not our own choice to work so; we were not allowed to leave till we had finished our work. Our being on piecework made us, perhaps, ready to stop, but we could not go whenever we wished.

The young ones breakfasted before they came: we, who began at 6 a.m., often had nothing to eat till 11 a.m.; but we did generally breakfast at about 8 a.m. Half an hour was allowed for that, and for tea at 4; an hour for dinner at 1 p.m.; and if we worked late we took some supper at 9 or 10 p.m. We often worked through the meal times, but the children did not. I think most of us ate our meals at the table where we worked.

The dust of the green, and the blue too, was bad; it used to fly about and get on our hands when we had to separate the "pieces"; if we had a cut it made it sore; we used to tie a handkerchief over our mouths and noses, so that nothing got down our throats. We had nothing to do with preparing or putting on the colours; men did that. We used to draw the poison out of our hands with soap and sugar.

Our fingers often got cut by the silk and wire; I have known a girl ill for a fortnight through sores made by winding the stalks.

I have been at other flower makers; at one where I was for six months, three years ago, there were 40 at work; I was the youngest, and was 17 then. We never worked longer than from 8 to 8; but I was not there in their busiest time.

(iv) Isabella Killick

Chairman.—What business are you engaged in?—On the trouser finishing. I have worked at it now about 22 years altogether; it is paid for now so terribly bad.

What class of work do you do?—Finishing.

Finishing trousers?—Yes.

And you have been in the business 22 years?—Yes.

How many can you finish in a day now?—I cannot do more than four.

Is there anybody working with you?—No, only myself; and I have got an afflicted husband; he is dying; I do not know whether he will be dead when I get back or not; he is in an infirmary. I have three children to support; the eldest 10 years of age, and the youngest three.

What do you get?—I get 4½ d., 3¾ d., and 5 d., up to 6 d.; it is in my book.

What do you earn a week?—I have to find my own materials; I cannot earn more than 1 s. 2 d. a day; and I have to find my own materials and fire and lighting out of it.

What materials have you to find?—For the twist holes, 4½ d. work, you have your twist to buy; there is gimp and soap, black cotton, white cotton, and red cotton, and black thread; or white thread if they are white buttons.

You mean that you are paid 1 s. 2 d., including all those articles?—I have trimmings to find out of that 1 s. 2 d.; if they are 3½ d. ones they are cotton holes, but if they are twist holes they are 4½ d.; the twist will cost you 1½ d. for the four sets of holes.

How much does it come to?—Altogether I do not clear 1 s. a day, not after finding my own trimmings, firing and all, because there are many trimmings to find; and then I have to work many hours to do that. I am up at six o'clock every morning, and never done till eight at night. I am obliged to get in at a quarter-past eight, because the door closes.

What do you pay out of that for rent?—Two shillings; and I have to support three children out of it; the eldest is only 10 years of age; there are three children, one 10, one seven, and one four years next July; that is the youngest.

Your husband is in an infirmary, you say?—Yes. I was there at eight o'clock this morning to see him; he is paralysed all on one side; he has been there nine weeks.

How long has he been laid up?—Three years the 10th of May he has been laid up. . . .

Do you get about the same amount of work all the year round?—No, because it falls off slack at a certain time of the year; about two months before Christmas it falls off, then it does not start again till a month after Christmas; about three months of the year is slack.

What do you get to do then?—I am glad to get anything to do, a bit of cleaning or washing; I cannot be without work, as I have three little ones to support. . . .

What is the food you get chiefly?—Chiefly, I get a herring and a cup of tea; that is the chief of my living, with the rent to pay, and three children eating very hearty. As for meat, I do not expect; I get meat once in six months.

Are there any others working in the same way where you live?—There is nobody in the same house that works as I work; I do not associate with any; I am very glad to get into the shop and out again as quickly as I can.

Lord Monkswell.—Do your neighbours ever give you anything?—No; I have nothing to live on but what I work for.

But I suppose you help one another if you have had a good week?—No, nothing of that at all.

Earl of Crawford and Balcarres.—I take it from what you said that you manage to clear 1 s. a day by your work after providing your materials?—After the trimmings.

Then there is 2 s. for rent?—Yes.

Therefore all you have is 5 s. a week really to live upon?—Yes.

And out of that you have to pay firing, and your living?—Yes, firing and lights.

69. French and American seamstresses petition their governments

Not all working women submitted in silence to the starvation wages paid them for their needlework. Collective action by women—even those who worked alone at home—occurred spontaneously generations before effective

sources: (i) Records of the Comité du Travail du Gouvernement Provisionnel, C. 2233, Archives Nationales, Paris. The editors are grateful to Professor S. Joan

trade unions were organized. These two petitions, one from Paris during the Revolution of 1848 and one from Philadelphia during the American Civil War, exhibit certain similarities: in both cases, the women were unafraid to petition in person, signing their names and addresses; in both cases, women appealed to the government to right injustices visited on them by private contractors and businessmen; and in both cases, women claimed special consideration because they were mothers left alone to support themselves and their offspring in inflationary times of war and crisis.

(i) Parisian garment workers, August 1848

Gentlemen:

Please consider the request of some poor working women. The convents and the prisons take all our work away from us; they do it for such a low price that we can't compete with them. Almost all of us are mothers of families. We have our keep, our nourishment and our lodgings to pay for and we are not able to make enough money to cover these expenses. The employers also wrong us by sending their garment-making orders out of Paris; thus we can find no work and are nearly reduced to begging. Therefore, gentlemen, we urge you to put an end to these injustices. All we want is work.

We hope, Gentlemen, that you will be good enough to consider our request. We salute you with respect.

[Signed by seven women, with their addresses]

(ii) Philadelphia seamstresses, July 1862

We the undersigned formerly doing sewing for the United States Arsenal at Philadelphia most respectfully remonstrate against the action of Col. Crossman in taking the work from us and giving it to contractors who will not pay wages in which we can live—many of us have husbands, fathers, sons & brothers now in the army and from whom we derived our support. Deprived of that as we are our only mode of living was by sewing and we were able by unceasing exertions to barely live at the prices paid by the Arsenal. The Contractors who are speculators offer about fifty per cent of the prices paid heretofore by the arsenal—we respectfully ask your attention to our case. We have all given satisfaction in the work we have done. Then why should the government money be taken from the families of the poor to enrich the wealthy speculator without any gain to the government.

Very Resp^y Yours &c
Anna Long Widow 5 children 121 Mois St.
Louisa Bastian 124 Mirris St.
Mary Hamelton 1673 Front St. Husband at war

[Some 100 signatures followed these—many with the indication that the women were widows with children or had husbands or sons in the army.]

Moon, California State University, Sacramento, for making this document available to us. (ii) Petition addressed to Hon. Edwin M. Stanton, Secretary of War (received July 29, 1862), N.A.F. 6730 A, National Archives, Washington, D.C.

70. Industrial poisoning in a New York sweatshop: Almira ――――

The farm girls who migrated to the cities of America to find work often ended up in small shops and factories where industrial poisoning slowly destroyed their health. Almira, the fur-sewer in this 1887 case study, was the victim of arsenic poisoning. Born in the 1860's in the rocky New Hampshire farm country, Almira was orphaned at the age of seventeen, and the local doctor foreclosed on the farm she inherited to recover the money her family owed him. She was left alone with forty dollars and some old furniture, yet elated by the prospect of a new life in New York, the city of her dreams. After five years working as a fur-sewer in a New York sweatshop, Almira married her hometown beau, Leander, now a New York clerk. Although her work had ruined her sight and her health, she continued to work as a fur-sewer until shortly after Leander's death from consumption. The dying Leander begged Almira not to degrade herself by becoming a domestic servant, but widowed, penniless, and nearly blind at twenty-two, she could do no other work. Almira's experience was not unique to America: Agnes Hafferman of London (Doc. 68.iii) also suffered industrial poisoning.

All this time I hadn't thought much what I'd do. Forty dollars seemed a big lot, enough for weeks ahead. I'd done most everything about a house, an' I could make everything I wore. I had only to look at a pattern an' I could go home an' cut out one like it. The dress I had on was cheap stuff, but when I looked at other folks's I saw it wasn't so much out o' the way. So I said, most likely some dressmaker would take me, an' I'd try my luck that way. This was before I got to Boston, an' I went round there all the afternoon before it was time to take the train, for the conductor told me just what to do, an' I hadn't a mite of trouble. I never do going to a strange place. I was half a mind to stay in Boston when I saw the Common an' the crowds of folks. I sat still there an' just looked at 'em, an' cried again for joy to think I'd got where there were so many. "But there'll be more in New York," I said, "an' there'll be sure to be plenty ready to do a good turn." I could have hugged 'em all. I didn't think then the time would ever come that I'd hate the sight of faces an' wish myself on top of the hill in the cobble-stones, but it did, an' it does now sometimes.

I went on board the boat that night sort of crazy. I'd gone an' got some sandwiches an' things at a place the conductor told me, an' I sat on the deck in the moonlight an' ate my supper. I'd been too happy to eat before, an' I was so happy then I could hardly keep still. There was a girl not far off, a kind of nice-looking girl, an' she watched me, an' at last she began to talk. In half an hour I knew all about her an' she about me. She was a Rhode Island girl an' had worked in a mill near Providence, an' gone to New York at last an'

SOURCE: Helen Stuart Campbell, "One of the Fur Sewers," reprinted in *Prisoners of Poverty: Women Wage-Workers, Their Trades and Their Lives* (Boston, 1889), pp. 140–48. Originally published in the *New York Tribune* in 1887.

learned fur-sewing. She said it was a good trade, an' she made ten an' twelve dollars a week while the season lasted an' never less than five. This seemed a mint of money, an' when she said one of their old hands had died, an' she could take me right in as her friend an' teach me herself, I felt as if my fortune was made.

Well, I went with her next day. She had a room in Spring Street, near Hudson,—an old-fashioned house that belonged to two maiden sisters; an' I went in with her the first night, an' afterward for a while had the hall bedroom. It didn't take me long to learn. It was a Jew place an' there were thirty girls, but he treated us well. For my part I've fared just as well with Jews as ever I did with Christians, an' sometimes better. I'd taken to Hattie so that I couldn't bear to think of leaving her, an' so I let my dressmaking plan go. But I'll tell you what I found out in time. These skins are all dressed with arsenic. The dealers say there's nothing poisonous about them, but of course they lie. Every pelt has more or less in it, an' the girls show it just as the artificial-flower girls show it. Your eyelids get red an' the lids all puffy, an' you're white as chalk. The dealers say the red eyes come from the flying hairs. Perhaps they do, but the lids don't, an' every fur-sewer is poisoned a little with every prick of her needle. What the flying hair does is just to get into your throat an' nose and everywhere, an' tickle till you cough all the time, an' a girl with weak lungs hasn't a chance. The air is full of fur, an' then the work-room is kept tight shut for fear of moths getting in. The work is easy enough. It's just an everlasting patchwork, for you're always sewing together little bits, hundreds of them, that you have to match. You sew over an' over with linen thread, an' you're always piecing out an' altering shapes. It's nothing to sew up a thing when you've once got it pieced together. If it's beaver, all the long hairs must be picked out, an' it's the same with sealskin. We made up everything; sable an' Siberian squirrel, bear, fox, marten, mink, otter, an' all the rest. There were some girls very slow in learning that only got a dollar a week, an' in the end four, but most of them can average about five. I was seventeen when I began, an' in a year I had caught all the knack there is to it, an' was an expert, certain of ten dollars in the season an' about six in between. It's generally piece-work, with five or six months when you can earn ten or twelve dollars even, an' the rest of the time five or six dollars. In the busiest times there'd be fifty girls perhaps, but this was only for two or three months, an' then they discharged them. 'T isn't a trade I'd ever let a girl take up if I could help it; I suppose somebody's got to do it, but there ought to be higher wages for those that do.

This went on five years. I won't take time telling about Leander, but he'd got to be a clerk at Ridley's an' had eight hundred dollars a year, an' we'd been engaged for two years, an' just waiting to see if he wouldn't get another rise. I knew we could manage on that. Leander was more ambitious than me. He said we ought to live in a showy boarding-house an' make our money tell that way, but I told him I was used to the Spring Street house, an' we could have a whole floor an' be snug as could be an' Hattie board with us. He gave in, an' it's well he did; for we hadn't been married six months before he had a hemorrhage an' just went into quick consumption. I'd kept right on with my trade, but I was pulled down myself an' my eyelids so swollen sometimes I could hardly see out of 'em. But I got a sewing-machine from money I'd saved, an' I took in work from a place on Canal Street,—a good one, too, that always paid fair. The trouble was my eyes. I'd used 'em up, an' they got so I couldn't see the needle nor sew straight, an' had to give up the sewing, an' then I didn't know which way to turn, for there was Leander. The old folks were up there still, wrastling with the stones, but poorer every year, an' I couldn't get him up there. Leander was patient as a saint, but he fretted over me an' how I was to get along.

"You're not to worry," says I. "There's more ways than one of earning, an' if my eyes is bad, I've got two hands an' know how to use 'em. I'll take a place an' do housework if I can't do nothing else."

You'd never believe how the thought o' that weighed on him. He'd wake me up in the night to say, "Now, Almiry, jest give up that thought an' promise me you'll try something else. I think I'd turn in my grave if I had to know you was slavin' in anybody's kitchen."

"What's the odds?" I said. "You have to be under orders whatever you do. I think it won't be a bad change from the shop."

He took on so, though, that to quiet him I promised him I wouldn't do it unless I had to, an' 'twasn't long after that that he died. Between the doctor's bill—an' he was a kind man, I will say, an' didn't charge a tenth of what he had ought to—an' the funeral an' all, I was cleaned out of everything. I'd had to pawn a month before he died, an' was just stripped. Sewing was no good. My eyes went back on me like everything else, an' in a fortnight I knew there wasn't anything for it but getting a place. I left such things as I had in charge of the old ladies an' answered an advertisement for "a capable girl willing to work."

Well, it was a handsome house an' elegant things in the parlors an' bedrooms, but my heart sunk when she took me into the kitchen. The last girl had gone off in a rage an' left everything, an' there was grease and dirt from floor to ceiling. It was a deep basement, with one window an' a door opening right into the area with glass set in it, an' iron bars to both; but dirty to that degree you couldn't see three feet beyond; cockroaches walking round at their ease an' water-bugs so thick you didn't know where to lay anything.

"You'll have things quite your own way," the lady said, "for I never come into the kitchen. Bridget attends to upstairs, but you attend to fires and the meals and washing and ironing, and I expect punctuality and everything well done."

"At least it sounds independent," I thought, and I made up my mind to try it, for the wages were fifteen dollars a month, an' that with board seemed doing well. Bridget came down presently. She was seventeen an' a pretty girl rather, but she looked fit to drop, an' fell down in a chair.

"It's the bell," she said. "The comin' an' goin' here niver ceases, an' when 'tisn't the front door it's her own bell, an' she'll jingle it or holler up the tube in the middle o' the night if she takes a notion."

I wouldn't ask questions, for I thought I should find out soon enough, so I said I'd like to go up to my room a minute.

"It's our room you'll mane,' she said, "There's but the one, an' it's hard enough for two to be slapin' on a bed that's barely the width o' one."

My heart sunk then, for I'd always had a place that was comfortable all my life, but it sunk deeper when I went up there. A hall bedroom, with a single bed an' a small table, with a washbowl an' small pitcher, one chair an' some nails in the door for hanging things; that was all except a torn shade at the window. I looked at the bed. The two ragged comfortables were foul with long use. I thought of my nice bed down at Spring Street, my own good sheets an' blankets an' all, an' I began to cry.

"You don't look as if you was used to the likes of it," Bridget said. "There's another room the same as this but betther. Why not ax for it?"

I started down the stairs an' came right upon Mrs. Melrose, who smiled as if she thought I had been enjoying myself.

"I'm perfectly willing to try an' do your work as well as I know how," I said, "but I must have a place to myself an' clean things in it."

"Highty-tighty!" says she. "What impudence is this? You'll take what I give you and be thankful to get it. Plenty as good as you have slept in that room and never complained."

"Then it's time some one did," I said. "I don't ask anything but decency, an' if you can't give it I must try elsewhere."

"Then you'd better set about it at once," she says, an' with that I bid her good-afternoon an' walked out. I had another number in my pocket, an' I went straight there; an' this time I had sense enough to ask to see my room. It was bare enough, but clean. There were only three in the family, an' it was a little house on Perry Street. There I stayed two years. They were strange years. The folks were set in their ways an' they had some money. But every day of that time the lady cut off herself from the meat what she thought I ought to have, an' ordered me to put away the rest. She allowed no dessert except on Sunday, an' she kept cake and preserves locked in an upstairs closet. I wouldn't have minded that. What I did mind was that from the time I entered the house till I left it there was never a word for me beyond an order, any more than if I hadn't been a human being. She couldn't find fault. I was born clean, an' that house shone from top to bottom; but a dog would have got far more kindness than they gave me. At last I said I'd try a place where there were children an' maybe they'd like me. Mrs. Smith was dumb with surprise when I told her I must leave. "Leave!" she says. "We're perfectly satisfied. You're a very good girl, Almira." "It's the first time you've ever told me so," I says, "an' I think a change is best all round." She urged, but I was set, an' I went from there when the month was up.

Well, my eyes stayed bad for sewing, an' I must keep on at housework. I've been in seven places in six years. I could have stayed in every one, an' about every one I could tell you things that make it plain enough why a self-respecting girl would rather try something else. I don't talk or think nonsense about wanting to be one of the family. I don't. I'd much rather keep to myself. But out of these seven places there was just one in which the mistress seemed to think I was a human being with something in me the same as in her. I've been underfed an' worked half to death in two of the houses. The mistress expected just so much, an' if it failed she stormed an' went on an' said I was a shirk an' good for nothing an' all that. There was only one of them that had a decently comfortable room or that thought to give me a chance at a book or paper now an' then. As long as I had a trade I was certain of my evenings an' my Sundays. Now I'm never certain of anything. I'm not a shirk. I'm quick an' smart, an' I know I turn off work. In ten hours I earn more than I ever get. But I begin my day at six an' in summer at five, an' it's never done before ten an' sometimes later. This place I'm in now seems to have some kind of fairness about it, an' Mrs. Henshaw said yesterday, "You can't tell the comfort it is to me, Almira, to have some one in the house I can trust. I hope you will be comfortable an' happy enough to stay with us." "I'll stay till you tell me to go," I says, an' I meant it.

71. The daily cares of Victorian writers

Even the most successful women authors of the nineteenth century found it difficult to reconcile the demands of their craft with the "small Lilliputian arrows of peddling cares" inherent in daily life. These selections from the writings of two of the best-known writers of the Victorian period give some sense of the obstacles that confronted the would-be author.

Elizabeth Gaskell (1810–65; Doc. 6.ii), the English novelist from whose letters the first selection is taken, was the mother of five children; indeed, she turned to writing to seek solace after the death of her only son, William. Her letters suggest that the claims of motherhood, although she wants to make them compatible with the demands of art—and insists that they can be so made—created difficulties and conflicts. Although Gaskell's letters imply that her work functioned chiefly as a "refuge," the proceeds from her novels in fact supplemented the modest income of her husband, a Unitarian minister.

Like Gaskell, Louisa May Alcott (1832–88), the celebrated New England author, was well acquainted with the interferences and distractions that plagued the writer. A spinster, Alcott became in turn teacher, nurse, seamstress, washerwoman, and servant, and finally an author, all in an effort to earn money to support her parents and sisters. Alcott's journal, from whose pages the second selection is taken, conveys a sense of the many interruptions suffered by the writer; it also suggests her pride in the independence she gained from money earned by her literary efforts.

SOURCES: (i) *The Letters of Elizabeth Gaskell*, ed. J. A. V. Chapple and Arthur Pollard (Cambridge, Mass., 1967), pp. 106–7, 693–96. (ii) *Louisa May Alcott: Her Life, Letters, and Journals*, ed. Ednah D. Cheney (Boston, 1889), pp. 266–75.

(i) Elizabeth Gaskell

[The first of the Gaskell selections consists of excerpts from a letter written to her good friend Eliza Fox in February 1850. The addressee of the second letter, dated Sept. 25, 1862, is unknown.]

One thing is pretty clear, Women must give up living an artist's life, if home duties are to be paramount. It is different with men, whose home duties are so small a part of their life. However we are talking of women. I am sure it is healthy for them to have the refuge of the hidden world of Art to shelter themselves in when too much pressed upon by daily small Lilliputian arrows of peddling cares; it keeps them from being morbid as you say; and takes them into the land where King Arthur lies hidden, and soothes them with its peace. I have felt this in writing, I see others feel it in music, you in painting, so assuredly a blending of the two is desirable. (Home duties and the development of the Individual I mean), which you will say it takes no Solomon to tell you but the difficulty is where and when to make one set of duties subserve and give place to the other. I have no doubt that the cultivation of each tends to keep the other in a healthy state,—my grammar is all at sixes and sevens I have no doubt but never mind if you can pick out my meaning. I think a great deal of what you have said.

Thursday.—I've been reading over yr note, and believe I've only been repeating in different language what you said. If Self is to be the end of exertions, those exertions are unholy, there is no doubt of *that*—and that is part of the danger in cultivating the Individual Life; but I do believe we have all some appointed work to do, whh no one else can do so well; Wh. is *our* work; what *we* have to do in advancing the Kingdom of God; and that first we must find out what we are sent into the world to do, and define it and make it clear to ourselves, (that's *the* hard part) and then forget ourselves in our work, and our work in the End we ought to strive to bring about. I never can either talk or write clearly so I'll ee'n leave it alone.

My dear Madam,

I have received your letter at this out of the way place, (where I shall not remain much longer, so *Plymouth Grove, Manchester* will be your best address, if you have to write again.) Your MSS has not been forwarded to me along with your letter; so at present I have no opportunity of judging of it's merits; when I have read it I will give you the best & truest opinion I can. I feel very sorry for you, for I think I can see that, at present, at least you are rather overwhelmed with all you have to do; and I think it possible that the birth of two children,—one so close upon another may have weakened you bodily, and made you more unfit to cope with your many household duties. Try—even while waiting for my next letter, to strengthen yourself by every means in your power; by being very careful as to your diet; by cold-bathing, by resolute dwelling on the cheerful side of everything; and by learning to œconomize strength as much as possible in all your household labours; for I dare say you already know how much time may be saved, by beginning any kind of work in good time, and not driving all in a hurry to the last moment. I hope (for instance,) you soap & soak your dirty clothes well for some hours before beginning to wash; and that you understand the comfort of preparing a dinner & putting it on to cook *slowly*, early in the morning, as well as having *always* some kind of sewing ready arranged to your hand, so that you can take it up at any odd minute and do a few stitches. I dare say at present it might be difficult for you to procure the sum that {may} is necessary to purchase a sewing machine; and indeed, unless you are a good workwoman to begin with, you will find a machine difficult to manage. But *try*, my dear, to con-quer your 'clumsiness' in sewing; there are thousand little bits of work, which no sempstress ever does so well as the wife or mother who knows how the comfort of those she loves depends on little pecularities which no one but she cares enough for the wearers to attend to. My first piece of advice to you would be *Get strong*—I am almost sure you are out of bodily health and that, if I were you, I would make it my first object to attain. Did you ever try a tea-cup full of *hop-tea* the first thing in the morning? It is a very simple tonic, and could do no harm. Then again try *hard* to arrange your work well. That is a regular piece of headwork and taxes a woman's powers of organization; but the reward is immediate and great. I have known well what it is to be both wanting money, & feeling weak in body and entirely disheartened. I do not think I ever cared for literary fame; nor do I think it *is* a thing that ought to be cared for. It comes and it goes. The exercise of a talent or power *is* always a great plea-sure; but one should weigh well whether this pleasure may not be obtained by the sacrifice of some duty. When I had *little* children I do not think I could have written stories, because I should have become too much absorbed in my *fictitious* people to attend to my *real* ones. I think you would be sorry if you began to feel that your desire to earn money, even for so laudable an object as to help your husband, made you unable to give your tender sym-pathy to your little ones in their small joys & sorrows; and yet, don't you know how you,—how every one, who tries to write stories *must* become absorbed in them, (fictitious though they be,) if they are to interest their readers in them. Besides viewing the subject from a solely artistic point of view a good writer of fiction must have *lived* an active & sympathetic life if she wishes her books to have strength & vitality in them. When you are forty, and if you have a gift for being an authoress you will write ten times as good a novel as you could do now, just because you will have gone through so much more of the interests of a wife and a mother.

All this does not help you over present difficulties, does it? Well then let us try what will—How much have you in your own power? How much must you submit to because it is God's appointment? You have it in your own power to arrange your day's work to the very best of your ability, making the various household arts into real studies (& there is plenty of poetry and asso-ciation about them—remember how the Greek princesses in Homer washed the clothes &c &c &c &c.) You would perhaps find a little book called The

Finchley Manual of Needlework of real use to you in sewing; it gives patterns and directions &c. Your want of strength may be remedied *possibly* by care & attention; if not, you must submit to what is God's ordinance; only remember that the very hardest day's bodily work I have ever done has never produced anything like the intense exhaustion I have felt after writing the "best" parts of my books.

All this letter is I fear disheartening enough: you must remember I have not seen your MSS as yet; & I can only judge of it from such a number of MSS sent me from time to time; and only *one* of these writers has ever succeeded in getting her writings published, though in several instances I have used my best endeavours on their behalf.

Have you no sister or relation who could come & help you for a little while till you get stronger,—no older friend at hand who would help you to plan your work so that it should oppress you as little as possible? If this letter has been of *any* use to you, do not scruple to write to me again, if I can give you help. I may not always be able to answer you as soon as I do now, for at home my life is very very much occupied, but I will always *try* & do so. And do my dear, always remember to ask God for light and help—for with Him all things are possible—and it almost astonishes one sometimes to find how He sends down answers to one's prayers in new bright thoughts, or in even more bright & lovely peace.

Your sincere though unknown friend,
E. C. Gaskell

(ii) Louisa May Alcott

August 1872.—May goes to Clark's Island for rest, having kept hotel long enough. I say "No," and shut the door. People *must* learn that authors have some rights; I can't entertain a dozen a day, and write the tales they demand also. I'm but a human worm, and when walked on must turn in self-defence.

Reporters sit on the wall and take notes; artists sketch me as I pick pears in the garden; and strange women interview Johnny as he plays in the orchard.*

It looks like impertinent curiosity to me; but it is called "fame," and considered a blessing to be grateful for, I find. Let 'em try it. . . .

October.—Went to a room in Allston Street, in a quiet, old-fashioned house. I can't work at home, and need to be alone to spin, like a spider. . . .

November.—Forty on the 29th. Got Father off for the West, all neat and comfortable. I enjoyed every penny spent, and had a happy time packing his new trunk with warm flannels, neat shirts, gloves, etc., and seeing the dear man go off in a new suit, overcoat, hat, and all, like a gentleman. We both laughed over the pathetic old times with tears in our eyes, and I reminded him of the "poor as poverty, but serene as heaven" saying.

Something to do came just as I was trying to see what to take up, for

---

* May and Nan (Anna), mentioned below, were Alcott's sisters; Johnny was her nephew.—EDS.

work is my salvation. H. W. Beecher sent one of the editors of the "Christian Union" to ask for a serial story. They have asked before, and offered $2,000, which I refused; now they offered $3,000, and I accepted.

Got out the old manuscript of "Success," and called it "Work." Fired up the engine, and plunged into a vortex, with many doubts about getting out. Can't work slowly; the thing possesses me, and I must obey till it's done. One thousand dollars was sent as a seal on the bargain, so I was bound, and sat at the oar like a galley-slave.

F. wanted eight little tales, and offered $35 apiece; used to pay $10. Such is fame! At odd minutes I wrote the short ones, and so paid my own expenses. "Shawl Straps," Scrap-Bag, No. 2, came out, and went well.

Great Boston fire; up all night. Very splendid and terrible sight.

December.—Busy with "Work." Write three pages at once on impression paper, as Beecher, Roberts, and Low of London all want copy at once.

[This was the cause of the paralysis of my thumb, which disabled me for the rest of my life.—L. M. A.]

Nan and the boys came to visit me, and break up the winter. Rested a little, and played with them. . . .

January 1873.—Getting on well with "Work;" have to go slowly now for fear of a break-down. All well at home.

A week at Newport with Miss Jane Stewart. Dinners, balls, calls, etc. Saw Higginson and "H. H." Soon tired of gayety, and glad to get home to my quiet den and pen.

Roberts Brothers paid me $2,022 for books. S. E. S. invested most of it, with the $1,000 F. sent. Gave C. M. $100,—a thank-offering for my success. I like to help the class of "silent poor" to which we belonged for so many years,—needy, but respectable, and forgotten because too proud to beg. Work difficult to find for such people, and life made very hard for want of a little money to ease the necessary needs.

February and March.—Anna very ill with pneumonia; home to nurse her. Father telegraphed to come home, as we thought her dying. She gave me her boys; but the dear saint got well, and kept the lads for herself. Thank God!

Back to my work with what wits nursing left me.

Had Johnny for a week, to keep all quiet at home. Enjoyed the sweet little soul very much, and sent him back much better.

Finished "Work,"—twenty chapters. Not what it should be,—too many interruptions. Should like to do one book in peace, and see if it wouldn't be good.

April.—The job being done I went home to take May's place. Gave her $1,000, and sent her to London for a year of study. She sailed on the 26th, brave and happy and hopeful. I felt that she needed it, and was glad to be able to help her.

I spent seven months in Boston; wrote a book and ten tales; earned $3,250 by my pen, and am satisfied with my winter's work.

May.—D. F. wanted a dozen little tales, and agreed to pay $50 apiece, if I give up other things for this. Said I would, as I can do two a day, and keep house between times. Cleaned and grubbed, and didn't mind the change. Let head rest, and heels and feet do the work.

Cold and dull; but the thought of May free and happy was my comfort as I messed about.

June and July.—Settled the servant question by getting a neat American woman to cook and help me with the housework.

Peace fell upon our troubled souls, and all went well. Good meals, tidy house, cheerful service, and in the P. M. an intelligent young person to read and sew with us. . . .

January 1874.—Mother quite ill this month. Dr. Wesselhoeft does his best for the poor old body, now such a burden to her. The slow decline has begun, and she knows it, having nursed her mother to the same end.

Father disappointed and rather sad, to be left out of so much that he would enjoy and should be asked to help and adorn. A little more money, a pleasant house and time to attend to it, and I'd bring all the best people to see and entertain *him*. When I see so much twaddle going on I wonder those who can don't get up something better, and have really good things.

When I had the youth I had no money; now I have the money I have no time; and when I get the time, if I ever do, I shall have no health to enjoy life. I suppose it's the discipline I need; but it's rather hard to love the things I do and see them go by because duty chains me to my galley. If I come into port at last with all sail set that will be reward perhaps.

Life always was a puzzle to me, and gets more mysterious as I go on. I shall find it out by and by and see that it's all right, if I can only keep brave and patient to the end. . . .

October.—Took two nice rooms at the Hotel Bellevue for the winter; May to use one for her classes. Tried to work on my book, but was in such pain could not do much. Got no sleep without morphine. Tried old Dr. Hewett, who was sure he could cure the woe. . . .

November.—Funny time with the publishers about the tale; for all wanted it at once, and each tried to outbid the other for an unwritten story. I rather enjoyed it, and felt important with Roberts, Low, and Scribner all clamoring for my "'umble" works. No peddling poor little manuscripts now, and feeling rich with $10. The golden goose can sell her eggs for a good price, if she isn't killed by too much driving.

December.—Better and busier than last month.

All well at home, and Father happy among his kind Westerners. Finish "Eight Cousins," and get ready to do the temperance tale, for F. offers $700 for six chapters,—"Silver Pitchers."

January 1875.— . . . Father flourishing about the Western cities, "riding in Louisa's chariot, and adored as the grandfather of 'Little Women,'" he says.

February.—Finish my tale and go to Vassar College on a visit. See M. M., talk with four hundred girls, write in stacks of albums and school-books, and kiss every one who asks me. Go to New York; am rather lionized, and run away; but things look rather jolly, and I may try a winter there some time, as I need a change and new ideas.

72. The trials of an English governess: Nelly Weeton Stock

Nelly Weeton Stock (1776–?1844) began work at the age of twelve, as-sisting her widowed mother in running a school. After her mother's death she decided to abandon the school for governessing, hoping thereby to be of financial help to her ne'er-do-well brother, whom she adored. The following excerpts from her letters and journal give a sense of her experiences as a governess, first with the family of Edward Pedder, for whom she worked from 1809 to 1811, and then from 1812 to 1814 with the family of Joseph Armitage. In September 1814, on the advice of her brother, she married Aaron Stock, a man whom she had known only a week (and who had bribed her brother £100 to press his case). Bullied, beaten, and imprisoned in the course of their marriage, she left him at last but could never obtain custody of her only child, Mary.

[Nellie Weeton to her brother, Dec. 9, 1809]
Never was I so anxious to hear from you, my dear Tom, as I have been the whole of this week. I begun to fear your letter would not arrive than after my departure from Liverpool, which event I expect to take place next Tues-day; and I wished to hear, that I might answer before I left, and inform you of the cause of my journey. I am going to be as companion to a Mrs. Pedder, about six miles beyond Kendal, somewhere bordering, or not far from the Lakes. Mr. Pedder (of whose family, near Preston, I have frequently heard you and my mother speak) has lately married a servant girl. He has taken her into retirement for a few years, until she becomes a little better fitted for the society he wishes hereafter to introduce her to, and has taken a little girl of eleven years old (by a former wife, I suppose), from school, intending to have her educated at home. . . .

I was, with Miss Winkley, drinking tea at a Mr. Nevett's, a bookseller in Castle Street, one evening a month or five weeks ago. A little before we left, Mrs. Winkley came to accompany us home, and said she had just seen a Newspaper in the shop; and informing us what she had been reading, acci-dently mentioned an advertisement for a Governess.
[Here is the advertisement, which she had clipped and enclosed:]

> WANTED, in the neighbourhood of Kendal, a GOVERNESS
> to superintend the Education of a Young Lady. None need
> apply but such as can give good references as to ability and
> character.—Apply to J. Gore.
> GORE'S General Advertiser. Liverpool. (Thursday).
> November 9, 1809.

. . . In a few days after I had written to you, an elderly gentleman called at Mrs. Winkley's shop, enquiring for me. She brought him down to the house. He had called in consequence of my application, he said, to Mr. Montgomery, with whom he was intimately acquainted. His name was Barton.

SOURCE: *Miss Weeton, Journal of a Governess*, ed. Edward Hall, 2 vols. (London, 1936–39), 1: 200–224 *passim*, 301–19 *passim*; 2 (reprint ed. New York, 1969): 57–62.

He lived at Walton, near Preston, and Mr. Pedder had requested him to insert the Advertisement in a Liverpool paper. He related several circumstances respecting the family he wished to engage me for; said I should be treated as an equal by them, more as a companion to Mrs. Pedder than as governess to Miss P., to assist her in regulating the management of a family such as Mr. P. wishes his to be. He enquired what salary I should expect. I answered, thirty guineas. He engaged me, and—I am going.

[Nellie Weeton to her friend Bessy Winkley, Dec. 28, 1809. She begins by describing her first evening at the Pedders' Home, Dove's Nest.]

Mr. and Mrs. Pedder were seated at their wine after dinner, Mrs. P. dressed in a pink muslin, with a very becoming head dress of the same. At supper we had two servants in livery attending, and some display of plate, silver nutcrackers, &c., and some things of which poor ignorant I knew not the use. I felt a little awkward, but as you may suppose, strove not to let it appear. I now feel much more at home, and quite comfortable. For more than a week I was far otherwise, not knowing exactly what was expected from me. I am now better acquainted with the task I have undertaken, and find it both an easy and agreeable one. Mr. and Mrs. Pedder treat me in a most pleasing, flattering manner. So far from making me feel any dependance, I am treated with so much deference, that I must endeavour to be cautious lest I thoughtlessly assume too much. Mr. P. is very good tempered in general, a little passionate sometimes. Mrs. P. is a most sweet tempered woman, and of a disposition upright and amiable in the extreme. I have had some instances of it that have delighted and astonished me. I am fortunate to have such an one under my care, for she is my pupil as well as Miss Pedder. The latter is not a pleasing child; far otherwise. Her fits, I think, have an effect upon her disposition. She has them very frequently, sometimes five in a day; seldom a whole day without. I don't feel so much alarmed with them as I expected. I have frequently to hold her in them. They seldom last five minutes.

I have to attend to the direction of the House, the table, &c., as well as literary studies; to assist in entertaining company in the parlour; and give directions to the servants. I am studying the art of carving, and learning, as far as books will teach me, as well as giving instructions. Mr. P. has a most excellent library.

Mrs. Pedder was a dairy maid at Darwen-Bank, Mr. P's house near Preston, when he fell in love with her. Her father heard of the connexion and fearing his daughter might be seduced, sent for her home. He lives near-by here. Mr. P. followed her, took her off to Gretna Green and married her. They lived some time at Darwen-Bank, and then took this house, where he intends to live retired than his wife (every way worthy her present rank, in my opinion), is fit to appear in the presence of his relations; and her improvement is so rapid, her application so close, and her disposition and understanding so superior, that a little time will make her all he wishes. He is a lucky fellow to have hit upon such an one. She is not eighteen yet. She expresses herself as much pleased with me, and satisfied with my attentions; and Mr. Barton told me, Mr. Pedder did the same.—How gratifying!

[Nellie Weeton's journal entry for Jan. 26, 1810]

The comforts of which I have deprived myself in coming here, and the vexations that occur sometimes during the hours of instruction with a child of such a strange temper to instruct, would almost induce me to give up my present situation, did not the consideration which brought me here, still retain me. O Brother! sometime thou wilt know perhaps the deprivations I have undergone for thy sake, and that thy attentions have not been such as to compensate them. For thy sake I have wanted food and fire, and have gone about in rags; have spent the flower of my youth in obscurity, deserted, and neglected; and now, when God has blessed me with a competence, have given up its comforts to promote thy interest in the world. Should I fail in this desire, should I not succeed!—what will recompense me?—God perhaps will bless me for the thought that was in my heart; and if I am rewarded in heaven—I am rewarded indeed! I will be patient—I will be resigned, and —with the help of the Power around me, I will persevere.

[Nellie Weeton to her brother, Sept. 15, 1810. Mr. Pedder's child was killed in a fire, but Weeton was asked to stay on as companion to Mrs. Pedder. The situation soon became intolerable, owing to Mr. Pedder's ungovernable temper.]

I am scarcely permitted either to speak or stir in his presence; nor ever to maintain any opinion different to his own. When in a violent passion (which is but too frequent), on the most trifling occasions he will sometimes beat and turn his wife out of doors. Twice she has run away to her father's—oh! brother, and then, such a house! Mr. P. roaring drunk and swearing horridly, and making all the men about the house drunk. I have thought at such times, I really could not bear to stay any longer, particularly when he has been in his violent passions with me, which has occurred six or seven times. As he at one time found fault with almost everything I did, I have ceased to do anything I am not asked to do. The consequence is, I have almost all my time to myself, as I do little else than sew for Mr. and Mrs. P. Mr. P. will have Mrs. P. take such an active part in the house, that she has little time for my instruction; and as my assistance in domestic concerns has not been required for 3 or 4 months back, I sit a great deal alone, chiefly employed at my needle. Whether Mr. P. means to keep me thus idle, or to dismiss me, I know not. Mrs. P's gentle and kind treatment of me makes me very comfortable, for in general, I see little of Mr. P. except at dinner.

[Nellie Weeton to her brother, Dec. 28, 1810]

How often do I wish that I could see you for a few weeks. I could tell you much that would exceed the limits of a letter—perhaps when Mr. and Mrs. P. go to Preston in the Spring, I may get a seat with them as far as there, if they go in a chaise—not that I think there is any chance of it either, for they always take such a load of luggage with them, when they go from home— perhaps I may come soon enough, for Mr. P., when he is in one of his violent fits of passion, often threatens to turn me out; so he does with his wife, or the servants. I am not worse treated than others; often better; but still I feel very uncomfortable when he talks in such a style. Were any person a spectator or a hearer when he goes on in such a manner, and were that person my bitterest enemy, still, if they spoke as their conscience dictates, I am certain they must say that there was scarcely the shadow of an error in my conduct, when I am so found fault with.

He will sometimes, as we sit after dinner, introduce some observations on Politics, History, Geography, and still more frequently on other subjects, almost too trifling to entertain *even a woman*. His memory is rather treacherous, and if I should unfortunately hold a different opinion to his, or appear to discover any incorrectness in his statement of facts or incidents, he does not forget it for the remainder of that day; and after he has stormed at me in the parlour, will walk into the kitchen and tell the servants that "Miss Weeton may appear to know more than he, but!—he knows better!" Which sound argument is enforced by a flourish of the arm, and a thwack with the thumb and middle finger.

If I listen to him in a kind of submissive silence, not venturing to speak lest I should give offence, he will attack me in high style for disrespect and ill-behaviour in not conversing with him; in short, in some humours, there is no pleasing him, and these humours will often hold for a week or a fortnight at once without intermission—if no visitors arrive; for then, whilst they stay, he is exactly the opposite character to what I have been describing; you would be astonished to see him act two parts so different. When any acquaintance is here, he treats me with a degree of deference and respect too much for him to offer, or me to receive, my situation considered.

[Nellie Weeton to Bessy Winkley Price, c. July 1812. Weeton had just become governess to the children of Joseph Armitage of High Royd, near Huddersfield.]

He and his wife are young people, not 30 yet, I dare say, either of them. Mr. A. is engaged in the woollen trade, has a handsome fortune of his own, and had another with his wife, though their parents are all living; at whose death, I suppose, they will have considerably more. They have no carriage, no in-door man-servant; there are four women servants. They kept a man till lately, but as Mr. Armitage's house at Lockwood was one of the first that was attacked by the Luddites a few months ago, he has not ventured since to keep a man in his house, as many gentlemen have been betrayed by their servants, who have been discovered to be of the Luddite party.* Mr. A. has but lately come to this house; he had only just got well settled in it, when I arrived. His father had long wanted him to come to it, but his wife and he objected to so very retired a situation. However, the affair at Lockwood (3 miles distant), and the threats of his father to leave the estate out of the family if he did not come to it now, induced him to comply; the house and lands, all together, are a very pretty present from the old gentleman; but

---

* The Luddites were workers who protested against industrialization and unemployment by breaking machines and rioting.—EDS.

the situation is too retired for a young man who has any relish for society. There has been a good deal of company since I came; but, though I dine or drink tea with them, I am obliged to leave the room so immediately after I have swallowed it, that I may truly be said to see little of them.

My time is totally taken up with the children; from 7 o'clock in the morning, till half past 7, or 8 at night. I cannot lie any longer than 6 o'clock in a morning; and, if I have anything to do for myself, in sewing, writing, &c., I must rise sooner. At 7, I go into the nursery, to hear the children their prayers, and remain with them till after they have breakfasted, when I go out with them whilst they play; and am often so cold, that I join in their sports, to warm myself. About half past 8, I breakfast with Mr. & Mrs. Armitage, and then return again to the children till 9, when we go into the school-room till 12. We then bustle on our bonnets, &c., for play, or a short walk. At One, we bustle them off again, to dress for dinner, to which we sit down at a quarter past; the children always dine with their parents. By the time dinner is well over, it is 2 o'clock, when we go into school, and remain till 5. Whilst I am at tea in the parlour, the children eat their suppers in the nursery. I then go to them, and remain with them till 7, either walking out of doors, or playing within, as the weather may permit. I then hear their prayers, and see them washed; at half past 7, they are generally in bed.

Mrs. Armitage conducts her house in so excellent a manner, that we are as punctual as the clock. I never have to wait of any one; and I take care that no one shall have to wait of me. It is the same with all in the house; break-fast, dinner, tea, or supper, are always within five minutes of the appointed time. The only thing I feel inclined to grumble at, is the being obliged to attend the children at their play in a morning, as they are only in the yard. I should voluntarily choose to do it sometimes, but the nursery maid, I should think, would be sufficient in general; however, I get a little air, and it will render me less subject to take colds; it will do me good, though I don't like it.

The children, though well ordered by their parents, when out of their sight are as unruly, noisy, insolent, quarrelsome, and ill-tempered a set, as I ever met with. I am beginning to get them to pay some respect to my man-dates, and perhaps by and bye, I may to my requests; but I assure you, I have had, and still have, a tough task to perform; and if Mr. & Mrs. Armitage had not given me every authority, in the most liberal manner, I must have de-spaired of doing any good. A few days ago, I felt a necessity of proceeding to some very severe methods; certain, almost, at the same time, I should meet the displeasure of Mr. & Mrs. A. in consequence, when they came to be informed; but how great was my satisfaction, when they expressed their approbation of the method and severity of punishment which I had inflicted. It has given me spirits to proceed with tenfold more confidence, and a greater desire to please them, than before. The little creatures are very affectionate to me already; and of the three younger ones, I think I can make something. Miss A., the eldest, is the bad sheep that infects the flock: punishment or reward make no lasting impression; I fear she is naturally depraved. Though 7 years of age, she has no ideas of common modesty; it is a wrong thing in parents to inure children to be stript entirely in the nursery, whilst washing. I am endeavouring to correct this, by degrees, as no innovation must be made suddenly that affects the mistress of the house or the servants.

I have begun to teach the children to dance; and a sweet boy of 5 years old, to write; and he does both, admirably. Their instruction, and sewing for Mrs. A., keep me very busy the whole of school-time; I begin again to know the value of minutes, and to be very careful to waste none of them.

[Nellie Weeton to her friend Mrs. Dodson, Aug. 18, 1812]

You don't know how much you are indebted for this scrawl; it has been almost the work of a week, my leisure moments are so very limited.

The children appear to have been allowed full liberty to a riotous degree; yet Mrs. A. seems to expect that I shall now, speedily, bring them into the exactest order . . . the task is a most arduous one! The eldest, a girl, is of that strange kind of temper, that she will purposely do the very thing that she thinks will excite most displeasure. I often wish that I could exchange her for one of yours. Of this girl, I shall never reap any credit, I fear; but the 2d, a boy, not six yet, will evince to his friends whether or no I possess any talents in the education of children. He is a fine little fellow, and understands, with great quickness, every thing I attempt to teach him. I have begun to instruct him in writing, and the elements of grammar and arithmetic; and they all learn to dance. I have four under my care.

Mr. and Mrs. A. are pleasant and easy in their temper and manners, and make my situation as comfortable as such a one can be; for it is rather an awkward one for a female of any reflection or feeling. A *governess* is almost shut out of society; not choosing to associate with servants, and not being treated as an equal by the heads of the house or their visiters, she must possess some fortitude and strength of mind to render herself tranquil or happy; but indeed, the master or mistress of a house, if they have any goodness of heart, would take pains to prevent her feeling her inferiority. For my own part, I have no cause of just complaint; but I know some that are treated in a most mortifying manner.

73. A French domestic recalls her family's years in service: Elise Blanc

The child of a family of servants at the château Prévange in the Bourbonnais, Elise Blanc (b. 1850's) was born and raised in central France. She never married but spent her adult years as a chambermaid, working first

SOURCE: "Madame Elise Blanc," in *Paysans par eux-mêmes*, ed. Emile Guillaumin (Paris, 1953), pp. 262–70. The editors are grateful to Nancy Fitch, University of California, Los Angeles, for calling our attention to this document.

*at the chateau and then accompanying the daughter of the household when
she married and moved away. The experiences Blanc describes in her memoirs
took place between 1860 and 1880. Her account offers a glimpse into the
twilight of a benevolent patriarchal mode of aristocratic French life, where
the privileges of rank were rarely questioned, but where the concept of mutual
obligation was also clearly understood by both the privileged and their
retainers.*

When I was seventeen, Madame la Marquise engaged me as a chambermaid. My parents made a great sacrifice in order to please their masters, for
there was plenty of work to be done at our house. Like my sister, I earned
20 francs per month plus keep: I was not well paid. Soon we left for Paris,
for —— rue de la Pompe, in Passy, where our *châtelains* kept an apartment.
How many letters and packages my father sent to this address!

The eldest of the *demoiselles* had just married M. de F—, who was an
officer stationed at Compiègne. My sister Antoinette had to accompany the
young household.

But it happened that I accompanied Madame to Compiègne for a while.
Then Antoinette and I wrote to our parents that we were together and in
good health.

It was Antoine [her younger brother] who wrote back. He told us the
news of the region and as always had something funny to say. [One] time he
wrote that he had been chosen as godfather for a newborn in the neighborhood. All three, with Papa and Mama, had attended the baptismal feast. For
this child, as for many others, my mother had served as midwife. She was an
expert in these things, and in spite of her many occupations, she was always
glad to be of service to the neighbor women.

It was she who was in charge of the chateau's poultry-yard. Sometimes
there were as many as sixty little white ducklings. There were also white and
black swans, Egyptian geese, and peacocks, whose young are very difficult to
raise.

My parents only received a very modest salary for their services, which
did not permit them to save much. Even so, there were some people who
were jealous of them; they were considered to be on too good terms with the
masters. They didn't worry much about that, though, in this case heeding
the advice given by the curate from his pulpit: "Let others say what they
will."

Their great joy was to see us all reunited. During our free hours on Sundays, we all played *boules;** even Mama took part. When there was a celebration in the area we would go for a while, escorted by my father. Despite
gray hair, he never missed a chance to try his luck at various games of chance;
frequently he was successful, and we would return home loaded down with
glasses, bowls, saucers, little vases, etc.

On occasion M. le Marquis watched us leave. My sister and I were coiffed

* Lawn bowling, a traditional French game.—EDS.

with little bonnets covered with lace and ribbons. One day he called out to the ladies, asking them to add a little flower to the bonnets of Toinette and Lisette: it was a cluster of Easter daisies, which was, I wager, very becoming.

We never stayed overnight at the chateau; our parents wouldn't have allowed it. And then, we had to return on time for church.

The illness of M. le Marquis, which we had always insisted was imaginary, became increasingly worse. This made him nervous and difficult. He wanted to go to Compiègne for the confinement of his daughter, Mme de F— and to take me along. I took advantage of this occasion to ask him, through my father, for a small raise. He refused. Both sides stubbornly refused to give in. As a result, I left the chateau and remained home for three years, where I was a great help to my parents.

During this period M. le Marquis died from his terrible malady, after suffering a great deal himself and greatly worrying the members of his family. Of the girls who succeeded me, none stayed long or were really satisfactory.

When my sister Antoinette got married they asked me to come back and offered me wages double those I had gotten before. I didn't think I could refuse.

On November 18 . . . my sister married a young man from the region, Jean D—. One hundred and twenty people came to the wedding, which was very animated and gay. All our masters attended. One of their cousins who was a member of the clergy officiated and gave a very nice speech. But my poor mother kept repeating: "If Lise gets married, I will never agree to invite so many people; it's really too much trouble . . ."

After their marriage the newlyweds entered the service of M. and Mme V. in our same town. On Sunday they came to spend some time at our house. . . .

Our grandmother, who had become senile, gave us a good deal of trouble. She stayed that way for several years more and finally succumbed after much suffering. Our Aunt Lise, who had been the cook at the chateau for many years, was, in her turn, cruelly afflicted by a general paralysis. Mama had to be with her a great deal in order to watch over her, and naturally her household work suffered a good deal. Sometimes Aunt Lise would send the maid over to get Mama at night, imagining that her mere presence would suffice to ease the suffering.

This state of affairs lasted a number of years. The ladies [of the chateau] gave her food and lodging along with a pension. She certainly would not have held on so long if she hadn't had this comfort, attentive care, and good nourishment. . . .

In the third year of their marriage, my sister and brother-in-law had a big baby boy whom they also called Antoine. My sister had a difficult childbirth. She was so weak afterward that she could not stand any noise, and we had to stop the clock whose ticking disturbed her too much. The child, who never stopped crying, was taken care of by Mama in another room.

Finally Antoinette recovered and the little one stopped crying long enough to grow steadily. . . . Later, the young couple returned to service at the Vs. . . . Each Sunday they came to our house to see their son. The child, who was large and vigorous, was very healthy and Mama cared for him lovingly. She would respond to his smallest desire, give him his bottle, and during the day she would take him for walks, give him baths, etc. The young parents were not able to enjoy seeing their baby make so much progress from one week to the next. They were worried about our brother Antoine's state, because he was visibly in decline. They could see it much better than my parents and I, who saw him every day. . . .

I was at Passy with the family when I received a message telling me that things were very bad for my brother. I left right away, fearing to find nothing but a corpse. But I had the joy of seeing him still alive, the unhappiness of being with him during his last moments, which were very calm.

Soon thereafter my sister was obliged to return home, for the doctor had forbidden her to continue her occupation as a cook. Her husband also left the service of the Vs . . . and came on as a gardener for Mme la Marquise.

Even so, this was the end of our gaiety and joyous celebrations. Meanwhile my nephew, little Antoine, became more and more interesting and amused us greatly. But he was suddenly struck by convulsions. How afraid we all were! Luckily, this was only a bad incident; he recovered and never had them again.

When his parents were installed as gardeners at the chateau, they took him with them. But every morning his grandfather could be seen hastening to bring him a bowl of fresh milk. When Mme la Marquise saw this scene from her window, she never forgot to call me. She knew that I loved Toinon, as she called him, very much, and that I was not the only one to spoil him. . . .

In spite of their age, my parents continued their tiring occupations with the same courage and devotion. People from the countryside would often say to my father: "Let someone else take your place; you certainly have enough for yourself."

Some believed that he was very rich. In reality, he was not well paid and since he had remained rigidly honest, he had only very modest savings. But sometimes, in jest, he let it be known that indeed he could live without doing anything. Mama, who under her white hair had retained the fine and regular features of her youth, got after him for bragging that way: "What good will these lies do you?"

"Well, it's to trick them—since they think I'm so rich!"

In the final analysis, my father thought himself happy as long as his tobacco pouch was full and he had a good bottle of wine on the lunch table.

The masters knew how scrupulous he was in performing his role, even though he had never brought a single poacher to trial—and they were not stingy with their esteem. Even so, his job as a guard, which he kept until his very old age, was a sad one.

Inside the chateau the methods of service changed around the turn of the century, just as the fashion in dress did. It seemed to me that the young heirs were far more demanding than the old dowager, and less cordial and familiar. How difficult it is when one gets older to change one's habits, just as it seemed harder to put up with their criticism. It got so bad that after the marriage of Mlle N—, I too left Prévange.

74. The diary of an English servant: Hannah Cullwick

Daughter and granddaughter of servants, Hannah Cullwick (1833–1909), born and raised in Shropshire, entered service at the age of eight. In her late teens, having lost both parents, Cullwick moved to London, where she took a variety of jobs, ranging from maid-of-all-work to cook. There she met the writer Arthur J. Munby, whom she later married and at whose behest she kept a diary. These two selections, taken from her entries for the year 1864, give a glimpse into the life of the Victorian servant and reveal the great gulf that separated the world below stairs from that above. Cullwick's repeated underscoring of her love for dirty work and degradation reflect the influence of Munby, who took a peculiar pleasure in hearing about her drudgery.

When this year began i was general servant to Mr. Foster the beer merchant at 22 Carlton Villas. i was kitchen-servant like, & did all the dirty work down stairs, besides the dining room & hall & steps & back stairs. There was 12 steps to the front door, & it took me ½ an hour to clean 'em crawling backwards, & often ladies & that come in while i was a doing 'em & their feet close to where my hands was on the steps. i liked that, & made foot-marks wi my wet hands on the steps like they did wi their wet feet. it made me think o the contrast, i clean'd all the boots & knives & some o the windows & the grates belonging to the dining room, kitchen & the room down stairs what the children play'd in & the nurse sat in to work & that—i had 3 or 4 pair o boots of a day & about 2 dozen knives & six forks—& i clean'd the watercloset & privy & the passage & all the rough places down stairs & my wages was 15 lbs a year. All that is my sort o work what i *love*, but i had to wait at breakfast, what i couldn't do well, cause there was no set time & i couldn't keep myself clean enough to go up any-time i the morning—to go before my betters & be star'd at, & the Missis told me once or twice of it. But i *couldnt* be clean, & besides i'd liefer be dirty, & no grand folks to stare at me. at last i got warning. the Missis said to me when i was clearing away the things "Hannah, your Master & me think you'd better leave & get a place where you've no waiting to do"—i look'd surprised, & she says "you're a good hard-working servant she says, & we like you, but that strap on your wrist* your Master cant bear to see it nor yet your arms all naked & black'd some-times &

* Cullwick wore a leather strap on her wrist as a sign of her bondage to Munby.
—EDS.

SOURCE: Derek Hudson, ed., *Munby, Man of Two Worlds: Life and Diaries of Arthur J. Munby* (London, 1972), pp. 184, 195–96.

you so dirty." i felt a bit hurt to be told i was too dirty, when my dirt was all got wi making things clean for *them*.

[The next passage was written when Cullwick had left the Fosters and had become a servant at Miss Knight's boarding house in Margate.]

i often thought of Myself & them, all they ladies sitting up stairs & talking & sewing & playing games & pleasing themselves, all so smart & delicate to what i am, though they was not real ladies the missis told me—& then *me* by myself in that kitchen, drudging all day in my dirt, & ready to do any thing for 'em whenever they rung for me—it seems like been a different kind o creature to them, but it's always so with ladies & servants & of course there *is* a difference cause their bringing up is so different—servants may feel it sharply & do sometimes i believe, but it's best not to be delicate, nor mind what work we do so as it's honest. i mean it's best to be really strong in body & ready for any sort o rough work that's useful; but keeping a soft & tender heart all while & capable o *feeling*. How shamed ladies'd be to have hands & arms like mine, & how weak they'd be to do my work, & how shock'd to touch the dirty things even, what i black my whole hands with every day—yet such things must be done, & the lady's'd be the first to cry out if they was to find nobody to do for 'em—so the lowest work i think is honourable in itself & the poor drudge is honourable too providing her mind isn't as coarse & low as her work is, & yet loving her dirty work too—both cause it's useful & for been content wi the station she is placed in. But how often poor servants have to bear the scorn & harsh words & proud looks from them above her which to my mind is very wicked & unkind & certainly most disheartening to a young wench. A good hard day's work of cleaning with a pleasant word & look from the Missis is to my mind the greatest pleasure of a servants life. There was two Miss Knights, & one was always in bed, & couldn't bear a bit o noise, so it was tiresome often to be stopp'd doing a job when i was doing it as quiet as ever i could, but i bore it patient knowing she was ill & that it vex'd the Missis so to have her disturb'd, & Miss Julia (the Missis) was the first real lady that ever talk'd to me, & she doing all the light part o cooking was a good deal wi me in the kitchen—she lent me a very nice book (The Footsteps o St. Paul), & said she was sure i sh^d not dirty it & I read it through wi a bit of paper under my thumb & give it her back as clean as when she give it me. She used to tell me things too about the moon & stars & fire & earth & about history that I knew not of & it surprised me, & she advised me to read the Bible now i was got older for that i may understand better than when i was younger—But she said it was difficult in some parts even to her & she'd study'd a great deal having bin a governess—And so I enjoy'd Miss Knight's company in the Kitchen & she sat one day ever so long seen me clean the paint, & she said she could watch me all day, there was something so very interesting in cleaning & that i seem'd to do it so hearty & i said i was really fond of it. But the poor thing couldn't wash a plate or a saucepan or peal a tato, nor even draw a cork of a bottle, which was unlucky for her, been so poor in pocket—& she *did* wish she could afford to give me more wages.

75. A social scientist describes the lives of Breton peasants: la famille Bihan

Frédéric Le Play (1806–82; Docs. 67, 102.i) categorized the Breton peasants in the following selection as part of the stable population. In 1851, when Le Play's assistant conducted this study, Brittany, one of the "backward" provinces of France, still possessed a strong peasant culture. The Breton family described here were traditional Catholic peasants who wore regional costume, distrusted doctors and state schools, and received a good part of their earnings in kind. Evidence of the conservative social ethos that Le Play and his associates brought to their investigations is visible in this document— they describe the wife, who actually spent more time in the fields than in the home, as concerned primarily with the household; and they provide no information about who tended the couple's two young children in her absence.

The worker lives in the commune of Penanvour, in the Quimper district (Finistère). . . . The principal products are cereal grains and potatoes. . . . All the inhabitants speak the Celtic or Breton language almost exclusively. They have kept their ancient national costume as well. . . . The women's costume has . . . been modified in consequence of the introduction of cotton fabrics and the low price of these products. . . .

The worker described in the present monograph belongs to the category of those who are on the way to becoming peasant landowners; he must therefore be regarded as in temporary sharecropping partnership with his employer, although he has worked for the man since childhood.

Civil Status of the Family

The family consists of the married couple and their two children, as follows:

1. Patern Le Bihan, head of the family, married for seven years, born in Penanvour, 32 years old
2. Yvonne Le Penru, his wife, born in Kerazan, 30 —
3. Mathurin Le Bihan, their elder son, born in Penanvour, 5 —
4. Jacquette Le Bihan, their daughter, born in Penanvour, 3 —

Religion and Moral Habits

The couple practices the Catholic religion. They perform their religious duties scrupulously and take part in communion and all the great festivals. They are sober and temperate. . . . They combine politeness with rustic manners, and in conformity with the old customs of the Breton peasant, they never fail to greet the stranger whom they meet in the fields. They show great tenderness and solicitude for their children, but they find it difficult to make up their minds to entrust them to the schoolmaster. Illiterate for

SOURCE: Armand-René Duchatellier, "Bordier de la Basse-Bretagne, ouvrier journalier, associé au patron," in Frédéric Le Play, *Les Ouvriers européens*, 4: *Les Ouvriers de l'occident, populations stables*, 2d ed. (Tours and Paris, 1877), pp. 336–45 *passim*, 252.

the most part and with little appreciation for the advantages of scholarly instruction, the peasants of lower Brittany fear, by sending their children to
school, to see them pick up bad habits and to lose respect for their parents.
Compared with the workers in the same condition in many other regions of
France, the agricultural day laborers of lower Brittany can be regarded as
having a tendency to save money. . . .

Hygiene and Health Service

. . . They rarely resort to doctors, and are ordinarily satisfied, in cases of illness, with traditional remedies and medicines prepared at home. . . .

Property
(excluding furniture and clothing)

Money placed to earn interest	600 f
. . .	
Domestic animals kept all year round, 2 cows	62 f
Domestic animals kept only part of the year,	
1 pig, average value 12 francs, kept for 2 months	2 f
Special materials for tasks and activities	6 f
For the cultivation of a field rented by the	
family.—1 spade, 3 f;—1 hoe, 3 f.	
Total Value of property	670 f

Subsidies

In lower Brittany one still finds a collection of subsidies that greatly
improves the condition of agricultural workers.* As soon as a young worker
is taken on as a hired hand by a landowner or a farmer, he is permitted to
put two heifers in the employer's herd, which will be fed and raised at no
expense. . . . After his marriage, having become a householder, the worker
still has the possibility of grazing his two cows on the uncultivated pasturelands that belong to the commune or to the landowner for whom he generally
works. These lands . . . also supply the family with free fuel to heat their
residence and the straw bedding necessary for the cows . . . Generally, at
harvest time, the landowners or their farmers give their day laborers several
gifts in kind. . . .

Tasks and Activities

Tasks of the worker.—The principal work of the worker is done by the
day for a landowner who exploits his own agricultural land. To this he
devotes 310 days per year.

His secondary tasks take up only a small proportion of his time. . . .

Tasks of the Wife.—The principal work of the woman involves looking
after the household. Agricultural work performed on the farm of a neighborhood landowner is the chief kind of secondary work and occupies about the
same number of days as the principal work. Her other occupations include

---

* These subsidies, or special privileges, appear to be remnants of medieval exchange customs between noble landowners and their peasant tenants.—EDS.

the cultivation of fields rented by the family, the gathering of fuel and straw on the pasturelands where the domestic animals graze, care of the domestic animals, the preparation and finishing of hemp, and finally, the making of bonnets, stockings, and some other clothing. . . .

Food and Meals

There are four meals in summer and three in winter. The principal foods are barley soup, buckwheat porridge or pancakes, and lastly, bread eaten with potatoes, milk, and butter. On some special occasions the family has more plentiful meals made up of meat, vegetables, cider, and eau-de-vie.

Dwelling, Furniture, and Clothing

Typically the one-story residences of these peasants consist of only a single room, which the family shares with their two cows. When the pig is kept in a shed that is completely separated from this room, and when decent care is taken to remove the manure, this arrangement has nothing unhygienic about it and is not nearly as unsound as one might first suppose. In the last few years the peasants have begun to appreciate the comforts of the household more; many of them have a tendency to decorate their houses and display a certain refinement in the choice and maintenance of their furnishings. These new tendencies are still little in evidence in the family described in the present monograph. Their personal property is among the simplest of those described in this volume. Even their clothing is consistent with their furnishings. On work days the man and the woman never wear stockings and have only large clogs lined with straw to protect their feet from moisture. . . .

Household linens: made up from a large piece of woven hemp fabric spun by the woman, and woven by a neighbor man in exchange for part of the thread. . . .

Clothing: . . . Children's clothing: made up in part from the old
clothing of the parents . . .
Total Value of furniture and clothing   149 f 35

Recreations

Religious services and the festival of the patron saint of the parish are the principal diversion from the ordinary work of the family. The favorite recreation of day laborers like this family is to take part in the local *Dévès-bras*, or *"grandes journées."* These are the names given to the festive "corvées" organized by a neighboring householder who wants a quick job done on some project that requires the help of a great number of workers. Examples would be clearing a piece of land, building a threshing floor for beating grain, and hauling a massive load. Payment for this work has the characteristics of a real celebration. The workers are copiously and substantially fed. The women, invited to the festivities that follow the work, bring along food, especially milk and butter. Never straying from the rules of temperance, the family described in the present monograph shares only moderately in the drinking that takes place on these occasions. . . . The worker takes much pleasure in smoking a moderate amount of tobacco, and the woman takes snuff.

Work Executed by the Family	Amount of Work in Days	
	Father	Mother
Principal work [of the man], executed by the day for a landowner:		
Tillage and earthwork	310	—
Principal work, particular to the woman, performed on behalf of the family:		
Household work: food preparation, child care, cleaning the house and furnishings, maintenance and washing of clothing and linens	—	105
Secondary work:		
Agricultural field work for a neighboring farmer	—	100
Cultivation of fields (10 ares) rented by the family	4	8
Care of household furnishings	2	—
Labor on the *grandes journées* . . . , done for the neighbors	8	—
Care of domestic animals	—	40
Gathering of fuel on the commons	—	20
Gathering of straw on the commons	—	10
Preparation (retting and stripping) of hemp	—	6
Spinning of hemp	—	25
Making of clothing (bonnets and stockings)	—	4
Total days for all members of the family	324	318

76. Work and play in antebellum Georgia

Before the Civil War the southern plantation system formed its own unique culture in which master and slave were linked by complex bonds. But the texture of the life varied vastly in a culture in which a plantation could mean a small farm where slave and master worked side by side or a huge estate where the owner and his human chattel had almost no contact. Indeed, the economic conditions on the plantation, the circumstances in which slaves lived and worked, and the character of the master all helped to shape the lives of slaves and to determine the harshness of their lot. Yet even the kindest master could not change the fact that slaves were property, totally subject to their master's will, and that slavery was an economic system in which the master was determined to extract the most work possible from his chattel.

SOURCES: All the selections come from *The American Slave: A Composite Autobiography*, ed. George P. Rawick (Westport, Conn., 1972), vols. 12 and 13: *Georgia Narratives*, as follows. (i), (ii), (iii), (vii), vol. 13, part 3: 71–72, 98–99; part 4, 103–4, 107–9, 156–57. (iv), (v), (vi), vol, 12, part 2: 266–68, 289–90, 347–48.

That work could take many forms besides field labor, from weaving cloth to making jelly. At times it wore the mask of play, as at a cornshucking or quilting, when the prize of whiskey, rather than the threat of the whip, spurred slaves to produce their utmost. For slave women, who bore a double burden, labor was never-ending: not only did they work from dawn to dusk in the fields, but they also performed their families' domestic chores; on a small plantation, they might have to cook and clean for the master's family after a day of work in the fields. The following selections, from the reminiscences of former slaves, give a sense of the plantation slave's experience: they show the richness of plantation culture, the close connection between work and play, the relation between nature and the rhythm of work, and the brutality of the slave system. Above all, they testify to the spirit and endurance of the American slave.

(i) Amanda McDaniel

Mr. Hale, our master, was not rich like some of the other planters in the community. His plantation was a small one and he only had eight servants who were all women. He wasn't able to hire an overseer and all of the heavy work such as the plowing was done by his sons. Mrs. Hale did all of her own cooking and that of the slaves too. In all Mr. Hale had eleven Children. I had to nurse three of them before I was old enough to go to the field to work. . . .

Our folks [the slaves] had to get up at four o'clock every morning and feed the stock first. By the time it was light enough to see they had to be in the fields where they hoed the cotton and the corn as well as the other crops. Between ten and eleven o'clock everybody left the field and went to the house where they worked until it was too dark to see. My first job was to take breakfast to those working in the fields. I used buckets for this. Besides this I had to drive the cows to and from the pasture. The rest of the day was spent in taking care of Mrs. Hale's young children. After a few years of this I was sent to the fields where I planted peas, corn, etc. I also had to pick cotton when that time came, but I never had to hoe and do the heavy work like my mother and sisters did.

(ii) William McWhorter

Dere warn't never no let-up when it come to wuk. When slaves come in from de fields atter sundown and tended de stock and et supper, de mens still had to shuck corn, mend hoss collars, cut wood, and sich lak; de 'omans mended clothes, spun thread, wove cloth, and some of 'em had to go up to de big house and nuss de white folks' babies. One night my ma had been nussin' one of dem white babies, and atter it dozed off to sleep she went to lay it in its little bed. De chid's foot cotch itself in Marse Joe's galluses dat he had done hung on de foot of de bed, and when he heared his baby cry Marse Joe woke up and grabbed up a stick of wood and beat ma over de head 'til he 'most kilt her. Ma never did seem right atter dat and when she died she still had a big old knot on her head.

(iii) Frances Willingham

Our overseer got all de slaves up 'fore break of day and dey had to be done et deir breakfast and in de field when de sun riz up. Dat sun would be down good 'fore dey got to de house at night.

When slaves come in from de fields at night de 'omans cleant up deir houses atter day et, and den washed and got up early next mornin' to put de clothes out to dry. Mens would eat, set 'round talkin' to other mens and den go to bed. On our place evvybody wukked on Saddays 'till 'bout three or four o'clock and if de wuk was tight dey wukked right on 'till night lak any other day.

(iv) Amanda Jackson

All of de slaves on de plantation worked in de fiel'—even de cook—dat is 'till time fer her to cook de meals. On dis plantation dey raised practically everything—corn, cotton, wheat, an' rye, an' a heap o' live stock. Dey wuz runnin' 'bout twenty-five or thirty plows all de time. Dere wuz one overseer.

Every mornin' de slaves had to git up an' by de time it wuz light enuff to see dey had to be in de fiel' workin'. . . . Dey knowed how to git you up alright—de overseer had a horn dat he blowed an' dem dat didn't wake up when de horn wuz blowed wuz called by some of de others in de quarters. . . . Dey wuz in de fiel' fore de sun rose an' dere 'till after it went down—fum sun to sun. De fiel' han's had one hour fer dinner—dem dat had families done dere own cookin' an' dere wuz a special cook fer de single ones. De women whut had families would git up soon in de mornin' 'fore time to go to de fiel' an' put de meat on to boil an' den day would come in at dinner time an' put de vegetables in de pot to cook an' when dey come home in de evenin' dey would cook some corn bread in de ashes at de fireplace.

All dat I could do den wuz sweep de yards, water de cows an' de chickens an' den go to de pasture to git de cows an' de calves—we had two pastures— one fer de calves an' one fer de cows. I had to git de cows so de womens could milk 'em.

All of de hard work on de plantation wuz done in de summertime. In rainy weather an' other bad weather all dat dey had to do wuz to shell corn an' help make cloth. As a rule ol' marster wuz pretty good to his slaves but sometimes some of 'em got whupped kinda bad fer not workin' an' stuff like dat—I seen 'im cut womens on dey shoulders wid a long whip 'till it looked like he wuz gonna cut de skin off'n 'im.

You had to do yo' own work on Saturdays an' Sundays—I 'members see-ing my po' mother wash her clothes on Sundays many times. We did'nt have no holidays except Sundays an' den we did'nt have nowhere to go except to church in de woods under a bush-arbor.

(v) Lina Hunter

I 'members dem old frolics us had, when harvest times was over, and all dat corn was piled up ready for de big cornshuckin'. Honey, us sho had big old times. Us would cook for three or four days gittin' ready for de feast dat was to follow de cornshuckin'. De fust thing dey done was 'lect a general to lead off de singin' and keep it goin' so de faster dey sung, de faster dey shucked de corn. Evvy now and den dey passed de corn liquor 'round, and dat holped 'em to wuk faster, and evvy Nigger dat found a red ear got a extra swig of liquor. Atter de sun went down dey wuked right on by de light of pine torches and bonfires. Dem old pine knots would burn for a long time and throw a fine bright light. Honey, it was one grand sight out dar at night wid dat old harvest moon a-shinin', fires a-burnin', and dem old torches lit up. I kin jus' see it all now, and hear dem songs us sung. Dem was such happy times. When all de corn was shucked and dey had done et all dat big supper, dey danced for de rest of de night.

Dey had logrollin's when dere was new ground to be cleared up. De menfolks done most of dat wuk, but de 'omans jus' come along to fix de big supper and have a good time laughin' and talkin' whilst de menfolks was doin' de wuk. Atter de logs was all rolled, dey et, and drunk, and danced 'till dey fell out. I'll bet you ain't never seed nothin' lak dem old break-downs and drag-outs us had dem nights atter logrollin's. Dey sho drug heaps of dem Niggers out.

When de harvest moon was 'most as bright as daylight us had cotton pickin's. Dem big crowds of slaves would clean out a field in jus' no time, and you could hear 'em singin' a long ways off whilst dey was a-pickin' dat cotton. Dey 'most allus had barbecue wid all de fixin's to enjoy when dey finished pickin' out de cotton, and den lots of drinkin' and dancin'. 'Bout dat dancin', Honey, I could sho cut dem corners. Dancin' is one thing I more'n did lak to do, and I wish I could hear dat old dance song again. *Miss Liza Jane*, it was, and some of de words went lak dis, "Steal 'round dem corners, Miss Liza Jane. Don't slight none, Miss Liza Jane. Swing your partner, Miss Liza Jane." Dere was heaps and lots more of it, but it jus' won't come to me now.

(vi) Estella Jones

At quiltin' bees, four folks wuz put at every quilt, one at every corner. Dese quilts had been pieced up by old slaves who warn't able to work in de field. Quiltin's always tuk place durin' de winter when dere warn't much to do. A prize wuz always give to de four which finished dere quilt fust. 'Freshments went 'long wid dis too.

Sometimes de grown folks all went huntin' for fun. At dem times, de women had on pants and tied dey heads up wid colored cloths.

Cake walkin' wuz a lot of fun durin' slavery time. Dey swept de yards real clean and set benches 'round for de party. Banjos wuz used for music makin'. De womens wore long, ruffled dresses wid hoops in 'em and de mens had on high hats, long split-tailed coats, and some of 'em used walkin' sticks. De couple dat danced best got a prize. Sometimes de slave owners come to dese parties 'cause dey enjoyed watchin' de dance, and dey 'cided who danced de best. Most parties durin' slavery time wuz give on Saturday night durin' work seasons, but durin' winter dey wuz give on most any night.

(vii) Addie Vinson

Long 'fore day, dat overseer blowed a bugle to wake up de Niggers. You could hear it far as High Shoals, and us lived dis side of Watkinsville. Heaps of folkses all over dat part of de country got up by dat old bugle. I will never forget one time when de overseer said to us chillun: "You fellows go to de field and fetch some corn tops." Mandy said: "He ain't talkin' to us 'cause us ain't fellows and I ain't gwine." Bless your sweet life, I runned and got dem corn tops, 'cause I didn't want no beatin'. Dem udder chillun got deir footses most cut off wid dem switches when dat overseer got to wuk to sho dem dey had to obey him. Dat overseer sho did wuk de Niggers hard; he driv' em all de time. Dey had to go to de field long 'fore sunup, and it was way atter sundown 'fore dey could stop dat field wuk. Den dey had to hustle to finish deir night wuk in time for supper, or go to bed widout it.

You know dey whupped Niggers den. Atter dey had done wukked hard in de fields all day long, de beatin' started up, and he allus had somepin in mind to beat 'em about. When dey beat my Aunt Sallie she would fight back, and once when Uncle Randall said somepin he hadn't oughta, dat overseer beat him so bad he couldn't wuk for a week. He had to be grez all over evvy day wid hoalin' ointment for a long time 'fore dem gashes got well. . . .

When slaves got in from de fields at night dey cooked and et deir supper and went to bed. Dey had done been wukin' since sunup. When dere warn't so much to do in de fields, sometimes old Marster let his Niggers lay off from wuk after dinner on Saddays. If de chinches was most eatin' de Niggers up, now and den de 'omans was 'lowed to stay to de house to scald evvything and clear 'em out, but de menfolkses had to go on to de field. On Sadday nights de 'omans patched, washed, and cut off peaches and apples to dry in fruit season. In de daytime dey had to cut off and dry fruit for Old Miss. When slaves got smart wid deir white folkses, deir marsters would have 'em beat, and dat was de end of de matter. Dat was a heap better'n dey does now days, 'cause if a Nigger gits out of place dey puts him on de chaingang.

When Aunt Patience led de singing at cornshuckin's, de shucks sho'ly did fly. Atter de corn was shucked dey fed us lots of good things and give us plenty of liquor. De way cotton pickin' was managed was dis: evvybody dat picked a thousand pounds of cotton in a week's time was 'lowed a day off. Mammy picked her thousand pounds evvy week.

77. Agricultural gang labor in England

Like dressmakers and milliners (Doc. 68.i), agricultural laborers in England worked long hours, in very rough conditions, with no bargaining power; moreover, the frequency of their employment depended on the vagaries of

SOURCE: Great Britain, *Parliamentary Papers*, 1867, XVI, Children's Employment Commission, 6th report, pp. 85, 89, 91–92, 147.

the English climate. The most notorious and arduous form of agricultural work was gang labor. In the 1860's Parliament began to inquire into the employment of children and women in agriculture, singling out the gang system for particular consideration. The disclosures of these investigations led to the curtailment of the worst abuses of that system. The following excerpts from the report of J. E. White, a parliamentary commissioner who inspected agricultural gangs in Norfolk, give insights into the lives of women who worked as gang laborers.

Female Labour in the Fields

Two Classes of.—This may be divided into two classes, that of the married women, and that of the single women.

Injurious effect on Married Women.—Being employed from 8 in the morning til 5 in the evening they return home tired and wearied, and unwilling to make any further exertion to render the cottage comfortable. When the husband returns he finds everything uncomfortable, the cottage dirty, no meal prepared, the children tiresome and quarrelsome, the wife slatternly and cross, and his home so unpleasant to him that he not rarely betakes himself to the public house, and eventually becomes a drunkard. The wife becomes indifferent about her personal appearance, neglectful of her domestic duties, and careless of her children. Those who visit the cottages of the labouring poor will invariably find misery and discomfort in those homes where the wife is employed in field labour, as compared with those where the wife stays at home and attends to her domestic duties. The moral and religious character of the female labourer in the fields is also worse. . . .

Injurious to Single Women and Girls.—This class of female labour generally consists of young girls who have been refractory and disobedient in schools, and who having been punished or threatened with punishment in consequence, are removed from the school by foolish mothers who back them in their disobedience. They are for the most part self-willed, headstrong, and idle, and these bad qualities are not eradicated but rather encouraged by their employment in field labour. They are fond of finery and amusements, and are often in consequence led into sin.

Another class of female labourers consist of those who having been thus brought up are seduced and become the mothers of illegitimate children. These take to this mode of labour for support, and because it affords them leisure time in which to seek amusement. They are their own mistresses, and are under no control or restraint; they labour when they please, and are idle when they please. With all these the fact that the field labour is not continuous, but that it takes place only at intervals, is a great inducement to their following this kind of employment instead of seeking domestic service. A girl or young woman who follows field labour is seldom really respectable, and is generally fond of gossip and idle amusements. Of course if they marry they make bad wives and careless mothers.

Physical Injury.—Those women who labour in fields become prematurely old, and are subject to many constitutional diseases, which either shorten their lives or render them dependent for the greater part of their lives on the Union for support.

The employment of women in field labour is injurious to them physically, morally, and religiously.

[White next offered in evidence the accounts of gang members he interviewed. All the parenthetical explanations are his.]

Elizabeth Dickson.—What I say is, these gangs should not be as they are. There are so many girls that they make lads at a loose hand, *i.e.*, leave them nothing to do. Then there is the girls coming home at dark; that is when the job is done. The gangs are drafted off, two (*i.e.*, workers) here, three there, and so on, so that the gangmaster cannot look after them, and is not to blame. I have gone with 20 in a morning, and seen only two perhaps come home with the man at night. Then girls will have bad language amongst themselves, though the man might wish to stop it, but there are so many together, 20 or 30 perhaps, that he can't keep them quiet. But in one gang (private) the man had the best rule, viz., that there should be no blackguarding, &c., or else he would pay them off. I have worked in gangs many years. . . .

My children were obliged to go to work very young, some before they were 7 years old. If you have nothing except what comes out of your fingers' end, as they say, it's no use, you must let them; they want more victuals.

My husband left me a widow with 11 children living, out of 15; nine of them being then under 16 years old, and three under 3 years, two being twins. The parish allowed me 3s. 4d. in money and goods (bread) according to the number of children, but not widow's pay. My Henry wasn't 8 years old, and when I asked, "What, will you turn him out?" they said, "Well, he's big enough, he must help as well as others."

Jemima was not more than two months, I think, over 6 years old when she went out. She said, "Mother, I want some boots to go to school," so I sent her out and saved up what she earned till it was enough to get them. She was a corpse from going in the turnips. She came home from work one day, when about 10½ years old, with dizziness and her bones aching, and died and was buried and all in little better than a fortnight. The doctor said it was a violent cold stuck in her bones. Children stooping down get as wet at top as below. They get wet from the rain too. Perhaps they may have [to] go out three or four times in a week and not earn 2d., not having made a quarter (of a day), and come home so soaked that the wet will run out of their things. I have often been obliged to take my flannel petticoat off and roll it round a girl's legs and iron it with a warming pan to take off the pain and misery of the bones and let her get to sleep.

One now living with me suffers very much in this way, and her legs swell below the knee and over the ankle, especially after a hard day's work. She says then her feet feel as if they were wrung, and if she takes her boots off she can't get them on again. The doctor said it was done when she was young from getting her feet wet so. I have suffered very much from rheumatism, but that was partly from doing washing at night, and then turning out with the gang by day; but I always considered a penny of my own better than 1,000l. to ask a gentleman. . . .

Some of the work is very hard, pulling turnips and mangolds, muck shaking, and when turnips are being put into the ground putting muck as fast as the plough goes along,—work which women and girls have sometimes to do. Drawing mangolds is the hardest; globe mangolds are fit to pull your inside out, and you often have to kick them up. I have pulled till my hands have been that swelled that you can't see the knuckles on them. I have come home so exhausted that I have sat down and cried; it would be an hour before I could pull my things off; and I have been obliged to have the table moved up to me because I could not move to it. When I have found the door locked I have lain down outside till the key came. At singling, the little ones cry out about their backs, and stand with their hands behind, so, saying "Oh, I must rest."

Rachel Claskson Gibson, Castleacre.—I can't speak up for any gangs; they ought all to be done away with. My children shan't go to one if I can help it, *i.e.*, as long as I and their father are alive, I hope, if we can keep them; one is 7, one 5. I believe that I am the same as many other people about this. There are a great many mothers who send their children into gangs who would not if they could help it, and they say so. Nothing comes amiss to children after they have been in them, no bad talk nor anything else. I know that a child if brought up in a gang is quite different from what it would have been if brought up otherwise; you would soon know that it had been out, especially if you were to talk to it. . . .

Gangs might be very well for boys, but never for girls. I did not go myself till I was 17 and could take care of myself. The coming home is the worst part, that's when the mischief is done, but this is hardly the master's fault. When they are hard at work they can't have bad language so much; but some will talk to set the others laughing, and the master can't be looking after all at once, and perhaps he believes that all is going right. There never was any good got out of gangs, neither in talk nor in the other way, and they never will be kept as they should. One man can never look after such a lot. I know that there is a great deal of badness done in the fields. As for the talk, you can't stand at your door but what you would have to shut your ears for it.

I don't think it proper that womenkind should go into the fields at all, in gangs or not, though I have done both. There would then be more in the houses to mind them. Harvest work is different; you are not under a gang-master, except that sometimes the tying has been done by a gang; and at harvest much more money can be made; a woman may make 2s. 3d. in a day, and that comes nice to any one.

But other work is different. I should just have liked you to have met that gang coming back this afternoon, with their great thick boots, and buskins on their legs, and petticoats pinned up; you might see the knees of some. A girl whom I took in to live, because she has no home to go to, came back to-day from the gang all dripping wet from the turnips. If you don't feel any hurt from the wet when you are young, you do afterwards, when you are old and the rheumatism comes on.

Ann Seal.—When I was young, 30 or 40 years ago, there were no gangs; it is a very bad thing that ever they came up. Two of my grandchildren, girls, work in gangs here now, and two of my daughters did. One, the mother of these two, went out when she was just turned 8; the other wasn't quite so old. My granddaughter Ellen began this summer soon after she was 7. They do all kinds of work, and have to find their own tools, *e.g.*, fork, hoe, reap-hook, puddle for thistles, &c. Wheat hoeing is very hard work. Yesterday and the day before one was knocking muck. The eldest gets 7d. a day, the young est 4d. They reckon to be on the ground at 8 a.m. The further they have to go the sooner they start off, commonly about 7. They think nothing of a mile. The little one has been to one place [?] miles off, and to another, four or five miles. I suppose Susan began at 10 years old, and has worked in four gangs here. She has had to go all six miles, that it is, several times. If they leave off at 5 they only let them have half an hour for dinner at noon instead of an hour as when they leave later. Sometimes, but only in summer, they make a quarter of a day over, *i.e.*, five quarters. They get tired, and sometimes their feet full of blisters. This summer they have had great blisters. Susan has said, "How the stubble runs into my feet." They have, too, to carry such loads of stones to fill the bucket. They make them work, and scold them and use a stick to make them, but not to injure them. I only know of one girl who was injured. The man hit her on the back, and she was laid up from it for years with sores in her back. My daughter saw it done.

At some work they can't keep dry. They come home wonderful wet, poor things, sometimes. It's ruination to girl's health, that it is. Susan is weak in the chest, and her head very bad, and she has been stopping at home for it several times. She was not delicate as a child, but became so after she got in these gangs. She got cold with wet feet and clothes, and being badly shod. The doctor says she ought not to go in field work at all. This year she should have gone to harvest to tie with her stepmother, but could not for her health. They complained how she had lost all 30s. by it.

I do not like gangs. They are very bad for the mind. Girls hear such shocking language. The eldest of the two can read. She picked it up at Sunday school. A gentleman paid 1d. a week for her to go to school, but they would not let the child go.

[White then continued his report with a case history of an assault on a young girl.]

The accounts contained in the following statements have been received as bearing on the alleged moral influences of gang work, and I do not feel justified in withholding them. . . .

"A.B., 13 years of age. . . . I know C— (the defendant) he is the gangmaster. I remember last Monday week. . . . Mr. C— pulled me down and pulled up my clothes, pulled up my clothes to my waist. I think there were a dozen in the gang, it was in the sight of the gang, we were sitting down to our dinners. . . . The other boys and girls in the gang were round me. I called out, the others laughed. He said, 'Open your legs more.' He had a stick, and I had not run away with it. I told my mother, not directly I got home (at night). I told her half an hour after. My mother spoke to me first. C— hurt my hand when I tried to get up. He was on me and I could not get up, he was laying on me flat, I was on my back on the ground. I don't know how long he was on me. He did not say anything to any of the others, the others saw it. C— has threatened to flog me, if we told any tales; this was before the assault."

[On cross examination by a solicitor the girl denied anything passing about "shaving." (See below.) A boy —— in the gang, aged 12, who was 100 yards off at the time, deposed that he only saw defendant "shave her and put his hand up her petticoats."—J. E. W.]

"——, a boy aged 10, brother of the girl. . . . I saw C— pulling the girls about and showing their backsides. He did it to my sister, and —— [two other girls named. The boy then confirms the facts and the words used by the defendant, as stated by the girl.—J. E. W.] I was four or five yards off. The boys and girls were all dining together. My sister's clothes were up not five minutes.

"——, 13 years [one of the two girls named by last witness.—J. E. W.] I work with C—'s gang. I was there one day last week. —— [the girl assaulted] took his stick. He got on her and rubbed her face. He did not pull up her clothes."

[Sentenced to two calendar months' hard labour.]

The document from which the above is taken appears to be a formal copy of the depositions, and was forwarded to me by a member of Parliament, with the remark "I am afraid they (cases) would come oftener before the magistrates if the children dared to speak." A gentleman who heard the case, and with whom I am acquainted, also forwarded his notes of it, from which it appears that the girl assaulted did not tell her mother till the latter asked about it, "from something which she had heard from a neighbour," and the girl is represented as stating "The same sort of thing has taken place with two other girls; with me once before." In this account some details are given more fully, and are by no means more favourable to the defendant. The writer of this last account speaks of "great pains taken to hush the matter up," and remarks, "It seems that on another occasion he threw himself upon her and rubbed his chin on her face. There was some confusion about the transaction of shaving and that for which the information was laid as to date. It will be seen that this evidence is somewhat "contradictory, though conclusive, however, of the practices alleged being common." The farmer employing the gangmaster, an old man of 72, and who had employed him "30 years, 25 wholly on his farm, had always found him a straightforward and upright man, and believed that he would act as a "father to the children." From this, and from the Return made from the parish, it appears that the above defendant is what is called a "private" gangmaster. The gang consisted of 14 or 15 young girls and boys, one of the latter 8 years old.

78. Farming in post–Civil War America

Farm management took many forms in America after the Civil War, from sharecropping in the South to homesteading in the West. In the first selection Cora Gillem remembers the sharecropping system in Arkansas right after the Civil War, when the freed slaves, left without land, mules, or tools, went back to work for their old masters in an exploitative system that often left them worse off materially than they had been under slavery. In the second selection, Julia Blanks, a former slave who was part black, part French, and part Native American, describes with relish the pleasures of ranch life in Texas, where game was plentiful and cattle ruled the range. The third selection is a bitter lament written by Mariam Peckham, a white homesteader in Kansas in the 1870's. In this excerpt from a letter to an aunt in the East, Peckham describes some of the hardships that especially beset the prairie farmers: the expense of the mechanized harvest, the crop losses from grasshoppers and other pests, and the depressed prices in the grain market.

(i) Cora Gillem

It was while she was in Little Rock that mama married Lee. After peace they went back to Helena and stayed two years with old mistress. She let them have the use of the farm tools and mules; she put up the cotton and seed corn and food for us. She told us we could work on shares, half and half. You see, ma'am, when slaves got free, they didn't have nothing but their two hands to start out with. I never heard of any master giving a slave money or land. Most went back to farming on shares. For many years all they got was their food. Some white folks was so mean. I know what they told us every time when crops would be put by. They said "Why didn't you work harder? Look. When the seed is paid for, and all your food and everything, what food you had just squares the account." Then they take all the cotton we raise, all the hogs, corn, everything. We was just about where we was in slave days.

When we see we never going to make anything share cropping, mother and I went picking. Yes ma'am, they paid pretty good; got $1.50 a hundred [weight?]. So we saved enough to take us to Little Rock.

(ii) Julia Blanks

I was fifteen years old the first time I married. It was almost a run-a-way marriage. I was married in San Antonio. . . . I was about twenty years old when I married the second time. I was married in Leon Springs the second time.

SOURCES: (i) *The American Slave: A Composite Autobiography*, ed. George P. Rawick, 9: *Arkansas Narratives* (Westport, Conn., 1972), part 3: 29–30. (ii)

Before we come out to this country from Leon Springs, they was wild grapes, dewberries, plums and agaritas, black haws, red haws. M-m-m! Them dewberries, I dearly love 'em. I never did see wild cherries out here. I didn't like the cherries much, but they make fine wine. We used to gather mustang grapes and make a barrel of wine.

After I married the second time, we lived on the Adams ranch on the Frio and stayed on that ranch fifteen years. We raised all our chillen right on that ranch. I am taken for a Mexkin very often. I jes' talk Mexkin back to 'em. I learned to talk it on the ranch. As long as I have lived at this place, I have never had a cross word about the chillen. All my neighbors here is Mexkins. They used to laugh at me when I tried to talk to the hands on the ranch, but I learned to talk like 'em.

We used to have big round-ups out on the Adams ranch. They had fences then. The neighbors would all come over and get out and gather the cattle and bring 'em in. Up at Leon Springs at that time they didn't have any fences, and they would have big round-ups there. But after we come out here, it was different. He would notify his neighbors they were goin' to gather cattle on a certain day. The chuck wagon was right there at the ranch, that is, I was the chuck wagon. But if they were goin' to take the cattle off, they would have a chuck wagon. . . .

On the Adams ranch, in the early days, we used to have to pack water up the bank. You might not believe it, but one of these sixty-pound lard cans full of water, I've a-carried it on my head many a time. We had steps cut into the bank, and it was a good ways down to the water, and I'd pack that can up to the first level and go back and get a couple a buckets of water, and carry a bucket in each hand and the can on my head up the next little slantin' hill before I got to level ground. I carried water that way till my chillen got big enough to carry water, then they took it up. When I was carryin' water in them big cans my head would sound like new leather—you know how it squeaks, and that was the way it sounded in my head. But, it never did hurt me. You see, the Mexkins carry loads on their heads, but they fix a rag around their heads some way to help balance it. But I never did. I jes' set it up on my head and carried it that way. Oh, we used to carry water! My goodness! My mother said it was the Indian in me—the way I could carry water. . . .

Another thing, we used to have big round-ups, and I have cooked great pans of steak and mountain orshters. Generally, at the brandin' and markin', I cooked up many a big pan of mountain orshters. I wish I had a nickel for ever' one I've cooked, and ate too! People from up North have come down there, and, when they were brandin' and cuttin' calves there, they sure did eat and enjoy that dinner.

The men used to go up to the lake, fishin', and catch big trout, or bass, they call 'em now; and we'd take big buckets of butter—we didn't take a

Ibid., 4: Texas Narratives, part 1: 99–100, 102–5. (iii) Letter from Mariam Peckham to her aunt, Nov. 5, 1876. The editors are grateful to Helen Jordan, Dewitt, N.Y., for permission to quote from this unpublished letter in her possession.

saucer of butter or a pound; we taken butter up there in buckets, for we sure had plenty of it—and we'd take lard too, and cook our fish up there, and had corn bread or hoe cakes and plenty of butter for ever'thing, and it sure was good. I tell you—like my husband used to say—we was livin' ten days in the week, then.

When we killed hogs, the meat from last winter was hung outside and then new meat, salted down and then smoked, put in there, and we would cook the old bacon for the dogs. We always kep' some good dogs there, and anybody'll tell you they was always fat. We had lots of wild turkeys and I raised turkeys, too, till I got sick of cookin' turkeys. Don't talk about deer! You know, it wasn't then like it is now. You could go kill venison any time you wanted to. But I don't blame 'em for passin' that law for people used to go kill 'em and jes' take out the hams and tenderloin and leave the other layin' there. I have saved many a sack of dried meat to keep it from spoilin'.

We would raise watermelons, too. We had a big field three mile from the house and a ninety-acre field right in the house. We used to go get loads of melons for the hogs and they got to where they didn't eat anything but the heart.

I used to leave my babies at the house with the older girl and go out horseback with my husband. My oldest girl used to take the place of a cowboy, and put her hair up in her hat. And ride! My goodness, she loved to ride! They thought she was a boy. She wore pants and leggin's. And maybe you think she couldn't ride!

After we left that ranch, we took up some state land. I couldn't tell you how big that place was. We had 640 [acres] in one place and 640 in another place; it was a good big place. After my husband got sick, we had to let it go back. We couldn't pay out. We only lived on it about four years.

(iii) Mariam Peckham

I tell you Auntie no one can depend on farming for a living in this country. Henry is very industrious and this year had in over thirty acres of small grain, 8 acres of corn and about an acre of potatoes. We have sold all our small grain (have not saved enough even to make our bread till next harvest) and it come to $100 now deduct $27.00 for cutting, $16.00 for threshing, $19.00 for hired help, say nothing of boarding your help, none of the trouble of drawing 25 miles to market and 25cts on each head for ferriage over the river and where is your profit. I sometimes think this a God forsaken country, the hoppers hurt our corn and we have ½ a crop and utterly destroyed our garden. If one wants trials, let them come to Kansas. I am ashamed to say so much, and don't very often. I never write anything of the kind now a days to Father Peckhams' folks for fear they will think me begging. . . .

Henry earns money to work at his trade more than on his farm. He has earned about $120 this summer, we could not possibly live if he did not. Yes, and hired girls' wages $15.00, but then there is a way through. It is hope against hope, when I begin to get discouraged and fretful I begin to sing as loud as I can holler. I have no neighbors near enough to hear me.

79. A New England teacher contemplates her work: Mary Lyon

Nowhere did teaching offer young women more possibilities for paid employment and institutional innovation than in nineteenth-century America. One of the most famous teachers of that era was Mary Lyon (1797–1849). Lyon grew up on a farm in western Massachusetts and attended several local academies in her quest for an education. She taught school for several years, beginning in 1817, and after several years' experience assisted her friend Zilpah Grant in founding private academies for young women in Londonderry, New Hampshire, and Ipswich, Massachusetts. In the midst of this work she found time to open a school of her own in her home town of Buckland, Massachusetts. The first two letters presented here were written in 1825, during Lyon's first two terms at Buckland, when she was not yet thirty. She wrote the third letter nine years later, after her experience at Ipswich and before she had decided to found another school, the one that gained her lasting fame—Mount Holyoke.

[Mary Lyon to her friend and fellow teacher Hannah Chickering, Feb. 21, 1825, Buckland, Mass.]

My school here consists of twenty-five young ladies. After so large a number had been admitted, I had some anxiety respecting it. I feared that I might attempt more uniformity about books than, considering the circumstances, would be expedient. I expected, also, a cold winter, and my design was to have the scholars study in school. And as I possess not much natural dignity, I could foresee my scholars crowding around the fire, some whispering, some idle, &c. I remembered that, several years ago,* I had a school of young ladies in this town, in which there was more whispering than in all the schools in which I have been engaged for the last three or four years. The fault then was mine, and I knew not but that the effects might be felt even now. . . .

At the commencement, I thought it best to assume as much artificial dignity as possible; so, to begin, I borrowed Miss Grant's plan to prevent whispering.† All, with one exception, strictly complied; and that was one of the first young ladies in age and improvement. It appeared altogether probable that the termination of this affair would be a matter of considerable importance in relation to her, her father's family, and perhaps to the school generally. But after I had passed a few almost sleepless nights about it, a kind Providence directed the result in a manner that seemed best calculated to promote the interests of the school; for at length she came cheerfully into the arrangement.

A circumstance in relation to the first set of compositions was somewhat trying. One pupil refused entirely to write; but I was assisted in leading her

* Probably in 1819, her first "select school," the year after her term at Amherst Academy.

† An honor system with daily reports.

SOURCE: Mary Lyon Through Her Letters, ed. Marion Lansing (Boston, 1937), pp. 58–61, 133–35.

to comply with the requirement. Some other things I *could* mention. Suffice it to say, that I have had just enough of such things to give me continual anxiety; but God in his providence has been very kind to me. Many events have terminated as I desired, when it seemed not at all in my power to control them. Perhaps I have generally been able to accomplish about what I have undertaken.

My school in many respects is very pleasant. I have but two or three pupils under sixteen years of age. With the exception of two or three, they are very studious. On the whole, I think it the best school I have ever had; the best, because the most profitable to its members; I do not mean the best in which I have been engaged. I have an opportunity this winter to see the value of what I gained at Derry [Londonderry].

[Mary Lyon to Zilpah Grant, Dec. 26, 1825, Buckland, Mass.]
My school is larger than I expected, having about fifty scholars. . . . My heart is pained to see so much important unaccomplished labor accumulating on my hands, and I have engaged an assistant. . . .

Fourteen of my scholars board in the family with me. Before I came here, and for the first week after, I had much anxiety about the arrangements for these young ladies. We have finally become settled, so that everything seems to go on well. The members of the school in the family have a table by themselves. As I was well aware that it would require more than an ordinary share of dignity to prevent too much, if not improper, conversation at meals, I thought it the safest to introduce some entertaining exercise. This requires an effort on my part which I had scarcely realized. I frequently think, "How *could* Miss G. take care of so many last summer?" But I recollect hearing you say that your first schools were as much your all as your one hundred pupils at Derry.

My spirits have been unusually unform for four weeks. I do not recollect an hour of depression. I consider this a blessing for which I ought to be thankful. . . .

The thought that some, who were beginning to think about their eternal interests, may here become so much absorbed in their studies, so much interested in the business of the school, as to exclude God from their hearts, is truly painful. I hope I may not be the instrument of hardening the hearts of those whom I tenderly love.

[Mary Lyon to her mother, May 12, 1834, Ipswich, Mass.]
I do not expect to continue my connection with Miss G. after this summer. I have for a great while been thinking about those young ladies who find it necessary to make such an effort for their education as I made, when I was obtaining mine. In one respect, from year to year, I have not felt quite satisfied with my present field of labor. I have desired to be in a school, the expenses of which would be so small, that many who are now discouraged from endeavoring to enjoy the privileges of this, might be favored with those which are similar at less expense.

The course of instruction adopted in this institution, and the course which I have endeavored to adopt when I have instructed among my native hills, I believe is eminently suited to make good mothers as well as teachers. I have had the pleasure of seeing many, who have enjoyed these privileges, occupying the place of mothers. I have noticed with peculiar interest the cultivated and good common sense, the correct reasoning, the industry and perseverance, the patience, meekness, and gentleness of many of them. I have felt, that if all our common farmers, men of plain, good common sense, could go through the country and witness these mothers in their own families, and compare them with others in similar circumstances, they would no longer consider the money expended on these mothers as thrown away.

Since I have lived to see so many of these ladies in their own families, I have felt more than ever before, that my field of labor was among the most desirable. I have felt that I could thank Him who has given me my work to do. O how immensely important is this work of preparing the daughters of the land to be good mothers! If they are prepared for this situation, they will have the most important preparation which they can have for any other; they can soon and easily become good teachers, and they will become, at all events, good members of society. The false delicacy, which some young ladies indulge, will vanish away as they see most of the companions of their childhood and youth occupying the solemn and responsible situation of mothers. It will no longer appear like a subject for which no care should be taken in the training of daughters.

While, in the good providence of God, I have been permitted to occupy a field of labor where I could aid in preparing some who must mould the character of future generations for their great work, I have not been quite satisfied. I have looked out from my quiet scene of labor on the wide world, and my heart has longed to see many enjoying these privileges, who cannot for the want of means. I have longed to be permitted to labor where the expenses would be less than they are here, so that more of our daughters could reap the fruits. Sometimes my heart has burned within me; and again I have bid it be quiet. I have sometimes speculated, and built airy castles, and again I have bid my mind dwell on sober realities. I have thought that there might be a plan devised by which something could be done. I have further thought, that if I could be released from all engagements and all encumbrances, perhaps I might in time find some way opened before me for promoting this good object. With this view, I decided some time since, if Miss Grant's health should be sufficiently restored, to propose a separation. That time has now come, and we have agreed to close our joint labors next fall. Miss Grant is to be absent through the summer term, to improve her strength, and we shall spend most of the vacation here together, in getting ready for the winter, and then I expect to leave this scene of labor forever.

I do not expect immediately to commence in any other field. I very much want six months or a year to read, write, plan, and do a thousand other things. I do not expect to be idle. This may seem like a wild scheme; but I cannot plead that it is a hasty one. I have had it under careful consideration two years or more, and for one whole year the question has been weighed by Miss Grant and myself. . . .

Perhaps you may inquire, what course I expect to take, and where is to be my future scene of labor. This I do not know. The present path of duty is plain. The future I can leave with Him who doeth all things well.

80. A French lay teacher describes village persecution: Mlle N—

This diary account was written by a young primary school teacher, who in 1892 was sent out by the public school authorities to teach the girls in a small community in Loir-et-Cher (Selles-Saint-Denis, population 1,200). Her experiences were by no means unique, for the young, single teacher encountered many problems during this period of increasing tension between Church and State in France. Above all, these women were strangers to the communities to which they were assigned. They were neither married nor nuns; thus they were rejected by the Catholic villagers but tendered little compensatory support either by their male counterparts in the villages or by the secular authorities. They were most often of humble birth, yet expected to exhibit a certain degree of gentility (but not too much). No wonder such women complained to Francisque Sarcey, a prominent literary figure, when in 1897 he launched an inquiry to test the accuracy of a recently published naturalistic novel—Léon Frapié's 'L'Institutrice'—concerning the public school teacher's plight. Theirs was hardly a situation calculated to make them effective in their assigned role as the female vanguard of the Republic, the purveyors of literacy, secular culture, and scientific ways of doing things to inhabitants of provincial villages.

July 1, 1892.—I have already been here one month. I have not been able to note down anything, because I am not yet set up; sometimes I think I never will be. And indeed, how can I move in properly? I have no kitchen, or rather the kitchen is also my schoolroom. Children sit on the ledge of the fireplace, which is blocked up. . . .

I remember well my arrival in the cart, at night, accompanied by two or three great devilish fellows . . . whom the mayor had sent, each with his own vehicle, to pick up the young lady and her bundle. . . . I sat amongst the firewood, one cord of which served me as a seat, en route to Selles-Saint-Denis, my new battlefield. Perhaps I will find death at the end. So much the better, life is so beautiful! . . .

As we rode along the road, stretched out like a long moonlit ribbon bordered by dark green, my companions smoked their vile pipes while they asked me the usual questions, "What province are you from? Where do you come from? Do you have family? Are you unmarried? Why aren't you married? How old are you?" etc. . . .

SOURCE: *Lettres d'institutrices rurales d'autrefois; rédigées à la suite de l'enquête de Francisque Sarcey en 1897*, ed. Ida Berger (Paris, [1961]), pp. 2–10.

When I arrived at Selles-Saint-Denis—it was past ten at night—the mayor had not yet gone to bed; he was waiting for me in order to give me the keys, and welcomed me with "good night."—The first driver took me to his place; he kept an inn. I had to sleep there until my furniture arrived. . . .

Finally I was at home. The house belonged to a rich farmer, and was ill-equipped to be a school. There was a little garden where the teacher who preceded me had taken care to destroy the half-grown crops so that I would not be able to enjoy them. . . .

Because I had no kitchen, I could not cook for myself. Therefore I arranged with the mistress of the big hotel to provide my meals for forty-five francs a month. In the morning they bring me breakfast at home; I am going to the hotel for the other two meals. There I sometimes enjoy the distraction of other dining companions. I am not too bored. . . .

Sept. 18, 1892.—It seems that I shock my colleagues more and more; they have never seen a teacher take her meals at an inn. The hostess . . . has asked me to eat at home.

It has cost me a great deal to go back to cooking and washing up. I have no vegetables and have to pay the mailman to bring me some from Salbris, or to do my shopping at Romorantin on market days. I don't want to patronize the other inns, which are real dumps.

Jan. 4, 1893.—Solitude, bitter cold, frosted walls in my rooms—nothing to read. . . . The class is a distraction for me, but how hard. Oh! that little Ch—, a true alcoholic's daughter. One could call her half-cracked. How she makes me suffer!

February 1893.—No courage to live . . . .

[No date, but after April 15].—This winter the mayor has received all the benedictions of Bacchus. Suddenly he has begun to speak to me in rather spicy language. And because I have kept silent out of respect for his office, he probably believes that I go along with his talk, and he continues his idiotic declarations, all in order to attract me to him, to make me fall into his arms. My gesture to him expressed my complete disgust. . . .

And now my innocent walks [in the neighboring woods] have become suspect. Madame L— has been spreading absurd rumors: that I go there for trysts.

Sept. 7, 1893.—Before shaking the dust of this rotten town off my feet forever, I want to go over the sufferings I have endured. I have not had the energy to write for a long time. These last three months have been hell. I wanted to die! Today I await my reassignment and the world begins to brighten.

How can I tell everything without offending modesty?

One day before the evening class, three pupils, whose names I would prefer to forget, said to me—probably with good intentions—Mademoiselle, if you only knew what Mandine D— said about you! Children, I would rather not kn . . .

[Undated entry].—Everything is packed. The carriages leave this evening.

Goodbye Selles-Saint-Denis where I have suffered so much. Goodbye, dear forest. Goodbye, my few friends. Goodbye, poor people who felt sorry for me.

Goodbye, children. I gave you my best. Goodbye to everyone. Farewell and forgiveness for everything.

81. The lot of New York shopgirls

The plight of shopgirls in the large cities of the late nineteenth century, where jobs for women were scarce, aroused great anxiety among urban reformers. One of the pioneer American social investigators, Helen Stuart Campbell (1839–1918), set out to bring public pressure to bear against the exploitation of these and other working women in a series of passionately indignant articles that ran in the 'New York Tribune' in 1887. The story of Almira —— (Doc. 70) was one of the articles in the series. In this selection Campbell records the voices of the employers and of the shopgirls themselves, as they tell their conflicting stories about working conditions in the new and growing department stores of New York City.

Why this army of women, many thousand strong, is standing behind counters, overworked and underpaid, the average duration of life among them as a class lessening every year, is a question with which we can at present deal only indirectly. It is sufficient to state that the retail stores of wellnigh every order, though chiefly the dry-goods retail trade, have found their quickness and aptness to learn, the honesty and general faithfulness of women, and their cheapness essentials in their work; and that this combination of qualities—cheapness dominating all—has given them permanent place in the modern system of trade. A tour among many of the larger establishments confirmed the statement made by employers in smaller ones, the summary being given in the words of a manager of one of the largest retail houses to be found in the United States.

"We don't want men," he said. "We wouldn't have them even if they came at the same price. Of course cheapness has something to do with it, and will have, but for my part give me a woman to deal with every time. Now there's an illustration over at that hat-counter. We were short of hands to-day, and I had to send for three girls that had applied for places, but were green— didn't know the business. It didn't take them ten minutes to get the hang of doing things, and there they are, and you'd never know which was old and which was new hand. Of course they don't know all about qualities and so on, but the head of the department looks out for that. No, give me women every time. I've been a manager thirteen years, and we never had but four

SOURCE: Helen Stuart Campbell, "Among the Shop-girls," reprinted in *Prisoners of Poverty: Women Wage-Workers, Their Trades and Their Lives* (Boston, 1889), pp. 173–81. Originally published as an article in the *New York Tribune* in 1887.

dishonest girls, and we've had to discharge over forty boys in the same time. Boys smoke and lose at cards, and do a hundred things that women don't, and they get worse instead of better. I go in for women."

"How good is their chance of promotion?"

"We never lose sight of a woman that shows any business capacity, but of course that's only as a rule in heads of departments. A saleswoman gets about the same right along. Two thirds of the girls here are public-school girls and live at home. You see that makes things pretty easy, for the family pool their earnings and they dress well and live well. We don't take from the poorer class at all. These girls earn from four and a half to eight dollars a week. A few get ten dollars, and they're not likely to do better than that. Forty dollars a month is a fortune to a woman. A man must have his little fling, you know. Women manage better."

"If they are really worth so much to you, why can't you give better pay? What chance has a girl to save anything, unless she lives at home?"

"We give as high pay as anybody, and we don't give more because for every girl here there are a dozen waiting to take her place. As to saving, she doesn't want to save. There isn't a girl here that doesn't expect to marry before long, and she puts what she makes on her back, because a fellow naturally goes for the best-looking and the best-dressed girl. That's the woman question as I've figured it out, and you'll find it the same everywhere."

Practically he was right, for the report, though varying slightly, summed up as substantially the same. Descending a grade, it was found that even in the second and third rate stores the system of fines for any damage soon taught the girls carefulness, and that while a few were discharged for hopeless incompetency, the majority served faithfully and well.

"I dare say they're put upon," said the manager of one of the cheaper establishments. "They're sassy enough, a good many of them, and some of the better ones suffer for their goings-on. But they ain't a bad set—not half; and these women that come in complaining that they ain't well-treated, nine times out of ten it's their own airs that brought it on. It's a shop-girl's interest to behave herself and satisfy customers, and she's more apt to do it than not, according to my experience."

"They'd drive a man clean out of his mind," said another. "The tricks of girls are beyond telling. If it wasn't for fines there wouldn't one in twenty be here on time, and the same way with a dozen other things. But they learn quick, and they turn in anywhere where they're wanted. They make the best kind of clerks, after all."

"Do you give them extra pay for over-hours during the busy season?"

"Not much! We keep them on, most of them, right through the dull one. Why shouldn't they balance things for us when the busy time comes? Turn about's fair play."

A girl who had been sent into the office for some purpose shook her head slightly as she heard the words, and it was this girl who, a day or two later, gave her view of the situation. The talk went on in the pretty, home-like parlors of a small "Home" on the west side, where rules are few and the atmosphere of the place so cheery that while it is intended only for those out of work, it is constantly besieged with requests to enlarge its borders and make room for more. Half a dozen other girls were near: three from other stores, one from a shirt factory, one an artificial-flower-maker who had been a shopgirl.

"When I began," said the first, "father was alive, and I used what I earned just for dressing myself. We were up at Morrisania, and I came down every day. I was in the worsted and fancy department at D—'s, and I had such a good eye for matching and choosing that they seemed to think everything of me. But then father fell sick. He was a painter, and had painter's colic awfully and at last paralysis. Then he died finally and left mother and me, and she's in slow consumption and can't do much. I earned seven dollars a week because I'd learned fancy work and did some things evenings for the store, and we should have got along very well. We'd had to move out a little farther, to the place mother was born in, because rent was cheaper and she could never stand the city. But this is the way it worked. I have to be at the store at eight o'clock. The train that leaves home at seven gets me to the store two minutes after eight, but though I've explained this to the manager he says I've got to be at the store at eight, and so, summer and winter, I have to take the train at half-past six and wait till doors are open. It's the same way at night. The store closes at six, and if I could leave then I could catch an express train that would get me home at seven. The rules are that I must stop five minutes to help the girls cover up the goods, and that just hinders my getting the train till after seven, so that I am not home till eight."

I looked at the girl more attentively. She was colorless and emaciated, and, when not excited by speaking, languid and heavy.

"Are you sure that you have explained the thing clearly so that the manager understands?" I asked.

"More than once," the girl answered, "but he said I should be fined if I were not there at eight. Then I told him that the girls at my counter would be glad to cover up my goods, and if he would only let me go at six it would give me a little more time for mother. I sit up late anyway to do things she can't, for we live in two rooms and I sew and do a good many things after I go home."

Inquiry a day or two later showed that her story was true in every detail and also that she was a valuable assistant, one of the best among a hundred or so employed. The firm gives largely to charitable objects, and pays promptly, and at rates which, if low, are no lower than usual; but they continue to exact this seven minutes' service from one whose faithfulness might seem to have earned exemption from a purely arbitrary rule—in such a case mere tyranny. The girl had offered to give up her lunch hour, but the manager refused; and she dared not speak again for fear of losing her place.

"After all, she's better off than I am or lots of others," said one who sat near her. "I'm down in the basement at M—'s, and forty others like me, and about forty little girls. There's gas and electric light both, but there isn't a breath of air, and it's so hot that after an hour or two your head feels baked and your eyes as if they would fall out. The dull season—that's from spring

to fall—lasts six months, and then we work nine and a half hours and Saturdays thirteen. The other six months we work eleven hours, and holiday time
till ten and eleven. I'm strong. I'm an old hand and somehow stand things,
but I've a cousin at the ribbon counter, the very best girl in the world, I do
believe. She always makes the best of things, but this year it did seem as if
the whole town was at that counter. They stood four and five deep. She was
penned in with the other girls, a dozen or two, with drawers and cases behind
and counter in front, and there she stood from eight in the morning till ten at
night, with half an hour off for dinner and for supper. She could have got
through even that, but you see there has to be steady passing in that narrow
space, and she was knocked and pushed, first by one and then by another, till
she was sore all over; and at last down she dropped right there, not fainting
but sort of gone, and the doctor says she's most dead and can't go back, he
doesn't know when. Down there in the basement the girls have to put on blue
glasses, the glare is so dreadful, but they don't like to have us. The only comfort is you're with a lot and don't feel lonesome. I can't bear to do anything
alone, no matter what it is."

A girl with clear dark eyes and a face that might have been almost beautiful
but for its haggard, worn-out expression, turned from the table where she
had been writing and smiled as she looked at the last speaker.

"That is because you happen to be made that way," she said. "I am always
happier when I can be alone a good deal, but of course that's never possible,
or almost never. I shall want the first thousand years of my heaven quite to myself, just for pure rest and a chance to think."

"I don't know anything about heaven," the last speaker said hastily, "but
I'm sure I hope there's purgatory at least for some of the people I've had to
submit to. I think a woman manager is worse than a man. I've never had
trouble anywhere and always stay right on, but I've wanted to knock some
of the managers down, and it ought to have been done. Just take the new superintendent. We loved the old one, but this one came in when she died, and
one of the first things she did was to discharge one of the old girls because she
didn't smile enough. Good reason why. She'd lost her mother the week before
and wasn't likely to feel much like smiling. And then she went inside the
counters and pitched out all the old shoes the girls had there to make it easier
to stand. It 'most kills you to stand all day in new shoes, but Miss T—
pitched them all out and said she wasn't going to have the store turned into
an old-clothes shop."

"Well, it's better than lots of them, no matter what she does," said another. "I was at H—'s for six months, and there you have to ask a man
for leave every time it is necessary to go upstairs, and half the time he would
look and laugh with the other clerks. I'd rather be where there are all women.
They're hard on you sometimes, but they don't use foul language and insult you
when you can't help yourself."

This last complaint has proved for many stores a perfectly well-founded
one. Wash-rooms and other conveniences have been for common use, and

many sensitive and shrinking girls have brought on severe illnesses arising sole-ly from dread of running this gantlet.

Here and there the conditions of this form of labor are of the best, but as a whole the saleswoman suffers not only from long-continued standing, but from bad air, ventilation having no place in the construction of the ordinary store. Separate dressing-rooms are a necessity, yet are only occasionally found, the sys-tem demanding that no outlay shall be made when it is possible to avoid it. Overheating and overcrowding, hastily eaten and improper food, are all causes of the weakness and anæmic condition so perceptible among shop and factory workers, these being divided into many classes. For a large proportion it can be said that they are tolerably educated, so far as our public-school system can be said to educate, and are hard-working, self-sacrificing, patient girls who have the American knack of dressing well on small outlay, and who have tastes and aspirations far beyond any means of gratifying them. For such girls the working-women's guilds and the Friendly societies—these last of English origin—have proved of inestimable service, giving them the opportunities long denied. In such guilds many of them receive the first real training of eye and hand and mind, learn what they can best do, and often develop a practical ability for larger and better work. Even in the lowest order filling the cheaper stores there is always a proportion eager to learn. But here, as in all ordinary methods of learning, the market is overstocked, and even the best-trained girl may sometimes fail of employment. Now and then one turns toward household service, but the mass prefer any cut in wages and any form of privation to what they regard as almost a final degradation.

82. 'Every woman is a nurse'

In the second half of the nineteenth century two gifted women—Florence Nightingale (1820–1910) and Clara Barton (1821–1912)—spearheaded the crusade to make nursing a respected profession for women. Both of these able and energetic women put superhuman effort into caring for wounded soldiers in dangerous and difficult battlefront conditions, Nightingale in the Crimean War and Barton in the Civil War. Although their wartime exploits made them famous, both paid the price afterwards with years of ill health. In their work and writings they stressed that nursing required not only compassion and the desire to help and heal, but great endurance and ingenuity—not to mention a strong stomach. Like Beeton's housewife, the good nurse, whether in the sick-room or at the battlefront, needed to be an organizing general, as well as a ministering angel.

In the first selection Nightingale warns women who are amateur nurses at home to take command of the sickroom, neglecting no detail. In the second

SOURCES: (i) Florence Nightingale, *Notes on Nursing* (New York, 1860), pp. 3, 35, 39–43. (ii) Percy H. Epler, *The Life of Clara Barton* (New York, 1915), pp. 37–59 *passim*, 399–401.

selection Barton writes to a friend about her Civil War experiences; her account bears out Nightingale's view that a good nurse had to have organizational skills. Barton also believed that the competent nurse-administrator should be flexible and clever at improvising, and indeed the American Red Cross, which she founded and directed for many years, ran very effectively by her principles, "No soliciting funds, no red tape, instantaneous action." The second selection concludes with a poem Barton composed hurriedly one afternoon in 1892 to read at a Washington banquet that evening. In bad verse, she makes sarcastic reference to the enormous obstacles army officers, doctors, and government bureaucrats placed in the path of the Civil War nurses as they struggled to get to the front. Nightingale would have applauded these sentiments.

(i) Florence Nightingale

The following notes are by no means intended as a rule of thought by which nurses can teach themselves to nurse, still less as a manual to teach nurses to nurse. They are meant simply to give hints for thought to women who have personal charge of the health of others. Every woman, or at least almost every woman, in England has, at one time or another of her life, charge of the personal health of somebody, whether child or invalid,—in other words, every woman is a nurse. Every day sanitary knowledge, or the knowledge of nursing, or in other words, of how to put the constitution in such a state as that it will have no disease, or that it can recover from disease, takes a higher place. It is recognized as the knowledge which every one ought to have— distinct from medical knowledge, which only a profession can have. . . .

All the results of good nursing, as detailed in these notes, may be spoiled or utterly negatived by one defect, viz.: in petty management, or in other words, by not knowing how to manage that what you do when you are there, shall be done when you are not there. The most devoted friend or nurse cannot be always *there.* Nor is it desirable that she should. And she may give up her health, all her other duties, and yet, for want of a little management, be not one-half so efficient as another who is not one-half so devoted, but who has this art of multiplying herself—that is to say, the patient of the first will not really be so well cared for, as the patient of the second. . . .

In institutions where many lives would be lost and the effect of such want of management would be terrible and patent, there is less of it than in the private house.*

---

* . . . But, as far as regards the art of petty management in hospitals, all the military hospitals I know must be excluded. Upon my own experience I stand, and I solemnly declare that I have seen or known of fatal accidents, such as suicides in *delirium tremens,* bleedings to death, dying patients dragged out of bed by drunken Medical Staff Corps men, and many other things less patent and striking, which would not have happened in London civil hospitals nursed by women. The medical officers should be absolved from all blame in these accidents. How can a medical officer mount guard all day and all night over a patient (say) in *delirium tremens?* The fault lies in there being no organized system of attendance. Were a trustworthy *man* in charge of each ward, or set of wards, not as office clerk, but as head nurse, (and head nurse

But in both, let whoever is in charge keep this simple question in her head (*not*, how can I always do this right thing myself, but) how can I provide for this right thing to be always done? . . .

How few men, or even women, understand, either in great or in little things, what it is the being "in charge"—I mean, know how to carry out a "charge." From the most colossal calamities, down to the most trifling accidents, results are often traced (or rather *not* traced) to such want of some one "in charge" or of his knowing how to be "in charge." A short time ago the bursting of a funnel-casing on board the finest and strongest ship that ever was built, on her trial trip, destroyed several lives and put several hundreds in jeopardy—not from any undetected flaw in her new and untried works— but from a tap being closed which ought not to have been closed—from what every child knows would make its mother's tea-kettle burst. And this simply because no one seemed to know what it is to be "in charge," or *who* was in charge. Nay more, the jury at the inquest actually altogether ignored the same, and apparently considered the tap "'in charge," for they gave as a verdict "accidental death."

This is the meaning of the word, on a large scale. On a much smaller scale, it happened, a short time ago, that an insane person burned herself slowly and intentionally to death, while in her doctor's charge and almost in her nurse's presence. Yet neither was considered "at all to blame." The very fact of the accident happening proves its own case. There is nothing more to be said. Either they did not know their business or they did not know how to perform it.

To be "in charge" is certainly not only to carry out the proper measures yourself but to see that every one else does so too; to see that no one either wilfully or ignorantly thwarts or prevents such measures. It is neither to do everything yourself nor to appoint a number of people to each duty, but to ensure that each does that duty to which he is appointed. This is the meaning which must be attached to the word by (above all) those "in charge" of sick. . . .

It is often said that there are few good servants now; I say there are few good mistresses now. As the jury seems to have thought the tap was in charge of the ship's safety, so mistresses now seem to think the house is in charge of itself. They neither know how to give orders, nor how to teach their servants to obey orders—*i.e.*, to obey intelligently, which is the real meaning of all discipline.

Again, people who are in charge often seem to have a pride in feeling that they will be "missed," that no one can understand or carry on their arrangements, their system, books, accounts, &c., but themselves. It seems to me that the pride is rather in carrying on a system, in keeping stores, closets, books, accounts, &c., so that any body can understand and carry them

---

the best hospital serjeant, or ward master, is not now and cannot be, from default of the proper regulations,) the thing would not, in all probability, have happened. But were a trustworthy *woman* in charge of the ward, or set of wards, the thing would not, in all certainty, have happened. In other words, it does not happen where a trustworthy woman is really in charge.

on—so that, in case of absence or illness, one can deliver every thing up to others and know that all will go on as usual, and that one shall never be missed.

(ii) Clara Barton

[In the period covered here, late August to mid-September 1862, the Union and Confederate armies met successively at Bull Run, Chantilly, Harpers Ferry, and Antietam.]

At 10 o'clock Sunday (August 31) our train drew up at Fairfax Station. The ground, for acres, was a thinly wooded slope—and among the trees on the leaves and grass, were laid the wounded who were pouring in by scores of wagon loads, as picked up on the field under the flag of truce. All day they came and the whole hillside was covered. Bales of hay were broken open and scattered over the ground like littering for cattle, and the sore, famishing men were laid upon it.

And when the night shut in, in the mist and darkness about us, we knew that standing apart from the world of anxious hearts, throbbing over the whole country, we were a little band of almost empty handed workers literally by ourselves in the wild woods of Virginia, with 3000 suffering men crowded upon the few acres within our reach.

After gathering up every available implement or convenience for our work, our domestic inventory stood 2 water buckets, 5 tin cups, 1 camp kettle, 1 stewpan, 2 lanterns, 4 bread knives, 3 plates, and a 2-quart tin dish, and 3000 guests to serve.

You will perceive by this, that I had not yet learned to equip myself, for I was no Pallas, ready armed, but grew into my work by hard thinking and sad experience. It may serve to relieve your apprehension for the future of my labors if I assure you that I was never caught so again. . . .

This finds us shortly after daylight Monday morning. Train after train of cars were rushing on for the wounded and hundreds of wagons were bringing them in from the field still held by the enemy, where some poor sufferers had lain three days with no visible means of sustenance. If immediately placed upon the trains and not detained, at least twenty-four hours must elapse before they could be in the hospital and properly nourished. They were already famishing, weak and sinking from loss of blood and they could ill afford a further fast of twenty-four hours. I felt confident that unless nourished at once, all the weaker portion must be past recovery before reaching the hospitals of Washington. If once taken from the wagons and laid with those already cared for, they would be overlooked and perish on the way. Something must be done to meet this fearful emergency. I sought the various officers on the grounds, explained the case to them and asked permission to feed all the men as they arrived before they should be taken from the wagons. It was well for the poor sufferers of that field that it was controlled by noble-hearted, generous officers, quick to feel and prompt to act.

They at once saw the propriety of my request and gave orders that all wagons would be stayed at a certain point and only moved on when every one had been seen and fed. This point secured, I commenced my day's work of climbing from the wheel to the brake of every wagon and speaking to and feeding with my own hands each soldier until he expressed himself satisfied. . . .

The rain continued to pour in torrents, and the darkness became impenetrable save from the lightning leaping above our heads and the fitful flash of the guns, as volley after volley rang through the stifled air and lighted up the gnarled trunks and dripping branches among which we ever waited and listened.

In the midst of this, and how guided no man knows, came still another train of wounded men, and a waiting train of cars upon the track received them. This time nearly alone, for my worn-out assistants could work no longer, I continued to administer such food as I had left. . . .

The departure of this train cleared the grounds of wounded for the night, and as the line of fire from its plunging engines died out in the darkness, a strange sensation of weakness and weariness fell upon me, almost defying my utmost exertion to move one foot before the other.

A little Sibley tent had been hastily pitched for me in a slight hollow upon the hillside. Your imaginations will not fail to picture its condition. Rivulets of water had rushed through it during the last three hours. Still I attempted to reach it, as its white surface, in the darkness, was a protection from the wheels of wagons and trampling of beasts.

Perhaps I shall never forget the painful effort which the making of those few rods, and the gaining of the tent cost me. How many times I fell from sheer exhaustion, in the darkness and mud of that slippery hillside, I have no knowledge, but at last I grasped the welcome canvas, and a well established brook which washed in on the upper side at the opening that served as door, met me on my entrance. My entire floor was covered with water, not an inch of dry, solid ground.

One of my lady assistants had previously taken train for Washington and the other worn out by faithful labors, was crouched upon the top of some boxes in one corner fast asleep. No such convenience remained for me, and I had no strength to arrange one. I sought the highest side of my tent which I remembered was grass grown, and ascertaining that the water was not very deep, I sank down. It was no laughing matter then. But the recollection of my position has since afforded me amusement. . . .

And thus the morning of the third day broke upon us, drenched, weary, hungry, sorefooted, sad-hearted, discouraged, and under orders to retreat. . . .

The enemy's cavalry skirting the hills, admonished us each moment, that we must soon decide to go from them or with them. But our work must be accomplished, and no wounded men once given into our hands must be left. And with the spirit of desperation, we struggled on.

At three o'clock an officer galloped up to me, with "Miss Barton, can you ride?" "Yes, sir," I replied.

"But you have no lady's saddle—could you ride mine?"

"Yes, sir, or without it, if you have blanket and surcingle."

"Then you can risk another hour," he exclaimed and galloped off.

At four he returned at a break-neck speed—and leaping from his horse said, "Now is your time. The enemy is already breaking over the hills, try the train. It will go through, unless they have flanked, and cut the bridge a mile above us. In that case I've a reserve horse for you, and you must take your chances to escape across the country."

In two minutes I was on the train. The last wounded man at the station was also on. The conductor stood with a torch which he applied to a pile of combustible material beside the track. And we rounded the curve which took us from view as we saw the station ablaze, and a troop of cavalry dashing down the hill. The bridge was uncut and midnight found us at Washington.

You have the full record of my sleep—from Friday night till Wednesday morning—two hours. You will not wonder that I slept during the next twenty-four. . . .

The patient endurance of [the] men was most astonishing. As many as could be were carried into the barn, as a slight protection against random shot. Just outside the door lay a man wounded in the face, the ball having entered the lower maxillary on the left side, and lodged among the bones of the right cheek. His imploring look drew me to him, when placing his finger upon the sharp protuberance, he said, "Lady, will you tell me what this is that burns so?" I replied that it must be the ball which had been too far spent to cut its way entirely through.

"It is terribly painful," he said. "Won't you take it out?"

I said I would go to the tables for a surgeon. "No! No!" he said, catching my dress. "They cannot come to me. I must wait my turn, for this is a little wound. You can get the ball. There is a knife in your pocket. Please take the ball out for me."

This was a new call. I had never severed the nerves and fibers of human flesh, and I said I could not hurt him so much. He looked up, with as nearly a smile as such a mangled face could assume, saying, "You cannot hurt me, dear lady, I can endure any pain that your hands can create. Please do it. It will relieve me so much."

I could not withstand his entreaty and opening the best blade of my pocket knife, prepared for the operation. Just at his head lay a stalwart orderly sergeant from Illinois, with a face beaming with intelligence and kindness, and who had a bullet directly through the fleshy part of both thighs. He had been watching the scene with great interest and when he saw me commence to raise the poor fellow's head, and no one to support it, with a desperate effort he succeeded in raising himself to a sitting posture, exclaiming as he did so, "I will help do that." Shoving himself along the ground he took the wounded head in his hands and held it while I extracted the ball and washed and bandaged the face.

I do not think a surgeon would have pronounced it a scientific operation, but that it was successful I dared to hope from the gratitude of the patient. . . .

At two o'clock my men came to tell me that the last loaf of bread had been cut and the last cracker pounded. We had three boxes of wine still unopened. What should they do?

"Open the wine and give that," I said, "and God help us."

The next instant, an ejaculation from Sergeant Field, who had opened the first box, drew my attention, and to my astonished gaze, the wine had been packed in nicely sifted Indian meal.

If it had been gold dust, it would have seemed poor in comparison. I had no words. No one spoke. In silence the men wiped their eyes, and resumed their work.

Of 12 boxes of wine which we carried, the first nine, when opened, were found packed in sawdust; the last three, when all else was gone, in Indian meal.

A woman would not hesitate long under circumstances like these.

This was an old farmhouse. Six large kettles were picked up, and set over fires, almost as quickly as I can tell it, and I was mixing water and meal for gruel.

It occurred to us to explore the cellar. The chimney rested on an arch, and forcing the door, we discovered three barrels and a bag. "They are full," said the sergeant, and rolling one into the light, found that it bore the mark of Jackson's Army. These three barrels of flour, and a bag of salt, had been stored there by the Rebel army during its upward march.

I shall never experience such a sensation of wealth, and competency again, from utter poverty to such riches.

All that night, my thirty men (for my corps of workers had increased to that number during the day), carried buckets of hot gruel for miles down the line to the wounded and dying where they fell.

This time, profiting by experience, we had lanterns to hang in and around the barn, and having directed it to be done, I went to the house, and found the surgeon in charge, sitting alone, beside a table, upon which he rested his elbow, apparently meditating upon a bit of tallow candle, which flickered in the center.

Approaching carefully, I said, "You are tired, Doctor." He started up with a look almost savage, "Tired! Yes, I am tired, tired of such heartlessness, such carelessness!" Turning full upon me, he continued: "Think of the condition of things. Here are at least 1,000 wounded men, terribly wounded, 500 of whom cannot live till daylight, without attention. That two inch of candle is all I have, or can get. What can I do? How can I endure it?"

I took him by the arm, and leading him to the door, pointed in the direction of the barn where the lanterns glistened like stars among the waving corn.

"What is that?" he exclaimed.

"The barn is lighted," I said, "and the house will be directly."

"Who did it?"

"I, Doctor."

"Where did you get them?"
"Brought them with me."
"How many have you?"
"All you want—four boxes."

He looked at me a moment—as if waking from a dream, turned away without a word, and never alluded to the circumstances, but the deference which he paid me was almost painful.

"The Women Who Went to the Field"

The women who went to the field, you say,
The women who went to the field; and pray,
What did they go for?—just to be in the way?
They'd not know the difference betwixt work and play.
And what did they know about war, anyway?
What could they do? of what use could they be?
They would scream at the sight of a gun, don't you see?
Just fancy them round where the bugle-notes play,
And the long roll is bidding us on to the fray.
Imagine their skirts 'mong artillery wheels,
And watch for their flutter as they flee 'cross the fields
When the charge is rammed home and the fire belches hot;
They never will wait for the answering shot.
They would faint at the first drop of blood in their sight.
What fun for us boys,—(ere we enter the fight),
They might pick some lint, and tear up some sheets,
And make us some jellies, and send on their sweets,
And knit some soft socks for Uncle's Sam's shoes,
And write us some letters, and tell us the news.
And thus it was settled, by common consent,
By husbands, or brothers, or whoever went,
That the place for the women was in their homes,
There to patiently wait until victory comes.
But later it chanced—just how no one knew—
That the lines slipped a bit, and some 'gan to crowd through;
And they went, where did they go?—Ah! where did they not?
Show us the battle,—the field,—or the spot
Where the groans of the wounded rang out on the air
That her ear caught it not, and her hand was not there;
Who wiped the death sweat from the cold, clammy brow,
And sent home the message " 'Tis well with him now"—?
Who watched in the tents whilst the fever fires burned,
And the pain-tossing limbs in agony turned,
And wet the parched tongue, calmed delirium's strife
Till the dying lips murmured, "My mother," "My wife?"
And who were they all?—They were many, my men;

Their records were kept by no tabular pen;
They exist in traditions from father to son,
Who recalls, in dim memory, now here and there one,
A few names were writ, and by chance live to-day;
But it's a perishing record, fast fading away.

    . . .

Did these women quail at the sight of a gun?
Will some soldier tell us of one he saw run?
Will he glance at the boats on the great western flood,
At Pittsburg and Shiloh, did they faint at the blood?
And the brave wife of Grant stood there with them then,
And her calm stately presence gave strength to his men.
And Marie of Logan; she went with them too,
A bride, scarcely more than a sweetheart, 'tis true.
Her young cheek grows pale when the bold troopers ride.
Where the "Black Eagle" soars she is close at his side,
She stanches his blood, cools the fever-burnt breath,
And the wave of her hand stays the Angel of Death;
She nurses him back, and restores once again
To both army and state the great Leader of men.
She has smoothed his black plumes and laid them to sleep
Whilst the angels above them their high vigils keep;
And she sits here alone, with the snow on her brow—
Your cheers for her, Comrades! Three cheers for her now.
And these were the women who went to the war.
The women of question; what did they go for?
Because in their hearts God had planted the seed
Of pity for woe, and help for its need;
They saw, in high purpose, a duty to do,
And the armor of right broke the barriers through.
Uninvited, unaided, unsanctioned ofttimes,
With pass, or without it, they pressed on the lines;
They pressed, they implored, 'till they ran the lines through,
And that was the "running" the men saw them do.
'Twas a hampered work, it's worth largely lost;
'Twas hindrance, and pain, and effort, and cost;
But through these came knowledge,—knowledge is power,—
And never again in the deadliest hour
Of war or of peace shall we be so beset
To accomplish the purpose our spirits have met.
And what would they do if war came again?
The scarlet cross floats where all was blank then.
They would bind on their "brassards" and march to the fray.
And the man liveth not who could say them nay;
They would stand with you now, as they stood with you then
The nurses, consolers, and saviours of men.

83. Textile workers in Leeds and Nottingham

In 1833 Parliament passed an act that forbade the employment of young children in textile mills and established an eight-hour workday for children over nine. This was the first major piece of industrial legislation enacted in England, but by the end of the century Parliament had passed a whole series of acts designed to regulate working conditions in factories and limit the hours of work. The Factory Act of 1833 grew out of the findings of royal commissioners who traveled throughout the textile districts seeking evidence about the factory system; the following depositions were given to commissioners investigating the cotton and woolen mills of Leeds and Nottingham. These accounts highlight the long hours and dangerous conditions of factory work. They not only provide valuable insights into the family structures of English mill workers, but also show how essential were the earnings of women and children to family economies. Although the act of 1833 curtailed the exploitation of young children, it led to the increased employment of young women like Hannah Goode and Eliza Marshall in the mills, and, ironically, hastened the breakup of the working-class family.

Hannah Goode.—I work at Mr. Wilson's mill. I attend the drawing-head.* I get 5s. 9d. It is four or five years since we worked double hours. We only worked an hour over then. We got a penny for that. We went in the morning at six o'clock by the mill clock. It is about half past five by our clock at home when we go in, and we are about a quarter too fast by Nottingham. We come out at seven by the mill. The clock is in the engine-house. It goes like other clocks. I think the youngest child is about seven. There are only two males in the mill. I dare say there are twenty under nine years. They go in when we do and come out when we do. The smallest children work at the cards, and doffing the spinning bobbins.† I work in that room. We never stop to take our meals, except at dinner. It has gone on so this six years and more. It is called an hour for dinner from coming out to going in. We have a full hour. Some stop in, if they have a mind. The men stop half an hour at dinner-time to clean the wheels. The children stop to clean their own work; that may take them five or ten minutes or so. That is taken out of the dinner-time. William Crookes is overlooker in our room; he is cross-tempered sometimes. He does not beat me; he beats the little children if they do not do their work right. They want beating now and then. He has a strap; he never beats them with any thing else, except his hand. The children are in a middling way as to goodness. I have sometimes seen the little children drop asleep or

* Or drawing-frame, a machine in which the slivers of wool from the carding machine were drawn out or attenuated.—EDS.

† The first job involved feeding the wool through leather-covered rollers studded with pointed wires to comb or clean it. A doffer removed the full bobbins or spindles of wool, which were then taken to other machines to be processed into thread.—EDS.

SOURCE: Great Britain, *Parliamentary Papers*, 1833, XX, Factory Inquiry Commission, 1st report, pp. C1 43, C1, 72–74, C2 20–21, C2 60.

so, but not lately. If they are catched asleep they get the strap. They are always very tired at night. I have weakened them sometimes to prevent Crookes seeing them; not very often, because they don't often go to sleep. Sometimes they play about the street when they come out; sometimes they go home. The girls often go home and sew. I sit up often till nine or ten o'clock at home, picking the spinners waste. I get 2½d. a pound for that. I can pick about half a pound a night, working very hard. I have known the people complain of their children getting beat. There is no rule about not beating the children. When the engine stops, all stops except the reeling. The reelers are all grown up. I can read a little; I can't write. I used to go to school before I went to the mill; I have since. I am sixteen. We have heard nothing in our mill about not working so long.

Mrs. Smith.—I have three children working in Wilson's mill; one eleven, one thirteen, and the other fourteen. They work regular hours there. We don't complain. If they go to drop the hours, I don't know what poor people will do. I suppose they'll take off the wages as well as the hours. I'd rather it continued as now. We have hard work to live as it is. It would make sad work with us. My husband is of the same mind about it. He works in the mill, and I am winding. My husband earns 12s. a week, I earn 2s., the eldest child 4s. 6d., second child 3s. 6d., third child 2s. 6d.; total 1l. 4s. 6d. Out of this we have to pay house-rent, fire, and clothes, and food, for six of us. We have never had parish help, but stood greatly in need of it last summer. My husband was six weeks ill of a bowel complaint; we pledged almost all our things to live; we got through without help; it was last summer; the things are not all out of pawn yet. I am sure taking two hours from the twelve we now work would much distress us, if, as I expect, our wages was reduced according: my husband thinks so; and we were talking about it to-day at dinner. He said he did not know how we should get on if there was any reducement. We reckoned it would take from my husband's wages 2s. a week, from the eldest child 9d., from the second 7d., from the youngest 5d.; total 3s. 9d. a week. This would lessen our comforts very much. We don't feel the number of hours too much now. We complain of nothing but short wages. I have never had any communication with Wilsons, or anybody belonging to the mill, about any questions being asked us. I heard of your being down here last night. Nothing has been said either before or since to me or my husband, that I know of, about questions being put to us. My children have been in the mill three years. I have no complaint to make of their being beaten. Mine never are beaten, nor fined neither. Never had any talk with Miller about that. Never told him I would rather they were beaten than fined. Never talked with him at all in my life. There are other Mrs. Smiths living about this neighbourhood. I have heard folks talk about his fining the children. I have never heard 'em say they'd rather have them beaten.

What is your own opinion about that?—Well, I'd rather have mine corrected on the spot than have 'em fined. If the children would not mind their work, fining wouldn't do them any good; they wouldn't care for it. Their parents would suffer for it. When they won't attend what are you to do with them? My children are never either fined or beaten. They mind their work as they should do.

But are the children not very tired with this work?—Well, they are tired at night; I generally try to get 'em to bed about nine o'clock. Sometimes they'd rather go on playing; sometimes very willing to go to bed. Sometimes fall asleep over supper. Often very tired.

Do you ever beg them off?—Never. Our comings in won't allow it; we can't give way to what they would like. Their appetite is not always good. One in particular fails; eleven years of age; the youngest; the doctor said he was in a consumption last year; but he is better and goes to work again. I think it comes partly of working in the mill; but he was always a sickly delicate child, I don't think it is much the case with people's children hereabout. I have often great difficulty to get 'em up in the morning. The first bell rings at half past four by the factory clock. They have 'em in by about five or half past. They give an hour for dinner, but call them in before the end of the hour. No time for breakfast or tea. They let 'em out at half past six. I reckon it about twelve hours on the whole. I have trouble to waken them up, but when wakened they are fit for their work, and always willing to go. I think it would do the youngest good to keep him at home; but we can't afford it, unless we could put him to something would suit his health better, and produce the same wages. The other two are quite healthy: one is a girl; the other a boy.

Eliza Marshall.—I live near the middle of Bayton Street, Top Close, in a cellar. I pay 1 s. a week for it. Nobody lives with us. I do nothing. I have no mother. I live with my little sisters. The youngest is going fifteen, and the other is sixteen. I am turned eighteen. My sisters work, one at Rush's, the other at Durham. I have 2s. 6d. a week from the town.

I was about nine when I went to Mr. Marshall's. It was the same week I came to Leeds. I did not stop there long. I worked in the screwing-room.* I screwed. Then I went to Burgess', what is now Warburton's, in Lady Lane now; it was in Meadow Lane when I went. I was put to learn to spin. They had only one room. It was a worsted mill. I was put to the one spindle frame. I was put at first with another to learn me, and in two or three weeks I was able to mind it myself. My next sister went with me; she was put to spin, too, at the one-spindle frame. I got 3s. at first, and then 3s. 6d. . . .

When Mr Warburton began, we went from five [A.M.] to nine [P.M.] We had over-money for that: it made a week of seven days. My standing wage then was 5s. 6d.: we reckoned that from six to seven. We gave over at five on Saturdays. I had 6s. odd when we worked this time. I forget the coppers. I had worked about a year with Burgess before he broke. I was not lame then. I had my strength very well. I had my health very well till I took from five to nine. My sister was very well too while we worked from six to seven. She began to fail, too, when we began the long hours. Mrs. Smith gave her some

---

* At a machine that formed the threads of nuts and bolts.—EDS.

strengthening plaister, and she is quite well now. I was turned ten when I began to work from five to nine. My sister was nine. There were older than me at Burgess'. Mr. Warburton picked us out, I suppose, because I was sharp at my work, a good hand: so was my sister. I was forced to go to work. I had no father, and my mother could not keep us without working. My mother is dead now. She died about half a year ago, since I was in London. I worked on at Warburton's till better than a year ago. I worked those hours all the time. We sometimes worked from six to seven, but it was mostly from five to nine. He has got nearly two rooms full now: when I left him, there were about fifteen hands or so. I went from there to the Infirmary. . . .

It was the work and hours together that hurt me, and always having to stop the flies* with my knee. I could stop it with my hand, but I had to hold it with my knee while I pieecened it.† It was having to crook my knee to stop the spindle that lamed me as much as any thing else. It is my right knee that is crooked: I don't know any other girls who have a crooked knee like mine. They were wearied at night. Another time I went to Durham's: I worked there two days. I worked there from six to seven, and had an hour to my dinner in that time. Mr. Warburton sent for me; I was going to have 6s. at Durham's, and Warburton asked me how much I wanted to have, and I thought happen if I had said 6s he would not have given it me, because he used to say I was not so sharp as I used to be; so I said 5s. 6d., and he agreed. I thought it was gainer, being some lame, and Durham's being so much farther. It was away over Leeds' Brigg, and Warburton's was close by us.

It was after I came back that he knocked me down. I was very weak, Sir, you know: I was soon knocked down. He came in one Saturday, and was so vexed with me for having left him. I was crying when he gave me my wage, and he said I was laughing at him, which was not true, and he took me down with his hand. . . . It was a common thing for him to beat the hands then. It was his knocking me down that made me cry. It was not at the time he knocked me down that he gave me my wage. I was crying when he gave my wage; I was crying all the afternoon at after. He had not struck me for a long time before. Not since I was little. He has strapped me many a time when I was lesser.

I think if I had gone on working only from six to seven, my lameness would not have come on at all. There is not much dust in a worsted mill. I took my meals with me. I generally took a bottle of coffee with me for breakfast, and warmed it at top of boiler. Sometimes with milk, sometimes not. For dinner sometimes bread and butter, sometimes cheese and bread, or a bit of meat. My mother used to cook it at night, and we warmed it there when we did not go home to dinner. I used to take no coffee at drinking time, only a bit of bread. Sometimes we did not live so well. We mostly had a bit of meat on Sunday and Monday, sometimes on other days. Some of the girls were better off than me, and some worse. When my sister and I worked together, we took

---

* The cylinders of the carding-machine.—EDS.
† The piecener joined (or pieced) the cardings together to make them into a continuous thread.—EDS.

our meals all in one. My sister staid at Warburton's after I left. The master turned her away, about a quarrel with another girl. He has heard of what I said in London, and came on to our house a good bit since. He said he had thought he had served me best of any girl in the mill; he asked, "Did I ever ill use you," and I said, "Yes Sir," because I had not told any thing but the truth. He did not seem angry; he said he would give me a job if I was better. He did not say any thing of his striking me down. If he denies it, I can face him with it, or any thing ever I have said. He knew I was ill with the lameness; he said he would give me some money, but he never has. He has never given me a farthing since I was unable to work for him. Neither to me nor any one for me, that I ever got. Sometimes I get better, and then again I can't hardly stir. I wash up for myself and for my sisters: I can sew too, but I can't get much to do. I was learning to be a dress-maker when my mother died. Miss Darley, of Timble Brigg, was learning me. I had to pay half a guinea for learning; I was only there a quarter of a year. I was to pay the half guinea for a year. My mother was taken very ill, and I had to mind her, and then I was very poorly, and in the Infirmary myself: I have never been able to go backwards and forwards since. She would take me back again, but I can't walk so far. The iron that I wear is so heavy. It supports me up, but I don't feel any stronger. She told me some time ago she would take me again if I could come, and I dare say she would be of the same mind yet. I tried a little since my mother died. I shouldn't like to flit [move] from where we are. We have lived there seven years among friends nigh at hand to help us, and I shouldn't like to leave them. I remember all I said when I was in London; it was all true. I happen might make a mistake, but not of my knowing. . . .

Both my sisters are working regular hours now, from six to seven:—No, I had forgot, one works at night now, she lays in bed day-times. That is the littlest. She works at Durham's. That is Simpson Fold Mill. I did not hear her say she had seen you there the other morning. I heard another girl say so, Nancy Simpson. My sister would have been there. She goes at seven and comes away at six. They have no seats to sit down all night. I believe they stop about twelve o'clock. She has been only working there a week about. She was working regular hours before at the same place. She was changed because she asked to work at night. She does not get more wages, but she thought she would. Some of the night hands get more than the day set. She never asked what she was to have, but only would they put her in the night set. She is very sorry now. She has not asked to be put back again. My sister goes to bed as soon as she comes home; about half-past six, and goes to bed. I left her at home asleep. She gets up about five or half-past. She takes some coffee and bread at home before she goes. When she worked days, if she was a quarter too late, they'd stop her wage till breakfast time. She'd not need then to work till after breakfast, at nine o'clock. She gets 4s. 6d. I never heard her say any thing about her night work, but I think she looks as if she did not like it. She says they sing all night to keep them awake. I think they don't fight them a deal there; I never heard no complaints from my sister about it. Her name is Marianne; she has never worked overtime since she went to Mr. Durham's, better than a year. She has been well. She has been poorly lately with this complaint, but she has never left her work. I don't think it too much for her. She does not get very good support, but still she keeps on at her work.

My other sister works in a worsted mill: it is partly a blue mill (I mean a cloth mill), Mr. Rush's; she has worked there a month. She does not give me her wages, she finds herself. She has 5s. She is a wild girl. She has nobody to master or mind her but me, and I have not strength. She was wildish when my mother lived. My little sister is a very good girl. The work is not too much for my second sister either. She has good strength.

I have been to a Sunday school, but I was too tired when I got to those long hours, and being so lame, I was not able to work on week days, and much less to go to school on Sundays. I was learning to write when I left. I think neither of my sisters can. I can read a little. If I had kept on from six to seven, and minding only one side, I could have gone to school well enough. I had six boxes and eight spindles in each. That was the same on each side. That is more than a girl can do, unless they are very strong: it was past my strength. It is being kept so much agait that tires so; with one side only I had more time to sit down. Mr. Warburton was not again that if the work was going well.

Elizabeth Strother.—I was working about eleven weeks ago in a mill for spinning woolen yarn, in the occupation of Mr. Nevins, at New Road End, Leeds. I was piecening for one of the mules.* There was an upright shaft at the back of the mule which I was piecening for in front, the mule was between me and the shaft while I was at my work. There is often occasion for the piecener to go to the back part of the mule when any thing is wrong during the work. This shaft was so placed that we could not go to the back part of the mule without passing close to it. It was placed very near the wall, and we had to pass between it and the wall; it was so close that we could not pass it with the shoulders turned breadthways; we had to turn and go sideways in passing it. I had been five years at the mill; but only five weeks at work at this mule; I was passing the shaft about twenty minutes to twelve at noon, when it caught hold of my apron first, and afterwards my petticoats, and whirled me round three or four times, when my clothes tore and gave way, and I was thrown to the ground: I did not receive any injury from the fall that I know of; but in whirling round with the shaft, my shoulder and arm, down to the elbow, got very much injured. My shoulder, I believe, was put out of joint; and I was told by my mother and the patients at the Infirmary, where I was taken sense-less, that Mr. Sharpe, the surgeon, did something to it and brought it into joint again. It gave me great pain both at the time of the accident happening and afterwards. Mr. Smith, the surgeon, has told me that the bones are all right now; that was about a month since, but I am not able to use it at all up to this time; I can move it very little in a forward and backward direction, as you see. My arm also, above the elbow, was a good deal crushed; the skin was not broken, nor the bone, but it appeared as if all blood had left it; that sensation did not continue long. They have not told me from what it is that I can't

* The mule was a machine that spun the thread.—EDS.

move my arm; Mr. Smith says he hopes it will get better in time. There was no reason why that shaft should not have been boxed up; it was boxed up the week afterwards.

84. Lives of American mill girls

Textile mills like those that first employed the educated young farm women of rural New England were established in the South after the Civil War, drawing poorer, less literate white women into the labor force. In both regions many women regretted the personal sacrifices involved in going into the mills, despite the importance of their wages for the family economy. In the first selection H. E. Back describes to a former co-worker, Harriet Hanson Robinson, her feelings about returning to the Lowell mills. The second selection comes from a Federal Writers' Project interview with Ann Kinley Waldrop, who was seventy-seven years old at the time (1939). Waldrop, described by the interviewer as a snuff-taking woman of Irish descent, entered the mills in Athens, Georgia, during the 1870's. After her marriage she and her husband tried farming, but they soon returned to Athens, where he worked in the boiler room at the Southern Mills while she raised their seven children.

(i) H. E. Back

Dear Harriet,   Sept. 7, 1846, Lowell, Mass.
    With a feeling which you can better imagine than I can describe do I announce to you the horrible tidings that I am *once more a factory girl*! yes; once more a factory girl, seated in the short attic of a Lowell boarding house with a half dozen of girls seated around me talking and reading and myself in the midst, trying to write to you, with the thoughts of so many different persons flying around me that I can hardly tell which are my own. . . . My friends and my mother had almost persuaded me to stay at home during the fall and winter but when I reached home I found a letter which informed me that Mr. Saunders was keeping my place for me and sent for me to come back as soon as I could and after reading it my Lowell fever returned and, come I would, and come I did, but now, "Ah! me. I rue the day" although I am not so homesick as I was a fortnight ago and just begin to feel more resigned to my fate. I have been here four weeks but have not had to work very hard for there are six girls of us and we have fine times doing nothing. I

SOURCES: (i) Letter from H. E. Back to Harriet Hanson Robinson, Sept. 7, 1846, Harriet Hanson Robinson Papers, The Arthur and Elizabeth Schlesinger Library on the History of Women in America, Radcliffe College. The editors are grateful to Allis Rosenberg Wolfe, New York City, for contributing this letter and to the Schlesinger Library for permission to publish it. (ii) "Life History of Mrs. Ann Waldrop," unpublished typescript, Federal Writers' Project Papers, Southern Historical Collection, Library of the University of North Carolina, Chapel Hill. The editors wish to thank Jerrold Hirsch, Chapel Hill, for bringing this document to our attention and to the Southern Historical Collection for authorizing publication.

should like to see you in Lowell once more but cannot wish you to exchange your pleasant home in the country for a factory life in the "great city of spindles." I hope you will learn to perform all necessary domestic duties while you have an opportunity for perhaps you may have an invitation from a certain dark eyed gentleman whom you mentioned in your letter to be mistress of his house his hand and heart and supposing such an event should take place then I will just take a ride some pleasant day and make you a visit when I will tell you more news than I can write—but I will not—anticipate

I almost envy your happy sundays at home. A feeling of loneliness comes over me when I think of *my home*, now far away; you remember perhaps how I used to tell you I spent my hours in the mill—in imagining myself rich and that the rattle of machinery was the rumbling of my charriot wheels but now alas that happy tact [?] has fled from me and my mind no longer takes such airy and visionary flights for the wings of my imagination have folded themselves to rest; in vain do I try to soar in fancy and imagination above the dull reality around me but beyond the roof of the factory I can not rise. . . .

You told me you had been gipsying a number of times but I hope you will not turn gipsy in imitating their wandering yet *happy* life; I say happy because any one must be happy while they are free to rove when and where they will among the green fields, by the running streams, in the debths of the forest, and in the pleasant valley with none to molest or make them afraid, so different from a city life. But enough of this now, for the good reason that I have no room to write it; do not think I am unhappy because I cannot wish you here, far from it, but I think you are happier *there*.

I forgot to tell you that Sarah Burton has left our dress room in old No. 2 to be married. I believe she is going to reside in Maine. I have no more that you would be interested in, to write. When you receive this letter I shall expect that *long* one you promised me do write it wont you.

Your friend H. E. Back

(ii) Ann Kinley Waldrop

I growed up in a mill. . . . I started to work when I was eleven years old to keep from having to go to school. Now I wish I had some learnin'. I never worked in no mill but the Athens Manufacturin' Company. Old man Bloomfield owned that mill then, and he paid me $9.30 a month. I done ever'thing there was to be done from sweepin' the floors and reelin' to spoolin' and spinnin'. You see, I just growed up in the mill. Them days you was 'lowed to go to work soon as you was big enough to do the work. 'Fore I was big enough to work myself, my oldest sisters worked there in that same mill, and I remember hearin' 'em. They said them niggers warn't right black; they was almost white. I reckon they was some white man's chillun. When I started to work the war had done freed the niggers, and white folks wouldn't let nigger women work in mills no more. Several nigger men worked in the mill when I did, but they just toted rope and done things like that what was too heavy for womenfolks to handle. I'm sure glad niggers are free, for if they warn't this mill down here would be filled up with 'em. . . .

I worked in the mill for 15 years. I didn't make no big money, but we got on a heap better, for things were lots cheaper. Ma and pa lived in a two-room house that belonged to the Gas Works, and they never had to pay no rent on it. Ma raised chickens, cows, and hogs. We just had plenty of the right sort of things to eat, and what rations and clothes we did have to buy didn't cost as much as they do now. Even snuff costs a lots less. Now it costs twice as much as it used to. . . .

You recollect I told you about startin' to work when I was 'leven years old to get out of havin' to go to school. Well, there didn't none of us amount to nothin'. There warn't no free schools then. It cost a dollar a head to send us, and pa 'lowed it would take too much money to school us, so we all went to work. . . .

No, I never worked in the mill no more after I got married, for when we lived near enough to the mill for me to work there, I was always tied down with a little one comin' on.

85. A French silk worker's apprenticeship contract

Following the silk workers' uprisings in Lyon during the 1830's, silk merchants sought to minimize labor problems and to increase their profits by moving their mills to the rural areas of southeastern France and employing women. For this new labor force they created a very different sort of manufacturing institution adapted from the world-famous example of the Lowell mills—in effect, a sort of industrial convent for girls. Managed by nuns and heavily mechanized, these new mills recruited young women from peasant families who were eager to accumulate savings for their dowries. By the late 1850's some forty thousand girls were employed in these convent-factories, despite the bitter yet impotent opposition of the male master weavers of Lyon.

The apprenticeship contract in this selection was used in the 1850's at the industrial convent at Tarare (Rhône), west of Lyon. The French social investigator and novelist Louis Reybaud (1799–1879), who published it in his book on the French silk industry, remarked of this type of contract: "The conditions in it are very strictly observed and questions of discipline, in these businesses, have an importance that will easily be understood."

MILLING, REELING, AND WARP-PREPARATION OF SILKS

Conditions of Apprenticeship

Art.1. To be admitted, young women must be between the ages of thirteen and fifteen, of good character and in good health, intelligent and industrious, and must have been vaccinated. They must present their birth certificate, a certificate of vaccination, and a trousseau.

source: Louis Reybaud, *Etudes sur le régime de manufactures: Condition des ouvrières en soie* (Paris, 1859), pp. 330–33.

Art. 2. Girls who are accepted by the establishment will be placed in milling, reeling, or warp preparation by the director, according to the needs of the establishment and their intelligence.

Art. 3. During the apprenticeship period, the pupil will be paid wages, fed, lodged, given heat and light, and laundry *for her body linen only*; she will also be furnished with aprons.

Art. 4. The pupil promises to be obedient and submissive to the mistresses charged with her conduct and instruction, as well as to conform to the rules of the establishment.

Art. 5. In case of illness the director will notify the father or guardian of the sick apprentice, and if her state necessitates a leave, it will be granted to her until her recovery.

Art. 6. If the sick pupil remains in the establishment, every care necessitated by her condition will be given to her.

Art. 7. In case of illness or any other serious cause that warrants her leaving, the apprentice who must absent herself from the establishment will be obligated to prolong her apprenticeship during a time equal to that of her absence.

Art. 8. The director alone has the right to authorize or refuse leaves. They will be granted only on the request of the father or guardian of the pupil.

Art. 9. Apprenticeship is for three consecutive years, *not including an obligatory trial month.* In order to encourage the pupil, she will be paid.

> 1st year: a wage of 40 to 50 francs
> 2nd year: "   "   " 60 to 75   "
> 3rd year: "   "   " 80 to 100 "

After the apprenticeship the wage will be established according to merit.

At the end of the apprenticeship, a gratuity of 20 francs will be given to the apprentice to reward her for her exactitude in fulfilling her engagements.

*Art.*10. The effective work time is twelve hours. Summer and winter, the day begins at 5 o'clock and ends at 7:15.

Breakfast is from 7:30 to 8:15; lunch is from 12:00 to 1:00; snack is from 5:00 to 5:30; supper is at 7:15.

After the second year, pupils will receive lessons in reading, writing, and arithmetic. They will be taught to sew and to do a little cooking.

Art. 11. As a measure of encouragement and with no obligation, it is established that at the end of each month the young people will be graded as follows:

> 1st class, gift for the month 1 fr. 50 c.
> 2nd class   1 " —
> 3rd class   50 c.
> 4th class   —

Each month a new classification will take place, and the young person will rise or fall according to her merit. This classification will be based on an overall evaluation of conduct, quantity and quality of work, docility and diligence, etc.

Art. 12. Wages are not due until the end of the year. They will be paid during the month following their due date. Gifts, incentive pay, and compensation for extra work will be paid each month.

Art. 13. Any apprentice who leaves the establishment before the end of her term, or who has been dismissed for bad conduct, conspiracy, rebellion, laziness, or a serious breach of the rules loses her rights to wages for the current year; beyond this, in such a case, the father or guardian of the pupil agrees to pay the director of the establishment the sum of one hundred francs to indemnify him for the non-fulfillment of the present agreement: half of this sum will be given to the *bureau de bienfaisance** in the pupil's parish.

Art. 14. If, during the first year, the apprentice is recognized as unfit, despite the agreement and in the interest of both parties the director reserves the right to send her away without indemnity.

Art. 15. The apprentice who leaves the establishment at the end of the first month under the pretext that she cannot get used to the place, will pay 50 centimes per day toward the costs she has occasioned, as well as her travel expenses.

Art. 16. On her arrival, the apprentice will submit to inspection by the house doctor. Any girl who has a skin disease or who is found to be sickly will not be accepted and will be sent away immediately at her own expense.

Contract

The undersigned _____ the manufacturer, and have made the following contract:

M. _____, having read and understood the conditions of apprenticeship stipulated above in sixteen articles, declares that he accepts them for _____ aged _____, present and consenting, and pledges to execute them and have them executed in all their contents by _____. M. _____, manufacturer, pledges likewise to execute the above conditions insofar as they concern him.

The present agreement is consented to for *Three years* beginning on _____.

Made and signed in duplicate _____

Father or Guardian	Director

P.S. Girls will not be admitted on Sundays or holidays.

86. Do women have a right to work?

In the 1860's, with the founding of the International Working Men's Association, or First International, the continuing controversy over women's

---

* A Catholic parochial organization responsible for social welfare.—EDS.

SOURCES: (i) "Compte rendu de J. Card," Session of Sept. 7, 1866, *La Première Internationale: Recueil des documents*, ed. Jacques Freymond (Geneva, 1962), 1:

right to work divided the workers' movement. The following selections show not only how heated these discussions had become within socialist circles, but also how French workers felt about women working for pay. In the first selection, taken from a report of the debates of the First Congress of the International in 1866, the followers of the worker-philosopher Pierre-Joseph Proudhon (1809–65) oppose any and all work for women outside the home. In the second selection Paule Mink (1839–1901), angered by the patriarchal absolutism of Proudhon's disciples, gives a compelling speech in Paris defending women's right to work. Mink went on to play a leading role in the first French workers' political party, the Parti Ouvrier Français, one of the few groups on the political Left to support consistently her cry that women should not be "condemned to inaction."

(i) The First International

M. Dupont reads the report of the London Central Committee concerning the work of women and children in the mills.

M. Coullery gives a fiery speech in favor of women's emancipation.* He exposes the miserable situation of the woman in today's society. She is almost inevitably doomed to prostitution. That is the most horrible aspect of proletarian life. He paints a somber picture of the woman's miseries, of the limited resources she can obtain through her work, of the ensuing demoralization, of the painful work for which she is not equipped and that perverts her sex; of the temptations and traps that, in such a situation, are laid everywhere for her by a corrupt parasitic class. Woman's place is in the home, near her children: she should watch over them and instill in them basic moral principles. Her mission is great; if we give her the place she deserves and if we ward off pernicious influences, she will become the bulwark of liberty and democracy.

M. Butter, delegate from the Magdeburg section, reads a passage from the *Précurseur*, the publication of the Genevan German section concerning the emancipation of women. The speaker maintains that a virtuous woman will always find a husband, and that is the only remedy against prostitution. It is in the interest of both sexes and of humanity that woman be assured an honorable position.

MM. Chemalé, Tolain, Fribourg, of the French delegation, propose that: From a physical, moral, and social viewpoint, women's work outside the home should be energetically condemned as a cause of the degeneration of the race and as one of the agents of demoralization used by the capitalist class.

Woman, these delegates say, has received from nature predetermined functions: her place is in the family! It is her job to raise children in their early years. Only the mother is capable of fulfilling that responsibility.

The delegates cite statistics that demonstrate the death rate of children

---

75–76. (ii) Paule Mink, "Le Travail des femmes: Discours pronouncé par Mme Paul [*sic*] Mink à la réunion publique du Vauxhall, le 13 juillet 1868," Rp 12236, Bibliothèque Nationale, Paris. The editors are grateful to Professor Marilyn J. Boxer, San Diego State University, for sending us a copy of this document.

* From the context, it is clear that M. Coullery means emancipation from paid labor outside the home.—EDS.

abandoned to wet nurses and infant asylums. Only the mother is capable of giving the child a moral education, of forming an upright man. Moreover, the woman is the bond, the attraction that keeps the man at home, makes him lead an orderly and moral life, and softens his manners. Such are the functions, such is the work incumbent on woman; to impose another on her is evil.

MM. Varlin and Bourdon are of a different opinion. They propose this resolution: For the women who work in the mills, lack of education, excessive work, minimal remuneration, and unhygienic working conditions are the true causes of their physical and moral decline; these causes can be eliminated by a better organization of work and by cooperation. Since women need to work in order to live honorably we should strive to ameliorate their work, not to suppress it.

This proposition is rejected by the majority, who adopt those of MM. Chemalé and Tolain. . . .

The Congress votes resolutions conforming to the propositions of the London Central Committee and the French delegations, condemning in principle the work of women in the mills as one of the causes of the degeneration of the human race and of demoralization; it likewise condemns excessive work by children.

(ii) Paule Mink

Many of you, Gentlemen, recognize no other duty for woman than that of being a wife, no other right than that of being a mother.

This is the feminine ideal, so you say. Ah! Let's have less of the ideal, thank you! Let's stay a bit more on practical ground, for these appeals to the ideal tend to destroy the best, most fruitful questions.

The ideal changes with the times. Our current ideal is that of perpetual and incessant progress; no theory these days can offer an ideal if it does not offer some progress.

Now, let's see whether your ideal constitutes progress. . . .

Women's work! This is one of the most vital questions of our time. This question carries with it the moral and even the physical regeneration of the future race.

But I am speaking here about a suitable kind of work, not this abusive exploitation that turns the worker in general and the poor woman in particular into a slave, the serf of modern society, the subject of speculation at pleasure.

Work constitutes a necessary law, which we must all obey under penalty of becoming weak and falling from grace. Everything in nature stirs itself and works; it is the sum of these activities, of these diverse aptitudes, that produces good and creates the sublime harmony of creatures and objects.

Why then does man not activate himself as nature does? Why should he deprive himself of one of the strengths that make up his individual humanity? Why not balance the diverse faculties of these two constituent elements of humanity: man and woman?

It has been suggested that work exhausts and kills, and the dissimilar appearance of woman in Bordeaux and Marseille and those in the manufacturing towns of Rouen, Lille, etc., has been invoked. One could perhaps point out the differences in hygiene of these places; for the first, the proximity to the sea; for the second, the deadly necessity of living in airless cellars with no space and no sunlight. But meanwhile let us admit that the difference in work has a good deal to do with the development of the first group of women and the withering of the second. Certainly in the latter case, the suffering is immense and the results are terrible! But where and when have excesses not been an evil? Can we then say, for all that, that the good cannot be found at a certain distance from this extreme without having to go all the way to the opposite extreme? Must one then conclude: Woman works too much, therefore she should not work at all, and let her avoid the wreckage produced by excessive work by plunging her into an enervation caused by idleness?

Let us rather ensure that women's salaries are raised, that they are commensurate with the product obtained, that they are raised in proportion to the cost of life's necessities. Then there will be no excess, no extreme sapping of strength leading inevitably to corruption, degeneration, and even to death.

It has been suggested that the excessive work of women causes a bastardization of the race. Certainly, excessive work—whether by woman or man—is an atrocious anomaly that ought to disappear. But we ourselves believe that the bastardization of the race can be attributed far more to the excessive vice and depravity produced by the faulty distribution of women's salaries, which leads so fatally to debauchery and all the evils it engenders.

Woman should not work, they say, because it will destroy her beauty and grace. Certainly this is a noble concern on the part of those whom we have too long spoken of as our lords and masters; but, we must admit that it doesn't seem to us that work necessarily destroys this beauty.

Normal work develops the body rather than wearing it out; it maintains one's skills in a happy state of activity; it maintains equilibrium among one's various physical faculties and expands them, giving to them a new fullness of life that is rarely encountered among those depressed, enervated, suffering, nearly invalid creatures who are condemned to idleness.

It is certainly all right to be concerned with physical beauty, but moral beauty should by no means be left entirely to one side. Now—and I will say it loudly—the only means of progress and perfection that has been given to us is work. Through work, the mind is developed, the heart is fortified, the level of intelligence is raised. Through work, suffering can be forgotten; through work, one can acquire additional energy for struggling and winning; through work, one can better withstand adversity, combat evil, and master life. . . .

By denying woman the right to work, you degrade her, you put her under man's yoke and deliver her over to man's good pleasure. By ceasing to make her a worker, you deprive her of her liberty and, thereby, of her responsibility (and this is why I insist so much on this issue), so that she no longer will be a free and intelligent creature, but will merely be a reflection, a small part of her husband.

Certainly there will come a time—and I hope it is not too far off—when our honor will come primarily from our work, where no one will be worth more than he produces. Then what will woman's role be if, inert and passive, she is entirely at the disposal of her husband? If she is forbidden to think of work? If she has no future apart from marriage? And if she is deprived forever of liberty and a life of her own?

Pardon me for dwelling at such length on this subject, but I believe it is the keystone. It is work alone that makes independence possible and without which there is no dignity. . . .

Oh! I understand very well the feelings that made you want to prohibit women from working. In theory, they are very noble and very praiseworthy. For so long your wives and daughters have been taken from you that you want to keep them with you in spite of everything. But let us not exaggerate. . . .

You say that wives and mothers should not work. This is all very well, but what of the others? All women are not wives and mothers; some could not be or did not want to be, some are not yet, others are no longer.

We must not sacrifice a large number of women to a form of social life that is, I admit, widespread but not completely universal.

How about the daughters, the widows, the women who have bad husbands or who have been abandoned—and that sometimes happens—what about them? Who will take care of them if woman is fatally condemned to inaction? . . .

Certainly it is essential that women produce goods and earn money, but it does not follow that her work must necessarily lower the salaries of men: equal pay for equal work, this is the only true justice.

87. Union sisters

The women who joined and organized trade unions in shops and factories during the last third of the nineteenth century needed special courage. Like their union brothers, they risked losing their jobs because of their organizing activities—indeed, workers who were not union members were often fired summarily for even speaking to union people. Although more exploited than men in every trade in which they worked, union women frequently found that their male colleagues were indifferent and even hostile to their aspirations.

These two selections document the struggles of two union organizers. In the first Leonora Barry (1849–1930), general investigator and director of the newly formed department of women's work of the Knights of Labor, reports at the union's 1887 and 1889 conventions about her activities among women workers. Chiding the delegates for the union's lack of attention to women's

SOURCES: (i) "Report of the General Investigator," *Proceedings of the General Assembly of the Knights of Labor,* 1887, pp. 1581–87; "Report of the General Investigator of Woman's Work and Wages," *ibid.,* 1889, pp. 1–14 *passim.* (ii) Great Britain, *Parliamentary Papers,* 1892, XXXV, Royal Commission on Labour, pp. 342–52 *passim.*

issues, she appeals to them in the name of their mothers, wives, and innocent daughters to help exploited working women. Barry, an Irish immigrant, knew from first-hand experience the perils of working life; as a widow, she supported herself and children by working in a hosiery mill in upstate New York. In the second selection Clara James, secretary of the Confectioners' Trade Union and a member of the London Trades Council, tells a Parliamentary commission in 1891 about her organizing activities. Although James points out the benefits unions have brought workers, her testimony underscores the ineffectiveness of over sixty years of factory legislation and the unhealthy and abusive conditions persisting in English factories.

(i) Leonora Barry

[Report of 1887]
General Master Workman and Members of the General Assembly:

One year ago the Knights of Labor, in convention assembled at Richmond, Va., elected me to a position of honor and trust—the servant and representative of thousands of toiling women. Not one of those present at that time realized the responsibility placed upon my shoulders and my incompetency to do justice to the position more thoroughly than myself. However, feeling that it was a cause of right and justice, therefore would receive the blessing and assistance of a just God, I was satisfied to become an instrument in His hands to further the good work among His creatures. On every occasion I have labored for the best interest of our noble Order, to the extent of my knowledge and ability. What the fruits of my work have been it is for those among whom I have labored to say.

Having no legal authority I have been unable to make as thorough an investigation in many places as I would like, and, after the discharge of Sister Annie Conboy from the silk mill in Auburn, in February last, for having taken me through the mill, I was obliged to refrain from going through establishments where the owners were opposed to our Order lest some of our members be victimized; consequently the facts stated in my report are not all from actual observation but from authority which I have every reason to believe truthful and reliable.

Upon the strength of my observation and experience I would ask of officers and members of the Order that more consideration be given, and more thorough educational measures be adopted on behalf of the working-women of our land, the majority of whom are entirely ignorant of the economic and industrial question which is to them of such vital importance; and they must ever remain so while the selfishness of their brothers in toil is carried to such an extent as I find it to be among those who have sworn to demand equal pay for equal work. Thus far in the history of our Order that part of our platform has been but a mockery of the principles intended. And, if those who pledged themselves to the support of this principle do not resolve to trample under foot their selfish personal ambition and for a time turn their attention to the poor down-trodden white slave, as represented by the women wage-workers of this country, then let us here and now wipe the twenty-second plank out of our platform, and no longer make a farce of one of the grandest principles of our Order.

Within the jurisdiction of our District Assemblies starvation and sin are knocking at, aye, and have gained entrance at the doors of thousands of the victims of underpaid labor. And the men who have pledged themselves to the "assistance of humanity" and the "abolition of poverty" are so engrossed in the pursuit of their own ambitious desires, that upon their ears the wail of woe falls unheeded, and the work of misery and destruction still goes on.

Men! ye whose earnings count from nine to fifteen dollars a week and up-ward, cease, in the name of God and humanity, cease your demands and griev-ances and give us your assistance for a time to bring some relief to the poor unfortunate, whose week's work of eighty-four hours brings her but $2.50 or $3 per week. When men make light of the condition of women wage-workers, and declare that there is no necessity of having any particular attention paid to them or effort on their behalf, there comes to us a strong suspicion that such an one is in the Order for "self alone" and not for the assistance of humanity.

Once more we appeal to you, brothers of the Knights of Labor, by your love for the sacred name of mother, by your protecting love and respect for your wives and daughters, to sustain your manly principles, to uphold the dignity of your strong, noble manhood, and assist to uproot the corrupt system that is making slaves—not alone of poverty, but slaves to sin and shame—of those who by the right of divine parentage we must all call sisters. . . .

Commencing under instructions from the General Executive Board, on October 26, 1886, I worked among the Local Assemblies of Little Falls, Fort Plain, Amsterdam, and Cohoes. . . .

I reached Pittsburg June 11, by invitation of L.A. 7228. Here would be a good place for some to come who are constantly talking of *women's sphere.* Women are employed in the manufacturing of barbed wire, underground cable cork works, pickle factories, bakeries, sewing of all kinds and all the other branches of business at which women are employed, elsewhere. I visited a large establishment, a part of which is to be fitted for the manufacturing of nails, at which women are to be employed. There are also many laundries here in which women are compelled to work, the number of hours constituting eight days in a week of ten hours per day, and for which they receive pay for a week's work of six days. Also, in a tailoring establishment here I found that whatever wages are made by the employee, she must pay her employer 50 cents per week for the steam-power which runs the machines. There is but little organization here among the women, consequently their condition is similar to that of all others who are unprotected—small pay for hard labor and long hours. While the cause of their lack of interest in organized labor is largely due to their own ignorance of the importance of this step, yet much blame can be attached to the neglect and indifference of their brother toilers within the jurisdiction of D.A. 3, who seem to lose sight of one important fact, that organization can never do the work it was intended to do until every competitor in the labor market can be taught its principles. Having assisted to renovate and revive Ladies' L.A. 7228, I have every reason to believe that it will continue to grow and flourish and achieve great success in the future.

[Report of 1889]
My understanding of the duties implied in my office was that I was to do everything in my power that would in my judgment have a tendency to educate and elevate the workingwomen of America and ameliorate their condition. Therefore, when I spoke to a public audience of American citizens, exposing existing evils and showing how, through the demands of Knighthood, they could be remedied, I felt that I was fulfilling the duties of my office. When I found a body of workingmen who were so blind to what justice demanded of them on behalf of women as to pass unanimously a resolution excluding women from our organization, I felt I was performing a sacred duty toward women by trying to enlighten those men and showing their mistake. When I found an opportunity of laying before other organizations of women the cause of their less fortunate sisters and mould a favorable sentiment, I felt I was doing that which is an actual necessity, as woman is often unconsciously woman's oppressor. With these, my honest convictions, I place my work of the past year in your hands. . . .

November 18, at Reading, Pa., I found but few women organized, although they were at one time, and received many material benefits from their connection with the organization. November 12 to 18 in Baltimore under the direction of D.A. 41. The situation here is even worse than at my last report of it. Ignorance, apathy and internal bickering, caused by petty jealousies, have done their work effectively and caused the death of many Locals, among which was the Barry Assembly. . . .

On March 8 I visited Laporte, Ind. March 9 held public meetings at Elkhart, Ind. On March 11, 12, and 13 held meetings in Springfield, Ohio. Quite a large number of women in the Order here, but no particular trade represented, the majority being housewives desirous of helping along the work of industrial reform that few feel the need of more than a workingman's wife. . . .

One of the many tales of injustice and cruel selfishness which I have listened to in my journeyings was told me here, and was as follows: A poor woman with one child to support was employed by the wife of a wealthy, flourishing merchant to do housecleaning. After a day's work of thirteen hours she was offered for her day's wages one of her employer's cast-off dresses; for fear of giving offense and thereby depriving herself of any more work she accepted, and with heavy heart returned home, where herself and child went supperless to bed. This is only one instance of many acts of criminal carelessness of people in comfortable circumstances, who know or care nothing for the helpless beings who perform their work. . . .

A custom is rapidly increasing in this country which means shame, dishonor and humiliation to womanhood, and I here and now appeal to every father within sound of my voice to be watchful and wary of his little daughter, if she be employed in any large establishment, or small one either, where she is made to understand that the price of her position is, that she "stand in with the boss." Many may ask why I do not give name and locality. First, because those who resent such pernicious approaches shrink from giving publicity to their humiliation, and those who do submit will not make their misfortunes public until, perhaps, they can no longer hide their shame. In very many instances facts were given that were blood-curdling, but no affidavit would be made, and neither myself or the Order was in a position to stand a libel suit, with all the power of wealth against us wherewith to influence a decision against honor and truth. . . .

It has been intimated that the Woman's Department was started on sentiment. Well, if so, it has turned out to be one of the most thoroughly practical departments in the Order. Without egotism I can safely say it has done as much effective work in cheering, encouraging, educating and instructing the women of this Order in the short year of its existence as was done by the the organization in the whole time of women's connection with it previous to its establishment. Ten thousand organized women to-day look to the Woman's Department for counsel, advice and assistance. It is their hope, their guiding star; and the free and full outpouring of sorrow-stricken and heavy-laden hearts, not alone of women and girls, but their heart-broken parents, that comes to the Woman's Department for consolation and comfort cannot be recorded here because that would be a breach of sacred confidence. However, it can be imagined with all its force from the expression of an anguish-stricken father, who, after relating the injustice done his little innocent daughter, said: "Oh, Sister Barry, I thank my God there is a hell where the punishment will be meted out that I am powerless to give."

(ii) Clara James

What is the number of the workpeople; have you any approximate idea of the number engaged in this trade?—In the East End there are about 2,000 or 3,000 women working in the trade.

In the confectionery trade?—In the confectionary trade; and in the south of London there are about the same number. There are some thousands of women working in the trade altogether. . . .

Your union applies only to the east of London, I understand?—To the east of London, but of course we take them from all parts of London.

How many women are there members of your union?—About 500 women I have now.

How is it that so few of them are members of the union, as compared with the aggregate number employed?—The women are afraid of joining the union; several of them have been dismissed for joining a trades union. I was dismissed for joining a trades union.

You were dismissed because you joined a trades union?—Yes. When the union was first started I was dismissed two days after I joined the union with two other girls.

How long was that since?—Two years ago, when the union was first started.

Now, what have you to say as to the causes of disputes in the confectionery trade?—The causes of disputes are low wages, fines, dismissal without notice, bad regulations, and obnoxious officials.

You say low wages; now, what are the wages that are prevailing in the confectionery trade?—The wages range from 5s. a week to 9s. 12s. is the highest paid to a weekly worker, and it is not often they get that. . . .

Now, what are the fines for?—Well, before the union was formed—it was formed two years ago—then the girls were dismissed constantly for joining the union, until at last they all left the union.

All left the union?—They all left the union because they were afraid of being dismissed. It was two years ago. Miss Black and I knew how the prices were going down, and we tried to form the union again. We called meetings, but the meetings were very small, as the girls were afraid to come, because the foremen came to the meetings to spy after the girls, and, of course, spoke about them when they went into work the next morning, and the girls were dismissed. That is a fact. At the meeting where they formed the union, 12 girls came. The whole of the time they were at the meeting they were looking out of the windows; they were really afraid of joining the union, because they knew that the foremen and forewomen were about, and would tell of them the next morning. But one girl came to the meeting, and she had been fined a shilling that day. Her wages were 6s. a week, and she had been fined 1s. She gave her name in first, and then the other girls joined in. . . .

Will you tell us what are the hours in these establishments?—The hours are generally from eight in the morning till seven at night.

From eight in the morning till seven?—Yes, and they have an hour for dinner. Before the union was formed they were not allowed to come out in the dinner hour. There are factories now where the girls are kept in all day long, and married women, too, are kept in the works from the time they go in in the morning to the time they go out at night—they are not allowed to go out in the dinner hour. . . .

There is a certain amount of machinery?—Yes. Before the union was formed the girls were not allowed to come out in the dinner hour, the girls in one factory had to sit and eat their meals in the room where the cocoa-nuts were smashed up; these cocoa-nuts were very often rotten, and they had to sit and eat their food with the stench of these rotten cocoa-nuts rising around them. I had two cases where girls were taken away with typhoid fever through the smell. . . .

What do you mean when you speak about obnoxious officials. There must be surely some people who are overlookers, forewomen, and so on, are there not?—The foremen and forewomen are, more often than not, the cause of much of the trouble. Masters often leave the management of the workers in their hands; the foremen frequently use very bad language, and the amount of petty tyranny is often very galling. The foremen have power to impose fines, and these are sometimes enormous, considering the wages. For instance, in one room, if there is a window broken, not only does the girl who broke it have to pay, but the whole of the girls working in the room are fined for this broken window. They impose fines for eating food, looking away from their work. They give them "drillings." Supposing a girl loses five minutes in the morning, or supposing she does not get to her work till 8 o'clock, the foreman can give her a fortnight's drilling if he likes. That means that he can keep this girl out for a fortnight without employing her, and then take her back when he chooses.

A fortnight's drilling they call it?—Yes.

And that means that her work and wages are suspended for a fortnight, then?—Yes.

What are the sanitary conditions of the buildings in which they work?— The sanitary conditions are bad, very bad. The pulp holes are left sometimes for a week or a fortnight before they are emptied. The pulp holes are where all the bad jam and the lemon peel is all thrown down into one place.

The refuse?—All the refuse, yes.

Do they give out bad smells?—Yes, they do. Then in one place the lavatories are all full of water. The floors are rotten, so that the rain gets in, and they are in a very bad condition. . . .

All these workshops and factories are under inspection, are they not?— Yes, I think they all are.

You have seen the factory inspector, have you not?—No.

You have been a worker for some years and you have not been accustomed to see the factory inspector?—I have never seen a factory inspector inside a factory.

What?—I have never seen a factory inspector inside a factory.

For how long have you been employed in this industry?—I have not worked at it so long as some of the girls who are in the Union. There is one girl here who has worked in the factory for 12 years and she has never seen an inspector inside the factory. . . .

What scale do your girls pay upon for belonging to the Union? What is the contribution?—Those who earn under 8s. pay 1d., and those who earn over 8s. pay 2d. per week.

Now, you spoke of girls being discharged because they were unionists, and I find in your proof you refer to girls discharged because they were delegates. Is that so?—Yes, it is so.

Are you quite clear that there are such cases?—Yes. I was referring to this girl who has been on the sick club for nine weeks. She was one of the committee of the Union in her factory. She has worked at this firm for 12 years, and has never had any complaint made against her before. When she went last week to the master to tell him that she was a little better, and that she was able to go back again to work, he told her that her place was filled up, and that he did not want to have anything more to do with her. This girl had never had any complaint made against her in the factory; the younger girls always looked to her for advice, and we can only think that the master has taken this opportunity of dismissing her because she is one of the leaders of the Union.

That is your conclusion?—In the same firm at one of the factories—the master owns three factories—six collectors (the girls who collect the Union money) have been dismissed one after the other, and the master now stands at one factory every Saturday, and has forbidden the girls to pay their Union money, or to pay club money, or any money whatever outside the room. He thinks by that that the girls will go off and not belong to the Union at all.

And you say the girls are afraid to belong to your Union?—The girls are afraid. I went to one factory—I was distributing bills, and asking the girls to come to a meeting—and the master came out to me and said: "My girls are treated properly, but if I catch any of them coming to your meetings I will dismiss the lot of them." I told him the girls had a right to go where they liked, or do what they liked, after the work was done. He said they should not come. He took hold of one girl and took the bill away from her, and he said if he caught her coming to the meeting he would dismiss her, and he also said he would put two hours more on to his worker's work if any of them were caught coming to the meeting. In almost every firm it is the same, the masters intimidate the women.

Is your Union conducted in its relations to employers and to non-unionists without being in any way offensive, or indulging in intimidation, or threats, or anything of that kind?—There are never any threats, and we have always tried as long as the Union has been formed to be fair to the masters. If girls break the rules, of course, we do not take the matter up at all; we try to get them work elsewhere. But we do find that the masters will not be fair towards the Union. . . .

Now, in order that this Commission may obtain clear and full knowledge of the conditions of working women engaged in your and similar industries, do you think that women sub-commissioners are desirable, and do you think that we shall get better evidence from them than we shall get from persons like yourself coming here?—I think if you get the proper working women you could get better evidence from them.

But do you think we could get the working women to come and tell their story here?—Yes, I think you could. . . .

Have you any remedy to suggest for this state of things?—A strong Trade Union will do a great deal, but the grievances will never be done away with until employers are compelled to recognize that they are working and wearing out human lives instead of mere machines. But it does not rest upon us to lay down here what form that compulsion shall take; it is for those who make the law.

Do you believe any law can prevent this decline in the wages and the advantage which inconsiderate employers will take of impoverished workpeople, if they are not in a Union; can anything prevent it?—I do not know.

Has your Union done anything at all to improve the condition of the workers?—They have. In one factory they have improved their condition a great deal. The fines there were very great. One girl there was fined 2s. 6d.— and that was the cause of a strike—for falling down in the dinner hour. They were not allowed to go out in the dinner hour there, and she got up for something and slipped down, and the forewoman said to her, "I will fine you

2s. 6d." The girl replied, "What am I to do; I cannot take 2s. 6d. home out of 5s., and say I have been fined the other 2s. 6d.; my parents will not believe me," but the forewoman told her that she would either have to pay this fine or that she would be dismissed.

That was the cause of a strike in that factory?—A strike was the result, yes. Those were the girls that went out of the Union because they were afraid of their master. He had a very bad name, and they said they were afraid to join the Union. That is the master that is now trying to break the Union up by degrees, and standing outside the factory each day when the wages are paid. The girls' wages are not sufficient for them to buy their clothes with ready money, so they have clubs. They will have, perhaps, a jacket club or a boot club. One girl will hold the club, and they will pay 3d. each until they have paid up, and that is how they got their clothes. But the master is standing outside the factory now, and he is forbidding those girls to have clubs. . . .

Do you attribute the smallness of the numbers to the terrorism exercised by the employers in preventing girls from joining the Union?—Yes. The master I am speaking about now has three factories; and the collectors one after another have always been dismissed. In one room where most of the committee girls were, there were 11 girls dismissed out of one room one night. One girl who had been there eight years, and had never had any complaint made against her, was dismissed. When I wrote to the master about it, and asked him if he would look into the case, as I did not think the girls had committed any offence, and if they had, would he look over it, as some of the girls were in very bad circumstances, he sent me word back by letter to say that he was quite surprised at my letter, that surely he had a right to dismiss or take on girls as he pleased, and he did not want to hear anything more about it. He said, however, when the Union was first started, he would be glad to see me in any little dispute of that kind. I went to him with one or two cases where the girls were dismissed, and at first he took the girls on again. Now, he won't see me.

So the girls are completely at the mercy of the masters in these places?—Yes; and in such a slack time nothing could be done.

That is the cause of the low rate of wages and the long hours?—Yes. If the girls come out on strike now, and any dispute takes place they will be dismissed, and their places filled up the next time he opens the factory. At Christmas time the factory is closed, and then he will send for them when he wants them. Meanwhile they are walking about looking for work elsewhere.

88. An American 'fallen woman' recalls her plight: Lucy Brewer

Lucy Brewer's narrative of her seduction, abandonment, and subsequent entrapment in a Boston brothel provides a rare glimpse into the way a prosti-

SOURCE: Lucy (Brewer) West [pseud. of Louisa Baker], *The Adventures of Lucy Brewer* (Boston, 1815), pp. 5–9, 13. The editors are grateful to Jonathan Katz

tute interpreted her own experiences. Brewer's motive for publishing her adventures—"To vindicate the principles of virtue and morality"—is reflected in her tone. Anticipating moral and public health reformers of the next generation, she portrayed herself as a victim of circumstances and condemned prostitution as a social threat. After escaping from the brothel in the disguise of a man, Brewer served for three years aboard the U.S. Navy frigate Constitution and received an honorable discharge without ever having her sex discovered.

I was born in a small town in the county of Plymouth in the State of Massachusetts—my real name is LUCY BREWER—at the age of sixteen I unfortunately became acquainted with a youth of respectable parentage, who resided within a short distance of my father's house—he at first pretended to harbour a very great share of love for me, solemnly declaring that I should one day become his wife—my parents were suspicious of his real views and admonished me for my credulity—but the artful tales of the vile and insinuating deceiver had made too great an impression—he saw my growing attachment for him, and by the most solemn promise of marriage, having lulled every suspicion asleep, obtained the forfeiture of the only gem that could render me respectable in the eyes of the world!—My vile seducer now threw off his mask of pretended affection for me, and in an exulting tone, declared that he had never really intended to make me his wife, and that I must never presume to trouble him with the fruits of my misplaced confidence!—thus after adding insult to injury, the wretch deserted me, and I never saw him from that time until since my return to my parents—I now too late began to repent of my folly in not adhering to the good advice of my parents and friends, as I was now likely soon to incur a disgrace, that would too very materially effect them, should it come to their knowledge—as the only means to avoid which, I formed the resolution to seek an assylum abroad, among strangers, where I might be permitted to remain until I could return with safety to my unsuspecting friends;—it was in the dead of a cold winter's night, that I accordingly (furnished with a small bundle of cloathing) quit the peaceful abode of my tender parents, and alone and unprotected, bent my course for Boston, where I arrived the succeeding day almost famished with cold and hunger! ...

Here I continued my application for a place and at 3 in the afternoon on the west side of the hill was so fortunate (as I then thought) to find the asylum sought for!—the good old lady (or rather nefarious witch) of the house, pretended to have great pity for me!—her darling daughters were requested to spare no pains to afford relief to the "poor female wanderer!"—warm tea and toast was served me, and every restorative administered. In the evening marm's "spotless flock" having withdrawn, the old beldam succeeded in drawing from me every particular relative to my situation, the reason of my deserting my parents, &c.—the old hag letting fall a few hypocritical tears, assured me that I might now consider my troubles at an end, that I should find her a

for informing us of this source, and to Professor George Behlmer, University of Washington, for securing a copy.

mother and her house an assylum until such time as I could with safety return to my friends—indeed so artfully did this "old fowl and her chickens" conceal from me every thing that could give rise to suspicion, that not until after my confinement, had I the most distant idea of the manner in which these vile harlots obtained their livelihood!—my infant not surviving its birth, and having obtained sufficient strength to return to my parents, from whom I now had been five months absent, I was making preparation to bid adieu to the hospitable mansion of my "good marm" when this old deceiver threw off the mask of pretended friendship, and by threatening me with exposure, and prosecution if I should presume to leave her house without discharging a debt which my sickness had incurred, compelled me to give up the idea of an immediate return.

From this moment this antiquated hag, and her not less cunning pupils began by degrees to unfold to me the important secret, which they had never before thought proper to disclose—no pains were spared to decoy me from the paths of virtue and innocence, and to fit me for their market! and O! must I add, to my everlasting shame, that they at length fully succeeded in their nefarious schemes, and rendered me the object they so much desired. I was soon pronounced a forward scholar by my arch preceptress, by whom I was taught—

> "How to entrap the armourous youth,
> And to send him pennyless from my bed!"

.   .   .

After a three years residence with these vile prostitutes, I became disgusted with their wretched habits, and was resolved to quit them at all hazards—accordingly, a short time after, a favourable opportunity offering, I, clad in a male suit, escaped from my "fair Shepherdess" unsuspected. . . .

Look around you, my dear Youth, and behold many a promising young person, plunged into wretchedness, whose ruin is to be ascribed to too great a love of pleasure; who has given way to the inclination, and precipitated himself into the habit of dissipation, till he has become deaf to all good advice—proof against admonition, intreaty and persuasion, and is now among the splendid ruins of human nature.—Let these instances warn you of your danger, and persuade you to devote some part of that time, which is spent in pursuit of unlawful pleasures, to reflection and consideration.

89. Regulating urban prostitution

Even before the nineteenth century the world's oldest profession was perceived as a serious social problem in burgeoning cities and port towns throughout the Western world. But in the Victorian period medical men,

SOURCES: (i) William Acton, *Prostitution Considered in its Moral, Social and Sanitary Aspects in London and other Large Cities, with Proposals for the Mitigation*

military authorities, and government officials, worried about the incidence of venereal disease, especially syphilis, among soldiers and sailors, blamed prostitution for the widespread and growing contagion. Municipal authorities, alarmed by the existence of an autonomous world of prostitutes, criminals, and thieves within their gates, scrutinized them with an eye to regulation. In 1836, as official concern was mounting, a pioneering monograph by the French doctor A.-J.-B. Parent-Duchatelet, 'De la prostitution dans la Ville de Paris,' captured the public imagination. It provided material for novelists and social reformers alike and served as a model for the subsequent investigations of William Acton in England and William Sanger in the United States. In contrast to the romantic or moralistic outpourings of novelists, the treatises by medical professionals focused on prostitutution as a problem in public health—an aspect of urban pathology to be recognized, controlled, and regulated by enlightened government.

Paris was the first city in the Western world to attempt to regulate prostitution by confining the trade to certain districts, licensing the women involved (whose numbers increased from 22,000 in 1815 to 52,000 in 1850), and subjecting them to regular medical inspections. The Paris regulations greatly interested reformers in England and America. In the first selection, the prominent British venereologist William Acton (1813–75; Doc. 37.ii) describes the system he had become familiar with while a medical resident in Paris. The publication of Acton's book in 1857 brought the evils of prostitution into public view in England and led directly to the passage of the Contagious Diseases Acts by Parliament in the 1860's. The second selection comes from Dr. William Sanger's 'History of Prostitution' (1858), which was commissioned by public health authorities in New York City. Sanger surveyed some 2,000 New York prostitutes in order to discover why individual women entered the trade. Like most nineteenth-century moral reformers, he emphasized economic want and seduction and seemingly discounted answers that pointed instead to individual inclination. The third selection is a license granted by the Union Army to a prostitute in Nashville, Tennessee, during the Civil War, shortly after the army had begun to regulate prostitutes in the garrison towns in an effort to avoid an epidemic among Union troops.

(i) William Acton

The great object of the system adopted in France is to repress private or secret, and to encourage public or avowed prostitution.

I may, however, as well premise by observing that the authorities of Paris by no means pretend to have established a control over the whole prostitution of that city. The *concubinaires* they cannot reach. The large sections of superior

and Prevention of its Attendant Evils. 2d ed. (London, 1870), pp. 100, 103–8. Originally published in 1857. (ii) William W. Sanger, The History of Prostitution: Its Extent, Causes and Effects throughout the World (New York, 1895), pp. 460–61, 488–91. Originally published in 1858. (iii) Certificate no. 193, Reports on Prostitutes in Nashville, File A, manuscript no. 388, Adjutant General's Office, records for the 1780's–1917 (RG 94), National Archives, Washington, D.C.

professional prostitutes, whom the French term *femmes galantes* and *lorettes*, evade them, as do also vast hordes of the lowest class of strumpets who throng the low quarters and the villages of the Banlieu. M. Antin, an official of the Assistance-Publique, estimated in 1856 that there were 20,000 females in Paris having no other ostensible means of subsistence, on whom a tax in aid of retreats from prostitution might be levied. . . .

The official registration of common prostitutes was first loosely set on foot in 1765, and re-organized in 1796, under the Convention. Through neglect it was inoperative until 1801; then, after reorganization, it fell gradually into desuetude until 1816, when the present mechanism was adopted, and has undergone slight change, except in 1828, when exhibition of her *acte de naissance* was first demanded of each person presenting herself for inscription, and the poll-tax was abolished.

The keepers of licensed houses acted formerly also as agents in collecting women into the grasp of the authorities; but this has been suppressed on obvious grounds, that if it were permitted they would become purveyors. The registration is now either on the voluntary demand of the female, or by requisition of the *Bureau des Mœurs*. On appearing before this tribunal, the candidate, after declaring her name, age, quality, birth-place, occupation, and domicile, is submitted to a searching examination, as follows. Is she married or single? Has she father and mother living, and what are their pursuits? Does she reside with them; if not, why not, and when did she leave them? Has she children? How long has she inhabited Paris, and can she be owned there? Has she ever been arrested, and if so, the particulars? Has she previously been a prostitute; if so, the details? Has she had any, and what, education? Has she had any venereal affection? Her motives for the step?

She next proceeds to the *Bureau Sanitaire*, is medically examined, and enrolled in that department. If found diseased, she is consigned to the Saint-Lazare Hospital forthwith. Steps are meanwhile taken to verify her replies at the *Bureau des Mœurs*, and formal communications are now made to the mayor of her native commune, with an appeal for the woman's redemption to her parents. . . .

Should the relatives of the girl be willing to receive her, she is remitted to them at the public cost. She, however, frequently refuses to disclose them, or is ignorant of their existence, and it rarely occurs that they reclaim her. If, as has happened, she be a virgin or a minor, she is consigned to a religious establishment. Should spleen or despair cause the step, and she show symptoms of good qualities, immediate attempts are made to change her intention, and she is often sent home, or placed in a reformatory at the public cost. If her parents reside in Paris they are communicated with. All, in fact, that the *Bureau des Mœurs* can do, I should in justice say, I believe to be done, to warn and restrain the female about to enrol herself in the ranks of public prostitution, and only when all has failed is the formality complied with. This formality, which takes the form of a colourable contract or covenant between the prostitute and the authorities, would seem to argue a sort of consciousness

on the part of the latter of the entire illegality of the proceedings throughout. . . .

This over, the individual is presumed at liberty to select the category of
prostitution in which she will be comprehended. If she is totally destitute, or
any arrangement to this effect had been previously entered into, she is registered to a certain licensed house, to whose licensed proprietress she becomes
a marked and numbered serf or chattel, to be used or abused, within certain
limitations, at discretion. If she has command of capital enough to furnish a
lodging of her own, she is provided with a ticket, or *carte* . . . on the reverse
of which are printed the following

Obligations and Restrictions Imposed on Public Women.

"Public women, *en carte*, are called upon to present themselves at the
dispensary for examination, once at least every fifteen days.

"They are called upon to exhibit this card on every request of police officers and agents.

"They are forbidden to practise the calling during daylight, or to walk
in the thoroughfares until at least half-an-hour after the public lamps are
lighted, or at any season of the year before seven o'clock, or after eleven P.M.

"They must be simply and decently clad, so as not to attract attention by
the richness, striking colours, or extravagant fashion of their dress.

"They must wear some sort of cap or bonnet, and not present them selves
bareheaded.

"They are strictly forbidden to address men accompanied by females or
children, or to address loud or anxious solicitations to any person.

"They may not, under any pretext whatever, exhibit themselves at their
windows, which must be kept constantly closed and provided with curtains.

"They are strictly forbidden to take up a station on the foot-pavement, to
form, or walk together, in groups, or to and fro in a narrow space, or to allow
themselves to be attended or followed by men.

"The neighbourhood of churches and chapels, within a radius of twenty-
five yards, the arcades and approaches of the Palais Royal, the Tuileries, the
Luxembourg, and the Jardin des Plantes, are interdicted.

"The Champs Elysées, the Terrace of the Invalides, the exterior of the
Boulevards, the quays, the bridges, and the more unfrequented and obscure
localities are alike forbidden.

"They are especially forbidden to frequent public establishments or private
houses where clandestine prostitution might be facilitated, or to attend *tables-
d'hôte*, reside in boarding-houses, or exercise the calling beyond the quarter
of the town they reside in.

"They are likewise strictly prohibited from sharing lodgings with a kept
woman, or other girl, or to reside in furnished lodgings at all without a permit.

"Public women must abstain when at home from anything which can give
ground for complaints by their neighbours, or the passers-by.

"Those who may infringe the above regulations, resist the agents of authority, or give false names or addresses, will incur penalties proportioned to the gravity of the case."

To recapitulate, then; the public women called *filles soumises, inscrites,* or *enregistrées,* over whom the *Bureau des Mœurs* of the prefecture of police has cast its net, are divided into two categories:—

1. Domiciled in, and registered to certain licensed houses, for whom the keepers of those houses are responsible.

2. Free prostitutes, who are responsible to the authorities direct.

The first, or *filles des maisons,* are known at the Bureaux by their number, and that of the house to which they are *inscrites,* and are termed by themselves *filles à numero.* Their health is inspected by the official medical staff, at the house of their inscription, once in every week. The second form two sub-classes—viz., women who have their own apartment and furniture, and others who, by special permit, live in furnished lodgings, &c. To all of these, who are termed *filles à carte,* or by the police *isolées,* a *carte,* or bill of health, from time to time is supplied, to which the *visa* of the medical officer of the *Bureau Sanitaire* is affixed at the health inspections for which they present themselves once every fifteen days, in compliance with obligation 1.

This sanitary department was placed upon its present footing in 1828. The medical staff consists of ten superior and ten assistant surgeons, and the number of inspections in 1854 was:—

At the dispensary	97,626
At the registered houses	53,404
At the depôt of the prefecture (which answers to a first-class police station here)	4,777

The inspection, for which the speculum is very frequently used, is performed with all the delicacy consistent with accuracy, and great despatch; the average time occupied being three minutes, which includes filling up the papers.

(ii) William Sanger

It has been frequently remarked, and as generally believed, in the absence of any satisfactory information on the subject, that a very large majority of the prostitutes in New York are of foreign birth; but the facts already developed . . . go far toward falsifying that opinion. The enumeration shows that five eighths only were born abroad, the dominions of Great Britain furnishing the largest proportion. . . .

But these numbers, being based upon the population of the several countries, gives but a very imperfect idea of the extent of vice among that portion of their people who have settled in America, and a more satisfactory comparison can be drawn from the records of emigration. Upon an examination of the arrivals in each year from the time the existing Board of Commissioners of Emigration was organized to the end of 1857 (a period of ten years), it is found that the numbers average two hundred and thirty thousand per annum, which gives a proportion of one prostitute to every two hundred and fifty emigrants. This is based upon the theory that one fourth of the abandoned women die or are otherwise removed from the city every year. To repeat this fact in plainer words: of every two hundred and fifty emigrants—men, women, and children, who land at our docks, at least one woman eventually becomes known as a prostitute. . . .

QUESTION. WHAT WAS THE CAUSE OF YOUR
BECOMING A PROSTITUTE?

Causes	Numbers
Inclination	513
Destitution	525
Seduced and abandoned	258
Drink, and the desire to drink	181
Ill-treatment of parents, relatives, or husbands	164
As an easy life	124
Bad company	84
Persuaded by prostitutes	71
Too idle to work	29
Violated	27
Seduced on board emigrant ships	16
" in emigrant boarding houses	8
Total	2,000

This question is probably the most important of the series, as the replies lay open to a considerable extent those hidden springs of evil which have hitherto been known only from their results. First in order stands the reply "Inclination," which can only be understood as meaning a voluntary resort to prostitution in order to gratify the sexual passions. Five hundred and thirteen women, more than one fourth of the gross number, give this as their reason. If their representations were borne out by facts, it would make the task of grappling with the vice a most arduous one, and afford very slight grounds to hope for any amelioration; but it is imagined that the circumstances which induced the ruin of most of those who gave the answer will prove that, if a positive inclination to vice was the proximate cause of the fall, it was but the result of other and controlling influences. In itself such an answer would imply an innate depravity, a want of true womanly feeling, which is actually incredible. The force of desire can neither be denied nor disputed, but still in the bosoms of most females that force exists in a slumbering state until aroused by some outside influences. No woman can understand its power until some positive cause of excitement exists. What is sufficient to awaken the dormant passion is a question that admits innumerable answers. Acquaintance with the opposite sex, particularly if extended so far as to become a reciprocal affection, will tend to this; so will the companionship of females who have yielded to its power; and so will the excitement of intoxication. But it must be repeated, and most decidedly, that without these or some other equally stimulating cause, the full force of sexual desire is seldom known to a virtuous woman. In the male sex nature has provided a more susceptible organization than in females, apparently with the beneficent design of repressing those evils which must result from mutual appetite equally felt by both. In other words, man is the *aggressive* animal, so far as sexual desire is involved. Were it otherwise, and the passions in both sexes equal, illegitimacy and prostitution would be far more rife in our midst than at present.

Some few of the cases in which the reply "Inclination" was given are herewith submitted, with the explanation which accompanied each return. C. M.: while virtuous, the girl had visited dance-houses, where she became acquainted with prostitutes, who persuaded her that they led an easy, merry life; her inclination was the result of female persuasion. E. C. left her husband, and became a prostitute willingly, in order to obtain intoxicating liquors which had been refused her at home. E. R. was deserted by her husband because she drank to excess, and became a prostitute in order to obtain liquor. In this and the preceding case, inclination was the result solely of intemperance. A. J. willingly sacrificed her virtue to a man she loved. C. L.: her inclination was swayed by the advice of women already on the town. J. J. continued this course from inclination after having been seduced by her lover. S. C.: this girl's inclination arose from a love of liquor. Enough has been quoted to prove that, in many of the cases, what is called willing prostitution is the sequel of some communication or circumstances which undermine the principles of virtue and arouse the latent passions. . . .

During the progress of this investigation in one of the lower wards of the city, attention was drawn to a pale but interesting-looking girl, about seventeen years of age, from whose replies the following narrative is condensed, retaining her own words as nearly as possible.

"I have been leading this life from about the middle of last January (1856). It was absolute want that drove me to it. My sister, who was about three years older than I am, lived with me. She was deformed and a cripple from a fall she had while a child, and could not do any hard work. She could do a little sewing, and when we both were able to get work we could just make a living. When the heavy snow-storm came our work stopped, and we were in want of food and coals. One very cold morning, just after I had been to the store, the landlord's agent called for some rent we owed, and told us that, if we could not pay it, we should have to move. The agent was a kind man, and gave us a little money to buy some coals. We did not know what we were to do, and were both crying about it, when the woman who keeps this house (where she was then living) came in and brought some sewing for us to do that day. She said that she had been recommended to us by a woman who lived in the same house, but I found out since that she had watched me, and only said this for an excuse. When the work was done I brought it home here. I had heard of such places before, but had never been inside one. I was very cold, and she made me sit down by the fire, and began to talk to me, saying how much better off I should be if I would come and live with her. I told her I could not leave my sister, who was the only relation I had, and could not help herself; but she said I should be able to help my sister, and that she would find some light sewing for her to do, so that she should not want. She talked a good deal more, and I felt inclined to do as she wanted me, but then I thought how wicked it would be, and at last I told her I would think about it. When I got home and saw my sister so sick as she was, and wanting many little things that we had no money to buy, and no friends to help us to, my heart almost broke. However, I said nothing to her then. I laid awake all night thinking, and in the morning I made up my mind to come here. I told her what I was going to do, and she begged me not, but my mind was made up. She said it would be sin, and I told her that I should have to answer for that, and that I was forced to do it because there was no other way to keep myself and help her, and I knew she could not work much for herself, and I was sure she would not live a day if we were turned into the streets. She tried all she could to persuade me not, but I was determined, and so I came here. I hated the thoughts of such a life, and my only reason for coming was that I might help her. I thought that, if I had been alone, I would sooner have starved, but I could not bear to see her suffering. She only lived a few weeks after I came here. I broke her heart. I do not like the life. I would do almost any thing to get out of it; but, now that I have *once done wrong*, I can not get any one to give me work, and I must stop here unless I wish to be starved to death."

This plain and affecting narrative needs no comment. It reveals the history of many an unfortunate woman in this city, and while it must appeal to every sensitive heart, it argues most forcibly for some intervention in such cases. The following statements of other women who have suffered and fallen in a similar manner will show that the preceding is not an isolated case. M. M., a widow with one child, earned $1.50 per week as a tailoress. J. Y., a servant, was taken sick while in a situation, spent all her money, and could get no employment when she recovered. M. T. (quoting her own words) "had no work, no money, and no home." S. F., a widow with three children, could earn two dollars weekly at cap-making, but could not obtain steady employment even at those prices. M. F. had been out of place for some time, and had no money. E. H. earned from two to three dollars per week as tailoress, but had been out of employment for some time. L. C. G.: the examining officer reports in this case, "This girl (a tailoress) is a stranger, without any relations. She received a dollar and a half a week, which would not maintain her." M. C., a servant, was receiving five dollars a month. She sent all her earnings to her mother, and soon after lost her situation, when she had no means to support herself. M. S., also a servant, received *one dollar a month wages*. A. B. landed in Baltimore from Germany, and was robbed of all her money the very day she reached the shore. M. F., a shirt-maker, earned one dollar a week. E. M. G.: the captain of police in the district where this woman resides says, "This girl struggled hard with the world before she became a prostitute, sleeping in station-houses at night, and living on bread and water during the day." He adds: "In my experience of three years, I have known *over fifty cases* whose history would be similar to hers, and who are now prostitutes."

(iii) Annie Johnson

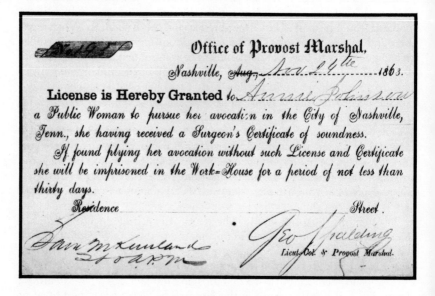

90. Prostitution and poverty in London

The specter of the hungry urban working girl being forced to take to the streets to supplement the meager wages paid in many shops and trades appalled more than one nineteenth-century social reformer. Jules Michelet wrote that the sight of men buying the favors of these starving, pathetic working women in the streets of Paris made him ashamed to be a man, and others, too, wrote with indignation about the plight of such women. Among these protesters, none was more eloquent than the French socialist-feminist Flora Tristan (1803–44; Doc. 58.i). In 1839 Tristan visited London with the express intention of investigating social problems concerning women. Guarded by two male companions armed with canes, she toured the Waterloo Road district, which was inhabited almost exclusively by prostitutes and pimps. She also managed to visit one of the "finishes," or gin-palaces, reputed to be the scene of unspeakable orgies. Her sense of shock runs through the following

SOURCES: (i) Flora Tristan, *Promenades dans Londres* (Paris and London, 1840), pp. 109–12, 117–20. The editors are indebted to Professor S. Joan Moon, California State University, Sacramento, for contributing this selection. (ii) *The Unknown Mayhew*, ed. Eileen Yeo and E. P. Thompson (London, 1971), pp. 147–49. Originally published in the London *Morning Chronicle*, Nov. 13, 1849.

selection from 'Promenades in London,' which she published in 1840. The second selection is a letter that appeared in the London 'Morning Chronicle' in 1849, one of a series submitted by Henry Mayhew (1812–87), a British social investigator who spent years studying the condition of the London poor. Among the most sensational revelations in Mayhew's letters were those accounts—like the one given here—that showed needlewomen forced into prostitution because of their extreme poverty. In the public outcry precipitated by Mayhew's letters, Lord Shaftesbury, a prominent Tory reformer, publicly suggested that this social evil might be remedied by subsidizing the emigration of such women.

(i) Flora Tristan

On the subject of finishes, I had been told about scenes of debauchery I had refused to believe.—I found myself in London for the fourth time, and had come with the firm intention of getting to know everything. Therefore I resolved to overcome my repugnance and go in person to one of these finishes, so that I could decide whether to believe the descriptions I had heard. The same friends who had accompanied me to Waterloo Road again offered to chaperone me.

It is truly a spectacle, one that better reveals the moral state of England than anything else one could say. . . .

From the outside these gin-places, tightly shut up, reveal nothing but sleep and silence, but scarcely has the porter opened the little gate by which the habitués enter than one is dazzled by an intense and brilliant light radiating from a thousand gas lamps.—On the first floor is an immense *salon* divided in half along its length. As in all English restaurants, on one side is a row of tables separated by wooden partitions; on both sides of each table are benches made up of sofas. On the other side, facing them, is a stage where the prostitutes, all dressed up, display themselves.—They entice the men with their glances and remarks.—When someone responds, they lead the elegant gentleman to one of the tables that are loaded with cold cuts, hams, poultry, pastries, and every kind of wine and liqueur.

The finishes are the temples that English materialism has raised to its gods!—The servants who clear the tables are richly dressed; the industrialist-owners of the establishment humbly greet the *male* guests who come there to exchange their gold for debauchery.

Around midnight the habitués begin to arrive. Several of these cabarets are the meeting places where high society or the aristocratic elite gather.— First the young lords lie down on the sofas, smoking and chatting with the girls; then, after they have had a few drinks, and the fumes of the champagne and the alcohol from the madeira have excited their brains, the illustrious scions of the English nobility, the very honorable members of Parliament, take off their jackets, loosen their ties, remove their waistcoats and suspenders.—They set up their *private boudoirs* in *a public cabaret.*—Why should they be ashamed?—don't they pay a great deal for the right to force their contempt on others? And as for the contempt they inspire, they could care less.—The orgy mounts to a climax; between four and five in the morning, it reaches its peak. . . .

In what a worthy manner these noble English lords use their immense fortunes! How handsome, how generous they are when they have lost control of their reason and offer fifty, a hundred guineas to a prostitute, if she will abandon herself to all the obscenities born of drunkenness.

In the finishes there are all sorts of amusements. One of the most relished is to get a prostitute so soused that she falls down dead drunk; then they force her to drink a mixture of vinegar, mustard, and pepper; this beverage almost always gives her horrible convulsions, and the twitching and contortions of the poor unfortunate woman provoke laughter and entertain *honorable society* ever so much!—Another diversion greatly enjoyed at these fashionable parties is to throw a glass of something on the girls who are lying dead drunk on the floor.—I have seen satin gowns that no longer have any color; they exhibit only a mess of stains—wine, *eau-de-vie*, beer, tea, coffee, cream, etc.—sketching a thousand fantastic forms, the mad artwork of the orgy. Oh! how could human beings descend so low! . . .

This life, which begins over again *every night*, is the only way these public women have to make money, for they have no chance with a starving Englishman—the starving Englishman is chaste to the point of prudery.

I have never been able to look at a prostitute without being moved by a surge of compassion for our societies, without contempt for their social organization and hate for those who dominate them. These latter, having no sense of decency, no respect for humanity, no love for their fellow creatures, reduce God's creature to the lowest degree of abjection!—lowering her below the level of the beast.

I can understand the brigand who holds up passers-by on the highways and loses his head to the guillotine; I can understand the soldier who continually risks his life and only receives one *sou* per day in exchange; I can understand the sailor who exposes his life to the fury of the seas; all three find in their vocation a somber and terrible poetry! But I cannot understand the prostitute: surrendering herself! annihilating both her will and her bodily feelings; sacrificing her body to brutality and suffering, and her soul to contempt! The prostitute is, for me, an impenetrable mystery.—I see in prostitution a horrible folly, or else it is so exceedingly sublime that my human self cannot even comprehend it. Risking death is nothing—but what a death awaits the prostitute! She is engaged to suffering, vowed to abjection! Physical tortures unceasingly repeated; a moral death each instant! *And self-contempt as well!!!*

I repeat—either it is sublime! Or it is madness!

Prostitution is the most hideous of the afflictions produced by the unequal distribution of the world's goods; this infamy stigmatizes the human species and bears witness against the social organization far more than does crime; prejudices, misery, helotism combine their baleful effects to bring about this revolting degradation. Certainly, if you had not imposed the virtue of chastity on woman without compelling man to observe it as well, she would not be repulsed by society for ceding to the feelings of her heart, and the seduced, wronged, abandoned girl would not be reduced to prostituting herself. Certainly, if you allowed her to receive the same education, to exercise the same jobs and professions as man, she would not be struck down by misery any more than he. Certainly, if you did not expose her to every abuse of strength due to the despotism of paternal power and the indissolubility of marriage, she would never be in the position of having to choose between oppression and infamy.

Virtue and vice suppose the freedom to choose between good and evil; but what can be the morals of a woman who is not even in possession of herself, who has nothing of her own, and who all her life has been trained to extricate herself from the arbitrary by ruse, from constraint by using her charms? And when she is tortured by misery, and sees that men are able to enjoy all goods, is it surprising that the art of pleasing in which she has been raised does not inevitably lead her into prostitution?

Thus, this monstrosity ought to be blamed on your social statute, and woman ought to be absolved! As long as she is subject to man's yoke or to prejudice, as long as she receives no professional education, as long as she is deprived of her civil rights, there can be no moral law for her! As long as she can obtain the enjoyment of goods only by the influence she exercises over passions, as long as there is nothing that belongs to her, and as long as she is dispossessed by her husband of all the property she acquired by her labor, or that her father gave her, as long as she can only assure herself of the use of her property and liberty by living as a celibate, there can be no moral law for her! And one can affirm that, until the day that women are emancipated, prostitution will spread and grow.

(ii) Henry Mayhew

During the course of my investigation into the condition of those who are dependent upon their needle for their support, I had been so repeatedly assured that the young girls were mostly compelled to resort to prostitution to eke out their subsistence, that I was anxious to test the truth of the statement. I had seen much want, but I had no idea of the intensity of the privations suffered by the needlewomen of London until I came to inquire into this part of the subject. But the poor creatures shall speak for themselves. I should inform the reader, however, that I have made inquiries into the truth of the almost incredible statements here given, and I can in most of the particulars at least vouch for the truth of the statement. Indeed, in one instance . . . I travelled nearly ten miles in order to obtain the character of the young woman. The first case is that of a good-looking girl. Her story is as follows:

"I make moleskin trowsers. I get 7d. and 8d. per pair. I can do two pairs in a day, and twelve when there is full employment, in a week. But some weeks I have no work at all. I work from six in the morning to ten at night; that is what I call my day's work. When I am fully employed I get from 7s. to 8s. a week. My expenses out of that for twist, thread, and candles are about 1s. 6d. a week, leaving me about 6s. per week clear. But there's coals to pay for out of this, and that's at the least 6d. more; so 5s. 6d. is the very outside of what I earn when I'm in full work. Lately I have been dreadfully slack; so we are every winter, all of us 'sloppers', and that's the time when we wants the most money. The week before last I had but two pair to make all the week; so that I only earnt 1s. clear. For this last month I'm sure I haven't done any more than that each week. Taking one week with another, all the year round I don't make above 3s. clear money each week. I don't work at any other kind of slop-work. The trowsers work is held to be the best paid of all. I give 1s. a week rent.

"My father died when I was five years of age. My mother is a widow, upwards of 66 years of age, and seldom has a day's work. Generally once in the week she is employed pot-scouring—that is, cleaning publicans' pots. She is paid 4d. a dozen for that, and does about four dozen and a half, so that she gets about 1s. 6d. in the day by it. For the rest she is dependent upon me. I am 20 years of age the 25th of this month. We earn together, to keep the two of us, from 4s. 6d. to 5s. each week. Out of this we have to pay 1s. rent, and there remains 3s. 6d. to 4s. to find us both in food and clothing. It is of course impossible for us to live upon it, and the consequences is I am obliged to go a bad way. I have been three years working at slop-work.

"I was virtuous when I first went to work, and I remained so till this last twelvemonth. I struggled very hard to keep myself chaste, but I found that I couldn't get food and clothing for myself and mother, so I took to live with a young man. He is turned 20. He is a tinman. He did promise to marry me, but his sister made mischief between me and him, so that parted us. I have not seen him now for about six months, and I can't say whether he will keep his promise or not. I am now pregnant by him, and expect to be confined in two months' time. He knows of my situation, and so does my mother. My mother believed me to be married to him. She knows otherwise now. I was very fond of him, and had known him for two years before he seduced me. He could make 14s. a week. He told me if I came to live with him he'd take care I shouldn't want, and both mother and me had been very bad off before. He said, too, he'd make me his lawful wife, but I hardly cared so long as I could get food for myself and mother.

"Many young girls at the shop advised me to go wrong. They told me how comfortable they was off; they said they could get plenty to eat and drink, and good clothes. There isn't one young girl as can get her living by slop work. The masters all know this, but they wouldn't own to it of course. It stands to reason that no one can live and pay rent, and find clothes, upon 3s. a week, which is the most they can make clear, even the best hands, at the moleskin and cord trowsers work. There's poor people moved out of our house that was making ¾d. shirts. I am satisfied there is not one young girl that works at slop work that is virtuous, and there are some thousands in the trade. They may do very well if they have got mothers and fathers to find them a home and food, and to let them have what they earn for clothes; then they may be virtuous, but not without. I've heard of numbers who have gone from slop work to the streets altogether for a living, and I shall be obligated to do the same thing myself unless something better turns up for me.

"If I was never allowed to speak no more, it was the little money I got by my labour that led me to go wrong. Could I have honestly earnt enough to have subsisted upon, to find me in proper food and clothing, such as is necessary, I should not have gone astray; no, never—As it was I fought against it as long as I could—that I did—to the last. I hope to be able to get a ticket for a midwife; a party has promised me as much, and, he says, if possible, he'll get me an order for a box of linen. My child will only increase my burdens, and if my young man won't support my child I must go on the streets altogether. I know how horrible all this is. It would have been much better for me to have subsisted upon a dry crust and water rather than be as I am now. But no one knows the temptations of us poor girls in want. Gentlefolks can never understand it. If I had been born a lady it wouldn't have been very hard to have acted like one. To be poor and to be honest, especially with young girls, is the hardest struggle of all. There isn't one in a thousand that can get the better of it. I am ready to say again, that it was want, and nothing more, that made me transgress. If I had been better paid I should have done better. Young as I am, my life is a curse to me. If the Almighty would please to take me before my child is born, I should die happy."

91. 'Unjustly accused of prostitution!': Ellen Vokes

Parliament enacted the Contagious Diseases Acts of 1864, 1866, and 1869 to check the spread of venereal disease among soldiers and sailors in English and Irish garrison and port towns. This legislation established procedures by which women whom the municipal authorities accused of being common prostitutes were registered, subjected to periodic medical examinations, and if found to have venereal disease, kept in a prison hospital for as long as six months. The definition of a "common prostitute" was vague and allowed the police broad discretionary powers; the accused woman bore the burden of proving her virtue. The C. D. Acts, which thus deprived poor women of their legal rights, functioned as socially repressive laws that served to control the behavior of lower-class women. Indeed, they offered a flagrant example of the double standard, leaving the male carrier of venereal disease free to spread the contagion and punishing the infected woman. The repeal of these acts became one of the chief goals of English feminists, and after a long and bitter campaign, all of them were removed from the statute books by the end of the century. The following testimony by Ellen Vokes, a domestic servant from a village near Southampton, illustrates the arbitrary manner in which authorities enforced the acts and used them to harass working-class women.

SOURCE: Great Britain, *Parliamentary Papers*, 1881, VIII, Report from the Select Committee on the Contagious Diseases Acts, pp. 478–80.

I, Ellen Vokes, of Peabody-road, Farnborough, in the county of South-ampton, do declare that I am 23 years of age, and am a domestic servant, and was in the service of Major Shaw of the 102nd Regiment, in Victoria-road, Aldershot, as cook until the 30th day of September 1880. I had been in the service of Major Shaw for 10 months, and received an excellent written char-acter from Mrs. Shaw on leaving. . . .

On leaving Major Shaw's service I went to reside with Mrs. Birchall in Peabody-road, Farnborough. Mrs. Birchall had formerly worked for my mother at Winchester, and on her suggesting I could assist her as a laundress she took me in until I could get another situation. Mrs. Birchall's husband was a soldier in the Royal Engineers.

I had difficulty in getting a situation, as in the autumn a great number of the officers go on leave; I remained at Mrs. Birchall's up to the 3rd of De-cember last (1880), and worked for her as a laundress, and managed her work during an illness which prevented her attending to her work.

While I was at Mrs. Birchall's a young man named Charles Richards, of the 60th Rifles, who was on provost duty, kept company with me, and I occasionally went out with him in the evening, and about once a week went with him to the North Camp Music Hall, a place of entertainment, not far from Peabody-road. On the night of the 3rd of December I went home to Mrs. Birchall's about nine o'clock, and I was surprised to find the door locked against me. I knocked for half an hour, but was not admitted; finding I could not get in I went to the house of Mrs. Hoffman, who also worked for Mrs. Birchall, and she kindly took me into their small house, and her husband slept in a chair during that night. On inquiring the following day for the cause of my being locked out I found that the police had been to Mr. Birchall and threatened him that if he did not get rid of me he would report him to his commanding officer and get him punished for harbouring a prostitute. This I heard to my great astonishment from Mrs. Sadler, who is Mrs. Birchall's sister, and living next door to her, and this was the first intimation that I had that the police were watching me or endeavouring to do me an injury. I can most sincerely say that I had given them no reason whatever for their endeavouring to get me turned out of Mr. Birchall's house, and his wife's service. Mrs. Sadler upon this took me into her house, and I got work at Mrs. Mills, another laun-dress living in Peabody-road. I continued to work for Mrs. Mills and to live at Mrs. Sadler's and am still working for Mrs. Mills and living with Mrs. Sadler.

The first time any police officer spoke to me was on the 7th of December, about seven o'clock in the evening. When I was going out of Mrs. Sadler's house I saw a policeman not in uniform at Mrs. Birchall's door; he said "You are the young woman I am looking for." I said "What do you want me for," and he said "I want you to be at the Metropolitan Police Station to-morrow morning at 10 o'clock." I said "What for?" He said "You will see when you get there, and remember I am a policeman in plain clothes; you know where it is, don't you?" And I said "No." He said "It is at Aldershot, at the corner of the Avenue-road." I said "I shall not go, I have done nothing." He then said "If you don't come I shall fetch you in my uniform, and it will nicely show you up going through the camp." I said "I am not going," and he said "If you don't come I shall fetch you," and he went off.

I met Mrs. Sadler in the road shortly after, and while telling her what had taken place the policeman came by, and she said it was policeman Banks, and she called him to her, and said to him "What have you been interfering with this young woman for; have you anything against her," and he then said "No, I wish I had." Mrs. Sadler said "What do you mean by stopping her"; he said "Oh, it is not that I have a case, but walls have ears." She said "Well have you heard anything," and he said "No, and it is not for me to tell what I hear"; I said to him "I shall not go to-morrow," and Mrs. Sadler said "You had better go and hear what it is all about, and you know they can prove nothing against you"; the policeman said "I have known brighter girls than you talk in this way, and I have known them drown themselves rather than come to our rules, and you can do the same if you like, it won't trouble me." I said "I will never come to your rules, and would sooner drown myself." Mrs. Sadler said "There should be no bother; she shall come, and I will come with her."

In the morning (8th December) Mrs. Sadler went with me to the Metropolitan Police Station, and the same policeman was waiting for me at the door, and he took me into a separate room where the inspector was. The Inspector asked me my name, and whether I lived at Farnborough. In answer to his questions I told him whose service I had been in, and my home was at Winchester, and that I had a mother but no father. He put two pieces of blue paper before me and told me to sign them; I said "Certainly not"; he said "Don't speak to me in that way, but sign the papers"; I said "The policeman told me yesterday I should know what I was to come here for, and now I wish to know"; he said "This is not a place for talking." I then turned to the policeman, and said "You told me I should know what I was to come here for, and now I am told this is not a place for talking." The policeman did not answer, and I said "I am not going to sign any papers. I want to know what I am called here for." The policeman said "I am not allowed to talk." The inspector read a statement the policeman had made to the effect that he had seen me talking to three different men of the 60th Rifles and a bandsman of the 82nd Regiment. I said to the policeman "Do you really say you have seen these men talking to me now." I said "You bring them forward." The inspector told me to be quiet, and to bring the men myself, and that I was to sign the papers, and go away quietly; I said "I would not." He said to the policeman "You must make a case against this woman, and we must make her sign." Mrs. Sadler told them as they ordered me out that I should not be wronged, and they then said we will summon her. After this a message was sent by the policeman, through Mr. Birchall, to Mr. Sadler, who is a pensioner from the 60th Rifles, that a report would be made against him if he did not turn me out of his house, and that he would lose his pension for harbouring a prostitute. From the time I was at the police station I found that the same policeman was constantly dogging my steps where I went, and I was told that he inquired of the various persons I spoke to whether they knew anything about me. On the 16th of December I had finished my work at Mrs. Mills about six o'clock, and the policeman came to Mrs. Sadler's, and she went to the door. He said "I want that young woman you have got in your house." She said "I will call her." He said "No you won't," and pushed past her and came into the room where Mr. Sadler was ill in bed. He pushed me, as I was going to the door, back on to the bed, and said "Here, my girl, is your summons," and he said to Mr. Sadler, as he lay in bed, "Mind, I have done for this girl, and I'll do for you, and get your pension taken away," and called the children to witness that he had told their father to get rid of me out of his house. Mr. Sadler said "It is lucky for you I am in bed or I would kick you out; you have no business in this house without a warrant." I placed the summons in the hands of Mr. Eve, solicitor, Aldershot, and instructed him to defend me, which he did before the county magistrates, in Petty Sessions at Aldershot, on the 23rd of December.

The information against me was made by Mr. Ody Wenham, the Superintendent of the Metropolitan Police for Aldershot, under the Contagious Diseases Act, and alleged that he had good cause to believe that I was a common prostitute, and resident, within the limits of a place to which the Act applied.

I was asked whether I would like the case heard publicly or in private, and I chose to have it heard privately.

The magistrates present were Major Birch (Chairman), Captain Elliott, F. H. Fitzroy, and Wm. Sherwin, Esqrs. The police-constable, Edward Banks, was sworn, and stated that he noticed me about the latter part of October last go into a house that was frequented by soldiers, and to which house he had seen prostitutes go.

On the 21st November, at eight o'clock in the evening, he saw me talking to a bandsman of the 82nd Regiment at the North Camp Hotel, and that the bandsman went with me to Mr. Beggs, a shoemaker, and that the bandsman remained there for 16 minutes, and at near 10 o'clock two soldiers came out of the same house for a minute and go back again, and in about five minutes left the house. That I left shortly after the two soldiers. That before I left the house Beggs said he would see if all was clear.

My solicitor objected to this statement and other statements as to what Beggs was alleged to have said. The policeman further stated he saw me on the 22nd November last with another woman ask two soldiers to treat us, and that on the 30th November he saw me at the music hall at North Camp Hotel and leave with an artilleryman, and return in 15 minutes, and that he watched me leave the hall with a 60th Rifleman and go to Beggs' house. That he watched me on the 4th, 6th, 9th, and 15th of December with men of the 60th Rifles, and the said bandsman. In cross-examination the policeman admitted that he could not say whether the private of the 60th Rifles was not the same soldier that he had seen me with on other occasions.

He had heard I was keeping company with Private Charles Richards of the 60th Rifles, and that I worked for my living at laundry work with Mrs. Birchall and Mrs. Mills. This was all the evidence against me. My solicitor, on my behalf, contended at great length that there was no evidence upon which the magistrates could assume that I was a common prostitute, and stated, as the fact was, that until within a month of my steps being watched by the police-man, I had been in respectable service of officers, at Aldershot and elsewhere, from the time I had left my mother's home some six years ago. That I had en-tered into each service with a good character, and left my last situation with the written character from Mrs. Shaw, which was produced. That on leaving my last situation I had entered the house of my friend, Mrs. Birchall, until I could get another situation, and worked hard for my living there until I was turned out of her house through the police. That other friends took me in and pro-tected me while I was working hard for my living. It was most improbable that a prudent, honest, and industrious girl, as I was proved to be on leaving Mrs. Shaw's service on the 30th September last, would so soon sacrifice a well-earned, honest character by leading a life of infamy, as the police wished them to believe.

The magistrates could not assume from the police evidence that I was pros-tituting myself when it was proved I was working hard for my living.

Unfortunately that morning the 60th Rifles had been ordered to Ireland, or it could have been shown by the young man Richards himself that he was keeping company with me, and was the man that was so frequently seen with me by the police.

Mrs. Sadler was called and proved she knew my mother, and had known me from a child, and the situations I had filled at Winchester and Aldershot, and that after leaving Mrs. Shaw's I had gone to live with and work for her sister, Mrs. Birchall. That I worked for Mrs. Birchall from morning till night, and went out occasionally in the evening with witness to the music hall, and that I conducted myself as an honest, prudent girl should do, not only during my stay at Mrs. Birchall's, but particularly since I had left there and resided with witness. That Charles Richards, a private in the 60th Rifles, and who was on provost duty, kept company with me, and was with her and me at the music hall when he could get off duty. On hearing this evidence the magis-trates retired, and on returning into court adjourned the case for the attendance of other witnesses for the defence. At the adjourned hearing, on the 30th De-cember, the court was again cleared; Mr. Marshall, from the office of the Na-tional Association,* was present, and was desired to leave by the police. My solicitor, Mr. Eve, strongly objected, and stated that Mr. Marshall was a friend of mine, and as such had as much right to remain in court as the police officers not in the case, and that if he were ordered out I would demand an open court. Mr. Marshall was allowed to remain. Mrs. Birchall was called on my behalf, and stated she had known me from a child, and that on my leaving Mrs. Shaw at the end of September she had offered me a home and work until I got a situation.

That during the time I lived with her I worked hard, and till late some nights, and conducted myself as an honest and prudent girl; occasionally I

* Presumably the National Association for the Repeal of the Contagious Diseases Acts, founded in 1869 and disbanded in 1886.—EDS.

went out of an evening after work was done, and generally from six till eight, sometimes till half-past nine. That I was keeping company with Private Richards of the 60th Rifles. In cross-examination Mrs. Birchall said that an artilleryman called on me once, but that she understood I did not wish to keep company with him, but with Richards, and that I was not out twice so late as 11. My solicitor offered to call Mr. Beggs to negative the statements of the policeman, but submitted that the evidence adduced was sufficient for my case.

The magistrates retired, and on returning into court the chairman said they were divided in opinion, but gave the defendant the benefit of the doubt.

I may say with reference to the artilleryman, referred to in the case, he wished to keep company when I was in service, and wanted to marry me when I went to live with Mrs. Birchall, but I declined his offer then for my own reasons, and he did not come to see me afterwards.

The bandsman of the 82nd Regiment was only a youth, and I talked to him as I knew him and his friends when living at home at Winchester.

Dated this 26th day of January 1881.   (signed) Ellen Vokes.

92. A French midwife becomes a doctor: Madeleine Brès

In the United States Elizabeth Blackwell (1821–1910; Doc. 37.iii) received her medical degree in 1849, after many difficulties in gaining admittance to an accredited school. But in England and France the opening of the medical profession to women took a generation longer. France did, however, have a world-famous school for midwives with an associated teaching hospital. (Blackwell studied there for a term in 1848; Suzanne Voilquin [c. 1800–1860; Doc. 35] also studied there.) Thus when the issue of admitting women to medical faculties arose in the 1860's, approval from the medical school was relatively easy to obtain—if, that is, one could get a baccalaureate, a prerequisite for admission to all professional schools. Madeleine Brès (1842–1925) was among the first women to sit for and pass the baccalaureate, which required the "unwomanly" mastery of Greek and Latin; and she was the first woman admitted to the Paris School of Medicine. She accomplished all this as the widowed mother of ten children. For many years, Brès remained exceptional in France; foreign women long outnumbered Frenchwomen in the French medical schools. In this article from an educational journal, Brès looks back on her life and career.

My father was a cartwright and worked for the nuns of the Nîmes hospital. Sometimes I accompanied him, and the sisters, who loved me, allowed me to bring poultices and herb teas to their patients. "What a good little doctor you would make!" said the chief doctor when he met me with my load. I was seven years old. As I grew up I never forgot that little phrase. My studies were scarcely elaborate. Until I was ten I had been with the sisters of La Calade at

SOURCE: "Une Bachelière d'autrefois," *Revue Universitaire*, 1921, part 2: 145–46.

Nîmes, where the schooling cost two *sous* per month. I did not really begin to learn anything until after the birth of my first child.

I had ten children and I survived them all! Our neighbor was a professor of Latin and Greek. Since he had no children, he often liked to fondle my baby, a handsome child. One day I confided my dream to him—to study, to become a doctor. He smiled: "First you must be schooled and pass your baccalaureate." This word, which I didn't know, did not discourage me. In a little bookstore I found a manual for the baccalaureate and bought it. I rapidly learned all that I could learn. My marvelous memory served me well. Touched by my zeal, my neighbor loaned me the *Epitome** and gave me lessons. I was twenty-eight years old when I became a *bachelière.* I was not successful in the first round, but did succeed in the second. More than ever I thought of medicine and wanted to specialize in the illnesses of women and children. At that time the minister of public instruction was Victor Duruy.

But in order to take the examination, I needed the endorsement of Empress Eugénie. She was quite interested in my project. She even said: "If this young woman is successful, I will found a school of medicine for women." But then came 1870!—

During the war [of 1870–71] I entered a hospital as a provisional intern. Fifty-seven shells landed there during the siege of Paris. I did not receive my doctorate until 1875, with a thesis I remember very well: "The Breast and Breast-Feeding." I was in attendance to Dr. Broca; for masters, I had Wurtz, Sainte-Claire-Deville, Sappey. In 1891 I founded a day-care center [*crèche*] in Paris. We called it *Ecole populaire d'hygiène,* the People's School of Hygiene, since mothers didn't like the word *crèche.* There I gave courses in child-raising and lessons in all sorts of things. We served some 7,000 children a year.

Then I opened an office for consultations on the Rue de Rivoli. For fifty years I was active as a gynecologist and pediatrician. I do not regret my life of struggle and work. Indeed, I can say I enjoyed it.

93. Women helping women: Benevolence and philanthropy

For centuries before the Victorian era, upper-class women had been engaged in charitable activities on behalf of the poor, usually under the auspices of religious bodies. But in the nineteenth century there was a great outburst of

---

* A preparatory text for the baccalaureate.—EDS.

SOURCES: (i) Elizabeth Fry, *Observations of the visiting, superintendence, and government of female prisoners* (London, 1827), pp. 1–8. (ii) Oeuvre des Liberées de Saint-Lazare recruitment brochure, 1878, Bibliothèque Marguerite Durand, Paris. (iii) "Hester Vaughan. Workingwomen's Meeting at Cooper Institute. A Plea for Mercy," *The World* (New York), Dec. 2, 1868. The editors wish to thank Professor Carol Turabin, Vassar College, for calling this article to our attention, and Professor Ellen DuBois, State University of New York, Buffalo, for her aid in identifying Mrs. Kirk.

philanthropic work, much of which was directed toward helping other women. For the women engaged in it, this work offered a legitimate way to exercise power and quickly brought them into contact with the world of public decision-making. It also contributed to the growth of a sense of sisterhood that, for some women, transcended socioeconomic boundaries.

Elizabeth Gurney Fry (1780–1845), devout Quaker and wife and mother of a large family, pioneered the reform of prison conditions for women in England and throughout continental Europe as well. Touched by the plight of the unfortunate in her London neighborhood, in 1817 she established an association aimed at improving the lot of female prisoners in the notorious Newgate prison. Her activities soon transcended personal benevolence, and she began to advocate the use of women to inspect, staff, and administer prisons as a way to better conditions for the female inmates. In the excerpt given here she offers her ideas about the role charitable "ladies" should play in helping their poor sisters.

During the next fifty years many women, following in Fry's footsteps, founded organizations and institutions to assist other women. In France one of the best known of these organizations was the Society for Released Female Prisoners of Saint-Lazare (Oeuvre des Libérées de Saint-Lazare), founded in 1869 by Mlle Michel du Grandpré. Its specific goal was to assist "salvageable" women—that is, those who were not jailed for prostitution—to return to the outside world armed with a skill that could provide them with a livelihood. The society attracted a number of Protestant women already active in female philanthropy and, like similar efforts in England and the United States, it quickly became a forcing-ground for a new generation of feminist leaders. In the second selection, a membership recruitment brochure dating from 1878, the society's activities are fully described.

Women's attempts to help members of their own sex quickly brought them into conflict with the male political establishment. In 1868 a group of prominent women's rights advocates convoked a meeting in New York City to demand a new trial for a Philadelphia woman who had been sentenced to death for infanticide. The convicted woman, Hester Vaughan, was a recent immigrant from England who had been abandoned by her husband and then raped by another man while working as a domestic servant. Vaughan had subsequently given birth to a child, which was found dead several days after the birth, and she was accused—on flimsy evidence—of murder. The third selection is a newspaper's text of a speech by Eleanor Kirk, a New York journalist, in which she recounts her visit to Vaughan in Moyamensing Prison, her discussions of the case with the prison inspector and the judge, and her analysis of the ingredients for a more equal justice for women. The intervention of Kirk and her colleagues was apparently effective, for six months later Hester Vaughan was quietly pardoned and then deported to England.

(i) Elizabeth Fry

I wish to make a few general remarks, which have long impressed me, respecting my own sex, and the place which I believe it to be their duty and privilege to fill in the scale of society. I rejoice to see the day in which so many women of every rank, instead of spending their time in trifling and unprofitable pursuits, are engaged in works of usefulness and charity. Earnestly is it to be desired that the number of these valuable labourers in the cause of virtue and humanity may be increased, and that all of us may be made sensible of the infinite importance of redeeming the time, of turning our talents to account, and of becoming the faithful, humble, devoted, followers of a crucified Lord, who went about DOING GOOD.

Far be it from me to attempt to persuade women to forsake their right province. My only desire is, that they should *fill that province well*; and, although their calling, in many respects, materially differs from that of the other sex, and may not perhaps be so exalted an one—yet a minute observation will prove that, if adequately fulfilled, it has nearly, if not quite, an equal influence on society at large.

No person will deny the importance attached to the character and conduct of a woman, in all her domestic and social relations, when she is filling the station of a daughter, a sister, a wife, a mother, or a mistress of a family. But it is a dangerous error to suppose that the duties of females end here. Their gentleness, their natural sympathy with the afflicted, their quickness of discernment, their openness to religious impressions, are points of character (not unusually to be found in our sex) which evidently qualify them, within their own peculiar province, for a far more extensive field of usefulness.

In endeavouring to direct the attention of the female part of society to such objects of Christian charity as they are most calculated to benefit, I may now observe that no persons appear to me to possess so strong a claim on their compassion, and on their pious exertions, as the helpless, the ignorant, the afflicted, or the depraved, of *their own sex*. It is almost needless to remark, that a multitude of such persons may be found in many of our public institutions.

During the last ten years much attention has been successfully bestowed by women on the female inmates of our *prisons*; and many a poor prisoner, under their fostering care, has become completely changed,—rescued from a condition of depravity and wretchedness, and restored to happiness, as a useful and respectable member of the community. Most desirable is it that such efforts should be pursued with patient perseverance wherever they have been already made, and that they should be gradually extended to all the prisons in the kingdom.

But a similar care is evidently required for our hospitals, our lunatic asylums, and our workhouses. It is quite obvious, that there are departments in all such institutions which ought to be under the especial superintendence of females. Were ladies to make a practice of regularly visiting them, a most important check would be obtained on a variety of abuses, which are far too apt to creep into the management of these establishments. Such a practice would be the means, not only of essentially contributing to the welfare of the afflicted sufferers, but of materially aiding those gentlemen, on whom devolves the government or care of the institutions. The Roman Catholic ladies, in many parts of the continent of Europe, have set us, in this respect, a bright and useful example; and the result of their care and attention, especially in the hospitals, has been found, in a high degree, salutary and beneficial. Nor have similar effects failed to be produced in the comparatively solitary instances in which women, in our own country, have been in the habit of regularly visiting the public abodes of poverty or disease. . . .

Much may be accomplished by the *union of forces.*—If, in every parish or district, such ladies, as desire to make the best use of their time, would occasionally meet together, in order to consider the condition of their neighbourhood, and would then divide themselves and allot the labours of Christian love to the several parties respectively, according to their suitability for different objects, the employment of but a small portion of their time would enable them to effect more extensive good than could previously have been thought possible; and, instead of being incapacitated for their domestic duties, they would often return to those duties, refreshed in spirit, and stimulated to perform them with increased cheerfulness, propriety, and diligence.

To revert, for a short time, to the subject of our public institutions, although I feel it a delicate matter so earnestly to insist on the point, I must now express my conviction, that few persons are aware of the *degree* in which the female departments of them stand in need of the superintending care of judicious ladies. So great are the abuses which exist in some of those establishments, that *modest* women dare not run the risk to which they would be exposed, did they attempt to derive from them the relief which they require. I would have this subject occupy the serious consideration of the benevolent part of the community. All reflecting persons will surely unite in the sentiment, that the female, placed in the prison for her crimes, in the hospital for her sickness, in the asylum for her insanity, or in the workhouse for her poverty, possesses no light or common claim on the pity and attention of those of her own sex, who, through the bounty of a kind Providence, are able *"to do good, and to communicate."*

May the attention of *women* be more and more directed to these labors of love; and may the time quickly arrive, when there shall not exist, in this realm, a single public institution of the kind, in which the degraded or afflicted females who may happen to be its inmates shall not enjoy the *efficacious superintendence of* the pious and benevolent of THEIR OWN SEX!

(ii) Oeuvre des Libérées de Saint-Lazare

Everyone knows the prison of Saint-Lazare. It is the sole prison for women in Paris. All the compromised women of the capital are incarcerated there; the accused, the convicts, and the juvenile delinquents, and also the loose-living woman.

The fallen women must be divided into two distinct categories: those who are guilty of some misconduct or are simply accused, who make up the First Section of Saint-Lazare, and those who are morally corrupt, who make up the Second. Until now few people have been aware of this distinction and, therefore, nobody has been concerned with either the accused or the convicts. All the shelters open to penitents are designed for loose women. Thus, a charity was needed that would concern itself with released prisoners, that is for those who have served their sentences and those who have been acquitted. This is the gap that the *Society for Released Female Prisoners of Saint-Lazare* ought to fill. This good work is primarily a work of rehabilitation, for when discharged prisoners are entirely abandoned to their fate on leaving prison, they almost invariably return, not to the First Section but to the Second, and sometimes they are lost forever [to prostitution].

In the life of any woman who has encountered the long arm of the law, there is a difficult, indeed a terrible moment. Is it the moment she is arrested? The moment of her return to Saint-Lazare? That of her conviction? No . . . certainly all those days must leave an ineradicable trace in the heart and life of each convict; but there is a moment that is still more terrible—that of her release. We have seen women swoon on stepping through the prison door, and greet their return to freedom with a cry of pain. Alas! How justified this cry of suffering is! How bitter the life that is open to the released prisoner can sometimes be! Ordinarily, her family will have nothing to do with her; she no longer has friends, or position, or shelter, and she nearly always passes the first night in a shabby furnished room. Since those detained at Saint-Lazare do not stay there long, they rarely leave with much money, and it scarcely suffices for their immediate needs.

During the time of their detention, their clothing has worn thin, since the prison only furnishes them with linens. The months go by; the proprietor of the lodgings they inhabit confiscates any furnishings to pay the unpaid rent; that which they have is dispersed or thrown away. If she is a businesswoman, her clients have left, the bills have arrived, and misery sets in. She thinks seriously of entering domestic service, but she cannot produce a certificate and cannot give a good reference. At that point she sees her position clearly; often there is no alternative left for her but to jump into the Seine or register as a prostitute.

In the face of this heartbreaking misery, a simple idea has emerged; it will already have occurred, Mesdames, to all of you who are reading this. There must be a charity for giving temporary support to all these unfortunate women, to give them shelter, food, clothing, and work, and to preserve them from an imminent fall.

The Society has an Administrative Council to watch over the interests of the released prisoners, a Judiciary Council for assisting them, a Medical Committee to offer them health care, a Work Committee for placing them, an Instructional Committee to help them complete their elementary schooling or finish their apprenticeship, a Vestry to furnish clothing to them, and a number of Lady Patronesses to look after them and see to their good conduct.

This *Society for the Released Female Prisoners of Saint-Lazare*, which is a protective society for women par excellence, cannot be the work of one person; it must be the work of all. The minuscule offering of the poor must contribute to it as well as the gold of the rich. If society has its lapses, it must know how to repair its faults and valiantly carry its obligations. Thus we make an appeal to all worthy women and to all men of goodwill to help us by all the means at their disposal. We ask not only for their charitable offering, but especially for the treasure of their pity and sympathy for our released prisoners, in order that henceforth there will be a place in the sun for repentance.

Memberships will be taken at 5, rue Albouy, at the Secretariat . . .

The obligatory membership fee is 5 francs a year, or 100 francs lifetime.

In 1877 the Society assisted 700 released prisoners.

We would greatly appreciate receiving old linens and old clothing for women and children for our Vestry.

(iii) Eleanor Kirk

When one week ago last evening, the motion was carried by the Working-women's Association in regard to petitioning Governor Geary for the pardon and release of the unfortunate English girl now under sentence of death for infanticide, it was certainly with the expectation of arousing a large amount of public feeling in her behalf; but we were entirely unprepared for so spontaneous and enthusiastic a demonstration. . . . The particulars of this story, as first publicly stated on this platform not long ago by Miss Dickinson, touched many a heart; and when it was decided to send a committee to Philadelphia to learn from the girl's own lips the sad particulars, not only did the association of workingwomen offer their means and time towards the furtherance of the grand object, but the women of the whole country—excuse me, with the exception of Pennsylvania—demanded an investigation of the case. On Thursday morning last Mrs. Dr. Lozier and myself, accompanied by Mr. Seward, knocked at the prison door of Moyamensing. The Hon. Mr. Chandler, former minister to Italy, and now acting as Prison Inspector, informed us that no visitors were admitted on this day. "Sir," said we, "we have come from New York on purpose to see and converse with Hester Vaughan." And then gave him our passports, which acted as a soporific upon his lordship. Thank God, for great names! They unlock the gates of trade to the deserving, unearth infamy and double-dealing, and waft, like a breeze from Araby the blest, joy and comfort to the poor prisoner. "Now, I warn you to be careful," said Mr. Chandler, as he walked by our side, "this is the long corridor. Hester's mind has been very much agitated lately by the visits of a certain woman who has very foolishly and wickedly held out hopes of pardon which can never be realized." We found afterwards that he referred to a Dr. Smith, a very successful female practitioner in Philadelphia, and one of the noblest women I have ever met. For the last five months she has been visiting Hester, and is the only woman in Philadelphia, during the long period of her incarceration, who has interested herself in the prisoner's behalf. Dr. Smith has been constant in season and out of season;

has laid the "facts" which she has from time to time gathered before the Governor, and kept the poor child from sinking into utter despondency. Do not, I beseech you, my friends, forget that there is *one* woman, at least, in Philadelphia, who loves her sex, and that one Dr. Smith. Imagine, if you please, a girlish figure; a sweet, intelligent face; soft, brown eyes; broad fore-head; warm earnest mouth, and you have a slight idea of Hester Vaughan. Her story is quickly told. She was born in Glostershire, England; well reared by respectable parents; married a man, a native of Wales, and came to this country full of hope and enthusiasm for the future. A few weeks, and Hester was deserted. Some other woman had a prior claim, it is supposed, and the scamp has never since been heard of. Then came the tug of war for Hester Vaughan, as for every other woman who, from what cause soever, finds herself compelled to fight the battle of life alone. Think of this young girl, a stranger in a strange land, with neither friend nor relative to advise or comfort. For several weeks she lived out as servant in a family at Jenkintown; was then recommended as dairy maid to another family, and here misfortune befel her. Overcome, not in a moment of weakness and passion, but by superior strength —*brute force*—Hester Vaughan fell a victim to lust and the gallows. That man also went his way. Three months after this terrible occurrence Hester removed to Philadelphia and hired a room there. She supported herself by little odd jobs of work from different families, always giving the most perfect satisfaction. During one of the fiercest storms of last winter she was without food or fire or comfortable apparel. She had been ill and partially unconscious for three days before her confinement, and a child was born to Hester Vaughan. Hours passed before she could drag herself to the door and cry out for assistance, and when she did it was to be dragged to a prison where she now lies with the near prospect of a halter. Is it not terrible that this victim of a man's craven lust should be thus foully dealt with while her seducer walks the earth free and unmolested? In this connection let me say that no amount of coaxing or entreaty will induce Hester Vaughan to name the man who thus cruelly wronged her. Since that time he has married. "If he were alone," said Hester, "I would ring his name through the whole country, but nothing will induce me to send terror and disgrace into the heart of an innocent trusting woman." Glorious Hester Vaughan! True as steel to her own sex. Dr. Lozier has in-formed you how she came to be accused of infanticide. This comes under the head of medical testimony, and as I am entirely at sea on that subject I can only give as my belief from all that I saw and heard at Philadelphia, that Hester Vaughan is no more guilty of infanticide than I am, and I am right sure that I never killed a baby in my life. There is a quiet womanly dignity about Hester Vaughan which immediately enlisted our sympathies. As we entered the cell she stood a little [to] one side, as if shrinking from curiosity seekers, but not-withstanding the advice of Mr. Chandler we managed in two minutes' time to make Hester feel that we were her friends, ready to assist her to life, liberty, and the pursuit of happiness if it could possibly be accomplished. The cell gave evidence of the most exquisite neatness and good taste. There was no evasion or circumlocution in her replies to our varied questionings. . . .

We were with her nearly two hours, and were every moment more impressed by her innocence and truthfulness. When we bade her good-by she said: "Ladies, I know you will do all for me that lies in your power, but my trust must be in God." It is said by Philadelphians that Hester Vaughan was not properly defended. Let me tell you about it. She had managed to save, by the strictest economy, $30; a grasping, avaricious lawyer, of Philadelphia, offered his services, and took from the poor child her last penny. During the long five months before her trial, this man never came to her cell, and the only conversation she ever had with him was in the open court. His name, my friends, is Goforth, and I propose that all such wretches go forth and return no more. (Applause.) When we came out on the corridor Mr. Chandler very kindly invited us to take a survey of the prison. Moyamensing is a credit to Pennsylvania—there is no mistake about that—and if there be one thing more than another which I firmly believe in, it is justice to all and honor to whom honor is due. At the door of each cell hangs a slate with the name of the occupant and the crime of which they are accused. On one was written Mary McClinkey—"R.C."—which, interpreted, means "riotous conduct." Ay! Didn't I know there was a man at the root of that trouble, said Mr. Chandler. What phase of riotous conduct was here exhibited? "Well," he replied, "this family is from Maine—very nice woman—and two lovely children. Her husband left her under very suspicious circumstances, and she followed him to Philadelphia, and then found he was living with another woman. Now, this wife became demonstrative and insisted that the father of her children support them. This was riotous conduct, my friends, with a "vengeance." Let us for a moment, to use a homely expression, put the boot on the other foot. If Mrs. McClinkey had left her husband and two children, and walked away with a paramour, not a court of justice in the land but would have acquitted the outraged husband should he have shot and killed both wife and paramour. Are we to dignify such legal partiality as this by the name of justice? A man may shoot down, in cold blood, the destroyer of his peace and he has only vindicated his wounded honor while if a woman protests even against such infernal proceedings she is locked up in a cell. (Immense applause.) "Woman has all the rights she wants," has she? Not while we have men empowered to make such laws as these. (Applause.) . . .

I had a very pleasant interview with Judge Ludlow, the man who pronounced the sentence of death upon poor Hester. "I do not think her a bad woman naturally," said the Judge; "she has an excellent face, but there was no other course open for me but the broad course of condemnation: she was, in the opinion of the jury, guilty of the murder of her child. Mrs. Kirk," he continued, quite earnestly, "you have no idea how rapidly the crime of 'infanticide' is increasing. Some woman must be made an example of. It is for the establishment of a principle, ma'am." Establishment of a principle indeed. I suggested to the Judge that he inaugurate the good work by hanging a few men, but strange to relate he has not been able to see in that light. Women of New York, women of America, turn your backs upon libertines. The victims of the fiends you will see upon all sides as you go from your respective houses. Be careful that the very arm you are now leaning on has not just wound itself around the waist of one of these fallen creatures, the touch of whose garment even you would consider the rankest contamination. And, above all things, my sisters, sustain, comfort, cheer, and defend each other. The very day that poor Hester was sentenced to be hung by her neck until she was dead, Orford Alexander, a colored man, was also sentenced for the murder of his wife. Hester, imprisoned for a man's diabolical lust, is so heinously guilty that she may not walk out on to the corridor near by the side of her cell, while Orford Alexander can work in the prison yard, have the benefit of out-door air, and exercise, and more than this, 20,000 of the most respectable citizens of Pennsylvania have petitioned Governor Geary for the man's pardon; and not one woman in Philadelphia, with the exception of Doctor Smith, has said a good word for Hester Vaughan.

94. Women reforming society through home and school

Philanthropy soon led to social action. This was especially true in nineteenth-century America, where women reformers tackled what they viewed as the great social problems of their nation—slavery, poverty, ignorance, and vice—with zest and missionary zeal. For some women, the crusade for a particular reform, be it temperance, social purity, or the vote, quickly became a religious calling that consumed their lives. Such crusaders were generally college educated, articulate, and convinced that reforms emanating from the home and school—the special domains of nineteenth-century women— would ultimately speed the triumph of justice and equality throughout the entire society. The following selections are excerpted from the speeches and writings of three prominent American educator-reformers, Frances E. Willard, Lucy Craft Laney, and Anna Julia Cooper.

The author of the first selection, Frances Elizabeth Caroline Willard (1839–98) grew up in a Methodist family on a frontier farm in Wisconsin. A schoolteacher and the first dean of women at Northwestern University, Willard became unhappy with academic life, left the university, and threw herself into temperance work. In 1879 she was elected national president of the Women's Christian Temperance Union, a post she held until her death. Willard had long wished to help other women, but it was only through her involvement with the WCTU that she found an effective way to do so— campaigning not only against alcohol but also in favor of other measures, including the vote, which she believed would improve women's condition.

SOURCES: (i) Frances E. Willard, "Woman's Work in Education," *National Education Association. Addresses and Proceedings* (Madison, Wis., 1884), pp. 162–66, 168. (ii) Lucy Craft Laney, "The Burden of the Educated Colored Woman," paper read at the Hampton Negro Conference No. III, July 1899, *Report* (n.p., 1899), pp. 37–42; quoted from *Black Women in American Life,* ed. Bert James Loewenberg and Ruth Bogin (University Park, Pa., 1976), pp. 297–301. (iii) Anna Julia Cooper, "Woman vs. the Indian," in *A Voice from the South* (Xenia, Ohio, 1892), pp. 120–26.

Willard's motto for the WCTU, "For God and Home and Native Land,"
could have served as the title of this speech, given during a "women's sym-
posium" at the 1884 National Education Association convention.

Lucy Craft Laney (1854–1933), author of the second selection, was born
to a free black family in Georgia. Thanks to the education her family gave
her, she entered Atlanta University, graduating in the first class in 1873. In her
subsequent teaching career, Laney founded schools for black children and took
a special interest in the education of girls. In this speech, delivered at the
Hampton Negro Conference in 1899, Laney argues that educated black wom-
en have a special mission to fulfill.

The third selection comes from the published writings of Anna Julia
Cooper (1859–1964). Like Laney, Cooper was a black woman, the daughter
of a North Carolina slave who had bought his freedom. She married an Epis-
copal minister when she was eighteen but found herself widowed two years
later. She then went north and worked her way through college at Oberlin,
graduating with distinction. Cooper served for many years as principal of a
black high school in Washington, D.C., and earned a doctorate from the
Sorbonne when she was over sixty. As the final selection eloquently attests, she
believed that women's voice must be heard in the affairs of the world.

(i) Frances E. Willard

Away back in ever so far, there were men that said that women must not
be taught, they must not go to the schools, for, if they do, it will change the
whole regime and plan of creation and be the very worst of all the curses that
ever afflicted humanity; but there were other men, like Horace Mann, who
said, "Nonsense, let the women sit down beside their brothers at the banquet
of Minerva even, as at their homesteads, they are seated beside us"; and then
women came forth and took their places in the academies and universities and
in the ranks of teachers, until two-thirds of our teachers are women to-day;
and if you want to find the gentlest and strongest and noblest types of women
look at the teachers of your native land. And I believe that this people love
these teachers because of the kindliness they have shown in the training of
your children, and I believe that our people would say that my verdict is correct; they would make no dissent therefrom.

And so the time went on, and you, our brothers, invaded our realm, and
we are not a bit jealous that you did, and we bring no words in the indictment
to your harm. With forceful and strong hands you built railroads and tun-
nelled mountains and carried forward your splendid endeavors, and then you
looked in on the realm of the household and what wonderful havoc you
made there. My mother has a quilt which she made in her country home on a
farm in western New York. She not only spun but wove the material that
enters into that wonderful composition, and she said to me it was just a play-
day from the spinning and the weaving for the family that they had to do. In
those days the women picked their own geese and did their own dyeing, and
here came the brotherhood, and they took the wash-tub and carried that out
of the house and built great laundries, and they set little nibbling fingers

at work on that weaving and spinning, and did it by steel fingers, and it did not tire the women's fingers any more, and they are going on at such a rate that I predict that they will soon have the cook-stove out of the house, and I am not sorry. I do not think we shall see so many dinners with a broiled lady at the head of the feast. I look for the time when the great caterer of the town shall require nothing of me but to stand in the back hall and put my lips to the telephone and order my dinner and it will come through the pneumatic tube. We are going on at just that rate: the wash-tub and cook-stove are not the *Lares* and *Penates* of the home. You, having done this, are welcome to go on and do more and more of it. Because you have accomplished so much already is the reason that women's hands are free to take up this splendid work of teaching, and these grand endeavors of philanthropy.

I am here to-night just thinking these things over because this is a woman's symposium, trying to think why it is there are so many women teachers and doctors and philanthropists. They are trying to do what? Since you have invaded the home and taken away so many of the cares and inconveniences of the past, women have made up their minds that the whole world shall be homelike; that we will go out into social life and try to make that more homelike; that we will go out into the professions and try to make them more homelike, and in the wide sphere of government try to prove that you need two heads in council as beside the hearth. So, if you think that it is a wandering from the sphere of woman, remember that women, by becoming teachers, have made the school-room far more homelike, and the little ones happier than they were ever made before.

Now, since I am a temperance worker, and since my whole endeavor in life is to build firm and deep foundations for the protection of the homes of the country that I love so much, I ask you as those loyal to the home as I am, those who are striving in your avocation, as I am in mine (and I once belonged to your own honored guild), I ask you to stand by us in our effort and our endeavor to so work upon the brain and heart of childhood that the children of our nation shall go forth forearmed and forewarned against the greatest enemy of home, and that is the liquor traffic, and the drink traffic, in this "land of the free and home of the brave."

. . . I am here as a temperance worker to remind you that we are doing grand service in your cause, for we women of the temperance society are out in a splendid fight for a clear brain. That is what we have set our hand to do. We come here to-night to ask your co-operation as women in this battle of home-building and home-protection. . . .

The brain is the skylight of the soul, it mirrors God's thought, but, oh, when it is cobwebbed with beer, when the impact of strong drink is put upon it, the brain can no more reflect the high and rational ideas that a man ought to entertain. Plutonian fires in the brain from alcoholic drinks render it impossible for the lighting up the Promethean fires so dear to the heart of the enthusiastic and earnest teacher; and so I come to you, kind friends, to speak about the fact that it is physiologically true that the impact of strong drink upon this delicate substance of the brain, the organ of thought, makes it physiologically impossible for a man to have as clear a perception of the fact that there is a God somewhere about, that there is a future somewhere ahead, that there are laws of God that interlace us everywhere, and we cannot escape them. . . .

We have everything to gain by the triumph of this scientific temperance work, and it is so practical; it goes to make the school-houses where the children can go from the mother's protection to the protection of the school-house. God hasten the day when with the guaranties of the State, and the majesty of law, and the dignity of science, the young people shall get a "thus saith nature," "thus saith reason," "thus saith physiology and hygiene," for the doctrine that it is best never to touch the products of the vineyard, the brewery, or the still. . . . .

I believe the time is coming when this shall be known as the great sister and mother country of Christendom. In my mind's eye I see two great statues as the emblems of the two great lines of thought the world has seen. The first is the Colossus at Rhodes; the second is Bartholdi's statue of the Goddess of Liberty. The first is the emblem of physical force; the second is the emblem of the subtle, spiritual force that lies back of the physical, the emblem of the new America. I have thought of that beautiful statue as it will soon stand on Bedloe's Island; I have thought of that regal and kindly and affluent presence as the type and symbol of American womanhood; I have thought of the emigrant ship as it shall come in. I have been at Castle Garden, and my heart has ached as I have seen them, the kind-faced Scandinavian so lonesome-like, and looked at the Celt with the home-ache in his honest heart, and seemed so sorry that the Emerald Isle was so far away. I have thought as they saw that gracious and benign presence that it would come into their hearts that America is a motherly country; that it is a home-like place; that into the activities of our time are coming those gracious, sweet, and tender influences which can only come when manhood and womanhood go forth side by side to make the nation a home. . . .

God grant that with all the scintillating brain of womanhood in this age we may each and all take for our motto, "Womanliness first, afterwards what you will."

(ii) Lucy Craft Laney

If the educated colored woman has a burden,—and we believe she has— what is that burden? How can it be lightened, how may it be lifted? What it is can be readily seen perhaps better than told, for it constantly annoys to irritation; it bulges out as did the load of Bunyan's Christian—ignorance— with its inseparable companions, shame and crime and prejudice. . . .

Ignorance and immorality, if they are not the prime causes, have certainly intensified prejudice. The forces to lighten and finally to lift this and all of these burdens are true culture and character, linked with that most substantial coupler, cash. We said in the beginning that the past can serve no further purpose than to give us our present bearings. It is a condition that confronts us. With this we must deal, it is this we must change. The physi-

cian of today inquires into the history of his patient, but he has to do especially with diagnosis and cure. We know the history; we think a correct
diagnosis has often been made—let us attempt a cure. We would prescribe:
homes—better homes, clean homes, pure homes; schools—better schools;
more culture; more thrift; and work in large doses; put the patient at once on
this treatment and continue through life. Can woman do this work? She can;
and she must do her part, and her part is by no means small.

Nothing in the present century is more noticeable than the tendency of
women to enter every hopeful field of wage-earning and philanthropy, and
attempt to reach a place in every intellectual arena. Women are by nature
fitted for teaching very young children; their maternal instinct makes them
patient and sympathetic with their charges. Negro women of culture, as
kindergartners and primary teachers have a rare opportunity to lend a hand
to the lifting of these burdens, for here they may instill lessons of cleanliness,
truthfulness, loving kindness, love for nature, and love for Nature's God.
Here they may daily start aright hundreds of our children; here, too, they
may save years of time in the education of the child; and may save many
lives from shame and crime by applying the law of prevention. In the kindergarten and primary school is the salvation of the race. . . .

The educated Negro woman, the woman of character and culture, is
needed in the schoolroom not only in the kindergarten, and in the primary
and the secondary school; but she is needed in high school, the academy,
and the college. Only those of character and culture can do successful lifting, for she who would mould character must herself possess it. Not alone in
the schoolroom can the intelligent woman lend a lifting hand, but as a public lecturer she may give advice, helpful suggestions, and important knowledge that will change a whole community and start its people on the upward
way. . . . The refined and noble Negro woman may lift much with this lever.
Women may also be most helpful as teachers of sewing schools and cooking
classes, not simply in the public schools and private institutions, but in
classes formed in neighborhoods that sorely need this knowledge. Through
these classes girls who are not in school may be reached; and through them
something may be done to better their homes, and inculcate habits of neatness and thrift. To bring the influence of the schools to bear upon these
homes is the most needful thing of the hour. Often teachers who have labored most arduously, conscientiously, and intelligently have become discouraged on seeing that society had not been benefited, but sometimes positively injured by the conduct of their pupils.

The work of the schoolroom has been completely neutralized by the training of the home. Then we must have better homes, and better homes mean
better mothers, better fathers, better born children. . . . As a teacher in the
Sabbath school, as a leader in young people's meetings and missionary societies, in women's societies and Bible classes our cultured women are needed
to do a great and blessed work. Here they may cause many budding lives to
open into eternal life. . . . The young people are ready and anxiously await
intelligent leadership in Christian work. The less fortunate women already

assembled in churches, are ready for work. Work they do and work they will; that it may be effective work, they need the help and leadership of their more favored sisters.

A few weeks ago this country was startled by the following telegram of southern women of culture sent to Ex-Governor Northen of Georgia, just before he made his Boston speech: "You are authorized to say in your address tonight that the women of Georgia, realizing the great importance to both races of early moral training of the Negro race, stand ready to undertake this work when means are supplied." But more startled was the world the next day, after cultured Boston had supplied a part of the means, $20,000, to read the glaring head lines of the southern press, "Who Will Teach the Black Babies?" because some of the cultured women who had signed the telegram had declared when interviewed, that Negro women fitted for the work could not be found, and no self-respecting southern white woman would teach a colored kindergarten. Yet already in Atlanta, Georgia, and in Athens, Georgia, southern women are at work among Negroes. There is plenty of work for all who have the proper conception of the teacher's office, who know that all men are brothers, God being their common father. But the educated Negro women must teach the "Black Babies;" she must come forward and inspire our men and boys to make a successful onslaught upon sin, shame, and crime.

(iii) Anna Julia Cooper

The cause of freedom is not the cause of a race or a sect, a party or a class,—it is the cause of human kind, the very birthright of humanity. Now unless we are greatly mistaken the Reform of our day, known as the Woman's Movement, is essentially such an embodiment, if its pioneers could only realize it, of the universal good. And specially important is it that there be no confusion of ideas among its leaders as to its scope and universality. All mists must be cleared from the eyes of woman if she is to be a teacher of morals and manners: the former strikes its roots in the individual and its training and pruning may be accomplished by classes; but the latter is to lubricate the joints and minimize the friction of society, and it is important and fundamental that there be no chromatic or other aberration when the teacher is settling the point, "Who is my neighbor?"

It is not the intelligent woman vs. the ignorant woman; nor the white woman vs. the black, the brown, and the red,—it is not even the cause of woman vs. man. Nay, 'tis woman's strongest vindication for speaking that *the world needs to hear her voice*. It would be subversive of every human interest that the cry of one-half the human family be stifled. Woman in stepping from the pedestal of statue-like inactivity in the domestic shrine, and daring to think and move and speak,—to undertake to help shape, mold, and direct the thought of her age, is merely completing the circle of the world's vision. Hers is every interest that has lacked an interpreter and a defender. Her cause is linked with that of every agony that has been dumb—every wrong that needs a voice.

It is no fault of man's that he has not been able to see truth from her standpoint. It does credit both to his head and heart that no greater mistakes have been committed or even wrongs perpetrated while she sat making tatting and snipping paper flowers. Man's own innate chivalry and the mutual interdependence of their interests have insured his treating her cause, in the main at least, as his own. And he is pardonably surprised and even a little chagrined, perhaps, to find his legislation not considered "perfectly lovely" in every respect. But in any case his work is only impoverished by her remaining dumb. The world has had to limp along with the wobbling gait and one-sided hesitancy of a man with one eye. Suddenly the bandage is removed from the other eye and the whole body is filled with light. It sees a circle where before it saw a segment. The darkened eye restored, every member rejoices with it.

What a travesty of its case for this eye to become plaintiff in a suit, *Eye vs. Foot.* "There is that dull clod, the foot, allowed to roam at will, free and untrammelled; while I, the source and medium of light, brilliant and beautiful, am fettered in darkness and doomed to desuetude." The great burly black man, ignorant and gross and depraved, is allowed to vote; while the franchise is withheld from the intelligent and refined, the pure-minded and lofty souled white woman. Even the untamed and untamable Indian of the prairie, who can answer nothing but "ugh" to great economic and civic questions is thought by some worthy to wield the ballot which is still denied the Puritan maid and the first lady of Virginia.

Is not this hitching our wagon to something much lower than a star? Is not woman's cause broader, and deeper, and grander, than a blue stocking debate or an aristocratic pink tea? Why should woman become plaintiff in a suit versus the Indian, or the Negro or any other race or class who have been crushed under the iron heel of Anglo-Saxon power and selfishness? If the Indian has been wronged and cheated by the puissance of this American government, it is woman's mission to plead with her country to cease to do evil and to pay its honest debts. If the Negro has been deceitfully cajoled or inhumanly cuffed according to selfish expediency or capricious antipathy, let it be woman's mission to plead that he be met as a man and honestly given half the road. If woman's own happiness has been ignored or misunderstood in our country's legislating for bread winners, for rum sellers, for property holders, for the family relations, for any or all the interests that touch her vitally, let her rest her plea, not on Indian inferiority, nor on Negro depravity, but on the obligation of legislators to do for her as they would have others do for them were relations reversed. Let her try to teach her country that every interest in this world is entitled at least to a respectful hearing, that every sentiency is worthy of its own gratification, that a helpless cause should not be trampled down, nor a bruised reed broken; and when the right of the individual is made sacred, when the image of God in human form, whether in marble or in clay, whether in alabaster or in ebony, is consecrated and inviolable, when men have been taught to look beneath the rags and grime, the pomp and pageantry of mere circumstance and have regard unto the celestial kernel uncontaminated at the core,—when race, color, sex, condition, are realized to be the accidents, not the substance of life, and consequently as not obscuring or modifying the inalienable title to life, liberty, and pursuit of happiness,—then is mastered the science of politeness, the art of courteous contact, which is naught but the practical application of the principle of benevolence, the back bone and marrow of all religion; then woman's lesson is taught and woman's cause is won—not the white woman nor the black woman nor the red woman, but the cause of every man or woman who has writhed silently under a mighty wrong. The pleading of the American woman for the right and the opportunity to employ the American method of influencing the disposal to be made of herself, her property, her children in civil, economic, or domestic relations is thus seen to be based on a principle as broad as the human race and as old as human society. Her wrongs are thus indissolubly linked with all undefended woe, all helpless suffering, and the plenitude of her "rights" will mean the final triumph of all right over might, the supremacy of the moral forces of reason and justice and love in the government of the nation.

God hasten the day.

95. 'Justice for women': Women help themselves

By the second half of the nineteenth century women on both sides of the Atlantic had come to believe that only through the vote would their interests be truly represented and their grievances remedied. In England and the United States women banded together to form suffrage organizations; but in France a few stalwart spirits petitioned the Chamber of Deputies to grant women votes. Hubertine Auclert (1848–1914), a gentlewoman from the Bourbonnais, spearheaded the campaign in that country, but until the early twentieth century she was virtually a voice crying in the wilderness. Auclert had joined Maria Deraismes (1828–94; Doc. 25.ii) in her quest to change the Civil Code and make it more equitable to women, but this work only left her convinced that without political power, women would remain impotent to effect any reform, whether legal or social. Thus, in 1881 she founded a newspaper, 'La Citoyenne,' to agitate for women's suffrage. In this selection, taken from the first issue of the paper, Auclert argues that suffrage is the keystone of all women's rights; unfortunately, male legislators turned a deaf ear to her pleas, and it was not until 1944 that French women won the vote.

Across the Channel the more fortunate Millicent Garrett Fawcett (1847–1929) lived to witness the enfranchisement of English women in 1918. As a young woman, Fawcett had watched John Stuart Mill introduce the first women's suffrage bill in the House of Commons, and for the next fifty years

SOURCES: (i) La Citoyenne, no. 1 (Feb. 13, 1881). The editors wish to thank Professor Steven C. Hause, University of Missouri, St. Louis, for making this selection available to us. (ii) Millicent Garrett Fawcett, "Women and Representative Government," Nineteenth Century, 78.14 (Aug. 1883): 285–91.

she served as one of the leaders of the English suffrage movement. One of the most capable and energetic women of her generation, Fawcett did not confine her activities to suffrage, but tried to help women in a variety of ways—whether by working to end the white slave traffic or seeking to make higher education available to women. Like Auclert, Fawcett believed that the voices of her sisters would be heard only when they achieved the status of voters, and in this selection, taken from an article written in 1883, she asks Parliament to give "equal justice to women."

(i) Hubertine Auclert

What do we mean by the civil emancipation of woman?

By civil emancipation of woman we mean the abrogation of a host of vexatious laws that put woman outside justice and outside common law.

It is, first of all, the absurd law that prohibits me, a woman, from owning the title or serving as publisher of this newspaper, even though I have more need than any man of a newspaper in order to denounce the abuses from which I suffer in my capacity as a woman.

It is the law on marriage that makes the married woman and her property the property of her husband.

It is the law of guardianship that, in order to exclude women (with the exception of the mother and her ancestors) from guardianship and family councils, does not hesitate to class them with criminals and the insane.

It is the humiliating law that, for purposes of giving verbal or written testimony, lumps women together with male idiots and men deprived by law of their civil rights. Women are not allowed to act as witness to the registration of a birth or a marriage, or the execution of an act of sale. What am I saying? A woman is not even allowed to attest to the identity of another woman for the notarization of a signature.

By the civil emancipation of woman, I mean, in a word, the abrogation of every one of these laws of exception that release men from responsibilities and weigh down women with the heaviest burdens.

Who can abolish the iniquitous laws that oppress women in civil life? The voters and the legislators, that is to say, only those who make the laws or who command that the laws be made. This point is well established.

Now, what do we mean by the political emancipation of woman? We mean women's receiving the right that confers the power to make laws: by itself, if one is elected deputy; by delegation, if one is a voter.

Thus, it is evident that political rights are for women the keystone that will give her all other rights.

When women are able to intervene in public affairs, their first concern will be to reform unjust legislation; their first act will be to use the right given them to change their situation.

But since woman does not have the power to weaken the laws that oppress her, whom can she count on to do it? On man? But it is man who has established the existing laws and these laws do not trouble him. On the contrary, they give him all the facilities to trouble us; thus, instead of suppressing these laws that enslave woman, man busies himself with creating laws that will further enlarge his horizons. In this country where there are seventeen million sovereigns—men—and more than seventeen million slaves—women—the reforms that men perceive as essential are the reforms that will grant them still more privileges.

This means that it is beyond any doubt that as long as woman does not possess this weapon—the vote—she will suffer the rule of masculine law. All her efforts to conquer her civil and economic liberties will be in vain.

What women need to free themselves from masculine tyranny—made law—is the possession of their share of sovereignty; they need the title of *citoyenne française*; they need the ballot.

The French citizeness: this means that woman invested with the highest social rights will, by freedom, have her dignity restored; by the sense of responsibility, her character enlarged.

The French citizeness will promptly rise out of her distressing economic situation; the State and the laws will no longer render her inferior; the schooling of woman being, like that of man, essentially useful, every career, every profession will be open to her; and whatever her work, woman will no longer see it deprecated under the ridiculous pretext that it was done by a woman.

The French citizeness will quintuple the effectiveness of her maternal influence; she will raise the child not for herself alone, or for itself, but for society. She will inculcate those private and public virtues that will contribute to the child's happiness and that of his fellow-creatures.

The woman invested with the highest social rights, the French citizeness, will have the power to endow generations with such a sweeping moral vision, that fraternity will replace egoism in human relationships, and harmony—the goal to which all aspire—will supplant the present conflict in society.

In as much as we believe that from the emancipation of woman will flow a source of good for all humanity, we can do no better than to consecrate all our efforts to this cause.

(ii) Millicent Garrett Fawcett

It is not necessary here to dwell at any length on the painful subject of laws that are unjust to women. No one who has ever given even a few minutes' attention to the subject will deny that there are many laws which, to use Mr. Gladstone's expression, give to women "something less than justice."* If it is necessary to quote examples, the inequality which the law has created between men and women in divorce suits furnishes one. The cruel law which gives a mother no legal guardianship over her children is another. I think there can be little doubt that if similar hardships had affected any represented class, they would long ago have been swept away. As it is, however, though the injustice of these and other laws affecting women is fully and almost universally recognised, year after year rolls by and nothing is done to remedy them. Here are matters almost universally admitted to involve

* William Gladstone was leader of the Liberal Party, a Prime Minister, and a prominent opponent of women's suffrage.—EDS.

injustice and wrong, and no one tries to remedy them. Why is this? It is because the motive power is wanting. Representation is the motive power for the redress of legislative grievances. If not what is the use of representation? People would be as well off without it as with it. But all our history shows the practical value of representation. Before the working classes were represented, trades-unions were illegal associations, and consequently an absconding treasurer of one of these societies was liable to no legal punishment. Not one man in a thousand attempted to justify such an iniquity, even when it was an established institution. It was a recognised injustice; but it was not till the working classes were on the eve of obtaining a just share of representation that the motive power for the redress of that injustice was forthcoming. The same thing can be said with regard to those laws which press unjustly on women. Hardly anyone defends them; it is not so much the sense of justice in parliament or in the country that is wanting, as the motive power which representation, and representation alone, in a self-governed country can give, to get a recognised wrong righted. . . .

A curious illustration of the absolute neglect so far as politics are concerned, of all who are not represented, or whom, it is expected, will be shortly represented, may be found in the accounts of the recent celebration of the Bright festival at Birmingham. The Liberals who assembled to do the honour to Mr. Bright which he so richly deserves,* enumerated, in honest pride, the main achievements of Mr. Bright's career; but they did not point to any chapter in the statute book and say, "Here he succeeded in changing a condition of the law that was oppressive to women." And this was so, although Mr. Bright has, on more than one occasion—as, for example on behalf of a bill enabling women to receive medical degrees—lifted his powerful voice in favour of justice being done to women. Matters which affect injuriously, or the reverse, unrepresented classes, lie outside what are called practical politics. The politicians' field of vision is entirely filled by those who are represented; the unrepresented are forgotten. So, again, when the Birmingham Liberals let their imagination range over what was to be expected and worked for in the future, no mention was made of anything being done for women. Their ideal seemed rather to be manhood as opposed to universal suffrage; that is, all men not being either paupers or felons to be admitted to political power, no matter how ignorant, how poor, how degraded, in virtue of their manhood; while all women are to be excluded in virtue of their womanhood. . . .

I have said that the sense of justice is not so much wanting as the motive power which will convert a passive recognition of the existence of wrong into an active determination to get that wrong righted. It must not, however, be forgotten, that without being consciously unjust or cruel, there is such a thing as a torpid sense of justice. As the ear gets deafened and the vision gets blurred by frequent misuse, so the sense of justice becomes feeble and dim by constant association with laws and customs which are unjust. To live in

* John Bright was a prominent Liberal and staunch advocate of franchise reform, —EDS.

a society whose laws give women "something less than justice," is apt to pervert the conscience, and make those whose imagination is not very active acquiesce in injustice as if it were part of the inevitable nature of things. Magistrates, for example, who sometimes punish men less severely for half-killing their wives than for stealing half-a-crown, are partly responsible for this faulty sense of justice, and may be partly regarded as the victims of it. We want—to use an expression of Mr. Matthew Arnold's—to call forth "a fresh flow of consciousness" on all these questions where the interests of women are concerned. We want to ask ourselves, and to set others to ask themselves, "Ought these things to be supported simply because they exist?" "Could we not come nearer to righteousness if we aimed at a higher ideal of justice?"

It will no doubt be argued by some, that while much yet remains to be done before the balance is adjusted, so as to give perfect justice to women, yet that much has already been done to improve their legal status, and that it is not too much to hope that in time all grievances will be redressed without giving women votes. The Married Women's Property Act, it is said, has redressed a great and crying evil;* why may not other evils be redressed in the same way? To such as use this argument it may be replied that, in the first place, the Married Women's Property Act would probably never have been introduced or heard of, if it had not been for the wider movement for the parliamentary representation of women. The women's suffrage societies, by constant and untiring efforts actively carried on for sixteen years, have done something to awaken that keener sense of justice to women to which reference has just been made. However, let it be supposed that this view of the history of the passing of the Married Women's Property Act is entirely erroneous, and let it be supposed that the Legislature have, of their own free will, quite unmoved by any representations made to them by women, been graciously pleased to say that married women may have what is their own. What right has any set of human beings to say to another, "I concede to you that piece of justice, and I withhold this, not because you ask for either, or can make me give you either, but because I choose to act so?" What is the policy, what is the sense, of compelling half the English people to hold their liberty on such terms as these? All this circumlocution is unnecessary and inexpedient. Give women the rights of free citizenship, the power to protect themselves, and then they will let their representatives know what they want and why they want it. They will find, no doubt—as other classes have found—that though the price of liberty is vigilance, the House of Commons will never turn a deaf ear to well-conceived measures of reform which are demanded by the constituencies. . . .

When the representatives of the present electorate undertake a further extension of the suffrage, we ask them to be true to their own principles, to be just—even to women—without fear. If women are not excluded from the

* The Married Women's Property Act, enacted in 1870, marked an important advance in the legal position of married women, giving the wife control of her personal property, earnings, and income.—EDS.

next Reform Bill, may we not anticipate the growth of new bonds of sympathy and union between men and women? Their lives will be less separated than they have hitherto been. It is one of the most disastrous things that can happen to a nation to have a great wall of separation, as regards opinion and feeling, grow up between men and women. . . .

Every circumstance which widens the education of women—their political, as well as their literary education—renders impossible the building up of that wall of separation. It may be said there is no danger of such a state of things in England; but if there is no danger of it, is it not because we have already gone so far along the road of giving equal justice to women? We have gone so far and with such good results there could hardly be a better reason for going further.

Part IV
The Older Woman

Introduction

Marilyn Yalom

When Robert Browning wrote his famous lines "Grow old along with me! / The best is yet to be, / The last of life, for which the first was made," he was undoubtedly not thinking about women. The poet's Victorian optimism is difficult enough to reconcile with the realities of old age for men, and virtually impossible when we consider the condition of older women in the nineteenth century. Neither men nor women were likely to survive what we have come to call middle age. As we see in the accompanying tables, life expectancy still hovered around the fifty-year mark as late as 1900 in England, France, and the United States; and old people were a statistically negligible part of the populations of all three countries through the whole of the century.

Although growing old was equally frightening to both men and women to the extent that it represented failing strength, more and more serious

LIFE EXPECTANCY AT BIRTH FOR FEMALES
IN ENGLAND, FRANCE, AND THE UNITED
STATES IN THE NINETEENTH CENTURY

Country	Years
England	
1838–54	41.8
1891–1900	47.8
France	
1817–31	40.8
1898–1903	49.1
United States	
1800	37.0[a]
1900	51.0

SOURCE: Louis I. Dublin and Alfred J. Lotka, *Length of Life: A Study of the Life Table* (New York, 1936), pp. 47–48, 57.

[a] Dublin and Lotka note that only meager and generally untrustworthy information is available for the U.S. as a whole until 1900. This figure is based on their judgment that the 1900 figure is reasonably reliable and their estimate that life expectancy for both sexes increased perhaps 14 years in the course of the 19th century.

PERCENT OF POPULATION AGE 65 AND ABOVE IN ENGLAND,
FRANCE, AND THE UNITED STATES, 1850–1970

Date	England[a]	France	United States
1850	4.6%	6.5%	—
1900	4.7	8.2	4.1%
1969/70	13.0	13.0	10.0

SOURCE: Peter Laslett, *Family Life and Illicit Love in Earlier Generations* (Cambridge, Eng., 1977), p. 195.
[a] Includes Wales.

diseases, and approaching death, it did not entail the same social and economic liabilities for men that it did for women. In the world of work, men continued to ply their trades and professions until death or debilitation, without the mandatory retirement that has become customary in our own time. Their position as head of a household was sanctioned by legal and religious authority. As widowers, they were expected to remarry, if only to provide a second mother for their children; and it was not uncommon for men to found families in their fifties and sixties. The virile patriarch-cum-venerable sage offered an idealized archetype for masculine old age, one that found its incarnation on both sides of the Atlantic in such exemplary figures as Henry Wadsworth Longfellow and Victor Hugo.

Women, on the other hand, usually had no comparable status to look forward to as they advanced in years. Growing old, they could not expect to progress into a position of power as, for example, Chinese and Japanese women do when they assume the role of mother-in-law. Their social status depended almost always on their fathers and husbands, less frequently on their children, and only in very rare instances, on themselves. Valued in early womanhood when they were "young and beautiful" and capable of bearing children, women had ample reason to envision with anxiety the time of life when they would be "old and ugly," barren, and often financially constrained.

Menopause was viewed as the gateway to old age through which a woman passed at the peril of her life. If she was fortunate enough to escape from a host of minor and major physical ills described in every medical treatise on the change of life (hot flashes, severe vaginitis, and the more life-threatening diseases of uterine and breast cancer), she might find an unexpected respite in the post-menopausal years. Yet even the liberation from menstruation and childbirth may not have been welcomed unambivalently. Given the Victorian obsession with woman as a reproductive creature, menopause marked the end of a primary sexual identity that was inextricably linked with motherhood.

Another disadvantage for women was the greater likelihood of their being widowed. Peter Stearns, in his study of old age in France, has found a steadily increasing differential between the number of widows and the number of widowers during the second half of the century.[1] In England and America, by the end of the century, the ratio of widows to widowers has been estimated

[1] Stearns 1976: 120.

to have been as high as two to one.[2] But whatever the statistics, it was generally agreed in all three countries that widows had a worse time of it than widowers. Since married women were usually dependent on their husbands, widowhood often represented an economic as well as an emotional catastrophe, especially in the cities, where both men and women were increasingly dependent on wages. Moreover, whereas a widower, young or old, was expected to remarry, the older widow in search of a spouse was not treated kindly by public opinion. Witness the malicious words of the American journalist Horace Greeley: "A widow of doubtful age will marry almost any sort of white man." In France, particularly in the provinces, widows over forty or forty-five were not expected to remarry, though, as Stearns reports, a minority had sufficient property or personal appeal to defy convention.

Women were generally considered old by the age of forty, even though many, most notably in America, still bore children during the fifth decade of life. The historian David Hackett Fischer reminds us that during the first two centuries of American history, a woman was typically involved in childbearing throughout the greater part of her adult life; her first baby was born within a year of marriage and her last when she was in her mid-forties.[3] Nevertheless, women over forty, whatever the number of their years or the condition of their ovaries, were frequently lumped together by popular wisdom and collectively disposed of like wilted produce. Our sample of representative nineteenth-century documents, ranging from the sphere of *belles lettres* to would-be scientific, medical, and popular advice literature, reveals the prevailing biases against older women, as well as an occasional defensive retort and helps us understand the cultural context in which these women experienced their later years.

Cultural Attitudes Toward Older Women

After forty a woman was expected to "act her age." Moral tracts and beauty manuals counseled her to behave and dress in a manner deemed suitable for the "decline of life." *The Female Aegis,* an anonymous work that appeared in London in 1798 and thereafter in numerous pirated editions, admonished older women to remember that "the spring and summer of life are past; autumn is far advanced; the frown of winter is already felt," and that they should forgo the "active pleasures" and "gay amusements of youth." In *The Arts of Beauty; or secrets of a lady's toilet,* published in America a half century later, the celebrated Irish-born adventuress Lola Montez (Doc. 97.ii) used a similar seasonal analogy, comparing the young girl to spring, the woman of twenty to summer, and allowing the woman of thirty to fifty an autumnal grandeur. But beyond that age she should "lay aside all such pretensions." Above all, paint and powder should not be used by "ladies who have passed the age of life when roses are natural to the cheek. A *rouged* old woman is a horrible sight—a distortion of nature's harmony."

[2] Laslett 1977: 189, 192; *Twelfth Census of the United States,* 1900, part 2, table 49, as cited by Dahlin n.d.
[3] Fischer 1978: 107.

Alongside this popular advice literature, authors of greater literary merit contributed their models, mostly negative, to the Victorian portrait gallery of elderly ladies. From Lord Byron in the early 1800's to W. S. Gilbert and Oscar Wilde in the last decades of the century, English novelists, poets, and playwrights specialized in satire on the woman of a "certain age," the woman who had "remained thirty-five for years," the woman who must resign her claim to beauty "after at the most, some forty years' lease."[4] Although Margaret Fuller (Doc. 97.i), the foremost female American intellectual in the first half of the century, asserted that such a woman had her own grandeur and looked "as a human being should at the end of forty years," she was also forced to concede that society was not very generous on the older woman's behalf. The most flattering appraisal she could hope for was, "How well she is preserved!"

The attitude voiced by most writers toward women over forty was predominantly one of faint ridicule if not outright contempt. In this respect, women were sometimes their own worst critics. The British journalist Eliza Lynn Linton, in a series of unsigned articles that appeared in the *Saturday Review* in 1868, mercilessly ridiculed the English woman past her prime. In one article (Doc. 97.iii) she chided her for acting and dressing inappropriately and for not attempting to find an interest outside herself. In a second piece she satirized the older woman who had in fact found an outside interest in the pursuit of archeology. The matron who cultivated her intellect, as Linton subsequently advised in a third article entitled "Beauty and Brains," was clearly damned if she did and damned if she didn't. Whatever she did, she must always remember that woman was "essentially a mother—that is, a woman who can forget herself . . . and find her best joy in the well-being of those about her." Self-effacement in harmony with the maternal instinct was proffered as the surest guide to harmony in the later years. Linton's ideal older woman, whose secret lay "in love, in purity, and in unselfishness," is representative of the conventional image of Victorian woman circumscribed within a middle-class frame.

Medical literature was no less saturated with prejudice that informed the treatment of women at menopause. Menopause was invariably linked to puberty in nineteenth-century medical thought, and both were considered periods of stress, marking the beginning and the end of women's sexual activity.[5] In France, where women of the privileged classes were essentially valued for their sexual and procreative functions, doctors describing the female climac-

---

[4] The three quoted phrases come, respectively, from Byron, *Beppo* (1818), stanza 22 ("She was not old, nor young, nor at the year / Which certain people call a 'certain age,' / Which yet the most uncertain age appears"); Oscar Wilde, *The Importance of Being Earnest* (1895), act 3 ("Thirty-five is a very attractive age—London society is full of women of the very highest virtue who have, of their own free choice, remained thirty-five for years"); and William Makepeace Thackeray, *The Virginians* (1857–59), chap. 73 ("'Tis hard with respect to Beauty, that its possessor should not have even a life-enjoyment of it, but be compelled to resign it after, at the most, some forty years' lease"). See also Byron's *Don Juan* (1822), canto vi, stanza 69: "A lady of a 'certain age,' which means / Certainly aged."

[5] Smith-Rosenberg 1974: 23–37.

teric often sound more like Renaissance poets than men of science. Listen to
Dr. Marc Colombat's elegy on women at the change of life: "Their features
are stamped with the imprint of age, and their genital organs are sealed with
the signet of sterility." He had no better advice to offer the menopausal woman than that of being moderate in her sexual life, since "love . . . may, at the
critical age, produce the greatest disturbance in the nervous system." The
woman no longer capable of procreation should resign herself to a relatively
chaste existence, avoiding "everything calculated to cause regret for charms
that are lost and enjoyments that are ended for ever."[6]

In England, where attention to the erotic was less single-minded, medical
practitioners emphasized the changes in character, rather than the loss of
sexual attractiveness, that accompanied the change of life. Doctors observed
a predisposition toward depression, melancholia, and hysteria, as well as the
lesser evils of querulousness and peevishness that have long been associated
with old age. In a widely read study on the change of life (Doc. 96.i), Dr.
Edward Tilt, betraying some impatience with menopausal women, advised
them to develop their moral qualities through the pursuit of charitable endeavors. This would help them negotiate the difficult period of menopause
and exert a favorable influence not only on their own mental and physical
well-being, but on society at large.

Activities for Older Women: Philanthropy, Religion, and Grandmothering

Whether women took up philanthropy for the reasons and benefits out-
lined by Dr. Tilt is highly questionable, but as the century progressed and
the expanding middle classes became increasingly affluent, many older wom-
en were able to involve themselves in charitable activities, especially in the
Anglo-American world. Married women who had done with child rearing
and single women of all ages found a socially acceptable outlet for their
energies and talents in projects that aided the poor, the sick, the aged, and
the "fallen." In urban areas of both England and America philanthropy
offered an arena outside the home wherein the feudal tradition of noblesse
oblige could be turned to the purpose of the growing nineteenth-century concern for social stability. Expanding their ancient role in charity, some older
women ventured into social and political causes. The American reformer
Eliza Farnham welcomed her post-menopausal years as a "golden age" of
social involvement and spiritual development (Doc. 96.ii). Elizabeth Cady
Stanton's lifelong pursuit of justice for women, as recounted in her autobiography, Eighty Years and More, demonstrated the validity of her belief
that "the hey-day of woman's life is on the shady side of fifty, when the vital
forces heretofore expended in other ways are garnered in the brain, when
their thoughts and sentiments flow out in broader channels, when philanthropy takes the place of family selfishness, and when from the depths of
poverty and suffering the wail of humanity grows as pathetic to their ears as
once was the cry of their own children."[7] Her vision was shared on the other

[6] Colombat 1850: 551–54 passim.
[7] Stanton 1898: 447.

side of the Atlantic by such activists as the English suffrage leaders Millicent Garrett Fawcett (Doc. 95.ii) and Emmeline Pankhurst, and by the members of the Oeuvre des Libérées de Saint-Lazare (Society for Released Female Prisoners of Saint-Lazare; Doc. 93.ii), all of whom increased their involvement in the feminist movement in their later years.

In England, France, and America, as in other predominantly Christian countries, women were also encouraged to turn to religion in old age in preparation for impending death. The French had a long-standing tradition of "retiring to the convent" when a woman was widowed, ailing, or simply tired of life. Before the French Revolution these "religieuses" were largely grandes dames who turned from the worldly to the otherworld in quest of personal salvation, but during the nineteenth century older women from a wider social and economic range entered the convent not so much to seek asylum as to devote themselves to the care of the sick and the education of the young. The much-read Mme Necker de Saussure (Doc. 99.ii) encouraged the woman of sixty to derive solace from the bitter realities of aging in the contemplation of God. She believed that a consideration of life after death would produce a "beneficial tranquilizing effect" on the Christian woman and those around her.

Yet philanthropy and religion were by no means the most popular models presented to older women. Most prescriptive literature focused heavily on women's maternal duties under the assumption that a natural metamorphosis would transform mothers into grandmothers. (This assumption did not take into account the significant number of women who were spinsters[8] and the high infant mortality rate that left many mothers childless in their later years.) A notable example of this "grandmother model" is found in Louis Aimé-Martin's influential book *The Education of Mothers* (Doc. 99.i). Waxing poetic on the joys of grandmotherhood, he advised women between the ages of forty-five and sixty whose reproductive powers had ended to welcome the role of grandmother: to become "a second mother," "the soul of a new society," and thus save themselves from the "sorrows of isolation, abandonment, and indifference." Aimé-Martin's eulogy to the grandmother may strike the modern reader as hopelessly sentimental, but it derives from a realistic appraisal of what we have come to call the empty-nest syndrome; it focuses, quite accurately, on the confused sense of identity and loss of self-worth to which older mothers are subject.

When we investigate the histories of individual women living in the nineteenth century, many of their lives appear to correspond to the models that were offered to them. Given the prevailing ideology of women as "relative creatures"[9] whose "natural" sphere was domestic, most women lived their adult lives in some form of service to others, generally fulfilling until death the duties of mother and grandmother. Becoming a grandmother could confer a certain desirable status, as evidenced by this excerpt from a Georgia

[8] As discussed in the Part II essay by Estelle Freedman and Erna Olafson Hellerstein.

[9] The term is Françoise Basch's (1974).

planter's letter to a male friend: "I have great pleasure in congratulating you on the birth of your granddaughter and of my niece. . . . I expect tomorrow to make the acquaintance of my young relative, and of felicitating Mrs. King on having attained to the dignity of a grandmother."[10] But the advent of grandchildren could also be the cause of new sorrows, since grandmothers were frequently called upon to nurse and sometimes to bury their infant grandchildren and, what was worse, their daughters and daughters-in-law who died in childbirth (Docs. 59.i–iii). The diaries of Susannah Hyde Braly, begun in 1867 when she was sixty-two years old, bear poignant testimonial to these and other anguishes (Doc. 101.i). The mother of seven live children (at least three others died in infancy) and numerous grandchildren, Braly dwells obsessively on her offspring and cannot reconcile herself to separation from them, whether through distance or through death.

Whereas in Europe the aged generally lived reasonably close to their children, Braly's situation was quintessentially American in the distances that separated family members. The tombstones in nineteenth-century California cemeteries tell the story of extreme migrations—people born in North Carolina or Boston laid to rest in Yountville and Santa Clara by children who did not know where they themselves would die. This uncertainty about where one would eventually die and the desire to be buried with one's family is reflected in a poem that appears, with variations, on several California tombstones:[11]

> This stone to my Mother I bequest
> To mark her last place of rest.
> And when I die if at home
> Inter my body near her tomb.

A few women were able to break out of the narrow domestic circle prescribed for old age. One was the illustrious French writer George Sand (Doc. 100), who had been scandalizing Europe since she was thirty. At the age of sixty-one she buried the most devoted of her many lovers; at the age of sixty-eight she confounded her doctors by bathing daily in an icy stream; and until her death at seventy-two she published two or three works a year, following the pattern of writing at night when her children, grandchildren, and houseguests had gone to bed. Her restless energy and unconventional behavior provoked censure, as witness these words attributed to her onetime friend Marie d'Agoult: "What I cannot forgive her . . . is her lack of style, the way she dresses, her coarse farces at Nohant and, at her age, her bohemian manners. . . . She has no excuse for remaining a *gamin* as she grows old."[12] But

---

[10] J. Hamilton Couper to Thomas Butler King, Jan. 15, 1846, William Audley Couper Papers, Southern Historical Collection, Library of the University of North Carolina, Chapel Hill.

[11] Taken from a grave in Yountville cemetery. The marker, signed Mrs. A. F. Grigsby, bears this inscription: "Sacred to the Memory of Leah, / Wife of Eli Coverdill / Born in Robinson Co. Tenn. / Sept. 14, 1822 / Died in Napa Co. / Feb. 18, 1862 / Aged 39 yrs. 5 Mos. & 4 Ds.

[12] Cited by Barret 1975: 82.

countless other women throughout Europe and America who read her works admired her extravagantly, though they were in no way able to emulate her in their own lives.

Similarly, the Englishwoman Harriet Martineau (Doc. 105) continued her career as a prodigious author of books, articles, and letters expounding unorthodox views on such traditionally "non-feminine" subjects as political economy, mesmerism, and agnosticism. At the age of seventy-four she greeted death with stoic relief because she had begun to perceive the loss of her faculties and was loath to become dependent on her retainers.

The Problem of Dependence

In the end, dependence could become the great leveler, joining an atypical woman like Martineau to the mainstream, and uniting the fates of rich and poor. Old people, men and women, faced with physical degeneration and imminent death, understandably fear dependence on children, relatives, servants, public and private institutions, charity—whatever they are forced to accept as replacements for their own resources. The nineteenth century dealt with the problem of dependence in a number of ways, some of which prefigure our own still-inadequate attempts to provide for the aged in their time of need.

In America it was the custom for one child, often the youngest daughter, to live at home, unmarried, caring for the parents when they could no longer care for themselves (Doc. 31). It was also common for widowed mothers to move in with their children, sometimes sequentially, as in the case of Lucy Crawford, who when she published her *History of the White Mountains* in 1846 (Doc. 104.ii), wrote that she had been "wandering about from place to place since 1837," finding a home with her children wherever she could be "most useful."[13] Similarly, elderly spinsters like Catharine Beecher (Doc. 21.i) moved about from relative to relative depending on who would have them.

In France the Civil Code stated explicitly that children owed support to their parents who were in want, and for the most part, French adults kept their parents at home. But there were numerous examples of the abuse of parents who were old and feeble (Doc. 102.i). Simone de Beauvoir, in her book *The Coming of Age*, reproduces several newspaper accounts from the years 1850–90 that reported the neglect, abuse, or outright murder of old mothers, fathers, and mothers-in-law.[14] Eugen Weber's more scholarly study of rural France provides further evidence of such practices; in peasant society aged parents no longer able to work were often treated with various shades of indifference, resentment, and even hatred "by grudging son and perhaps vengeful daughter-in-law who wished them dead and sometimes drove them to it."[15]

For the aged poor, regardless of sex, dependence was a harrowing experi-

[13] Morse 1978: 225–26.
[14] Beauvoir 1972: 288–94.
[15] Weber 1976: 176.

ence. To be old and poor in the nineteenth century usually meant extreme hardship and physical deprivation. The descriptions of the Nottingham lace makers in the 1840's and the Stepney paupers in the 1890's (Docs. 98.ii, 103.i) suggest that the condition of the aged poor in England continued to be similarly wretched through the century, despite the efforts of novelists and reformers like Frances Power Cobbe and Elizabeth Gaskell to call attention to their plight (Docs. 13, 71.i).

Some poor old women in rural France and England, and even in America, were subject to a special form of abuse reserved for "witches." Itinerant beggars, herbalists, and eccentrics of any type incurred the insults of Christian brothers and sisters on whom it would have been incumbent to offer alms instead of curses and graveside prayers instead of desecration (Docs. 104.ii–iv).

Such archaic attitudes persisted mostly in the countryside. Elsewhere more enlightened minds began to provide institutional care for the aged poor, especially in the cities. Early in the century old-age homes began to be founded in eastern America, many along religious and class lines. Certain religious institutions, like St. Luke's Episcopal Home for Aged Women in New York City, were reserved for women from better families; a specific provision stated that only "needy gentlewomen" were admitted. There were also old-age homes for the less fortunate, public institutions supported by state and local governments. These offered varying degrees of care, ranging from the minimal to the merely adequate, but even in the relatively good ones, the inmates generally felt disgraced by the notion of ending their days in the poorhouse. Fischer cites the example of a widow in the town of Easton, Massachusetts, whose husband had been an influential citizen of the town. When he died and she had no relatives to take her in, she was forced at the age of eighty-seven to enter a public old-age home, where she spent her last days braiding straw in order to pay for her own funeral.[16]

In England the problem of the aged poor became a topic of public debate by the end of the century, partially as a result of the work of Charles Booth, an enterprising social scientist (Doc. 103.i). The reports of private citizens and government officials called attention to an increasing number of destitute old men and women, many of whom received assistance from public funds. In 1892 approximately one in four persons over sixty-five was classified as a "pauper" (Doc. 103.ii). The term applied equally to "indoor paupers" living at public expense in workhouses (some 68,000 males and 46,000 females) and "outdoor paupers" receiving medical and financial aid at state dispensaries (some 95,000 males and 192,000 females).

The ratio of male to female among those receiving some form of public charity was one to one-and-a-half. Thus, more aged females were officially recorded as needy than their male counterparts. Several explanations for the greater incidence of female destitution among the aged come immediately to mind. If widowed, the aged woman usually lost her sole means of financial support, whereas the widower lost "only" a housekeeper. Married or single,

[16] Fischer 1978: 152.

the working woman's wages were so low as to render her unable to "set aside" for old age.

It is also significant that despite the disproportion in the number of elderly women receiving public aid, men far outnumbered women in the "indoor pauper" category. Elderly men suffering from sickness, the loss of a job or a spouse, or some other personal catastrophe seem to have required a more complete form of institutional care than their female counterparts. Women, traditionally accustomed to caring for their own creaturely needs, seem to have been more capable of surviving on their own, outside of the workhouse, however meager their means of survival.

Another view of women's greater ability to survive outside the poorhouse is provided by the historian Michel Dahlin. In America in the late nineteenth century, she notes, women were more often cared for by children and by private charity than men. Dahlin cites the following from an 1896 almshouse report to explain in part why society was more tolerant of the dependence of older women than older men, and so, more inclined to grant them charity: "It must be said . . . that the world recognizes the inevitable dependence of women by considering it a most disgraceful thing for relatives or children to allow an old woman to go to the almshouse. On the other hand, men are supposed to have had their chance to lay up money, and if they have not done so they must take the consequences."[17]

Women's "natural dependence" could, in this instance, work to their advantage in old age. As Dahlin points out, old women were more welcome in the home because they continued to make themselves useful as babysitters and housekeepers, whereas old men were more likely to be viewed as useless and "in the way" by their daughters and daughters-in-law.

On the basis of the sources we have examined, it is possible to offer a few generalizations about the lives of older women in the nineteenth century. But they are offered tentatively, in the awareness that research into the history of old age has just begun.

Some modernization theorists have argued that older people lost status in the nineteenth century as the new industrial economy came to value younger workers more than older ones. Fischer, for example, identifies a deterioration in American attitudes toward the aged by citing an increase in derogatory terms for old men beginning in the early nineteenth century (e.g. old fogy, old goat, baldy, oldster). But he also points out that similarly derogatory terms for women have a longer history. Words such as hag, nag, and witch can be traced back to Chaucer and Shakespeare.[18] In this instance, Fischer's theory of history seems to be based on a male model that does not take sufficiently into account differences in gender.

Although it is not within the scope of this essay, it is tempting to argue that earlier eras devalued older women at least as much as, if not more than, the nineteenth century, and that one should look back to the Middle Ages,

[17] Dahlin 1978.
[18] Fischer 1978: 90–94.

and probably to classical antiquity, for the double root of sexism and ageism in the Western world. The written word testifies to an almost universal lack of esteem for women in their later years. For centuries the twin expressions "young and beautiful" "old and ugly" have summed up the social attitudes that women could expect to encounter in youth and in old age.

The nineteenth century seems to have added nothing new to this dichotomy, though more subtle forms of caricature replaced the old hags and foul witches of medieval fables and the faded beauties of Renaissance poetry. By the nineteenth century Western civilization had progressed to the point where old women were simply depicted as ridiculous, especially middle- and upper-class women who would not stay put in the asexual, self-effacing, all-nurturing role that society had mandated for them.

Working-class women, on the other hand, did find themselves at the mercy of an industrializing economy that not only valued younger workers more than older ones, but effectively hastened the aging process through the devastating regime of twelve-, fourteen-, and sixteen-hour workdays. Yet paid employment outside the home, however minimal, may still have offered older women a chance to support themselves or earn supplementary income at a time of life when their only alternative was to endure the charity or abuse of kinfolk or to repair to the poorhouse.

Under favorable conditions age conferred increased respect, freedom, and even social power. But on the whole the liabilities of old age seem to have outweighed the advantages. In addition to the fears of illness and death to which all old people in all times are subject, women in the nineteenth century often lost status and encountered severe economic hardship as they grew old. Despite recent attention in the Western world to the condition of "senior citizens," we have yet to see enough change in the circumstances surrounding old age so as to consider the nineteenth-century woman's experience past history.

Documents 96-106

96. The change of life

Physicians taught that menopause was physically risky and emotionally harrowing, marking, as it did, the end of women's years of motherhood and of their sexual attractiveness. This medical view of menopause permeated the extensive hygienic advice literature. The following selections, both from roughly mid-century, challenge that view. Although the first author, John Edward Tilt (1815–93), one of the founding fellows of the Obstetrical Society of London, voices the conventional wisdom when he writes that the change of life unhinges the female nervous system and deprives women of their personal charms, he is also at pains to remind older women that age has its own beauty, and that they, too, can find useful and meaningful lives. In the second selection, Eliza Farnham (1815–64), an American prison reformer and lecturer, criticizes the standard view of menopause as one that has made women associate the change of life with death. What this transition really signifies, Farnham claims, is a rest from the unstinting labors of maternity, a vacation from self-sacrifice that women should welcome, not dread.

(i) Edward Tilt

During the c. [change] of life, the nervous system is so unhinged, that the management of the mental and moral faculties requires great attention, and often taxes the ingenuity of the medical confidant. The study of the patient's character will teach him, however, what occupation and pursuit is most likely to engross her mind, and effectually replace those of former times. If he be not prepared to be at once a divine, a moralist, and a philosopher, without ceasing to be a physician, his medicines will, in some cases, be of little use. It cannot be wondered at that the full conviction that age has stamped them with its first irrevocable seal, should cast a gloom over the imagination; but in well-trained minds it will soon be dispelled, by the knowledge that this epoch proclaims an immunity from the perils of childbearing and the tedious annoyances of a monthly restraint.

SOURCES: (i) Edward Tilt, *The Change of Life in Health and Disease: A Practical Treatise on the Nervous and Other Affections Incidental to Women at the Decline of Life*, 2d ed. (London, 1857), pp. 128–31. (ii) Eliza Farnham, *Woman and Her Era* (New York, 1864), 1: 62–65.

The natural good sense of many will show them how the notion that after this period little remains to console women for the anxieties and troubles of life, is a *pagan* idea, suited to the position allotted to them in the civilization of Greece and Rome, where they were seldom considered worth more than to amuse men and to bring forth children; but this cannot apply to women after their social emancipation by the doctrines of Christianity. They should be shown that the importance of their position after the great change, may be inferred by the length of time allotted to them after its occurrence, and the singular immunity from disease which is often observed after that period. They should be reminded that many intimate sources of pleasure are attached to every age, but that it would be unfair to ask of one period the pleasures allotted to another. . . .

Besides the vast improvement in health, it must not be thought that the c. of life implies the loss of all personal attractions. The beauty of youth charms; that of mature age excites admiration; but in many women there is at the c. of life and long after, an autumnal majesty so blended with amiability, that it fascinates all who approach them. To those fired with a little noble ambition, it may be safely said, that the home government of society, from Almack's down to the lowest of our social strata, offers a wide field of employment to women after this period of life. Many never think of cultivating their minds until they find their influence fading with their charms, and then set about acquiring a less perishable empire, and employ this period of freedom in literary pursuits. Others govern with discretion that circle of society, limited or extensive, in which they have been placed; becoming the guides, the supports, and mainstays of both sexes in the difficulties of life. Indeed, it would not be too much to say, that in no dwelling can the discordant elements of society be harmoniously blended without the authority willingly conceded to age and sex. . . . Those acquainted with French society at the present time will remember the influence of the late Mme. Recamier over a large circle of talented friends; and during my residence in Paris I have myself frequently witnessed the benign influence of Mme. Swichine prompting those around her to what was great and noble; guiding many in the difficult paths of life; healing wounds caused by inexperience; and making many bless her for the happiness they now enjoy. This brings me to the noblest motive to be offered to the laudable ambition of women—that of doing the greatest amount of good to the greatest number of their fellow-creatures. Time dulls the eye, robs the cheek of its bloom, delves furrows in the forehead, but cannot quell the seraphic fire burning in the heart of women, prompting them to deeds of charity, and to heal the deep wounds which afflict society. Those who have attained their sunset without having been granted the anxious though desirable vicissitudes of wedded life, even if destitute of relatives, or unfortunate in friendship, may still find in the various forms of unmerited affliction which fill our country cottages, or the hovels of our populous cities, that whereon to expend a warmth of feeling, an energy of self-sacrifice, which the sophisticated state of society has not permitted to flow into their natural and more graceful channels. Why then should some women, sensible in everything else, be unable to accept their new position, and, instead of kind and charitable, become, at this period, peevish, harsh, dismal, and viewing everything through a jaundiced veil?

The most distressing appeals to medical sympathy are made by those who, when unnerved by the c. of life, find themselves alone in the world, bereft, when most needed, of the solace of filial piety, or the gushing sympathies of conjugal affection. One can only at first, respond to such appeals, with a sympathizing look and a silent pressure of the hand; but should tears burst their bonds, lightening the suffering spirit of half its load, sweeping away black sorrow, disquietude, and trembling doubts, then it may be hinted that time steals even sorrows from the heart, doubtless because they are sweeter than joy, and that after a brief period nothing will remain but calm judgment and the unmoved remembrance of past goodness, where it was once thought that impassioned love and devoted tenderness must be eternal. The best mode of affording relief is to discover some kind of occupation capable of engrossing the sufferer's attention, such as music, gardening, the education of a relative or of an adopted child, or the management of a school, or some other charity. The continued friction of social duties will, in time, rub off the asperities of character, and restore peace and tranquillity to the troubled spirit. Every effort should be made, in such a case, to prevent brooding and self-absorption, for the mind may gaze so long on one object that the moral vision may become affected with the same disorder which befalls the bodily eye when fixed too long on one colour, surrounding objects losing their own colours, and shining only with unnatural tints.

(ii) Eliza Farnham

To be a Woman is to suffer, thus far in the human career. Each of us knows this, and it is not hidden from the noblest men. Yet, though disappointment has shocked, pain has wrung, and grief exhausted her life, the fountain has refilled itself after every drain, from those invisible springs whose deeply-hidden sources even she perchance knows not. Finding that they are, she is thankful; with secret thrills that sound down to the depths of her nature, she takes conscious possession of her riches and moves along her way. From year to year of the thirty or forty that make her middle period, she has accepted life as it came, sustaining herself as best she could when the revolving wheel carried her down, and, as she rose, reaching out to draw others up to her own elevation. The men who set out on the road with her, the husband, brother, friends, are excused if they grow hard, or bitter, or resistant, between the upper and the nether mill-stone, even though they be less bruised than she; but no provision is made for her becoming so. She is counted on to be steadily hopeful, sustaining, compassionate, helpful, loving. The average Woman is so. She is the concrete of those elements in the human society of all ages.

She stands at this portal, now, which separates her past and present from a future that is unknown to her, and that is made forbidding by the theory she has received of it. No wonder that she looks upon these gates, as the condemned upon the door which is next to open the way to his scaffold—that she counts sadly every step which brings her nearer to them—that she would fain convince herself and the world that she is yet far off; thirty-five instead of forty-five; fresh with youth instead of cosmetics; gay from happiness instead of simulation. For that awful future! Wherein it is not mysterious it is worse; insulting, neglectful, chilling. And, whatever its aspect to her, the near approaches to it are through trials of soul and sense that call for the most delicate consideration, the deepest tenderness, the finest sympathy of the spirit. It is the winding up of a set of functions, the most august of her gifts—of a circuit of nerve-activities, and the transfer of the finer powers, capacities, and sensibilities involved in them, from the corporeal to the psychical level. All this does not take place without perturbations of heart, and nerve, and brain, hard to bear at the best—appalling at times, in the darkness wherein she has to grope her lonely way. First come those fluctuating movements, the ebb of the currents from center to circumference, the earliest hint given by Nature that she is preparing to suspend their centripetal action. But this of the corporeal is only the symbol of a corresponding spiritual action. In the Maternal period centralization was the necessary policy, since Maternity is of a rank to subordinate all contemporary powers, and make them legitimately subservient to itself. Now this function is to pass away from her. The powers which co-worked with it may remain, many of them even in augmented degree, for years, but their direction is to be changed.

Three reasons appear for this change. Doubtless there are many others, did we understand them, but three are apparent; two which concern the race and one the individual. First, the species is to be protected against the wide-spread calamity which must fall upon it were this office continued into the dotage of Woman, as paternity is to Man. Second, Society, according to its advancement, needs other service from Woman; calls her to other fields in these years, having need of her there, as we shall see by-and-by. Third, the individual is to have a period of repose from the taxes and cares which Maternity lays upon her—a period when the powers are ripened for growth, and when life, through the fullness of experience, has become a majestic, flowing river, whose current passion and sense are no more to lash into foam or break into roaring rapids. Or a lofty mountain is it? whose calm summit has pierced the clouds and now rises in grand repose above their changing, shifting haste and fury. After the earnest, self-sacrificing, absorbing struggles of the maternal years, this season fitly comes—a sabbath interlude of harmony and peace, to be followed by Heaven. Let any woman to whom Maternity has been what it ought to be in the feminine life, the paramount interest, aim, and office of its two or three middle decades, consider what it would be to go on giving herself thus in that unstinted measure, up to the full term of her years—all the self-sacrifice continuing, all the cares, solicitudes, responsibilities, going on so till sixty or seventy, and she will readily see how beneficient is its suspension, and also how much more her self-hood is involved in it than is that of Man in paternity. Each life has yielded of itself according to the demands upon it: one in self-gratification, the other in self-giving; one in self-love, the other in loving. Instead, therefore, of repining at the change which finally suspends this office to her, she will receive it as a just due—especially if she has been so happy as to give herself freely, wholly, intelligently, loyally, to its fulfilling—and feel her life made richer, not poorer, by its coming.

97. Three writers discuss aging and appearance

Victorian women were greatly concerned about the changes age wrought upon their personal appearance. In these selections three women writers discuss popular prejudices about the "fading charms" of women over forty and advise their sisters how to age gracefully. In the first selection Margaret Fuller (1810–50), the most prominent American female intellectual of her generation, defends the mature woman against the poet's indifference and society's ridicule. She offers women classical heroines as role models for their later years. Like Fuller, the celebrated Irish-born courtesan Lola Montez (1818–61) draws on classical models to recommend that women dress appropriately for their age. Montez, a renowned Parisian beauty and mistress to the King of Bavaria, takes a harsh view of older women who attempt to preserve by artificial means the beauty of their youth. Yet she is not above offering women a "safe" recipe for removing the grey from their hair. In the third selection the British journalist Eliza Lynn Linton (1822–98) ridicules society women's resistance to aging and condemns their attempts to hide the signs of age with thick cosmetics and desperate flirtations.

(i) Margaret Fuller

See a common woman at forty; scarcely has she the remains of beauty, of any soft poetic grace which gave her attraction as Woman, which kindled the hearts of those who looked on her to sparkling thoughts, or diffused round her a roseate air of gentle love. See her, who was, indeed, a lovely girl, in the coarse, full-blown dahlia flower of what is commonly matron-beauty, "fat, fair, and forty," showily dressed, and with manners as broad and full as her frill or satin cloak. People observe, "How well she is preserved!" "She is a fine woman still," they say. This woman, whether as a duchess in diamonds, or one of our city dames in mosaics, charms the poet's heart no more, and would look much out of place kneeling before the Madonna. She "does well the honors of her house,"—"leads society,"—is, in short, always spoken and thought of upholstery-wise.

Or see that care-worn face, from which every soft line is blotted,—those faded eyes, from which lonely tears have driven the flashes of fancy, the mild

SOURCES: (i) Margaret Fuller, *Woman in the Nineteenth Century* (Boston, 1855), pp. 99–101. Originally published in 1845. (ii) Lola Montez [pseud. of Marie Dolores Eliza Rosanna Gilbert], *The Arts of Beauty; or secrets of a lady's toilet* (New York, 1858), pp. 74–75, 93–94. (iii) [E. Lynn Linton], "La Femme passée," *The Saturday Review*, 26.663 (July 11, 1868): 49–50.

white beam of a tender enthusiasm. This woman is not so ornamental to a tea-party; yet she would please better, in picture. Yet surely she, no more than the other, looks as a human being should at the end of forty years. Forty years! have they bound those brows with no garland? shed in the lamp no drop of ambrosial oil?

Not so looked the Iphigenia in Aulis. Her forty years had seen her in anguish, in sacrifice, in utter loneliness. But those pains were borne for her father and her country; the sacrifice she had made pure for herself and those around her. Wandering alone at night in the vestal solitude of her imprisoning grove, she has looked up through its "living summits" to the stars, which shed down into her aspect their own lofty melody. At forty she would not misbecome the marble.

Not so looks the Persica. She is withered; she is faded; the drapery that enfolds her has in its dignity an angularity, too, that tells of age, of sorrow, of a stern resignation to the *must*. But her eye, that torch of the soul, is untamed, and, in the intensity of her reading, we see a soul invincibly young in faith and hope. Her age is her charm, for it is the night of the past that gives this beacon-fire leave to shine. Wither more and more, black Chrysalid! thou dost but give the winged beauty time to mature its splendors!

Not so looked Victoria Colonna, after her life of a great hope, and of true conjugal fidelity. She had been, not merely a bride, but a wife, and each hour had helped to plume the noble bird. A coronet of pearls will not shame her brow; it is white and ample, a worthy altar for love and thought.

(ii) Lola Montez

But as beauty of form and complexion varies in different women, and is still more various in different ages, so the styles in dress should assume characters corresponding with all these circumstances. . . .

The best school to teach a woman taste in dress is the Pantheon of ancient Rome. First behold the lovely Hebe; her robes are like the air, her motion is on the zephyr's wing. That may be woman's style until she is twenty. Then comes the beautiful Diana. The chaste dignity of womanhood and intelligence pervades the whole form, and the very drapery which enfolds it, harmonizes with the modest elegance, the buoyant strength of ripened health, which give elastity and grace to every limb. That is woman from twenty to thirty. Then comes Juno or Minerva, standing forth in the combined power of beauty and wisdom. "At this period she gradually lays aside the flowers of youth, and arrays herself in the majesty of sobriety, or in the sober beauty of simplicity. Long ought to be the reign of this commanding epoch of woman's age, for from thirty to fifty she may most respectably maintain her station on the throne of matron excellence,"* and still be lawfully admired as a beautiful woman. But beyond this age, it becomes her to lay aside all such pretensions, and, by her "mantle of grey," gracefully acknowledge her entrance into the "vale of years." What can be more disgusting than a painted

---

* Montez does not identify the sources of the quotes in her text.—EDS.

and bepowdered old woman, just "trembling on the brink of the grave, and yet a candidate for the flattery of men?" . . .

How to Color Grey Hair

A great many compounds, which are of a character most destructive to the hair, are sold in the shape of hair-dyes, against which ladies cannot be too frequently warned. These, for the most part, are composed of such things as poisonous mineral acids, nitrate and oxide of silver, caustic alkalies, lime, litharge and arsenic. The way these *color* the hair is simply by *burning* it, and they are very liable to produce a disease of the hair which increases ten-fold the speed of growing grey. One patent hair-dye was proved on analysis, to be a preparation of hydrophosphuret of ammonia, a most filthy ingredient, which, besides its villainous smell, would cause immediate suffocation if inhaled by the lungs. All these patent compounds rot the hair, if they do no greater mischief.

An old physician and chemist at Lisbon gave a charming Parisian lady of my acquaintance, whose hair was turning grey, on one side of her head after a severe sickness, a recipe for a hair dye which proved to be of astonishing efficacy in coloring the faded hair a beautiful and natural black. The following is the recipe for making it.

Gallic acid	10 grs.
Acetic acid	1 oz.
Tincture of sesqui-chloride of iron	1 oz.

Dissolve the gallic acid in the tincture of sesqui-chloride of iron, and then add the acetic acid. Before using this preparation, the hair should be thoroughly washed with soap and water. A great and desirable peculiarity of this dye is that it can be so applied as to color the hair either *black* or the lighter shade of brown. If *black* is the color desired, the preparation should be applied while the hair is moist, and for *brown* it should not be used till the hair is perfectly dry. The way to apply the compound is to dip the points of a fine tooth comb into it until the interstices are filled with the fluid, then gently draw the comb through the hair, commencing at the roots, till the dye has perceptibly taken effect. When the hair is entirely dry, oil and brush it as usual.

(iii) Eliza Lynn Linton

Without doubt it is a time of trial to all women, more or less painful according to individual disposition, when they first begin to grow old and lose their good looks. Youth and beauty make up so much of their personal value, so much of their natural *raison d'être*, that when these are gone many feel as if their whole career was at an end, and as if nothing was left to them now that they are no longer young enough to be loved as girls are loved, or pretty enough to be admired as once they were admired. For women of a certain position have so little wholesome occupation, and so little ambition for anything, save indeed that miserable thing called "getting on in society," that they cannot change their way of life with advancing years; they do not attempt to find interest in things outside themselves, and independent of the mere personal attractiveness which in youth constituted their whole pleasure of existence. This is essentially the case with fashionable women, who have staked their all on appearance, and to whom good looks are of more account than noble deeds; and, accordingly, the struggle to remain young is a frantic one with them, and as degrading as it is frantic. With the ideal woman of middle age—that pleasant woman, with her happy face and softened manner, who unites the charms of both epochs, retaining the ready responsiveness of youth while adding the wider sympathies of experience—with her there has never been any such struggle to make herself an anachronism. Consequently she remains beautiful to the last, far more beautiful than all the pastes and washes in Madame Rachel's shop could make her. . . . What she has lost in outside material charm—in that mere *beauté du diable* of youth—she has gained in character and expression; and, not attempting to simulate the attractiveness of a girl, she keeps what nature gave her—the attractiveness of middle age. And as every epoch has its own beauty, if women would but learn that truth, she is as beautiful now as a matron of fifty, because in harmony with her years, and because her beauty has been carried on from matter to spirit, as she was when a maiden of sixteen. This is the ideal woman of middle age, met with even yet at times in society—the woman whom all men respect, whom all women envy, and wonder how she does it, and whom all the young adore, and wish they had for an elder sister or an aunt. And the secret of it all lies in truth, in love, in purity, and in unselfishness.

Standing far in front of this sweet and wholesome idealization is *la femme passée* of to-day—the reality as we meet with it at balls and fêtes and afternoon at homes, ever foremost in the mad chase after pleasure, for which alone she seems to think she has been sent into the world. Dressed in the extreme of youthful fashion, her thinning hair dyed and crimped and fired till it is more red-brown tow than hair, her flaccid cheeks ruddled, her throat whitened, her bust displayed with unflinching generosity, as if beauty was to be measured by cubic inches, her lustreless eyes blackened round the lids, to give the semblance of limpidity to the tarnished whites—perhaps the pupil dilated by belladonna, or perhaps a false and fatal brilliancy for the moment given by opium, or by eau de cologne, of which she has a store in her carriage, and drinks as she passes from ball to ball; no kindly drapery of lace or gauze to conceal the breadth of her robust maturity, or to soften the dreadful shadows of her leanness—there she stands, the wretched creature who will not consent to grow old, and who will still affect to be like a fresh coquettish girl when she is nothing but *la femme passée*—*la femme passée et ridicule* into the bargain. There is not a folly for which even the thoughtlessness of youth is but a poor excuse into which she, in all the plenitude of her abundant experience, does not plunge. Wife and mother as she may be, she flirts and makes love as if an honourable issue was as open to her as to her daughter, or as if she did not know to what end flirting and making love lead in all ages.

If we watch the career of such a woman, we see how, by slow but very sure degrees, she is obliged to lower the standard of her adorers, and to take up at last with men of inferior social position, who are content to buy her patronage by their devotion. To the best men of her own class she can give nothing that they value; so she barters with snobs who go into the transaction with their eyes open, and take the whole affair as a matter of exchange, and *quid pro quo* rigidly exacted. Or she does really dazzle some very young and low-born man who is weak as well as ambitious, and who thinks the fugitive regard of a middle-aged woman of high rank something to be proud of and boasted about. That she is as old as his own mother—at this moment selling tapes behind a village counter or gathering up the eggs in a country farm—tells nothing against the association with him; and the woman who began her career of flirtation with the son of a duke ends it with the son of a shopkeeper, having between these two terms spanned all the several degrees of degradation which lie between giving and buying. She cannot help herself; for it is part of the insignia of her artificial youth to have the reputation of a love affair, or the pretence of one, if even the reality is a mere delusion. When such a woman as this is one of the matrons, and consequently one of the leaders in society, what can we expect from the girls? What worse example could be given to the young? . . .

What good in life does this kind of woman do? All her time is taken up, first in trying to make herself look twenty or thirty years younger than she is, and then in trying to make others believe the same; and she has neither thought nor energy to spare from this, to her, far more important work than is feeding the hungry or nursing the sick, rescuing the fallen or soothing the sorrowful.

98. A lifetime of work in England and France

Women of the working class did not know the luxury of worrying about grey hair and fading beauty; for them, old age offered no respite from unceasing labor, as the following selections show. When the French reformer Flora Tristan (1803–44; Docs. 58.i, 90.i) visited Nîmes in the early 1840's, she was outraged to find a washerwoman of some fifty years of age who, by local custom, was still plying her trade, as she had done since she was a girl, standing in befouled water up to her waist. In the 1830's and 1840's Parliamentary investigators in England recorded the testimonies of older women who, despite illness and infirmity, had to keep at their jobs in factories and workshops in order to survive. Although many of these women describe grueling hours and unspeakable working conditions, some, remarkably, seem to have kept both health and spirit, no matter how unrelenting the toil.

SOURCES: (i) Flora Tristan, *Le Tour de France: Journal inédit (1843–1844)* (Paris, 1973), pp. 216–17. The editors wish to thank Dr. Sandra Dijkstra, University of California, Los Angeles, for contributing this selection. (ii) Great Britain, *Parliamentary Papers*, 1833, XX, Factory Inquiry Commission, 1st Report, pp. B1

(i) The washerwomen of Nîmes

Imagine a hole, dignified with the title of pool, scooped out in the middle of a public square (whose name I don't know)—this hole must be about sixty feet wide, one hundred feet long, and forty feet deep. You get down to it by a staircase. . . . There are two *lavoirs* [washing troughs] that run the entire length of it, but are less than a foot wide. . . . In all [other] *lavoirs* the stone on which the washerwoman washes slopes into the water so that she can scrub her linens in the water. The washerwoman is on her knees or standing (as in the boats at Paris), and thus washes her linens on the sloping stone. This is so evident that all country women who set up a *lavoir* themselves, whether on the banks of a river or a stream, put down a sloping stone behind which they kneel. Well! In Nîmes things happen backwards. It is not the laundry that is in the water, no, it is the washerwoman who is in the water up to the waist—and the laundry is out of the water. The washerwoman washes on a stone, the tip of which slants out of the water. At least 300 to 400 washerwomen in Nîmes are thus condemned to pass their lives with their bodies in water up to the waist, and in a water that is poisonous because it is befouled with soap, potash, soda, bleach, and grease, and finally with all kinds of dyes such as indigo, madder red, saffron, etc. etc. Thus in order to earn their bread many women are condemned to uterine illnesses, to acute rheumatism, to painful pregnancies, to miscarriages, in short, to every imaginable evil! . . . If a convict were condemned to suffer for only eight days the torture these unfortunate women have endured for the past 300 years since the *lavoir* was constructed!—Philanthropists would be unable to find enough words to protest against this atrocity! The press would hurl a terrible anathema against the government that would dare to kill men thus, day by day, hour by hour! . . . But as for these miserable washerwomen, who have committed no crime, who work day and night, who courageously dedicate their health, their life, to the service of humanity, who are women, who are mothers . . . Well! They find not one philanthropist, not one journalist, who protests on their behalf. . . .

I stayed at the Hôtel du Gard and my casement window faced out on that *lavoir*. Thus, I could see these women every day. Good God, what work! . . . When it rained, they were exposed to the rain (in the tiniest village, the *lavoirs* are always covered). These miserable washerwomen no longer looked like human beings, habitually being in the water had bloated them—professional washerwomen are always very fat and deformed . . .

These women work with an extraordinary courage—day and night they are at the *lavoir*. I could hear their beaters all night. Several times I got up in the night to see how many were there—15, 20, 30 were there washing with unbelievable vigor. Wishing to know the reason for this night washing, I stopped two of them in the street who answered me politely and gave me, in very bad French, all the explanations I desired: Those who do the laundry

---

88, C1 23, C2 22; 1843, XIV, Children's Employment Commission, pp. c 6, f 39–40, f 133.

and wish to have water that is less dirty wash "at night"—1) they are sure to avoid the dyers,—2) they will also avoid the rag peddlers who come to wash all kinds of very filthy linen—3) they can choose the best places. . . .

The old washerwoman who spoke to me looked more like a slug than a woman. She appeared to be seventy years old but was only fifty-one. Her daughter, nineteen years old, was very pale—she seemed so unwell, so weak, so crushed—that she aroused pity. The poor mother seemed to be very touched by her daughter's state. "Oh! madame, our conditions are really harsh, always in the water . . . there are a good many strong ones who cannot get used to it"—She deplored her daughter's weak constitution, but limited herself to that. She did not dream of blaming those who condemned her daughter to rot in the sludge. . . . It is clear that she had seen her mother wash in the sludge, that she herself has washed there for thirty years, that she thinks her daughter must wash there. Poor people! Thus do they continue from century to century, enduring the same cruelties, the same abuse.

(ii) Older English working women

Anny Williams, Staffordshire pottery worker, age forty-one.—I have worked as a potter altogether 20 years; I have worked in this employ about 4 years. I am married, and have one girl who works on the same premises; I have two rooms in this department, and have 6 persons working with me; we never have children working with us. We receive our ware from the ovens in the dusty and rough state; our business is to scour it with sand-paper and stone; this occupation is very unhealthy, it stuffs a person up very much in the stomach; not many scourers live long; it takes some off sooner than others; none of us are ill now, except that we *all* feel overloaded upon the chest; sometimes we cough very much, especially in the morning when we first begin. We are paid by the piece, and earn upon the average 8s. or 9s. a-week. These rooms are spacious and have the means of ventilation. Particles of dust, as in the sifting-room adjoining the sagger-room and oven, flying in all directions; the air is loaded with it.

Sarah Caby, Birmingham button maker, age forty-four.—Reads and writes a little. Works at drilling pearl buttons. Has been in trade 15 years. Worked before that in this manufactory at the gilt and plating trade. Former is worse for health. The pearl dust lies at the chest. Her breathing is very bad in the morning. Has had constant pain in the side since she has worked at the pearl-button trade. These effects are common to all the mechanics in this business. Is only able to work 6 hours a-day because she is not able to stand it longer. The regular hours are from 8 A.M. till 7 P.M. One hour is allowed for dinner and half an hour for tea. Works by the piece.

Mrs. Fortescue, Nottingham cotton spinner, age forty-nine.—I went into a factory when I was six years old. It was Mr. Robinson's of Papplewick; it was a mill for *spinning cotton*. The hours were from six to seven, with an hour for dinner; no other time allowed. I was then eleven years. I then went to James Robinson's, where we had the same hours. I staid there two years until I was married at the age of nineteen; and continued there afterwards; altogether twenty years at Robinson's. This also was a mill for *spinning cotton.* I began with carding, roving, &c., and came to spinning and doubling. I was then at Farnifield's of Edingley for thirteen months. From thence we came here. I am a reeler at these mills now. I begin work at six, and work till nine. I am now forty-nine years of age. My health continued very good until long after I was married; but within these ten years it has failed me. I am much subject to sick head-ache, and am generally weaker. I still keep up these long hours, and work with the young women. I have borne seven children in my time. I think I don't look much amiss for forty-nine; many people have said that. I keep pretty well as sharp as the young ones. But I think I should have been stronger if I had not had so much hard work. I was eleven years in the carding-room. The cotton-flues flying about were very bad. I could not help the cotton getting mixed with my food. I have eaten a good deal of it in my time. I am not tired of my work, to say so, 'till half past nine.

Mary Walters, Nottingham lace embroiderer, age forty-nine.—Is married. Cannot read or write; went when a child to the Exchange Sunday school. Has been a lace-runner ever since she was "a little bit of a thing that could stand on two bricks to reach the frame"; works generally from 5 A.M. till 9 or 10 P.M.; "she can't sit longer, because she is a poor creature now," has about one hour for dinner and half an hour for breakfast and tea; works for an agent, and earns on an average 2s. 6d. a-week; this is as much as she can get, and that with hard work. Does not know how much is paid at the warehouse for the work. There is a ticket on the lace with the name of the proprietor; no price is marked. Her sight has suffered a great deal; this happens generally to runners; she cannot see what o'clock it is across her room; her eyes are getting worse. . . .

Has a son 20 years old, who works in the brickyard, but who has had no employment this winter; he tried the lead-mills, but this made him so ill, she thought he would have died; if this son could get work, she should have more time to attend to her family; as it is, everything is neglected, "through being tied to the piece so."

Has eight children, five of whom are at home and three married; has lost one child of scarlet fever; her husband is a journeyman shoemaker; he has not half work; her eldest daughter, 18, is at a warehouse, and is the best off for employment; earns 5s; the next are two boys, 15 and 13 years old; they are employed in a part of the stocking business, but it is very poor indeed; the eldest may earn 3s. and the youngest 1s. 6d. after the expenses are paid; the youngest girl, nine years, has been a chevener two years, and earns 1s. 6d. a-week at full work; she goes at 7 A.M. and comes home at 9 P.M.; the work tires her sight so much, that witness has been obliged to buy her a pair of spectacles.

Pays for house-rent 2s. 3d. a-week.

Sarah Siddons, Leicester woolen worker, age fifty-eight.—We two have worked here since the factory began.* I find this work suit my health very

* Siddons has reference here to a woman co-worker.—EDS

well. I suppose you are inquiring about making us work less hours, but I am afraid if we work less hours we shall get less wages; and it is quite as much as we can do now to get along. . . . I can stand the work of twelve hours well enough, and I don't want to work more.

Elizabeth Hodges, Bruton silk worker, age seventy-three.—How long have you lived in Bruton?—I was born and bred here.

How long have you worked in the silk-mills?—About sixty-four years.

How long have you worked for Mr. Ward?—I have worked for him, and his father before him, fifty-four years.

Has your health been good all your life?—Yes, very good.

Had you ever swelled legs by standing so long?—Never; until I became old. . . .

Do you think there is a kindly good feeling between the masters and the people they employ?—Yes, I am sure there is; both my master and his family.

When the people are sick, are they looked after by the masters?—Yes; they send doctors, and go themselves to see them.

99. Two influential French prescriptions on roles for the older woman

Two widely read French moralists of the 1830's who wrote for and about women agreed that older women often undergo a devastating crisis and a loss of identity when their children grow up. In the first selection Louis Aimé-Martin (1786–1847), a history professor at the Ecole Polytechnique in Paris who wrote popular books on moral issues, advocates that women between forty-five and sixty try to find meaning in the role of grandmother and thereby sustain a firm bond with their daughters and their daughters' children. The author of the second selection, Albertine-Adrienne Necker de Saussure (1766–1841; Doc. 10.i), suggesting a less secular role for women over sixty, recommends a spiritual model of religious retreat for old women as they approach death. Necker was herself over sixty when she wrote these passages.

(i) Louis Aimé-Martin

A woman grows old; the homage of the world forsakes her; but she has children; she nurses, she educates, she basks in the warm rays of these young creatures, who are born to love her. Nevertheless, there is an hour marked out both by Nature and the Gospel, in which the child must leave its mother; the son to receive his wife, the daughter to receive her husband. The maternal nest is no longer large enough; the birds fly away, the brood is dispersed. Other rocks are wanting to the eagle, other shades to the dove, other

SOURCES: (i) Louis Aimé-Martin, *The Education of Mothers; or the civilization of mankind by women*, tr. Edwin Lee (Philadelphia, 1843), pp. 78–82. Originally published in Paris in 1834. (ii) Albertine-Adrienne Necker de Saussure, *The Study of the Life of Woman* (Philadelphia, 1844), pp. 264–67, 277–78, 281–82. Originally published in Paris in 1838.

loves to all. It is then that the poor mother, oppressed with feelings hitherto unknown, finds her task finished, perceives her own isolation, sees a blank in the future, and knows no longer how to employ life. Here indeed is a profound evil, though hitherto unnoticed by moralists!

This feeling, which devours her, and which has not a name; this feeling, which saddens her in beholding her daughters happy and in a happiness which springs not from herself, cannot be jealousy, cannot be selfishness, or even regret of the past; and yet we detect in it every appearance of them. The salons of Paris yet resound with the history of Madame de Bal . . . , a pious and charitable woman, resplendent in all the graces of second youth, who threw herself into a cloister to avoid witnessing the happiness of her two daughters, whose education she had carefully directed. "What!" said she, "strangers to supplant me in my daughters' affections! Twenty years of tenderness and devotion to be effaced by a few days of delirium! To be left thus alone, to be forgotten by my children, and to have my sufferings even held in derision! I dare not interrogate myself; my feelings affright me; they resemble envy. But can I be jealous of the affections of my daughters?" A sad question, but one which almost every mother might address to herself, at the fatal hour when a husband separates her from her daughter. Let us leave the unreflecting to accuse Nature of a monstrosity, the whole cause of which is to be found in our false system of education. We have pointed out the evil; we must now look for the remedy. The evil is in believing that the mission of the mother has terminated the moment that she is deprived by some stranger of the attentions of her daughters. For the remedy,—it consists in the discovery of the true mission of the grandmother, that is to say, in the discovery of all the joys which she can diffuse, of all the benefits which she can confer.

It is but too true that marriage weakens, at least in appearance, those sweet ties which unite the daughter to the mother. But how shall this be otherwise? Unhappy mothers! before you accuse Nature, have courage to ask yourselves what you have done to prepare for a revolution so complete in the existence of this feeble creature? Yesterday she was a timid child, living only in the affection of her mother; to-day she is a woman, who imparts happiness, and whose caprices are deified by love. The young girl obeyed, the young wife commands; and, in this rapid transition from innocence to pleasure, from submission to empire, you wonder that vanity, delirium of the senses, pride, and, more than these, love, have wrought their accustomed effects.

But this evil, which you deplore, and which it had been so easy to avert, is but a transient effervescence. The mother will soon recover her daughter; she will find her again, happy or unhappy, (no matter,) she will find her daughter again, to console, to enlighten, to love her. Consolations and love are the life of the maternal heart.

Thus then the mother, far from being transformed into an useless and passive being, after the marriage of her children, becomes the guardian angel of her new family. Careless of the charms which yet remain to herself, freed from domestic anxieties, having renounced the world and its frivolities, she finds herself again in the midst of her beloved ones, whom she enriches with the treasures of her experience. She alone understands attentive devotedness, kind foresights; she alone possesses that goodness which nothing exhausts, and that unfailing tact, which, taking its rise in love, can comprehend or divine all griefs. See her at her daughter's side on every approach of indisposition; how she foresees the accidents, how she guards against the uneasinesses, the disgusts, that threaten her! What tender confidings! What sweet ministrations! What cares, which she alone knows the exact moment to alleviate! At length come the first pains, which cause the young husband to fly, but which chain the mother more closely to the bed of her daughter. There is also another woman, who awaits the new-born and handles it with indifference; it is the nurse, who only acts in her vocation. But with what transport does the grandmother receive the innocent creature! how she broods over it with her looks, how she cherishes it with her love! Oh, she is doubly a mother; she has recovered both the emotions of her youth and the joys of maternity. There she is, all tenderness, bustle, and trepidation; she watches over the child's slumbers, comprehends its least cries, anticipates all its wants, and divines all its instincts. The young wife, exhausted and suffering, scarce dares, in her inexperience, to touch the fragile creature; but the grandmother, radiant with joy, raises it to the maternal bosom, and, having placed it at this source of life, brings back the distracted husband to the bed of suffering, and in the fulness of maternal feeling thus doubled, pours over these three beings the treasures of her benediction. Oh, then all pains are forgotten, and, as in the first days of the Creation, the family prospers and increases under the eye of the Almighty. Then come the physical cares, necessary alike to the health of the mother and to the life of the child; missions of prudence and devotedness, which demand a long experience aided by much love, and which a young wife can learn only from her mother. For instance, there is not a wife, who, at the cradle of her babe, does not give way to the most restless inquietude. The slightest accident throws her into a fever, the feeblest cry alarms her. Hearken to her; she is recounting sad stories, and, in the vivacity of her anguish, becomes exhausted without comfort to herself or good to the child. Not so with the grandmother; she is less alarmed, because she has more experience; and then she is acquainted with the symptoms, she has secrets of her own for alleviating them; then she is patient, she can wait; and it is a fact worthy of attention, that, in all the ills of infancy, Nature calls more for our patience than for our remedies. The best physician of infancy is patience. . . .

Such is the almost divine mission of the grandmother. It is to accomplish this mission, that God has endowed women in the decline of life, with so much courage and sensibility. In proportion to the wretchedness of her, who, forgetting her lost freshness of youth, and laden with finery, runs after the vain homage that flies her, is that woman's glory, who, though still beautiful, is seen surrounded by her children and grandchildren. Thus the woman between forty-five and sixty, instead of withering away in solitude, becomes the soul of a new society. Every young household claims her and makes a holiday of her presence, for wherever she turns her steps, moral power and tender consolations are in her train. It is thus that families, true to the laws of Nature, find, within themselves, their pleasures, their glory, their instruction and their support. All is linked together in the moral, as it is in the physical world; and the grandmother is not only the joy, but the light of childhood. It is through her that the daughters resemble their mother, and that the sons, in marrying, carry into the conjugal mansion the virtues which they have practised under the maternal roof. . . .

From all this two conclusions are to be drawn: the first, that women are not unhappy in growing old, except when they misunderstand their twofold mission of mother and grandmother; the second, that society, in the present day, shaken even to its foundations, can only be re-established by means of the family, and that the family itself cannot acquire true elevation except by the maternal influence.

(ii) Albertine-Adrienne Necker de Saussure

During the long interval which separates youth from old age, the decline of life may not have been much perceived. A woman who has retained her strength unimpaired, may only have observed the course of time by the gradual loss of her external advantages. But when she arrives at the age of sixty, she cannot help knowing that many alterations have taken place in her situation, and in her soul. Nothing around her is what it has been. The concerns of human life have been presented to her in a variety of aspects, and the changing scenes which she has witnessed have all produced some effect upon her. Impressions no doubt natural, directed, perhaps from above, by Him who orders all things, have caused in succeeding each other great modifications in her interior existence. She must at the same time judge what she has been, and what she has become, in order to guide herself with safety on the remaining portion of the route which remains for her to travel over. What has passed before her eyes with respect to this earth? One whole generation has been engulfed. She has seen fall around her, one by one, those ancient trees of the forest, by whose shade her youth was sheltered; now her head is uncovered, and independently of the bitter regrets that cruel and irreparable losses have excited, she experiences a sort of awe in finding herself in the first line face to face with death. . . .

Such is the effect of old age when the idea is presented in all its force to the woman who finds herself upon the threshold of that period of life. She soon acknowledges that the best lot, in this world, is that of mothers of families; and no doubt whatever happiness they derive from it comes from their children. Yet, how often it happens that a silent sadness weighs down that life of the heart so active in a mother! During mature life the part of a woman was still important; but the habit of consulting her diminishes in proportion as she advances towards old age. She is supposed ill informed in many respects. Care is taken to spare her anxiety by concealing what may happen in future. After having been the centre of interests she becomes, to those around her, only that of their cares and attentions. Her own sentiments remain unchanged; but she does not venture to manifest them as formerly. It is not without timidity that she exercises some influence. Her personal consideration must *now* be *evidently* supported by reason and morality. There is no possibility of acting by means of charm—by the vivacity of impressions; all must be weighed in a just balance; a system of delicate reserve is also necessary; and it becomes at last evident that grown-up children are only dearer friends—often more devoted to us than others—but whose rights it is equally necessary to respect. There has been an exchange of parts. *We* now depend upon *them*. In our old age they love us still, but we are no longer necessary to them. With them every thing may go on without us; and so it should be: but for us nothing can go on well without them. There remain the grandchildren—the delights of old age—cherished objects bestowed by Heaven to embellish our latter days; but we enjoy without possessing them. They do not belong to us; and if maternal love is here in all its tenderness, it has not the energetic and absorbing sentiment of responsibility. No doubt it is still a blessing to have them to love; and although our affection is trammelled in many ways by the absence of authority, although we often sigh to find ourselves almost useless to them, there is sometimes established between them and us a true intimacy, and the two generations are mingled together in our hearts. Then, when there arises a third generation, when new and charming little beings have for us an irresistible attraction, the pleasure with which we contemplate them is mingled with much sadness. We shall not witness their future life, their pleasures are strangers to ours; they seem to move in a world that we have left, and (except the chance of a sympathy which is very rare) there seems to be a transparent glass between them and us. We see, then, that a woman who has arrived at the entrance of old age, discovers very soon that all the ties of this life— altered by time—have still the power to make us suffer, but not that of making us happy; and that they would leave us a prey to deep melancholy, if we were unable to take a more elevated view of the whole of life. We must die: such is the solution of all things. We must die to the world, and live in eternity. And with what careful arrangement (at least in the circumstances I have described) this life and this death have been blended! Both begin and grow insensibly. Already we have seen them in presence of each other in our earlier days. At twenty we no longer experienced the joys of childhood; at forty the emotions of twenty had passed by; but sentiments ever new, and unknown hopes were constantly arising within us. It is thus that withered leaves and flowers fall from the tree in the spring, but new germs are constantly unfolding: a principle of dissolution and a renovating principle constantly show themselves in us. For the body, it is death that triumphs: for the soul, life asserts supremacy.

The work of God that we are now called to second, consists in freeing our immortal soul from the narrow ties that held it captive here. This work cannot be accomplished without tearing; but if through inevitable regrets, the soul acknowledges that the rupture of each tie advances her deliverance, she gains vigour. When detached from many interests we find it more easy to rise towards God. . . .

Here, as elsewhere, men are seen to rise in old age to a height that women rarely attain. But women are, perhaps, in general, less subject to decay of mind. The really great evils of advanced age, the drying up of the heart, and the usurpations of physical instincts, do not readily reach them, at least in the affluent class. Too dependent not to be always occupied about others, they preserve the affections of the heart; accustomed to small evils, they bear greater ones with more patience; and ignoble tastes having been early subdued, rarely acquire power over them. A course of life in general pure, a separation from business, and, therefore, from intercourse with corrupt people, preserve them from that contempt for the human species, which sometimes lays waste the best hearts, and paralyses their good impulses.

So there is little moral numbness in women, and if their minds sometimes appear to become narrow, this is the effect of a continuity of monotonous pursuits which have limited the sphere of its action. The instrument has rusted for want of use, but is not worn out. So, also, they rather retain their old defects than contract new ones. A frivolity and a vanity, often ridiculous, give them absurd pretensions, and a constant desire to produce effect. But this is life out of place rather than death; since the necessity of the approbation of others is always a bond of union with them. Preserving to the last, some of the interests of youth, they are still susceptible of enjoyments that most men no longer experience. But if, thanks to their flexible organization, their portion in old age is better than that of men, should they not regard with a profound compassion the fate of beings who have been so long their superiors, and consecrate their remaining strength to those to whom providence has allied them? Is it not now their destination to alleviate evils to which men are unaccustomed, to soothe their pride, which spurns the idea of dependence, to soften by dint of affection, hearts which might become dry and hard? Ah! let us do them justice, they do this with a zeal, a devotedness which are admirable, that even coldness does not weary; with a care so delicate and tender that they reanimate the soul while seeking only to soothe the evils inseparable from old age. . . .

What remains for the aged woman but to take a tender interest in what surrounds her, to be a benevolent spectator and nothing more?

As to herself, it would not suit her to exercise active influence. Too much responsibility would be attached to the measures that she might recommend. Her right, and her duty, especially if she is a mother, is to pronounce her opinion against the slightest wrong. But with regard to social arrangements she would do well to be on the reserve. Too prone to be severe with respect to interests that she no longer feels, or disposed to extreme indulgence when she wishes to make herself agreeable, she is not in a position to see correctly. Objects of comparison are wanting to enable her to judge of what has nothing absolute in itself. Besides, who knows whether the contradiction that her advice would meet with, might not excite in her feelings of displeasure—

and whether self-love, which never dies, would not be awakened in her bosom? We rarely disturb embers nearly extinguished without seeing the little coals light up again.

Constant religious duties, the exact order that at every age, a woman should observe in her own affairs, some needle-work, some attention to the preservation of her faculties, which would enable her, if an occasion should arise, to be of use to others, or at least, to avoid being troublesome, would fully employ her time, and preserve to her, a degree of independence. Let her beware of a restless activity, of that disposition to meddle with every thing which renders the best intentions liable to the imputation of a desire to play a part, to the last. Nothing is so injurious to respectability, and to the state of the soul.

The element of old age should be a calm which arises from the absence of selfishness, and from internal amelioration. While enjoying that repose, one is still useful without thinking of being so, an example is given, an influence operates, the thoughts which are expressed have their weight, and good sentiments are diffused. When a perfect harmony has long reigned between a mother and those around her, her last days are full of sweetness. Satisfied that all the intentions of her connexions are right, their conduct proper and judicious, she takes delight in seeing the machinery that she has wound up, go on of its own accord, without the necessity of touching it.

It sometimes seems to her that her soul has already passed the boundaries of earth, and that she contemplates all things from on high.

100. George Sand cheerfully faces old age

Not all older women accepted the prescriptive models offered them by moralists. One of the most vigorous, unconventional women in the nineteenth century, the French writer George Sand (1804–76; Docs. 26.i, 60), evinced in old age the same vitality and exuberance that had characterized her earlier years. In the following excerpts from the correspondence between Sand and her close friend, the novelist Gustave Flaubert (who was seventeen years her junior), Sand's letters exude optimism, a love of life, and joy in her grandchildren, whereas Flaubert's reveal him as old, worn out, and irritated with everyone and everything. Unlike Flaubert, Sand embraced life, as well as literature, and extracted from both a wisdom for old age.

[Sand to Flaubert, July 5, 1872, Nohant]
I must write to you today. Sixty-eight years old. Perfect health in spite of the cough, which lets me sleep now that I am plunging daily in a furious little torrent, cold as ice. It boils around the stones, the flowers, the great grasses in a delicious shade. It is an ideal place to bathe.

We have had some terrible storms: lightning struck in our garden; and

SOURCE: *The George Sand–Gustave Flaubert Letters*, tr. Aimée L. McKenzie (New York, 1921), pp. 255–338 *passim.*

our stream, the *Indre*, has become like a torrent in the Pyrenees. It is not unpleasant. What a fine summer! The grain is seven feet high, the wheat fields are sheets of flowers. The peasant thinks that there are too many; but I let him talk, it is so lovely! I go on foot to the stream, I jump, all boiling hot, into the icy water. The doctor says that is madness. I let him talk, too; I am curing myself while his patients look after themselves and croak. I am like the grass of the fields: water and sun, that is all I need. . . .

The other day we discovered, about three leagues from here, a wilderness, an absolute wilderness of woods in a great expanse of country, where not one hut could be seen, not a human being, not a sheep, not a fowl, nothing but flowers, butterflies and birds all day.

[Flaubert to Sand, July 12, 1872, Bagnères de Luchon]
I have been here since Sunday evening, dear master, and am no happier than at Croisset, even a little less so, for I am very idle. They make so much noise in the house where we are, that it is impossible to work. Moreover, the sight of the bourgeois who surround us is unendurable. I am not made for travelling. The least inconvenience disturbs me. Your old troubadour is very old, decidedly! Doctor Lambron, the physician of this place, attributes my nervous tendencies to the excessive use of tobacco. To be agreeable I am going to smoke less; but I doubt very much if my virtue will cure me! . . .

This letter is stupid. But they are making such a noise over my head that it is not clear (my head).

In the midst of my bewilderment, I embrace you and yours also. Your old blockhead who loves you.

[Sand to Flaubert, Aug. 31, 1872, Nohant]
My old troubadour, here we are back again at home, after a month passed, just as you said, at Cabourg, where chance more than intention placed us. We all took wonderful sea baths. . . . We have returned in splendid health, and we are glad to see our old Nohant again, after having been glad to leave it for a little change of air.

I have resumed my usual work, and I continue my river baths, but no one will accompany me, it is too cold. As for me, I found fault with the sea for being too warm. Who would think that, with my appearance and tranquil old age, I would still love *excess*? My dominant passion on the whole is my [granddaughter] Aurore. My life depends on hers. She was so lovely on the trip, so gay, so appreciative of the amusements that we gave her, so attentive to what she saw, and curious about everything with so much intelligence, that she is real and sympathetic company at every hour. Ah! how *unliterary* I am! Scorn me, but still love me.

I don't know if I shall find you in Paris when I go there for my play. I have not arranged with the Odéon for the date of its performance.

[Sand to Flaubert, March 15, 1873, Nohant]
Well, my old troubadour, we can hope for you very soon, I was worried about you. I am always worried about you. To tell the truth, I am not happy

over your ill tempers, and your *prejudices*. They last too long, and in effect they are like an illness, you recognize it yourself. Now, forget; don't you know how to forget? You live too much in yourself and you get to consider everything in relation to yourself. If you were an egoist, and a conceited person, I would say that it was a normal condition; but with you who are so good and so generous it is an anomaly, an evil that must be combated. Rest assured that life is badly arranged, painful, irritating for everyone; but do not neglect the immense compensations which it is ungrateful to forget.

That you get angry with this or that person, is of little importance if it is a comfort to you; but that you remain furious, indignant for weeks, months, almost years, is unjust and cruel to those who love you, and who would like to spare you all anxiety and all deception.

You see that I am scolding you; but while embracing you, I shall think only of the joy and the hope of seeing you flourishing again. We are waiting for you with impatience, and we are counting on Tourgueneff* whom we adore also.

I have been suffering a good deal lately with a series of very painful hemorrhages; but they have not prevented me from amusing myself writing tales and from playing with my *little children*. They are so dear, and my big children are so good to me, that I shall die, I believe, smiling at them. What difference does it make whether one has a hundred thousand enemies if one is loved by two or three good souls? Don't you love me too, and wouldn't you reproach me for thinking that of no account? When I lost Rollinat,† didn't you write to me to love the more those who were left? Come, so that I may *overwhelm* you with reproaches; for you are not doing what you told me to do.

We are expecting you, we are preparing a mid-Lent fantasy; try to take part. Laughter is a splendid medicine. We shall give you a costume; they tell me that you were very good as a pastry cook at Pauline's!‡ If you are better, be certain it is because you have gotten out of your rut and have distracted yourself a little. Paris is good for you, you are too much alone yonder in your lovely house. Come and work, at our house; how perfectly easy to send on a box of books!

Send word when you are coming so that I can have a carriage at the station at Chateauroux.

[Sand to Flaubert, Nov. 6, 1874, Nohant. Sand has just turned seventy.]
I was in Paris from the 30th of May to the 10th of June, you were not there. Since my return here, I have been ill with the grippe, rheumatic, and often absolutely deprived of the use of my right arm. I have not the courage to stay in bed: I spend the evening with my children and I forget my little miseries which will pass; everything passes. That is why I was not able to write to you, even to thank you for the good letter which you wrote to me

* The Russian novelist Ivan Turgenev.—EDS.
† François Rollinat, an attorney and lifelong friend of Sand's.—EDS.
‡ Pauline Viardot, a famous singer.—EDS.

about my novel. In Paris I was overwhelmed by fatigue. That is the way I am growing old, and now I am beginning to feel it; I am not more often ill, but now, illness *prostrates* me more. That is nothing, I have not the right to complain, being well loved and well cared for in my nest. I urge [my son] Maurice to go about without me, since my strength is not equal to going with him.

[Sand to Flaubert, Dec. 8, 1874, Nohant]

Poor dear friend, I love you all the more because you are growing more unhappy. How you torment yourself, and how you disturb yourself about life! for all of which you complain, is life; it has never been better for anyone or in any time. One feels it more or less, one understands it more or less, one suffers with it more or less, and the more one is in advance of the age one lives in, the more one suffers. We pass like shadows on a background of clouds which the sun seldom pierces, and we cry ceaselessly for the sun which can do no more for us. It is for us to clear away our clouds.

You love literature too much; it will destroy you and you will not destroy the imbecility of the human race. Poor dear imbecility, that, for my part, I do not hate, that I regard with maternal eyes: for it is a childhood and all childhood is sacred. What hatred you have devoted to it! what warfare you wage on it!

You have too much knowledge and intelligence, you forget that there is something above art: namely, wisdom, of which art at its apogee is only the expression. Wisdom comprehends all: beauty, truth, goodness, enthusiasm, in consequence. It teaches us to see outside of ourselves, something more elevated than is in ourselves, and to assimilate it little by little, through contemplation and admiration.

But I shall not succeed in changing you. I shall not even succeed in making you understand how I envisage and how I lay hold upon *happiness*, that is to say, the acceptation of life whatever it may be! There is one person who could change you and save you, that is father Hugo;* for he has one side on which he is a great philosopher, while at the same time he is the great artist that you require and that I am not. You must see him often. I believe that he will quiet you: I have not enough tempest in me now for you to understand me. As for him, I think that he has kept his thunderbolts and that he has all the same acquired the gentleness and the compassion of age.

See him, see him often and tell him your troubles, which are great, I see that, and which turn too much to *spleen*. You think too much of the dead, you think that they have too soon reached their rest. They have not. They are like us, they are searching. They labor in the search.

Every one is well, and embraces you. As for me, I do not get well, but I have hopes, well or not, to keep on still so as to bring up my grandchildren, and to love you as long as I have a breath left.

[Sand to Flaubert, May 7, 1875, Nohant]

You leave me without news of you? You say that you prefer to be forgot-

* The novelist Victor Hugo, who was two years older than Sand.—EDS.

ten, rather than to complain ceaselessly, as it is very useless and since you will not be forgotten; complain then, but tell us that you are alive and that you still love us. . . .

We are all well here. I am better since it is not cold any more, and I am working a great deal. I am also doing many water colors, I am reading the *Iliad* with Aurore, who does not like any translation except Leconte de Lisle's, insisting that Homer is spoiled by approximate renderings.

The child is a singular mixture of precocity and childishness. She is nine years old and so large that one would think her twelve. She plays dolls with passion, and she is as *literary* as you or I, meanwhile learning her own language which she does not yet know.

Are you still in Paris in this lovely weather? Nohant is now *streaming* with flowers, from the tips of the trees to the turf; Croisset must be even prettier, for it is cool, and we are struggling with a drought that has now become chronic in Berry. But if you are still in Paris, you have that beautiful Parc Monceau under your eyes where you are walking, I hope, since you have to. Life is at the price of walking!

Won't you come to see us? Whether you are sad or gay, we love you the same here, and we wish that affection meant something to you, but we shall give it to you, and we give it to you without conditions.

I am thinking of going to Paris next month, shall you be there?

[Flaubert to Sand, May 10, 1875, Croisset]
A wandering gout, pains that go all over me, an invincible melancholy, the feeling of "universal uselessness" and grave doubts about the book that I am writing, that is what is the matter with me, dear and valiant master. Add to that worries about money with melancholic recollections of the past, that is my condition, and I assure you that I make great efforts to get out of it. But my will is tired. I cannot decide about anything effective! Ah! I have eaten my white bread first, and old age is not announcing itself under gay colors. Since I have begun hydrotherapy, however, I feel a little less like a *cow*, and this evening I am going to begin work without looking behind me. . . . It is true that I am endowed with an absurd sensitiveness; what scratches others tears me to pieces. Why am I not organized for enjoyment as I am for suffering!

The bit you sent me about *Aurore* who is reading Homer, did me good. That is what I miss: a little girl like that! But one does not arrange one's own destiny, one submits to it. I have always lived from day to day, without plans for the future and pursuing my end (one alone, literature) without looking to the right or to the left. Everything that was around me has disappeared, and now I find I am in a desert. In short, the element of distraction is absolutely lacking in me. One needs a certain vivacity to write good things! What can one do to get it again? How can one proceed, to avoid thinking continually about one's miserable person? The sickest thing in me is my humor: the rest doubtless would go well. You see, dear, good master, that I am right to spare you my letters. Nothing is as imbecile as the whiners.

101. The cares of two California women

Prescriptive literature may have emphasized the tranquility and contentment that women should aspire to as they grew old, but the journals of older women reveal that old age rarely brought release from cares and anxieties. The writings of the California pioneer Susannah Hyde Braly (1805–97), wife of a Presbyterian minister and mother of seven, express her deep concern for her children and her unhappiness at separating from them. In the following diary entries, written when she was sixty-four and living at Lawrence Station, near San Jose, Braly laments the departure of her son James for distant Oregon and seeks solace in religion for her distress. Like Braly, Eleanor Brittain (1834–1907; Doc. 62.ii) found that old age guaranteed neither peace of mind nor a life of ease. A widow with three daughters to care for, Brittain married Charles Knowlton, a house painter, and in 1876, at the age of forty-two, gave birth to a fourth daughter, Olive. She separated from her husband, a wastrel and drunkard, in 1882, and for the next eleven years worked at a variety of trades to support herself and her youngest daughter. These excerpts from her journal, written between 1883 and 1893, depict her efforts to make a living, and show with what courage and good humor an older woman could face economic uncertainty.

(i) Susannah Hyde Braly

Jan. 12.—Rained last night—clear this morning all at work—James and family has just started for the cars—bin with us a few days—Oh how things change, only a few years ago and my little children was happy around us— and so is life—and so it will be till we leave this world.

Jan. 18.—Clear—We are all well today. What few there is of us to gather now—from a large family down to one chile—and that is Eusebius— what changes in a few years. Nothing of note today Pa went to Mountain View—Sebe [Eusebius] to school. Soald some dryed apples today.

Jan. 19.—Clear and very cold—everything is mooving on smoothly on the farm—how pleasant it is when we are well and ought to be happy but Pa and I both feeld oald age creeping on us. I am so stiff I find I cannot moove as I use to—Lord grant that we ma be fully ripe for a neather world— and our family with us.

Jan. 20.—Clear and cold no change in bisness. All at work the crop is going in nicely So Pa sais—we are all well—as people of our age is generally I reckon. I do hope we may live to some good purpes while we do live.

Jan. 22.—A little cloudy. I have bin very bissy to day—they killed hogs

SOURCES: (i) Susannah Hyde Braly Diaries, 1867–96, MS 210, The Manuscript Collection of the California Historical Society Library, San Francisco. (ii) Journal of Eleanor Fitzgerald Brittain Knowlton, VMS 128, The Manuscript Collection of the California Historical Society Library, San Francisco. (As in the earlier Brittain document, we have added periods and capital letters here and there in the entries as an aid to the reader.) The editors are grateful to Karl Feichtmeir for guiding us to this journal, and to the California Historical Society for permission to quote from both these sources.

yesterday—and this morning I have rendered out the lard, and to day I have made a kettle of soap—I feeld thankfull that we are all well anuff to attend to our bissness—may the good Lord grant us health while we live—and bring us to heaven at last.

Feb. 12—After sutch a terable storm we have a pretty morning—Pa got home yesterday evening—grate dammage done by the rain—Pa bring me word that our Dear James is going to Oregon and take his family—I felt so bad about it I could not sleep—none but a mother nows how it feels to give up a dear child.

Feb. 15.—The sun is just rizing it look very beautifull—Monday morning is always a buisy time—Sebe is leaving for school—Pa is going to town. . . . James and family is comming today—oh how sad I feeld over it James has become resless and thinks of going to Oregon I hope the Lord may direct other wise.

Feb. 16.—Clear and pleasant—James and family is here. I have had no talk with James as yet about the moove to Oregon—I wish to have a good long talk with him pretty soon I do hope he may give it out yet—I have just got back from M Sutherlands—they are quite sick there.

Feb. 17.—Clear and pleasant—nothing of interest today whatever—all—for whitc I try to feeld thankfull. I often wish I had somthing of interest to record—if it was something good—I find that James is in my mind all the time now I do hope he will stay in this cuntry yet.

Feb. 18.—Very heavy fog this morning—we are all as well as common—for witch I feeld very thankfull. . . . James and family is here—the littlefolks makes the house reather merry—I love so mutch to have them here.

Feb. 24.—The weather continues very fine—last evening my Dear Sucky got home once more*—but they are going away this evening—we expect several of our children to dine with us to day—we have prepared a fine turkey—Sarah Ann is here and her too little girls—Lizzie and George—James went to town—His family was here.

Feb. 25.—This is a beautiful day—and I am pretty mutch alone and I feeld all cast down it seems to be pretty certin that James and family is going to leave soon for Oregon—not likely that I will see them again soon if ever—I ask for grace—to bear up—and then again I bid Sucky good by last evening—may the Lord help poor me.

Feb. 26.—Clear and pleasant—I wish my mind was so—but I acnoledge it is fare from it—for reasons I cannot explain—I do most earnestly ask my kind heavenly Father for grase sufficient to meet all my trials—and further I ask him to accept of my dear children—as they are scattering over this coald heirted world.

Feb. 27.—The weather is very pleasant—but my troubles increas—I do feeld so cast down—nothing but light from above can brake this gloom—This morning I bid farewell to my Dear James that has bin so dear to me all his childhood and manhood life—but he is gone—may God go with him—Pa and Sebe went to the city.

* Sucky and the others named here were her children.—EDS.

March 8.—Thick clouds or fog I scarsely no what to write this morning I find I cannot or do not controle my mind I find it is almost continnealy runing after my children by day and by night a sleep or a wake—I dream of them—I awake and feeld so lonely I scarsly no what to do—I then look up and ask the Lord to have pity on me—even me.

March 17.—I have been cleaning out my old book case—I come across menny oald realicks that brings to mind former days and oh how sad—I find every one of the childrens names in books—God only knows how I doo feeld.

March 18.—The sun is shining this morning the wind is still south more rain I reckon—I had a dream last night—meeting James and his family—as I was kissing them I awoke oh how lonely I felt—and do yet—how we do cling to our dear ones—I ask the question dose our kind heavenly Father remember us as we do our dear children—I hope he dose—I cast myself on him.

March 20.—My mind has been very occupied all night . . . as I grow older I sleep less—and my mind runs back to my childhood and home and then my travels—and my Dear Parents—and then my marriage relation and then my children.

March 23.—I am very anxious to get a letter from James—I think of him almost constantly—perhaps moore than I ought to. I reckon I will get more reckensiled by and by.

March 26.—Some appearance of rain—I scarsly no what to say today— by no means well—and then I feeld so lonely when I compear the preasant with the past—all alone here today—not a soul on the place save my self— I wonder if all oald people feeld just as I do—I often find myself looking at the oald with sorrow—and the young with pity.

(ii) Eleanor Brittain Knowlton

1883, Lakeport. I am now at the Mound Cottage Hotel. Mr. Wells is a friend of mine and said I could stop there untill I got my house repared and it would not cost me anything. 15th of April I went to help a lady for a little while one day. She gave me one dollar. The first of May I commenced to repare my house and worked every day I could at one dollar and helf a day untill the 21st of June. I went to take care of a lady in confinement. I got a good price and Olive's board. Staid untill the 25th of July. Came home on the 26th. Now my house is newly repared and Furnished and tonight the 29th all paid for. The 1st of August we are going to Cloverdale to see Mrs. McConithy. She has written to me to come that she would pay me 35 dollars amonth and Olives board.

1883–84, Lakeport.—I may get two or three boarders for company but I wont go from home any more. It is Dec the first. I have two young men to board and room for the winter Mr. Labor and Mr. Stockton. They seem at home and pleased. Mr. Labor is a Bankers son from Wis. Stocton is going to school. It is now Christmas and they have given us presents. I got an extry good dinner for them. Well another New Year is near at hand. I hope I will have as good luck as I have this year. It is New Yearsday 1884 and I shall continue to stay home and keep boarders. I only want enough to buy food and cloths.

1887, Lakeport.—My health is still poor. I have had Dr. Downs and White both to see me and they both advise me to make a change of climate and rest. That I was passing through a change of life which is common for all women.

1888–93, San Jose.—This is now Christmas, and we are in our home and quite comfortable. I have had a chance to make a few dollars this winter. Enough to buy wood and provisions with out using what I had on hands.

This is now new years day 1889. I am now going to content my self untill spring. In the meantime I will quilt some quilts and do some sewing which I will need if I get something to do during The summer. And I am going to have my house lined and papered new also painted and a well bored. It is now summer. My house is all done well bored and I am going to work in the fruit at Bowman's caniry as a day hand for a dollar a day through the fruit season and when the fruit season is over I will follow nursing and confine women. I had one case while I was working for Bowman's but I was allowed to put another woman in my place untill I could come back. My patient was Mr. Anberry's wife. Some of the Doctors found out that I had confined her and was nursing her and told Anberry to tell me to come to Dr. Cusnow's office they wanted to see me. I went and as I had no business with any of the Doctors and was in a hurry to get back to My patient I finaly said Gentlemen I understand you wanted to see me. If so I would like you to make your business known as I am in a hurry. Dr. Cusnow said yes we have learned Anberry had a baby a few days ago. I said no Indeed he did not. But his wife gave birth to a fine Boy and I attended her and the mother and baby are both doing well. They then said did you know you were laying your self liable to a fine. I told them I had not given a thought concerning the matter, that I had followed that business in other towns in this state and had never been stoped. But Gentlemen I am a widow woman have one little girl to support and I feel I am competent to do what I have done but if you say quit I will do so as I don't wish to do anything unlawful. They said no they did not wish to stop me gave me a book to put the birth and names of the baby's to fill out and said at anytime I had a difficult case any one of the board would come If I would send for them. I thanked them and went back to Mr. Anberrys. This is the year 1889 and I followed nursing and working in the fruit between times until my health give way and I was compelled to take a rest. I have followed the same business untill the year 1893.

102. Quarreling with Grandma: Old women live with their children

The presence of three generations within a single, often cramped household did not always create the tender scenes of familial harmony envisioned

SOURCES: (i) M. P. A. Toussaint, "Bordier-Vigneron de l'Aunis (France)," in Frédéric Le Play, *Les Ouvriers européens*, 6: *Les Ouvriers de l'occident, popula-*

by Louis Aimé-Martin (Doc. 99.i), as these two selections reveal. The first describes the household of a vineyard worker in an Atlantic coastal village near La Rochelle, investigated in the late 1850's for Frédéric Le Play's study of European workers (Docs. 67, 75). The household had four members: the worker, who was fifty-eight, and his fifty-year-old wife, their thirteen-year-old son, and the wife's mother, aged seventy, who had given her house, barns, gardens, and vineyard to the couple when they married fifteen years earlier. For this act of generosity, the old woman was rewarded with a tiny grain shed over the kitchen to sleep in while her daughter and son-in-law occupied her former bedroom; she was provided only with wretched and tattered clothing, and was handled roughly when her son-in-law came home drunk. In the meantime, the old woman had to work all the day through, tending the cow, harvesting snails, and doing housework. Because of just such histories, many French peasant proverbs warned against relinquishing property to one's children.

The second selection is excerpted from a letter written in 1906 to "Aunt Jennie," an advice columnist in an American agricultural magazine, 'Progressive Farmer.' In it, Nellie Taylor, a North Carolina farmer's wife about whom little is known, bewails her difficult domestic situation. Married to a man twenty-one years her senior (who, as she notes, never left home), she lives on his parents' farm with him and his now feeble father and stepmother, aged eighty-five and seventy-nine, respectively. Nellie's problem is her stepmother-in-law, who is jealous of the children by her husband's first marriage and resents giving up her control of her household and farm to her stepson and to Nellie, his wife, whom she criticizes incessantly.

(i) Anne P—

Civil Status of the Family

The family consists of four persons, as follows:

1. Antoine F—, head of the family, married for the second time 15 years ago, 58 years old
2. Marie P—, his wife, 50 —
3. Etienne F—, their only son, 13—
4. Anne P—, the wife's mother, 70 —

Religion and Moral Habits

The worker gets drunk frequently; he beats his wife and mistreats his mother-in-law. Moreover, the married couple have no respect for the old woman; often they even deny her the right to speak. . . .

---

tions désorganisées, 2d ed. (Tours and Paris, 1878), pp. 143–73 passim. (ii) Letter from Ellen (Nellie) Taylor of Magnolia, N.C., to "My Dear Aunt Jennie," April 23, 1906, Leonidas Lafayette Polk Papers, Southern Historical Collection, Library of the University of North Carolina, Chapel Hill. The editors wish to thank the SHC for permission to publish this letter.

The Family's Rank

The worker belongs to the category of worker-landowners; as a matter of fact, he owns a house with a garden and a vineyard. But he is not very attached to this property, which he did not acquire by saving and which came to the couple from his widowed mother-in-law. . . .

The owner of the vineyard who employs him believes the worker to be one of the best vinedressers in the neighborhood. . . . His wife devotes herself to tending a milk cow that she rents; its care absorbs a good part of her and her mother's time; as a consequence the housework is badly neglected. . . .

Property

Real estate: representing the personal property of the worker's mother-in-law, which she relinquished to the married couple when she came to live with them, 2,100 francs

1. Living quarters.—house, consisting of a ground floor and a first floor, 800f;—stable attached to the house, 140f;—pigsty, 60f. Total, 1,000f.

2. Rural property.—garden of 3 ares, 100f;—vineyard of 32 ares, 1,000f. —Total, 1,100f.

Tasks and Activities

. . . *Work of the wife*. The wife's principal work is managing the cow. She gathers a part of the grass to feed it; she milks it and takes the milk to town to sell. Besides this, she busies herself with the housework and the preparation of food. As secondary tasks, she raises a pig whose products will be used by the family. She makes bread; bleaches and maintains the linens and clothing for the family; gathers shellfish at the seashore; cultivates the small garden; and even helps her husband in the vineyard that belongs to the family.

Work of the wife's mother. The wife's mother goes once or twice a day, depending on the season, to graze the cow on the commons and to gather fresh grass. She also works at harvesting snails in the vineyard. Finally, she helps her daughter with all the household tasks. . . .

Housing, Furniture, and Clothing

. . . In the first room is a wooden staircase that leads to an upper room where the couple's bed is installed. Above the kitchen is a little room that serves as a granary and where the wife's mother sleeps. These two rooms, the first 2 meters high, the second only 1.80 meters [roughly 6.5 and 5.9 feet, respectively], are both lit by a casement window. The house is not kept properly; the walls are rarely whitewashed. . . .

Clothing of the wife (53f 75)

1. Sunday clothing.—1 cotton camisole, 3f;—1 skirt of drugget, 7f;—2 underslips in coarse drugget, 10f—1 cotton apron, 2f;—1 *corselette*, 3f;—1 scarf of colored cotton, 1f;—2 pair of wool stockings, 3f;—2 pair of cotton

stockings, 2f;—1 piqué bonnet lined with mousseline, 3f 50;—6 cotton pocket handkerchiefs, 2f;—1 pair of shoes, 3f.—Total, 39f 50.

2. Work clothing.—Old Sunday clothing (for a keepsake), 0;—1 cotton camisole, 1f;—1 skirt of drugget, 1f 50;—1 gray cloth apron, 1f;—2 cotton headdresses, 1f;—1 pair clogs decorated with nails, of 75;—6 linen blouses, half worn out, 9f.—Total 14f 25. . . .

Clothing of the wife's mother: all very old and nearly worn out (2of 45).

2 camisoles, 3f;—2 skirts of drugget, 3f;—1 old cloak of coarse wool cloth, 5f;—1 gray cloth apron, 1f 20;—2 pair of woolen stockings, 1f 50;— 1 pair of clogs, 50c;—3 blouses, 4f 50;—1 headdress of cotton and linen for summer, 75c;—1 headdress of wool for winter, 1f.—Total, 2of 45.

History of the Family

. . . The worker remained a widower for a number of years, then he married the domestic servant of the landowner for whom he worked. This woman, born to a family of small vinegrowers, had shown herself since childhood to be grossly materialistic. When she was about fifteen, she found a place as a domestic in La Rochelle. In this position she acquired new tastes and inclinations that verged on the immoral; then, not liking her situation with her masters, she accepted the proposals of marriage made to her by Antoine F—. She was not unaware of the bad background of the man she was marrying; but she hoped to have enough influence over him to reform him. Unfortunately she did not succeed. . . . The quarrels began and blows followed. Since then, the two spouses never cease their reciprocal mistreatment; it has become a habit with them.

The estate of the worker's father consisted of a house and two small fields. The worker sold this property before his second marriage for 600 francs, which he spent on debaucheries as soon as he received it. . . . The wife's mother owned a house, a garden, and a vineyard; she turned the property over to her daughter at the time of her marriage to the worker, and came to live with the newlyweds. Since then the couple have saved nothing that would permit them to add to this property. Moreover, their pretensions do not go that far; they don't think of bettering their lot; and they live from day to day.

(ii) Nellie Taylor

Well Aunt Jennie you trusted me with your troubles and I must trust you with mine. As every sweet have a drop of bitter. My husband is twenty one years older than myself. He is one of the best men in his family I ever saw. If he has ever felt worried with me in the eight years we have been married I have never known it. And he is so ready and willing to help me about the house. His mother died when he was a child. She left two boys and one girl. Soon after the war ended father married a second wife, she was a widow with one child. The children were all taken home together. In a few years there were three more, one boy and two girls. One of the girls died at six, and the other lived to get grown, and died. That left her one son, *and her daughter* who soon married. Willie their youngest left home before he was free, and the other two of the first wifes children married, so that left Mord *my husband* the only one left at home. He has staid right here all this *long long* time and worked for them. And hasent had a single thing only what he lived on. And for several years they have been dependent for they are both old and feeble. We do all in our power to make them comfortable. We are nothing but common poor farmers but we live comfortable and happy except one thing and that is *this and the secret* I am *trusting you with*. She cant be *suited* with any thing on earth. Father told me not long ago that he had been living with her now forty years. And he had never been able to do the first thing that was right. She will be seventy nine next month, and you know she cant do much. I do every thing I can for her. And has for eight years. And I have never done any thing to please her yet. Since she has not been able to take the responsibility of the house and its surroundings, I am just compelled to take charge myself. Father has given up every thing to us to manage as we see best, and has told *me to go* ahead and pay no attention to what she says. But you know that is hard to do, still I do my best. And the poor old creature cant even appreciate my hard endevers to work for and take care of her. And very often tells me how offensive it is for me to come in and take possession of her house. She is a constant reader of the Bible and professes to be a great christion and any one who does not know would think she is the best woman on earth. But oh, my they don't know. She does not love the first children and therefore she doesnt love me. I think where the big trouble lie is this. She is afraid her son will not get every thing and the older ones will get something she wants him to have. Aunt Jennie Please dont let any one see this or they may think I am *curious* as the children say for writing such to a stranger but you do not feel like a stranger to me, altho I have never seen you.

103. The economic realities of old age in England

By the end of the century the plight of the aged poor had become a public issue in England: in the early 1890's a Royal Commission investigated pauperism among the aged, and two private citizens, Charles Booth and Geoffrey Drage, published separate accounts of cases they had found, together with plans to improve the condition of those who were both poor and old. Although neither Booth nor Drage directed his research specifically toward women, their studies contain valuable statistical data and many descriptions of Englishwomen whose last years were spent in extreme poverty.

Charles Booth (1840–1916), shipowner and author of the monumental social study 'Life and Labour of the People in London,' publicly advocated the introduction of old age pensions in 1891, and his help in converting

SOURCES: (i) Charles Booth, *Pauperism and the Endowment of Old Age* (London, 1892), pp. 39, 57–58, 67, 69, 78–79. (ii) Geoffrey Drage, *The Problem of the Aged Poor* (London, 1895), pp. 40–42.

public opinion to this cause was invaluable in securing the passage of the Old Age Pensions Act in 1908. In the first selection, taken from his study of pauperism, Booth presents case studies of poor old women in the Stepney district of London who were forced to seek public relief at the parish workhouse at Bromley. In the second selection Geoffrey Drage (1866–1955), a civil servant whose book was published some three years after Booth's pioneering work, describes the fate in store for working women in Coventry and Birmingham when they become too old to continue their labors.

(i) The Stepney paupers

Mrs. Bennett is a widow and blind and 73 years old. While her husband lived she and he hawked bathbricks and hearthstone, and earned about 6s. a week. In December 1884 she asked for medicine for her husband, and the doctor's order was renewed in January 1885. In February he grew worse, and when visited was found very ill in a small and dirty ill-smelling room with bed on floor. He died before he could be moved to the sick asylum. In May the widow asked for admission to the house. She looked ill, dirty, and miserable. She was admitted at Bromley.

Eliza English is a widow, now 83, whose husband (a stone mason) died 16 years before her application for relief. He was in no club, and had made no provision for her. She supported herself by charing until she was struck with paralysis. She stated that since then for 4 years she had lived with a daughter, and helped her at tailoring. She had no furniture of her own. It had been disposed of when she and her husband had both been in hospital 16 years before. No order appears to have been made. After an interval of 7 years she again applied, stating that her son had helped her, but insufficiently, and could do so no longer. Her daughter was unkind, a terrible drunkard, pawning her children's clothes for drink. The daughter said that her mother was troublesome and drank. The relieving officer found the house very dirty. The woman was admitted to Bromley.

Jane Neville, age 73, is a widow. Her husband was a tidesman, and applied in 1877 for medical relief for his wife, who was ill. In 1880 he himself had medical attendance for rheumatism, and shortly after his wife was again very ill. The Charity Organisation Society had assisted him in the winter of 1879, but had ceased to do so, as the result of their inquiries about him were not satisfactory. He applied several times for medicines in 1880, and was sent to Bromley in 1881. The landlady of these people stated that they drank and begged; but they do not seem to have been great drinkers, and the man has not been seen drunk. The woman was sent to the sick asylum for a time. In August 1882 the man applied for out-relief, but obtained only a medical order. In 1883, however, he was sent to the sick asylum. He had done no work for 4 months. In February 1883 both man and wife were sent to Bromley. She came out twice in 1884, but had to return, her legs being so bad, and she was sent to the sick asylum to have them treated. The man died in October 1887.

Mrs. Hart is another case. She is 68 and a widow, and had done canvas work. In 1882 she said she had done no work for 7 or 8 weeks, and had sold most of her furniture. She was then admitted to Bromley House, but came out the following August and went to live with her sister, Mrs. Harfield, who is 4 years older than herself, and engaged in the same work. The old women worked and lived together till 1884 (with an interval of a few months, when Mrs. Hart was in the house again). In 1884 Mrs. Hart injured herself carrying some canvas, and was found by the relieving officer lying on the floor apparently in great pain. She was sent to the sick asylum, and on coming out and being unable to work, took refuge at Bromley, where she has remained, except for one short visit to her sister. Mrs. Harfield fell ill in 1886, and application was made on her behalf. The relieving officer found her very ill, and several of the neighbours were with her. The place was clean and comfortable, and medical relief was given. Two years later Mrs. Harfield (then 71) applied, saying she was destitute and could not keep herself. She had no furniture and her landlady could not keep her any longer. Mrs. Hart had a son who used to work at the docks, but he lost his right leg and became chargeable in 1880. He is dead now. She has a married daughter who does not seem to help.

Mrs. Marston, born in 1816 and a widow since 1867, earned her living by washing, but had become helpless, and had been supported for some time by her daughter, the wife of a dock labourer with two children. The daughter applied for her mother's admission in 1885. She could not manage to keep her mother any longer. They had only one room, and she was expecting to be confined.

Old Mrs. Stimson has been asking for assistance ever since 1877. It has been usually refused, her case being thought one for the "House."* Nevertheless she has struggled on, and is now 75. She obtains some food from her daughters, and does needlework to pay the rent. Her room is reported very untidy, but her personal character is good; she is honest and hard working. She was given 2s. 6d. a week for a while, but is considered a "Poor Law case."

(ii) The old working women of Coventry and Birmingham

With regard to the wages received by women workers, and their ability to provide for sickness and old age, special evidence was given by Miss Hurlston, who has made a particular investigation of the conditions of working women in the neighborhood of Coventry. . . . Out of these wages it is at present impossible for them as a rule to make provision for old age, although they are insured "against sickness and death, as a rule," by joining some club or society. "In nearly all instances there are compulsory payments in the factories. They are compelled to subscribe to hospital funds, and generally to a sick club fund in connection with the works themselves." "But as to old age and old age pension nothing is done?"—"Nothing is ever done; it is impossible for them to do it." If, however, a pension scheme were open to them in which they were required to make a small weekly payment, the witness believes that "emphatically, yes, they would." This contribution could not

* Presumably the parish workhouse.—EDS.

exceed 2d. a week, and they would not be able to pay an initial lump sum premium. "Except where a girl or a woman belongs to what I should call a rather high status, that is, is the daughter of the more highly skilled artisans, where the parents could afford to board and lodge her free of expense, then it is possible that she may save; otherwise, never." The witness expressed the same opinion with regard to the lower grade of domestic servants, although "there are exceptional cases in the higher grade of domestic servants where I should think it is quite possible. . . . . There is a very large number of domestic servants in the Midlands who are employed at a very low rate of wages, you know; and I do not see how they could possibly put much aside. . . . . You find a very great number of them coming under £10 a year. I think you would find £8 a year very much nearer the average." The returns which Mr. Chamberlain secured from Birmingham contained information as to the previous occupations of the female paupers. Out of 710 women who were in receipt of relief, 331 gave as their previous occupation "house work," meaning thereby that they kept house for their husbands. Mr. Chamberlain maintains that as the majority of aged pauperism is female pauperism, and as women have seldom any opportunity of saving for themselves, if they keep house for their husbands, "it is cruel to say that aged pauperism is mainly due to the paupers themselves." Another of the previous occupations of the female paupers was that of "domestic service." In this, Mr. Chamberlain maintains, women fare exceedingly badly. "It is the custom," he says, "for domestic servants to move about from place to place at intervals of one or two years or so. The consequence is that they do not remain in any one place sufficiently long to estabtablish a claim on their employers. They ultimately become aged, when employers cease to be willing to employ them; consequently, they come on the rates. I have known servants who were perfectly happy in a comfortable service and who said so, but at the same time expressed a desire for a change. 'They wanted to see,' as they say, 'more of the world.' Well, it may be very foolish, but after all you cannot charge it against them as an offence." Mr. Charles Booth does not appear to take quite such a sweeping view of the case as Mr. Chamberlain. He bears out the latter's statements, however, with regard to the large proportion of female aged pauperism, attributing it to the fact that women are less financially responsible and have less control over the purse. The ratio of female paupers to male paupers appears to be 146 to 100.

104. Witches, healers, beggars, and outcasts

The crone, feared and revered for her power to heal and hurt, was a familiar figure in legend and story before the nineteenth century; indeed, in

SOURCES: (i) Walter Cline, Rachel S. Commons, and May Mandelbaum, *The Sinkaietk or Southern Okanagon of Washington*, ed. Leslie Spier (Menasha, Wis., 1938), p. 160. (ii) *Lucy Crawford's History of the White Mountains*, ed. Stearns Morse (Boston, 1978), pp. 47–48. (iii) Mary Boykin Chesnut, *A Diary*

societies where old people were the repository of traditional wisdom and local history, the aged possessed real power. By the nineteenth century, with rapid social and technological change and a great increase in the numbers of the elderly, this picture had begun to change. Although old women continued to be venerated by certain isolated groups, far more were likely to suffer the indignity of neglect—they had become merely burdensome and pathetic.

The old women portrayed in these selections range from the powerful to the helpless. In the first an Indian woman, Lucy Joe, reputed by her tribe to be a shaman, tells an anthropologist about the animal power of a nineteenth-century ancestor of the Southern Okanagons of Washington State. This tribe believed that such power, acquired in childhood, stayed with a person for life as long as he or she did not abuse it, and served as a source of strength and a guardian spirit. The second selection documents the healing abilities of Granny Stalbard, an old woman who lived in the White Mountains of New Hampshire in the 1840's and who had learned how to use medicinal roots and herbs from the Indians. The subject of the third selection, also from America, is Milly Trimlin, a lonely old Southern woman who, as a purported witch, was thrice removed from church burial grounds by the local populace. In the fourth selection Athénaïs Michelet (1828–99; Doc. 2) recalls a childhood encounter in the south of France with a wandering beggar woman, who was also said to be a witch. Finally, two selections, one from Moses Grandy's narrative about his life as a slave in the nineteenth century, and the other by a French traveler in Louisiana in the early years of the century, reveal the utter helplessness of elderly slave women left uncared for and in some cases virtually turned out to die when their useful days of work were past.

(i) Sikuntaluqs

Power was often brought into play at the fisheries. Michel's father told the people during a winter dance that he intended to go salmon fishing near Malott. When the season came they all helped him to make the weir. People came from Nespelem, Kartaro, Sanpoil, and near Chelan. After they had caught a few salmon, dried them, and distributed them among the families, the salmon stopped running. Most of the fishermen then moved away, leaving only a few at the weir. Michael's grandmother, who had salmon power, cleaned the weir and sat down near it. She sang no songs; she just "thought about her power" and went away. Very late that night the salmon began to run again and by the next morning they had filled the weir. The people took them out, but salmon came up abundantly for several days afterward.

Lucy Joe told the following anecdote which, she said, shows that the peo-

from Dixie, ed. Ben Ames Williams (Boston, 1949), p. 542. (iv) Mme Jules Michelet, The Story of My Childhood, tr. Mary Frazier Curtis (Boston, 1867), pp. 38–42. (v) Narrative of the Life of Moses Grandy, Late a Slave in the United States of America. Sold for the Benefit of His Relations Still in Slavery (Boston, 1844), pp. 32–33. (vi) Berquin-Duvallon, Travels in Louisiana and the Floridas, in the Year, 1802, Giving a Correct Picture of Those Countries, tr. John Davis (1806), pp. 90–92. Originally published in Paris in 1803.

ple long ago really did have power. Nmaskwist, her father's sister's son, once made a salmon weir at Malott. At first it was unproductive. Nmaskwist's grandmother, Sikuntaluqs, said, "I'm going to the weir." She walked along the weir to the opposite bank of the river and lay down there. Soon after sunset she heard the kingfisher . . . flying over the camp. She thought, "Now we're going to eat." She lay there and slept. The salmon came. By daybreak a great many had been caught in the weir, and she called to the people, "Your weir is going to overflow." Then the fishermen all ran down with their spears and other equipment, without stopping to put on their shoes, and took out two hundred salmon. When they had got these, the weir broke. Sikuntaluqs took off her moccasins and went swimming just above it. The people said to her, "What's the matter with you? You shouldn't swim up there." But that was her power. She replied, "I was the one that made the salmon come. It's all right if I take a swim." When other camps heard that the fishing was so good there, they came from Nespelem, Similkameen, and other distant places. In the evening Sikuntaluqs lay down again and "fixed the weir." In the morning a kingfisher was found dead on the bank, and the weir was full of salmon. The kingfisher must have been Sikuntaluqs' guardian spirit. When she sang, she said, "I'm an eagle and its little sister, the kingfisher."

Though women should not come within half a mile of a salmon weir, those who had salmon power, or who were attended by a man who had such power, could do so with impunity.

(ii) Granny Stalbard

There happened to be at my house then, a Mrs. Stalbard, who is known in our country and bore the name of Granny Stalbard, whose head was whitened with more than eighty years; who ought to be remembered for the good she had done, and many sufferings and hardships she endured to assist others in distress, and who seemed to be raised for the same end for which she lived in those days. She was an old Doctress woman; one of the first female settlers in Jefferson, and she had learned from the Indians the virtues of roots and herbs, and the various ways in which they could be made useful. Now the old lady said it was best to examine this wound and have it properly dressed; but as it had stopped bleeding I told her I thought it better to let it remain as it then was; but she thinking she was the elder, and knew better, unwrapped it, and it soon set bleeding afresh, and it was with difficulty she now stopped it. She, however, went into the field, plucked some young clover leaves, pounded them in a mortar, and placed them on my wound; this stopped the blood so suddenly that it caused me to faint; this was a new thing to me—a large stout man to faint!—which made me feel rather queerly, but there was no help for it. This wound laid me up pretty much the rest of the summer, but still we persevered, and these men, with some others, finished cutting the path through the woods. So it is that men suffer various ways in advancing civilization, and through God, mankind are indebted to the labors of men in many different spheres of life.

(iii) Milly Trimlin

Today H. Lang told me that poor Sandhill Milly Trimlin was dead; that as a witch she had been denied Christian burial. Three times she was buried in consecrated ground at different church yards, and three times she was dug up by a superstitious horde and put out of their holy ground. Where her poor old ill-used bones are lying now I do not know. I hope her soul is faring better than her body. She was a good, kindly creature. Everybody gave Milly a helping hand. She was a perfect specimen of the the Sandhill tackey race, sometimes called country crackers. Her skin was yellow and leathery, and even the whites of her eyes were bilious in color. She was stumpy and strong and lean, hard-featured, horny-fisted.

(iv) An old French beggar woman

The old women who were called witches tramped about the country, and were ugly enough to frighten one. They came among those troops of beggars who are so much dreaded at lonely farm-houses. They knew themselves to be feared, and looked grim, on purpose to appear more savage. Their dry, yellow locks straggled from under their torn caps; and they muttered to themselves as they walked, as if they held communion with spirits. They paused in front of animals and trees, gesticulating with sticks. I had seen them coming to the barn; and rudely pushing the gate open. I heard their quavering voices; their sharp, discordant laughter. I saw their glittering eyes under their wrinkled, frowning brows; with a diabolical expression, in which the old women of southern lands excel. Our farm-servant, Mélette, pretended to know the peculiar power of each of these hags. She would say, aside, "This one will burn our hay-rick."—"Janille, shut the door; there is one that has got a bad word for your sick mother."—"Last night I saw the Black Witch coming down; and now she is knocking at the door."—"Ah! our good master is laying up misfortunes by calling in these beggars. Philibert had a calf with two heads, because his children mocked at old *Boiler*. Don't laugh, naughty child: she can cast *the evil eye*; and perhaps you will be bewitched yourself."

. . . There was one old woman, who preserved the vigor of twenty devils in her little, emaciated frame. She never walked: she ran. She peeped into every thing. She examined everybody, without speaking. Her lips were tightened over her toothless jaws; her piercing eyes seemed to go through one's body. When she had looked at every thing, and put her sharp nose in all the corners, she either went out, or sat down, without saying "good day," or "good bye." She took her bread or her money as something due; and threw a sidelong glance, which I thought full of malevolence. She was the terror of the country. Our old Mélette crossed herself three times when she saw this woman coming round the corner. Jeanneton, the washerwoman, called out, "Children, shut the door: if she should even *look* at me, she will spoil my wash."

I always ran and hid myself when it was her turn to come. The malicious old thing perceived this, and missed coming on her day. My father said, "The witch has not come: she must be ill." He was mistaken; for the spiteful creature was well enough. I forgot all about her, and was walking up and down with my knitting, when she rose from behind a hedge. "Good heavens!" I cried; "the witch!"—"Yes, miss," she answered; "the witch: you'll see, you'll see"; and she ran at me, brandishing her stick. I stood rooted to the spot, while she rocked herself backwards and forwards with delight at my terror. I raised my arms imploringly, and said, "Madame, don't bewitch me."—"Oh yes, madame! you are afraid, eh? Take this." And she touched me with her stick. I thought it was all over with me,—that I was changed to a beast; and my terror was overwhelming. The woman burst out laughing, and went off without asking for any thing.

Old men were much less formidable to me than old women, and I observed that Mélette took little notice of them. Those who passed for sorcerers came to us in a merry mood, after sundry glasses of wine drunk on the road. As they seemed to be good fellows, I was not afraid to talk to them.

My father presided at the almsgiving; and, under shelter of his presence, I examined the countenances of our old beggars, as I offered them bread and wine. I distinguished between those who laughed and those who were melancholy; and I liked the latter best. I was attracted particularly by one who did not beg in harsh tones, like the others; but had dim eyes, and an unusual timidity. I longed to know why she, who had the power of an enchanter, should look so sad. . . . If I should find her indulgent to me, I would tell her all my troubles; and then, if I dared, would beg her to come in the night, and leave a pretty changeling in place of my little doll. But I never got a chance to speak to her; for, her alms received, she made a respectful salutation, and went away alone across the fields.

To teach myself to be brave, I visited a dark, dark passage, which our servant said was haunted. The slightest noise, the creaking of the floor, made me shake like an aspen leaf; but I persevered, my teeth firmly set, saying to myself, "Who's afraid?" After two or three experiments, I thought myself above all fear, and was ready for the witch at any day or hour. How should I meet her? Sometimes I imagined a pretty speech, while I showed her the unfortunate child in my arms. Sometimes I decided upon saluting her with great respect, to show that I was not like other rude children. Another time I would inquire after her health, and slip my luncheon into her hand. No: that would be too bold, by far. If she should bewitch my hand? No: better not touch her at all.

At last the day of her usual visit arrived, and I had come to no decision. I was no longer afraid, only a little choked in the throat. With a great sigh to blow out the words, I called out, "Witch." She made no reply. I began again: "Witch, I desire—." Silence again. I was ready to take flight; but, in a voice broken by sobs, I said, "Look, witch!" and held out the dolly. She looked at me silently a long while, but not in anger. "Child," she said at last, "you call me a witch. Who taught you to call me so? Don't you know that the aged poor are called so in derision? Your father is an old man: nobody calls *him* names,—because he is rich." And then, in harsher accents, she continued, "If I were indeed a fairy, I should not be here, holding out my hand for charity."

I began to comprehend how I had wounded her; and I was grieved and ashamed.

(v) Moses Grandy's mother

When my mother became old, she was sent to live in a little lonely log-hut in the woods. Aged and worn-out slaves, whether men or women, are commonly so treated. No care is taken of them, except, perhaps, that a little ground is cleared about the hut, on which the old slave, if able, may raise a little corn. As far as the owner is concerned, they live or die, as it happens; it is just the same thing as turning out an old horse. Their children, or other near relations, if living in the neighborhood, take it by turns to go at night with a supply saved out of their own scanty allowance of food, as well as to cut wood and fetch water for them: this is done entirely through the good feelings of the slaves, and not through the masters' taking care that it is done. On these night-visits, the aged inmate of the hut is often found crying on account of sufferings from disease or extreme weakness, or from want of food or water in the course of the day: many a time, when I have drawn near to my mother's hut, I have heard her grieving and crying on these accounts: she was old and blind too, and so unable to help herself. She was not treated worse than others: it is the general practice.

(vi) Old Irrouba

[The slaves'] smoky huts admit both wind and rain. An anecdote offers itself to my pen on this subject, which will exhibit the frigid indifference of the colonists of Louisiana towards every thing that interests humanity. Being on a visit at a plantation on the Mississippi, I walked out one fine evening in winter, with some ladies and gentlemen, who had accompanied me from the town, and the planters at whose house we were entertained. We approached the quarter where the huts of the negroes stood. "Let us visit the negroes," said one of the party; and we advanced towards the door of a miserable hut, where an old negro woman came to the threshold in order to receive us, but so decrepit as well as old, that it was painful for her to move.

Notwithstanding the winter was advanced, she was partly naked; her only covering being some old thrown away rags. Her fire was a few chips, and she was parching a little corn for supper. Thus she lived abandoned and forlorn; incapable from old age to work any longer, she was no longer noticed.

But independently of her long services, this negro woman had formerly suckled and brought up two brothers of her master, who made one of our party. She perceived him, and accosting him, said, "My master, when will you send one of your carpenters to repair the roof of my hut? Whenever it rains, it pours down upon my head." The master lifting his eyes, directed them to the roof of the hut, which was within the reach of his hand. "I will think of it," said he.—"You will think of it," said the poor creature. "You always say so, but never do it."—"Have you not," rejoined the planter, "two grandsons who can mend it for you?"—"But are they mine," said the old woman, "do they not work for you, and are you not my son yourself? who suckled and raised your two brothers? who was it but Irrouba? Take pity then on me, in my old age. Mend at least the roof of my hut, and God will reward you for it."

I was sensibly affected; it was *le cri de la bonne nature*. And what repairs did the poor creature's roof require? What was wanting to shelter her from the wind and rain of heaven? A few shingles!—"I will think of it," repeated her master, and departed.

105. An Englishwoman welcomes death: Harriet Martineau

One of the prominent "bluestockings" of the Victorian period, Harriet Martineau (1802–76; Doc. 30) supported herself on the proceeds from her numerous books and articles. Martineau suffered from ill health throughout her life and in 1854 developed heart disease, which her doctors predicted would soon prove fatal; despite this incurable illness, she continued her prodigious literary activities for the next twenty-two years. Although brought up a Unitarian, Martineau became an agnostic, believing, as she wrote in her 'Autobiography,' in the "eternal and irreversible laws, working in every department of the universe, without any interference from any random will, human or divine." In the following letters written to close friends a month before her death, Martineau calmly, and with a certain relief, contemplates death, firmly rejecting the Christian notion of salvation.

[Harriet Martineau to Maria Weston Chapman, May 17, 1876]

My dearest Friend,—I must try to keep up our correspondence to the latest moment, however painful the aspect of my letter may be to your eyes. J— tells me that our last letter will have prepared you for whatever we must tell you now of my condition. I hope she is right, and that it will not overtake you with a surprise if I find myself unable to pour out as I have always hitherto done. Dearest friend, I am *very ill*. I leave it to J— to show you how nearly certain it is that the end of my long illness is at hand. The difficulty and distress to me are the state of the head. I will only add that the condition grows daily worse, so that I am scarcely able to converse or to read, and the cramp in the hands makes writing difficult or impossible; so I must try to be content with the few lines I can send, till the few days become none. We believe that time to be near; and we shall not attempt to deceive you about it. My brain feels under the constant sense of being *not myself*, and the in-

SOURCE: *Harriet Martineau's Autobiography and Memorials of Harriet Martineau*, ed. Maria Weston Chapman (Boston, 1877), 2: 555–57.

troduction of this new fear into my daily life makes each day sufficiently trying to justify the longing for death which grows upon me more and more. I feel sure of your sympathy about this. You enter into my longing for rest, I am certain; and when you hear, some day soon, that I have sunk into my long sleep, you will feel it as the removal of a care, and as a relief on my account.

On my side I have suffered much anxiety on your account; and if you can tell me that you are no longer suffering physically under the peculiar feebleness that attends bronchial mischief, you will make me happier than any thing else could make me. Farewell for to-day, dearest friend! While I live I am your grateful and loving, H. M.

[Harriet Martineau to Henry Atkinson, May 19, 1876. A close friend of Martineau's, Atkinson was, like her, an agnostic and a believer in mesmerism.]

Dear Friend,—My niece J— and also my sister have been observing that you ought to be hearing from us, and have offered to write to you. You will see at once what this means; and it is quite true that I have become so much worse lately that we ought to guard against your being surprised, some day soon, by news of my life being closed. I feel uncertain about how long I *may* live in my present state. I can only follow the judgment of unprejudiced observers; and I see that my household believe the end to be not far off. I will not trouble you with disagreeable details. It is enough to say that I am in no respect better, while all the ailments are on the increase. The imperfect heart-action immediately affects the brain, causing the suffering which is worse than all other evils together,—the horrid sensation of not being quite myself. This strange, dreamy *non-recognition of myself* comes on every evening, and all else is a trifle in comparison. But there is a good deal more. Cramps in the hands prevent writing, and most other employment, except at intervals. Indications of dropsy have lately appeared: and after this, I need not again tell you that I see how fully my household believe that the end is not far off. Meantime I have no cares or troubles beyond the bodily uneasiness, (which, however, I don't deny to be an evil). I cannot think of any future as at all probable, except the "annihilation" from which some people recoil with so much horror. I find myself here in the universe,—I know not how, whence, or why. I see every thing in the universe go out and disappear, and I see no reason for supposing that it is not an actual and entire death. And for *my* part, I have no objection to such an extinction. I well remember the passion with which W. E. Forster said to me, "I had rather be damned than annihilated." If he once felt five minutes' damnation, he would be thankful for extinction in preference. The truth is, I care little about it any way. Now that the event draws near, and that I see how fully my household expect my death pretty soon, the universe opens so widely before my view, and I see the old notions of death and scenes to follow to be so merely human,—so impossible to be true, when one glances through the range of science,—that I see nothing to be done but to wait, without fear or hope or ignorant prejudice, for the expiration of life. I have no wish for further experience, nor have I any fear of it. Under the weariness of illness I long to be asleep; but I have not set my mind on any state. I wonder if all this represents your notions at all. I should think it does, while yet we are fully aware how mere a glimpse we have of the universe and the life it contains.

About all I wish to escape from the narrowness of taking a mere human view of things, from the absurdity of making God after man's own image, &c.

But I will leave this, begging your pardon for what may be so unworthy to be dwelt on. However, you *may* like to know how the case looks to a friend under the clear knowledge of death being so near at hand. My hands are cramped, and I must stop. My sister is here for the whole of May, and she and J—— are most happy together. Many affectionate relations and friends are willing to come if needed (the Browns among others),—if I live beyond July. . . .

So good by for to-day, dear friend!

Yours ever,

H. M.

P.S. I am in a state of amazement at a discovery just made; I have read (after half a lifetime) Scott's "Bride of Lammermoor," and am utterly disappointed in it. The change in my taste is beyond accounting for,—almost beyond belief.

106. The rituals of death

Though death has commonly been viewed as the "great equalizer," the rituals surrounding it magnify differences in social and economic status, and often make sexual distinctions explicit. Consider, for example, the itemized lists in the first two selections—an inventory of the assets of the deceased Widow Drouet of France and a breakdown of the funeral expenses for Miss Emma Smith of England. Little is known of the seventy-nine-year-old Drouet, who died in rural France in 1851; but she left behind so meager a list of personal possessions as to suggest an impoverished old age and a pauper's

SOURCES: (i) "Enventair de la veuve Drouet," manuscript 44–294, Archives de la Musée des Arts et Traditions Populaires, Paris, as cited in Eugen Weber, *Peasants into Frenchmen: The Modernization of Rural France, 1870–1914* (Stanford, Calif., 1976), pp. 526–27. (ii) Receipt presented to the estate of Miss Emma Smith by R. H. Perkins, upholsterer and cabinet manufacturer, Jan. 20, 1859, for expenses incurred Nov. 3, 1858, Special Collections, Green Library, Stanford University. (iii) *Etiquette à suivre pour les deuils, dont les assortimens se trouvent chez NAUD, Rue du Dragon, No. 42, au magasin d'étoffes de deuil* (Paris, n.d.). (iv) Death announcement for Françoise-Victoire de la Forte, 1852, original in the possession of Marilyn Yalom. (v) *Treasures from David Fulton's Strong Box,* comp. John Wichels (privately printed, 1976), Napa County Historical Library, Napa, Calif. (vi) Inscription on Harriet Mill's tombstone, as reproduced in *The Amberley Papers,* ed. Bertrand and Patricia Russell (London, 1937), 1: 305.

funeral. By contrast, the abundant papers documenting the death of Emma Smith of Southampton a few years later testify to the attentions of family, friends, servants, and a personal physician; and as the document shows, she was laid to rest with all the pomp and circumstance befitting a cousin of the second Marquess of Northampton. In the third selection the author of a French booklet on mourning etiquette matter-of-factly sets out two distinctly different procedures to be followed for husbands and wives. This booklet was for the guidance of the upper classes, but there is something of the same tone in certain French peasant customs—for example, in some villages of the south, the convention of tolling the bells longer for a dead man than for a woman.

In addition to the differences wrought by social position and sex, cultural differences are manifest in funeral notices and tombstones. Even in death Frenchwomen were entangled in a web of kinship; as we see in the fourth selection, the name of Françoise-Victoire de la Forte, of Lyon, is practically lost in the list of mourners to whom she was related. By contrast, the propriety that demanded a stiffly formal funeral notice like that of Mary A. Fulton of California—a widow and mother of two grown daughters—seems to distance the deceased from their families. Finally, as the last selection shows, tombstones could provide a means of making a public statement about the deceased. This somewhat unorthodox tombstone inscription of Harriet Taylor Mill, wife of the British philosopher and feminist John Stuart Mill, is unusual both in its length and in the intensity of its praise. Such graveyard paeans were rare, even for men.

(i) La veuve Drouet's estate

a pothook
tongs and andirons
a candlestick
2 bad chairs
a table and a kneading trough
a chest
3 plates and 3 spoons and 2 forks
1 platter and 1 pot

9 bad shirts
3 corsets
3 bad dresses
body of the deceased with her dress
a wooden bed with curtains
2 blankets, 1 for the bed and 1 for self
a feather mattress and a bolster
3 sheets and a bad canvas bag

(ii) Miss Emma Smith's funeral expenses

	£	s	d		£	s	d
Stout Elm Shell lind, Flannel	3	3	–	Brass engraved Shield Plate	1	12	6
Mattrass and pillow	1	10	–	3 Crape Bands and Scarfs			
Wool to fill in Corpse	–	7	6	for Gentlemen, 28/	4	4	–
Fine Flannel Robe and				9 Armozine Bands and			
Cap Trimd	1	10	–	Scarfs, the Revd Hanison			
Stout Mill Lead Coffin	9	–	–	Davis & Usborn, Mr.			
Stout Elm Outside Coffin				Tyler, Mr Wm and Mr.			
covered fine, Blk Cloth [?]				Dumper Senr & J^r The			
Furniture naild & plate	8	10	–	Undertaker			
Carriage of 3 Coffins Solder-				& Assistant, 42/-	18	18	–
ing down, etc. etc	1	10	–	12 Pair Kidd Gloves, 3/9	2	5	–

	£	s	d
5 Silk Hoods for Female Mourners	3	10	–
8 Pair Kidd Gloves for dr & Nurses, 2/9	1	2	–
16 Silk Bands for 10 Bearers, 2 Mutes and 4 Drivers, 10/6	8	8	
16 Pair Gloves, 1/6	1	4	–
8 Silk Bands for Coachmen, Footman, 2 Gardeners, Plumber, Bricklayer, Clerk & Sexton, 14/–	5	12	–
8 Pair Leather Gloves, 2/6	1	–	–
Silk for 2 Mutes Staves	2	10	–
Pair Kidd Gloves for Mrs. Pestor	–	2	9
Undertaker & Assistants attendance	–	–	–
Use of Best Silk Velvet Pall	1	1	–
Use of Velvets for Hearse and 10 Horses, of 4 Hammer Cloths, of 10 Trancheons & Wands, of Drivers Coats	4	13	6
Use of Pair Mutes Cloaks, of Pair Mutes Staves	–	–	–
Use of Best Ostrich Plumes for Hearse and 10 Horses	4	15	–
Pair Bridges	–	11	6
Hearse and 4 Horses, 3 Coaches with Pairs	7	10	–
4 Drivers, 10 Bearers and 2 Mutes	5	12	–
Fees at Peartree	5	18	–
Brick Vault	3	12	6
£	109	12	3

(iii) Etiquette for mourning

For a Husband

In Paris, this type of mourning lasts one year and six weeks. In the provinces, it can be prolonged according to individual desire or custom. The first four and a half months: dress of wool and Saint-Cyr light wool; ruffled bonnet, black and white or completely black crepe; the bonnet is scarcely worn any longer except indoors. Outside: a crepe hat without ornamentation, and a crepe veil.

Crepe neckerchief, crepe collar with a wide hem, wool stockings, silk or beaver gloves.

The next three months: dress of floss silk, grenadine cloth, Naples cloth, taffeta, black crepe, etc.; neckerchief, bonnet and hat of black gauze; silk stockings, leather gloves.

The next three months: dress of levantine cloth, satin, gauze, muslin, black twill; black hat decorated with satin or black flowers, black gauze neckerchief, black silk stockings, black leather gloves.

The next three months, Half-Mourning: silk, linen or muslin dress, which may be gray or black, black and white, or gray with black ornaments; gray and black or white and black hat; white gauze neckerchief, white stockings, gray or black leather gloves, or white gloves embroidered with black.

The servants should be dressed in heavy mourning.

For a Wife

All one's attire in woolen cloth and cashmere for six months, mourning band on the hat, bronze buckles; the first three months: wool stockings, black beaver gloves.

The servants should be dressed in heavy mourning.

(iv) Françoise-Victoire de la Forte's death announcement

M. and Mme Jules de la Forte and their children; M. and Mme Clément de la Forte and their children; M. and Mme Edouard de la Forte and their child; M. and Mme de la Murette and their child; Mme Pamphile de Rosière and her children; M. and Mme de St. Genest; M. le Baron and Mme la Baronne de Silans; M. le Comte and Mme la Comtesse de Caussans; M. Léon de Laval; M. and Mlle Prunelle have the honour of informing you of the painful loss that they have just suffered in the person of Madame Françoise Victoire de la Forte, née de Rosière, their mother, mother-in-law, grandmother, sister-in-law, aunt, great-aunt and cousin, deceased the 26th of March, 1852.

Pray for her.

(v) Mary A. Fulton's funeral notice

FUNERAL NOTICE.

FRIENDS AND ACQUAINTANCES OF THE LATE

Mrs. Mary A. Fulton,

Are respectfully invited to attend her funeral which will take place from the family residence, on Fulton lane, St. Helena, to-morrow, Thursday, December 21st, 1893, at 2 o'clock P. M.

(vi) Harriet Taylor Mill's tombstone inscription

To the beloved Memory
of
Harriet Mill
The dearly beloved & deeply regretted
Wife of John Stuart Mill.
Her great and loving heart
Her noble Soul
Her clear, powerful, original and
Comprehensive Intellect
Made her the Guide & Support
The Instructor in Wisdom
And the example in Goodness
As she was the sole earthly delight
Of those who had the happiness to belong to her.
As earnest for all public good
As she was generous and devoted
To all who surrounded her.
Her Influence has been felt
In many of the greatest
Improvements of the Age
And will be in those still to come.
Were there even a few hearts and intellects
Like hers
This earth would already become
The hoped-for heaven.
She Died
To the irreparable loss of those who survive her
At Avignon. Nov. 3, 1858.

Reference Matter

Works Cited in the Introductions

Abbott, Edith. 1924. *Women in Industry: A Study in American Economic History*. 2d ed. New York. 1969 reprint edition available.

Agulhon, Maurice, Gabriel Desert, and Robert Specklin. 1976. *Apogée et crise de la civilisation paysanne, 1789–1914*. Paris.

Anderson, Michael. 1971. *Family Structure in Nineteenth-Century Lancashire*. Cambridge, Eng.

Andrews, William D., and Deborah C. Andrews. 1974. "Technology and the Housewife in Nineteenth-Century America," *Women's Studies*, 2.3: 309–28.

Ariès, Philippe. 1962. *Centuries of Childhood: A Social History of Family Life*. Tr. Robert Baldick. New York.

Aron, Jean-Paul, and Roger Kempf. 1978. *Le Pénis et la démoralisation de l'occident*. Paris.

Atkinson, Paul. 1978. "Fitness, Feminism, and Schooling," in Sara Delamont and Lorna Duffin, eds., *The Nineteenth-Century Woman: Her Cultural and Physical World*. London.

Banks, Joseph A. 1954. *Prosperity and Parenthood: A Study of Family Planning Among the Victorian Middle Classes*. New York.

Banks, Joseph A., and Olive Banks. 1964. *Feminism and Family Planning in Victorian England*. New York.

Barker-Benfield, G. J. Ben. 1973. "The Spermatic Economy: A Nineteenth-Century View of Sexuality," in Michael Gordon, ed., *The American Family in Social-Historical Perspective*. New York.

Barret, André. 1975. *Nadar: 50 photographies de ses illustres contemporains*. Paris.

Basch, Françoise. 1974. *Relative Creatures: Victorian Women in Society and the Novel*. Tr. Anthony Rudolf. New York.

Basch, Norma. 1979. "Invisible Women: The Legal Fiction of Marital Unity in Nineteenth-Century America," *Feminist Studies*, 5.2 (Summer): 346–66.

Beauvoir, Simone de. 1972. *The Coming of Age: The Study of the Aging Process*. Tr. Patrick O'Brian. New York.

Berguès, Hélène, et al. 1960. *La Prévention des naissances dans la famille, ses origines dans les temps modernes*. Paris.

Bernard, Richard M., and Maris A. Vinovskis. 1977. "The Female School Teacher in Ante-Bellum Massachusetts," *Journal of Social History*, 10.3 (Spring): 332–45.

Bidelman, Patrick Kay. 1975. "The Feminist Movement in France: The

Formative Years, 1858–1889." Ph.D. dissertation, Michigan State University.

———. 1976. "The Politics of French Feminism: Léon Richer and the Ligue Française pour le Droit des Femmes, 1882–1891," *Historical Reflections*, 3.1 (Summer): 93–120.

———. 1977. "Maria Deraismes, Léon Richer, and the Founding of the French Feminist Movement, 1866–1878," *Third Republic/Troisième République*, 3–4 (Spring–Fall): 20–73.

Biraben, Jean-Noël. 1966. "Communication sur l'évolution de la fécondité en Europe occidentale," *Official Documents of the European Population Conference*, vol. 1. Strasbourg.

Blackwell, Elizabeth. 1895. *Pioneer Work in Opening the Medical Profession to Women*. New York. 1977 reprint edition available under the title *Opening the Medical Profession to Women: Autobiographical Sketches*.

Boserup, Ester. 1970. *Woman's Role in Economic Development*. New York.

Bourgeois-Pichat, Jean. 1965. "The General Development of the Population of France Since the Eighteenth Century," in D. V. Glass and D. E. C. Eversley, eds., *Population in History: Essays in Historical Demography*. Chicago.

Boxer, Marilyn J., and Jean H. Quataert, eds. 1978. *Socialist Women: European Socialist Feminism in the Nineteenth and Early Twentieth Centuries*. New York.

Branca, Patricia. 1974. "Image and Reality: The Myth of the Idle Victorian Woman," in Mary S. Hartman and Lois Banner, eds., *Clio's Consciousness Raised: New Perspectives on the History of Women*. New York.

———. 1975. *Silent Sisterhood: Middle-Class Women in the Victorian Home*. Pittsburgh.

———. 1975. "A New Perspective on Women's Work: A Comparative Typology," *Journal of Social History*, 9.2 (Winter): 129–53.

Bridenthal, Renate. 1976. "The Dynamics of Production and Reproduction in History," *Radical America*, 10.2 (March–April): 3–11.

Bridenthal, Renate, and Claudia Koonz, eds. 1977. *Becoming Visible: Women in European History*. Boston.

Burnham, Dorothy. 1978. "The Life of the Afro-American Woman in Slavery," *International Journal of Women's Studies*, 1.4 (July–Aug.): 363–77.

Cantor, Milton, and Bruce Laurie, eds. 1977. *Class, Sex, and the Woman Worker*. Westport, Conn.

Chambers-Schiller, Lee. 1978. "The Single Woman Reformer: Conflict Between Family and Vocation, 1830–1860," *Frontiers*, 3 (Fall): 41–48.

Charrier, Edmée. 1931. *Evolution intellectuelle féminine*. Paris.

Chatelain, Abel. 1970. "Les Usines internats et les migrations féminines dans la région lyonnaise," *Revue d'histoire économique et sociale*, 48.3: 373–94.

Chevalier, Louis. 1973. *Laboring Classes and Dangerous Classes during the First Half of the Nineteenth Century*. Tr. Frank Jellinek. New York. Originally published in Paris in 1958.

Christ, Carol. 1977. "Victorian Masculinity and the Angel in the House," in Martha Vicinus, ed., *A Widening Sphere: Changing Roles of Victorian Women*. Bloomington, Ind.

Clarke, Edward H. 1889. *Sex in Education; or, a Fair Chance for the Girls*. 5th ed. Boston. Originally published in 1873.

Coale, Ansley J., and Melvin Zelnik. 1963. *New Estimates of Fertility and Population in the United States*. Princeton, N.J.

Colombat, Marc. 1850. *A Treatise on the Diseases and Special Hygiene of Females*. Tr. Charles D. Meigs. Philadelphia.

Cominos, Peter T. 1963. "Late Victorian Sexual Respectability and the Social System," *International Review of Social History*, (2 parts), 8.1: 18–48; 8.2: 216–50.

————. 1973. "Innocent Femina Sensualis in Unconscious Conflict," in Martha Vicinus, ed., *Suffer and Be Still: Women in the Victorian Age*. Bloomington, Ind.

Cone, Helen Grey. 1891. "Women in Literature," in Annie Nathan Meyer, ed., *Woman's Work in America*. New York. 1972 reprint edition available.

Conway, Jill. 1971. "Women Reformers and American Culture," *Journal of Social History*, 5.2 (Winter): 164–77.

Cott, Nancy F. 1977. *The Bonds of Womanhood: "Woman's Sphere" in New England, 1780–1835*. New Haven, Conn.

————. 1978. "Passionlessness: An Interpretation of Victorian Sexual Ideology, 1790–1850," *Signs*, 4.2 (Winter): 219–36.

Dahlin, Michel. 1978. "Perspectives on Family Life of the Elderly in 1900." Paper presented at the Pacific Coast Branch meeting of the American Historical Association, San Francisco, Aug. 17.

————. N.d. "The Problem of Old Age, 1890–1929." Ph.D. dissertation in progress, Stanford University.

Davidoff, Leonore. 1973. *The Best Circles: Women and Society in Victorian England*. Totowa, N.J.

————. 1974. "Mastered for Life: Servant and Wife in Victorian and Edwardian England," *Journal of Social History*, 7.4 (Summer): 406–28.

————. 1976. "The Rationalization of Housework," in Sheila Allen and Diana Barker, eds. *Dependence and Exploitation in Work and Marriage*. New York.

————. 1979. "Class and Gender in Victorian England: The Diaries of Arthur J. Munby and Hannah Cullwick," *Feminist Studies*, 5.1 (Spring): 87–141.

Davis, Angela. 1972. "Reflections on the Black Woman's Role in the Community of Slaves," *Massachusetts Review*, 13.1–2 (Winter–Spring): 81–100.

Davis, Katharine Bement. 1929. *Factors in the Sex Life of Twenty-Two Hundred Women*. New York. 1972 reprint edition available.

Davis, Natalie Zemon. 1972. "Women in the Labor Force in Early Modern Europe." Paper presented at the Pacific Coast Branch meeting of the American Historical Association, Santa Barbara, Aug. 26.

————. 1977. "Ghosts, Kin, and Progeny: Some Features of Family Life in Early Modern France," *Daedalus*, 106 (Spring): 87–114.

Degler, Carl N. 1974. "What Ought to Be and What Was: Women's Sexuality in the Nineteenth Century," *American Historical Review*, 79.5 (Dec.): 1467–90.

Delamont, Sara. 1978. "The Contradictions in Ladies' Education," in Sara Delamont and Lorna Duffin, eds., *The Nineteenth-Century Woman: Her Cultural and Physical World*. London.

de Mause, Lloyd. 1974. "The Evolution of Childhood," *History of Childhood Quarterly*, 1.4 (Spring): 503–75.

————. 1976. "The Formation of the American Personality Through Psychospeciation," *Journal of Psychohistory*, 4.1 (Summer): 1–30.

Dickinson, Susan E. 1891. "Women in Journalism," in Annie Nathan Meyer, ed., *Women's Work in America*. New York. 1972 reprint edition available.

Donnison, Jean. 1976. "Medical Women and Lady Midwives. A Case Study in Medical and Feminist Politics," *Women's Studies*, 3.3: 229–50.

————. 1977. *Midwives and Medical Men: A History of Inter-Professional Rivalries and Women's Rights*. New York.

Douglas, Mary. 1973. *Natural Symbols: Explorations in Cosmology*. London.

Dublin, Thomas. 1979. *Women at Work: The Transformation of Work and Community in Lowell, Massachusetts, 1826–1869*. New York.

Dubois, Ellen. 1978. *Feminism and Suffrage: The Emergence of an Independent Women's Movement in America, 1848–1869*. Ithaca, N.Y.

Ehrenreich, Barbara, and Deirdre English. 1978. *For Her Own Good: 150 Years of the Experts' Advice to Women*. Garden City, N.Y.

Ellis, Sarah Stickney. 1843. *The Mothers of England*. London.

Evans, Richard J. 1977. *The Feminists: Women's Emancipation Movements in Europe, America, and Australasia, 1840–1920*. London.

Faragher, Johnny, and Christine Stansell. 1975. "Women and Their Families on the Overland Trail, 1842–1867," *Feminist Studies*, 2.2–3: 150–66.

Fischer, David Hackett. 1978. *Growing Old in America: The Bland-Lee Lectures Delivered at Clark University, Expanded Edition*. New York. Originally published in 1976.

Flexner, Eleanor. 1971. *Century of Struggle: The Woman's Rights Movement in the United States*. New York.

Foner, Philip S., ed. 1977. *The Factory Girls: A Collection of Writings on Life and Struggles in the New England Factories of the 1840's*. Urbana, Ill.

Foucault, Michel. 1977. *Discipline and Punish: The Birth of the Prison*. Tr. Alan Sheridan. New York.

————. 1978. *The History of Sexuality*, vol. 1: *An Introduction*. Tr. Robert Hurley. New York.

Franklin, Jill. 1975. "Troops of Servants: Labour and Planning in the Country House, 1840–1914," *Victorian Studies*, 19.2 (Dec.): 211–39.

Freedman, Estelle B. 1981. *Their Sisters' Keepers: Women's Prison Reform in America, 1830–1930*. Ann Arbor, Mich.

Gathorne-Hardy, Jonathan. 1972. *The Rise and Fall of the British Nanny*. London.

Gauldie, Enid. 1974. *Cruel Habitations: A History of Working-Class Housing, 1780–1918*. London.

Genovese, Eugene D. 1976. *Roll, Jordan, Roll: The World the Slaves Made*. New York.

Gilbert, Sandra M., and Susan Gubar. 1979. *The Mad Woman in the Attic: The Woman Writer and the Nineteenth-Century Literary Imagination*. New Haven, Conn.

Gillis, John R. 1979. "Servants, Sexual Relations, and the Risks of Illegitimacy in London, 1801–1900," *Feminist Studies*, 5.1 (Spring): 142–73.

Gordon, Linda. 1974. "Voluntary Motherhood: The Beginnings of Feminist

Birth Control Ideas in the United States," in Mary S. Hartman and Lois Banner, eds., *Clio's Consciousness Raised: New Perspectives on the History of Women*. New York.

———. 1976. *Woman's Body, Woman's Right: A Social History of Birth Control in America*. New York.

Grabell, Wilson H., Clyde V. Kiser, and Pascal K. Whelpton. 1973. "A Long View," in Michael Gordon, ed., *The American Family in Social-Historical Perspective*. 1st ed. New York.

Gréville, Mme Henry [pseud. of Alice Durand]. 1884. Report on French literary women, in Theodore Stanton, ed., *The Woman Question in Europe*. New York. 1970 reprint edition available.

Guilbert, Madeleine. 1966. *Les Femmes et l'organisation syndicale avant 1914*. Paris.

Guiral, Pierre, and Guy Thuillier. 1978. *La Vie quotidienne des domestiques en France au XIXe siècle*. Paris.

Gutman, Herbert G. 1976. *Work, Culture, and Society in Industrializing America: Essays in American Working-Class and Social History*. New York.

———. 1977. *The Black Family in Slavery and Freedom, 1750–1925*. New York. Reprint of 1976 edition.

Hajnal, John. 1965. "European Marriage Patterns in Perspective," in D. V. Glass and D. E. C. Eversley, eds., *Population in History: Essays in Historical Demography*. Chicago.

Hall, G. Stanley. 1904. *Adolescence*. Vol. 1. New York.

Haller, John S., Jr., and Robin M. Haller. 1974. *The Physician and Sexuality in Victorian America*. Urbana, Ill.

Hartman, Mary S. 1977. *Victorian Murderesses: A True History of Thirteen Respectable French and English Women Accused of Unspeakable Crimes*. New York.

Hellerstein, Erna Olafson. 1976. "French Women and the Orderly Household, 1830–1870," *Proceedings of the Western Society for French History*, 3: 378–89.

———. 1980. "Women, Social Order, and the City: Rules for French Ladies, 1830–1870." Ph.D. dissertation, University of California, Berkeley.

Hewitt, Margaret. 1975. *Wives and Mothers in Victorian Industry*. Westport, Conn. Originally published in London in 1958.

Holcombe, Lee. 1973. *Victorian Ladies at Work: Middle-Class Working Women in England and Wales, 1850–1914*. Hamden, Conn.

Horn, Pamela. 1975. *The Rise and Fall of the Victorian Servant*. New York.

Houghton, Walter E. 1957. *The Victorian Frame of Mind, 1830–70*. New Haven, Conn.

Howe, Julia Ward, ed. 1874. *Sex and Education: A Reply to Dr. E. H. Clarke's Sex in Education*. New York. 1972 reprint edition available.

Hufton, Olwen. 1975. "Women and the Family Economy in Eighteenth-Century Europe," *French Historical Studies*, 9.1 (Spring): 1–22.

Hume, Leslie Parker Bryant. 1979. "The National Union of Women's Suffrage Societies, 1897–1914." Ph.D. dissertation, Stanford University.

Humm, Rosamond Olmstead, ed. 1978. *Children in America: A Study of Images and Attitudes* (exhibit catalog). Atlanta.

Johansson, Sheila Ryan. 1977. "Sex and Death in Victorian England," in

Martha Vicinus, ed., *A Widening Sphere: Changing Roles of Victorian Women*. Bloomington, Ind.

Juster, Norton, ed. 1979. *So Sweet to Labor: Rural Women in America, 1865–1895*. New York.

Kamerman, Sheila B. 1979. "Work and Family in Industrialized Societies," *Signs*, 4.4 (Summer): 632–50.

Kamm, Josephine. 1965. *Hope Deferred: Girls' Education in English History*. London.

Katz, Jonathan. 1976. "Passing Women: 1782–1920," in Katz, ed., *Gay American History: Lesbians and Gay Men in the U.S.A., A Documentary*. New York.

Katzman, David M. 1978. *Seven Days a Week: Women and Domestic Service in Industrializing America*. New York.

Kerber, Linda. 1976. "The Republican Mother: Women and the Enlightenment—An American Perspective," *American Quarterly*, 28.2 (Summer): 187–205.

Klaich, Dolores. 1974. *Woman Plus Woman: Attitudes Toward Lesbianism*. New York.

Kleinberg, Susan J. 1976. "Technology and Women's Work: The Lives of Working Class Women in Pittsburgh, 1870–1900," *Labor History*, 17.1 (Winter): 58–72.

Knibiehler, Yvonne. 1976a. "Le Discours médical sur la femme," *Romantisme: Revue du Dix-Neuvième Siècle*, 13–14: 41–55.

———. 1976b. "Les Médecins et la 'nature féminine' au temps du Code Civil," *Annales: Economies, Sociétés, Civilisations*, 31.4 (July–Aug.): 824–45.

Kovacevic, Ivanka, and S. Barbara Kanner. 1970. "Blue Book into Novel: The Forgotten Industrial Fiction of Charlotte Elizabeth Tonna," *Nineteenth Century Fiction*, 25: 152–73.

Langer, William L. 1975. "Origins of the Birth Control Movement in England in the Early Nineteenth Century," *Journal of Interdisciplinary History*, 5.4 (Spring): 669–86.

Lasch, Christopher. 1965. *The New Radicalism in America, 1889–1963 (The Intellectual as a Social Type)*. New York.

Laslett, Peter. 1973. "Age at Menarche in Europe Since the Eighteenth Century," in Theodore K. Rabb and Robert I. Rotberg, eds., *The Family in History: Interdisciplinary Essays*. New York.

———. 1977. *Family Life and Illicit Love in Earlier Generations*. Cambridge, Eng.

Le Play, Frédéric. 1878. *Les Ouvriers européens*, vol. 6: *Les Ouvriers de l'occident. Populations désorganisées, égarées par la nouveauté, méprisant la tradition*. 2d ed. Tours and Paris.

Lerner, Gerda. 1977. *The Female Experience: An American Documentary*. Indianapolis, Ind.

Leroy-Beaulieu, Paul. 1873. *Le Travail des femmes au XIXe siècle*. Paris.

Lesselier, Claudie. 1978. "Employées de grands magasins à Paris (avant 1914)," *Le Mouvement Social*, 105 (Oct.–Dec.): 109–26.

Liddington, Jill. 1977. "Rediscovering Suffrage History," *History Workshop*, 4 (Autumn): 192–202.

Lipinska, Melanie. 1900. *Histoire des femmes médicins.* Paris.

Loewenberg, Bert J., and Ruth Bogin, eds. 1976. *Black Women in Nineteenth-Century American Life: Their Words, Their Thoughts, Their Feelings.* College Park, Pa.

McBride, Theresa M. 1976. *The Domestic Revolution: The Modernization of Household Service in England and France, 1820–1920.* New York.

———. 1978. "A Woman's World: Department Stores and the Evolution of Women's Employment, 1870–1920," *French Historical Studies,* 10.4 (Fall): 664–83.

———. 1979. "Servants, Sexual Relations, and the Risks of Illegitimacy in London, 1801–1900," *Feminist Studies,* 5.1 (Spring): 142–73.

McGregor, Oliver Ross. 1957. *Divorce in England, a Centenary Study.* London.

McLaren, Angus. 1974. "Some Secular Attitudes Toward Sexual Behavior in France, 1760–1860," *French Historical Studies,* 8.4 (Fall): 604–25.

———. 1975. "Doctor in the House: Medicine and Private Morality in France, 1800–1850," *Feminist Studies,* 2.2–3: 39–54.

———. 1976. "Sex and Socialism: The Opposition of the French Left to Birth Control in the Nineteenth Century," *Journal of the History of Ideas,* 37.3 (July–Sept.): 475–92.

MacLeod, Anne S. 1975. *A Moral Tale: Children's Fiction and American Culture, 1820–1860.* Hamden, Conn.

Manton, Jo. 1965. *Elizabeth Garrett Anderson.* New York.

Marcus, Steven. 1966. *The Other Victorians: A Study of Sexuality and Pornography in Mid-Nineteenth Century England.* New York.

Meyers, Peter V. 1979. "Professionalization and Gender: Secular Elementary School Teachers in the Belle Epoque." Paper presented at the Society for French Historical Studies meeting, Pittsburgh, March 31.

Michelet, Jules. 1873. *Woman (Le Femme).* Tr. J. W. Palmer, M.D. New York. Originally published in Paris in 1860.

Middleton, Lucy, ed. 1977. *Women in the Labour Movement: The British Experience.* London.

Mitchell, Juliette. 1966. "Women: The Longest Revolution," *New Left Review,* 40 (Dec.): 11–37.

Modell, John, and Tamara K. Hareven. 1973. "Urbanization and the Malleable Household: An Examination of Boarding and Lodging in American Families," *Journal of Marriage and the Family,* 35.3 (Aug.): 467–79.

Moers, Ellen. 1977. *Literary Women.* New York.

Mohr, James C. 1978. *Abortion in America: The Origins and Evolution of National Policy.* New York.

Morse, Stearns, ed. 1978. *Lucy Crawford's History of the White Mountains.* Boston.

Moses, Claire Goldberg. 1978. "The Evolution of Feminist Thought in France, 1829–1889." Ph.D. dissertation, George Washington University, Washington, D.C.

Neff, Wanda Fraikin. 1929. *Victorian Working Women.* New York.

Niethammer, Carolyn. 1977. *Daughters of the Earth: The Lives and Legends of American Indian Women.* New York.

Noonan, John T. 1966. *Contraception: A History of Its Treatment by the Catholic Theologians and Cannonists.* Cambridge, Mass.

Oakley, Ann. 1974. *Woman's Work: A History of the Housewife, Past and Present*. New York.

Offen, Karen M. 1973. "The 'Woman Question' as a Social Issue in Republican France Before 1914," unpublished manuscript.

———. 1977. "The 'Woman Question' as a Social Issue in Nineteenth-Century France: A Bibliographical Essay," *Third Republic/Troisième République*, 3–4 (Fall): 238–99.

O'Neill, William. 1971. *The Woman Movement: Feminism in the United States and England*. Chicago.

———. 1973. *Divorce in the Progressive Era*. New York.

Pearsall, Ronald. 1969. *The Worm in the Bud: The World of Victorian Sexuality*. New York.

Perrot, Michelle. 1976. "L'Eloge de la ménagère dans le discours des ouvriers français au XIXe siècle," *Romantisme: Revue du Dix-Neuvième Siècle*, 13–14: 105–21.

———. 1977a. "Workers and Machines in France During the First Half of the 19th Century," *Proceedings of the Western Society for French History*, 5: 198–217.

———. 1977b. "L'Usine et sa discipline au 19e siècle." Paper presented at the University of California, Berkeley, Nov.

Peterson, M. Jeanne. 1973. "The Victorian Governess: Status Incongruence in Family and Society," in Martha Vicinus, ed., *Suffer and Be Still: Women in the Victorian Age*. Bloomington, Ind.

Petrie, Glen. 1971. *A Singular Iniquity: The Campaigns of Josephine Butler*. New York.

Pinchbeck, Ivy. 1930. *Women Workers and the Industrial Revolution, 1750–1850*. London. 1975 reprint edition available.

Pleck, Elizabeth H. 1976. "Two Worlds in One: Work and Family," *Journal of Social History*, 10.2 (Winter): 178–95.

———. 1979. "Wife-Beating in Nineteenth-Century America," *Victimology*, 4.1: 60–74.

Pope, Barbara Corrado. 1976. "Maternal Education in France, 1815–1848," *Proceedings of the Western Society for French History*, 3: 368–77.

Potter, David M. 1959. "American Woman and the American Character," reprinted 1973 in *History and American Society: Essays of David M. Potter*, ed. Don Fehrenbacher. New York.

Rapp, Rayna, Ellen Ross, and Renate Bridenthal. 1979. "Examining Family History," *Feminist Studies*, 5.1 (Spring): 174–200.

Reddy, William M. 1975. "Family and Factory: French Linen Weavers in the Belle Epoque," *Journal of Social History*, 8.2 (Winter): 102–12.

Riegel, Robert. 1968. "Changing American Attitudes Toward Prostitution (1800–1920)," *Journal of the History of Ideas*, 29.3 (July–Sept): 437–52.

Rigby, Elizabeth. 1848. "Vanity Fair—and Jane Eyre," *Quarterly Review*, 84.167 (Dec.): 153–85.

Roberts, Ann. 1976. "Mothers and Babies: The Wetnurse and Her Employer in Mid-Nineteenth Century England," *Women's Studies*, 3.3: 279–93.

Robertson, Priscilla. 1974. "Home As a Nest: Middle-Class Childhood in Nineteenth-Century Europe," in Lloyd de Mause, ed., *The History of Childhood*. New York.

Rosen, Andrew. 1974. *Rise Up, Women!: The Militant Campaign of the Women's Social and Political Union.* London.

Rotella, Elyce J. 1979. "Women's Labor Force Participation and the Growth of Clerical Employment in the United States, 1870–1930," *Journal of Economic History,* 39.1 (March): 331–33. Summary of Ph.D. dissertation, University of Pennsylvania, 1977.

Roubin, Lucienne. 1977. "Male Space and Female Space Within the Provençal Community," in Robert Forster and Orest Ranum, eds., *Rural Society in France. Selections from the Annales: Economies, Sociétés, Civilisations.* Tr. Elborg Forster and Patricia Ranum. Baltimore.

Ruskin, John. 1865. "Of Queen's Gardens," in *Sesame and Lilies.* London.

Ryan, Mary P. 1975. *Womanhood in America: From Colonial Times to the Present.* New York.

Sahli, Nancy. 1979. "Smashing: Women's Relationships Before the Fall," *Chrysalis,* 8 (Summer): 17–27.

Schupf, Harriet Warm. 1974. "Single Women and Social Reform in Mid-Nineteenth Century England: The Case of Mary Carpenter," *Victorian Studies,* 17.3 (March): 301–17.

Schwarz, Judith. 1979. "Yellow Clover: Katharine Lee Bates and Katharine Coman," *Frontiers,* 4.3 (Spring): 59–67.

Scott, Anne Firor. 1970. *The Southern Lady from Pedestal to Politics, 1830–1930.* Chicago.

Scott, Joan W., and Louise A. Tilly. 1975. "Women's Work and the Family in Nineteenth-Century Europe," *Comparative Studies in Society and History,* 17.1 (Jan.): 36–64.

Ségalen, Martine, ed. 1973. *Mari et femme dans la France rurale traditionnelle.* Exhibit catalog. Paris.

Shorter, Edward. 1973. "Female Emancipation, Birth Control, and Fertility in European History," *American Historical Review,* 78.3 (June): 605–40.

———. 1974. "Différences de classe et sentiment depuis 1750: l'exemple de la France," *Annales: Economies, Sociétés, Civilisations,* 29.4 (July–Aug.): 1034–57.

———. 1975. *The Making of the Modern Family.* New York.

Showalter, Elaine. 1977. *A Literature of Their Own: British Women Novelists from Brontë to Lessing.* Princeton, N.J.

Sigsworth, E. M., and T. J. Wyke. 1972. "A Study of Victorian Prostitution and Venereal Disease," in Martha Vicinus, ed., *Suffer and Be Still: Women in the Victorian Age.* Bloomington, Ind.

Simon, Jules. 1861. *L'Ouvrière.* Paris.

Sklar, Kathryn Kish. 1973. *Catharine Beecher: A Study in American Domesticity.* New Haven, Conn.

Smelser, Neil J. 1959. *Social Change in the Industrial Revolution.* Chicago, Ill.

———. 1967. "The Industrial Revolution and the British Working-Class Family," *Journal of Social History,* 1.1 (Fall): 17–35.

Smith, Bonnie Gene Sullivan. 1975. "The Women of the Lille Bourgeoisie, 1850–1914," Ph.D. dissertation, University of Rochester (N.Y.).

Smith, Daniel Scott. 1974. "Family Limitation, Sexual Control, and Domestic Feminism in the United States," in Mary S. Hartman and Lois

Banner, eds., *Clio's Consciousness Raised: New Perspectives on the History of Women.* New York.

——. 1978. "Parental Power and Marriage Patterns: An Analysis of Historical Trends in Hingham, Massachusetts," in Michael Gordon, ed., *The American Family in Social-Historical Perspective.* Rev. ed. New York.

Smith, Daniel Scott, and Michael S. Hindus. 1975. "Premarital Pregnancy in America, 1640–1971: An Overview and Interpretation," *Journal of Interdisciplinary History,* 5.4 (Spring): 537–70.

Smith, F. Barry. 1977. "Sexuality in Britain, 1800–1900: Some Suggested Revisions," in Martha Vicinus, ed., *A Widening Sphere: Changing Roles of Victorian Women.* Bloomington, Ind.

Smith-Rosenberg, Carroll. 1972. "The Hysterical Woman: Some Reflections on Sex Roles and Role Conflict in Nineteenth-Century America," *Social Research,* 39.1 (Winter): 652–78.

——. 1974. "Puberty to Menopause: The Cycle of Femininity in Nineteenth-Century America," in Mary S. Hartman and Lois Banner, eds., *Clio's Consciousness Raised: New Perspectives on the History of Women.* New York.

——. 1975. "The Female World of Love and Ritual: Relations Between Women in Nineteenth-Century America," *Signs,* 1.1 (Autumn): 1–29.

——. 1976. "A Richer and a Gentler Sex." Paper presented at the Berkshire Conference on Women's History, Bryn Mawr (Pa.) College, June.

Solden, Norbert C. 1978. *Women in British Trade Unions, 1874–1976.* Dublin.

Stage, Sarah. 1979. *Female Complaints: Lydia Pinkham and the Business of Women's Medicine.* New York.

Stanton, Elizabeth Cady. 1898. *Eighty Years and Mores: Reminiscences, 1815–1897.* New York. 1971 reprint edition available.

Stearns, Peter N. 1976. *Old Age in European Society: The Case of France.* New York.

Strachey, Ray. 1928. *"The Cause": A Short History of the Woman's Movement in Great Britain.* London. 1969 reprint edition available.

Strickland, Charles E. 1973. "A Transcendentalist Father: The Child-Rearing Practices of Bronson Alcott," *History of Childhood Quarterly,* 1.1 (Summer): 4–51.

Strober, Myra H., and David B. Tyack. 1979. "Sexual Asymmetry in Educational Employment: Male Managers and Female Teachers." Draft report 79–C1, Institute for Research on Educational Finance and Governance, Center for Educational Research, Stanford University.

Strumingher, Laura. 1978. *Women and the Making of the Working Class: Lyon, 1830–1870.* Toronto.

Sullerot, Evelyne. 1966. *Histoire de la presse féminine.* Paris.

——. 1968. *Histoire et sociologie du travail féminin.* Paris.

Sumner, Helen L. 1910. *History of Women in Industry in the United States: Report on the Conditions of Women and Child Wage Earners in the United States.* Washington, D.C. 1974 reprint edition available.

Sussman, George D. 1975. "The Wet-Nursing Business in Nineteenth-Century France," *French Historical Studies,* 9.2 (Fall): 304–28.

——. 1977. "The End of the Wet-Nursing Business in France, 1874–1914," *Journal of Family History,* 2.3 (Fall): 237–58.

Taylor, Gordon Rattray. 1953. *Sex in History: The Story of Society's Changing Attitudes to Sex Throughout the Ages.* London. 1973 reprint edition available.

Thompson, E. P. 1963. *The Making of the English Working Class.* New York.

————. 1967. "Time, Work-Discipline, and Industrial Capitalism," *Past and Present,* 38 (Dec.): 56–97.

Tilly, Louise A. 1978. "Women and Collective Action in Industrializing France, 1870–1914," unpublished manuscript.

Tilly, Louise A., and Joan W. Scott. 1978. *Women, Work, and Family.* New York.

Tilly, Louise A., Joan W. Scott, and Miriam Cohen. 1976. "Women's Work and European Fertility Patterns," *Journal of Interdisciplinary History,* 6.3 (Winter): 447–76.

Tyack, David B. 1974. *The One Best System: A History of American Urban Education.* Cambridge, Mass.

Van de Walle, Etienne. 1974. *The Female Population of France in the Nineteenth Century.* Princeton, N.J.

Vanoli, Dominique. 1976. "Les Ouvrières enfermées: Les Convents soyeux," *Les Révoltes Logiques,* 2 (Spring–Summer): 19–39.

Walkowitz, Judith. 1977. "The Making of an Outcast Group: Prostitutes and Working Women in Nineteenth-Century Plymouth and Southampton," in Martha Vicinus, ed., *A Widening Sphere: Changing Roles of Victorian Women.* Bloomington, Ind.

Walkowitz, Judith R., and Daniel J. Walkowitz. 1974. "We Are Not Beasts of the Field: Prostitution and the Poor in Plymouth and Southampton Under the Contagious Diseases Act," in Mary S. Hartman and Lois Banner, eds., *Clio's Consciousness Raised: New Perspectives on the History of Women.* New York.

Walsh, Mary Roth. 1978. *"Doctors Wanted: No Women Need Apply." Sexual Barriers in the Medical Profession, 1835–1975.* New Haven, Conn.

Walters, Ronald E. 1974. *Primers for Prudery: Sexual Advice to Victorian America.* Englewood Cliffs, N.J.

Watt, Ian. 1957. *The Rise of the Novel: Studies in Defoe, Richardson, and Fielding.* London.

Weber, Eugen. 1976. *Peasants into Frenchmen: The Modernization of Rural France, 1870–1914.* Stanford, Calif.

Wells, Robert V. 1979. "Women's Lives Transformed: Demographic and Family Patterns in America, 1600–1970," in Carol Ruth Berkin and Mary Beth Norton, eds., *Women of America: A History.* Boston.

Welter, Barbara. 1966. "The Cult of True Womanhood, 1820–1860," *American Quarterly,* 18.2 (Summer): 151–74.

Wertz, Richard W., and Dorothy C. Wertz. 1977. *Lying-In: A History of Childbirth in America.* New York.

Weston, Elisabeth. 1979. "Prostitution in Paris in the Later Nineteenth Century: A Study of Political and Social Ideology." Ph.D. Dissertation, State University of New York, Buffalo.

White, Cynthia L. 1970. *Women's Magazines, 1693–1968.* London.

Wohl, Anthony, ed. 1978. *The Victorian Family: Structure and Stresses.* New York.

Wood, Ann Douglas. 1971. "The 'Scribbling Women' and Fanny Fern: Why Women Wrote," *American Quarterly*, 23.1 (Spring): 3–24.

———. 1972. "The War Within a War: Women Nurses in the Union Army," *Civil War History*, 18.3 (Sept.): 197–212.

Woody, Thomas. 1929. *History of Women's Education in the United States.* 2 vols. New York. 1966 reprint edition available.

Wrigley, E. A. 1969. *Population and History*. New York.

Zeldin, Theodore. 1973. *France, 1848–1945*, vol. 1: *Ambition, Love, and Politics*. New York.

Acknowledgments

Docs. 1.iv, 5. *Mémé Santerre*, by Serge Grafteaux, by permission of Jean-Pierre Delarge, Editeur. Copyright © 1975 by Editions du Jour.

Docs. 1.vi, 48, *Caroline Clive: From the Diary and Family Papers of Mrs. Archer Clive*, ed. Lady Mary Clive, by permission of David Higham Associates, Ltd. Copyright © 1949 by The Bodley Head, Ltd.

Docs. 1.vii, 4, 66. *Love Lies Bleeding*, by Helen Smith Jordan, courtesy of Helen Smith Jordan, Dewitt, N.Y., and Henry Chaffee Abell, Inchelium, Wash. Copyright © 1979 by Helen Smith Jordan.

Docs. 3, 12. Reprinted from *Two Quaker Sisters: From the Original Diaries of Elizabeth Buffum Chace and Lucy Buffum Lovell*, with the permission of Liveright Publishing Corporation. Copyright © 1937 by Liveright Publishing Corporation. Copyright renewed 1964 by Malcolm R. Lovell.

Docs. 6.ii, 71.i. *The Letters of Elizabeth Gaskell*, ed. J. A. V. Chapell and Arthur Pollard, by permission of Manchester University Press and by courtesy of Harvard University Press. Copyright © 1966 by Manchester University Press; copyright © 1967 by Harvard University Press.

Doc. 6.iii. *Longtime Californ': A Documentary Study of an American Chinatown*, by Victor G. and Brett de Bary Nee, by permission of Pantheon Books, a division of Random House, Inc. Copyright © 1973 by Houghton Mifflin Co.

Docs. 7.iii–iv, 29.iii, 33.ix, 42, 53.i–vii, 53.ix, 76.i–vii, 78.i–ii. Material reprinted from *The American Slave: A Composite Autobiography*, edited by George P. Rawick and used with the permission of the publisher, Greenwood Press, a division of Congressional Information Service, Inc., Westport, Conn.

Doc. 16. *The Brontës: Their Lives, Friendships and Correspondence*, ed. Thomas James Wise and John Alexander Symington, by permission of Basil Blackwell, Oxford. Copyright © 1932 by Basil Blackwell Publishers, Ltd.

Doc. 20. *An Autobiography*, by Annie Besant, by permission of Ernest Benn, Ltd. Copyright © 1893 by T. Fisher Unwin.

Doc. 22. *Autobiography of St. Thérèse of Lisieux*, tr. Ronald Knox. Copyright © 1958 by P. J. Kenedy & Sons.

Doc. 28. Selections from the Jullien Family Letters, National Archives, Paris, tr. Barbara Corrado Pope, by permission of Barbara Corrado Pope. Translation copyright © 1978 by Barbara Corrado Pope.

Doc. 43.i. *The Ladies of Alderly*, by Nancy Mitford, by permission of A. D. Peters & Co., Ltd. Copyright © 1938 by Chapman and Hall.

Doc. 46.ii. *Dearest Child: Letters Between Queen Victoria and the Princess Royal, 1858–61*, ed. Roger Fulford, by permission of Evans Brothers, Ltd. Copyright © 1964 by Evans Brothers, Ltd.

Doc. 47. Georgiana Bruce Kirby Diary, by permission of the California Historical Society Library. San Francisco.

Doc. 49.i. Lenoir Family Papers, courtesy of the Southern Historical Collection, Library of the University of North Carolina at Chapel Hill, and Dr. James L. Lenoir, Metairie, La.

Doc. 50. *The Amberley Papers*, ed. Bertrand and Patricia Russell, by permission of George Allen & Unwin (Publishers), Ltd. Copyright © 1937 by The Hogarth Press, Ltd.

Doc. 59.iii. Fries-Shaffner Papers, courtesy of the Southern Historical Collection, Library of the University of North Carolina at Chapel Hill, and Dr. Louis DeS. Shaffner, Winston-Salem, N.C.

Doc. 72. *Miss Weeton: The Journal of a Governess*, ed. Edward Hall, by permission of Oxford University Press and by courtesy of Augustus M. Kelly (Publishers). Copyright © 1936 by Oxford University Press.

Doc. 73. *Paysans par eux-mêmes*, by Emile Guillaumin, by permission of Editions Stock. Copyright © 1953 by Editions Stock.

Doc. 74. *Munby, Man of Two Worlds*, by Derek Hudson, by courtesy of Gambit and by permission of John Murray (Publishers), Ltd. Copyright © 1972 by John Murray, Ltd.

Doc. 82.ii. *The Life of Clara Barton*, by Percy Epler, by permission of Macmillan Publishing Co., Inc. Copyright © 1915 by Macmillan Publishing Co., Inc.

Doc. 100. Reprinted from *The George Sand–Gustave Flaubert Letters*, tr. Aimee McKenzie, with the permission of Liveright Publishing Corporation. Copyright © 1921 by Boni & Liveright, Inc. Copyright renewed 1949 by Aimee L. McKenzie.

Doc. 104.i *The Sinkaietk or Southern Okanagon of Washington*, by Walter Cline, Rachel S. Commons, May Mandelbaum, Richard H. Post, and L. V. W. Walters, ed. Leslie Spier, courtesy of George Banta Publishing Company, Menasha, Wis.

Doc. 104.ii. *Lucy Crawford's History of the White Mountains*, ed. Stearns Morse, by courtesy of Appalachian Mountain Club. Copyright © 1978 by Appalachian Mountain Club.

Doc. 104.iii. *A Diary from Dixie*, by Mary Boykin Chesnut, ed. Ben Ames Williams, courtesy of Houghton Mifflin Co. Copyright © 1949 by Houghton Mifflin Co.

Index